T0203023

Lecture Notes in Computer Science   14357

Founding Editors

Gerhard Goos
Juris Hartmanis

Editorial Board Members

Elisa Bertino, *Purdue University, West Lafayette, IN, USA*
Wen Gao, *Peking University, Beijing, China*
Bernhard Steffen, *TU Dortmund University, Dortmund, Germany*
Moti Yung, *Columbia University, New York, NY, USA*

The series Lecture Notes in Computer Science (LNCS), including its subseries Lecture Notes in Artificial Intelligence (LNAI) and Lecture Notes in Bioinformatics (LNBI), has established itself as a medium for the publication of new developments in computer science and information technology research, teaching, and education.

LNCS enjoys close cooperation with the computer science R & D community, the series counts many renowned academics among its volume editors and paper authors, and collaborates with prestigious societies. Its mission is to serve this international community by providing an invaluable service, mainly focused on the publication of conference and workshop proceedings and postproceedings. LNCS commenced publication in 1973.

Huchuan Lu · Wanli Ouyang · Hui Huang ·
Jiwen Lu · Risheng Liu · Jing Dong · Min Xu
Editors

Image
and Graphics

12th International Conference, ICIG 2023
Nanjing, China, September 22–24, 2023
Proceedings, Part III

 Springer

Editors
Huchuan Lu (iD)
Dalian University of Technology
Dalian, China

Hui Huang (iD)
Shenzhen University
Shenzhen, China

Risheng Liu (iD)
Dalian University of Technology
Dalian, China

Min Xu (iD)
University of Technology Sydney
Sydney, NSW, Australia

Wanli Ouyang (iD)
University of Sydney
Sydney, NSW, Australia

Jiwen Lu (iD)
Tsinghua University
Beijing, China

Jing Dong (iD)
Institute of Automation, CAS
Beijing, China

ISSN 0302-9743   ISSN 1611-3349 (electronic)
Lecture Notes in Computer Science
ISBN 978-3-031-46310-5   ISBN 978-3-031-46311-2 (eBook)
https://doi.org/10.1007/978-3-031-46311-2

© The Editor(s) (if applicable) and The Author(s), under exclusive license
to Springer Nature Switzerland AG 2023

This work is subject to copyright. All rights are reserved by the Publisher, whether the whole or part of
the material is concerned, specifically the rights of translation, reprinting, reuse of illustrations, recitation,
broadcasting, reproduction on microfilms or in any other physical way, and transmission or information
storage and retrieval, electronic adaptation, computer software, or by similar or dissimilar methodology now
known or hereafter developed.
The use of general descriptive names, registered names, trademarks, service marks, etc. in this publication
does not imply, even in the absence of a specific statement, that such names are exempt from the relevant
protective laws and regulations and therefore free for general use.
The publisher, the authors, and the editors are safe to assume that the advice and information in this book
are believed to be true and accurate at the date of publication. Neither the publisher nor the authors or the
editors give a warranty, expressed or implied, with respect to the material contained herein or for any errors
or omissions that may have been made. The publisher remains neutral with regard to jurisdictional claims in
published maps and institutional affiliations.

This Springer imprint is published by the registered company Springer Nature Switzerland AG
The registered company address is: Gewerbestrasse 11, 6330 Cham, Switzerland

Paper in this product is recyclable.

Preface

These are the proceedings of the 12th International Conference on Image and Graphics (ICIG 2023), which was held in Nanjing, China, on September 22–24, 2023. The Conference was hosted by China Society of Image and Graphics (CSIG), organized by Nanjing University of Posts & Telecommunications, co-organized by Nanjing University of Science & Technology and Nanjing University of Information Science and Technology, supported by Springer.

ICIG is a biennial conference that focuses on innovative technologies of image, video, and graphics processing and fostering innovation, entrepreneurship, and networking. ICIG 2023 featured world-class plenary speakers, exhibits, and high-quality peer-reviewed oral and poster presentations.

CSIG has hosted the series of ICIG conference since 2000. Details about the past conferences are as follows:

Conference	Place	Date	Submitted	Proceedings
First (ICIG 2000)	Tianjin, China	August 16–18	220	156
Second (ICIG 2002)	Hefei, China	August 15–18	280	166
Third (ICIG 2004)	Hong Kong, China	December 17–19	460	140
4th (ICIG 2007)	Chengdu, China	August 22–24	525	184
5th (ICIG 2009)	Xi'an, China	September 20–23	362	179
6th (ICIG 2011)	Hefei, China	August 12–15	329	183
7th (ICIG 2013)	Qingdao, China	July 26–28	346	181
8th (ICIG 2015)	Tianjin, China	August 13–16	345	170
9th (ICIG 2017)	Shanghai, China	September 13–15	370	172
10th (ICIG 2019)	Beijing, China	August 23–25	384	183
11th (ICIG 2021)	Haikou, China	December 26–28	421	198

For ICIG 2023, 409 submissions were received and 166 papers were accepted. To ease the search for a required paper in these proceedings, the accepted papers have been arranged into different sections according to their topic.

We sincerely thank all the contributors, who came from around the world to present their advanced work at this event. We would also like to thank all the reviewers, who carefully reviewed all submissions and made their valuable comments for improving the accepted papers. The proceedings could not have been produced without the invaluable efforts of the members of the Organizing Committee, and a number of active members of CSIG.

September 2023

Huchuan Lu
Wanli Ouyang
Hui Huang
Jiwen Lu
Risheng Liu
Jing Dong
Min Xu

Organization

Organizing Committee

General Chairs

Yaonan Wang	Hunan University, China
Qingshan Liu	Nanjing University of Posts & Telecommunications, China
Ramesh Jain	University of California, Irvine, USA
Alberto Del Bimbo	University of Florence, Italy

Technical Program Chairs

Huchuan Lu	Dalian University of Technology, China
Wanli Ouyang	University of Sydney, Australia
Hui Huang	Shenzhen University, China
Jiwen Lu	Tsinghua University, China

Organizing Committee Chairs

Yuxin Peng	Peking University, China
Xucheng Yin	University of Science and Technology Beijing, China
Bo Du	Wuhan University, China
Bingkun Bao	Nanjing University of Posts & Telecommunications, China

Publicity Chairs

Abdulmotaleb El Saddik	University of Ottawa, Canada
Phoebe Chen	La Trobe University, Australia
Kun Zhou	Zhejiang University, China
Xiaojun Wu	Jiangnan University, China

Award Chairs

Changsheng Xu   Institute of Automation, CAS, China
Shiguang Shan   Institute of Computing Technology, CAS, China
Mohan Kankanhalli   National University of Singapore, Singapore

Publication Chairs

Risheng Liu   Dalian University of Technology, China
Jing Dong   Institute of Automation, CAS, China
Min Xu   University of Technology Sydney, Australia

Workshop Chairs

Yugang Jiang   Fudan University, China
Kai Xu   National University of Defense Technology,
                                   China
Zhu Li   University of Missouri, USA
Oliver Deussen   Universität Konstanz, Germany

Exhibits Chairs

Qi Tian   Huawei Cloud, China
Wu Liu   JD.COM, China
Weishi Zheng   Sun Yat-sen University, China
Kun Xu   Tsinghua University, China

Tutorial Chairs

Weiwei Xu   Zhejiang University, China
Nannan Wang   Xidian University, China
Shengsheng Qian   Institute of Automation, CAS, China
Klaus Schöffmann   Klagenfurt University, Austria

Sponsorship Chairs

Xiang Bai   Huazhong University of Science and Technology,
                                   China
Mingming Cheng   Nankai University, China

Finance Chairs

Lifang Wu	Beijing University of Technology, China
Yubao Sun	Nanjing University of Information Science & Technology, China
Miao Hong	CSIG, China

Social Media Chairs

Zhenwei Shi	Beihang University, China
Wei Jia	Hefei University of Technology, China
Feifei Zhang	Tianjin University of Technology, China

Local Chairs

Jian Cheng	Institute of Automation, CAS, China
Xiaotong Yuan	Nanjing University of Information Science & Technology, China
Yifan Jiao	Nanjing University of Posts & Telecommunications, China

Website Chairs

Rui Huang	Chinese University of Hong Kong, Shenzhen, China
Jie Wang	Nanjing University of Posts & Telecommunications, China

Area Chairs

Yuchao Dai	Xi Peng	Yong Xia
Yulan Guo	Boxin Shi	Shiqing Xin
Xiaoguang Han	Dong Wang	Feng Xu
Tong He	Lijun Wang	Jia Xu
Gao Huang	Limin Wang	Kun Xu
Meina Kan	Nannan Wang	Yongchao Xu
Yu-Kun Lai	Xinchao Wang	Junchi Yan
Li Liu	Xinggang Wang	Shiqi Yu
Huimin Lu	Yunhai Wang	Jian Zhang
Jinshan Pan	Baoyuan Wu	Pingping Zhang
Houwen Peng	Jiazhi Xia	Shanshan Zhang

Additional Reviewers

Bingkun Bao
Yulong Bian
Chunjuan Bo
Zi-Hao Bo
JIntong Cai
Zhanchuan Cai
Mingwei Cao
Jianhui Chang
Yakun Chang
Bin Chen
Guang Chen
Hongrui Chen
Jianchuan Chen
Junsong Chen
Siming Chen
Xiang Chen
Xin Chen
Ziyang Chen
Jinghao Cheng
Lechao Cheng
Ming-Ming Cheng
Jiaming Chu
Hainan Cui
Yutao Cui
Enyan Dai
Tao Dai
Jisheng Dang
Sagnik Das
Xinhao Deng
Haiwen Diao
Jian Ding
Wenhui Dong
Xiaoyu Dong
Shuguang Dou
Zheng-Jun Du
Peiqi Duan
Qingnan Fan
Yongxian Fan
Zhenfeng Fan
Gongfan Fang
Kun Fang
Sheng Fang
Xianyong Fang

Zhiheng Fu
Wei Gai
Ziliang Gan
Changxin Gao
Qing Gao
Shang Gao
Zhifan Gao
Tong Ge
Shenjian Gong
Guanghua Gu
Yuliang Gu
Shihui Guo
Yahong Han
Yizeng Han
Yufei Han
Junwen He
Mengqi He
Xiaowei He
Yulia Hicks
Yuchen Hong
Ruibing Hou
Shouming Hou
Donghui Hu
Fuyuan Hu
Lanqing Hu
Qiming Hu
Ruimin Hu
Yang Hu
Yupeng Hu
Bao Hua
Guanjie Huang
Le Hui
Chengtao Ji
Naye Ji
Xiaosong Jia
Xu Jia
Chaohui Jiang
Haoyi Jiang
Peng Jiang
Runqing Jiang
Zhiying Jiang
Leyang Jin
Yongcheng Jing

Hao Ju
Yongzhen Ke
Lingshun Kong
Jian-Huang Lai
Yu-Kun Lai
Xingyu Lan
Yang Lang
Wentao Lei
Yang Lei
Baohua Li
Bocen Li
Boyang Li
Chao Li
Chenghong Li
Dachong Li
Feng Li
Gang Li
Guanbin Li
Guorong Li
Guozheng Li
Hao Li
Hongjun Li
Kunhong Li
Li Li
Manyi Li
Ming Li
Mingjia Li
Qifeng Li
Shifeng Li
Shutao Li
Siheng Li
Xiaoyan Li
Yanchun Li
Yang Li
Yi Li
Ying Li
Yue Li
Yunhao Li
Zihan Li
Dongze Lian
Jinxiu Liang
Junhao Liang
Tian Liang

Zhengyu Liang	Zhongjin Luo	Jing Tan
Zhifang Liang	Yunqiu Lv	Jiajun Tang
Bencheng Liao	Junfeng Lyu	Jin Tang
Zehui Liao	Youwei Lyu	Shiyu Tang
Chuan Lin	Chunyan Ma	Minggui Teng
Feng Lin	Fengji Ma	Yao Teng
Qifeng Lin	Huimin Ma	Yanling Tian
Weilin Lin	Tianlei Ma	Zhigang Tu
Wenbin Lin	Xinke Ma	Matthew Vowels
Xiaotian Lin	Qirong Mao	Bo Wang
Yiqun Lin	Yuxin Mao	Dong Wang
Jingwang Ling	Wei Miao	Dongsheng Wang
Qiu Lingteng	Yongwei Miao	Haiting Wang
Aohan Liu	Weidong Min	Hao Wang
Chang Liu	Jiawen Ming	Jingyi Wang
Cheng-Lin Liu	Weihua Ou	Jinjia Wang
Haolin Liu	Jinshan Pan	Jinting Wang
Jingxin Liu	Yun Pei	Jinwei Wang
Jinyuan Liu	Zongju Peng	Junyu Wang
Kenkun Liu	Hongxing Qin	Lijun Wang
Lei Liu	Liangdong Qiu	Longguang Wang
Long Liu	Xinkuan Qiu	Meng Wang
Meng Liu	Yuda Qiu	Miao Wang
Min Liu	Zhong Qu	Peizhen Wang
Qingshan Liu	Weisong Ren	Pengjie Wang
Risheng Liu	Nong Sang	Rui Wang
Shengli Liu	Guangcun Shan	Ruiqi Wang
Shiguang Liu	Linlin Shen	Ruotong Wang
Shuaiqi Liu	Zhiqiang Shen	Shengjin Wang
Songhua Liu	Jiamu Sheng	Shijie Wang
Wei Liu	Jun Shi	Tao Wang
Wenrui Liu	Zhenghao Shi	Xiaoxing Wang
Wenyu Liu	Zhenwei Shi	Xin Wang
Xuehu Liu	Chengfang Song	Xingce Wang
Yiguang Liu	Jiechong Song	Yili Wang
Yijing Liu	Jifei Song	Yingquan Wang
Yipeng Liu	Yong Song	Yongfang Wang
Yong Liu	Zhengyao Song	Yue Wang
Yu Liu	Qingtang Su	Yun Wang
Yunan Liu	Jiande Sun	Zi Wang
Zhenguang Liu	Long Sun	Hongjiang Wei
Zilin Lu	Xuran Sun	Shaokui Wei
Weiqi Luo	Zhixing Sun	Xiu-Shen Wei
Yong Luo	Gary Tam	Ziyu Wei
Zhaofan Luo	Hongchen Tan	Shuchen Weng

Zhi Weng
Qian Wenhua
Jianlong Wu
Lianjun Wu
Tao Wu
Yadong Wu
Yanmin Wu
Ye Wu
Yu Wu
Yushuang Wu
Di Xiao
Yuxuan Xiao
Jin Xie
Jingfen Xie
Jiu-Cheng Xie
Yutong Xie
Jiankai Xing
Bo Xu
Hongming Xu
Jie Xu
Xiaowei Xu
Yi Xu
Mingliang Xue
Xiangyang Xue
Difei Yan
Xin Yan
Yichao Yan
Zizheng Yan
Bin Yang
Cheng Yang
Jialin Yang
Kang Yang
Min Yang

Shuo Yang
Shuzhou Yang
Xingyi Yang
Xue Yang
Yang Yang
Yiqian Yang
Zhongbao Yang
Chao Yao
Chengtang Yao
Jingfeng Yao
Chongjie Ye
Dingqiang Ye
Jingwen Ye
Yiwen Ye
Xinyu Yi
Xinyi Ying
Di You
Bohan Yu
Chenyang Yu
Jiwen Yu
Runpeng Yu
Songsong Yu
Danni Yuan
Yang Yue
Lin Yushun
Qingjie Zeng
Qiong Zeng
Yaopei Zeng
Yinwei Zhan
Dawei Zhang
Guozhen Zhang
Jianpeng Zhang
Jiawan Zhang

Jing Zhang
Mingda Zhang
Pengyu Zhang
Pingping Zhang
Xiao-Yong Zhang
Xinpeng Zhang
Xuanyu Zhang
Yanan Zhang
Yang Zhang
Ye Zhang
Yuanhang Zhang
Zaibin Zhang
ZhiHao Zhang
Jie Zhao
Sicheng Zhao
Yuchao Zheng
Shuaifeng Zhi
Fan Zhong
Chu Zhou
Feng Zhou
JiaYuan Zhou
Jingyi Zhou
Tao Zhou
Yang Zhou
Zhanping Zhou
Minfeng Zhu
Mingli Zhu
Mingrui Zhu
Xu Zhu
Zihao Zhu
Shinan Zou

Contents – Part III

Computer Graphics and Visualization

Compression, Transmission, Retrieval

Computer Vision and Pattern Recognition

Adaptive Fine-Grained Region Matching for Image Harmonization

Liuxue Ju[1], Chengdao Pu[1], Fang Gao[2], and Jun Yu[1($\boxtimes$)]

[1] University of Science and Technology of China, Hefei, China
{juliuxuet,puchengdao}@mail.ustc.edu.cn, harryjun@ustc.edu.cn
[2] Guangxi University, Nanning, China
fgao@gxu.edu.cn

Abstract. Image harmonization aims to generate composite images that are visually consistent by adjusting the foreground to be compatible with the background. However, previous image harmonization methods overlook the fact that in a real image, the appearance (e.g., illumination, color temperature, saturation, hue, and texture) of different regions can vary significantly depending on content and position. For each foreground region, the background regions related to it should be taken as major references to adjust its appearance. To address this, a fine-grained appearance translation strategy is designed in this work. When adjusting the appearance of each foreground region, our method pays more attention to the background regions that are more relevant to it based on content similarity and position information. Furthermore, a multi-scale feature calibration strategy is introduced to adaptively calibrate the fine-grained features. Finally, an adaptive reconstruction strategy is proposed to further improve the harmonization result. Extensive experiments show our method significantly reduces parameters and achieves state-of-the-art performance compared with previous methods.

Keywords: Image harmonization · Appearance translation · Content similarity · Position information

1 Introduction

Image composition technology is essential for image editing and data enhancement [1–3]. It aims to paste the foreground object of one image onto another background image to generate a realistic and high-quality composite image. However, due to varying shooting conditions (e.g., weather, season, and time of day), the appearance (e.g., illumination, color temperature, saturation, hue, and texture) of the foreground and background varies. This often results in composite images that appear unrealistic. To solve this problem, image harmonization is introduced. It ensures that the foreground is more compatible with the background by preserving the structure and semantic information of the foreground while adjusting its appearance to match the background environment.

© The Author(s), under exclusive license to Springer Nature Switzerland AG 2023
H. Lu et al. (Eds.): ICIG 2023, LNCS 14357, pp. 3–15, 2023.
https://doi.org/10.1007/978-3-031-46311-2_1

Recently, a variety of deep learning-based image harmonization methods have been proposed from different perspectives, such as attention mechanism [2], semantic information [4,5], domain verification discriminator [6,7], reflectance and illumination [8–10], and style transfer [11,12]. However, the existing methods ignore that in a real image, the distance and content similarity between local regions can affect the differences in their appearance features, and the differences will be more significant because of the lower content similarity and the further distance. Taking Fig. 1 (a) as an example, the foreground floodlight appears twice in the background. It is easy to distinguish the foreground floodlight as a composite, because it is different from the background floodlights in appearance distribution. The model should pay more attention to the distribution of local appearance features of both regions. Meanwhile, the two floodlights in the background have subtle differences in appearance. Therefore, the appearance features distribution of the foreground floodlight should be closer to the closer floodlight in the background than the further floodlight.

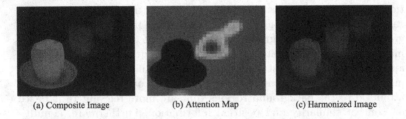

(a) Composite Image   (b) Attention Map   (c) Harmonized Image

Fig. 1. Illustration of adjusting each foreground region according to its most referential background regions. As shown in the "Attention Map", our method successfully focuses on the floodlights in the background, in which the closer floodlight gets more attention than the further floodlight. Besides, the harmonized result is more realistic.

Based on the above observations, we think that for each foreground region, the closer background regions with similar content can provide more reference information. In this paper, (1) we design an adaptive region-matching appearance translation strategy, which finer-grained adjusts the foreground features. Specifically, we align each foreground region with the matching background regions in a learned deep neural network (DNN) feature space, and then adjust the fine-grained features as it retains more detailed structural information. Considering that there may be significant differences in appearance between different regions, we separately unfold the foreground and background into overlapping patches. To adaptively adjust the appearance of each foreground patch, we first normalize the sum of content similarity and position information between it and all background patches to obtain the corresponding weight of each background patch. Then, we weigh the appearance information of all background patches to the foreground patch. In this way, the visual appearance of each foreground patch is jointly determined by its associated background patches. (2) To increase the effectiveness of data in the network, we capture the information under different receptive fields by adjusting the dilation rate [13] of the convolution, and then calibrate the original features using a gating mechanism. (3) In image harmonization, we coordinate the encoder output with the original input instead of generating the foreground [4,6–8,11] directly, which is conducive to preserving the basic structure and semantic information. (4) Besides, our model improves the performance of the baseline model by adding few parameters, which mainly come from the 3×3 convolutions in the multi-scale feature calibration strategy. The main contributions of our work are four-fold as follows:

- We design an adaptive patches-to-patches translation strategy in appearance by matching the closer background regions with similar content, which is the first to consider both content similarity and position information.
- To increase the effective information, we use the multi-scale dilated convolution and the gating mechanism to calibrate features.
- To reduce the error by image reconstruction in the decoder, we calibrate the learned foreground features by alpha blending with adaptive weighting.
- Our method achieves competitive performance using fewer parameters on the benchmark dataset.

2 Related Work

Traditional image harmonization methods focus on the transmission of handmade low-level feature statistics summarized in the background to the foreground, such as color statistics [1,14], gradient information [15–17] and multiscale feature statistics [18]. Recently, more deep learning-based methods have improved the authenticity of composite images. DIH [4] is the first to propose an end-to-end training method for image harmonization. S^2AM [2] designs a spatial-separated attention to learn foreground and background features respectively. DoveNet [6] proposes a domain verification discriminator and adopts adversarial training. BargainNet [7] designs a domain code extractor to capture background domain information to guide the foreground. According to the intrinsic image theory, IIH [8] disentangles composite images into reflectance and illumination based on an autoencoder, and DHT [9] and DHT+ [10] design Transformer [19] based frameworks. RainNet [11] regards the mean and standard deviation of feature statistics as appearance information and transfers them from the background features to the normalized foreground features. Zhu et al. [12] adaptively shift and scale each foreground feature based on the similarity between foreground and background features. These methods ignore the appearance differences between different regions, even though background regions with the same content but different positions provide different reference information.

3 Methodology

3.1 Overall Framework

Image harmonization is to input a composite image $I_c = I_f \times M + I_b \times \bar{M}$ with the corresponding foreground mask M, and output the harmonized image $\tilde{I}$ by using the background to adjust the foreground, where I_f, I_b, and $\bar{M} = 1 - M$ denote the foreground image, background image, and background mask. Its goal is to train a generator G to generate the harmonized image $\tilde{I}$, where $\tilde{I} = G(I_c, M)$. To achieve this goal, we introduce multi-scale feature calibration (MFC), adaptive patches-to-patches translation (APTP) and adaptive reconstruction layer for improving the performance of basic networks. As demonstrated in Fig. 2, the composite image and foreground mask are concatenated and input to the U-Net [20] for features encoding and decoding. Then the decoder output and the composite image are input to the adaptive reconstruction layer to generate the harmonized image. In which, MFC extracts multi-scale features during encoding, and APTP does appearance transfer of foreground features during decoding.

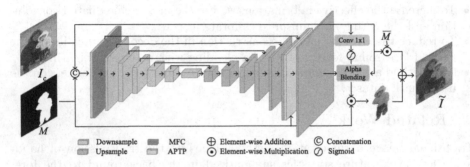

Fig. 2. The overall framework of our method.

3.2 Multi-scale Feature Calibration (MFC)

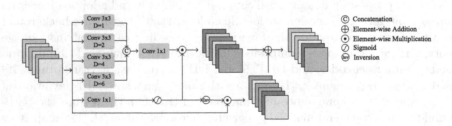

Fig. 3. Multi-scale feature calibration (MFC).

To enhance the valid information in the data, we use a gating mechanism to calibrate the original features by multi-scale fusion features. As demonstrated in Fig. 3, we first load the input features F_{in} into dilate convolution layers with different dilation rates in parallel to extract different-scale features. Next, the different-scale features are concatenated according to the channels, and input to the 1×1 convolution layer to obtain the multi-scale fusion features F_m with the same number of channels as F_{in}. Then, the input features are input into the

1×1 convolution layer with the Sigmoid function to obtain the feature weights α of each position. Finally, the calibrated features F_{out} are obtained by weighted summation of input features F_{in} and multi-scale fusion features F_m in Eq. (1). In this paper, we use four 3×3 dilate convolutions with dilation rates of $\{1, 2, 4, 6\}$.

$$F_{out} = F_m \times \alpha + F_{in} \times (1 - \alpha). \tag{1}$$

3.3 Adaptive Patches-to-patches Translation (APTP)

In appearance transfer, both RainNet [11] and Zhu et al. [12] ignore that in a real image, the differences in appearance between different regions can become more significant with lower content similarity and further distance. To effectively adjust the foreground of a composite image, we adaptively adjust each foreground region by the appearance of relevant background regions according to content similarity and position information. Specifically, we first calculate the content similarity between all foreground and background regions, and then weighted transfer the appearance of the background regions to each foreground region according to the content similarity and position information, as shown in Fig. 4.

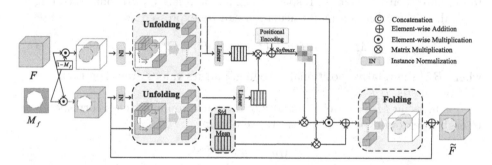

Fig. 4. Adaptive patches-to-patches translation (APTP).

Let $F \in \mathbb{R}^{H \times W \times C}$ be the features of the decoder layer and $M_f \in \mathbb{R}^{H \times W \times 1}$ be the adjusted foreground mask, where H, W, and C represent the height, weight and channel number of F respectively. To obtain information about the appearance and content of each background region, we first unfold the background features $F \times (1 - M_f)$ into multiple patches $F_b = \{F_{b,n}\}_{n=1}^K$ with the stride of (d, d) and the patch size of $s \times s \times C$. Besides, the background mask is also unfolded into corresponding patches $M_b = \{M_{b,n}\}_{n=1}^K$. According to the appearance information of each region can be represented by its statistics, while the normalized region contains content information [21], we use the mean $\mu = \{\mu_n\}_{n=1}^K \in \mathbb{R}^{K \times C}$ and standard deviation $\sigma = \{\sigma_n\}_{n=1}^K \in \mathbb{R}^{K \times C}$ of each background patch to represent its own appearance information.

$$\mu_n = \frac{1}{\sum\limits_{h,w} M_{b,n}^{h,w}} \sum_{h,w} F_{b,n}^{h,w} \times M_{b,n}^{h,w}, \tag{2}$$

$$\sigma_n = \sqrt{\frac{1}{\sum\limits_{h,w} M_{b,n}^{h,w}} \sum_{h,w} \left(F_{b,n}^{h,w} - \mu_n\right)^2 \times M_{b,n}^{w,h} + \epsilon}, \tag{3}$$

where n is a sequence number, and (h,w) is a location within the patch.

To obtain content features of the foreground $F \times M_f$ and background $F \times (1 - M_f)$, we apply IN [22] to them respectively. Besides, we unfold the content features of the foreground and background into content features $C_f = \{C_{f,n}\}_{n=1}^{K}$ of the corresponding foreground patches and the content features $C_b = \{C_{b,n}\}_{n=1}^{K}$ of the corresponding background patches. For conveniently calculating, we squeeze content features of the foreground and background patches into corresponding foreground content tokens $f = \{f_n \in \mathbb{R}^{1 \times C}\}_{n=1}^{K}$ and background content tokens $b = \{b_n \in \mathbb{R}^{1 \times C}\}_{n=1}^{K}$ with a linear projection respectively to calculate the content similarity between foreground and background regions.

Next, we use the attention map between foreground and background patches to measure their correlation. Inspired by [23], the relative positional encoding is applied, so the attention map calculation can be expressed as

$$Map = Softmax(f \odot b^T + B) \in \mathbb{R}^{K \times K}, \tag{4}$$

where B is the relative positional encoding, and its values are taken from learnable parameter $\bar{B} \in \mathbb{R}^{(2K-1) \times (2K-1)}$.

Then, using Map to weigh μ and σ of the background patches corresponding to each foreground patch respectively, we obtain

$$E = Map \odot \mu \in \mathbb{R}^{K \times C}, \tag{5}$$

$$S = Map \odot \sigma \in \mathbb{R}^{K \times C}, \tag{6}$$

where, E and S are the mean and standard deviation required for foreground patches, respectively.

We transfer the appearance information to the content features C_f of each foreground patch, and the features of foreground patch $\tilde{F}_f = \left\{\tilde{F}_{f,n}\right\}_{n=1}^{K}$ after appearance transfer are

$$\tilde{F}_{f,n,h,w} = C_{f,n,h,w} \times \sigma_n + \mu_n, \tag{7}$$

where, (n, h, w) is a location within the nth feature patch.

Finally, we reconstruct the transferred foreground patches into the whole foreground. For the foreground patches with overlapping parts, we use the average strategy to process.

3.4   Adaptive Reconstruction Layer

Image harmonization aims to adjust the foreground of a composite image while retaining the basic structure and content information. For a composite image I_c and its foreground mask M, previous generative methods of image harmonization [4, 6–8, 11] usually use a decoder to directly predict the foreground. Inspired by [5], we design a simple yet effective calibrator further improve the harmonization result, as shown in Fig. 2. Using β obtained by inputting the composite image I_c into a 1×1 convolution with the Sigmoid function, we adopt the decoder output I' and the composite image I_c to performer alpha blending.

$$\tilde{I}_f = I' \times \beta + I_c \times (1 - \beta), \tag{8}$$

$$\tilde{I} = \tilde{I}_f \times M + I_c \times (1 - M), \tag{9}$$

where, $\beta \in [0, 1]$ is the per-pixel parameter to smartly borrow information from the input image.

4   Experiments

4.1   Settings

To demonstrate the effectiveness of our method, we perform experiments on the benchmark dataset iHarmony4 [6], which consists of four sub-datasets (i.e., HCOCO, HAdobe5K, HFlickerd, and Hday2night). Meanwhile, our method is also evaluated on 99 real composite images provided by [4]. Following [8–10], we use Mean-Squared Error (MSE), Foreground Mean-Squared Error (fMSE), and Peak Signal-to-Noise Ratio (PSNR) as evaluation metrics. Our model is trained for 140 epochs with Adam optimizer [24] and input images are resized as 256×256. The learning rate is initialized with 0.001 and divided by 10 at epochs 110, and 130. In the image harmonization task, we only adjust the foreground. Following [5], which considers the area of the foreground region, we adopt fMSE loss as our loss function.

Table 1. Quantitative comparison across four sub-datasets of iHarmony4.

Sub-dataset	HCOCO		HAdobe5k		HFlickr		Hday2night		All		
Evaluation metric	PSNR↑	fMSE↓	PSNR↑	fMSE↓	PSNR↑	fMSE↓	PSNR↑	fMSE↓	PSNR↑	fMSE↓	Param.↓
Input composite	33.99	996.59	28.52	2051.61	28.43	1574.37	34.36	1409.98	31.78	1376.42	–
DoveNet [6]	36.50	555.34	35.89	384.17	31.01	833.73	35.86	1066.58	35.69	545.72	54.76 M
RainNet [11]	36.59	535.39	36.21	320.43	31.33	751.12	36.12	852.08	35.88	502.49	54.75 M
BargainNet [7]	37.11	397.60	36.13	279.81	31.46	700.61	35.95	830.23	36.17	404.89	58.74 M
IIH [8]	37.82	361.94	36.61	259.05	32.10	638.35	37.06	740.6	36.81	369.64	40.86 M
DHT [9]	38.99	286.58	37.05	243.05	33.55	464.72	37.03	627.11	37.78	299.92	26.52 M
DHT+ [10]	39.22	274.66	37.17	242.57	33.55	471.09	36.38	736.54	37.94	295.56	21.77 M
Ours	**39.29**	**264.65**	**38.83**	**165.49**	**33.75**	**438.32**	**37.96**	**583.66**	**38.51**	**260.87**	**8.51 M**

4.2   Comparison with Current Methods

To illustrate performance, we compare our method with DoveNet [6], Rain-Net [11], BargainNet [7], IIH [8], DHT [9] and DHT+ [10] on iHarmony4. Our model achieves the highest performance with the fewest parameters in Table 1.

Quantitative Comparison. Table 1 shows the quantitative results of different harmonization methods in each sub-dataset. We use pre-trained other state-of-the-art methods to obtain the results for comparison. We can observe that our method outperforms other methods on all sub-datasets. Compared to the most recent method DHT+ [10], our method brings 0.57 dB improvement in terms of PSNR, and 34.69 improvement in terms of fMSE. Besides, following [6], we also investigate the quantitative results of different methods in different foreground ratio ranges (i.e., 0% ~ 5%, 5% ~ 15%, and 15% ~ 100%). As shown in Table 2, our method outperforms other methods on all foreground ratio ranges.

Table 2. Quantitative comparison in each foreground ratio on iHarmony4.

Foreground ratios	0% ~ 5%		5% ~ 15%		15% ~ 100%		0% ~ 100%	
Evaluation metric	PSNR↑	fMSE↓	PSNR↑	fMSE↓	PSNR↑	fMSE↓	PSNR↑	fMSE↓
DoveNet [6]	39.24	602.03	34.09	487.76	29.21	482.13	35.69	545.72
RainNet [11]	39.27	579.88	34.57	410.56	29.43	429.91	35.88	502.49
BargainNet [7]	39.40	449.31	34.84	360.43	30.13	353.23	36.17	404.89
IIH [8]	40.10	408.09	35.54	326.29	30.55	330.75	36.81	369.64
DHT [9]	40.85	344.29	36.69	249.96	31.82	255.00	37.78	299.92
DHT+ [10]	40.97	335.45	36.88	250.80	32.01	254.98	37.94	295.56
Ours	**41.77**	**298.54**	**37.08**	**221.19**	**32.54**	**219.53**	**38.51**	**260.87**

Qualitative Comparison. Given a composite image from the test set, the harmonized results generated by DoveNet [6], RainNet [11], IIH [8], DHT [9], DHT+ [10] and ours are shown in Fig. 5. Among the five grounds of images, the last three groups have background regions related to the foreground in content, and our method performs better on these composite images by referring to these background regions. In the first and second groups without clear reference, our method benefits from the position information successfully harmonizing the composite images. Compared with other methods, our method achieves better visual consistency between foreground and background, and our harmonized images are visually closer to the ground-truth real images.

4.3   Ablation Study

We take a U-Net [4,6,7,11] alike network as our baseline model, which directly predicts the foreground. We use "Base" and "ABase" to denote the baseline model and baseline model with adaptive reconstruction layer respectively. We

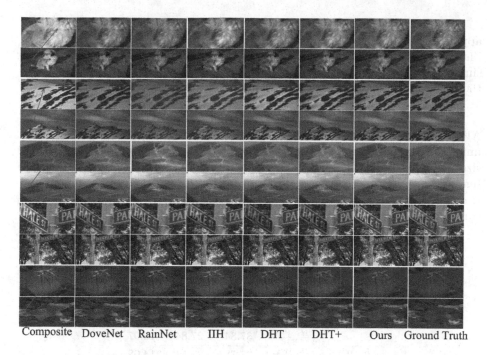

Composite DoveNet RainNet   IIH   DHT   DHT+   Ours Ground Truth

Fig. 5. Qualitative comparison on iHarmony4. We have enlarged local regions.

illustrate the effectiveness of MFC, APTP, and the adaptive reconstruction layer as shown in Table 3. Compared with "Base", "ABase" brings performance improvement of 1.65 dB in PSNR, 12.04 in MSE, and 99.72 in fMSE. When MFC is added, the fMSE value is reduced from 332.88 to 280.59. When APTP is used, the fMSE value is reduced from 332.88 to 309.00. Adding MFC and APTP, the fMSE value is reduced from 332.88 to 260.87.

Table 3. Ablation study on iHarmony4. APTP* denotes APTP without positional encoding, and APTP+ denotes APTP without content similarity.

Evaluation metric	PSNR↑	MSE↓	fMSE↓
Base	35.60	42.82	432.60
ABase	37.25	30.78	332.88
ABase+MFC	38.05	25.37	280.59
ABase+RAIN [11]	37.32	30.02	331.47
ABase+PTL [12]	37.58	27.23	314.13
ABase+APTP*	37.84	27.99	314.68
ABase+APTP+	37.44	28.07	321.18
ABase+APTP	37.86	27.41	309.00
ABase+MFC+APTP	**38.51**	**23.35**	**260.87**

To prove the effectiveness of content similarity and position information in appearance transfer, we compare APTP with RAIN of RainNet [11], PTL of Zhu et al. [12], APTP without positional encoding, and APTP without content similarity, respectively, as shown in Table 3. Note that we are adding them to the decoder layer at 128×128 resolution, and adding MFC to the encoder layer at 128×128 resolution.

Besides, we investigate how the size and stride of unfolding patches in our APTP influence the performance. Table 4 shows the experimental results of unfolding the whole region into patches with different patch sizes and stride sizes on "ABase+APTP". Overlapping patches help capture more accurate content and position information and richer appearance information for match and transfer than non-overlapping patches. Smaller patch size and smaller stride size can help our model achieve higher performance.

Table 4. Influence of the patch and stride size on iHarmony4.

Patch size	Stride size	PSNR↑	MSE↓	fMSE↓
$(\frac{H}{4}, \frac{W}{4})$	$(\frac{H}{4}, \frac{W}{4})$	37.48	28.50	318.88
	$(\frac{H}{8}, \frac{W}{8})$	37.75	28.73	316.61
	$(\frac{H}{16}, \frac{W}{16})$	37.84	27.84	312.07
$(\frac{H}{8}, \frac{W}{8})$	$(\frac{H}{8}, \frac{W}{8})$	37.78	27.51	314.08
	$(\frac{H}{16}, \frac{W}{16})$	37.60	27.51	310.76
	$(\frac{H}{32}, \frac{W}{32})$	**37.86**	**27.41**	**309.00**

4.4   User Study on Real Composite Images

Sometimes, PSNR and fMSE can't correctly reflect visual perception. Following [6,11], we conduct user study on 99 real-world composited images released by DIH [4]. We invite 15 volunteers and ask them to choose the most realistic images from the original composite image and results generated by DoveNet [6], RainNet [11], and ours. The total number of votes is 1485. As shown in Table 5, our method obtains more votes than other methods, which proves that our method not only performs best in PSNR, and fMSE but also can generate more realistic images than other methods according to manual judgment. Besides, as shown in Fig. 6, although there is no ground truth image as a reference, we can still observe our method performs better in visual consistency.

Table 5. Comparison under user study on 99 real-world composited images.

Method	Input	DoveNet	RainNet	Ours
Votes↑	178	331	367	**609**
Preference↑	12.0%	22.3%	24.7%	**41.0%**

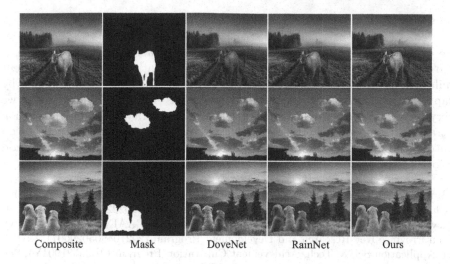

Composite   Mask   DoveNet   RainNet   Ours

Fig. 6. Example results on 99 real-world composited images.

4.5 Visualization of Attention Map

As shown in Fig. 7, we further demonstrate the effectiveness of our APTP strategy by visualizing the attention results. We can see that in the first and second columns, our method successfully focuses on the regions where the foreground object appears in the background. In the last column, the foreground object does not appear in the background, and our method focuses on the background regions near the foreground object due to the relative position.

Fig. 7. Visualization of attention map in APTP.

5   Conclusion

The existing image harmonization models ignore that the significant appearance differences of different regions are affected by relative distance and content similarity. We propose to transfer the appearance of each foreground region by adaptively matching the background regions. For each foreground region, we query its related background regions by content similarity and relative position to transfer its appearance. Besides, we design the multi-scale feature calibration strategy and adaptive reconstruction strategy. Experiments prove our method performs favorably on both iHarmony4 and real-world composited images.

Acknowledgements.. This work was supported by the Natural Science Foundation of China (62276242), National Aviation Science Foundation (2022Z071078001), CAAI-Huawei MindSpore Open Fund (CAAIXSJLJJ-2021-016B, CAAIXSJLJJ-2022-001A), Anhui Province Key Research and Development Program (202104a05020007), USTC-IAT Application Sci. & Tech. Achievement Cultivation Program (JL06521001Y), Sci. & Tech. Innovation Special Zone (20-163-14-LZ-001-004-01).

References

1. Xue, S., Agarwala, A., Dorsey, J., et al.: Understanding and improving the realism of image composites. ACM Trans. Graph. (TOG) **31**(4), 1–10 (2012)
2. Cun, X., Pun, C.M.: Improving the harmony of the composite image by spatial-separated attention module. IEEE Trans. Image Process. **29**, 4759–4771 (2020)
3. Zhang, L., Wen, T., Min, J., et al.: Learning object placement by inpainting for compositional data augmentation. In: ECCV, pp. 566–581 (2020)
4. Tsai, Y.H., Shen, X., Lin, Z., et al.: Deep image harmonization. In: CVPR, pp. 2799–2807 (2017)
5. Sofiiuk, K., Popenova, P., Konushin, A.: Foreground-aware semantic representations for image harmonization. In: WACV, pp. 1619–1628 (2021)
6. Cong, W., Zhang, J., Niu, L., et al.: DoveNet: deep image harmonization via domain verification. In: CVPR, pp. 8391–8400 (2020)
7. Cong, W., Niu, L., Zhang, J., et al.: BargainNet: background-guided domain translation for image harmonization. In: ICME, pp. 1–6 (2021)
8. Guo, Z., Zhang, H., Jiang, Y., et al.: Intrinsic image harmonization. In: CVPR, pp. 16362–16371 (2021)
9. Guo, Z., Gao, D., Zhang, H., et al.: Image harmonization with transformer. In: ICCV, pp. 14850–14859 (2021)
10. Guo, Z., Gou, Z., Zhang, B., et al.: Transformer for image harmonization and beyond. IEEE Trans. Pattern Anal. Mach. Intell. **45**, 12960–12977 (2022)
11. Ling, J., Xue, H., Song, L., et al.: Region-aware adaptive instance normalization for image harmonization. In: CVPR, pp. 9357–9366 (2021)
12. Zhu, Z., Zhang, Z., Lin, Z., et al.: Image harmonization by matching regional references. arXiv preprint arXiv:2204.04715 (2022)
13. Yu, F., Koltun, V.: Multi-scale context aggregation by dilated convolutions. arXiv preprint arXiv:1511.07122 (2015)
14. Reinhard, E., Adhikhmin, M., Gooch, B., et al.: Color transfer between images. IEEE Comput. Graph. Appl. **21**(5), 34–41 (2001)

15. Jia, J., Sun, J., Tang, C.K., et al.: Drag-and-drop pasting. ACM Trans. Graph. (TOG) **25**(3), 631–637 (2006)
16. Tao, M.W., Johnson, M.K., Paris, S., et al.: Error-tolerant image compositing. Int. J. Comput. Vision **103**, 178–189 (2013)
17. Pérez, P., Gangnet, M., Blake, A.: Poisson image editing. ACM Trans. Graph. (TOG) **22**(3), 313–318 (2003)
18. Sunkavalli, K., Johnson, M.K., Matusik, W., et al.: Multi-scale image harmonization. ACM Trans. Graph. (TOG) **29**(4), 1–10 (2010)
19. Vaswani, A., Shazeer, N., Parmar, N., et al.: Attention is all you need. In: NeurIPS, pp. 6000–6010 (2017)
20. Ronneberger, O., Fischer, P., Brox, T.: U-net: Convolutional networks for biomedical image segmentation. In: MICCAI, pp. 234–241 (2015)
21. Huang, X., Belongie, S.: Arbitrary style transfer in real-time with adaptive instance normalization. In: ICCV, pp. 1501–1510 (2017)
22. Ulyanov, D., Vedaldi, A., Lempitsky, Y.: Instance normalization: The missing ingredient for fast stylization. arXiv preprint arXiv:1607.08022 (2016)
23. Liu, Z., Lin, Y., Cao, Y., et al.: Swin transformer: hierarchical vision transformer using shifted windows. In: ICCV, pp. 9992–10002 (2021)
24. Kingma, D.P., Ba, J.: Adam: a method for stochastic optimization. arXiv preprint arXiv:1412.6980 (2014)

Inscription-Image Inpainting with Edge Structure Reconstruction

Haonan Liu, Xuelei He, Jiaxin Zhu, and Xiaowei He[✉]

Xi'an Key Lab of Radiomics and Intelligent Perception, School of Information
Sciences and Technology, Northwest University, Xi'an, Shaanxi, China
hexw@nwu.edu.cn

Abstract. Textual relics are particularly crucial for understanding history because they provide written records of past societies and their development. However, inscriptions and calligraphy works are susceptible to varying degrees of pollution or damage, which can cause the characters to be blurry, unclear, or even partially missing, thereby affects the recorded information. Compared with natural images, handwritten ancient inscription images have higher similarity, obvious structural features, clear edges, and explicit semantics. Image restoration techniques have made significant progress, but in textual images areas, they often lack an understanding of the overall structure of the characters and the standardization of stroke details, which can result in unsatisfactory restoration results. An inscription-image inpainting method has been proposed for the automated restoration of damaged inscriptions based on edge detection module and generative adversarial networks, taking into account the characteristics of ancient Chinese inscriptions. The edge detection module used to collect the edge information of the characters' strokes and lead the network to learn the structure and semantics of the characters. Moreover, a perceptual loss is adopted to enhance the detailed information of features which help to restore characters' details. A dataset of ancient inscriptions was created from publication, and experiments on this dataset showed that our method has better restoration quality than common natural image restoration methods.

Keywords: Digitization of ancient inscription · Image inpainting · Edge detection · Text restoration

1 Introduction

Among the numerous existing cultural relics, textual artifacts are particularly crucial for understanding history. Writing has recorded thousands of years of human civilization and history, playing a key role in the inheritance and development of civilization. However, with the passage of time, some inscriptions and paintings have suffered varying degrees of damage during the process of transmission, such as aging, dampness, stains, animal bites, erosion by wind and rain, and human damage. These factors have made the characters blurry, unclear, or even

© The Author(s), under exclusive license to Springer Nature Switzerland AG 2023
H. Lu et al. (Eds.): ICIG 2023, LNCS 14357, pp. 16–27, 2023.
https://doi.org/10.1007/978-3-031-46311-2_2

partially missing. Traditional manual restoration methods for these artifacts are not only complicated and time-consuming, but also require scarce professionals with historical and restoration knowledge to complete, which are prone to errors. In recent years, with the rapid development of artificial intelligence and image technology, restoration of damaged cultural relics can be completed on digital images after digitization of cultural relics information. Therefore, how to use the latest technological means to digitize and restore these damaged images is of great significance. Traditional image inpainting methods mainly include patch-based methods [3,19] and diffusion-based methods [11,22]. The diffusion-based image restoration mainly involves gradually spreading the pixel information around the damaged area in the image, synthesizing new textures to fill the missing parts. This method is difficult to learn from distant information and restore semantical texture structures in the missing area. Patch-based image restoration assumes that the damaged area of the image has similar content to the visible area. It searches for the most matching patch in the visible area, and copies the information to fill the missing area. However, when the damaged area of the image is a completely independent small entity or an unstructured partial damage, patch-based methods may become difficult to handle. In the field of traditional methods for text image restoration, Hamza H et al. [6] focus their discussion on the use of Self Organizing maps (SOM) for this project. Bannigidad P et al. [1] proposed a new novel approach for restoration of degraded Kannada handwritten paper inscription (hastaprati) using the combination of special local and global binarization techniques, by eliminating of non-uniformly illuminated background.

Deep learning-based image restoration technology has become the mainstream image restoration algorithm because it can learn and extract image features through deep convolutional neural networks, as well as learn prior knowledge of images. It has achieved remarkable results in restoring natural images. Compared with natural images, ancient inscriptions have several obvious characteristics: Firstly, the part of the character image that contains actual semantic information is relatively small, and there is often a large amount of useless background in the image. Only the middle character information part needs to be focused on. Secondly, the structure of the character image is clear and relatively fixed, and there is clear semantic differentiation between different characters. Therefore, the restored result must maximize the restoration of the original character structure, and the details of the strokes should be as clear and precise as possible. Unlike natural images, which sometimes need to restore multiple results, the restoration of character images has only one correct solution. To sum up, it is a very meaningful research topic to explore character structural repair based on deep learning and improve the accuracy of character image inpainting. Duan et al. [24] proposed a character image irregular interference restore method based on partial convolution to address the problem of misreading caused by irregular interference and page adhesion in text. a generative adversarial networks with dual discriminator (D2GAN) is designed by Chen et al. [20] to restore missing part in ancient Yi characters. Zhang et al. [27] designed a stone inscription image denoising model based on multiscale feature fusion and introduced Charbonnier loss function to improve this image denoising model. Su et al. [2] proposed a method for repairing ancient books based on a dual generative adversarial network, which can repair damaged characters to a certain extent while restoring textures. In addition, they proposed a sample based method for restoring ancient texts. Zheng et al. [23] Inspired by human's imitation writing behavior, proposed a two-branch structure character restoration network EA-GAN (Example Attention Generative Adversarial Network), which fuses reference examples. By referring to the features of the example character, the damaged character can be restored accurately even when the damaged area is large.

The above method has achieved good results in repairing standard text. However, the ancient inscriptions targeted in this article still have characteristics such as diverse character types, different writing styles for the same character, and irregular structures compared to standard Chinese characters, making it difficult to include all character categories in the dataset and unable to use standard examples as prior knowledge to guide model training. This presents new challenges to text restoration.

In this article, we designed an algorithm and model structure based on the characteristics of Chinese ancient inscriptions and proposed a ancient inscription image restoration algorithm based on edge detection and generative adversarial networks. In order to complete the missing structural features of the characters and restore the overall structure of the characters, we added an image edge information acquisition module to collect the stroke edge information of the characters to assist the network in learning the structure and semantics of the characters. To make the repaired characters details clear and recognizable, we used perceptual loss to enhance the detail information of the output features. We created a dataset of ancient inscriptions and conducted experiments on this dataset, which showed that our method has better repair quality compared to currently common inpainting method.

2   Related Work

With the maturity of research on artificial intelligence and image processing, restoration algorithms based on deep learning models are constantly being proposed. D. Pathak et al. first proposed the Context Encoder [17], a network model trained to repair missing pixels in images. Since then, people have continuously improved upon this method to enhance the quality of image restoration. To reduce the area of blurred regions, Iizuka et al. [8] proposed a method that reduces the number of downsampling layers and replaces fully connected layers with dilated convolution layers. Additionally, this method introduces an additional local discriminator constraint to ensure local consistency in the restored image. Liu et al. [13] proposed a Partial Convolution method that effectively addresses texture blur and inconsistency problems. Yu et al. [25] proposed a texture attention-based restoration method that can finely restore the texture of damaged areas. The first stage uses dilated convolutions and reconstruction loss for coarse repair, while the second stage introduces a Contextual Attention Layer in the network, which uses features surrounding the image to enhance the texture details of the damaged area. Liu et al. [15] also perform rough repairs in the first stage, and in the second stage, they embed a Coherent Semantic Attention mechanism in the decoder layer of the Unet [18] architecture network while using the VGG [21] network to minimize feature differences in the image background for optimized output. Yu et al. [26] proposed dynamically updating gated convolutions to replace partial convolutions, improving the rationality of updating damaged window regions and solving the problem of non-backward propagation in hard updates of partial convolutions. Liu et al. [14] proposed a mutually-encoded decoder for joint restoration, using the deep and shallow convolutional neural network features of the encoder to respectively represent the structure and texture of the input image. Nazeri et al. [16] were inspired by the working style of artists:'lines first, color next', and proposed a two-stage adversarial model, EdgeConnect, which includes an edge generator followed by an image completion network. The edge generator generates edges of the missing area of the image, and then the image completion network fills in the image with the edges as a prior. Liao et al. [12] introduced a consistency prior between semantics and texture to increase the texture constraints of restoration. They modeled the prior and then performed corresponding interleaved optimization of image restoration and semantic segmentation from coarse to fine, effectively alleviating texture confusion. Hui et al. [7] proposed a Dense Multi-scale Fusion Network (DMFN) for fine-grained image restoration, which adds a new multi-scale fusion module to the generator to obtain larger and more effective receptive fields through dense combinations of dilated convolutions, combining self-guided regression loss functions and geometric constraint terms to enhance the semantic details of images and obtain more reasonable semantic spatial locations, significantly improving the quality of generated images. Guo et al. [5] proposed a new dual-stream network for image restoration, dividing image restoration into two sub-tasks: texture synthesis and structural reconstruction, so that they can better leverage each other to generate more reasonable images.

These methods mentioned above mostly utilize networks such as GAN [4]. The concept of GAN was proposed by Ian Goodfellow in 2014 and since then, various variants have emerged and been applied in various fields related to artificial intelligence. For example, Isola P [9] proposed PatchGAN, whose discriminator uses convolution to map the input to an N × N matrix instead of fully connected layers. Each element in the matrix represents the discrimination of a local region (i.e., patch) in the original image. Xij represents the probability that each patch is a true sample, the final output of the discriminator is obtained by averaging Xij. This ensures that the discriminator focuses more on the structural details of each local region.

The inscription image inpainting model in this paper is designed based on the GAN network structure.

3   Inscription-Image Inpainting with Edge Structure Reconstruction

3.1   Network Model

Our inpainting method adopts the complete model architecture of rough and refined networks, which use encoder-decoder networks and generative adversarial networks as the fundamental structures. Figure 1 shows the complete framework of the network.

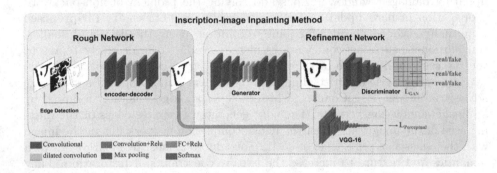

Fig. 1. Overview of our framework

The input of the coarse network is a Inscription image I with irregularly shaped holes, along with the corresponding edge image I-edge obtained using edge detection algorithms and a mask M that identifies the missing pixel locations. Due to the high randomness in the number, position, and shape of the irregular holes, simply inputting the missing image I can easily cause the generator to confuse the holes and background noise within the character itself with the actual parts that need to be repaired. Therefore, I-edge and M are used as auxiliary conditional information and input into the network. Here, I has a size of 512×512, I-edge is a binary image that corresponds to the text shape edges in I, and M is a single-channel binary mask with the same width and height as I. The value of each pixel on M is 0 or 1, which corresponds to either a complete or a missing pixel in the image. M is concatenated with I and I-edge in the channel dimension to form a 4-channel [I, M] and [I-edge, M], which are input into the encoder-decoder to output the repair results I-rough. I-rough is then concatenated with M to form [I-rough, M] and input into the generator of the refinement network to obtain the repaired image I-inpaint $=$ G([I-rough, M]). The input of the discriminator D is the repaired image I-inpaint and the corresponding complete image I-gt, where D scores both of them separately in an attempt to distinguish between the two.

The refinement network is a GAN-based structure that uses adversarial loss to optimize the overall repair capability of the network. Usually, the last layer of the discriminator in a GAN network is a fully connected layer that can only give the probability (a number between 0 and 1) of the entire repaired image being true or false. However, due to the particularity of inscription images, where there are fewer semantically meaningful parts and the background noise is large and has the same color as the hole, using the entire image for true or false discrimination can easily lead to a higher probability of being true and cause the network to prematurely overfit, which affects the repair accuracy. To ensure local consistency in inscription images, this paper chooses to use a PatchGAN structure as the discriminator instead of a traditional discriminator.

3.2   Loss

In our method, the loss function consists of three parts: Gan loss, reconstruction loss and perceptual loss.

Reconstruction Loss. The adversarial loss guides the generator to produce reasonable restoration results to deceive the discriminator, while the reconstruction loss guides the generator to produce restoration results that are closer to the ground truth image. In this paper, we adopt the SmoothL1Loss, which combines the advantages of both L2 loss and L1 loss. Regardless of the difference between the predicted value and the ground truth, the gradient can be kept stable in a small state:

$$L(x,y) = \frac{1}{n}\sum_{i=1}^{n}\begin{cases} 0.5 * (y_i - f(x_i))^2, \ if \ |y_i - f(x_i)| < 1 \\ |y_i - f(x_i)| - 0.5, \ otherwise \end{cases} \tag{1}$$

Perceptual Loss. In general, character images have high similarity, and the difference between different characters is reflected in the details of strokes. In other words, character images have a relatively consistent style. To improve the restoration accuracy of ancient inscriptions, it is necessary to measure the differences between high-dimensional features and maintain the consistency between the restored character and the original character in high-dimensional features. The perceptual loss [10], which is commonly used in the field of style transfer research, is suitable for measuring the restoration effect of character images with consistent styles. The perceptual loss uses a pre-trained network (usually VGG) to extract features output from different layers and calculate the feature loss between corresponding layers:

$$L_{feat}^{\phi,j}(\hat{y},y) = \frac{1}{C_j H_j W_j}\|\phi_j(\hat{y}) - \phi_j(y)\|_2^2 \tag{2}$$

where j represents the jth layer of the network, and Cj, Hj, and Wj represent the number of channels and width height of the jth layer, ϕ For the loss network. Our method adopts a pretrained VGG16 network. Extract the output features from each convolutional layer of the original image and the output image in the VGG16 network, and construct perceptual loss. Finally, the complete loss function of our method consists of the weighted sum of Gan loss, reconstruction loss and perceptual loss:

$$L = \lambda_1 L_{GAN} + \lambda_2 L_{SmoothL1} + \lambda_3 L_{perceptual} \tag{3}$$

4   Experiments

4.1   Dataset

Currently, there are few research studies on the restoration of ancient Chinese inscriptions or even characters image restoration worldwide. The mainstream text datasets are mainly used in the field of text recognition, and the languages are mainly English and Latin letters. There are few Chinese language datasets, and there is no recognized standard dataset. Therefore, we constructed a dataset of ancient inscriptions and conducted experiments based on it. The inscriptions dataset we built contains more than 21,000 single-character images, which were photographed and scanned from the book "Jin Wen Bian" published by Zhonghua Book Company. We marked and segmented different characters in each page using text boxes, and then performed preprocessing such as binarization and resizing each character image to 512 × 512.

The irregular mask-covered image dataset used in our study was NVIDIA's Irregular Mask Dataset: Testing Set, which is the most widely used mask dataset in the field of image restoration. These two datasets were combined to form the damaged inscription image to be restored.

4.2   Experimental Procedure

The model was implemented using the Pytorch framework. The input images to the network were all 512 × 512, and the model was trained for 60 epochs with a learning rate of 2e–4, batch size of 1, and loss function coefficients λgan, λsl1, λpl of 1, 100, and 10 respectively. The entire network was trained using the dataset mentioned in 4.1, with 6000 images used as the training set. The generator G was first fixed, and the discriminator D was optimized to maximize its discrimination accuracy. Then, the discriminator D was fixed, and the generator G was optimized to generate fake data G(z) that mimicked the real data x such that the discriminator D could not correctly identify the data source. These two steps were repeated alternately to train both the discriminator and the generator, gradually improving their performance. Once the discriminator's discrimination ability reached a certain level and could not correctly identify the data source, it was considered that the generator G had learned the distribution of real data, and the final Generative Adversarial Network (GAN) model was obtained.

5   Experimental Results and Analysis

The experiments were conducted on the inscription dataset mentioned in 4.1. To explore the restoration effect of the proposed method under different damaged areas, the test images were divided into five categories based on the percentage of the damaged area in the core glyph area (not the entire image), namely 0–15%, 15–30%, 30–45%, 45–60%, and above 60%, and the proposed method was compared with the existing image restoration methods such as CA (context attention) [19], MED (mutual encoder-decoder) [24], EC (edge connect) [25], and GC (gated convolution) [23]. The experimental results demonstrated that the proposed method could achieve better restoration results and outperform existing restoration methods in terms of SSIM [31] and PSNR indicators.

5.1 Comparative Experiments

In the following comparative experiments, our method is compared with four other mainstream image inpainting methods: CA (context attention), MED (mutual encoder-decoder), EC (edge connect), and GC (gated convolution). The experiments aim to prove the superiority of our proposed method from two aspects: qualitative comparison and quantitative analysis.

Figure 2 shows the experimental results of our proposed method and the other four methods on the inscription dataset. The columns in Fig. 2 from left to right are the real image (GT), the input damaged inscription image (Input), the inpainting results of the MED, CA, GC, and EC models, and the inpainting results of our method (Ours).

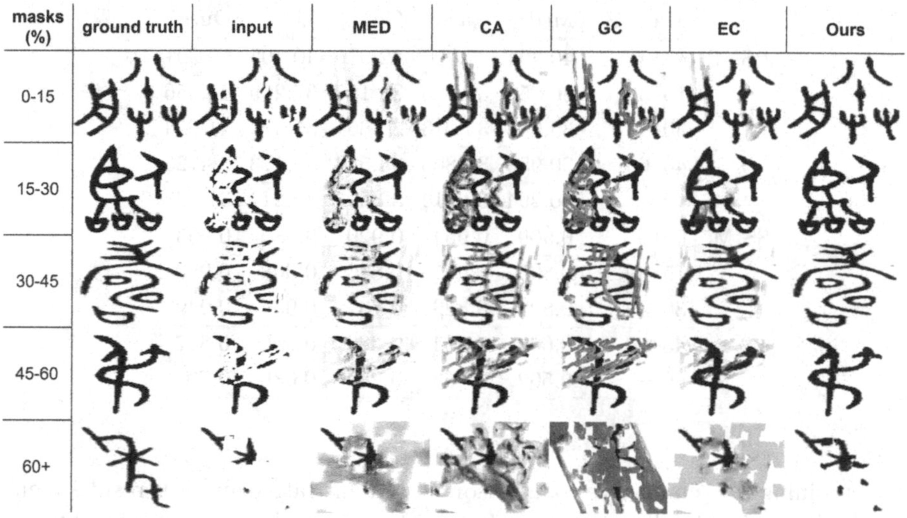

Fig. 2. Example cases of qualitative comparison

Visually, the restored local areas of the first three inpainting methods have inconsistent colors and textures with the surrounding areas, and the restored area details of EC are blurred, all having significant differences from the original image. In comparison, our method achieved better restoration results, with higher consistency in both structure and texture details with the original image. Besides, The results show that our method can correctly restore the damaged area and make the character recognizable when the glyph structure is intact. However, when the damaged area gradually increases until the main structure of the inscription is severely damaged, the repair effect of our method becomes less ideal, possibly because when the image area is severely damaged, the effective information around the damaged area is too sparse, and the model cannot accurately infer the semantics of these pixels, resulting in a lack of reliable basis for repairing missing pixels.

In addition to the qualitative analysis of the restoration results, this experiment also used two commonly used evaluation metrics in the image inpainting field, PSNR (peak signal to noise ratio) and SSIM (structural similarity), for quantitative analysis. The larger the values of these metrics, the better the restoration effect and similarity with the original image. The results are shown in Table 1. From the data in the table, it can be seen that both metrics of this paper's method outperform other algorithms under different levels of damage, which also to some extent reflects the effectiveness of this method.

Table 1. Comparison of different approaches including MED (mutual encoder-decoder), CA (context attention), GC (gated convolution), EC (edge connect) and our approach.

	Mask(%)	Med	Ca	Gc	Ec	Ours
PSNR	0–15	40.404	37.707	42.070	40.405	50.391
	15–30	36.859	35.215	38.157	37.269	43.056
	30–45	35.042	34.013	36.651	35.479	41.054
	45–60	30.953	30.805	33.524	31.123	38.125
	60+	30.294	30.214	32.995	30.214	37.328
SSIM	0–15	0.969	0.954	0.920	0.982	0.995
	15–30	0.895	0.905	0.840	0.968	0.980
	30–45	0.822	0.829	0.732	0.934	0.949
	45–60	0.669	0.564	0.382	0.796	0.827
	60+	0.569	0.463	0.284	0.636	0.704

Combining the qualitative comparison and quantitative analysis results mentioned above, it is fully demonstrated that our method is superior to the other four mainstream natural image inpainting method in restoring ancient inscriptions.

5.2   Ablation Study

To demonstrate the effectiveness of our method in improving the inpainting performance, this section conducts corresponding ablation experiments, which test the restoration results and evaluation metrics of the model under two conditions: without using character edges as priors and without adding perceptual loss. The visual results and evaluation metrics are shown in Fig. 3 and Table 2 respectively. From the experimental results, it can be observed that adding either character edges or perceptual loss alone can improve the restoration quality to some extent, while adding both can achieve even better performance.

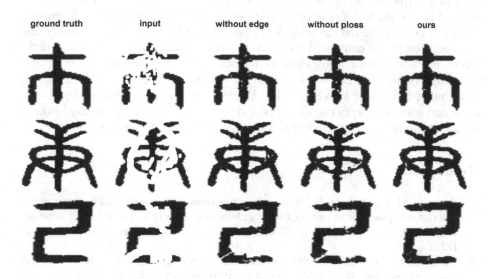

Fig. 3. Example cases of ablation study

Table 2. Quantitative ablation study

	Mask(%)	Without edge	Without perceptual loss	Ours
PSNR	0–15	48.520	47.707	50.391
	15–30	42.894	42.631	43.056
	30–45	40.121	40.596	41.054
	45–60	38.301	37.886	38.125
	60+	38.407	37.031	37.328
SSIM	0–15	0.902	0.944	0.995
	15–30	0.859	0.946	0.980
	30–45	0.770	0.908	0.949
	45–60	0.623	0.792	0.827
	60+	0.441	0.667	0.704

6   Conclusions

This paper proposes an ancient inscriptions image inpainting method based on edge detection and generative adversarial networks for the specific characteristics of ancient inscriptions, such as structural similarity, clear edges, and explicit semantics. This method is a deep exploration based on existing natural image inpainting methods and is improved based on the problems encountered in inscription image inpainting. By learning the edge contours and structural features of inscription images to restore damaged areas, a complete and correct ancient inscriptions image is obtained. By adding reconstruction loss and perceptual loss to the GAN, the restoration accuracy of the generator is improved, resulting in accurate details and clear edges in the restored image. Finally, the proposed method is compared with several mainstream image inpainting methods on a self-built ancient inscriptions dataset. The experiment results show that the proposed method has better visual effects and outperforms other methods in terms of SSIM and PSNR metrics. However, when the damaged area is too large and severely affects the inscription structure, the proposed method cannot guarantee good restoration results. This will be our future research direction.

References

1. Bannigidad, P., Gudada, C.: Restoration of degraded kannada handwritten paper inscriptions (hastaprati) using image enhancement techniques. In: 2017 International Conference on Computer Communication and Informatics (ICCCI), pp. 1–6. IEEE (2017)
2. Benpeng, S., Xuxing, L., Weize, G., Ye, Y., Shanxiong, C.: Restoration of ancient Chinese characters using dual generative adversarial networks. Vis. Inf. 6(1), 26–34 (2022)
3. Fan, Q., Zhang, L.: A novel patch matching algorithm for exemplar-based image inpainting. Multimedia Tools Appl. 77, 10807–10821 (2018)
4. Goodfellow, I., et al.: Generative adversarial networks. Commun. ACM 63(11), 139–144 (2020)
5. Guo, X., Yang, H., Huang, D.: Image inpainting via conditional texture and structure dual generation. In: Proceedings of the IEEE/CVF International Conference on Computer Vision, pp. 14134–14143 (2021)
6. Hamza, H.: Segmentation and restoration of images of old books (2004)
7. Hui, Z., Li, J., Wang, X., Gao, X.: Image fine-grained inpainting. arXiv preprint arXiv:2002.02609 (2020)
8. Iizuka, S., Simo-Serra, E., Ishikawa, H.: Globally and locally consistent image completion. ACM Trans. Graph. (ToG) 36(4), 1–14 (2017)
9. Isola, P., Zhu, J.Y., Zhou, T., Efros, A.A.: Image-to-image translation with conditional adversarial networks. In: Proceedings of the IEEE Conference on Computer Vision and Pattern Recognition, pp. 1125–1134 (2017)
10. Johnson, Justin, Alahi, Alexandre, Fei-Fei, Li.: Perceptual losses for real-time style transfer and super-resolution. In: Leibe, Bastian, Matas, Jiri, Sebe, Nicu, Welling, Max (eds.) ECCV 2016. LNCS, vol. 9906, pp. 694–711. Springer, Cham (2016). https://doi.org/10.1007/978-3-319-46475-6_43
11. Li, K., Wei, Y., Yang, Z., Wei, W.: Image inpainting algorithm based on tv model and evolutionary algorithm. Soft. Comput. 20, 885–893 (2016)
12. Liao, L., Xiao, J., Wang, Z., Lin, C.W., Satoh, S.: Image inpainting guided by coherence priors of semantics and textures. In: Proceedings of the IEEE/CVF conference on computer vision and pattern recognition. pp. 6539–6548 (2021)

13. Liu, G., Reda, F.A., Shih, K.J., Wang, T.C., Tao, A., Catanzaro, B.: Image inpainting for irregular holes using partial convolutions. In: Proceedings of the European conference on computer vision (ECCV). pp. 85–100 (2018)
14. Liu, H., Jiang, B., Song, Y., Huang, W., Yang, C.: Rethinking image inpainting via a mutual encoder-decoder with feature equalizations. In: Computer Vision-ECCV 2020: 16th European Conference, Glasgow, UK, August 23–28, 2020, Proceedings, Part II 16. pp. 725–741. Springer (2020)
15. Liu, H., Jiang, B., Xiao, Y., Yang, C.: Coherent semantic attention for image inpainting. In: Proceedings of the IEEE/CVF International Conference on Computer Vision. pp. 4170–4179 (2019)
16. Nazeri, K., Ng, E., Joseph, T., Qureshi, F.Z., Ebrahimi, M.: Edgeconnect: Generative image inpainting with adversarial edge learning. arXiv preprint arXiv:1901.00212 (2019)
17. Pathak, D., Krahenbuhl, P., Donahue, J., Darrell, T., Efros, A.A.: Context encoders: Feature learning by inpainting. In: Proceedings of the IEEE conference on computer vision and pattern recognition. pp. 2536–2544 (2016)
18. Ronneberger, O., Fischer, P., Brox, T.: U-net: Convolutional networks for biomedical image segmentation. In: Medical Image Computing and Computer-Assisted Intervention-MICCAI 2015: 18th International Conference, Munich, Germany, October 5–9, 2015, Proceedings, Part III 18. pp. 234–241. Springer (2015)
19. Ružić, T., Pižurica, A.: Context-aware patch-based image inpainting using markov random field modeling. IEEE Trans. Image Process. **24**(1), 444–456 (2014)
20. Shanxiong, C., Shiyu, Z., Hailing, X., Fujia, Z., Dingwang, W., Yun, L.: A double discriminator gan restoration method for ancient yi characters. Acta Automatica Sinica **48**(03), 853–864 (2014)
21. Simonyan, K., Zisserman, A.: Very deep convolutional networks for large-scale image recognition. arXiv preprint arXiv:1409.1556 (2014)
22. Sridevi, G., Srinivas Kumar, S.: Image inpainting based on fractional-order nonlinear diffusion for image reconstruction. Circuits Systems Signal Process. **38**, 3802–3817 (2019)
23. Wenjun, Z., Benpeng, S., Ruiqi, F., Xihua, P., Shanxiong, C.: Ea-gan: restoration of text in ancient chinese books based on an example attention generative adversarial network. Heritage Science **11**(1), 1–13 (2023)
24. Ying, D., Hua, L., Yuquan, Q., Qingzhi, D.: Research on irregular interference restoration algorithm for text image based on partial convolution. Computer Engineering and Science **43**(09), 1634–1644 (2014)
25. Yu, J., Lin, Z., Yang, J., Shen, X., Lu, X., Huang, T.S.: Generative image inpainting with contextual attention. In: Proceedings of the IEEE conference on computer vision and pattern recognition. pp. 5505–5514 (2018)
26. Yu, J., Lin, Z., Yang, J., Shen, X., Lu, X., Huang, T.S.: Free-form image inpainting with gated convolution. In: Proceedings of the IEEE/CVF international conference on computer vision. pp. 4471–4480 (2019)
27. Zhang, H., Qi, Y., Xue, X., Nan, Y.: Ancient stone inscription image denoising and inpainting methods based on deep neural networks. Discret. Dyn. Nat. Soc. **2021**, 1–11 (2021)

RatiO R-CNN: An Efficient and Accurate Detection Method for Oriented Object Detection

Chengdao Pu[1], Liuxue Ju[1], Fang Gao[2], and Jun Yu[1(✉)]

[1] University of Science and Technology of China, Hefei, China
{puchengdao,juliuxuet}@mail.ustc.edu.cn, harryjun@ustc.edu.cn
[2] Guangxi University, Nanning, China
fgao@gxu.edu.cn

Abstract. In recent years, oriented object detection has attracted much attention as an emerging branch of computer vision. Compared with objects in natural images, the oriented objects are distributed in any direction, and their ground truth bounding boxes have an extensive range of aspect ratios. In this paper, we propose a two-stage oriented object detection framework called RatiO R-CNN, which has good accuracy and efficiency on oriented object detection datasets. Specifically, we used a new anchor box generation method, RotateGA, to adapt to the characteristics of oriented detection datasets. We design a length ratio loss function to solve the deformation problem of the predicted boxes obtained by regression so that we can generate oriented proposals efficiently and accurately in the RPN phase. In the second stage, we propose a dynamic-oriented R-CNN head, which adjusts the IoU threshold and regression loss during the training process by adapting to the quality of the samples. Our model achieved the best results on the DOTA v1.0 dataset (77.82%mAP50, 49.44%mAP75), proving the validity of our model.

Keywords: Object Detection · Oriented Object · Aerial Images

1 Introduction

Oriented object detection, as a branch of object detection tasks, has recently received increasing attention. Compared with the datasets used for conventional object detection recognition, typical oriented-object datasets such as aerial object detection datasets have an extensive range of target aspect ratios and a precise orientation.

Unlike the standard horizontal object detection model that uses horizontal bounding boxes, the oriented object detector uses oriented bounding boxes with rotation angles to locate and classify targets. As shown in Fig. 1, this approach can effectively overcome the problem of overlapping detection boxes and more accurately label the location of oriented targets. Most existing advanced oriented object detection methods are divided into three main ideas: one-stage detection, two-stage detection, and anchor-free detection.

© The Author(s), under exclusive license to Springer Nature Switzerland AG 2023
H. Lu et al. (Eds.): ICIG 2023, LNCS 14357, pp. 28–40, 2023.
https://doi.org/10.1007/978-3-031-46311-2_3

Fig. 1. Horizontal bounding boxes versus oriented bounding boxes for the same aerial image. For densely arranged targets with orientation, the horizontal detection method has problems such as overlapping detection boxes.

The current application of oriented object detection has put forward higher and higher requirements for the detection boxes and ground truth boxes' IoU accuracy. The existing detectors need to be improved for this, and there is room for improvement in the mAP75 index that reflects the higher-order accuracy. In order to solve this problem, we studied the reasons for the poor performance of the existing region-proposals-based oriented detectors in terms of higher-order accuracy.

Due to the wide range of oriented object aspect ratios and the representation of oriented bounding boxes, the IoU of targets with large aspect ratios is easily affected by angular variations. After RROI Align, it affects the accuracy of the second-stage prediction. Therefore, the quality of the proposal output from the RPN network in the first stage significantly impacts the final detection results, and no model yet focuses on this point. In the second stage training process, the quality of the input oriented proposals is continuously optimized with the training process; and the number of positive samples is also increasing. The fixed IoU threshold can not balance the number of positive samples in the early stages of training with the quality of positive samples in the later stages of training, resulting in less-than-perfect model accuracy.

Based on the above shortcomings, we propose RatiO R-CNN, an oriented object two-stage detection framework, with the following main contributions.

- In the RPN stage, in order to improve the fitting ability of anchor boxes to oriented object datasets, we propose RotateGA to replace the currently most widely used sliding window anchor box generation method. For the model that encodes oriented boxes as parameter offsets for regression to obtain oriented proposals, we design ratio loss, to address the problems in converting oriented proposals.
- We propose a dynamic oriented R-CNN head in the second stage of the model. After extracting the oriented proposal generated in the RPN stage by RRoI Align, the oriented dynamic R-CNN head continuously adjusts the IoU threshold and the shape of the loss function dynamically according to the quality of the proposals. In this way, the classifier and the regressor in the second stage can adapt to the changes in the distribution of candidate boxes.

– Combining the above improvement modules, we propose the RatiO R-CNN, which exhibits advanced performance on the DOTA dataset. Experiments prove that our model plays a good role in oriented object detection in high-precision scenes.

2 Related Work

Oriented object detection has received much attention as a branch of object detection. There is an inconsistency between the final classification confidence and localization accuracy of traditional detection models that rely on horizontal boxes. To solve this problem, existing oriented target detection models replace the horizontal bounding box with an oriented bounding box that contains an offset angle parameter [2].

The proposal-based two-stage object detection framework is the mainstream of existing oriented object detectors. RRPN [11] applies a simple idea for oriented proposal generation, i.e., generating a large number of pre-defined rotated anchor boxes with different scales, aspect ratios, and angles for each anchor point. The oriented boxes are effectively detected. In contrast, the large number of anchor boxes generated leads to slow detection and wasted computational resources.

In order to obtain high-quality rotational ROIs with a small number of anchor boxes, Ding et al. proposed RoI Transformer [2]. The main idea of RoI Trans is to abandon the complex and expensive direct generation of rotational RoIs, and first generate low-cost horizontal RoIs by traditional RoI generation, and then learn rotational RoIs from the horizontal RoIs generated by RPN network through a fully connected layer. ReDet's [5] approach is to introduce rotation invariance in the feature extraction stage and can extract completely rotation invariant features. Oriented R-CNN [17] generates an approximate rotated frame by giving a new way of encoding the rotated frame, which significantly reduces the cost of RPN network to generate proposals. However, since the predicted vector is not necessarily a rectangle after decoding, it needs to be directly stretched to become a rectangle proposal. This will produce some unavoidable loss of accuracy in angle and scale with the ground truth box.

3 RatiO R-CNN

To address the current problems in oriented object detection, we propose RatiO R-CNN. The specific structure of the model is shown in Fig. 2(a). The model consists of two stages: RatiO-RPN and dynamic oriented R-CNN head. The input images is first passed through the backbone with FPN [9], and five levels of features $\{P2, P3, P4, P5, P6\}$ are extracted. The RPN stage of the model outputs oriented proposals efficiently and accurately with the extracted feature map and the pre-defined anchor boxes as inputs. In the second stage, we use a dynamic oriented R-CNN head with dynamic hyperparameters to classify and regress the proposals output in the first stage more finely. In the following, we describe our model in detail.

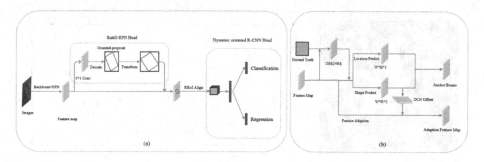

Fig. 2. (a) The specific process of RatiO R-CNN. (b) Schematic diagram of the structure of RotateGA.

3.1 RotateGA

To make the generation of level anchor boxes more suitable for the characteristics of rotated targets, we proposes a anchor box generation network called RotateGA for rotated object detection, based on the existing anchor box generation method Guided Anchoring [15] in horizontal object detection. It is used to generate anchor boxes suitable for rotated object datasets, and to better match the feature extraction of the feature map with the anchor boxes generated by the network. As shown in Fig. 2(b), the module determines the position of the generated anchor box by predicting the probability for each position on the feature map, and performs anchor box shape regression for the corresponding position to obtain the required anchor box. In order to ensure the consistency of the anchor boxes, the module introduces a feature adaptive module.

3.2 RatiO-RPN

In the original R-CNN model, four parameters (x, y, w, h) are used for the representation of a horizontal proposal. To generate oriented proposals, many existing models provide different approaches. We first give the representation of the oriented bounding boxes used by our model.

The Representation of Oriented Bounding Boxes. We use a representation scheme of oriented objects that uses external rectangular boxes with offsets to encode and decode oriented bounding boxes. As shown in Fig. 3(a), for an oriented bounding box, we encode it as $(x, y, w, h, \Delta\alpha, \Delta\beta)$. (x, y) is its centroid coordinate, w and h are the width and height of its external horizontal box, $\Delta\alpha$ is the horizontal coordinate of its topmost vertex v_2 offset from x, and $\Delta\beta$ is the vertical coordinate of its rightmost vertex v_3 offset from y.

Thus, we can encode and decode oriented objects. This way, we can obtain the oriented bounding boxes by directly regressing the offset, which greatly reduces the cost of prediction box generation.

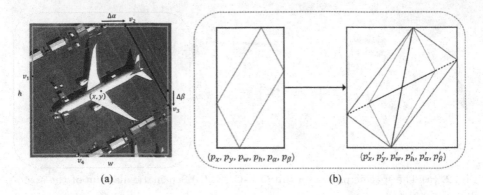

Fig. 3. (a) The representation of oriented bounding boxes. (b) The process of converting oriented proposals to rectangles.

RatiO RPN Network. The classification branch of the RatiO RPN network is similar to the Faster R-CNN, in which we only perform a binary prediction of whether or not the anchor box includes an oriented object. For our input feature maps, the classification network outputs predicted foreground and background scores for each anchor box. The regression branch of the RPN network outputs offsets $P(p_x, p_y, p_w, p_h, p_\alpha, p_\beta)$ for each anchor box. According to our encoder, we decode this anchor box with the corresponding offset to generate a predictive oriented proposal for this anchor frame at the current scale of features.

$$\begin{cases} \Delta\alpha_p = p_\alpha \cdot w_p, \Delta\beta_p = p_\beta \cdot h_p \\ w_p = w_a \cdot e^{p_w}, h_p = h_a \cdot e^{p_h} \\ x_p = p_x \cdot w_a + x_a, y_p = p_y \cdot h_a + y_a \end{cases} \quad (1)$$

In Eq. 1, the decoded $(x_p, y_p, w_p, h_p, \Delta\alpha_p, \Delta\beta_p)$ defines an oriented bounding box. The classification phase of RatiO-RPN is similar to the original faster R-CNN. Another convolutional layer trains it by evaluating the fore-and-aft view scores of each oriented bounding box, which is not shown here.

Lossfunction. In the training phase of RatiO RPN, we assign a label to each anchor box, with 0 as a negative sample and 1 as a positive sample. We assign labels to samples using the same approach as Faster R-CNN, with thresholds of 0.7 and 0.3.

In the RPN phase, we expect to improve the quality of the output oriented proposals by training the regression network; however, the oriented proposals regressed by offset have a problem: its shape is a parallelogram with high probability. As shown in Fig. 3(b), to perform the RROI Align operation, we need to transform it into a rectangle by stretching its shorter diagonal until the two diagonals are equal. This operation will result in the encoding $P(p_x, p_y, p_w, p_h, p_\alpha, p_\beta)$ obtained from the regression not corresponding to the actual output of the oriented proposal, leading to inadequate training of the regression network. Also, since the rotation angle of oriented proposals is defined as the angle between its longer side and the x-axis, direct stretching will enormously impact the rotation angle, which will affect the quality of the positive and negative samples for the second stage of training.

We propose a new loss function to solve the problem of accuracy loss. As shown in Fig. 3(b), we want the oriented proposals obtained by regression to be a rectangle as much as possible, which can reduce the accuracy loss caused by deformation. To achieve this, we introduce the loss of the aspect ratio of the external horizontal box and the loss of the diagonal length ratio in the regression loss function of the FPN stage. We expect that the regressor generates the same aspect ratio of the external frame as the aspect ratio of the horizontal ground truth, and the diagonal of the generated proposal is as equal as possible, i.e., satisfying Eq. 2 and 3.

$$\Delta\alpha_p^2 + 0.25 \cdot h_p^2 = \Delta\beta_p^2 + 0.25 \cdot w_p^2 \tag{2}$$

$$\frac{e^{g_h} \cdot h_a}{e^{g_w} \cdot w_a} = \frac{e^{p_h} \cdot h_a}{e^{p_w} \cdot w_a} \tag{3}$$

Based on the above considerations, we define the classification loss L_{cls} and the regression loss L_{reg} as shown in Eq. 4 and 5.

$$L_{cls} = \frac{1}{N} \sum_{i=1}^{N} F_{cls}(l_i, l_i^*) \tag{4}$$

$$L_{reg} = \frac{1}{N} \sum_{i=1}^{N} F_{reg}(P_i, G_i) + \frac{\lambda}{N} \sum_{i=1}^{N} F_{reg}(\lambda_i, \lambda_i^*) \tag{5}$$

In the formula, i represents the index of the anchor, and N is the total number of samples in a small batch. l_i is the output of the RatiO RPN classification branch, the probability that the oriented proposal belongs to the foreground, l_i^* is the assigned label for this anchor box. Equation 6 gives the definition of the offset encoding loss for the regression part; $G_i(g_x, g_y, g_w, g_h, g_\alpha, g_\beta)$ is the supervision offset of the ground-truth box relative to the i-th anchor, and $P_i(p_x, p_y, p_w, p_h, p_\alpha, p_\beta)$ is the vector of offset predicted by the regression network relative to the i-th anchor box. F_{cls} is the Cross-Entropy loss and F_{reg} is the Smooth L1 loss.

$$\begin{cases} p_\alpha = \Delta\alpha_p/w_p & p_\beta = \Delta\beta_p/h_p \\ p_w = log(w_p/w_a) & p_h = log(h_p/h_a) \\ p_x = (x_p/x_a)/w_a & p_y = (y_p/y_a)/h_a \\ g_\alpha = \Delta\alpha_g/w_g & g_\beta = \Delta\beta_g/h_g \\ g_w = log(w_g/w_a) & g_h = log(h_g/h_a) \\ g_x = (x_g/x_a)/w_a & g_y = (y_g/y_a)/h_a \end{cases} \tag{6}$$

We design the ratio loss for the regression part of the loss, as shown in Eq. 7. The newly introduced Smooth L1 loss between $\lambda_i(\lambda_r, \lambda_d)$ and $\lambda_i^*(\lambda_r^*, \lambda_d^*)$ makes

Eq. 2 and 3 tend to hold. The loss between λ_r and λ_r^* represents the degree of deformation of the external rectangular box. λ_d and λ_d^* are the ratios of the two diagonals of the prediction box relative to the sum of the diagonal lengths, respectively. To avoid letting the ratio loss dominate the backpropagation of the training process, we set a weight of $\lambda = 0.2$ for it after comparison experiments.

$$\begin{cases} \lambda_r = g_h - p_h, \lambda_r^* = g_w - p_w \\ d_1 = 4p_\alpha^2 \cdot w_p^2 + h_p^2 \\ d_2 = 4p_\beta^2 \cdot h_p^2 + w_p^2 \\ \lambda_d = d_1/(d_1 + d_2), \lambda_d^* = d_2/(d_1 + d_2) \end{cases} \tag{7}$$

Finally, the total loss function of the RatiO-RPN stage takes the form shown in Eq. 8. By introducing ratio loss, we can generate proposals at a lower cost while significantly improving the accuracy of providing oriented proposals in the first stage.

$$L_{total} = L_{cls} + L_{reg} \tag{8}$$

3.3   Dynamic Oriented R-CNN Head

The second stage of Ratio R-CNN takes the feature maps of the four levels $\{P2, P3, P4, P5\}$ and the oriented proposals generated by the RPN stage as input. Each proposal is converted into a fixed-size feature vector after RRoI ALIGN and then transformed by a fully connected layer. Two fully combined layers are used for category and location prediction. In the R-CNN stage, the probabilities of the category output have a total of K+1 categories, containing K example categories and background categories.

In the following, we will specify our proposed dynamic oriented R-CNN head.

Dynamic Oriented R-CNN Head. In object detection, the task of classification is annotated with ground truth bounding boxes in the image, so a certain strategy is needed to divide the samples for training the classifier. The current most popular model assigns positive and negative samples by setting some fixed thresholds on the Intersection-over-Union (IoU) of the ground truth bounding boxes and the predicted bounding boxes. However, current rotation object detection methods do not take into account both the quantity and quality of positive samples during the early and late stages of training.

To solve this problem, we introduce a dynamic oriented r-cnn head. Specifically, for the training of the classification network, we calculate the maximum IoU values for each RoI and all ground truth bounding boxes in the training phase and select the maximum 100 values on each image, take the average value as the current IoU threshold T_{now}, which is updated every 100 iterations. The specific label assignment is shown in Eq. 9. In this way, when assigning samples, we can consider both the number of positive samples in the pre-training period and the quality of positive samples in the post-training period.

$$Lable = \begin{cases} 1, if & maxIoU(b, G) \geq T_{now} \\ 0, if & maxIoU(b, G) < T_{now} \end{cases} \tag{9}$$

As shown in Eq. 10, we use the same dynamic idea to train the regression network. As the training proceeds, we continuously adjust the shape of Smooth L1 loss to accelerate the saturation of gradient magnitude by introducing dynamic β_{now}. The specific calculation process is as follows. After every 100 iterations, we calculate the regression labels E of the proposals and their target ground truth during training, select 20 minimum values from them, and use the median of them to update the β_{now}. With the newly introduced dynamic smooth l1 loss, we can improve the gradient of the loss function in the later stage of training and thus train more effectively.

$$smooth_{L1}(x, \beta_{now}) = \begin{cases} 0.5|x|^2/\beta_{now}, & if \ |x| < \beta_{now} \\ |x| - 0.5\beta_{now}, & otherwise \end{cases} \tag{10}$$

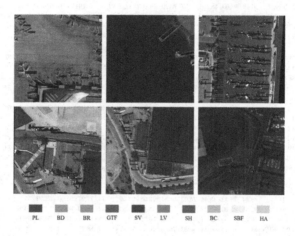

PL BD BR GTF SV LV SH BC SBF HA

Fig. 4. Examples of detection results for the DOTAv1.0 dataset generated by RatiO R-CNN. For the detection results of instances of different categories, we use different colored boxes to indicate them.

4   Experiments and Analysis

4.1   Experimental Environment and Dataset

We built our model on the MMRotate [24] platform, using a single RTX 3090 for training and inference. We used ResNet50 [6] and Swin-Tiny [10], both pretrained on ImageNet, as our backbone. To evaluate our proposed model, we conducted comprehensive experiments on the most widely used dataset in oriented object detection dataset DOTAv1.0 [16] for full-scale experiments.

The DOTA dataset is a large dataset for aerial image object detection, containing a total of 2806 aerial images, ranging in size from 800*800 to 4000*4000, with a total of 188282 annotated instances in poly format with coordinates of four vertices. The dataset contains 15 target types that are of most interest in remotely sensed images. As with the existing models, we use the trainval set for training, test on the test set, and generate test results to upload to the evaluation server on the official DOTA website for evaluation. The test uses the mean Average Precision with 0.5 IoU threshold(mAP50) and the mean Average Precision with 0.75 IoU threshold (mAP75) as the evaluation metric. Figure 4 shows some examples of detection results for the DOTAv1.0 dataset generated by RatiO R-CNN.

Table 1. Comparison with state-of-the-art methods on the DOTAv1.0 dataset. **Bolded text**: top two performances in single scale training and multi scale training.

Method	Backbone	PL	BD	BR	GTF	SV	LV	SH	TC	BC	ST	SBF	RA	HA	SP	HC	mAP50
Single Scale																	
One-Stage																	
DAL [12]	R-101-FPN	88.61	79.69	46.27	70.37	65.89	76.10	78.53	90.84	79.98	78.41	58.71	62.02	69.23	71.32	60.65	71.78
RSDet [14]	R-152-FPN	90.10	82.00	53.80	68.50	70.20	78.70	73.60	91.20	87.10	84.70	64.30	68.20	66.10	69.30	63.70	74.10
R3Det [20]	R-152-FPN	89.49	81.17	50.53	66.10	70.92	78.66	78.21	90.81	85.26	84.23	61.81	63.77	68.16	69.83	67.17	73.74
S2A-Net [4]	R-50-FPN	89.11	82.84	48.37	71.11	78.11	78.39	87.25	90.83	84.90	85.64	60.36	62.60	65.26	69.13	57.94	74.12
R3Det-DCL [19]	R-152-FPN	89.78	83.95	52.63	69.70	76.84	81.26	87.30	90.81	84.67	85.27	63.50	64.16	68.96	68.79	65.45	75.54
Anchor-Free																	
PIOU [1]	DLA-34 [?]	80.90	69.70	24.10	60.20	38.30	64.40	64.80	90.90	77.20	70.40	46.50	37.10	57.10	61.90	64.00	60.50
DRN [13]	H-104 [?]	89.71	82.34	47.22	64.10	76.22	74.43	85.84	90.57	86.18	84.89	57.65	61.93	69.30	69.63	58.48	73.23
CFA [3]	R101-FPN	89.26	81.72	51.81	67.17	79.99	78.25	84.46	90.77	83.40	85.54	54.86	67.75	73.04	70.24	64.96	75.05
Oriented RepPoints [8]	R-50-FPN	87.02	83.17	54.13	71.16	80.18	78.40	87.28	90.90	85.97	86.25	59.90	70.49	73.53	72.27	58.97	75.97
Two-Stage																	
SCRDet [21]	R-101-FPN	89.98	80.65	52.09	68.36	68.36	60.32	72.41	90.85	87.94	86.86	65.02	66.68	66.25	68.24	65.21	72.61
FAOD [7]	R-101-FPN	90.21	79.58	45.49	76.41	73.18	68.27	79.56	90.83	83.40	84.68	53.40	65.42	74.17	69.69	64.86	73.28
RoI-Trans [2]	R-101-FPN	88.65	82.60	52.53	70.87	77.93	76.67	86.87	90.71	83.83	82.51	53.95	67.61	74.67	68.75	61.03	74.61
Gliding Vertex [18]	R-101-FPN	89.64	85.00	52.26	77.34	73.01	73.14	86.82	90.74	79.02	86.81	59.55	70.91	72.94	70.86	57.32	75.02
Oriented-RCNN [17]	R-101-FPN	88.86	83.48	55.27	76.92	74.27	82.10	87.52	90.90	85.56	85.33	65.51	66.82	74.36	70.15	57.28	76.28
ReDet [5]	ReR-50-ReFPN	88.79	82.64	53.97	74.00	78.13	84.06	88.04	90.89	87.78	85.75	61.76	60.39	75.96	68.07	63.59	76.25
RatiO-RCNN(ours)	R-50-FPN	89.26	82.24	55.41	74.31	78.52	81.97	87.66	90.89	86.61	84.27	64.42	66.05	73.23	70.79	59.34	**76.33**
RatiO-RCNN(ours)	Swin-T-FPN	89.17	83.39	55.33	75.24	79.45	84.51	87.88	90.90	86.84	86.60	67.96	69.60	76.28	71.95	62.25	**77.82**
Multi Scale																	
RoI Trans	R-101-FPN	88.64	78.52	43.44	75.92	68.81	73.68	83.59	90.74	77.27	81.46	58.39	53.54	62.83	58.93	47.67	69.56
Gliding Vertex	R-101-FPN	89.64	85.00	52.26	77.34	73.01	73.14	86.82	90.74	79.02	86.81	59.55	70.91	72.94	70.86	57.32	75.02
S2A-Net	R-50-FPN	88.89	83.60	57.74	81.95	79.94	83.19	89.11	90.78	84.87	87.81	70.30	68.25	78.30	77.01	69.58	79.42
ReDet	ReR-50-ReFPN	88.81	82.48	60.83	80.82	78.34	86.06	88.31	90.87	88.77	87.03	68.65	66.90	79.26	79.71	74.67	80.10
Oriented-RCNN	R-101-FPN	90.26	84.74	62.01	80.42	79.04	85.07	88.52	90.85	87.24	87.96	72.26	70.03	82.93	78.46	68.05	80.52
KFIoU [22]-RoI Trans	Swin-T	89.44	84.41	62.22	82.51	80.10	86.07	88.68	90.90	87.32	88.38	72.80	71.95	78.96	74.95	75.27	**80.93**
RatiO-RCNN(ours)	R-50-FPN	89.25	85.51	61.38	79.47	79.44	84.19	89.34	90.91	87.41	87.56	71.88	68.33	80.25	76.23	69.48	80.04
RatiO-RCNN(ours)	Swin-T-FPN	89.38	85.71	61.36	83.23	79.16	86.03	88.06	90.90	87.12	87.49	72.68	72.26	78.29	78.38	72.42	**80.83**

4.2 Comparison to State-of-the-Arts

We trained the RatiO-RCNN method on the DOTAv1.0 dataset and compared it with some existing oriented object detectors. Table 1 compares our model on the DOTA dataset with mAP50 as a benchmark against some state-of-the-art methods, and Table 2 compares the comparison on DOTAv1.0 for the higher accuracy metric mAP75. On the DOTAv1.0 dataset, our method achieves 77.82% mAP50 under the single-scale training condition, with an improvement of 1.54% compared to State-of-the-Art. Under the multi-scale training condition, we achieve the second-best result(80.83%). For the metric mAP75, which reflects the fineness of the model detection, we achieved the best results for both single-scale

Table 2. Comparison results of accuracy metrics for mAP75 on the DOTAv1.0 dataset.* represents multi-scale training. **Bolded text**: top two performances.

Method	Backbone	mAP75
S2A-Net	R50	35.60
Oriented Reppoints	Swin-T	43.07
RoI-Trans	R101	40.24
Oriented-RCNN	R50	45.76
KFIoU.-RoI-Trans*	R50	52.53
RatiO-RCNN	R50	47.83
RatiO-RCNN*	R50	**55.40**
RatiO-RCNN	Swin-T	49.44
RatiO-RCNN*	Swin-T	**56.35**

and multi-scale training(49.44% and 56.35%), with an improvement of 3.68%, 3.04% compared to state-of-the-art, respectively.

4.3 Ablation Study

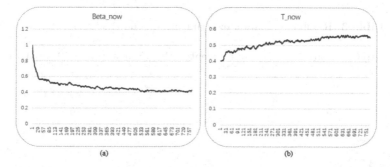

Fig. 5. (a) The curve of the change of Beta_now. (b) The curve of the change of T_now.

We conducted ablation experiments on the DOTAv1.0 dataset with Swin-T as the backbone under single-scale training, and the results are shown in Table 3. The ratio loss we designed leads to the improvement of both mAP50 and mAP75; the main contribution of the dynamic oriented R-CNN head we introduced is to improve the quality of positive samples during model training, which leads to a larger improvement of mAP75; the results of the parameter changes are shown in Fig. 5, which provides strong evidence that the proposed module achieves its intended purpose. Figure 6(a) shows the changes in the regression loss during the RPN training stage before and after the introduction of the RotateGA module. It

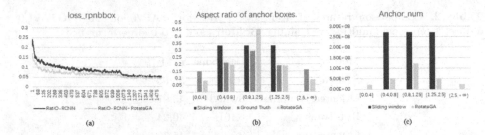

Fig. 6. (a) Comparison of loss_rpnbbox before and after the introduction of RotateGA. (b) Comparison of anchor box shape distribution before and after the introduction of RotateGA. (c) Comparison of the number of generated anchor boxes before and after the introduction of RotateGA.

can be observed that after the introduction of RotateGA, the loss is significantly reduced, indicating that the module can effectively improve the accuracy of the candidate regions. Figure 6(b) and (c) respectively show the comparison of the shape and quantity of anchor boxes before and after the introduction of RotateGA. It can be seen that after the introduction of RotateGA, the quantity and shape of anchor boxes are more appropriate, which helps to improve the detection accuracy.

The results of the ablation experiments show that our model effectively improves the accuracy of oriented object detection.

Table 3. Results of ablation experiments on the DOTAv1.0 dataset

RotateGA	RatioLoss	Dynamic oriented RCNN head	mAP50	mAP75
			75.67	46.87
✓			75.93	47.32
✓	✓		77.39	47.76
✓	✓	✓	77.82	49.44

5   Conclusions

In this paper, we propose a practical two-stage oriented object detection framework named RatiO R-CNN to address some shortcomings of existing models. In the RatiO R-CNN framework, we proposed RotateGA to replace the currently most widely used sliding window anchor box generation method; we suggest a ratio loss for the encoding form of rotation detection frame in the RPN stage, which reduces the accuracy loss of the model when generating oriented proposals and improves the training effect of the RPN network. In the second stage, we introduced a dynamic oriented R-CNN head, which adjusts the positive sample threshold and regression loss function form according to the sample quality in the training process. It can better balance the sample difference between the early and late stages of training. The model is extensively evaluated on DOTAv1.0 dataset. The experimental results show that the method has excellent detection ability for oriented objects and significantly improves over existing oriented object detection methods.

Acknowledgement. This work was supported by the Natural Science Foundation of China (62276242), National Aviation Science Foundation (2022Z071078001), CAAI-Huawei MindSpore Open Fund (CAAIXSJLJJ-2021-016B, CAAIX SJLJJ-2022-001A), Anhui Province Key Research and Development Program (202104a05020007), USTC-IAT Application Sci. & Tech. Achievement Cultivation Program (JL06521001Y), Sci. & Tech. Innovation Special Zone (20-163-14-LZ-001-004-01).

References

1. Chen, Z., et al.: PIoU Loss: towards accurate oriented object detection in complex environments. In: Vedaldi, A., Bischof, H., Brox, T., Frahm, J.-M. (eds.) ECCV 2020. LNCS, vol. 12350, pp. 195–211. Springer, Cham (2020). https://doi.org/10.1007/978-3-030-58558-7_12

2. Ding, J., Xue, N., Long, Y., Xia, G.S., Lu, Q.: Learning roi transformer for oriented object detection in aerial images. In: Proceedings of the IEEE/CVF Conference on Computer Vision and Pattern Recognition, pp. 2849–2858 (2019)

3. Guo, Z., Liu, C., Zhang, X., Jiao, J., Ji, X., Ye, Q.: Beyond bounding-box: convex-hull feature adaptation for oriented and densely packed object detection. In: Proceedings of the IEEE/CVF Conference on Computer Vision and Pattern Recognition, pp. 8792–8801 (2021)

4. Han, J., Ding, J., Li, J., Xia, G.S.: Align deep features for oriented object detection. IEEE Trans. Geosci. Remote Sens. **60**, 1–11 (2021)

5. Han, J., Ding, J., Xue, N., Xia, G.S.: Redet: a rotation-equivariant detector for aerial object detection. In: Proceedings of the IEEE/CVF Conference on Computer Vision and Pattern Recognition, pp. 2786–2795 (2021)

6. He, K., Zhang, X., Ren, S., Sun, J.: Deep residual learning for image recognition. In: Proceedings of the IEEE Conference on Computer Vision and Pattern Recognition, pp. 770–778 (2016)

7. Li, C., Xu, C., Cui, Z., Wang, D., Zhang, T., Yang, J.: Feature-attentioned object detection in remote sensing imagery. In: 2019 IEEE International Conference On Image Processing (ICIP), pp. 3886–3890. IEEE (2019)

8. Li, W., Chen, Y., Hu, K., Zhu, J.: Oriented reppoints for aerial object detection. In: Proceedings of the IEEE/CVF Conference on Computer Vision and Pattern Recognition, pp. 1829–1838 (2022)

9. Lin, T.Y., Dollár, P., Girshick, R., He, K., Hariharan, B., Belongie, S.: Feature pyramid networks for object detection. In: Proceedings of the IEEE Conference on Computer Vision and Pattern Recognition, pp. 2117–2125 (2017)

10. Liu, Z., et al.: Swin transformer: hierarchical vision transformer using shifted windows. In: Proceedings of the IEEE/CVF International Conference on Computer Vision, pp. 10012–10022 (2021)

11. Ma, J., Shao, W., Ye, H., Wang, L., Wang, H., Zheng, Y., Xue, X.: Arbitrary-oriented scene text detection via rotation proposals. IEEE Trans. Multimedia **20**(11), 3111–3122 (2018)

12. Ming, Q., Zhou, Z., Miao, L., Zhang, H., Li, L.: Dynamic anchor learning for arbitrary-oriented object detection. In: Proceedings of the AAAI Conference on Artificial Intelligence, vol. 35, pp. 2355–2363 (2021)
13. Pan, X., et al.: Dynamic refinement network for oriented and densely packed object detection. In: Proceedings of the IEEE/CVF Conference on Computer Vision and Pattern Recognition, pp. 11207–11216 (2020)
14. Qian, W., Yang, X., Peng, S., Yan, J., Guo, Y.: Learning modulated loss for rotated object detection. In: Proceedings of the AAAI conference on artificial intelligence, vol. 35, pp. 2458–2466 (2021)
15. Wang, J., Chen, K., Yang, S., Loy, C.C., Lin, D.: Region proposal by guided anchoring. In: Proceedings of the IEEE/CVF Conference on Computer Vision and Pattern Recognition, pp. 2965–2974 (2019)
16. Xia, G.S., et al.: Dota: A large-scale dataset for object detection in aerial images. In: Proceedings of the IEEE Conference on Computer Vision and Pattern Recognition, pp. 3974–3983 (2018)
17. Xie, X., Cheng, G., Wang, J., Yao, X., Han, J.: Oriented r-cnn for object detection. In: Proceedings of the IEEE/CVF International Conference on Computer Vision, pp. 3520–3529 (2021)
18. Xu, Y., et al.: Gliding vertex on the horizontal bounding box for multi-oriented object detection. IEEE Trans. Pattern Anal. Mach. Intell. **43**(4), 1452–1459 (2020)
19. Yang, X., Hou, L., Zhou, Y., Wang, W., Yan, J.: Dense label encoding for boundary discontinuity free rotation detection. In: Proceedings of the IEEE/CVF Conference on Computer Vision and Pattern Recognition, pp. 15819–15829 (2021)
20. Yang, X., Yan, J., Feng, Z., He, T.: R3det: refined single-stage detector with feature refinement for rotating object. In: Proceedings of the AAAI Conference on Artificial Intelligence, vol. 35, pp. 3163–3171 (2021)
21. Yang, X., et al.: Scrdet: towards more robust detection for small, cluttered and rotated objects. In: Proceedings of the IEEE/CVF International Conference on Computer Vision, pp. 8232–8241 (2019)
22. Yang, X., et al.: The kfiou loss for rotated object detection. arXiv preprint arXiv:2201.12558 (2022)
23. Zhang, H., Chang, H., Ma, B., Wang, N., Chen, X.: Dynamic R-CNN: towards high quality object detection via dynamic training. In: Vedaldi, A., Bischof, H., Brox, T., Frahm, J.-M. (eds.) ECCV 2020. LNCS, vol. 12360, pp. 260–275. Springer, Cham (2020). https://doi.org/10.1007/978-3-030-58555-6_16
24. Zhou, Y., et al.: Mmrotate: a rotated object detection benchmark using pytorch. In: Proceedings of the 30th ACM International Conference on Multimedia, pp. 7331–7334 (2022)

Student Classroom Behavior Detection Based on YOLOv7+BRA and Multi-model Fusion

Fan Yang[1], Tao Wang[1], and Xiaofei Wang[2]($\boxtimes$)

[1] Chengdu Neusoft University, Chengdu 611844, China
Yang.Fan@nsu.edu.cn
[2] School of Films and Animation of the College of Chinese and ASEAN Arts,
Chengdu University, Chengdu 610106, China
wangxiaofei@cdu.edu.cn

Abstract. Accurately detecting student behavior in classroom videos can aid in analyzing their classroom performance and improving teaching effectiveness. However, the current accuracy rate in behavior detection is low. To address this challenge, we propose the Student Classroom Behavior Detection system based on YOLOv7+BRA (YOLOv7 with Bi-level Routing Attention). We identified eight different behavior patterns, including standing, sitting, talking, listening, walking, raising hands, reading, and writing. We constructed a dataset, which contained 11,248 labels and 4,001 images, with an emphasis on the common behavior of raising hands in a classroom setting (Student Classroom Behavior dataset, SCB-Dataset). To improve detection accuracy, we added the biformer attention module to the YOLOv7 network. Finally, we fused the results from YOLOv7 CrowdHuman, SlowFast, and DeepSort models to obtain student classroom behavior data. We conducted experiments on the SCB-Dataset, and YOLOv7+BRA achieved an mAP@0.5 of 87.1%, resulting in a 2.2% improvement over previous results. Our SCB-dataset can be downloaded from: https://github.com/Whiffe/SCB-dataset.

Keywords: YOLOv7+BRA · Student Classroom Behavior ·
SCB-dataset · Bi-level Routing Attention

1 Introduction

Behavior detection technology [1] has enabled the analysis of student behavior in class videos. It provides information on the classroom status and learning performance of students, making it an essential tool for teachers, administrators, students, and parents in schools. In traditional teaching models, teachers find it challenging to monitor the learning situation of every student, which limits their understanding of the effectiveness of their teaching methods. School administrators rely on on-site observations and student performance reports to identify educational problems. Parents rely on communication with teachers and students

© The Author(s), under exclusive license to Springer Nature Switzerland AG 2023
H. Lu et al. (Eds.): ICIG 2023, LNCS 14357, pp. 41–52, 2023.
https://doi.org/10.1007/978-3-031-46311-2_4

to understand their child's learning situation. Therefore, utilizing behavior detection technology to accurately detect and analyze student behavior can provide comprehensive and accurate feedback for education and teaching.

Existing student behavior detection algorithms can be classified into three categories: video-action-recognition-based [2], pose-estimation-based [3], and object-detection-based [4], with the latter being a promising solution due to recent breakthroughs. Although video-based detection allows for the recognition of continuous behavior, it requires a large number of annotated samples such as in the AVA dataset [5] for SlowFast [6] detection which includes 1.58M annotations. Video behavior recognition is still under development, and in some cases, actions can only be determined by context or scene alone as seen in UCF101 [7] and Kinetics400 [8]. Pose-estimation algorithms obtain joint position and motion information but are not adequate for detecting behavior in overcrowded classrooms. Based on the challenges at hand, an object-detection-based approach, such as YOLOv7 [9], has been employed to analyze student behavior in this paper.

One-stage and two-stage object detection frameworks have shown impressive results on public datasets [10,11]. However, classical methods perform poorly in real classroom environments due to large scale variations among different positions, particularly between front and back rows, resulting in scale variations of nearly 25 times. Occlusion between students is also a significant issue in classroom behavior detection compared to popular object detection datasets like MS COCO [12]. Additionally, there are significant differences in hand-raising behavior in different environments, among different people, and from different angles.

In this work, we explore the effectiveness of computer vision techniques in automatically analyzing student behavior patterns in the classroom. Specifically, we focus on hand-raising behavior and have developed a large-scale dataset of labeled images for analysis. The dataset fills a gap in current research on detecting student behavior in classroom teaching scenarios. We have conducted extensive data statistics and benchmark tests to ensure the quality of the dataset, providing reliable training data.

YOLOv7 is one of the best one-stage object detection algorithms currently available, and we attempted to train it on our dataset for better detection results. However, we found that the original version of YOLOv7 still had some room for improvement after training - for example, it would misidentify other actions as raising hands and fail to detect smaller hand-raising actions. Therefore, we incorporated a dynamic sparse attention module called Bi-Level Routing Attention (BRA), which successfully improved detection performance.

Our main contributions are as follows:

(1) This paper constructed a dataset of students raising hands in classrooms, enabling better research into classroom behavior detection. Moreover, the SCB-dataset fills a gap in behavior datasets in the educational field. The YOLOv7 object detection algorithm was used to train and test the dataset, producing satisfactory results with high practical value. This work lays a foundation and

provides a reference for further research into object detection algorithms in student classroom behavior detection.

(2) This paper proposes an improved model, named YOLOv7+BRA. We added a Bi-Level Route Attention module to the model to give it dynamic query-aware sparsity. Experimental results show that our method successfully improves detection accuracy and reduces false detection rates.

(3) This paper utilizes a fusion of multiple models including YOLOv7 Crowd-Human, SlowFast, DeepSort, and YOLOv7+BRA to detect and obtain student behavior data during classroom sessions, providing essential data for further analysis of student behavior in the classroom. These contributions lay the foundation for future research in the field of student classroom behavior analysis.

2 Related Works

Student Classroom Behavior Dataset
Recently, many researchers have utilized computer vision to automatically detect student classroom behaviors. However, the limited availability of open student behavior datasets in the education field limits the application of video behavior detection. Researchers have proposed unpublished datasets, such as ActRec-Classroom [13] with 5,126 images across five categories, a large-scale student behavior dataset [14] containing hand-raising, standing, and sleeping samples from thirty schools, and a comprehensive dataset [15] capturing videos of 128 classes in different disciplines and in 11 classrooms. These datasets are from real monitoring data and cannot be made public.

Students Classroom Behavior Detection
Increasingly, researchers are turning to mature object detection techniques for student behavior recognition, such as YAN Xing-ya's method [4] leveraging deep learning with the YOLOv7 detection algorithm and the BetaPose lightweight pose recognition model. ZHOU Ye [16] proposed a method utilizing the Faster R-CNN detection framework for detecting student behaviors in crowded classrooms. To address scale variations and data category imbalances, the approach incorporates feature pyramid and prime sample attention mechanisms.

Attention Mechanisms
Attention is a crucial mechanism that can be utilized by various deep learning models in different domains and tasks. The beginning of the attention mechanisms we use today is often traced back to their origin in natural language processing [17]. The Transformer model proposed in [18] represents a significant milestone in attention research as it demonstrates that the attention mechanism alone can enable the construction of a state-of-the-art model. Recently, sparse attention has gained popularity in the realm of vision transformers due to the remarkable success of the Swin transformer [19]. Several works endeavor to make the sparse pattern adaptable to data, including DAT [20], TCFormer [21], and DPT [22]. Additionally, BiFormer [23] proposes a new dynamic sparse attention approach via bi-level routing to enable a more flexible allocation of computations with content awareness.

Student Behavior Detection System

Various methods and technologies can be used to detect student classroom behavior. Ngoc Anh B et al. [24]. developed a computer vision-based application to identify students paying attention in the classroom. Lin et al. [25]. proposed a student behavior recognition system based on skeleton pose estimation and person detection. Trabelsi et al [26]. used machine learning to train models for student behavior detection, incorporating facial expression recognition for attention detection. Yang [27] proposed using YOLOv5, SlowFast and Deep Sort [28] for detecting spatiotemporal behavior. Combining different methods and technologies, such as skeleton pose estimation, person detection, and facial expression recognition, and spatiotemporal behavior detection, can improve recognition accuracy and efficiency for student behavior detection.

3 SCB-Dataset

Understanding student behavior is crucial for comprehending their learning process, personality, and psychological traits, and is important in evaluating the quality of education. The hand-raising behavior is an essential indicator of classroom participation quality. However, the lack of publicly available datasets poses a significant challenge for AI research in the field of education.

To address this issue, we developed a publicly available dataset that focuses on hand-raising behavior. This dataset presents unique characteristics and challenges due to the complexity and specificity of educational settings, providing new opportunities for researchers. The dataset was constructed using real-world videos obtained from the bjyhjy and 1s1k websites, ensuring its representativeness and realism in reflecting the complexity of student behavior.

I dense environments   II pixel differences   III similar behaviors

Fig. 1. Challenges in the student hand-raising behavior dataset include dense environments, similar behaviors, and pixel differences.

The classroom environment presents challenges for detecting hand-raising behavior due to the dense population and variation in student positions, as shown in Fig. 1 I and II. There is also visual similarity between hand-raising and other behavior classes, further complicating detection as seen in Fig. 1 III.

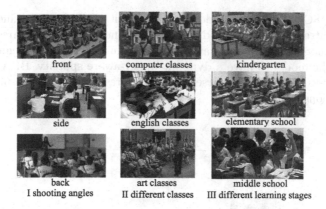

front   computer classes   kindergarten

side   english classes   elementary school

back   art classes   middle school
I shooting angles   II different classes   III different learning stages

Fig. 2. Challenges in the student hand-raising behavior dataset include varying shooting angles, class differences, and different learning stages.

The images of the hand-raising behaviors were captured from varying angles in our dataset, including front, side, and back views (Fig. 2 I). Additionally, the classroom environment and seating arrangement can vary, which adds complexity to the detection task (Fig. 2 II). Hand-raising behaviors also differ across learning stages from kindergarten to high-school, creating challenges for detection (Fig. 2 III).

We conducted a statistical analysis on the SCB-dataset, which comprised 4001 images with an average of 2.81 individuals with annotations in each image.

4   YOLOv7+BRA

Given the challenges of dense environments, pixel differences and similar student behaviors, we selected YOLOv7 as the foundational model due to its comprehensive consideration of speed and accuracy. This lightweight one-stage object detection algorithm has an inference speed of 6.9 ms per image, allowing for a frame rate of over 140fps, which is suitable for real-time monitoring requirements in student classroom behavior detection.

Generally, one-stage object detection models can be divided into three parts: backbone, neck and head. The purpose of the backbone is to extract and select features, the neck is to fuse features, and the head is to predict results. However, YOLOv7 only retains the backbone and head parts because it proposes an Extended efficient layer aggregation networks (E-ELAN) module to replace various FPNs and PANs commonly used for feature fusion in the neck. Additionally, the Model scaling operation is common in concatenation-based models, which increases the input width of the subsequent transmission layer. Therefore, YOLOv7 proposes the compound scaling up depth and width method.

Although YOLOv7 is considered one of the top object detection models, we found it challenging to handle occlusions and distinguish similar actions when detecting the SCB-dataset. To address these limitations, we introduced the bi-level routing attention (BRA) module, which is a novel dynamic sparse attention that enables more flexible computation allocation and content awareness (Fig. 3). This allows the model to have a dynamic query-aware sparsity. BRA filters out irrelevant key-value pairs at a coarse region level, resulting in only a small portion of routed regions remaining.

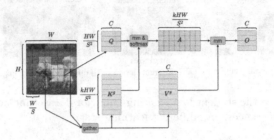

Fig. 3. Bi-level Routing Attention.

BRA can be divided into three steps. First, a feature map is input, divided into several regions, and query, key, and value are obtained through linear mapping. Second, an adjacency matrix is used to build a directed graph to identify participating relationships between different key-value pairs, indicating the regions in which given regions should participate. Finally, a routing index matrix is applied to apply fine-grained token-to-token attention to regions. As shown in Fig. 3, by aggregating key-value pairs within the top k related windows, BRA leverages sparsity to avoid computations in the least important areas, with only GPU-friendly dense matrix multiplications being utilized.

Figure 4 displays the structure of our modified YOLOv7+BRA model, which includes the BRA module placed in the final portion of the backbone. When introducing the BRA module, we considered three placement options: (1) replacing all convolutions with convolutions that include BRA; (2) placing BRA in the head section; (3) placing BRA in the backbone section. The first option would lead to a very large model that is difficult to train, impacting inference speed. Given that the attention mechanism's role is to have the model focus on specific areas rather than the entire image, we perceive this as part of feature extraction and thus placed it in the backbone section.

5   Student Classroom Behavior Detection System

The student classroom behavior detection system (Fig. 5) consists of three parts: continuous behavior detection, non-continuous behavior detection, and the fusion of behavior detection results with student IDs.

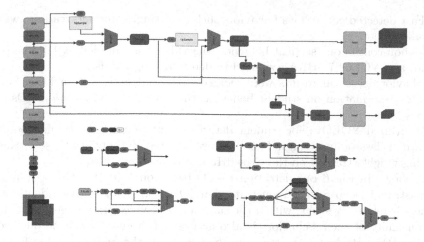

Fig. 4. The architecture of YOLOv7+BRA.

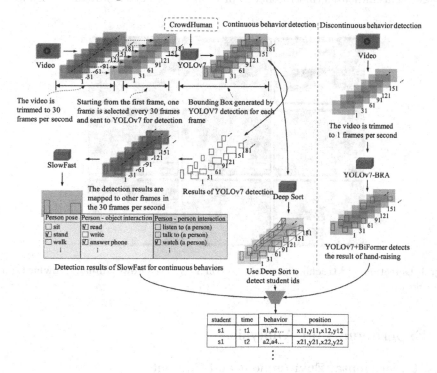

Fig. 5. Process of Student Classroom Behavior Detection System.

To detect continuous student behavior, we sampled the video at 30 frames per second and used YOLOv7 with weights trained on the CrowdHuman dataset [29] to detect student behaviors at every 30 frames. The detection results were sent to Deep Sort and SlowFast for mapping to other frames within the same second.

SlowFast detected continuous behaviors such as sitting, standing, reading, writing, talking, etc.

For non-continuous student behavior, the video was sampled at 1 frame per second, and YOLOv7+BRA was used to detect raising hands.

Behavior detection results were merged with student IDs from Deep Sort, providing information on student behavior, time, location, and student IDs for analysis.

We utilized YOLOv7 for student detection, but found it performed poorly in crowded classroom settings. Therefore, we adapted YOLOv7 to these settings by using weights trained on the CrowdHuman dataset.

As shown in Fig. 6 our detection results based on YOLOv7 CrowdHuman, SlowFast, and Deep Sort demonstrate that ID tracking for both students and teachers is relatively stable within the same angle of video frames. Additionally, the continuity of their behaviors is also accurate. However, it can be observed that the ID of students and teachers changes when the angle of video frames changes. This indicates that further improvements are needed in our future work.

Fig. 6. Detection and tracking results based on YOLOv7 CrowdHuman, SlowFast, and Deep Sort.

6   Experiment and Analysis

6.1   Experimental Environment and Content

Experiments were performed using an NVIDIA GeForce RTX 2080 Ti GPU with Ubuntu 20.04.2 and Python 3.8. We used PyTorch version 1.8.1 with CUDA version 10.1 to train the models.

The SCB-dataset was used and split into training and validation sets at a 4:1 ratio. We conducted experiments to compare the detection accuracy and performance of YOLOv7+BRA against various models of YOLOv7 and YOLOv5.

Training involved three parts: first, training various YOLOv7 network architectures, then training the YOLOv5m network architecture, and finally training the YOLOv7+BRA network architecture. For training the model, we set the epoch to 150, batch size to 8, and image size to 640 × 640. We use a pre-trained model for training.

6.2 Experimental Results and Analysis

For our training, we utilized various YOLOv7 network architectures such as YOLOv7-tiny, YOLOv7, YOLOv7-X, YOLOv7-W6, YOLOv7-E6 and, we employed YOLOv7+BRA and YOLOv5m network structures. The results of our experiments are outlined in Fig. 7, with Precision denoted as "P" and Recall denoted as "R".

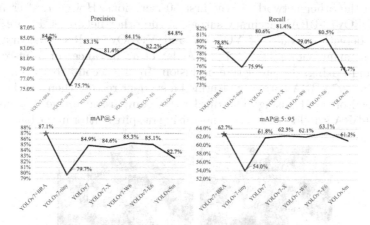

Fig. 7. Evaluation of hand-raising on SCB-dataset.

From Fig. 7, it can be seen that YOLOv7+BRA has higher Precision results than the YOLOv7 series models. Looking at the mAP@0.5 results, the YOLOv7+BRA model outperforms YOLOv7 series models and YOLOv5m model, with a difference of 2.2% over the second-place model. In terms of mAP@0.9, the YOLOv7+BRA model outperforms all other YOLO series models except for YOLOv7-E6, which has a much more complex network structure and requires more training time, YOLOv7+BRA also outperforms the YOLOv5m model in this regard.

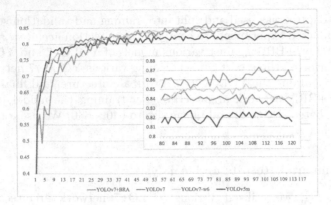

Fig. 8. Comparison of mAP@0.5 Results for Each Network's Training Iterations.

Figure 7 displays the training results of mAP@0.5 for YOLOv7+BRA, YOLOv7, YOLOv7-w6, and YOLOv5m. YOLOv7+BRA's accuracy is initially lower than the other networks in the first 30 iterations. However, after 70 iterations, YOLOv7+BRA's accuracy surpasses the other networks. Figure 9 compares the detection results of YOLOv7 and YOLOv7+BRA. The first row's comparison image shows YOLOv7+BRA detecting instances of front-row students's hand-raising, despite severe occlusion. In the second row's comparison image, YOLOv7+BRA correctly identified a student resting their hand on their head instead of hand-raising. The third row's comparison image demonstrates YOLOv7+BRA's ability to detect hand-raising despite clutter in the background.

YOLOv7   YOLOv7+BRA

Fig. 9. Comparison of detection results between YOLOv7 and YOLOv7+BRA models.

7   Conclusion

This paper emphasizes the importance of detecting student behavior in classroom videos and presents the Student Classroom Behavior Detection system based on YOLOv7+BRA. We identified eight behavior patterns, constructed a dataset of over 4,000 images with 11,248 labels, and improved detection accuracy using the bi-level routing attention module. The fusion of multiple models effectively obtained student behavior data during classroom sessions. This paper's contributions include the SCB-dataset and improved YOLOv7+BRA model, providing a foundation for future developments in student behavior detection and benefiting students' educational outcomes. Future work should increase the quantity and category of behavior datasets, use diverse networks as reliable references, and address limitations in DeepSort's performance changes.

References

1. Zhu, Y., Li, X., Liu, C., et al.: A comprehensive study of deep video action recognition. arXiv preprint arXiv:2012.06567 (2020)
2. Huang, Y., Liang, M., Wang, X., et al.: Multi-person classroom action recognition in classroom teaching videos based on deep spatiotemporal residual convolution neural network. J. Comput. Appli. **42**(3), 736 (2022)
3. He, X., Yang, F., Chen, Z., et al.: The recognition of student classroom behavior based on human skeleton and deep learning. Mod. Educ. Technol. **30**(11), 105–112 (2020)
4. Yan, X., Kuang, Y., Bai, G., Li, Y.: Student classroom behavior recognition method based on deep learning. Comput. Eng. https://doi.org/10.19678/j.issn.1000-3428.0065369
5. Gu, C., Sun, C., Ross, D.A., et al.: Ava: a video dataset of spatio-temporally localized atomic visual actions. In: Proceedings of the IEEE Conference on Computer Vision and Pattern Recognition, pp. 6047–6056 (2018)
6. Feichtenhofer, C., Fan, H., Malik, J., et al.: Slowfast networks for video recognition. In: Proceedings of the IEEE/CVF International Conference on Computer Vision, pp. 6202–6211 (2019)
7. Soomro, K., Zamir, A.R., Shah, M.: UCF101: A dataset of 101 human actions classes from videos in the wild. arXiv preprint arXiv:1212.0402 (2012)
8. Carreira, J., Zisserman, A.: Quo vadis, action recognition? a new model and the kinetics dataset. In: Proceedings of the IEEE Conference on Computer Vision and Pattern Recognition, pp. 6299–6308 (2017)
9. Wang, C.Y., Bochkovskiy, A., Liao, H.Y.M.: YOLOv7: trainable bag-of-freebies sets new state-of-the-art for real-time object detectors. arXiv preprint arXiv:2207.02696 (2022)
10. Ren, S., He, K., Girshick, R., et al.: Faster r-cnn: towards real-time object detection with region proposal networks. In: Advances in Neural Information Processing Systems, vol. 28 (2015)
11. Redmon J, Farhadi A. Yolov3: an incremental improvement. arXiv preprint arXiv:1804.02767 (2018)
12. Lin, T.-Y., et al.: Microsoft COCO: common objects in context. In: Fleet, D., Pajdla, T., Schiele, B., Tuytelaars, T. (eds.) ECCV 2014. LNCS, vol. 8693, pp. 740–755. Springer, Cham (2014). https://doi.org/10.1007/978-3-319-10602-1_48

13. Fu. R., Wu, T., Luo, Z., et al.: Learning behavior analysis in classroom based on deep learning. In: 2019 Tenth International Conference on Intelligent Control and Information Processing (ICICIP), pp. 206–212. IEEE (2019)

14. Zheng, R., Jiang, F., Shen, R.: Intelligent student behavior analysis system for real classrooms. In: ICASSP 2020–2020 IEEE International Conference on Acoustics, Speech and Signal Processing (ICASSP), pp. 9244–9248. IEEE (2020)

15. Sun, B., Wu, Y., Zhao, K., et al.: Student class behavior dataset: a video dataset for recognizing, detecting, and captioning students' behaviors in classroom scenes[J]. Neural Comput. Appl. **33**, 8335–8354 (2021)

16. Zhou, Y.: Research on Classroom Behaviors Detection of Primary School Students Based on Faster R-CNN. Sichuan Normal University (2021). https://doi.org/10.27347/d.cnki.gssdu.2021.000962

17. Bahdanau, D., Cho, K., Bengio, Y.: Neural machine translation by jointly learning to align and translate. arXiv preprint arXiv:1409.0473 (2014)

18. Vaswani. A., Shazeer, N., Parmar, N., et al.: Attention is all you need. In: Advances in Neural Information Processing Systems 30 (2017)

19. Liu, Z., Lin, Y., Cao, Y., et al.: Swin transformer: Hierarchical vision transformer using shifted windows. In: Proceedings of the IEEE/CVF International Conference on Computer Vision, pp. 10012–10022 (2021)

20. Xia, Z., Pan, X., Song, S., et al.: Vision transformer with deformable attention. In: Proceedings of the IEEE/CVF Conference on Computer Vision and Pattern Recognition, pp. 4794–4803 (2022)

21. Zeng, W., Jin, S., Liu, W., et al.: Not all tokens are equal: human-centric visual analysis via token clustering transformer. In: Proceedings of the IEEE/CVF Conference on Computer Vision and Pattern Recognition, pp. 11101–11111 (2022)

22. Chen, Z., Zhu, Y., Zhao, C., et al.: Dpt: deformable patch-based transformer for visual recognition. In: Proceedings of the 29th ACM International Conference on Multimedia, pp. 2899–2907 (2021)

23. Zhu, L., Wang, X., Ke, Z., et al.: BiFormer: Vision Transformer with Bi-Level Routing Attention. arXiv preprint arXiv:2303.08810 (2023)

24. Ngoc Anh, B., Tung Son, N., Truong Lam, P., et al.: A computer-vision based application for student behavior monitoring in classroom. Appl. Sci. **9**(22), 4729 (2019)

25. Lin, F.C., Ngo, H.H., Dow, C.R., et al.: Student behavior recognition system for the classroom environment based on skeleton pose estimation and person detection. Sensors **21**(16), 5314 (2021)

26. Trabelsi, Z., Alnajjar, F., Parambil, M.M.A., et al.: Real-time attention monitoring system for classroom: a deep learning approach for student's behavior recognition. Big Data Cognitive Comput. **7**(1), 48 (2023)

27. Yang, F.: A Multi-Person Video Dataset Annotation Method of Spatio-Temporally Actions. arXiv preprint arXiv:2204.10160 (2022)

28. Wojke, N., Bewley, A., Paulus D.: Simple online and realtime tracking with a deep association metric. In: 2017 IEEE International Conference on Image Processing (ICIP), pp. 3645–3649. IEEE (2017)

29. Shao, S., Zhao, Z., Li, B., et al.: Crowdhuman: A benchmark for detecting human in a crowd. arXiv preprint arXiv:1805.00123 (2018)

Tiny-YOLOv7: Tiny Object Detection Model for Drone Imagery

Pengchao Cheng[1,2], Xu Tang[2(✉)], Wenqi Liang[2], Yu Li[1,2], Wei Cong[2], and Chuanzhi Zang[1]

[1] School of Artificial Intelligence, Shenyang University of Technology,
Shenyang 10142, China
{chengpengchao,liyu1}@sia.cn
[2] State Key Laboratory of Robotics, Shenyang Institute of Automation Chinese
Academy of Sciences, Shenyang 110016, China
{tangxu,liangwenqi,congwei}@sia.cn

Abstract. With the rapid development of drones, tiny object detection in drone-captured scenarios has become a challenge task. However, the altitude of the drone changes while flying lead to the scale of the object changes dramatically. In addition, drones flying quickly cause motion blur on the densely tiny objects. In order to address the two issues mention above, we propose Tiny-YOLOv7. In order to detect multi-scale objects, we replace the original prediction heads with transformer prediction heads. For the motion blur issue, we propose DBS module to extract more visual elements and maintain computational cost of model. The DBS module consists of Dynamic Region-Aware Convolution (DRConv), Batch Normalization and Silu modules. On scenarios with dense objects, we additionally incorporate the Convolutional Block Attention Model (CBAM) to find the attention region of dense objects. Tiny-YOLOv7 is an effective and elegant method for handing tiny object detection. We validate our model through extensive experiments on VisDrone2021 and DOTA-v1.0 datasets. The results show that our method obtains remarkable improvements over the other models. In VisDrone2021 dataset, the mAP result of our method is 39.22%, which is higher than SOTA method by 1.07%. Furthermore, experiments on dataset DOTA-v1.0 demonstrate generalization of the propose model.

Keywords: Tiny object detection · Transformer · Attention mechanism

1 Introduction

Drones, or general UAVs, equipped with cameras have been fast deployed to a wide range of applications, including agricultural, aerial photography, fast delivery, and surveillance [9,11,17]. In this work, we pay attention to improving the performance of tiny object detection on drone-captured scenarios.

© The Author(s), under exclusive license to Springer Nature Switzerland AG 2023
H. Lu et al. (Eds.): ICIG 2023, LNCS 14357, pp. 53–65, 2023.
https://doi.org/10.1007/978-3-031-46311-2_5

Recent years, a considerable number of researchers have applied deep convolutional neural networks to aerial object detection [1,6,23]. Meanwhile, varies new aerial datasets (*i.e.* VisDrone2021 [3] and DOTA-v2.0 [10]) are available that can be utilized to validate models and substantially promote the development of tiny object detection application. Nonetheless, the majority of the existing tiny object detection models do not perform well in real-world scenarios. In practice, there are various issues with tiny object detection in drone-captured scenarios, as illustrated in Fig. 1. First and foremost, because the altitude of the drone is continually changing, the scale of the object in the image may fluctuate dramatically. The second issue is that images obtained by the aircraft may appear hazy between frames as it flies quickly, causing feature loss of tiny objects. The third issue is that the distribution of tiny objects in the image is significantly imbalanced due to the wider viewing angle of the drone.

(a) Multi-scale   (b) Motion Blur   (c) Maldistribution

Fig. 1. Three major issues of tiny object detection on drone-captured images. Figure a shows the different flying heights of drone result in multiple scales of the same object, Fig. b represents that the image becomes blurry since the drone is moving quickly. Figure c denotes the distribution of object is uneven in the image.

Among the object detection work, the YOLO series is better suited to the needs of real-time detection. In this paper, we present Tiny-YOLOv7, an enhanced model based on YOLOv7 [19], to increase tiny object recognition performance on drone-captured scenarios, where tiny object denotes a target area less than 80 pixels in a 256×256 picture. We employ the original backbone of YOLOv7 to extract the features of the objects in the images. Then in the Neck, enhance the performance of model to locate regions of the image with densely tiny objects, we incorporate CBAM [20] to generate the attention map. In addition, we propose DBS module, replace standard convolution with Dynamic Region-Aware Convolution (DRConv) [4] to improve representation ability of convolution and maintain computational cost of the model. Last but not least, in the Head, we employ transformer prediction heads to detect difficult tiny objects preferably. In the drone scenario, our proposed model is more suitable for tiny object detection.

To conclude, our main contributions are as follows:

(1) We employ transformer prediction heads in place of the original prediction heads. In complicated environments, the transformer prediction head is better suited to detect difficult tiny objects than original prediction heads.

(2) We propose DBS module to improve representation ability of convolution and maintain computational cost of the model.

(3) We incorporate CBAM to find the attention region of dense objects on scenarios with dense objects. The lightweight CBAM enhances the performance of model to find region of interest with negligible computational overhead.

(4) On VisDrone2021 test-dev dataset, the proposed model achieves 39.22% mAP, outperforming the SOTA method by 1.07%. On DOTAv-1.0 dataset, the proposed model shows optimal performance, the mAP result of the model is 80.4%.

2   Related Work

2.1   Object Detection

Object detection based on CNN is significantly superior to the traditional object detection. CNN-based detectors are divided into two categories: anchor-based and anchor-free detectors [5]. Specially, anchor-based detectors can be categorized into one-stage and two-stage. In this work, we adopt the well-known YOLO series in our investigation since one-stage is more capable of satisfying the needs of real-time detection.

Anchor-Based Detector. Faster R-CNN [16] is a classic work of object detection, which introduces a regional proposal network (RPN) and considerably enhances the detection performance by sharing full image convolution information with the detection network. Thereafter, the researchers continue to expand on their study [2,13]. The one-stage detectors directly predicts categories in the image, and is faster than the two-stage detection. [12] extends vertebrae and the neck to achieve the most advanced real-time accuracy performance.

Anchor-Free Detector. There are some drawbacks in anchor-free detectors because of the variety of object shapes and positions. However, this frequently results in enormous numbers of anchors and costs more calculation time. CenterNet [24] utilizes key-point estimates to find the central point and revert back to other object attributes, which is simpler, faster, and more accurate than the corresponding anchor-based detector. In [18], authors propose a more straightforward and adaptable detection framework, namely fully convolutional one-stage object detector (FCOS). The per-pixel prediction method is used to tackle the object detection problem.

2.2 Tiny Object Detection in Aerial Images

Object detection has always been a hot topic for researchers, but objects in the drone images have numerous issues, including multiple spatial scales, blurring motion, and unequal distribution. This presents a great challenge to the tiny objects detection. Researchers have offered a variety of models to address this problem. SSD [15] proposes a single deep neural network to recognize tiny objects in images. The network combines predictions from many feature maps at different resolutions to tackle objects of varied sizes naturally. FPN [14] proposes a deep convolutional networks that has an intrinsic multi-scale, pyramidal hierarchy, which allows for the construction of feature pyramids. These feature extractors exhibit a considerable improvement in specific applications when using feature pyramids. In [22], the authors establish the capability of global context information through context aggregation based on diverse regions, which effectively delivers high quality outcomes in scene resolution tasks and uses the pyramid pool module and the suggested pyramid scene parsing network (PSPNet). Due to convolutional neural network CNN-based methods are nearly never appropriate for detecting tiny objects, [7] proposes Sig-NMS to lessen the chance of losing a tiny objects. The non-maximum suppression (NMS) has replaced by Sig-NMS in the stage of region proposal network.

3   The Proposed Method

3.1   Overview of Tiny-YOLOv7

We apply the backbone of original version YOLOv7 as our backbone. In the Neck, as shown in Fig. 2. We incorporate CBAM to extract the features taken from the backbone network, that makes it easier to recognize tiny objects in images. Furthermore, in the CBS module, the normal convolution module replaced by DRConv, DRConv not only improves the representation of convolution, but also maintains the computational cost, which plays an important role in improving the detection performance.

As a result of the extremely large image size of drone, the object detection process of model can be quite time-consuming. We employ three transformer prediction heads, that can capture global information and rich contextual information, therefore, the new detection head will be quicker and more effective than the original. The introduction of more modules is in the lower right corner of Fig. 2. For more details, refer to [19].

3.2   Transformer Encoder Block

Compared to standard convolution block, transformer encoder blocks can record extensive contextual information as well as global data, that is beneficial for detecting densely occluded objects. The Vision Transformer [8] as an inspiration, we apply transformer encoder blocks in the Neck and Head as shown in Fig. 2. There are two primary sub-layers in every transformer encoder: multi-head attention and feed forwards modules. In Fig. 3. Between each sub-layer, the residual connection is used to prevents network degradation. The transformer encoder block improves the capacity to record various local data. Additionally, it can investigate how feature representation interacts with self-attention systems.

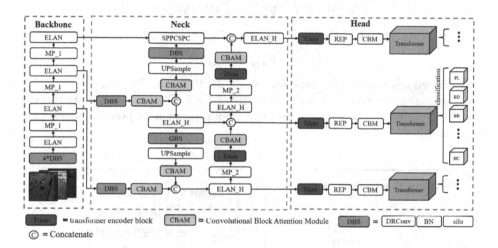

Fig. 2. The overview of Tiny-YOLOv7. a) In the Backbone, we first employ four DBS modules, the standard convolution replaced by DRConv to form a new DBS module. b) In the Neck, we integrate CBAM and transformer encoder block. c) In the Head, we employ three transformer prediction heads to output the categories of predictions.

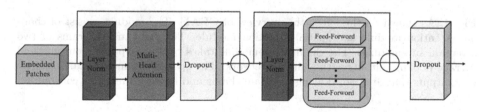

Fig. 3. The overview of transformer encoder block, which has two primary modules: self-attention module and feed forward neural network. The residual connection apply in self-attention module and feed forward neural network, LayerNorm helps model converge well and Dropout prevents model over fitting.

3.3 Convolutional Block Attention Module

Undetectable geographic backgrounds cover a significant portion of drone images. To assist the model in concentrating on useful objects, we utilize CBAM help to extract areas of attention. CBAM is a straightforward but powerful attention module, that has two sequential sub-modules: channel and spatial. Given an intermediate feature map $\mathbf{F} \in R^{C \times H \times W}$ as input, $\mathbf{M_c} \in R^{C \times 1 \times 1}$ and $\mathbf{M_s} \in R^{1 \times H \times W}$ are 1D channel attention map and 2D spatial attention map respectively is illustrated in Fig. 4. The channel attention and the spatial attention are computed as:

$$
\begin{aligned}
\mathbf{M_c}(\mathbf{F}) &= \sigma(\mathrm{MLP}(\mathrm{AvgPool}(\mathbf{F})) + \mathrm{MLP}(\mathrm{Max\,Pool}(\mathbf{F}))) \\
&= \sigma\left(\mathbf{W_1}\left(\mathbf{W_0}\left(\mathbf{F}_{\mathbf{avg}}^{\mathbf{c}}\right)\right) + \mathbf{W_1}\left(\mathbf{W_0}\left(\mathbf{F}_{\max}^{\mathbf{c}}\right)\right)\right)
\end{aligned}
\tag{1}
$$

$$
\begin{aligned}
\mathbf{M_s}(\mathbf{F}) &= \sigma\left(f^{7 \times 7}([\mathrm{AvgPool}(\mathbf{F}); \mathrm{MaxPool}(\mathbf{F})])\right) \\
&= \sigma\left(f^{7 \times 7}\left(\left[\mathbf{F}_{\mathbf{avg}}^{\mathbf{s}}; \mathbf{F}_{\max}^{\mathbf{s}}\right]\right)\right),
\end{aligned}
\tag{2}
$$

where σ denotes the sigmoid function, $\mathbf{W_0} \in R^{C/r \times C}$ and $\mathbf{W_1} \in R^{C \times C/r}$. $f^{7 \times 7}$ is a convolution operation with the filter size of 7×7. $\mathbf{F}_{\mathbf{avg}}^{\mathbf{s}}$ and $\mathbf{F}_{\max}^{\mathbf{s}}$ are spatial context descriptors obtained by average- pooling and max-pooling operations respectively.

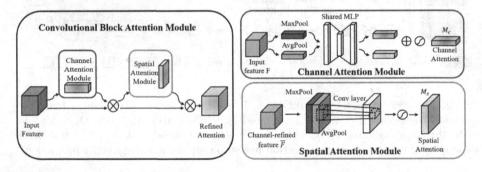

Fig. 4. As shown on the left is the overview of CBAM. The module consist of channel attention module and spatial attention module. The right are diagrams of two attention sub-modules. The channel sub-module takes both max-pooling outputs and average-pooling outputs with a shared network. The spatial sub-module takes similar two outputs that are pooled along the channel axis and forward them to a convolution layer.

3.4 Dynamic Region-Aware Convolution

As shown in Fig. 5, DRConv is divided into standard convolution and local convolution. In [4], the input of standard convolution can be denoted as $X \in R^{M \times N \times P}$, where M, N, P mean height, width and channel respectively. And $A \in R^{M \times N}$,

$Y \in R^{M \times N \times Q}$, $W \in R^p$ are spatial dimension, the output and standard convolutional filters respectively. For the q-th channel of output feature, related feature map is

$$Y_{m,n,q} = \sum_{p=1}^{P} X_{m,n,p} * W_t^{(q)} \quad (m,n) \in A, \tag{3}$$

Moreover, $*$ is 2D convolution operation. We use $W \in R^{M \times N \times P}$ to identify the filters that are spatially independent in the basic local convolution and define a guided mask $M = \{A_0, \ldots, A_{m-1}\}$ to represent the regions divided from spatial dimension. In the region just one filter is shared A_t, $t \in [0, m-1]$. M is learned from the input features according to the data dependency mechanism. We denote the filters of the regions as $W = [W_0, \ldots, W_{m-1}]$, the filter $W_t \in R^C$ is corresponding to the region A_t. Hence the expression for the q-th output feature map is

$$Y_{m,n,g} = \sum_{p=1}^{P} X_{m,n,p} * W_{t,p}^{(q)} \quad (m,n) \in A_t, \tag{4}$$

where $W_{t,p}^{(q)}$ is the p-th channel of the $W_t^{(q)}$ and (u, v) represents one of the points in region A_t. In addition, here the point (u, v) is related to the center of convolutional filter if the kernel size is larger than 1×1. That means a filter with kernel size 3×3 or 5×5 will extract features from bordering regions that are adjacent.

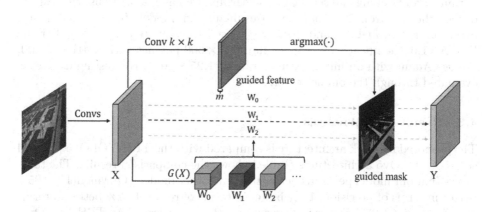

Fig. 5. The architecture of dynamic region-aware convolution. We obtain guided feature from X with $k \times k$ convolution and get m filters from filter generator module $G(\cdot)$. The spatial dimension is divided into m regions as guided mask shows. Filter W_0, W_1, W_2 are individual for every region. Moreover, filters are shared in this region and we implement $k \times k$ convolution with related filter in these regions of X to output Y.

4   Experiment

4.1   Dataset

The VisDrone2021 [3] is used in experiments to evaluate our method, the dataset contain 10 categories, the majority of the categories were pedestrians and cars, the maximal resolution of images is 2000×1500. There are 6471 images for training, in addition, validation set and testing set are 548 and 3190 images, respectively.

The DOTA-v1.0 [21] dataset contains 2,806 aerial images with a wide variety of scales, orientations, and shapes of objects. The image resolution ranges from 800×800 to 4000×4000. The fully-annotated images contain 188,282 instances. The DOTA-V1.0 has 15 categories: Plane, Baseball Diamond (BD), Bridge, Ground Track Field (GTF), Small Vehicle (SV), Large Vehicle (LV), Ship, Tennis Court (TC), Basketball Court (BC), Storage Tank (ST), Soccer-Ball Field (SBF), Roundabout (RA), Harbor (HA), Swimming Pool (SP) and Helicopter (HC).

4.2   Experiment Setup

The code for the implementation of the suggested architecture is written in the PyTorch1.7.1 framework. All of our models use two NVIDIA Titan Xp GPUs for training and testing. In order to save training time, we adopt part of the pre-training model of YOLOv7 as adopted in the training stage and train all models for 100 epochs. The image input size is 640×640. Moreover, we select a Adam optimizer for training and set the initial learning rate as $1e-3$, We use the testset-dev of the VisDrone2021 dataset to evaluate our model. In the experiment, precision, recall, $mAP_{0.5}$ and $mAP_{0.5:0.95}$ used to evaluate our models. For the DOTA-v1.0, the images are cropped into 600×600 patches with a stride of 100. We use Adam with an initial learning rate of 1.25×10^{-4}, the testing dataset is evaluated through the online server.

4.3   Results and Analysis

The proposed network architecture is compared with the TPH-YOLOv5 [25] and series of YOLOv5 architectures. Table 1 shows the comparison results. The table shows that our model performs better than the other models. Our model is 0.05% better in terms of precision, 1.5% better in terms of recall, 1.32% better in terms of $mAP_{0.5}$ and 1.07% better in terms of $mAP_{0.5:0.95}$ scores than TPH-YOLOv5, which is the second-best results. Our model represents excellent performance on the VisDrone2021 dataset compared to other YOLO series model.

Open aerial dataset DOTA-v1.0 receives numerous challenges from two-stage and one-stage models due to its openness. As illustrated in the Table 2, the second row of the table is the two-stage models, the next row of the table is a one-stage models, our results are in the last row. Since our model is based on one-stage, it does not produce the best outcomes, but the results of the experiment demonstrate that our model performs well in terms of generalization. For the one-stage models, we achieved optimal performance, the mAP result of the our model are 80.4%, which is better than previous SOTA method (GDW) by 0.2%.

Table 1. Comparison results between ours and other methods on VisDrone2021 test-dev, the red word means optimal.

Method	$mAP_{0.5:0.95}(\%)$	$mAP_{0.5}(\%)$	P(%)	R(%)
YOLOv5n	13.34	26.16	36.17	28.20
YOLOv5s	18.06	33.18	45.25	33.77
YOLOv5m	21.84	37.88	50.07	37.87
YOLOv7	23.98	43.46	51.55	45.72
THP-TOLOv5	38.15	59.18	66.59	54.96
Ours	**39.22**	**60.50**	**66.64**	**56.46**

We give various metrics during training and validation in Fig. 6 after each epoch. We train our model for 100 epochs, the model gradually converges after 50 epoch. Ultimately, the precision of result is 66.64%, the recall of result is 56.46%, the $mAP_{0.5}$ of result is 60.5% and the mAP of result is 39.22%.

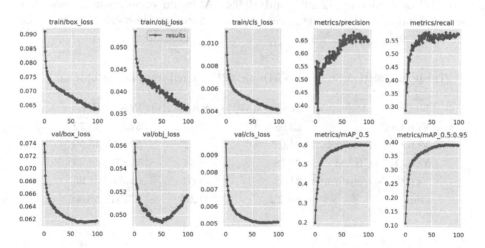

Fig. 6. Visualization of various metrics with the number of epochs during training and validation

In addition, we provide some visualizations of the results. Figure 7 depicts some of the output of our model on some of the test photos from the Vis-Drone2021 and DOTA-v1.0 datasets. Our model adapts well to the size, background, and motion constraints in the drone-captured scenario.

Table 2. Performance comparisons on DOTA-v1.0 HBB Task.

Method	mAP	PL	BD	BR	GFT	SV	LV	SH	TC	BC	ST	SBF	RA
DH-RSIA	83.1	89.1	87.4	66.2	81.8	80.0	86.6	89.2	93.9	89.3	88.1	73.5	69.4
dh-dota	81.5	87.5	87.0	65.9	81.2	79.6	79.3	87.3	93.9	89.3	86.2	72.1	68.1
pcalab	81.0	90.4	86.1	63.5	82.2	78.4	82.6	86.3	90.8	88.7	87.2	69.6	68.9
yangxue	80.7	90.1	87.0	63.9	74.8	84.0	83.6	87.7	90.8	87.6	86.9	73.8	66.0
STJU-Det	80.0	90.1	86.2	64.6	71.5	76.8	78.1	87.5	90.7	87.4	87.6	70.8	68.9
RetinaNet-DCL	74.1	89.1	84.1	49.3	50.2	70.4	58.1	78.0	90.9	86.6	86.8	68.0	67.3
R^3 Det	76.5	**89.8**	83.8	48.1	66.8	78.8	83.3	87.8	90.8	85.4	85.5	65.7	62.7
YOLOv5m-CSL	77.0	89.4	84.5	49.3	65.3	**81.2**	84.4	88.9	90.7	87.7	**87.9**	61.8	66.1
YOLOv5m-BCL	78.0	89.4	85.0	49.2	66.0	81.0	84.6	88.7	90.6	88.0	87.9	65.0	68.3
GWD	80.2	89.7	85.0	59.3	**82.2**	78.9	**84.8**	87.7	90.2	86.5	86.9	**73.5**	67.8
Ours	**80.4**	87.9	**85.9**	62.4	82.1	80.1	83.1	**89.2**	92.5	**88.6**	87.0	71.3	**68.6**

4.4 Ablation Study

In this section, we implement an ablation study and explore the effects of transformer prediction heads, CBAM and dynamic region-aware convolution on the results, respectively. From Table 3, we can observe that CBAM increases $mAP_{0.5}$ and mAP of model by 5.26% and 3.14%. DRConv makes only modest improvements to model performance, transformer prediction head increases $mAP_{0.5}$ and mAP of model by 12.14% and 10.6%. Ablation experiment shows that ensembled-modules play an significant role in improving the performance of the proposed model.

Table 3. Ablation Study on VisDrone2021, the red word means optimal.

Method	$mAP_{0.5:0.95}(\%)$	$mAP_{0.5}(\%)$	P(%)	R(%)
YOLOv7	23.98	43.46	51.55	45.72
YOLOv7+DRConv	24.09	44.52	52.34	45.99
YOLOv7+CBAM	27.48	48.44	58.67	48.33
YOLOv7+transformer	34.58	55.60	61.33	55.93
Ours	**39.22**	**61.05**	**67.51**	**56.46**

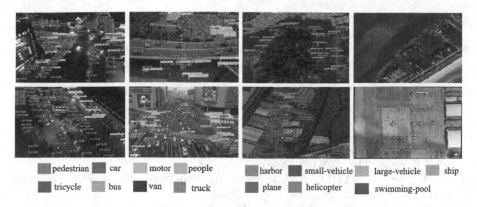

| | pedestrian | | car | | motor | | people | | | harbor | | small-vehicle | | large-vehicle | | ship |
| | tricycle | | bus | | van | | truck | | | plane | | helicopter | | swimming-pool | | |

Fig. 7. Visualization images of our model on the VisDrone2021 and DOTA-v1.0 datasets.

5 Conclusion

In this study, we incorporate the most sophisticated modules in YOLOv7, such as transformer encoder block, CBAM and DRConv. The modules mention about, greatly enhance the detection performance of YOLOv7. On the Vis-Drone dataset, our model performed better than existing YOLO series models. Experiments on the dataset DOTA-v1.0 demonstrate generalization of the model. According to the most recent study, the issues of object detection of UAVs at various heights have not been totally solved, and we are considering adding prompt words in future work.

References

1. Betti, A., Tucci, M.: YOLO-S: a lightweight and accurate YOLO-like network for small target selection in aerial imagery. Sensors **23**(4), 1865 (2023)
2. Cai, Z., Vasconcelos, N.: Cascade R-CNN: delving into high quality object detection. In: Proceedings of the IEEE Conference on Computer Vision and Pattern Recognition, pp. 6154–6162 (2018)
3. Cao, Y., et al.: VisDrone-DET2021: the vision meets drone object detection challenge results. In: Proceedings of the IEEE/CVF International Conference on Computer Vision, pp. 2847–2854 (2021)
4. Chen, J., Wang, X., Guo, Z., Zhang, X., Sun, J.: Dynamic region-aware convolution. In: Proceedings of the IEEE/CVF Conference on Computer Vision and Pattern Recognition, pp. 8064–8073 (2021)
5. Ding, J., et al.: Object detection in aerial images: a large-scale benchmark and challenges. IEEE Trans. Pattern Anal. Mach. Intell. **44**(11), 7778–7796 (2021)
6. Doloriel, C.T.C., Cajote, R.D.: Improving the detection of small oriented objects in aerial images. In: Proceedings of the IEEE/CVF Winter Conference on Applications of Computer Vision, pp. 176–185 (2023)
7. Dong, R., Xu, D., Zhao, J., Jiao, L., An, J.: Sig-NMS-based faster R-CNN combining transfer learning for small target detection in VHR optical remote sensing imagery. IEEE Trans. Geosci. Remote Sens. **57**(11), 8534–8545 (2019)

8. Dosovitskiy, A., et al.: An image is worth 16x16 words: transformers for image recognition at scale. arXiv preprint arXiv:2010.11929 (2020)

9. Gu, J., Su, T., Wang, Q., Du, X., Guizani, M.: Multiple moving targets surveillance based on a cooperative network for multi-UAV. IEEE Commun. Mag. **56**(4), 82–89 (2018)

10. Huang, Z., Li, W., Xia, X.G., Tao, R.: A general gaussian heatmap label assignment for arbitrary-oriented object detection. IEEE Trans. Image Process. **31**, 1895–1910 (2022)

11. Kellenberger, B., Marcos, D., Tuia, D.: Detecting mammals in UAV images: best practices to address a substantially imbalanced dataset with deep learning. Remote Sens. Environ. **216**, 139–153 (2018)

12. Li, C., et al.: YOLOV6 V3. 0: a full-scale reloading. arXiv preprint arXiv:2301.05586 (2023)

13. Li, Y., Chen, Y., Wang, N., Zhang, Z.: Scale-aware trident networks for object detection. In: Proceedings of the IEEE/CVF International Conference on Computer Vision, pp. 6054–6063 (2019)

14. Lin, T.Y., Dollár, P., Girshick, R., He, K., Hariharan, B., Belongie, S.: Feature pyramid networks for object detection. In: Proceedings of the IEEE Conference on Computer Vision And Pattern Recognition, pp. 2117–2125 (2017)

15. Liu, W., et al.: SSD: single shot MultiBox detector. In: Leibe, B., Matas, J., Sebe, N., Welling, M. (eds.) ECCV 2016. LNCS, vol. 9905, pp. 21–37. Springer, Cham (2016). https://doi.org/10.1007/978-3-319-46448-0_2

16. Ren, S., He, K., Girshick, R., Sun, J.: Faster R-CNN: towards real-time object detection with region proposal networks. In: Advances in Neural Information Processing Systems, vol. 28 (2015)

17. Shao, Z., Li, C., Li, D., Altan, O., Zhang, L., Ding, L.: An accurate matching method for projecting vector data into surveillance video to monitor and protect cultivated land. ISPRS Int. J. Geo Inf. **9**(7), 448 (2020)

18. Tian, Z., Shen, C., Chen, H., He, T.: FCOS: fully convolutional one-stage object detection. In: Proceedings of the IEEE/CVF International Conference on Computer Vision, pp. 9627–9636 (2019)

19. Wang, C.Y., Bochkovskiy, A., Liao, H.Y.M.: YOLOV7: trainable bag-of-freebies sets new state-of-the-art for real-time object detectors. arXiv preprint arXiv:2207.02696 (2022)

20. Woo, S., Park, J., Lee, J.-Y., Kweon, I.S.: CBAM: convolutional block attention module. In: Ferrari, V., Hebert, M., Sminchisescu, C., Weiss, Y. (eds.) ECCV 2018. LNCS, vol. 11211, pp. 3–19. Springer, Cham (2018). https://doi.org/10.1007/978-3-030-01234-2_1

21. Xia, G.S., et al.: DOTA: a large-scale dataset for object detection in aerial images. In: The IEEE Conference on Computer Vision and Pattern Recognition (CVPR), June 2018

22. Zhao, H., Shi, J., Qi, X., Wang, X., Jia, J.: Pyramid scene parsing network. In: Proceedings of the IEEE Conference on Computer Vision and Pattern Recognition, pp. 2881–2890 (2017)

23. Zhen, P.: Towards accurate oriented object detection in aerial images with adaptive multi-level feature fusion. ACM Trans. Multimed. Comput. Commun. Appl. **19**(1), 1–22 (2023)

24. Zhou, X., Wang, D., Krähenbühl, P.: Objects as points. arXiv preprint arXiv:1904.07850 (2019)
25. Zhu, X., Lyu, S., Wang, X., Zhao, Q.: TPH-YOLOV5: improved YOLOV5 based on transformer prediction head for object detection on drone-captured scenarios. In: Proceedings of the IEEE/CVF International Conference on Computer Vision, pp. 2778–2788 (2021)

Revisiting TENT for Test-Time Adaption Semantic Segmentation and Classification Head Adjustment

Xuanpu Zhao, Qi Chu[✉], Changtao Miao, Bin Liu, and Nenghai Yu

University of Science and Technology of China, Hefei, China
{qchu,flowice,ynh}@ustc.edu.cn, miaoct@mail.ustc.edu.cn

Abstract. Test-time adaption is very effective at solving the domain shift problem where the training data and testing data are sampled from different domains. However, most test-time adaption methods made their success on classification tasks while object detection and segmentation tasks usually have more applications in the real world. Meanwhile, methods that update the model at test-time which is a main branch in test-time adaption (e.g., TENT [1], a typical method of this branch) only update the backbone, and the classification head remains unchanged. Though the classification head trained by the training data behaves well on the source domain, it is not guaranteed to be effective for a new domain and a new backbone. In our work, we re-weight the entropy of pixels in an image and adopt SAR [2] to overcome the instability in online adaption. Experiment results show that the segmentation method in TENT becomes more efficient and stable thanks to these improvements. For the classification task, we propose to use T3A [3] to update the backbone and finetune the classification head in the meantime based on TENT, which boosts the classification accuracy by a large margin.

Keywords: Test-time adaption · Semantic segmentation · Classification head

1 Introduction

Deep learning models have achieved astounding performance. However, these successes are built on the basis that the data in the source and target domains are sampled from the same distribution. Dan Hendrycks et al. [4] discovered that deep learning models suffer from severe performance degradation when the training (source) data differ from the testing (target) data, which is known as the domain shift problem.

The general approaches to solve this problem include domain adaptation, domain generalization, and test-time adaptation. Domain adaptation aims to finetune the model trained on the source domain using data from the target domain. However, it is usually not possible to get data from the target domain

© The Author(s), under exclusive license to Springer Nature Switzerland AG 2023
H. Lu et al. (Eds.): ICIG 2023, LNCS 14357, pp. 66–77, 2023.
https://doi.org/10.1007/978-3-031-46311-2_6

in advance because we have no way to anticipate the target domain in most scenarios. Therefore the setting of domain generalization is not quite realistic.

In the field of domain generalization [5], scholars train the model on multiple source domains in order to get a model with strong generalization ability and they hope the model can generalize well to the unknown target domain. However, as Dubey et al. [6] point out, the optimal model learned from training domains may still be far from being optimal for an unseen target domain.

Unlike domain adaptation and domain generalization, test-time adaption adapts the model trained on the source domain at test time. One major strategy in test-time adaption is to update the model using unlabeled data seen at test time [1,7,8]. Wang et al. [1] proposed a fully test-time adaption method of this strategy. They take the entropy of the classification model as a loss function and minimize it at test time and extend their method from classification to semantic segmentation. However, they only update the backbone and ignore the classification head which remains unchanged at test time. Although the classification head behaves well on the source domain, it is not guaranteed to be effective for the target domain and a new backbone. In addition, they didn't consider the imbalance of the pixels' category which may impair the adaption when updating the segmentation model.

In our work, we raise a series of measures to resolve the mentioned drawbacks of TENT. For segmentation, we re-weight pixels' entropy to solve the imbalance of the pixel's category. We further overcome the instability existing in the online adaption of the segmentation with SAR [2]. For classification, we adopt a test-time classifier adjustment module (T3A) [3] which allows the update of the backbone and fine-tuning of the classification head both to happen at test time.

2   Related Work

Domain Adaption. Domain adaptation solves the domain shift method by leveraging unlabeled target data. The main methods include domain invariant learning, generative models, and self-training. Domain invariant learning methods learn invariant features for the source and target domains by imposing an adversarial loss [9], minimizing the domain distribution distance [10] or correlation distance [11]. Applying data augmentation with generative models can also reduce domain gap using image-to-image translation [12], style transfer [13], or hybrid methods that integrate with domain invariance learning methods [14]. Self-training methods [15] select target data predictions with high confidence and convert them into pseudo labels. These methods then iterate the fine-tuning and pseudo-labeling procedures until convergence.

Domain Generalization. A central branch algorithm is domain-invariant feature learning, which learns invariant representations using multiple source domains to improve model robustness on unseen or continuously changing environments [11,16]. Another branch is meta-learning-based methods [17–19], which divide the available domains into meta-train-domains and meta-test-domain and regulate the model trained in meta-train-domains to be useful for the meta-test-domain.

Test-Time Adaption. One major strategy is to update the model at test time. Yu Sun et al. [7] propose to use the rotation prediction task [20], or the MAE [21], as the self-supervised auxiliary task. Dequan Wang et al. [1] propose to adapt the model by minimizing entropy while testing (TENT), which does not require adding additional structure to the model in the training phase or changing the training procedure of the model as Yu Sun et al. [7] do. Some scholars discover that the statistic in the Batch Normalization layer carries information about the domain and propose to take advantage of the running mean and running variance in the Batch Normalization layer of test data [22,23]. Other scholars choose to adapt the data instead of the model. They convert data from the target domain back to the source domain using the diffusion model or the energy-based model. [24,25].

3 Methodology

3.1 Semantic Segmentation

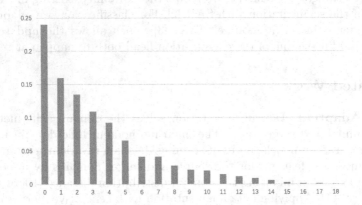

Fig. 1. We show the distribution of the number of different kinds of pixels in the Cityscapes dataset. A few classes occupy most of the data, while most classes have a small number of examples.

Re-Weighting. Dequan Wang et al. [1] update the semantic segmentation model at test time by minimizing the entropy of pixels over an image. However, as shown in Fig. 1, the autonomous driving dataset usually has a distribution with a long tail, which can cause deep long-tailed learning problems [26].

We use a simple method to solve the problem: we assign weights to different pixels based on the number of pixels of different categories in each image:

$$L_{rew} = \sum_{i=1}^{N} \frac{1}{19 \cdot M_i} \cdot H_i(\hat{y}). \tag{1}$$

In the Eq. (1), N represents total number of pixels within an image and $H_i(\hat{y})$ represents the entropy of the i th pixel, $H_i(\hat{y}) = -\Sigma_c p(\hat{y}_c) \log p(\hat{y}_c)$ where $p(\hat{y}_c)$ is the probability given by the model. 19 is the total number of classes in the dataset and M_i is the number of pixels that have the same class with the i th pixel. It should be clarified that the 'class' in M_i is obtained by prediction of the semantic segmentation model instead of a label, which is not available at the test time. This simple re-weighting method boosts the performance largely.

SAR for Online Adaption. We notice some instability in the online adaption process. As shown in Fig. 2(a), the mIoU for each image goes up at the beginning but encounters two obvious downtrends later. This downtrend can make the model collapse (to assign almost all probability to a single class, which does happen in the classification model updated with entropy minimization [2]).

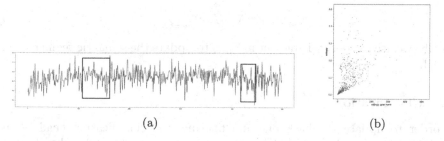

(a)	(b)

Fig. 2. (a) Change of mIoU for each image in online adaption. (b) Joint distribution.

Shuaicheng Niu et al. [2] attribute this instability in the online adaption of TENT [1] to some samples with excessive gradients of entropy to the model parameters (they call these samples noisy samples) and proposed a series of strategies (SAR) to overcome the instability within the online updation of the classification model in TENT. Using their method, we extend further to surmount the instability in the online updation of the semantic segmentation model.

As shown in Fig. 2(b), most of the noisy samples can be filtered out by removing those with entropy greater than a certain threshold, and then the model is updated using the sharpness-aware minimization method [27] to enhance the robustness of the model to the few remaining noisy samples.

In detail, for each image, the pixels with entropy greater than the threshold E are first filtered out, then the total entropy of the image is obtained using the re-weighting method among the remaining pixels

$$H(\omega) = \sum_{i=1}^{N} \frac{1}{19 \cdot M_i} \cdot H_i(\omega; \hat{y}), \tag{2}$$

where ω is the model parameters and $\hat{y}$ is the prediction probability. According to sharpness-aware minimization, we define the loss function as:

$$L(\omega) = \max_{\|\xi\|_2 \leq \rho} [H(\omega + \xi) - H(\omega)] + H(\omega) = \max_{\|\xi\|_2 \leq \rho} H(\omega + \xi). \tag{3}$$

In Eq. 3, ρ is hyperparameters, and $\max_{\|\xi\|_2 \leq \rho}[H(\omega + \xi) - H(\omega)]$ can be interpreted as the sharpness of the entropy surface. To get ξ^* that maximizes $H(\omega + \xi)$, we expand it using Taylor expansion and retain only first-order term

$$\xi^*(\omega) \approx arg \max_{\|\xi\|_2 \leq \rho} [H(\omega) + \xi^T \nabla_\omega H(\omega)] = arg \max_{\|\xi\|_2 \leq \rho} \xi^T \nabla_\omega H(\omega). \tag{4}$$

According to the solution of the dual norm problem

$$arg \max_{\|\xi\|_2 \leq \rho} \xi^T \nabla_\omega H(\omega) = \rho \cdot sgn(\nabla_\omega H(\omega)) \cdot \frac{\|\nabla_\omega H(\omega)\|}{\|\nabla_\omega H(\omega)\|_2}. \tag{5}$$

Substitute this result back into $L(\omega)$, differentiate and discard the second term:

$$\nabla_\omega L(\omega) \approx \nabla_\omega H(\omega)|_{\omega + \hat{\xi}(\omega)}. \tag{6}$$

Finally, we use the derived gradient in Eq. 6 to update the semantic segmentation model.

3.2 Classification

In order to update the backbone and finetune the classification head in the meantime, we get the pseudo-label of coming data x using the classification head obtained in the training phase

$$\hat{y} = arg \max_{y_k} q_\omega(Y = y_k|z) = \frac{exp(z \cdot \omega^k)}{\sum_j exp(z \cdot \omega^j)}, \tag{7}$$

where z is the feature produced by the backbone $z = f_\theta(x)$. The feature of x is preserved as the candidate samples for the predicted class:

$$S_t^k = \begin{cases} S_{t-1}^k \cup \{\frac{z}{\|z\|}\}, & if \ \hat{y} = y^k \\ S_{t-1}^k, & else. \end{cases} \tag{8}$$

In the queue, the M samples with the lowest entropy from candidate samples of each class are selected as the final samples

$$S_t^k = \{z \mid z \in S_t^k, H_\omega(\hat{Y}|z) \leq \alpha_k\}. \tag{9}$$

The centers of all final samples in each class are used as weights to form a new classification head and the probability of x belonging to each class is predicted by the new classification head.

$$c^k = \frac{1}{|S^k|} \sum_{z \in S_t^k} z \tag{10}$$

$$p(Y = y_k | z) = \frac{exp(z \cdot c^k)}{\sum_j exp(z \cdot c^j)} \tag{11}$$

This probability is used to calculate the entropy and the obtained entropy is back-propagated through the new classification head to update the backbone. Eventually, the category of x is predicted by the updated backbone and new classification head.

The New Classification Head Versus the Old One. We come to the question that should we use the old classification head obtained in the training phase or the new one derived from T3A to calculate the entropy and backpropagate it. If we calculate entropy and minimize it using the old classification head, entropy becomes lower from the perspective of the old classification head but may be still high for the new one. Based on this analysis, we propose that minimizing the entropy by the old classification head and predicting the class with the new one can not improve the performance and even make the entropy minimization method invalid. Thus, we minimize the entropy and predict the class both on the new classifier.

4 Experiment

For semantic segmentation, We train the DeepLabV3+ [28] model on the GTAV [29] training set and test it on the Cityscapes [30] validation set in both online and offline adaption. For classification, we employ experiments on PACS [31] and CIFAR-10/CIFAR-10-C [4]. Our implementation is in PyTorch based on the code from DeepLabV3+, Tent, and T3A. We run all of our experiments on a single NVIDIA TITAN XP GPU.

Datasets. The GTAV dataset was reconstructed by Stephan Richter and Vibhav Vineet et al. [29] from the video game GTAV, a video game that renders realistic cityscapes under different weather conditions. The Cityscapes dataset [30], contains a variety of stereoscopic video sequences recorded from street views of 50 different cities, with high quality 5,000 pixel-level annotations in addition to the larger 20,000 weakly annotated frames. CIFAR-10 comprises 10 classes, with a training set of 50,000, and a test set of 10,000 in total. CIFAR-10-C [4] is obtained by simulating real-world corruptions on the test set of CIFAR-10. PCAS [31] comprises four domains (art, cartoons, photos, sketches), containing 9, 991 examples of 7 classes.

Implementation Details. We test the DeepLabV3+ model pre-trained on the GTAV training set provided by Sungha Choi et al. [32] and test it on the Cityscapes validation set. For offline adaption, the baseline model obtained in the training phase is updated 10 times with per image (with both original and re-weighted entropy). For online adaption, the model is updated (with re-weighted entropy) only once per image and kept for the next image. For classification, we train the classification model on the CIFAR-10 training set and test it on CIFAR-10-C, level 5. Then we train the classification model on the art painting and photo domains respectively and test them on the other three domains in PACS. We minimize the entropy with both the old classification head from the source domain and the new one derived from T3A to show that the latter choice is better. Our networks are equipped with batch normalization. For Cityscapes, we can only use running mean and variance estimated in the training phase because the model is updated with a single image. For CIFAR-10-C and PACS, however, we estimate the running mean and variance using batch data since data comes in the form of the batch.

Optimization. We use the Adam with a learning rate of 5×10^{-5} and 5×10^{-6} in online and offline adaption respectively to optimize the DeepLabV3+ model. For TENT/TENT+T3A tested on CIFAR-10-C, we optimize by Adam and set the learning rate at 0.001. For TENT/TENT+T3A on PACS, we optimize by SGD with momentum and the learning rate is 0.001.

Backbone and Hyperparameters. For DeepLabV3+ and the classification model tested on PACS, we use residual networks [33] with 50 layers (R-50). For the model tested on CIFAR-10/CIFAR-10-C, we use the R-26 architecture. The threshold of the entropy E is set to be 0.4. The hyperparameters in sharpness-aware minimization ρ is 0.01.

4.1   Results

Figure 3 shows the semantic segmentation results of DeepLabV3+ updated offline and online respectively. Figure 4 shows the change of mIoU of the 500 images in the validation set of the Cityscapes dataset. Figure 5 visualizes the offline adaption with re-weighting on an example image. Table 1, 2, 3 and 4 summarize the results on CIFAR-10-C and PACS. For the experiment on PACS, we train the model on the photo and art painting domains respectively, and test the model on the other three domains (indicated by P → A, C, S and A → P, C, S).

Tent Improves the mIoU by a Large Margin by Re-Weighting the Entropy of Pixels. Figure 3 shows that although using the entropy of all pixels directly can improve the performance of the segmentation model, the improvement is limited. But by re-weighting each pixel's entropy according to the number of different classes, we can boost the mIoU largely. As Fig. 5 shows, in ten iterations the algorithm impresses the noise on the road tremendously and recovers the motorbike on the left and traffic sign on the right gradually.

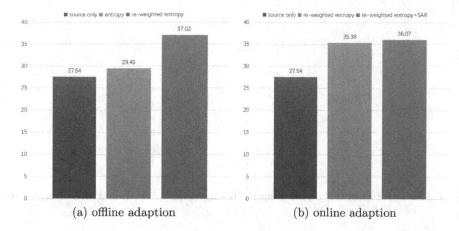

(a) offline adaption   (b) online adaption

Fig. 3. (a) mIoU of source only model, model adapted with entropy minimization and re-weighted entropy minimization. (b) mIoU of the source-only model, model adapted with re-weighted entropy minimization and re-weighted entropy minimization+SAR.

Table 1. Test accuracy on CIFAR-10-C, level 5, ResNet-26.

	gau	sho	imp	def	gla	mot	zoo	sno	fro	fog	bri	con	ela	pix	jpe
baseline	28.3	33.9	26.4	57.8	44.2	62.3	59.1	70.6	56.3	58.8	88.2	40.2	71.1	42.9	67.1
T3A	36.7	41.2	32.7	61.0	49.7	65.6	64.5	71.4	60.3	64.5	88.2	45.5	73.5	53.3	68.9
TENT	75.2	76.5	67.0	88.1	68.2	86.3	89.2	84.1	83.8	86.3	92.1	87.9	78.0	82.7	75.8
TENT+T3A (new cls)	78.0	79.8	71.1	88.7	70.9	87.8	89.6	85.4	85.0	87.4	92.3	89.2	79.7	84.6	79.0

Table 2. Test accuracy on CIFAR-10-C, level 5, ResNet-26.

	gau	sho	imp	def	gla	mot	zoo	sno	fro	fog	bri	con	ela	pix	jpe
TENT+T3A (old cls)	74.6	76.3	66.4	87.4	67.4	85.6	88.7	83.6	83.2	85.8	91.8	87.3	77.6	82.2	74.9
TENT+T3A (new cls)	78.0	79.8	71.1	88.7	70.9	87.8	89.6	85.4	85.0	87.4	92.3	89.2	79.7	84.6	79.0

SAR Restrains the Instability Existing in Online Adaption. Re-weighting entropy and then updating the model improves the mIoU by a large margin, but some instability exists in online adaption which can crash the model. As Fig. 3 shows, the downtrends are well overcome after using SAR. Figure 2(b) shows that SAR improves the mIoU further.

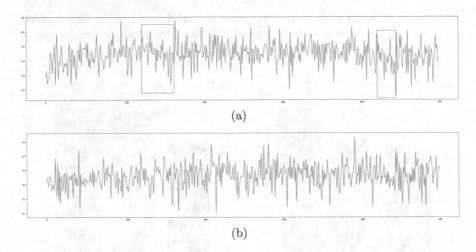

(a)

(b)

Fig. 4. Change of mIoU for online adaption before using SAR (a) and after using SAR (b).

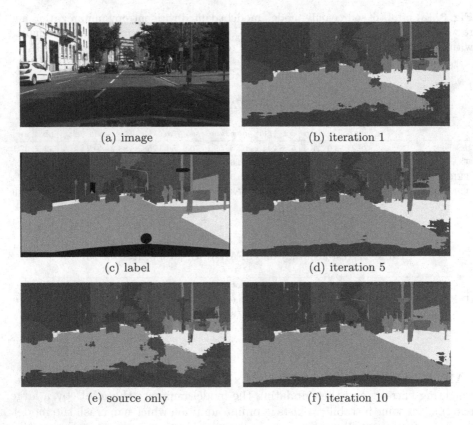

(a) image   (b) iteration 1

(c) label   (d) iteration 5

(e) source only   (f) iteration 10

Fig. 5. Visualization of offline adaption with re-weighting.

Table 3. Test accuracy on PACS, ResNet-50.

	P → A	P → C	P → S	A → P	A → C	A → S
baseline	72.6	28.9	30.1	97.1	60.1	49.7
T3A	76.5	70.7	48.2	98.8	76.9	66.0
TENT	75.0	62.3	47.0	98.0	72.7	62.4
TENT+T3A (new cls)	77.8	73.6	50.2	98.9	78.6	66.1

Table 4. Test accuracy on PACS, ResNet-50.

	P → A	P → C	P → S	A → P	A → C	A → S
TENT+T3A (old cls)	75.5	68.1	46.1	98.6	76.1	67.6
TENT+T3A (new cls)	77.8	73.6	50.2	98.9	78.6	66.1

T3A Boosts the Performance of TENT. Table 1 shows the performance of TENT and TENT+T3A on the CIFAR-10-C dataset, level 5. The average classification accuracy of the TENT+T3A (new cls) model is 83.06%, surpassing TENT (81.42%) and T3A (58.46%). Results on PACS are summarized by Table 3. For the model trained on the photo domain, the average accuracy of TENT is 61.42% on the other three domains. T3A reaches 65.13% while TENT+T3A (new cls) reaches 67.22%. For the model trained by the art painting domain, the average accuracy of TENT is 77.66% on the other three domains. T3A reaches 80.77% while TENT+T3A (new cls) reaches 81.19%.

The Choice of the Classification Head Matters. Minimizing entropy through the old classifier can not guarantee entropy also goes down on the new classification head obtained by T3A, which may impair the performance of TENT. It's shown in Table 2 and Table 4 that the classification accuracy becomes lower (more obvious in Table 2) if minimize through the old classification head instead of the new one.

5   Conclusion

In this paper, we improve the test-time segmentation method proposed by TENT by re-weighting the entropy of pixels and using the method of SAR. For classification, we adopt T3A to finetune the classification head which is generally ignored in current methods. We hope our paper can encourage researchers in this domain to pay more attention to detection and segmentation tasks as well as the classification head.

Acknowledgements. This work is supported by the National Natural Science Foundation of China (No. 62272430) and the Fundamental Research Funds for the Central Universities.

References

1. Wang, D., Shelhamer, E., Liu, S., Olshausen, B., Darrell, T.: Tent: fully test-time adaptation by entropy minimization. arXiv preprint arXiv:2006.10726 (2020)
2. Niu, S., et al.: Towards stable test-time adaptation in dynamic wild world. arXiv preprint arXiv:2302.12400 (2023)
3. Iwasawa, Y., Matsuo, Y.: Test-time classifier adjustment module for model-agnostic domain generalization. Adv. Neural. Inf. Process. Syst. **34**, 2427–2440 (2021)
4. Hendrycks, D., Dietterich, T.: Benchmarking neural network robustness to common corruptions and perturbations. arXiv preprint arXiv:1903.12261 (2019)
5. Blanchard, G., Lee, G., Scott, C.: Generalizing from several related classification tasks to a new unlabeled sample. In: Advances in Neural Information Processing Systems, vol. 24 (2011)
6. Dubey, A., Ramanathan, V., Pentland, A., Mahajan, D.: Adaptive methods for real-world domain generalization. In: Proceedings of the IEEE/CVF Conference on Computer Vision and Pattern Recognition, pp. 14340–14349 (2021)
7. Sun, Y., Wang, X., Liu, Z., Miller, J., Efros, A., Hardt, M.: Test-time training with self-supervision for generalization under distribution shifts. In: International Conference on Machine Learning, pp. 9229–9248. PMLR (2020)
8. Gandelsman, Y., Sun, Y., Chen, X., Efros, A.: Test-time training with masked autoencoders: Adv. Neural. Inf. Process. Syst. **35**, 29374–29385 (2022)
9. Ganin, Y., et al.: Domain-adversarial training of neural networks. J. Mach. Learn. Res. **17**(1), 2030–2096 (2016)
10. Long, M., Cao, Y., Wang, J., Jordan, M.: Learning transferable features with deep adaptation networks. In: International Conference on Machine Learning, pp. 97–105. PMLR (2015)
11. Sun, B., Saenko, K.: Deep CORAL: correlation alignment for deep domain adaptation. In: Hua, G., Jégou, H. (eds.) ECCV 2016, Part III. LNCS, vol. 9915, pp. 443–450. Springer, Cham (2016). https://doi.org/10.1007/978-3-319-49409-8_35
12. Bousmalis, K., Silberman, N., Dohan, D., Erhan, D., Krishnan, D.: Unsupervised pixel-level domain adaptation with generative adversarial networks. In: Proceedings of the IEEE Conference on Computer Vision and Pattern Recognition, pp. 3722–3731 (2017)
13. Dundar, A., Liu, M.-Y., Wang, T.-C., Zedlewski, J., Kautz, J.: Domain stylization: a strong, simple baseline for synthetic to real image domain adaptation. arXiv preprint arXiv:1807.09384 (2018)
14. Chen, Y.-C., Lin, Y.-Y., Yang, M.-H., Huang, J.-B.: CrDoCo: pixel-level domain transfer with cross-domain consistency. In: Proceedings of the IEEE/CVF Conference on Computer Vision and Pattern Recognition, pp. 1791–1800 (2019)
15. Zou, Y., Yu, Z., Vijaya Kumar, B.V.K., Wang, J.: Unsupervised domain adaptation for semantic segmentation via class-balanced self-training. In: Ferrari, V., Hebert, M., Sminchisescu, C., Weiss, Y. (eds.) ECCV 2018. LNCS, vol. 11207, pp. 297–313. Springer, Cham (2018). https://doi.org/10.1007/978-3-030-01219-9_18
16. Li, H., Pan, S.J., Wang, Kot, A.C.: Domain generalization with adversarial feature learning. In: Proceedings of the IEEE Conference on Computer Vision and Pattern Recognition, pp. 5400–5409 (2018)
17. Li, D., Yang, Y., Song, Y.-Z., Hospedales, T.: Learning to generalize: meta-learning for domain generalization. In Proceedings of the AAAI Conference on Artificial Intelligence, vol. 32 (2018)

18. Balaji, Y., Sankaranarayanan, S., Chellappa, R.: Metareg: towards domain generalization using meta-regularization. In: Advances in Neural Information Processing Systems, vol. 31 (2018)
19. Li, Y., Yang, Y., Zhou, W., Hospedales, T.: Feature-critic networks for heterogeneous domain generalization. In: International Conference on Machine Learning, pp. 3915–3924. PMLR (2019)
20. Gidaris, S., Singh, P., Komodakis, N.: Unsupervised representation learning by predicting image rotations. arXiv preprint arXiv:1803.07728 (2018)
21. He, K., Chen, X., Xie, S., Li, Y., Dollár, P., Girshick, R.: Masked autoencoders are scalable vision learners. In: Proceedings of the IEEE/CVF Conference on Computer Vision and Pattern Recognition, pp. 16000–16009 (2022)
22. Li, Y., Wang, N., Shi, J., Liu, J., Hou, X.: Revisiting batch normalization for practical domain adaptation. arXiv preprint arXiv:1603.04779 (2016)
23. Zou, Y., Zhang, Z., Li, C.L., Zhang, H., Pfister, T., Huang, J.B.: Learning instance-specific adaptation for cross-domain segmentation. In: Avidan, S., Brostow, G., Cissé, M., Farinella, G.M., Hassner, T. (eds.) ECCV 2022, Part XXXIII. LNCS, vol. 13693, pp. 459–476. Springer, Cham (2022). https://doi.org/10.1007/978-3-031-19827-4_27
24. Gao, J., Zhang, J., Liu, X., Darrell, T., Shelhamer, E., Wang, D.: Back to the source: diffusion-driven test-time adaptation. arXiv preprint arXiv:2207.03442 (2022)
25. Xiao, Z., Zhen, X., Liao, S., Snoek, C.G.M.: Energy-based test sample adaptation for domain generalization. arXiv preprint arXiv:2302.11215 (2023)
26. Zhang, Y., Kang, B., Hooi, B., Yan, S., Feng, J.: Deep long-tailed learning: a survey. arXiv preprint arXiv:2110.04596 (2021)
27. Foret, P., Kleiner, A., Mobahi, H., Neyshabur, B.: Sharpness-aware minimization for efficiently improving generalization. arXiv preprint arXiv:2010.01412 (2020)
28. Chen, L.-C., Zhu, Y., Papandreou, G., Schroff, F., Adam, H.: Encoder-decoder with atrous separable convolution for semantic image segmentation. In: Ferrari, V., Hebert, M., Sminchisescu, C., Weiss, Y. (eds.) ECCV 2018. LNCS, vol. 11211, pp. 833–851. Springer, Cham (2018). https://doi.org/10.1007/978-3-030-01234-2_49
29. Richter, S.R., Vineet, V., Roth, S., Koltun, V.: Playing for data: ground truth from computer games. In: Leibe, B., Matas, J., Sebe, N., Welling, M. (eds.) ECCV 2016, Part II. LNCS, vol. 9906, pp. 102–118. Springer, Cham (2016). https://doi.org/10.1007/978-3-319-46475-6_7
30. Cordts, M., et al.: The cityscapes dataset for semantic urban scene understanding. In: Proceedings of the IEEE Conference on Computer Vision and Pattern Recognition, pp. 3213–3223 (2016)
31. Li, D., Yang, Y., Song, Y.-Z., Hospedales, T.M.: Deeper, broader and artier domain generalization. In: Proceedings of the IEEE International Conference on Computer Vision, pp. 5542–5550 (2017)
32. Choi, S., Jung, S., Yun, H., Kim, J.T., Kim, S., Choo, J.: RobustNet: improving domain generalization in urban-scene segmentation via instance selective whitening. In: Proceedings of the IEEE/CVF Conference on Computer Vision and Pattern Recognition, pp. 11580–11590 (2021)
33. He, K., Zhang, X., Ren, S., Sun, J.: Deep residual learning for image recognition. In: Proceedings of the IEEE Conference on Computer Vision and Pattern Recognition, pp. 770–778 (2016)

Single Image Dehazing
with Deep-Image-Prior Networks

Hongyan Wang[1]([⊠]), Xin Wang[2], and Zhixun Su[3]

[1] Dalian University of Foreign Language, Dalian, China
wanghongyan@dlufl.edu.cn
[2] Beijing Huawei Digital Technologies Co., Ltd., Beijing, China
[3] Dalian University of Technology, Dalian, China

Abstract. Most conventional dehazing methods focus on separately estimating key parameters (e.g., the transmission map and the atmospheric light) based on the atmospheric scattering model to generate haze-free images, which may face the limitation of error accumulation. With the advance of deep learning technologies, employing deep neural networks (DNNs) to conduct haze removal becomes popular dehazing methods recently. Most DNNs-based methods automatically learn haze-free image or key parameters in the atmospheric scattering model in end-to-end manners, which heavily rely on training models on dataset. This work aims to recover haze-free images directly by DNNs without any time-consuming training process on dataset or cascading parameter estimation steps. In this paper, haze removal is achieved in Maximum-a-Posterior (MAP) framework based on an exist re-formulation of the atmospheric scattering model, which only involves one integrated variable. The proposed MAP framework is connected with DNN by two self-supervised generative networks—two deep-image-prior (DIP) networks, which are present for modeling the deep priors of the haze-free image and the integrated variable. We further investigate the statistical property of the integrated variable and propose handcrafted regularizers to better constrain the integrated variable. By iteratively updating two networks, solutions of the haze-free image and the integrated variable can be solved jointly. Experiments on both synthesized and real hazy images show that the proposed method performs competitively to state-of-the-art dehazing methods in terms of PSNR, SSIM and visual evaluations.

Keywords: Image dehazing · All-in-one model · Deep image prior

1 Introduction

The existence of haze may lead to annoying photographing experience in the outdoors. As the medium is turbid, the captured images usually exhibit poor color contrast and fidelity. In consumer/computational photography, removing the haze effect from a hazy image for good image quality is one of the most fundamental requirement. For many practical visual tasks, like outdoor video

© The Author(s), under exclusive license to Springer Nature Switzerland AG 2023
H. Lu et al. (Eds.): ICIG 2023, LNCS 14357, pp. 78–90, 2023.
https://doi.org/10.1007/978-3-031-46311-2_7

tracking and object recognition, inputting hazy images would result in undesired results, even with the state-of-the-art tracking and recognizing algorithms.
Hence, image dehazing is of significant investigation value.

The research on image dehazing has been witnessed remarkable progress over
the past two decades. Some methods [17,27] focus on improving color contrast
in the aspect of image enhancement without utilizing any cue from imaging
degradation process. However, this kind of methods tend to generate unpleased
outputs which may contain artifacts. In contrast, quite a number of dehazing
methods are proposed based on a physical hazy image formation model, a.k.a.,
the atmospheric scattering model. It is proposed by [15] and can be expressed
mathematically as

$$I(x) = t(x)J(x) + (1 - t(x))A, \tag{1}$$

where I denotes one hazy image, J denotes the corresponding haze-free image to
be recovered, A denotes the global atmospheric light, t denotes the transmission
map, and x is the pixel index. This model indicates that J will be decided if
both t and A are known. Accordingly, many methods propose to estimate these
two physical parameters and then generate the haze-free image via inverting (1).

Apart from estimating the global atmospheric light A, estimating the transmission map t from (1) is highly ill-posed. To reduce the ill-posedness of the
problem, various statistical priors of natural images have been explored and
exploited [1,4,5,8,16,24,25,28]. However, these statistical priors do not hold in
special cases, then an inaccurate t may be obtained. As the transmission map
describes the attenuation ratio, such an inaccurate t would cause an undesired
dehazing result J. Moreover, many conventional dehazing methods (e.g., [8])
estimate the global atmospheric light A based on a known transmission map t.
The non-joint estimation of t and A may lead to error accumulation and amplification occurred in the dehazed result J.

Recently, deep learning has also been introduced to cope with image dehazing, in the view of the powerful representation ability of DNNs. A typical
line is to implicitly learn the map between the hazy image and the haze-free
image in end-to-end manners [3,12–14,32]. Also, plenty of DNNs-based methods [2,6,18,22,30,31] propose to learn the key physical parameters based on
the degradation model (1). To address error accumulation incurred by separately estimating strategy, Li et al. [10] propose to remove haze based on a
re-expressed version of model (1), by computing one newly integrated variable.
Compared with conventional prior-based methods, one advantage of these DNNs-
based methods is that no hand-crafting step is required in the whole dehazing
process. Despite having achieved varying degrees of success, most of DNNs-based
methods suffer from unsatisfied generalization performance, due to inherent limitations in collecting training image pairs.

In this paper, we propose to adopt self-learning generative network for image
dehazing. To bypass the separately estimation of each physical parameter, we
employ the re-formulation of (1) proposed in [10] and jointly estimate the haze-
free image and an integrated variable defined by t and A. The proposed method
is self-supervised and does not require any training process on dataset.

Main contributions of this work can be summarized as:

1. We propose MAP-based neural dehazing framework which has two branches: haze-free image recovering and the integrated variable estimating. Two self-supervised DIP networks [29] are employed for both of them to capture deep priors. No training process on dataset is required, leading to relatively cheap computational cost compared with most existing DNNs-based dehazing methods.
2. Our neural dehazing formulation is also based on the statistical properties of the integrated variable. A jointly optimizing algorithm is present, in which we provide an unconstrained optimization model respect to the haze-free image and a constrained optimization model with respect to the integrated variable.
3. Experimental results on synthesized and real-world datasets demonstrate that the proposed method achieves competitive performance with state-of-the-art dehazing methods.

2   Related Work

In this section, we briefly review two representative categories of single image dehazing methods. One is prior-based methods, and the other is DNNs-based methods.

Prior-Based Methods.   Recovering a haze-free image by (1) given only a hazy image is rather challenging. To make the problem tractable, many methods adopt the strategy of first estimating parameters in (1) based on priors and then generating a haze-free image by inverting (1). Tan [28] proposes a local contrast maximization methods based on the observation that the clear images usually exhibit high local contrast compared to corresponding hazy images. In [4], haze removal is achieved based on the assumption that the transmission map and surface shading are locally uncorrelated. He et al. [8] propose dark channel prior (DCP), that the pixel intensities in non-haze regions tend to be low in at least one color channel, to estimate the transmission map. Meng et al. [16] estimate the transmission map by optimizing the inherent boundary constraint with weighted L_1-norm contextual regularization based on DCP. Fattal [5] proposes to dehaze a hazy image based on a generic regularity in natural images, that pixels of small image patches typically exhibit a one-dimensional distribution in RGB color space, namely color-line prior. Zhu et al. [33] propose a linear color attenuation prior (CAP) for haze removal based on the difference of the brightness and the saturation between haze-free images and hazy images. Berman et al. [1] introduce a non-local color prior that colors in an entire clear image can be well approximated by a few hundred distinct colors. These methods have demonstrated impressive dehazing results in the case of priors holding well.

DNNs-Based Methods. The past two decades have witnessed the increasing popularity of DNNs-based dehazing methods. In the recent literature, many researchers adopt DNNs to learn the map between hazy images and haze free-images or estimate key parameters in (1). Cai et al. [2] design a three-layer convolutional neural networks (CNNs), named DehazeNet, to estimate the transmission map. Ren et al. [22] propose a Multi-Scale CNN (MSCNN) to achieve the transmission map estimating and refining. To address the error accumulation and amplification problem, Li et al. [10] propose to bypass the separately key parameters estimation, and design AoD-Net for image dehazing based on an equivalent model of (1)—the all-in-one model. Yang et al. [30] propose to estimate the transmission map, the atmospheric light and the dehazed result by employing generative adversarial networks (GANs) on unpaired training datasets. Liu et al. [14] design an end-to-end trainable grid network, named GridDehazeNet, to recover haze-free image directly. Qu et al. [20] propose to generate haze-free image via GAN independent of physical model (1). Li et al. [12] propose to remove haze by conditional generative adversarial network (cGAN) with an encoder and decoder architecture. Single image dehazing is also realized by the marriage of neural networks and image layer decomposition [6,18], in which the transmission map and the atmospheric light are viewed as different layers. Other attempts on single image dehazing include fusion strategy [23] and transfer strategy [7], etc. Although these DNNs-based methods have achieved promising results, improving generalization performance of DNNs-based methods on real-world hazy images is still a bottleneck problem.

3   Modelling and Optimization

In this section, we first review an existing re-formulated version of model (1), the all-in-one model [10]. Then we introduce our MAP-based neural dehazing method, including problem formulation, network architecture, and optimizing scheme.

3.1   The All-in-One Model and MAP-Based Formulation

By unifying the $t(x)$ and A into one multiplier factor $K(x)$, the model (1) has the following equivalent expression, which has been introduced in [10]:

$$J(x) = K(x)I(x) - K(x) + b, \tag{2}$$

where

$$K(x) = \frac{I(x) - A + t(x)(A - b)}{t(x)(I(x) - 1)}, \tag{3}$$

and b is the constant bias being set as 1 by default.

Based on (2), the goal of image dehazing is to seek a pair of J and K from the observed I. To reach this goal, we propose an optimization model under the classical MAP framework associated with two regularizers:

$$\arg\min_{J,K} \|K \odot (I - 1) + b - J\|_2^2 + \alpha\phi(J) + \beta\varphi(K) \tag{4}$$

where K, I and J are of vector form, $\phi(J)$ and $\varphi(K)$ denote the priors on haze-free image J and the integrated variable K. α and β are trade-off parameters, and $\odot$ represents the element-wise multiplication operator.

Following the idea of plenty of existing regularization methods, the regularizers in (4) (especially $\phi(J)$) should be handcrafted with certain explicit expressions based on statistical priors, and then minimizing (4) would output the recovered J and K. This paper is not completely one of such methods. In this paper, we attempt to estimate K and J jointly in a self-supervised learning manner, as introduced in the following subsections.

(a)   (b)   (c)   (d)

(e)   (f)   (g)

Fig. 1. (a) A clear image in NYU2 dataset [26]. The second column ((b) and (e)): two synthetic hazy images. The third column ((c) and (f)): visualizations of K. The last column ((d) and (g)): intensity distributions of K.

3.2   Neural Dehazing Formulation

We note that the architecture of DIP generative network [29] has demonstrated excellent ability to learn deep low-level image prior, as evidenced in [6,21]. This inspires us to employ two generative networks $\mathbb{G}_K$ and $\mathbb{G}_J$ for solving (4). The proposed neural dehazing formulation can be expressed as:

$$\min_{\mathbb{G}_K, \mathbb{G}_J} \|\mathbb{G}_K(n_K) \odot (I - 1) + b - \mathbb{G}_J(n_J)\|_2^2, \qquad (5)$$

where n_K and n_J denote the initialized noisy inputs which both obey the uniform distribution.

There is no explicit $\phi(J)$ and $\varphi(K)$ in (5) because deep priors can be captured automatically by $\mathbb{G}_K$ and $\mathbb{G}_J$. Despite that the formulation (5) implies a theoretical feasibility for neural dehazing, there is still one issue to be addressed. That is the scale ambiguity between $J - b$ and K. The all-in-one model (2) indicates that $K \odot (I - 1) = J - b$. Then, for a scale factor s (typically, $s \neq 0$), $sK \odot (I - 1) = s(J - b)$, i.e., both $(K, J - b)$ and $(sK, s(J - b))$ satisfy the model (2). One practical technique to deal with the scale ambiguity is to impose scale constraint on K. Hence, we investigate the statistical distribution of K on synthetic dataset (NYU2 [26]). One example is shown in Fig. 1.

As can be seen in Fig. 1, each $K(x)$ is non-negative, since $J(x) - b$ (b is set to be 1 by default) and $I(x) - 1$ are both non-positive. $K(x)$ is of large probability to be larger than 1, and some $K(x)$ values lie near zero. We note that for the image degraded by thick haze concentration shown in Fig. 1(e), the values of $K(x)$ are not very large (less than 4 and peaked at about 2.4, see Fig. 1(g)), even though there is no evidence that $K(x)$ is bounded. To meet the above observations, our neural dehazing optimization model is modified by imposing two regularizers over variable K:

$$\min_{\mathbb{G}_J, \mathbb{G}_K} \|\mathbb{G}_K(n_K) \odot (I - 1) + b - \mathbb{G}_J(n_J)\|_2^2$$
$$+ \lambda \|\mathbb{G}_K(n_K)\|_2^2 + \mu \|1 - 0.5\mathbb{G}_K(n_K)\|_2^2, \tag{6}$$

where λ and μ are trade-off parameters.

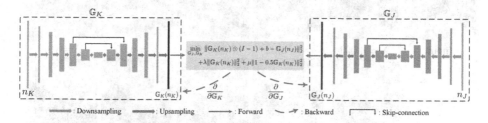

Fig. 2. Brief illustration of the architecture of our method.

3.3 Network Architecture and Optimization

Although K is not a natural image, the structure of K has close relationship with haze-free image J (see Fig. 1 (c) and (f)). Thus, we choose two similar generative network to recover J and K. A brief illustration of our whole network is shown in Fig. 2, where two encoder-decoder architectures with few skip-connections are employed. There are mainly three kinds of module operations in each generative-network branch: downsampling, upsampling, and skip-connection. One downsampling is implemented by the operators in the order of convolution (with strides), batch normalization (BN), LeakyReLU, convolution (without strides), BN, and LeakyReLU. One upsampling contains BN, convolution (without strides), BN, LeakyReLU, convolution (without strides), BN, LeakyReLU, bilinear upsampling operations. In comparison, the structure of one skip-connection is relative simple, which contains convolution (without strides), BN, and LeakyReLU.

The proposed neural dehazing method is a self-supervised one which requires no training dataset. Two noisy images n_K and n_J (both uniform distribution) are required for initializations. The solutions of the optimization model (6) can be obtained by self-supervised learning algorithm [29]. We learn $\mathbb{G}_J$ and $\mathbb{G}_K$ jointly, i.e., the learning process of each DIP network is independent under the guidance of (6). Automatic differentiation technique [19] and ADAM algorithm [9] are essential for our learning process.

4   Discussion and Experiments

In this section, we provide quantitative evaluations and visual experimental results compared with state-of-the-art dehazing methods. 8 representative dehazing algorithms, including 4 prior-based dehazing methods [1,8,16,33] and 4 DNNs-based dehazing methods [2,6,10,22], are selected for comparison. All the experiments are conducted on an Nvidia GTX 1080Ti GPU based on PyTorch. It takes about 186 seconds to recover a 460×620 color image.

Fig. 3. Results under different settings of the two parameters λ and μ. Setting of the other parameter: the first row: $\mu = 0.1$, the second row: $\lambda = 0.01$.

4.1   Experimental Settings

Network Settings. Each DIP generative network requires random noise (uniform distribution) as initialization. One is the initialization of $\mathbb{G}_K$, and the other is that of $\mathbb{G}_J$. Both of them are of $8 \times W \times H$ size, where $W \times H$ is the size of hazy image in one channel. The batch size is set to be 1. The ratio of downsampling is 0.5 (i.e., upsampling ratio is 2). The number of channels of one encoder-decoder architecture are 8, 8, 16, 32, 64, 128, 256, 128, 64, 32, 16, 8, 3. The learning rate is set to be 0.001.

λ and μ. There are two parameters in model (6), λ and μ. To better show the role of them, we report several results on a hazy image under different settings. As shown in Fig. 3, large λ favors a relative white dehazing result, and large μ favors a high contrast image. In our experiments, λ and μ are chosen empirically from $[0.001, 0.1]$ and $[0.05, 0.5]$, according to the different level of haze concentration.

The Max Number of Iterations. The proposed algorithm stops when reaching the max number of iterations. We set the max number of iterations to be 3000 empirically, and setting more iterations leads to a visually and quatitively similar dehazing result. We show the changes of energy value, PSNR and SSIM during 8000 iterations in Fig. 4, using an image for example. As can be seen, with the increase of iterations, the dehazing result generated by the proposed algorithm becomes more and more pleasing. A final solution can be recovered after no less than 2000 iterations.

Evaluation Criterions. PSNR and SSIM, which are commonly utilized in dehazing methods, are selected for quantitative evaluations on synthetic images. Evaluations on real-world images mainly rely on subjectively visual quality, as ground-truth haze-free images are usually unavailable.

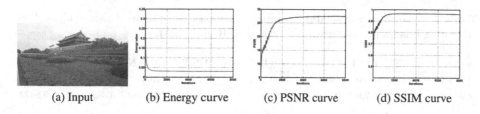

(a) Input   (b) Energy curve   (c) PSNR curve   (d) SSIM curve

Fig. 4. Quantitative evolution of the proposed self-learning framework along with the increase of iterations, in terms of energy value, PSNR, and SSIM.

4.2 Comparisons with AoD-Net [10] and Double-DIP [6]

The most related dehazeing methods of this work is AoD-net [10] and Double-DIP [6]. Hence, we provided some discussions in this subsection.

Comparisons with AoD-net [10]. Both AoD-net and our method are based on the all-in-one model (2). Both two methods do not require to estimate t and A in different sub-optimizations separately. While AoD-net is an end-to-end dehazing method which needs time-consuming training process on dataset, our method is a self-supervised one initialized by random noises. The architecture of AoD-net is built with convolutional neural network (CNN), and our architecture consists of two "hourglass" (or encoder-decoder) type of generative networks.

Comparisons with Double-DIP [6]. DIP generative network [29] is backbone network of both Double-DIP and our method to automatically capture deep priors. Double-DIP is a unified framework for several image restoration tasks based on image layer decomposition. For image dehazing task, Double-DIP employs two DIP networks to estimate two layers—J layer and A layer, and another DIP network to estimate the mixing mask t. In comparison, our method contains two DIP networks to generate K and J, being not so complicated as Double-DIP.

See Table 1 for quantitative comparisons (on dataset [11]), and see Fig. 5 and Fig. 6 for visual comparisons to [6,10].

4.3   Experiments on Synthetic Datasets

Dataset. We note a benchmark dataset RESIDE is proposed in [11], which contains 1, 3990 hazy/haze-free image pairs in total. 10 levels of the haze conditions are adopted to synthesize hazy images. Following [11], we utilize 13,000 pairs of images to train networks for the supervised learning based methods [2,10,22]. For fairly comparison and demonstrating convincing evaluation results, additional 500 pairs of indoor images from the Synthetic Objective Testing Set (SOTS, subset of RESIDE) are chosen for testing, as [6] and our method need no training process on dataset. The quantitative evaluations is reported in Table 1. Our results reach the highest value of average PSNR. The results of AoD-Net [10] reach the highest value of average SSIM, and ours is in the second place. As visual evaluations are rather important, we show two examples in Fig. 5 for visual comparisons.

Table 1. Quantitative evaluations compared with state-of-the-art dehazing algorithms on testing images [11] in terms of average PSNR and SSIM.

Metric	DCP	BCCR	CAP	NLD	DehazeNet	MSCNN	AoD-Net	Double-DIP	Ours
Ave PSNR	16.62	16.88	19.05	17.29	21.14	17.57	19.06	17.42	**21.20**
Ave SSIM	0.8179	0.7913	0.8364	0.7489	0.8472	0.8102	**0.8504**	0.8068	0.8473

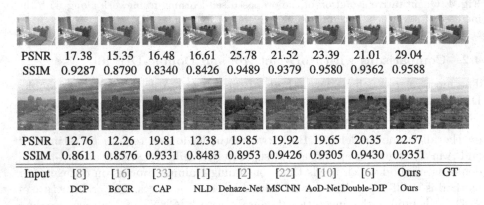

PSNR	17.38	15.35	16.48	16.61	25.78	21.52	23.39	21.01	29.04
SSIM	0.9287	0.8790	0.8340	0.8426	0.9489	0.9379	0.9580	0.9362	0.9588

PSNR	12.76	12.26	19.81	12.38	19.85	19.92	19.65	20.35	22.57
SSIM	0.8611	0.8576	0.9331	0.8483	0.8953	0.9426	0.9305	0.9430	0.9351

Input	[8]	[16]	[33]	[1]	[2]	[22]	[10]	[6]	Ours	GT
	DCP	BCCR	CAP	NLD	Dehaze-Net	MSCNN	AoD-Net	Double-DIP	Ours	

Fig. 5. Visual and quantitative comparisons of indoor and outdoor examples.

4.4   Experiments on Real Hazy Images

In addition to quantitative measurements, subjective visual quality is of great significance to evaluate the performance of a dehazing algorithm. We show several real-world hazy images in Fig. 6 (a). The dehazing results of them recovered by 9 algorithms are shown in Fig. 6 (b)–(j). Our results are relatively desired against the others in mainly two aspects: little unrealistic artifacts and small amount of haze residual. Particularly, our results is more pleasing than Fig. 6 (b) and (i), which supports that our joint estimating method based on all-in-one model is superior to separately parameters estimating methods [6,8].

4.5 Limitations

We hold the opinion that the handcrafted global constraints we imposed on K are rather rough. In fact, imposing proper scale constraints over K is challenging. The ratio value $K(x) = \frac{J(x)-b}{I(x)-1}$ (we set $b = 1$) is possible to be very large, especially for some "white" pixels. As our handcrafted regularizers force $K(x)$ to be near 0 or 2, the proposed method may be less effective to generate an accurate K in this case, giving rise to an unpleased dehazing result. Figure 7 shows one failure example.

Even being penalized by roughly handcrafted regularization, the proposed optimization model (6) facilitates the algorithm to generate convincing results on many synthetic and real-world images compared with SOTA dehazing methods, as demonstrated in Sect. 4.3 and Sect. 4.4. Elaborately handcrafting regularizers over K to improve performance might be one of our future work.

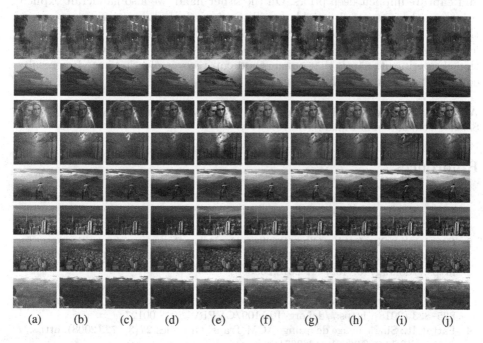

(a)   (b)   (c)   (d)   (e)   (f)   (g)   (h)   (i)   (j)

Fig. 6. Visual comparisons on several real-world examples. (a) Input. (b) DCP [8]. (c) BCCR [16]. (d) CAP [33]. (e) NLD [1]. (f) DehazeNet [2]. (g) MSCNN [22]. (h) AoD-Net [10]. (i) Double-DIP [6]. (j) Ours.

(a) Input   (b) Our result   (c) DCP [8]

Fig. 7. One failure case of a real-world hazy image. In comparison, the dark channel prior based method [8] generates visually desired result, as shown in (c).

5 Conclusion

In this work, we propose a neural dehazing method in MAP framework based on the all-in-one expression of the atmospheric scattering model. On one hand, we adopt two DIP generative networks to connect our neural dehazing formulation and capture implicit deep priors. On the other hand, we also handcraft explicit priors on the integrated variable based on statistical observations to overcome the scale ambiguity problem. The networks are trained jointly by self-supervised learning algorithm, initialized by random noises sampled from uniform distribution. Experiments shows that our method can recover pleasing haze-free results compared with state-of-the-art methods.

Acknowledgements. This work has been partially supported by National Natural Science Foundation of China (No. 61976041).

References

1. Berman, D., Treibitz, T., Avidan, S.: Non-local image dehazing. In: Computer Vision and Pattern Recognition, pp. 1674–1682 (2016). https://doi.org/10.1109/CVPR.2016.185
2. Cai, B., Xu, X., Jia, K., Qing, C., Tao, D.: DehazeNet: an end-to-end system for single image haze removal. IEEE Trans. Image Process. **25**(11), 5187–5198 (2016). https://doi.org/10.1109/TIP.2016.2598681
3. Engin, D., Genç, A., Ekenel, H.K.: Cycle-dehaze: enhanced CycleGAN for single image dehazing. In: Computer Vision and Pattern Recognition Workshops, pp. 825–833 (2018). https://doi.org/10.1109/CVPRW.2018.00127
4. Fattal, R.: Single image dehazing. ACM Trans. Graphics **27**(3), 72 (2008). https://doi.org/10.1145/1360612.1360671
5. Fattal, R.: Dehazing using color-lines. ACM Trans. Graphics **34**(1), 13:1–13:14 (2014). https://doi.org/10.1145/2651362
6. Gandelsman, Y., Shocher, A., Irani, M.: "Double-DIP": unsupervised image decomposition via coupled deep-image-priors. In: Computer Vision and Pattern Recognition, pp. 11026–11035 (2019). https://doi.org/10.1109/CVPR.2019.01128

7. Guo, C., Yan, Q., Anwar, S., Cong, R., Ren, W., Li, C.: Image dehazing transformer with transmission-aware 3d position embedding. In: Computer Vision and Pattern Recognition, pp. 5802–5810 (2022). https://doi.org/10.1109/CVPR52688.2022.00572
8. He, K., Sun, J., Tang, X.: Single image haze removal using dark channel prior. IEEE Trans. Pattern Anal. Mach. Intell. **33**(12), 2341–2353 (2011). https://doi.org/10.1109/TPAMI.2010.168
9. Kingma, D.P., Ba, J.: Adam: a method for stochastic optimization. In: International Conference on Learning Representations (2015), arxiv.org/abs/1412.6980
10. Li, B., Peng, X., Wang, Z., Xu, J., Feng, D.: AOD-Net: all-in-one dehazing network. In: International Conference on Computer Vision. pp. 4780–4788 (2017). https://doi.org/10.1109/ICCV.2017.511
11. Li, B., et al.: Benchmarking single-image dehazing and beyond. IEEE Trans. Image Process. **28**(1), 492–505 (2019). https://doi.org/10.1109/TIP.2018.2867951
12. Li, R., Pan, J., Li, Z., Tang, J.: Single image dehazing via conditional generative adversarial network. In: Computer Vision and Pattern Recognition, pp. 8202–8211 (2018). https://doi.org/10.1109/CVPR.2018.00856
13. Liu, W., Hou, X., Duan, J., Qiu, G.: End-to-end single image fog removal using enhanced cycle consistent adversarial networks. IEEE Trans. Image Process. **29**, 7819–7833 (2020). https://doi.org/10.1109/TIP.2020.3007844
14. Liu, X., Ma, Y., Shi, Z., Chen, J.: GridDehazeNet: attention-based multi-scale network for image dehazing. In: International Conference on Computer Vision, pp. 7313–7322 (2019). https://doi.org/10.1109/ICCV.2019.00741
15. McCartney, E.J.: Optics of the atmosphere: Scattering by molecules and particles 1 (1976)
16. Meng, G., Wang, Y., Duan, J., Xiang, S., Pan, C.: Efficient image dehazing with boundary constraint and contextual regularization. In: International Conference on Computer Vision, pp. 617–624 (2013). https://doi.org/10.1109/ICCV.2013.82
17. Narasimhan, S.G., Nayar, S.K.: Contrast restoration of weather degraded images. IEEE Trans. Pattern Anal. Mach. Intell. **25**(6), 713–724 (2003). https://doi.org/10.1109/TPAMI.2003.1201821
18. Pan, J., et al.: Learning dual convolutional neural networks for low-level vision. In: Computer Vision and Pattern Recognition, pp. 3070–3079 (2018). https://doi.org/10.1109/CVPR.2018.00324
19. Paszke, A., et al.: Automatic differentiation in pytorch. In: Neural Information Processing Systems Autodiff Workshop (2017). https://openreview.net/pdf?id=BJJsrmfCZ
20. Qu, Y., Chen, Y., Huang, J., Xie, Y.: Enhanced pix2pix dehazing network. In: Computer Vision and Pattern Recognition, pp. 8160–8168 (2019). https://doi.org/10.1109/CVPR.2019.00835
21. Ren, D., Zhang, K., Wang, Q., Hu, Q., Zuo, W.: Neural blind deconvolution using deep priors. In: Computer Vision and Pattern Recognition, pp. 3338–3347 (2020). https://doi.org/10.1109/CVPR42600.2020.00340
22. Ren, W., Liu, S., Zhang, H., Pan, J., Cao, X., Yang, M.: Single image dehazing via multi-scale convolutional neural networks. In: European Conference on Computer Vision, pp. 154–169 (2016). https://doi.org/10.1007/978-3-319-46475-6_10
23. Ren, W., et al.: Gated fusion network for single image dehazing. In: Computer Vision and Pattern Recognition, pp. 3253–3261 (2018). https://doi.org/10.1109/CVPR.2018.00343

24. Schechner, Y.Y., Narasimhan, S.G., Nayar, S.K.: Instant dehazing of images using polarization. In: Computer Vision and Pattern Recognition, pp. 325–332 (2001). https://doi.org/10.1109/CVPR.2001.990493
25. Shwartz, S., Namer, E., Schechner, Y.Y.: Blind haze separation. In: Computer Vision and Pattern Recognition, pp. 1984–1991 (2006). https://doi.org/10.1109/CVPR.2006.71
26. Silberman, N., Hoiem, D., Kohli, P., Fergus, R.: Indoor segmentation and support inference from RGBD images. In: European Conference on Computer Vision, pp. 746–760 (2012). https://doi.org/10.1007/978-3-642-33715-4_54
27. Stark, J.A.: Adaptive image contrast enhancement using generalizations of histogram equalization. IEEE Trans. Image Process. **9**(5), 889–896 (2000). https://doi.org/10.1109/83.841534
28. Tan, R.T.: Visibility in bad weather from a single image. In: Computer Vision and Pattern Recognition (2008). https://doi.org/10.1109/CVPR.2008.4587643
29. Ulyanov, D., Vedaldi, A., Lempitsky, V.S.: Deep image prior. Int. J. Comput. Vision **128**(7), 1867–1888 (2020). https://doi.org/10.1007/s11263-020-01303-4
30. Yang, X., Xu, Z., Luo, J.: Towards perceptual image dehazing by physics-based disentanglement and adversarial training. In: Association for the Advancement of Artificial Intelligence, pp. 7485–7492 (2018)
31. Zhang, H., Patel, V.M.: Densely connected pyramid dehazing network. In: Computer Vision and Pattern Recognition, pp. 3194–3203 (2018). https://doi.org/10.1109/CVPR.2018.00337
32. Zhang, H., Sindagi, V., Patel, V.M.: Multi-scale single image dehazing using perceptual pyramid deep network. In: Computer Vision and Pattern Recognition Workshops, pp. 902–911 (2018). https://doi.org/10.1109/CVPRW.2018.00135
33. Zhu, Q., Mai, J., Shao, L.: A fast single image haze removal algorithm using color attenuation prior. IEEE Trans. Image Process. **24**(11), 3522–3533 (2015). https://doi.org/10.1109/TIP.2015.2446191

Learning Sparse Neural Networks with Identity Layers

Mingjian Ni[1], Guangyao Chen[1], Xiawu Zheng[2], Peixi Peng[1], Li Yuan[1], and Yonghong Tian[1(✉)]

[1] Peking University, Beijing 100871, China
{sccdnmj,gy.chen,pxpeng,yuanli-ece,yhtian}@pku.edu.cn
[2] Peng Cheng Laboratory, Shenzhen 518055, China
zhengxw01@pcl.ac.cn

Abstract. The sparsity of Deep Neural Networks is well investigated to maximize the performance and reduce the size of overparameterized networks as possible. Existing methods focus on pruning parameters in the training process by using thresholds and metrics. Meanwhile, feature similarity between different layers has not been discussed sufficiently before, which could be rigorously proved to be highly correlated to the network sparsity in this paper. Inspired by interlayer feature similarity in overparameterized models, we investigate the intrinsic link between network sparsity and interlayer feature similarity. Specifically, we prove that reducing interlayer feature similarity based on Centered Kernel Alignment (CKA) improves the sparsity of the network by using information bottleneck theory. Applying such theory, we propose a plug-and-play **CKA**-based **S**parsity **R**egularization for sparse network training, dubbed CKA-SR, which utilizes CKA to reduce feature similarity between layers and increase network sparsity. In other words, layers of our sparse network tend to have their own identity compared to each other. Experimentally, we plug the proposed CKA-SR into the training process of sparse network training methods and find that CKA-SR consistently improves the performance of several State-Of-The-Art sparse training methods, especially at extremely high sparsity. Code is included in the supplementary materials.

Keywords: Network sparsity · Inter-layer feature similarity · Network compression

1 Introduction

Deep Neural Networks (DNNs) achieve great success on many important tasks, including but not limited to computer vision and natural language processing. Such accurate solutions highly rely on overparameterization, which results in a tremendous waste of resources. A variety of methods are proposed to solve such issues, including model pruning [6,7,10] and sparse training [2,4,14,22]. Sparse training aims to train a sparse network from scratch, which reduces both training and inference expenses.

© The Author(s), under exclusive license to Springer Nature Switzerland AG 2023
H. Lu et al. (Eds.): ICIG 2023, LNCS 14357, pp. 91–102, 2023.
https://doi.org/10.1007/978-3-031-46311-2_8

A recent study [15] shows the close relation between overparameterization and interlayer feature similarity (*i.e.* similarity between features of different layers, as shown in Fig. 1(a)). Specifically, overparameterized models possess obviously greater similarity between features of different layers. Concluding from the facts above, we know that both interlayer feature similarity and network sparsity are deeply related to overparameterization. Inspired by this, we utilize the interlayer feature similarity to increase network sparsity and preserve accuracy at a high level, namely by adopting similarity methods to solve sparsity problems.

Following this path, we survey similarity measurements of features, including Canonical Correlation Analysis (CCA) [8,11,16] and Centered Kernel Alignment (Linear-CKA and RBF-CKA) [12], etc. Among these measurements, CKA measurement is advanced and robust, for it reliably identifies correspondences between representations in networks with different widths trained from different initializations. Theoretically, CKA measurement has many good properties, including invariance to orthogonal transform and isotropic scaling, and close correlation with mutual information [23]. The advantages of CKA make it possible to propose robust methods to solve sparsity problems with interlayer feature similarity.

To this end, we propose **CKA**-based **S**parsity **R**egularization (CKA-SR) by introducing the CKA measurement into training loss as a regularization term, which is a plug-and-play term and forces the reduction of interlayer feature similarity. Besides, we further prove that the proposed CKA-SR increases the sparsity of the network by using information bottleneck(IB) theory [18,20,21, 23]. Specifically, we mathematically prove that our CKA-SR reduces the mutual information between the features of the intermediate and input layer, which is one of the optimization objectives of the information bottleneck method. Further, we prove that reducing the mutual information above is equivalent to increasing network sparsity. By these proofs, we demonstrate the equivalence of reducing interlayer feature similarity and increasing network sparsity, which heuristically investigates the intrinsic link between interlayer feature similarity and network sparsity.

To validate the proposed CKA-SR, we conduct experiments on several advanced sparse training methods, such as Lottery Ticket Hypothesis (LTH) [4], Gradient Signal Preservation (GraSP) [22], Dual Lottery Ticket Hypothesis (DLTH) [2], and Random Sparse Training [14]. Specifically, we introduce our CKA-SR regularization to the training process of these sparse training methods and thus achieve consistent performance gains across these methods. Moreover, we introduce CKA-SR to the training and finetuning process of network pruning methods such as l1-norm filter pruning [13], non-structured weight-level pruning [7], and knapsack channel pruning [1], and thus achieve performance improvements. In short, CKA-SR boosts the performance of sparse training and network pruning methods. Appendix and codes are included in the supplementary materials. See them in https://anonymous.4open.science/r/Learning-Sparse-Neural-Networks-with-Identity-Layers-9369.

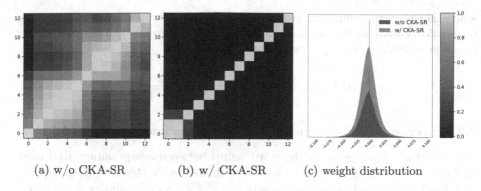

(a) w/o CKA-SR   (b) w/ CKA-SR   (c) weight distribution

Fig. 1. Reduction of interlayer feature similarity with CKA-SR. (a) Interlayer feature similarity visualization of baseline models. (b) Interlayer feature similarity visualization of models pre-trained with CKA-SR. (c) Comparison of weight distribution between baseline and CKA-SR models.

Our contributions are four-fold:

- We heuristically investigate the intrinsic link between interlayer feature similarity and network sparsity. To the best of our knowledge, we are the first to find that reducing interlayer feature similarity directly increases network sparsity.
- Theoretically, we prove the equivalence of interlayer feature similarity reduction, interlayer mutual information reduction, and network sparsity increment.
- We proposed Identity Layers Regularization (ILR) with few-shot samples increases network sparsity and weakens overparameterization by explicitly reducing interlayer feature similarity. Specifically, we implement ILR as CKA-SR.
- Experimentally, our CKA-SR regularization term increases network sparsity and improves the performance of multiple sparse training methods and several pruning methods.

2   Related Works and Preliminaries

2.1   Centered Kernel Alignment

Here we provide the formalization of Centered Kernel Alignment (CKA). For the feature map $X \in \mathbb{R}^{n \times p_1}$ and feature map $Y \in \mathbb{R}^{n \times p_2}$ (where n is the number of examples, while p_1 and p_2 are the number of neurons), we use kernels k and l to transform X and Y into K and L matrices, where the elements are defined as: $K_{ij} = k(x_i, x_j), L_{ij} = l(y_i, y_j)$. Further, the formalization of CKA-based similarity measurement $\mathcal{F}$ of K and L matrices could be formulated as:

$$\mathbf{CKA}(K, L) = \frac{\mathrm{HSIC}(K, L)}{\sqrt{\mathrm{HSIC}(K, K)\mathrm{HSIC}(L, L)}} \qquad (1)$$

where HSIC is the empirical estimator of Hilbert-Schmidt Independence Criterion [5]. Then, the formalizations of CKA-based similarity measurement for linear kernel $k(x, y) = x^T y$ is as follows:

$$\mathbf{CKA}_{Linear}(X, Y) = \frac{||Y^T X||_F^2}{||X^T X||_F ||Y^T Y||_F} \qquad (2)$$

2.2 Interlayer Feature Similarity of Overparameterized Models

Nguyen *et al.* [15] investigate the relationship between overparameterized models and similar feature representations. Specifically, wide ResNets, deep ResNets and ResNets trained on small datasets possess extremely similar feature representations between adjacent layers, named block structure. Then they infer an empirically verified hypothesis that *overparameterized models possess similar feature representations*. Besides, similar observations also appear in ViT [3] based architectures. We may conclude that such block structure is a common problem in different architectures. This prompts us to explore the potential benefits of reducing interlayer feature similarity and learning sparse neural networks with identity layers.

3   Methodology

3.1   Sparsity Regularization Based on Centered Kernel Alignment

As discussed above, the interlayer feature similarity of overparameterized models motivates us to learn sparse neural networks with identity layers. We choose Centered Kernel Alignment (CKA) as the basis of our method, for it's widely applied to measuring feature similarity of different layers. On the other side, the high similarity of layers indicates the overparameterization of Deep Neural Networks. Hence, CKA similarity measurement could be regarded as a scale of overparameterization. This reminds us of directly reducing this measurement to solve overparameterization problems. Even more remarkable, CKA owns many excellent properties, including robustness, invariance to orthogonal transformation, and invariance to scale transformation. These properties make CKA ideal for designing a regularization term to solve overparameterization problems.

Specifically, we add a CKA-based regularization term to the training loss function. For a model with empirical loss (cross-entropy loss) $\mathcal{L}_{\mathcal{E}}$, the training loss with CKA-SR is formalized as:

$$\mathcal{L} = \mathcal{L}_{\mathcal{E}} + \mathcal{L}_{\mathcal{C}} = \mathcal{L}_{\mathcal{E}} + \beta \cdot \sum_{s=1}^{S} \sum_{i=0}^{N_s} \sum_{j=0, j \neq i}^{N_s} w_{ij} \mathbf{CKA}_{Linear}(X_i, X_j) \qquad (3)$$

where $\mathcal{L}_{\mathcal{C}}$ is CKA-SR and β is the weight of $\mathcal{L}_{\mathcal{C}}$. S is the number of stages in the network. For networks with only one stage such as DeiTs, N_s is the total number of layers. And for networks with several stages such as ResNets, N_s is the number of layers in each stage s. w_{ij} is the weight of CKA measurement between the ith

and the jth layer, and it's optional. X_0 is the input representation and X_i is the output representation of the ith layer.

The $\mathcal{L}_C$ part in Eq.(3) forcibly reduces the sum of the pairwise similarity of all layers in the network, *i.e.* forcibly reduces the interlayer similarity of the network.

3.2   Theoretical Analysis

Approximate Sparsity. To further explore the relationship between the Frobenius norm of weight matrix and network sparsity, we expand sparsity to approximate sparsity. We define ϵ-sparsity (*i.e.*, approximate sparsity) of a neural network as follows:

$$S_\epsilon = \frac{|\{w|w \in \mathbb{W} \wedge |w| < \epsilon\}|}{|\mathbb{W}|} \qquad (4)$$

where ϵ is a number close to zero, $\mathbb{W}$ is the set consisting of all parameters of the network's weight matrix, $|\mathbb{W}|$ is the total number of parameters, and $\{w|w \in \mathbb{W} \wedge |w| < \epsilon\}$ is the set consisting of small parameters (*i.e.*, parameters with an absolute value smaller then ϵ) of the weight matrix.

In Eq. (4), S_ϵ represents the proportion of network parameters that approach 0. We define this as ϵ-sparsity of the network. Further, we prove that ϵ-sparsity and sparsity (*i.e.*, proportion of network parameters that equal 0) of neural networks are approximately equivalent in practice. Our theory is formulated as Theorem 1. See the detailed proof of Theorem 1 in the Appendix.

Theorem 1. *The ϵ-sparsity and the sparsity of neural networks are approximately equivalent.*

Information Bottleneck. The information bottleneck (IB) theory proposed by Tishby *et al.* [20] is an extension of the rate distortion theory of source compression. This theory shows a trade-off between preserving relevant label information and obtaining efficient compression. Tishby *et al.* [21] further research the relationship between information bottleneck theory and deep learning. They interpret the goal of deep learning as an information-theoretic trade-off between compression and prediction. According to the principles of information bottleneck theory, for a neural network $Y = f(X)$ with input X and output Y, the best representation of intermediate feature map $\hat{X}$ captures the relevant features and ignores the irrelevant features (features that have little contribution to the prediction of Y) at the same time. This process is called "compression". One of its minimization objectives is as follows:

$$L = I(X; \hat{X}) - \alpha I(\hat{X}; Y) \qquad (5)$$

where $I(X; \hat{X})$ is the mutual information between input X and intermediate representation $\hat{X}$, $I(\hat{X}; Y)$ is the mutual information between intermediate representation $\hat{X}$ and output Y, and α is a weight parameter for adjusting their proportions.

Minimizing the Mutual Information. Firstly, we prove that our CKA-SR is continuous and optimizable in Theorem 2, which makes it possible to minimize CKA-SR in machine learning. See the detailed proof of Theorem 2 in the Appendix. Then we prove that minimizing CKA-SR minimizes the mutual information $R = I(X; \hat{X})$ between the intermediate and input representation. Besides, the $\alpha I(\hat{X}; Y)$ part of Eq. (5) is implicitly optimized through the cross entropy loss $\mathcal{L}_\mathcal{E}$. Thus, we prove that our method minimizes the optimization objective in Eq. (5), *i.e.*, our CKA-SR method conforms to the principles of information bottleneck theory, and it's beneficial to the representation compression process. Our theory is formulated as Theorem 3.

Theorem 2. *$\mathcal{L}_\mathcal{C}$ is continuous and optimizable.*

Theorem 3. *Minimizing $\mathcal{L}_\mathcal{C}$ minimizes the mutual information $R = I(X; \hat{X})$ between intermediate representation $\hat{X}$ and input representation X.*

To prove Theorem 3, we first review Lemma 1 and Lemma 2 from [23] as follows. Following [23], we assume that $X \sim \mathcal{N}(\mathbf{0}, \Sigma_X)$ and $Y \sim \mathcal{N}(\mathbf{0}, \Sigma_Y)$, *i.e.*, feature maps X and Y follow Gaussian distribution.

Lemma 1. *Minimizing the distance between $X^T Y$ and zero matrix is equivalent to minimizing the mutual information $I(X; Y)$ between representation X and Y.*

Lemma 2. *Minimizing $\mathbf{CKA}_{Linear}(X, Y)$ is equivalent to minimizing $I(X; Y)$.*

These two lemmas illustrate the relationship between the CKA similarity measurement and information theory. That is, *minimizing the CKA similarity between two feature representations is equivalent to minimizing the mutual information between them.* Based on these two lemmas, we prove Theorem 3. See the detailed proof of the two lemmas and Theorem 3 in the Appendix.

Theorem 3 connects CKA-SR with information bottleneck theory. In short, *minimizing CKA-SR is equivalent to optimizing the optimization objective $I(X; \hat{X})$ of information bottleneck theory.*

Increasing the Sparsity of Neural Networks. Further, starting from the information bottleneck theory, we prove that CKA-SR increases the network sparsity, formulated as Theorem 4.

Theorem 4. *Minimizing $R = I(X; \hat{X}) \Leftrightarrow$ Minimizing $||W||_F^2 \Leftrightarrow$ Increasing the approximate sparsity of network $\Leftrightarrow$ Increasing network sparsity.*

Proof. According to Theorem 3, CKA-SR minimizes $R = I(X; \hat{X})$ for any X. Further, combining this with Lemma 1, for any X, CKA-SR minimizes the distance between $X^T \hat{X}$ and 0 matrix. For a fully-connected layer, we have $\hat{X} = W^T X + b$. Hence, due to the discussions above, we have: for any X, CKA-SR minimizes the distance between $X^T(W^T X + b) = X^T W^T X + X^T b$ and 0 matrix. We take an orthogonalized X. Due to the unitary invariance (*i.e.*, orthogonal invariance in the real number field) of Frobenius norm, $\|W\|_F^2$ equals to $\|X^T W^T X\|_F^2$. Therefore, minimizing the distance between $X^T W^T X + X^T b$ and 0 matrix is equivalent to minimizing $\|X^T W^T X\|_F^2$ and further equivalent to minimizing $\|W\|_F^2$.

The above minimization of $\|W\|_F^2$ minimizes the norm of parameter values in weight matrix W, thus making the values more concentrated around 0 value. This increases the network's approximate sparsity (defined earlier in this article). Further, according to Theorem 1, the approximate sparsity and sparsity are approximately equivalent. So we prove that the above minimization of $\|W\|_F^2$ increases the network sparsity.

Theorem 4 connects the optimization objective of information bottleneck theory with network sparsity, thus connecting CKA-SR with network sparsity. In short, *CKA-SR models are more sparse.* We validate this conclusion with our experimental results. Figure 1(c) compares parameter distribution between CKA-SR and baseline models. It's evident that the absolute value of CKA-SR network parameters is more concentrated around 0.

4 Experiments

4.1 Implementations

Datasets and Backbone Models. We validate the effectiveness of our CKA-SR method on image classification, network pruning, and advanced sparse training. We use ResNet18, ResNet20, ResNet32 and ResNet50 [9] as backbones to conduct extensive experiments on CIFAR-10, CIFAR-100 and ImageNet datasets.

Implementations. We implement our CKA-SR as a regularization of the loss function. We develop a plug-and-play CKA-SR class in PyTorch and plug it into various pre-training and sparse training codes. Because CKA-SR is a regularization of layerwise parameters instead of feature maps themselves, we could utilize few-shot samples of each batch (*generally 8 samples when the batch size is 128 or 256*) to compute CKA-SR. This reduces the computational complexity, thus reducing training expenses. Precisely, we strictly follow the experimental settings of the pruning [1,7,13] and sparse training methods [2,4,14,22] and make fair comparisons with them using CKA-SR. The total number of epochs, batch size, optimizer, weight decay, and learning rates all stay the same with the methods to be compared with.

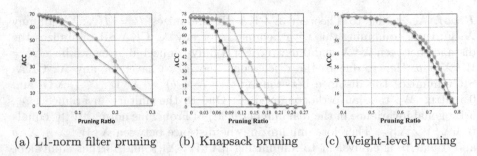

(a) L1-norm filter pruning   (b) Knapsack pruning   (c) Weight-level pruning

Fig. 2. Performances of several pruning methods with CKA-SR. The red lines represent CKA-SR models and the blue lines represent baseline models. (a) Performances of L1-norm filter pruning with ResNet18 on ImageNet. (b) Performances of knapsack channel pruning with ResNet50 on ImageNet. (c) Performances of non-structured weight-level pruning with ResNet50 on ImageNet. (Color figure online)

4.2   Pre-training with CKA-SR

As previously proved, our CKA-SR increases network sparsity. So we validate the performance of CKA-SR in network pruning tasks. We directly prune models pre-trained with CKA-SR on large-scale datasets such as ImageNet. We carry out experiments on several pruning methods and find that our method is effective. As shown in Fig. 2, at the same pruning ratio, CKA-SR models outperform baseline models.

Structured Pruning. Following the setting of [13], we perform filter pruning on models pre-trained with CKA-SR without finetuning. Specifically, we prune the filter according to the L1-Norm. The relationship between the pruning ratio and performance is shown in Fig. 2(a). When a few filters are pruned, the performance reduction of CKA-SR models is significantly smaller than that of baseline models.

As a State-Of-The-Art method for channel pruning, we perform Knapsack channel pruning [1] on models pre-trained with CKA-SR and achieve higher classification accuracy. The results of Knapsack pruning (w/o finetuning) are shown in Fig. 2(b). When a few channels are pruned, the performance reduction of CKA-SR models is much smaller than that of baseline models, which means CKA-SR models possess much higher sparsity.

Non-structured Pruning. We perform non-structured weight-level pruning [7] according to the absolute values of individual weights and compare the performance between baseline ResNet models and pre-trained ResNets with CKA-SR. The relationship between pruning ratio and performance is shown in Fig. 2(c). It could be concluded that when massive weights are pruned, the performance reduction of CKA-SR models is smaller than that of baseline models.

Generally, pre-trained models with CKA-SR outperform baseline models in both structured and non-structured pruning methods.

4.3   Sparse Network Training with CKA-SR

We conduct extensive experiments on several State-Of-The-Art sparse training methods. For fair comparisons, our experiments follow the same settings and backbones of these methods [2, 4, 14, 22]. Note that we conduct experiments on extremely high sparsity (such as 99.8%) settings in GraSP [22], Random sparse training [14], and DLTH [2]. From Table 1, we can find that CKA-SR consistently improves the performance at different levels of sparsity ratios in LTH [4], GraSP [22], Random sparse training [14], and DLTH [2].

LTH. Lottery Ticket Hypothesis (LTH) [4] is proposed to train a sparse network from scratch, which states that any randomly initialized dense network contains sub-networks achieving similar accuracy to the original network. We plug our CKA-SR into the training process of LTH. We use the code implemented for LTH by [19], adopt ResNet32 as the backbone, and apply sparsity ratios from 0.70 to 0.98 for fair comparisons. The results are given in the first row of Table 1.

GraSP. Gradient Signal Preservation (GraSP) [22] proposes to preserve the gradient flow through the network during sparse training. We plug our CKA-SR into the sparse training process of GraSP, adopt ResNet32 as the backbone, and apply sparsity ratios from 0.70 to 0.998. The results are given in the second row of Table 1.

Random Sparse Training. As one of the newest and State-Of-The-Art sparse training methods, it has been proven that sparse training of randomly initialized networks can also achieve remarkable performances [14]. We plug our CKA-SR into the random sparse training process, adopt ResNet20 as the backbone, and apply sparsity ratios from 0.70 to 0.998. The results are given in the third row of Table 1.

DLTH. As one of the newest and State-Of-The-Art LTH-based sparse training methods, Dual Lottery Ticket Hypothesis (DLTH) [2] proposes to randomly select subnetworks from a randomly initialized dense network, which can be transformed into a trainable condition and achieve good performance. We apply our CKA-SR to the training process of the DLTH method, adopt ResNet20 as the backbone, and apply sparsity ratios from 0.70 to 0.998. The results are given in the final row of Table 1.

As shown in Table 1, our CKA-SR can be plugged into multiple sparse training methods and improves the model performance consistently. The CKA-SR is effective consistently at different sparse networks, especially at extremely high sparsity. For GraSP, CKA-SR achieves more than 4.0% of performance improvement at sparsity 99.5% and 6.0% at sparsity 99.8%.

Table 1. The accuracy (%) when plugging CKA-SR to different sparse training methods on CIFAR-100 from scratch. (LTH is broken when sparsity ratio is larger than 0.99 due to destruction of the structure.)

Backbone	Method	Sparsity					
		0.70	*0.85*	*0.90*	*0.95*	*0.98*	*0.998*
ResNet32	LTH [4]	72.28	70.64	69.63	66.48	60.22	✘
	+CKA-SR	**72.67**	**71.90**	**70.11**	**67.07**	**60.36**	✘
ResNet32	GraSP [22]	71.98	70.22	69.19	65.82	59.46	12.19
	+CKA-SR	**72.19**	**70.25**	**69.28**	**66.29**	**59.49**	**18.44**
ResNet20	Random [14]	65.42	60.37	56.96	47.27	33.74	2.95
	+CKA-SR	**65.60**	**60.86**	**57.25**	**48.26**	**34.44**	**3.32**
ResNet20	DLTH [2]	67.63	65.33	62.90	57.33	48.08	19.32
	+CKA-SR	**67.95**	**65.80**	**63.19**	**57.99**	**49.26**	**20.81**

4.4   Ablation Studies

Ablation Study of Regularization Term. Savarese *et al.* [17] develop a regularization-based sparse network searching method named Continuous Sparsification. This method introduces L_0 Regularization into sparse training. We compare our CKA-SR with L_0 Regularization theoretically and experimentally. Theoretically, CKA-SR and L_0 regularization regularize networks from different granularity levels. L_0 regularization regularizes networks from the individual parameter level, while CKA-SR regularizes networks from the layer level. These regularizations from different granularity levels could work together. Experimentally, we conduct sparse training experiments with ResNet18 on CIFAR-10 using the official code of the CS method. We find that our CKA-SR is able to replace L_0 regularization and achieves better performance. Besides, combining CKA-SR and L_0 improves performance by 0.4%, demonstrating that our CKA-SR could cooperate with other regularizations. The results are shown in Table 2.

Table 2. Ablation study of regularization terms

Settings	CKA-SR Only	L_0 Only	CKA-SR+L_0
Top1-Acc	91.63	91.56	91.92

Ablation Study of Hyperparameter β. We conduct the ablation study of hyperparameter β with Random Sparse Training [14] method on CIFAR-10 dataset. Taking ResNet20 model at a sparsity of 0.95 and adjusting the weight hyperparameter β of our CKA-SR, we get the results shown in Table 3.

Table 3. Ablation study of hyperparameter β

β	0	1e−05	5e−05	2e−04	8e−04	1e−03	2e−03	5e−03
Top1-Acc	84.16	84.69	84.42	84.40	**85.03**	84.82	84.08	83.86

We conclude that multiple values of hyperparameter β between 1e−05 and 1e−03 increase the performance of sparse networks. However, when the hyperparameter β becomes too large, it would weaken the succession of information through layers, thus causing a reduction in performance. That is to say, there is a trade-off between the identity of layers and the succession of information through layers. In the view of sparsity, there is a trade-off between high sparsity and ideal performance.

5 Conclusion

Our work reveals the relationship between overparameterization, network sparsity, and interlayer feature similarity. We thus propose to use the robust and advanced CKA similarity measurement to solve the overparameterization issue. Specifically, we propose a plug-and-play sparsity regularization named CKA-SR which explicitly reduces interlayer similarity. Theoretically, we reveal the equivalence of reducing interlayer similarity and increasing network sparsity, thus proving the CKA-SR increases network sparsity. Experimentally, our CKA-SR consistently improves the performances of several State-Of-The-Art sparse training methods and several pruning methods. Besides, our CKA-SR outperforms former regularization methods. In the future, considering our limitations of expenses to manually select hyperparameters and calculate loss, we will continue to investigate the cooperation of multiple regularizations in sparse training and reduce the expenses of sparse training.

References

1. Aflalo, Y., Noy, A., Lin, M., Friedman, I., Zelnik, L.: Knapsack pruning with inner distillation. arXiv preprint arXiv:2002.08258 (2020)
2. Bai, Y., Wang, H., Tao, Z., Li, K., Fu, Y.: Dual lottery ticket hypothesis. arXiv preprint arXiv:2203.04248 (2022)
3. Dosovitskiy, A., et al.: An image is worth 16x16 words: transformers for image recognition at scale. arXiv preprint arXiv:2010.11929 (2020)
4. Frankle, J., Carbin, M.: The lottery ticket hypothesis: finding sparse, trainable neural networks. arXiv preprint arXiv:1803.03635 (2018)
5. Gretton, A., Bousquet, O., Smola, A., Schölkopf, B.: Measuring Statistical Dependence with Hilbert-Schmidt Norms. In: Jain, S., Simon, H.U., Tomita, E. (eds.) ALT 2005. LNCS (LNAI), vol. 3734, pp. 63–77. Springer, Heidelberg (2005). https://doi.org/10.1007/11564089_7
6. Han, S., Mao, H., Dally, W.J.: Deep compression: Compressing deep neural networks with pruning, trained quantization and huffman coding. arXiv preprint arXiv:1510.00149 (2015)

7. Han, S., Pool, J., Tran, J., Dally, W.: Learning both weights and connections for efficient neural network. In: Advances in Neural Information Processing Systems 28 (2015)

8. Hardoon, D.R., Szedmak, S., Shawe-Taylor, J.: Canonical correlation analysis: an overview with application to learning methods. Neural Comput. **16**(12), 2639–2664 (2004)

9. He, K., Zhang, X., Ren, S., Sun, J.: Deep residual learning for image recognition. In: Proceedings of the IEEE Conference on Computer Vision and Pattern Recognition. pp. 770–778 (2016)

10. He, Y., Liu, P., Wang, Z., Hu, Z., Yang, Y.: Filter pruning via geometric median for deep convolutional neural networks acceleration. In: Proceedings of the IEEE/CVF Conference on Computer Vision and Pattern Recognition, pp. 4340–4349 (2019)

11. Hotelling, H.: Relations between two sets of variates. In: Breakthroughs in statistics, pp. 162–190. Springer (1992). https://doi.org/10.1007/978-1-4612-4380-9_14

12. Kornblith, S., Norouzi, M., Lee, H., Hinton, G.: Similarity of neural network representations revisited. In: International Conference on Machine Learning, pp. 3519–3529. PMLR (2019)

13. Li, H., Kadav, A., Durdanovic, I., Samet, H., Graf, H.P.: Pruning filters for efficient convnets. arXiv preprint arXiv:1608.08710 (2016)

14. Liu, S., et al.: The unreasonable effectiveness of random pruning: Return of the most naive baseline for sparse training. In: International Conference on Learning Representations (2021)

15. Nguyen, T., Raghu, M., Kornblith, S.: Do wide and deep networks learn the same things? uncovering how neural network representations vary with width and depth. arXiv preprint arXiv:2010.15327 (2020)

16. Ramsay, J., ten Berge, J., Styan, G.: Matrix correlation. Psychometrika **49**(3), 403–423 (1984)

17. Savarese, P., Silva, H., Maire, M.: Winning the lottery with continuous sparsification. Adv. Neural. Inf. Process. Syst. **33**, 11380–11390 (2020)

18. Saxe, A.M., et al.: On the information bottleneck theory of deep learning. J. Stat. Mech: Theory Exp. **2019**(12), 124020 (2019)

19. Su, J., et al.: Sanity-checking pruning methods: Random tickets can win the jackpot. Adv. Neural. Inf. Process. Syst. **33**, 20390–20401 (2020)

20. Tishby, N., Pereira, F.C., Bialek, W.: The information bottleneck method. arXiv preprint arxiv:physics/0004057 (2000)

21. Tishby, N., Zaslavsky, N.: Deep learning and the information bottleneck principle. In: 2015 IEEE Information Theory Workshop (ITW), pp. 1–5. IEEE (2015)

22. Wang, C., Zhang, G., Grosse, R.: Picking winning tickets before training by preserving gradient flow. arXiv preprint arXiv:2002.07376 (2020)

23. Zheng, X., et al.: An information theory-inspired strategy for automatic network pruning. arXiv preprint arXiv:2108.08532 (2021)

Dense Small Object Detection Based on Improved Deep Separable Convolution YOLOv5

Yiwei Ben[✉] and Xiaofei Li

College of Telecommunications and Information Engineering, Nanjing University of Posts and
Telecommunications, Nanjing, China
63726790@qq.com

Abstract. Aiming at the limited detection ability of YOLOv5 target detector
when dealing with dense small targets, an improved YOLOv5 target detection
method YOLOV5-G based on improved depth-wise separable convolution was
proposed. The YOLOV5-G adds a prediction head based on the original YOLOv5
to improve the detection performance of small objects; The original loss function
is changed to α-CIoU to obtain more accurate boundary box regression. The standard convolution module in the neck of the model is replaced by a hybrid convolution composed of standard convolution and depth-wise separable convolution.
Compared with the original model using all the standard convolution modules,
the calculation amount is reduced and the detection performance of the model is
improved. Attention mechanism and lightweight module supplement each other,
enables the attention mechanism to work better. Simulation experiments were
conducted on CrowdHuman dataset, and the experimental results showed that
YOLOv5-G increased by 3.1% compared with the original YOLOv5.

Keywords: attention mechanism · depth-wise separable convolution · intensive
small target detection · loss function · YOLOv5

1 Introduction

With the rapid development of information technology and the continuous accumulation
of a large amount of image and video data in the era of big data, the ability of computers
to process information has been constantly improving. As a result, neural networks have
achieved rapid development in the field of computer vision, and related research results
continue to emerge, which can be implemented and deployed in industry, leading a new
wave of artificial intelligence development. Pedestrian detection, as one of the classic
problems in computer vision, is also the foundation of many other visual tasks and has
extremely wide application scenarios. For example, in the field of autonomous driving,
pedestrian detection is the basis for surrounding environment perception, emergency
avoidance, and driving behavior selection; in the field of intelligent video surveillance,
pedestrian detection is the basis for pedestrian tracking, re-identification, and pedestrian
flow statistics; in the field of industrial automation robots, pedestrian detection is the

© The Author(s), under exclusive license to Springer Nature Switzerland AG 2023
H. Lu et al. (Eds.): ICIG 2023, LNCS 14357, pp. 103–115, 2023.
https://doi.org/10.1007/978-3-031-46311-2_9

basis for human motion recognition, behavior prediction to avoid office staff, and safe operation.

Pedestrian detection algorithms can be divided into two categories: those based on deep learning theory and those based on traditional digital image processing techniques. Early pedestrian detection algorithms were limited by computer resources and used many manual feature selections when generating bounding boxes, resulting in reduced accuracy and generalization performance. In the past decade, with the rise of Convolutional Neural Networks (CNNs), pedestrian detection technology has continued to advance. Compared with traditional methods, algorithms based on deep learning theory can extract richer semantic information, resulting in significant improvements in accuracy and generalization performance. Currently, mainstream pedestrian detection algorithms mainly use deep learning-based object detection architectures for training and inference, which can be divided into one-stage models and two-stage models. One-stage object detection models aim to obtain the position information and confidence of the desired detection target with only one stage, while two-stage object detection models require two stages to finally determine the position information and confidence of the desired detection target. Classic two-stage object detection models include R-CNN [1], Fast R-CNN [2], and Faster R-CNN [3], while one-stage object detection models mainly include YOLO [4], SSD [5], and RetinaNet [6]. Because one-stage object detection models only need one step to obtain detection results, they have faster inference speed and are more in line with industrial application requirements, making them the mainstream models in pedestrian detection tasks.

YOLO [7], or "You Only Look Once" is an object detection model proposed by Joseph Redmon and his team in 2016. It is a one-stage detection model that directly predicts bounding boxes and class probabilities from the whole image, rather than using a two-stage approach that generates region proposals first. YOLO divides the input image into a grid of cells and predicts bounding boxes for each cell. Each cell is responsible for predicting only one object that falls inside it, making it a faster and more efficient model than two-stage detectors. Then came Yolov2 [8] and YOLOv3 [9]. YOLOv2 was proposed in 2017, which improved the original YOLO model by introducing batch normalization [10] and a new feature extraction network called Darknet-19. In 2018, YOLOv3 was proposed, which further improved the model by introducing a multi-scale feature extraction network called Darknet-53 and using anchor boxes to handle different object sizes. YOLOv4 [11], proposed in 2020, used a new feature extraction network called CSPDarknet-53 and introduced various advanced techniques, such as the mosaic data augmentation, self-adaptive anchor calculation, and focus mechanism, to improve the model's performance.Finally, YOLOv5 was proposed in 2020, which introduced several novel features, such as the cross-stage partial connection (CSP [12]) structure, and achieved state-of-the-art performance with a much faster training speed and smaller model size than previous versions. YOLOv5 [13] also features a new data augmentation technique called CutMix, which combines two images to create a new image, improving the model's generalization ability.Overall, YOLO and its variants have significantly contributed to the development of object detection technology and are widely used in various applications, including robotics, autonomous vehicles, and video surveillance systems.

However, accurately distinguishing pedestrians in crowded environments remains a challenge. While current pedestrian detection algorithms can achieve good detection accuracy in simple scenarios, their performance in crowded areas such as shopping malls, train stations, and popular tourist attractions is often unsatisfactory. In these scenarios, dense occlusion of targets is often present, and common object detection algorithms may have a high rate of missed detections, making it difficult to directly apply them in these complex real-world scenarios.

This article proposes a new object detection method, YOLOv5-G, to address the issue of poor performance in detecting dense crowds of people using the YOLOv5 object detector. YOLOv5-G improves the detection of small objects by adding an additional prediction head to the original YOLOv5 model. The loss function is also modified to α-CIoU to achieve more accurate bounding box regression. Additionally, the standard convolution module in the neck of the model is replaced with a hybrid convolution module composed of standard and depthwise separable convolutions, which reduces computation while improving detection performance compared to the original model that only uses standard convolution modules. The attention mechanism and lightweight modules complement each other, allowing the attention mechanism to work better. Simulation experiments on the CrowdHuman [14] dataset show that YOLOv5-G achieves a 3.1% improvement in AP compared to the original YOLOv5.

2 Improved YOLOv5-G Algorithm

2.1 YOLOv5-G Network Structure

The YOLOv5-G network structure proposed in this article is shown in Fig. 1. It mainly includes improvements to the multi-scale detection head, improvements to the standard convolution module, and the introduction of corresponding G3 modules and attention mechanism CBAM.

2.2 Improvement of Multi-Scale Detection Head

The YOLOv5 object detection continues the design of using FPN and PAN structures that have been commonly used in recent years. It is intended to perform object detection on three feature maps of different scales, with downsampling factors set to 32, 16, and 8, respectively. Each output scale is preset with 3 anchor boxes. The feature map with the lowest resolution is obtained by deep network convolution and has the largest local receptive field, which is conducive to the detection of large objects. The sizes of the anchor boxes are (116 × 90), (156 × 198), and (373 × 326). Moreover, the anchor box sizes of the feature map with medium resolution are (30 × 61), (62 × 45), and (59 × 119). Furthermore, the feature map with the highest resolution is obtained by shallow network convolution and has the largest local receptive field, which is conducive to the detection of large objects. The sizes of the anchor boxes are (10 × 13), (16 × 30), and (33 × 23).

Considering the problems of small target size and mutual occlusion in dense pedestrian datasets, even the feature map with the highest resolution will lose its feature and

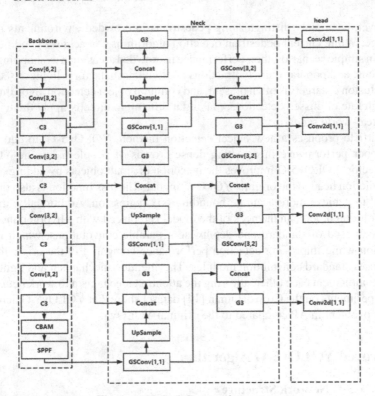

Fig. 1. YOLOv5-G network structure.

position information. Therefore, in order to obtain more fine-grained and comprehensive feature information, this paper adds one more scale to the existing three scales of feature map detection in YOLOv5. The improved object detector will detect objects on four feature maps of different sizes, with downsampling factors set to 32, 16, 8, and 4, respectively. Finally, 12 anchor boxes are obtained on the four scales of feature maps, which are: anchor boxes for super small objects with sizes of (5×6), (8×14), and (15×11); anchor boxes for small objects with sizes of (10×13), (16×30), and (33×23); anchor boxes for medium objects with sizes of (30×61), (62×45), and (59×119); anchor boxes for large objects with sizes of (116×90), (156×198), and (373×326). This design makes the detection of smaller targets more accurate.

The basic principle of introducing multi-scale detection is to fuse the various feature maps extracted at different levels to different degrees. When the feature map to be detected contains both high-level semantic information and object contour and position information, it is more conducive to improving the performance of the object detector. Therefore, this paper improves the detection of 3 scales of features in YOLOv5s to 4 scales of features. The specific details are shown in Fig. 2.

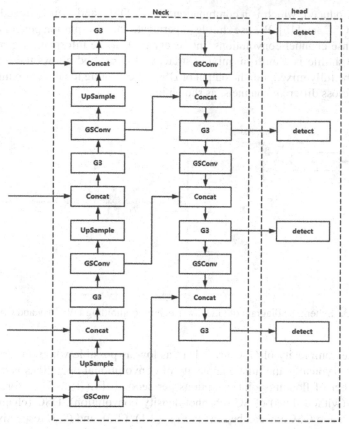

Fig. 2. On the basis of the existing detection of 3 feature maps with different scales in YOLOv5, one more scale is added in the improved object detector. The detector will now perform detection on 4 feature maps with different sizes.

2.3 Improvement of Standard Convolution

Traditional Standard Convolution (SC) has a large number of parameters and computations, which is not ideal for real-time applications. To address this issue and make more models feasible, researchers have gradually considered model lightweighting. Lightweight design effectively reduces the high computational cost at present. Currently, this is mainly achieved by using Depth-wise Separable Convolution [15] (DSC) operations to reduce the number of parameters and floating-point operations. Although it greatly improves the speed of the detector, the lower accuracy of these models is worrisome, which is due to the disadvantage of DSC: in the calculation process, the channel information of the input image is separated. SC calculates dense channel convolutions, while DSC calculates sparse channel convolutions, which leads to DSC having lower feature extraction and fusion capabilities than SC. Moreover, the feature maps generated only by transforming the output channel of DSC are still "depth-separated". To make the output of DSC as close as possible to SC and achieve the same effect, a new method has been introduced, which is a combination of SC, DSC, and shuffle mixed convolution, called GSConv [16]. We use shuffle to permeate the information generated by SC, which is dense channel convolutions, into every part of the information generated by DSC. Since shuffle is a uniform mixing strategy, this method allows the information from SC to be fully mixed into the output of DSC, exchanging local feature information uniformly across different channels, as shown in Fig. 3.

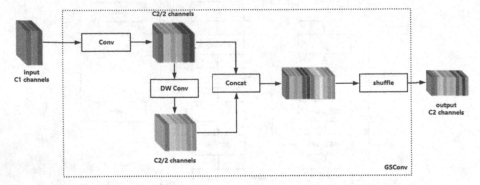

Fig. 3. Schematic diagram of GSconv structure, combining DWConv and Conv.

The time complexity of GSConv is kept as low as possible while preserving these connections. Typically, the time complexity of convolutional operations is determined by the number of floating-point operations per second (FLOPS). Therefore, the time complexity (without bias) of SC (channel-density convolution), DSC (channel-sparse convolution), and GSConv can be seen in Eqs. (2.1), (2.2), and (2.3) respectively:

$$SC \sim O(W \cdot H \cdot K_l \cdot K_2 \cdot C_1 \cdot C_2) \tag{2.1}$$

$$DSC \sim O(W \cdot H \cdot K_l \cdot K_2 \cdot 1 \cdot C_2) \tag{2.2}$$

$$GSConv \sim O\left(W \cdot H \cdot K_l \cdot K_2 \cdot (C_1 + 1) \cdot \frac{1}{2} \cdot C_2\right) \tag{2.3}$$

The computation complexity of GSConv is about 50% of SC ($0.5 + 0.5C1$, the closer the C1 value is to 50%, the closer the ratio), but its contribution to the model learning ability is equivalent to or even better than the latter in some scenarios. This module will further reduce the computation complexity of the model, providing assistance for practical implementation in the industry.

2.4   G3 Module

In this paper, the authors improved the original network structure by replacing the C3 modules with G3 modules, which reduced the computational complexity while improving the model accuracy. The authors suggest using GSConv to process the connected feature maps in the neck because there is less redundant and repeated information, and compression is not needed. The advantage of GSConv is more apparent for lightweight detectors because it enhances the non-linear expressive power through the addition of DSC layers and shuffle. However, simply replacing all Conv modules with GSConv in the network model will increase the network depth and resistance to data flow, leading to increased inference time. Therefore, it is better to use GSConv only in the neck because the feature maps have become sufficiently thin (with maximum channel dimensions and minimum width and height dimensions) and the transformation has become mild when they reach the neck network. Specifically, the authors replaced SC with GSConv and replaced the original BottleNeck in C3 with GSBottleNeck, as shown in Fig. 4. Unlike the general practice of retaining some Conv modules in the C3 module, this paper replaces all of them with GSConv. This approach is better combined with the attention mechanism described below to reduce computational complexity while increasing model accuracy.

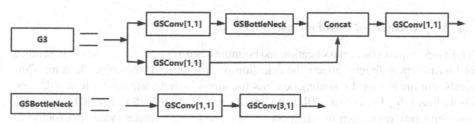

Fig. 4. The G3 module, different from the VoVGSCSP [17], replaces all Conv modules in the original C3 module with GSConv modules without preserving any of them.

2.5 Attention

Attention plays a crucial role in human perception, where the visual system does not attempt to process the entire image at once, but rather utilizes local glimpses to focus on the interesting and salient parts, in order to better capture and extract the image information. In the field of computer vision, the Convolutional Block Attention Module (CBAM [18]) is a lightweight attention module that almost does not increase the computational complexity of the model. The structure of CBAM is shown in Fig. 5 and consists of two main modules: channel attention module and spatial attention module. The feature maps are adaptively refined by CBAM in every convolutional module of the deep neural network.

As mentioned earlier, G3 module uses GSConv to replace all Conv modules in the original C3 module. The combination of CBAM and GSConv allows the attention mechanism of CBAM to be combined with the weight-sharing mechanism of GSConv, thereby improving the perceptual and generalization capabilities of the model while maintaining its computational efficiency. Specifically, the attention mechanism of CBAM can help the network to more accurately focus on important feature map regions, thereby better utilizing the weight-sharing mechanism of GSConv. On the other hand, the weight-sharing mechanism of GSConv can reduce the model's parameter count, thereby reducing the risk of overfitting and making it easier for CBAM to learn useful features. Therefore, the combination of CBAM, GSConv, and G3 can enhance each other, thereby improving the model's expressive power and generalization ability and achieving outstanding performance.

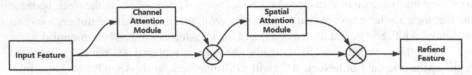

Fig. 5. The CBAM structure, combined with the G3 module mentioned earlier, enhances the network performance.

2.6 Improvement of Loss Function

YOLOv5 employs both classification and bounding box regression losses, and the choice of loss function directly affects the detection performance of the object detector. Currently, commonly used bounding box loss functions include Smooth L1 loss, IoU loss, GIoU loss [19], DIoU loss [20], and CIoU loss [21]. YOLOv5 utilizes CIoU loss for bounding box regression.IoU is a commonly used performance evaluation metric in object detection tasks, which evaluates the accuracy of the prediction based on the degree of overlap between the ground truth box and the predicted box. Its formula is shown in Eq. (2.4).

$$IoU = \frac{|A \cap B|}{|A \cup B|} \tag{2.4}$$

In the context of object detection, A represents the ground truth bounding box, and B represents the predicted bounding box.

When there is no overlap between A and B, the Intersection over Union (IoU) value is always 0. This limitation becomes apparent at such times, as IoU cannot clearly indicate the distance between the two boxes. Furthermore, even when the IoU is the same, there may be various different overlap situations. To overcome this limitation, the Generalized Intersection over Union (GIoU) loss was proposed.The formula for GIoU is shown in Eq. (2.5):

$$GIoU = IoU - \frac{|A_C - U|}{A_C} \tag{2.5}$$

In the GIoU formula, A_C represents the area of the smallest closed bounding box that encompasses both the ground truth box and the predicted box, while U represents the area of the union of the two boxes.

The DIoU loss is an improvement over the IoU loss that enhances the stability of bounding box regression. It takes into account the distance between the centers of the ground truth box and the predicted box, the degree of overlap between the two boxes, and the size of the boxes. The formula for DIoU is shown in Eq. (2.6):

$$\text{DIoU} = \text{IoU} - \frac{\rho^2(b, b^{gt})}{c^2} \tag{2.6}$$

Researchers further improved the DIoU loss by introducing the CIoU loss, which takes into account the aspect ratio of the bounding boxes. The calculation process of the CIoU loss is shown in Eqs. (2.7) and (2.8):

$$v = \frac{4}{\pi^2}\left(\arctan\frac{w^{gt}}{h^{gt}} - \arctan\frac{w}{h}\right)^2 \tag{2.7}$$

$$L_{\text{CIoU}} = 1 - \text{IoU} + \frac{\rho^2(b, b^{gt})}{c^2} + \alpha v \tag{2.8}$$

In the proposed method, the CIoU loss is used as the basis for the α-IoU [22] loss function, as shown in Eq. (2.9). The parameter α is a weight coefficient that takes into account the similarity in aspect ratio between the ground truth and predicted bounding boxes. When $\alpha > 1$, the loss and gradient for high-IoU targets are increased, which improves the accuracy of bounding box regression. The parameter α can be adjusted as a hyperparameter to achieve different levels of bounding box regression accuracy. In most cases, $\alpha = 3$ performs well and is advantageous for learning at high-IoU values. The α-IoU loss family can be easily used to improve the performance of object detectors without introducing additional parameters or increasing training and inference time in clean or noisy environments.

$$\mathcal{L}_{\alpha\text{-CIoU}} = 1 - IoU^\alpha + \frac{\rho^{2\alpha}(b, b^{gt})}{c^{2\alpha}} + (\beta v)^\alpha \tag{2.9}$$

3 Experimental Results and Analysis

In order to verify the effectiveness of YOLOv5-G proposed in this paper, experiments were conducted on the CrowdHuman dataset, as shown in Fig. 6, selecting human bodies as detection targets. The server GPU version used was GeForce GTX 1080 Ti, with Ubuntu version 20.04 and CUDA version 11.2. Each training was conducted for a total of 300 epochs with mosaic data augmentation. The batch size used in the experiment was 32. First, ablation experiments were conducted to study the contributions of the improved network structure and loss function to YOLOv5-G, and then YOLOv5-G was compared with other object detection algorithms in comparative experiments.

3.1 Ablation Experiments

To validate the effectiveness of various strategies proposed in YOLOv5-G, ablation experiments are conducted on the CrowdHuman dataset. The experimental results are shown in Table 1. α-CIoU($\alpha = 3$) represents using the CIoU loss function of the α-IoU

Fig. 6. CrowdHuman dataset.

Table 1. Ablation experiments

Method	$AP_{0.5}$	$AP_{0.5:0.95}$
YOLOv5s	0.844	0.522
YOLOv5s + α-CIoU(α = 3)	0.863	0.547
YOLOv5s + α-CIoU(α = 3) + GSConv	0.864	0.548
YOLOv5s + α-CIoU(α = 3) + GSConv + G3	0.866	0.551
YOLOv5s + α-CIoU(α = 3) + GSConv + G3 + 4detector	0.872	0.551
YOLOv5s + α-CIoU(α = 3) + GSConv + G3 + 4detector + CBAM	0.875	0.555

series instead of the original CIoU loss function, with α = 3. GSConv represents replacing the original Conv in the neck with the Group Shuffle Convolution. G3 represents using the G3 module instead of the original C3 module. 4detector represents using 4 detection heads. CBAM represents the attention mechanism module.

The results showed that using the α-IoU(α = 3) loss function improved the $AP_{0.5}$ and $AP_{0.5:0.95}$ metrics by 1.9% and 2.6%, respectively, compared to using the original YOLOv5 loss function on the CrowdHuman dataset. This is because the α-IoU loss function increases the loss and gradient of high IoU targets, improving the regression accuracy of bounding boxes and accelerating the learning rate when the IoU is high. Adding the CBAM attention mechanism to the backbone network reduced the $AP_{0.5}$ and $AP_{0.5:0.95}$ metrics by 0.2% and 0.9%, respectively. The GSConv optimization reduced the GFLOPs from 16.5 to 15.4 while maintaining accuracy. The addition of the G3 module further improved accuracy while reducing the GFLOPs to 13.4, which is advantageous for deployment on embedded devices. Adding a small detection head to form a 4-detector model increased the $AP_{0.5}$ to 87.2%. Finally, adding the attention mechanism while incorporating G3 and changing the neck network's Conv to GSConv enabled the attention mechanism to work better. The final YOLOv5-G model improved the $AP_{0.5}$ and $AP_{0.5:0.95}$ metrics by 3.1% and 3.2%, respectively, compared to the original YOLOv5. Fig 7 and 8 show the comparison between before and after improvement, and it is clear that the YOLOv5-G object detector is more accurate, with significantly fewer redundant boxes and improved detection performance.

Fig. 7. YOLOv5 detection result.

Fig. 8. YOLOv5-G detection result.

3.2 Comparative Experiments

We compared YOLOv5-G with other state-of-the-art object detection algorithms and the results are shown in Table 2. It is evident that our proposed model outperforms the other models in terms of accuracy and detection speed.

Table 2. Comparative experiments

Method	$AP_{0.5}$	$AP_{0.5:0.95}$
YOLOv5-G	0.875	0.555
PS-RCNN	0.860	0.547
Faster RCNN	0.850	0.534
Adaptive NMS	0.847	0.533
IterDet	0.844	0.533

4 Conclusion

In this paper, we propose a novel object detection method, YOLOv5-G, based on improved depth-wise separable convolution to address the limitation of YOLOv5 in detecting dense small objects. YOLOv5-G enhances the detection of small objects by adding an additional prediction head and employs the α-IoU loss function for more accurate bounding box regression. The standard convolution module in the model's neck is replaced with a mixed convolution module composed of standard and depth-wise separable convolution, which reduces the computational burden and improves the model's detection performance compared to the original model that uses only standard convolution modules. The attention mechanism and lightweight module complement each other, allowing the attention mechanism to function better. Simulation experiments on the CrowdHuman dataset demonstrate that YOLOv5-G achieves significant improvements over the original YOLOv5 model.

References

1. Girshick, R., Donahue, J., Darrell, T., et al.: Rich feature hierarchies for accurate Object detection and semantic segmentation. In: Proceedings of the IEEE Conference on Computer Vision and Pattern Recognition, pp. 580–587. IEEE Computer Society (2013)
2. Li, J., Liang, X., Shen, S.M., et al.: Scale-aware fast R-CNN for pedestrian detection. IEEE (2015). https://doi.org/10.1109/TMM.2017.2759508
3. Ren, S., He, K., Girshick, R., et al.: Faster R-CNN: towards real-time object detection with region proposal networks. IEEE Trans. Pattern Anal. Mach. Intell. **39**(6), 1137–1149 (2017)
4. Redmon, J., Divvala, S., Girshick, R., et al.: You only look once. In: Unified, Real-Time Object Detection, pp. 799–788. IEEE (2016)
5. Chikawa, T., Haradome, H., Hachiya, J., et al.: Diffusion-weighted MR imaging with a single-shot echoplanar sequence: detection and characterization of focal hepatic lesions. Ajr. Am. J. Roentgenol. **170**(2), 397–402 (1998)
6. Lin, T.Y., Goyal, P., Girshick, R., et al.: Focal loss for dense object detection, pp. 2980–2988. arXiv e-prints (2017)
7. Ballester, P., Araú, R.M.: On the performance of GoogLeNet and AlexNet applied to sketches. In: AAAI. AAAI Press (2016)
8. Zhang, J., Huang, M., Jin, X., et al.: A real-time Chinese traffic sign detection algorithm based on modified YOLOv2. Algorithms **10**(4), 127 (2017)
9. Redmon, J., Farhadi, A.: YOLOv3: an incremental improvement. arXiv e-prints (2018)
10. Ioffe, S., Szegedy, C.: Batch normalization: accelerating deep network training by reducing internal covariate shift, pp. 448–456. JMLR.org (2015)
11. Bochkovskiy, A., Wang, C.-Y., Liao, H.-Y.M.: YOLOv4: optimal speed and accuracy of object detection. arXiv preprint arXiv:2004.10934 (2020)
12. Xie, S., Girshick, R., Dollár, P., Tu, Z.: Aggregated residual transformations for deep neural networks. In: Proceedings of the IEEE Conference on Computer Vision and Pattern Recognition , pp. 1492–1500 (2017)
13. Wang, C., Zhang, X., Yu, K., Yang, B., Liu, X., Wang, C.: YOLOv5: a unifying framework for object detection. In: Proceedings of the European Conference on Computer Vision (ECCV), pp. 641–657 (2020)
14. Ren, S., He, K., Girshick, R., Sun, J.: CrowdHuman: a benchmark for detecting human in a crowd. In: ECCV (2018)

15. Chollet, F.: Xception: deep learning with depthwise separable convolutions. In: 2017 IEEE Conference on Computer Vision and Pattern Recognition (CVPR). IEEE (2017)
16. Zhang, X., Zhou, X., Lin, M., et al.: ShuffleNet: an extremely efficient convolutional neural network for mobile devices (2017)
17. Li, H., Li, J., Wei, H., et al.: Slim-neck by GSConv: a better design paradigm of detector architectures for autonomous vehicles. arXiv preprint arXiv:2206.02424 (2022)
18. Park, J., Woo, S., Lee, J.Y., et al.: BAM: bottleneck attention module (2018). https://doi.org/10.48550/arXiv.1807.06514
19. Rezatofighi, H., Tsoi, N., Gwak, J.Y., et al.: Generalized intersection over union: a metric and a loss for bounding box regression In: IEEE/CVF Conference on Computer Vision and Pattern Recognition (CVPR) , pp 658–666. IEEE (2019)
20. Zheng, Z., Wang, P., Liu, W., et al.: Distance-IoU Loss: faster and better learning for bounding box regression. arXiv (2019)
21. Zheng, Z., Wang, P., Ren, D., et al.: Enhancing geometric factors in model learning and inference for object detection and instance segmentation. IEEE Trans. Cybern. **52**, 8574–8586 (2020)
22. He, J., Erfani, S., Ma, X., et al.: Alpha-IoU: a family of power intersection over union losses for bounding box regression. Adv. Neural Inf. Process. Syst. **34**, 20230–20242 (2021)

A Multimodal Text Block Segmentation Framework for Photo Translation

Jiajia Wu[1,2]([✉]), Anni Li[2], Kun Zhao[2], Zhengyan Yang[2], Bing Yin[2], Cong Liu[1], and Lirong Dai[1]

[1] University of Science and Technology of China, Hefei, China
congliu2@iflytek.com, lrdai@ustc.edu.cn
[2] IFLYTEK Research, Hefei, China
{jjwu,anni3,kunzhao4,zyyang13,bingyin}@iflytek.com

Abstract. Nowadays, with the vigorous development of OCR (Optical Character Recognition) and machine translation, photo translation technology brings great convenience to people's life and study. However, when translating the content of an image line by line, the lack of contextual information in adjacent semantic-related text lines will seriously influence the actual effect of translation, making it difficult for people to understand. To tackle the above problem, we propose a novel multimodal text block segmentation encoder-decoder model. Specifically, we construct a convolutional encoder to extract the multimodal representation which combines visual, semantic, and positional features together for each text line. In the decoder stage, the LSTM (Long Short Term Memory) module is employed to output the predicted segmentation sequence inspired by the pointer network. Experimental results illustrate that our model outperforms the other baselines by a large margin.

Keywords: Text block segmentation · Multimodal fusion · Pointer network

1 Introduction

In recent years, photo translation technology has brought great convenience to people's life and study, so that people can understand the information on signs and menus when they are in a foreign country. Photo translation technology is mainly composed of three modules: text detection [11,31,32], text recognition [19,20,30] and machine translation [3,4,22]. First, the text detection method is performed on the input image to get the coordinates of bounding boxes for all text lines in the image. Then, text recognition is applied on each text line patch. Finally, the recognized text of each line should be put into a machine translation, and the results are combined to obtain the predicted translation of the entire image. With the widespread application of deep learning techniques [8,24], especially the maturity of neural network-based end-to-end sequence modeling techniques [3,20], the three techniques mentioned above have achieved high accuracy in their respective scenarios.

© The Author(s), under exclusive license to Springer Nature Switzerland AG 2023
H. Lu et al. (Eds.): ICIG 2023, LNCS 14357, pp. 116–127, 2023.
https://doi.org/10.1007/978-3-031-46311-2_10

However, previous translation systems usually translate the content of each text line independently, resulting in the lack of context information, which seriously affect the actual effect of the translator. As a result, people are likely to obtain translations that are not smooth, fluent or even difficult to understand. For instance, the second line of a paragraph in the document scene may be just only a part of a complete sentence. It is possible to be related to the first line and the third line. If we translate the recognition result of the second line alone, the transcription could be obscure, incomplete or unsatisfactory because the context in the upper part and the lower part of the sentence is missing. The proposed text block segmentation technology is exactly to solve this problem. Through the segmentation model, the text lines containing semantic relationships are grouped into a text block and then translated by a translator, which can greatly improve the user's actual experience and the related evaluation indicators of photo translation technology. Figure 1 shows an example of a non-text segmented image and a text segmented image.

(a)   (b)

Fig. 1. (a) The results of scene text detection, which are the input of a translation system without text block segmentation. (b) The results of the proposed method, which are the input of a translation system with text block segmentation. Different blocks are represented by different colors. (Color figure online)

In this paper, we propose a novel multimodal encoder-decoder text block segmentation model to separate the text blocks with semantic relationship for photo translation in order to tackle the problem as mentioned above. In the encoder stage, to make better use of multimodal information, we employ a convolutional network to extract and fuse multimodal features, including the visual embedding, text embedding and position embedding to improve the model accuracy. The multimodal features of all text lines together with the start symbol, delimiter symbol and end symbol flag vector are combined to form a candidate feature queue. In the decoder stage, the text line index at each moment is predicted by calculating the similarity between the feature output from a LSTM [6] module and all of the features in the decoding candidate queue. When the delimiter symbol is decoded, it means that the prediction of a text block ends, and the prediction of the next text block starts. When the end symbol is decoded or the maximum decoding length is reached, the whole decoding process ends.

Our contributions are summarized as follows. First, we present an novel framework for text block segmentation task aiming at clustering semantic-related text lines to merge a complete sentence, which can greatly improve photo translation performance. Second, we fully utilize the multimodal features to improve model accuracy. Finally, we design quantitative sequence evaluation to demonstrate the rationality and feasibility of our model in four different languages.

2   Related Works

In this section, we describe the previous work related to the proposed method, including text detection, text recognition and sequence modeling.

2.1   Text Detection

Text detection methods usually adopt similar ideas as in general object detection methods such as Faster R-CNN [18], Cascade R-CNN [5] and YOLO [17]. However, some differences between them are notable. For example, the shape of a text box can be arbitrary while the shape of an object box is usually rectangular and text lines are usually dense while objects are usually relatively sparse. In order to handle above problems, semantic segmentation methods [13,26,33] are applied to text detection which usually achieve good results.

2.2   Text Recognition

In the early days, text recognition methods were based on segmentation, then recognize segments through character models and merge them through language model. Since segmentation is not accurate in handwriting scene and complex backgrounds, the state of the art methods are often end-to-end without segmentation. The key of the end-to-end method is how to align the feature sequence and label sequence. The CTC-based methods align them through CTC loss [19], ACE [28] uses aggregate cross entropy loss and encoder-decoder methods [20] make use of the attention mechanism to align feature sequence and label sequence.

2.3   Sequence Modeling

Sequence modeling has been widely researched in many fields. In natural language processing, RNN-based Sequence-to-Sequence model [3] is often used in machine translation task and in computer vision, encoder-decoder based model [29] is often used in image caption task. However, these methods can not solve the permutation problem where the size of outputs depends on the inputs directly. Pointer Network [25] and attention map loss [27] which uses an attention mechanism to find the proper units from the input sequence as outputs and these methods are often applied in text summarization [1], visual question answering(VQA) [2] and text re-organization [10] which brings insightful idea for text block segmentation.

3 Method

In this section, we illustrate the main architecture of our method, including a multimodal encoder and a dynamic decoder based on the LSTM [6] modules. Specifically, In Sect. 3.1, we elaborate how visual, semantic and positional features are extracted respectively by the encoder. In Sect. 3.2, we describe the global LSTM decoder with a dynamic vocabulary. The whole architecture is shown in the Fig. 2.

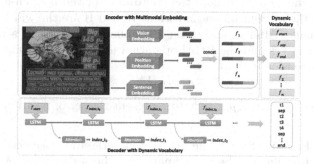

Fig. 2. The architecture of the proposed method, including the multimodal embedding and the LSTM-based decoder with dynamic vocabulary.

3.1 Encoder with Multimodal Embedding

Formally, we define the annotated text line set of the image is $\tau = \{t_1, t_2, ..., t_n\}$ where t_i refers to the ith text line. The target of the encoder is to get the embedding feature set of all of the text lines, which is defined as $F = \{f_1, f_2, ..., f_n\}$.

The Embedding of Vision. First, the input image is resized to 1280 along the long side. Then a Resnet50 [8] based backbone followed by a FPN [12] module is used to extract the visual feature of the input image. After obtaining the whole image feature, a ROI-Align [7] module can be employed to extract the visual feature of each text line in terms of the labeled bounding box. Finally, we flatten the visual features of every text line and put them into a linear projection head to convert them to a fixed dimension d_v. As a result, we can get the visual embedding set $V = \{v_1, v_2, ..., v_n\}, v_i \in R^{d_v}$.

The Embedding of Sentence. We build a RNN-based language model [14] for sentence embedding. First, the input content of each text line is segmented into tokens through tokenizer. Then the initial embeddings of these tokens should be put into the language model one by one. Finally, the last hidden vector of dimension d_w is extracted as the embedding of the whole text line. The embeddings of all text lines of the input image can be represented as $W = \{w_1, w_2, ..., w_n\}, w_i \in R^{d_w}$.

The Embedding of Position. The location information is very essential for our task as most text lines belonging to one block are adjacent to each other in position. We encode the position embedding for each text region via the normalized coordinates of upper left corner and lower right corner of the text line bounding box, which is calculated as below:

$$l_i = \left(\frac{x_1^i}{W}, \frac{y_1^i}{H}, \frac{x_2^i}{W}, \frac{y_2^i}{H} \right) \tag{1}$$

where (x_1^i, y_1^i) and (x_2^i, y_2^i) denote the coordinate of the bottom-left and top-right corner of the ith text line region while W and H are the width and height of the input image. After acquiring the normalized coordinates, a projection g with two linear layers and the ReLU operation are applied to map the vectors to a specific dimension d_p:

$$p_i = g(l_i) \tag{2}$$

we use $P = \{p_1, p_2, ..., p_n\}, p_i \in R^{d_p}$ to represent the set of position features.

Multimodal Fusion. So far, the visual, semantic and positional embedding vector of each text line on the input image have been extracted. At the end of the encoder, the feature vectors of the above three modalities are combined with a simple cascading operation which can be simply explained as follows:

$$f_i = concat(v_i, w_i, p_i) \tag{3}$$

where $f_i \in R^{d_f}, d_f = d_v + d_w + d_p$.

3.2 Decoder with LSTM

The dynamic vocabulary is composed of the the output feature vectors of the encoder and three extra learnable flag vectors, which can be interpreted as $D = \{f_{start}, f_{sep}, f_{end}, f_1, f_2, ..., f_n\}$. It is shown in Fig. 2 and the dimension of each element is equal to d_f. Further, the f_{start} vector is used as the input of the LSTM decoder at time 0, the f_{sep} vector stands for the separation between different text blocks and the f_{end} vector means that decoding process has ended.

The architecture of the decoder is cascading of LSTM modules which are usually used to solve sequence problems [23]. The whole decoding process is in an autoregressive pattern. The dynamic vocabulary is set to the decoding range of the decoder at each time step. At time step t, the hidden state of LSTM is considered as h_t. The attention score between the hidden vector and the feature in decoding range is calculated as below:

$$a_{t,i} = \frac{h_t \cdot f_i}{d_f} \tag{4}$$

where f_i means the ith feature vector in the dynamic vocabulary. After obtaining the attention scores of all vectors in the dictionary, a softmax function is utilized to normalize the scores:

$$\mathbf{s}_{t,i} = \frac{exp(a_{t,i})}{\sum_l a_{t,l}} \tag{5}$$

According to the result of Eq. 5, the feature with argmax index will be selected as the final decoding result at step, then this feature will be removed from dynamic vocabulary for avoiding repeated prediction of the same text line in the decoding sequence. The decoder repeats the above operations until the end symbol is decoded or the maximum decoding length is reached.

At each time step during decoding, we compute the cross-entropy loss between the one-hot groundtruth and the predicted probability distribution via Eq. 6:

$$L(\theta) = -\sum_t \sum_i y_{t,i} log s_{t,i} + (1 - y_{t,i}) log(1 - s_{t,i}) \tag{6}$$

where y_t refers to the label at time step t and θ is the weight of the model.

Suppose the final decoding sequence is $\{t_1, t_3, sep, t_2, end\}$. It means that text line t_1 and text line t_3 should be linked together as a block and text line t_2 is a block. Generally speaking, for every text block in the image, the text lines in the block are combined in the reading order to get a semantically complete sentence. Then the sentence is fed into a translator which gains the full contextual information.

4   Experiments

In this section, we set up experiments to evaluate our proposed method via the accuracy of the model and the translation performance. Specifically, the training and testing data are presented in Sect. 4.1 and the training details are shown in Sect. 4.2. In Sect. 4.3, we represent how to build a rule-based baseline and a detection-based baseline. In Sect. 4.4 we give the evaluation metrics and the result of our model will be presented in Sect. 4.5.

4.1   Dataset

We collected some images of natural scenes in multiple languages, including Kazakh, Russian, Uyghur and Vietnamese. These images are annotated and splited into train set, validation set and test set. Each image in the dataset has hierarchical labels, including text line and text block. The annotation of text line contains the coordinates of the text bounding box and the transcription. While the annotation of the text block contains the coordinates of the block bounding box and the transcription. The mapping between text block and text line are also stored according to the IOU matching.

The image number of training sets and testing sets for each language is shown in Table 1. What's more, we train four models for each language mentioned above respectively with language-specific training data and test the result in each language separately.

Table 1. The number of training and testing images in four language.

language	trainset	valset	testset
Kazakh	12540	500	563
Russian	13881	500	428
Uyghur	19747	500	513
Vietnamese	23484	500	575

4.2 Training

For encoder, the ResNet50 along with a FPN module is employed as our visual backbone. The dimension of the visual feature vectors is equal to 256 while the dimension of semantic and position embedding is 128. As a result, the multimodal feature's dimension is 512. For decoder, the dimension of LSTM's hidden state is 512 and we use two cascaded LSTM cells as the base architecture of the decoder.

We use an Adam [9] optimizer with weight decay 0.0005 and the initial learning rate $1e-4$. Then the learning rate is reduced by the CosineAnnealing schedule [21] epoch by epoch. The model is trained for 20 epochs in total and we set the batchsize to 16.

4.3 Baseline

We compare our method with the following two baselines, one is a rule-based clustering method and the other is a two-stage detection method. The former text clustering method is in terms of the position rules which is the most direct way. First, all the text lines on the input image are rearranged from top to bottom and then from left to right. After that, the separate flag is inserted between the sorted text lines when the distance of two adjacent text lines is greater than the preset threshold. For the latter baseline, we utilize the popular Faster R-CNN [18] architecture which is a state-of-the-art method to detect the bounding box of each text block directly.

4.4 Evaluation Metrics

We use two metrics to evaluate the performance of the model. One is the accuracy of the text block and the other is the BLEU [16] score of the translation task.

The accuracy score can be computed by the ratio of the number of text blocks whose text lines are perfectly matched with the label. For instance, if the text block label of the input image is $[[t_1, t_2], [t_5], [t_4], [t_3]]$ and the inference sequence after postprocess is $[[t_1, t_2], [t_3, t_4], [t_5]]$, then the number of matching correctly is 2 which stands for the length of the subset $[[t_1, t_2], [t_5]]$. It is worth noting that the text lines in the text block need to maintain the correct reading order which is required to form the right sentence, whether in annotation or prediction. In addition, we take no account of the order between diverse text blocks because it is not necessary for translation.

4.5 Results and Analysis

The main result of the accuracy score is depicted in Table 2. We compare the accuracy of our proposed method with the rule-based baseline and the Faster R-CNN baseline in test dataset of four different languages. Our approach exceeds the two baselines by a large margin. In fact, the rule-based baseline is very sensitive to the threshold which we will make a detailed analysis later while the Faster R-CNN network requires complex post-processing such as NMS [15] and sorting the matched lines in each block according to a positional rule. In addition, these two baseline methods do not use semantic features, and basically perform text block segmentation based on the visual distance of text lines. It is less effective for text block segmentation that is semantically close but visually distant or semantically not close but visually close. Compared to them, the proposed algorithm makes full use of multimodal information, not only has advantages in the performance, but also does not depend on the appropriate threshold and post-processing.

After obtaining the block of text, we join the content in the same text block and feed the contextual sentence into a translation engine. Table 3 presents the BLEU-2 score and BLEU-4 score between the annotated translation and the predicted translation under multiple settings. Single line setting refers to directly translating each text line without dividing them into text blocks, which is a common practice in previous photo translation systems. While annotation setting means we use the label of text block and the result under this setting represents the upper limit of our model. When considering the results in Table 2 and Table 3 comprehensively, our method outperforms other methods obviously and is very close to the upper limit on the BLEU score.

Table 2. Text block segmentation accuracy between baseline and our method on the test set of four different languages.

Method	Kazakh	Russian	Uyghur	Vietnamese
Rule	46.73	43.64	47.57	45.05
Faster R-CNN	62.41	58.09	64.09	73.04
Our method	79.86	78.10	79.80	87.59

Table 3. The BLEU scores of translation on test data of four languages.

Method	Kazakh		Russian		Uyghur		Vietnamese	
	BLEU-2	BLEU-4	BLEU-2	BLEU-4	BLEU-2	BLEU-4	BLEU-2	BLEU-4
Single line	46.48	32.05	64.31	50.64	65.70	51.23	62.27	46.30
Rule	49.08	34.97	66.38	53.13	67.71	53.99	64.91	50.62
Faster R-CNN	56.59	45.17	74.07	63.73	75.72	64.89	68.55	56.63
Our method	56.97	45.60	74.86	65.07	76.29	65.57	68.82	57.00
Annotation	57.29	46.21	75.99	66.63	76.75	66.23	69.25	57.65

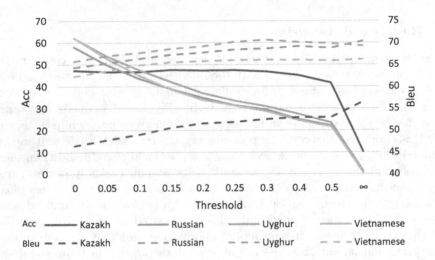

Fig. 3. Text block segmentation accuracy and BLEU-2 scores of the rule-based method under different thresholds.

We test the effect of different thresholds on the rule-based baseline. We use a certain proportion of the mean line height of text lines in the last text block along with the current line as the threshold for judging whether insert a separate flag before the current text line. All text lines have been sorted in advance. If two text lines are arranged left and right, a certain proportion of the mean line width is used as the separation threshold. Here, we define the former proportion as $ratio_h$ while the latter as $ratio_w$ and suppose $ratio_h = 2 * ratio, ratio_w = ratio$. Intuitively, the larger the $ratio$ is, the more the text lines tend to aggregate while the smaller the $ratio$ is, the more the text lines tend to separate. We compare text block segmentation accuracy and the BLEU score as the threshold changes in Fig. 3, where 0 represents that we consider every text line as a text block, and ∞ represents that all text lines in the image are aggregated together into a single block. The threshold we used in Table 2 and Table 3 is 0.1 for balance accuracy and BLEU score.

We also test ablation experiments based on different modal features. Here, we conduct ablation studies over the Vietnamese test data. Because visual information is very important in natural scenes, the basic network is constructed only via the visual embedding. Then, the position embedding and the semantic embedding are added to the network successively. The accuracy score and the translation BLEU score of the above three model are shown in Table 4. As we can see, the embedding of each mode play a positive role in the proposed network.

Table 4. Ablation studies of the three modal feature embedding.

Modal type	Acc	BLEU-2	BLEU-4
Vision only	78.17	67.89	55.45
Vision+Position	83.08	68.51	56.56
Vision+Position+Semantic	87.59	68.82	57.00

Some visualization results are shown in Fig. 4. It can be found the advantage of our model is that it can segment sentences accurately by using multimodal information, so as to provide complete contextual information for translation.

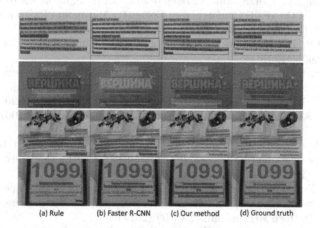

(a) Rule   (b) Faster R-CNN   (c) Our method   (d) Ground truth

Fig. 4. Comparative visualization results between our proposed method and other methods.

5   Conclusions

In this study, we propose a novel multimodal framework for text block segmentation. This framework improves model accuracy through fusion of multimodal information and attention mechanism. It makes use of a LSTM decoder to predict text block segmentation result. In addition, we introduce quantitative evaluation to measure the effect of the proposed method. Our model outperforms the baselines both on text block segmentation accuracy and translation accuracy. As for future work, we will try to combine unsupervised pre-trained model to improve text block segmentation accuracy.

References

1. Allahyari, M., et al.: Text summarization techniques: a brief survey. arXiv preprint arXiv:1707.02268 (2017)
2. Antol, S., et al.: VQA: visual question answering. In: Proceedings of the IEEE International Conference on Computer Vision, pp. 2425–2433 (2015)
3. Bahdanau, D., Cho, K.H., Bengio, Y.: Neural machine translation by jointly learning to align and translate. In: 3rd International Conference on Learning Representations, ICLR 2015 (2015)
4. Caglayan, O., et al.: Cross-lingual visual pre-training for multimodal machine translation. In: arXiv preprint arXiv:2101.10044 (2021)
5. Cai, Z., Vasconcelos, N.: Cascade R-CNN: delving into high quality object detection. In: Proceedings of the IEEE Conference on Computer Vision and Pattern Recognition, pp. 6154–6162 (2018)
6. D'Informatique, D.E., Ese, N., Esent, P., Au, E., Frasconi, P.P.: Long short-term memory in recurrent neural networks. EPFL (2001)
7. He, K., Gkioxari, G., Dollár, P., Girshick, R.: Mask R-CNN. In: Proceedings of the IEEE International Conference on Computer Vision, pp. 2961–2969 (2017)
8. He, K., Zhang, X., Ren, S., Sun, J.: Deep residual learning for image recognition. In: Proceedings of the IEEE Conference on Computer Vision and Pattern Recognition, pp. 770–778 (2016)
9. Kingma, D.P., Ba, J.: Adam: A method for stochastic optimization. arXiv preprint arXiv:1412.6980 (2014)
10. Li, L., Gao, F., Bu, J., Wang, Y., Yu, Z., Zheng, Q.: An end-to-end OCR Text Re-organization sequence learning for Rich-Text detail image comprehension. In: Vedaldi, A., Bischof, H., Brox, T., Frahm, J.-M. (eds.) ECCV 2020. LNCS, vol. 12370, pp. 85–100. Springer, Cham (2020). https://doi.org/10.1007/978-3-030-58595-2_6
11. Liao, M., Shi, B., Bai, X., Wang, X., Liu, W.: Textboxes: a fast text detector with a single deep neural network. In: Thirty-First AAAI Conference on Artificial Intelligence (2017)
12. Lin, T.Y., Dollar, P., Girshick, R., He, K., Hariharan, B., Belongie, S.: Feature pyramid networks for object detection. In: 2017 IEEE Conference on Computer Vision and Pattern Recognition (CVPR) (2017)
13. Long, S., Ruan, J., Zhang, W., He, X., Wu, W., Yao, C.: TextSnake: a flexible representation for detecting text of arbitrary shapes. In: Proceedings of the European Conference on Computer Vision (ECCV), pp. 20–36 (2018)
14. Mikolov, T., Karafilćt, M., Burget, L., Cernock, J., Khudanpur, S.: Recurrent neural network based language model. In: Interspeech, Conference of the International Speech Communication Association, Makuhari, Chiba, Japan, September (2015)
15. Neubeck, A., Van Gool, L.: Efficient non-maximum suppression. In: 18th International Conference on Pattern Recognition (ICPR 2006). vol. 3, pp. 850–855. IEEE (2006)
16. Papineni, K., Roukos, S., Ward, T., Zhu, W.J.: BLEU: a method for automatic evaluation of machine translation. Proceedings of the 40th annual meeting of the Association for Computational Linguistics, pp. 311–318 (2002)

17. Redmon, J., Divvala, S., Girshick, R., Farhadi, A.: You only look once: unified, real-time object detection. In: Proceedings of the IEEE Conference on Computer Vision and Pattern Recognition, pp. 779–788 (2016)
18. Ren, S., He, K., Girshick, R., Sun, J.: Faster R-CNN: towards real-time object detection with region proposal networks. In: Advances in Neural Information Processing Systems, pp. 91–99 (2015)
19. Shi, B., Bai, X., Yao, C.: An end-to-end trainable neural network for image-based sequence recognition and its application to scene text recognition. IEEE Trans. Pattern Anal. Mach. Intell. **39**(11), 2298–2304 (2016)
20. Shi, B., Wang, X., Lyu, P., Yao, C., Bai, X.: Robust scene text recognition with automatic rectification. In: Proceedings of the IEEE Conference on Computer Vision and Pattern Recognition, pp. 4168–4176 (2016)
21. Smith, L.N., Topin, N.: Super-convergence: very fast training of neural networks using large learning rates. Artif. Intell. Mach. Learn. Multi-Domain Oper. Appl. **11006**, 369–386 (2019)
22. Stĺẑn, A., Berard, A., Besacier, L., Gallĺe, M.: Multilingual unsupervised neural machine translation with denoising adapters. In: Empirical Methods in Natural Language Processing (2021)
23. Sutskever, I., Vinyals, O., Le, Q.V.: Sequence to sequence learning with neural networks. In: NIPS (2014)
24. Vaswani, A., Shazeer, N., Parmar, N., Uszkoreit, J., Jones, L., Gomez, A.N., Kaiser, Ł., Polosukhin, I.: Attention is all you need. In: Advances in Neural Information Processing Systems, pp. 5998–6008 (2017)
25. Vinyals, O., Fortunato, M., Jaitly, N.: Pointer networks. In: Advances in Neural Information Processing Systems, pp. 2692–2700 (2015)
26. Wang, W., et al.: Shape robust text detection with progressive scale expansion network. In: Proceedings of the IEEE Conference on Computer Vision and Pattern Recognition, pp. 9336–9345 (2019)
27. Wu, J., et al.: A multimodal attention fusion network with a dynamic vocabulary for textVQA. Pattern Recogn. **122**, 108214 (2022)
28. Xie, Z., Huang, Y., Zhu, Y., Jin, L., Liu, Y., Xie, L.: Aggregation cross-entropy for sequence recognition. In: Proceedings of the IEEE Conference on Computer Vision and Pattern Recognition, pp. 6538–6547 (2019)
29. Xu, K., et al.: Show, attend and tell: neural image caption generation with visual attention. In: International Conference on Machine Learning, pp. 2048–2057 (2015)
30. Yan, R., Peng, L., Xiao, S., Yao, G.: Primitive representation learning for scene text recognition. In: Proceedings of the IEEE/CVF Conference on Computer Vision and Pattern Recognition, pp. 284–293 (2021)
31. Zhou, X., et al.: EAST: an efficient and accurate scene text detector. In: Proceedings of the IEEE Conference on Computer Vision and Pattern Recognition, pp. 5551–5560 (2017)
32. Zhu, Y., Chen, J., Liang, L., Kuang, Z., Jin, L., Zhang, W.: Fourier contour embedding for arbitrary-shaped text detection. In: Proceedings of the IEEE/CVF Conference on Computer Vision and Pattern Recognition, pp. 3123–3131 (2021)
33. Zhu, Y., Du, J.: TextMountain: accurate scene text detection via instance segmentation. Pattern Recogn. **110**, 107336 (2020)

End-to-End Multilingual Text Recognition Based on Byte Modeling

Jiajia Wu[1,2]([⊠]), Kun Zhao[2], Zhengyan Yang[2], Bing Yin[2], Cong Liu[1], and Lirong Dai[1]

[1] University of Science and Technology of China, Hefei, China
congliu2@iflytek.com, lrdai@ustc.edu.cn
[2] IFLYTEK Research, Hefei, China
{jjwu,kunzhao4,zyyang13,bingyin}@iflytek.com

Abstract. Nowadays, multilingual text recognition is more and more widely used in computer vision. However, in practical applications, the independent modeling of each language cannot make full use of the information between different languages and consumes hardware resources very much, which makes the unified modeling of multiple languages very necessary. A natural approach to unified multilingual modeling is to combine modeling units (characters, subwords, or words) from all languages into a large vocabulary, and then use a sequence-to-sequence approach to modeling. However, this vocabulary is often very large making modeling difficult. In this paper, we propose a byte-based multilingual text recognition method, which makes the vocabulary size only 256, which effectively solves the problem of unified modeling. The experiments show that our method effectively utilizes the information between different languages and outperforms the baseline of independent modeling by a large margin.

Keywords: multilingual · end-to-end text recognition · unified modeling · byte modeling

1 Introduction

In recent years, multilingual text recognition [1,9,21] as show in Fig. 1 has brought people a lot of convenience, such as photo translation for tourists. Text recognition usually uses a sequence-to-sequence modeling approach to transcribe text images into text. The usual practice of multilingual text recognition is to model each language independently and the modeling units of each language are usually characters [22,24], sub-words [15,16,20] or words [10]. With the development of deep learning technology, independent modeling can achieve high recognition accuracy with sufficient training data.

However, data in many languages is difficult to collect and expensive to label. It makes independent modeling unable to achieve high recognition accuracy. Many languages belong to the same language family and the character structure is relatively close. It is very important to make the information between different language data complement each other to improve the recognition accuracy.

© The Author(s), under exclusive license to Springer Nature Switzerland AG 2023
H. Lu et al. (Eds.): ICIG 2023, LNCS 14357, pp. 128–137, 2023.
https://doi.org/10.1007/978-3-031-46311-2_11

Combining all language data together for unified modeling is an effective way to complement information.

A common unified modeling approach is to combine all language vocabularies into a large vocabulary, combine all language training data together, and then perform sequence-to-sequence modeling. This approach works well when there are not many languages involved in unified modeling. However, as more and more languages are involved in modeling and the combined vocabulary becomes larger, model training will become very difficult.

In this paper, we propose a multilingual recognition method based on byte modeling. In this framework, the label of all languages are represented as Unicode bytes [3] and bytes are used as a unified modeling unit for all languages. Byte modeling enables the vocabulary size to be fixed to 256, which solves large vocabulary problem in unified modeling. In addition, independent modeling consumes a lot of hardware resources when the engine is deployed and unified modeling can effectively solve this problem.

Our contributions are summarized as follows. First, we present an byte modeling framework for multilingual text recognition aiming at multilingual unified modeling, which can greatly improve recognition accuracy when training data is not enough. Second, we do detailed experimental analysis and specific case studies on five different languages to analyze the advantages of byte modeling.

(a) Multilingual images   (b) The results of multilingual recognition

Fig. 1. (a): Multilingual images. (b): The result text of the multilingual text recognition.

2   Related Works

In the early days, text recognition methods were based on over segmentation [13,26] and merge them through language model [4,14]. In the recent years, end-to-end approaches have become popular such as CTC-based method [6,17], aggregation-based method [27] and encoder-decoder method [18]. These methods typically use characters, sub-words or words for sequence modeling. In multilingual text recognition, unified modeling is used to alleviate data scarcity problem which combine modeling units from all languages into a large vocabulary. In speech recognition and machine translation, bytes are used for sequence modeling [12,25] which brings insightful idea for multilingual unified modeling text recognition.

3   Method

The proposed end-to-end multilingual byte modeling method for multilingual text recognition is based on unicode byte encoding [5] to represent text sequences. The unicode byte encoding splits a single character into multiple bytes as the target of text decoding, and the text recognition model is based on the sequence-to-sequence Long Short-Term Memory(LSTM) [8] method as shown in Fig. 2, which encodes the input image into high-dimensional features, and then classifies the target sequence according to the unicode byte vocabulary step by step.

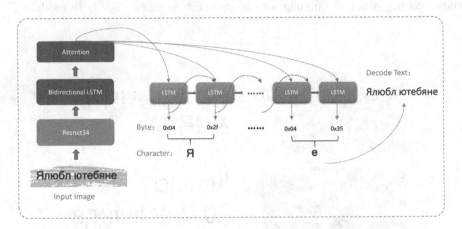

Fig. 2. The byte modeling framework for multilingual text recognition based on unicode byte encoding. It includes convolutional network, LSTM encoder network and LSTM decoder network.

3.1   Unicode Byte Encoding

Unicode is a character encoding scheme that sets a uniform and unique binary encoding for each character in each language to achieve cross-language and cross-platform text conversion. As shown in Fig. 3, each character is composed of multiple bytes to form Unicode encoding. The proposed Unicode byte encoding strategy is to split characters to form multiple single bytes, so each character can be composed of multiple single-byte encoding composition. One byte stores

8-bit unsigned numbers, and the range of stored values is 0–255. For multiple languages, the characters of different languages are represented by a single byte, so the size of the generated vocabulary is fixed at 256. This scheme is called unicode byte encoding.

Unlike character encoding [22,24], subword encoding [15,16,20] and whole word encoding [10], byte encoding is a very fine-grained way of encoding text. For whole-word encoding, a large dictionary will be generated, which is a huge overhead in the process of calculating cross-entropy at the classification layer. At the same time, due to the existence of low-frequency words, there is a serious long-tail problem. In order to alleviate this problem, the BPE subword-based [16] method combines characters to form subwords according to the frequency of different characters appearing together. The subwords themselves contain certain semantic relations, which shows certain advantages in the recognition of a single language or a small number of languages, but this method does not solve the problem of too large vocabulary. Character-based text encoding is a common approach for most languages, the size of the character vocabulary will also increase accordingly for the multilingual text recognition with the increase of the number of languages, and the distribution of the number of characters in different languages is also inconsistent, which leads to an increase in the computational complexity and recognition difficulty of the model classification. Byte encoding eliminates the inherent category differences of languages and reduces the decoding range to 256. Based on the characteristics of context in the sequence decoding process, the decoded byte sequences are highly correlated. Text characters can be generated by grouping bytes to recover its own semantic information.

The Unicode byte encoding fixes the classification dictionary to 256, which does not change with the increase of the number of languages, so that the text recognition model can be easily generalized to different languages, which is beneficial to the deployment and application of the model. In addition, the meaning of the characters themselves is broken because the characters are divided into different bytes. It makes the model pays more attention to the contextual relationship of the text which enhancing the semantic extraction ability of the model.

3.2   Encoder-Decoder Text Recognition

The byte modeling for text recognition model is based on encoder-decoder framework with attention mechanism [2]. Compared with the CTC-based text recognition scheme [17] which focuses on the alignment of characters and pixels, the encoder-decoder network is an implicit language model that can learn more language prior knowledge. For multilingual text recognition, it may contain multiple languages, such as Korean, Chinese, English, Spanish, etc. These languages have different language characteristics, and the Unicode byte encoding compromises character information. Therefore, the encoder-decoder network is more suitable for the text recognition with Unicode byte encoding.

The network is composed of three main modules as show in Fig. 2, including convolutional network, LSTM encoder network and LSTM decoder network. The

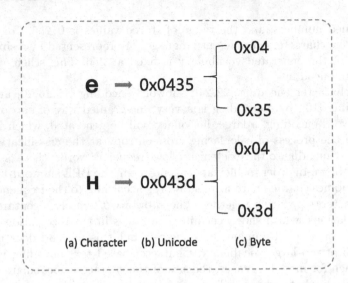

Fig. 3. The Unicode byte encoding. The Unicode encoding of characters is split into multiple bytes.

convolutional network is based on ResNet [7] which contains 5 ResNet blocks. The image is input to the convolutional network for extracting features $E_c \in R^{L \times D_c}$, where L represents the length of features, and D_c is the dimension of the features. Specifically, the width is downsampled by a factor of 8 to ensure sufficient sequence length for text decoding, and the height is downsampled by a factor of 64 to 1-dimensional space for sequence encoding. The LSTM encoder network consists of 1 bidirectional LSTM layer with 256 hidden units, which used to learn the inter-sequence context features E_l.

$$E_l = \{E_{l,0}, E_{l,1}, ..., E_{l,L}\}, E_{l,i} \in R^{D_l} \tag{1}$$

where $E_{l,i}$ represents the output features of $i-th$ length with D_l dimension in the encoder.

In the decoder stage, two-layer LSTM with 512 hidden units is used to decode the targets. Additive coverage attention [23] is used to learn the alignment between the input image features and the output target Unicode byte units. The calculation process is as follows:

$$q_t = f(concate(y_{t-1}, h_t)) \tag{2}$$

$$e_{ij} = a(E_{l,i}, q_j) \tag{3}$$

$$\alpha_{ij} = \frac{exp(e_{ij})}{\sum_{k=1}^{T} exp(e_{ik})} \tag{4}$$

$$v_t = \sum_{k=1}^{L} \alpha_{kt} E_{l,k} \tag{5}$$

where y_{t-1} is the text embedding of the previous time, and the h_t is the hidden state of the LSTM deocder at the current t time. $f(\cdot)$ and $a(\cdot)$ denotes the linear operation. q_t represents the query vector of attention . v_t is the contextual features based on attention mechanism.

Finally, the contextual features of the LSTM decoder and the embedding of the previous time are spliced together to the linear classification layer. and the entire recognition model is trained by calculating the cross entropy loss. We compute the cross-entropy loss between the one-hot groundtruth and the predicted probability distribution to train the model. In the test stage, the decoded byte units are spliced together to generate multilingual text recognition results.

4 Expriments

In this section, we evaluate the proposed method with encoder-decoder text recognition network on 5 different languages, namely Spanish(SP), Portuguese(PO), Korean(KO), Kazakh(KA), and Vietnamese(VI). Specifically, the datasets are presented in Sect. 4.1 and the training details are shown in Sect. 4.2. In Sect. 4.3, The experimental results and analysis are described in detail.

4.1 Datasets

Experiments are conducted on 5 collected natural scene multilingual datasets. In order to ensure that the text recognition model is more practical, the collected natural scenes include road signs, instructions, commodity packaging, books, etc. The labeled datasets are divided into train set and test set. The train set includes 50w images of the textlines, and the test set includes 2.5w images of the textlines. The language-specific details can be found in Table 1.

Table 1. The number of train and test images in different language.

language	Train	Test
Kazakh	100000	4443
Korean	100000	5970
Spanish	100000	7182
Vietnamese	100000	4407
Portuguese	100000	5774

4.2 Implementation Details

The network architecture for the text recognition is show in fig. The resnet module has 34 convolutional layers as the backbone network, and each convolutional layer uses kernel with a 3×3 spatial extent. Note that it is trained on Imagenet as pretraining parameters. For LSTM encoder and decoder networks, we use random parameter initialization sampled from gaussian distribution with 0.01 standard deviation. Given a input image, through the convolutional network, the height is downsampled to 1, and the context information is extracted through the LSTM encoding network. Then, the byte sequence is gradually solved by the LSTM decoding network based on the attention mechanism. Finally the byte sequence is combined to restore semantic text.

We use a Adam [11] optimizer with weight decay 0.0005 and the initial learning rate $2e - 4$. Then the learning rate is reduced by the CosineAnnealing schedule [19] epoch by epoch. The batchsize is set to 32 and the text recognition is trained with 16 epochs in total.

We calculate the word accuracy(Wacc) according to the edit distance as the evaluation criterion of the recognition model. The calculation process is as follows:

$$Wacc = (N - D - S - I)/N \tag{6}$$

where N represents the total number of labeled words. According to the edit distance algorithm, D denotes the number of deleted words, S denotes the number of replacement words, and I denotes the number of inserted words.

4.3 Results and Analysis

The multilingual recognition model based on Unicode byte encoding randomly mixes the training data of 5 languages (Korean, Kazakh, Portuguese, Spanish and Vietnamese) during the training process, and the dictionary is 256. In addition, two sets of comparative experiments are conducted. The first group is to train the text recognition model of each language separately based on Unicode byte encoding, and the second group is to train the recognition model of each language based on character encoding. Unlike Unicode byte encoding that has a fixed dictionary size, the size of the character dictionary varies with different languages. For example, the dictionary size of Korean characters is 4265, and the dictionary size of Portuguese characters is 924. The specific-language values are shown in the Table 2. All model training strategies remain the same, and the specific experimental results are shown in the following table:

Table 2. Scene text recognition accuracies(%) in different language.

Language	Multi Byte	Byte	UC	Dictionary
Kazakh	90.13	86.15	85.78	842
Korean	90.41	83.98	86.16	4265
Spanish	92.31	89.36	89.96	517
Vietnamese	89.28	75.41	86.41	1115
Portuguese	92.15	86.10	89.44	924

In the Tabel 2. The "Multi Byte" denotes the multilingual text recognition model based on Unicode byte encoding. "Byte" and "UC" represent models trained separately for each language based on bytes and characters respectively. The last column of data shows the size of the dictionary modeled for each language character, and there are obvious differences in the number of characters in different languages, which is easy to cause the problem of language category imbalance.

From the experimental results, the accuracy of the proposed byte modeling for multilingual text recognition model is about 5% higher than the single byte and uc results, which means that mixed training of multiple languages is good for modeling language contextual semantic relations. In the case of less language training data, mixing multiple languages together and using Unicode byte encoding can significantly improve the recognition effect of each language. In addition, the Unicode byte encoding has a fixed dictionary size and is more mobile, and new language recognition capabilities can be added at any time without adding a dictionary.

In addition, we compared the differences in the recognition results of the three groups of experiments. As shown in the Fig. 4, the multilingual byte model effectively reduces the replacement errors of recognition. It shows that sharing the same dictionary in different languages can improve the model accuracy effectively.

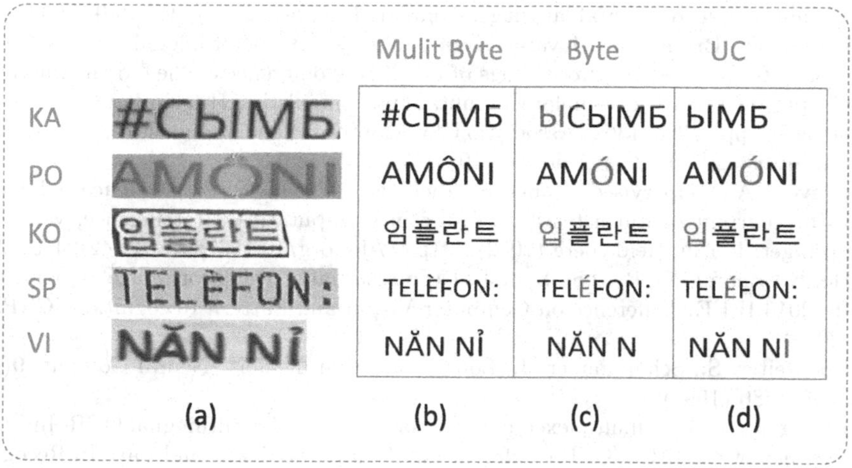

Fig. 4. Example of multilingual recognition results. (a): Multilingual images. (b): The result text of the proposed byte modeling for multilingual text recognition. (c): The result text of the independent text recognition model for each language based on Unicode byte encoding. (d) The result text of the independent text recognition model for each language based on character encoding. And the characters marked in red indicate substitution errors based on edit distance (Color figure online)

5   Conclusion

In this study, we propose a novel end-to-end multilingual byte modeling method for text recognition. We model text via a sequence of Unicode bytes for each character. The use of bytes allows us to build a unified model for multilingual text recognition with fixed vocabulary size of 256. The experiments show that our method outperforms the baseline of independent modeling by a large margin. As for future work, we will explore the use of additional byte-based language models to improve the performance of byte-based multilingual unified modeling for text recognition.

References

1. del Agua, M.A., Serrano, N., Civera, J., Juan, A.: Character-based handwritten text recognition of multilingual documents. In: Torre Toledano, D., et al. (eds.) IberSPEECH 2012. CCIS, vol. 328, pp. 187–196. Springer, Heidelberg (2012). https://doi.org/10.1007/978-3-642-35292-8_20
2. Bahdanau, D., Cho, K., Bengio, Y.: Neural machine translation by jointly learning to align and translate. In: International Conference on Learning Representations (2015)
3. Bettels, J., Bishop, F.A.: Unicode: a universal character code. Digit. Tech. J. **5**(3), 21–31 (1993)
4. Brown, P.F., Della Pietra, V.J., Desouza, P.V., Lai, J.C., Mercer, R.L.: Class-based n-gram models of natural language. Comput. Linguist. **18**(4), 467–480 (1992)
5. Gillick, D., Brunk, C., Vinyals, O., Subramanya, A.: Multilingual language processing from bytes. In: Proceedings of the 2016 Conference of the North American Chapter of the Association for Computational Linguistics: Human Language Technologies, pp. 1296–1306. Association for Computational Linguistics, San Diego, California (2016). https://doi.org/10.18653/v1/N16-1155
6. Graves, A.: Supervised sequence labelling. in: supervised sequence labelling with recurrent neural networks. Studies in Computational Intelligence, vol. 385. Springer, Berlin, Heidelberg (2012). https://doi.org/10.1007/978-3-642-24797-2_2
7. He, K., Zhang, X., Ren, S., Sun, J.: Deep residual learning for image recognition. In: 2016 IEEE Conference on Computer Vision and Pattern Recognition (CVPR) (2016)
8. Hochreiter, S., Schmidhuber, J.: Long short-term memory. Neural Comput. **9**(8), 1735–1780 (1997)
9. Huang, J., et al.: A multiplexed network for end-to-end, multilingual OCR. In: Proceedings of the IEEE/CVF Conference on Computer Vision and Pattern Recognition, pp. 4547–4557 (2021)
10. Jean, S., Cho, K., Memisevic, R., Bengio, Y.: On using very large target vocabulary for neural machine translation (2014)
11. Kingma, D., Ba, J.: Adam: A method for stochastic optimization. Computer Science (2014)
12. Li, B., Zhang, Y., Sainath, T., Wu, Y., Chan, W.: Bytes are all you need: End-to-end multilingual speech recognition and synthesis with bytes. In: ICASSP 2019– 2019 IEEE International Conference on Acoustics, Speech and Signal Processing (ICASSP), pp. 5621–5625. IEEE (2019)

13. Ma, L.L., Liu, C.L.: On-line handwritten Chinese character recognition based on nested segmentation of radicals. In: 2009 Chinese Conference on Pattern Recognition, pp. 1–5. IEEE (2009)
14. Mikolov, T., Karafiát, M., Burget, L., Cernocký, J., Khudanpur, S.: Recurrent neural network based language model. In: Interspeech. vol. 2, pp. 1045–1048. Makuhari (2010)
15. Mikolov, T., Sutskever, I., Deoras, A., Le, H.S., Kombrink, S., Cernocký, J.H.: Subword language modeling with neural networks (2011)
16. Sennrich, R., Haddow, B., Birch, A.: Neural machine translation of rare words with subword units. In: Proceedings of the 54th Annual Meeting of the Association for Computational Linguistics (Volume 1: Long Papers), pp. 1715–1725. Association for Computational Linguistics, Berlin, Germany (2016). https://doi.org/10.18653/v1/P16-1162
17. Shi, B., Bai, X., Yao, C.: An end-to-end trainable neural network for image-based sequence recognition and its application to scene text recognition. IEEE Trans. Pattern Anal. Mach. Intell. 39(11), 2298–2304 (2016)
18. Shi, B., Yang, M., Wang, X., Lyu, P., Yao, C., Bai, X.: Aster: an attentional scene text recognizer with flexible rectification. IEEE Trans. Pattern Anal. Mach. Intell. 41(9), 2035–2048 (2018)
19. Smith, L.N., Topin, N.: Super-convergence: Very fast training of neural networks using large learning rates (2017)
20. Snyder, B., Barzilay, R.: Unsupervised multilingual learning for morphological segmentation. In: Proceedings of ACL-08: HLT, pp. 737–745. Association for Computational Linguistics, Columbus, Ohio (2008)
21. Tian, S., et al.: Multilingual scene character recognition with co-occurrence of histogram of oriented gradients. Pattern Recogn. 51, 125–134 (2016)
22. Tiedemann, J.: Character-based PSMT for closely related languages. In: Proceedings of the 13th Annual Conference of the European Association for Machine Translation. European Association for Machine Translation, Barcelona, Spain (2009)
23. Tu, Z., Lu, Z., Yang, L., Liu, X., Hang, L.: Modeling coverage for neural machine translation. In: Proceedings of the 54th Annual Meeting of the Association for Computational Linguistics (Volume 1: Long Papers) (2016)
24. Vilar, D., Peter, J.T., Ney, H.: Can we translate letters? In: Proceedings of the Second Workshop on Statistical Machine Translation, pp. 33–39. Association for Computational Linguistics, Prague, Czech Republic (2007)
25. Wang, C., Cho, K., Gu, J.: Neural machine translation with byte-level subwords. In: Proceedings of the AAAI Conference on Artificial Intelligence. vol. 34, pp. 9154–9160 (2020)
26. Wang, Q.F., Yin, F., Liu, C.L.: Handwritten Chinese text recognition by integrating multiple contexts. IEEE Trans. Pattern Anal. Mach. Intell. 34(8), 1469–1481 (2011)
27. Xie, Z., Huang, Y., Zhu, Y., Jin, L., Liu, Y., Xie, L.: Aggregation cross-entropy for sequence recognition. In: Proceedings of the IEEE Conference on Computer Vision and Pattern Recognition, pp. 6538–6547 (2019)

Disentangled Shape and Pose Based on Attention and Mesh Autoencoder

Tao Wu and Xiaoning Song$^{(\boxtimes)}$

Jiangnan University, Wuxi 214122, China
6213113123@stu.jiangnan.edu.cn, x.song@jiangnan.edu.cn

Abstract. Deep 3D morphable models are widely applied in computer vision and graphics applications, including 3D reconstruction, pose estimation, and 3D pose transfer. The ability to decompose 3D data into shape and pose is essential in these applications. However, accurate and robust disentanglement of shape and pose remains a challenging task, as meshes with pose or shape labels are lacking. To alleviate this issue, we introduce A-MeshNet, an innovative approach that employs AFA module and Mesh Auto-encoder for unsupervised disentanglement of human mesh and high-precision human mesh reconstruction. Our approach builds a new mesh auto-encoder based on the AFA module for effective feature aggregation. We demonstrate that our proposed A-MeshNet achieves superior performance than state-of-the-art approaches on various benchmarking datasets.

Keywords: Mesh Auto-encoder · Attention Mechanism · Unsupervised Learning · 3D Pose Transfer

1 Introduction

The 3D morphable model has extensive applications in various vision tasks, including body tracking, pose estimation, and animation. The existing 3D morphable models can be categorized into linear and non-linear models. Most of the traditional models are linear models [1] [2], which are based on traditional linear approaches such as PCA [3]. Linear models like SMPL Model [4], Frank model [5] for bodies, MANO model [6] for hands, FLAME [7] for faces, are extensively used for various fields. Despite their popularity, the limited expressiveness of linear techniques makes it challenging to represent and fit complex human body shapes, poses, and large-scale motion deformations. With the strong non-linear fitting ability of neural networks, deep 3D morphable models [8] [9] have become increasingly popular. The non-linear model based on the neural network has shown better performance in fitting various human body shapes and postures in complex real-world scenarios.

Supported by National Social Science Foundation of China(21&ZD166); Natural Science Foundation of Jiangsu Province, China(BK20221535).

© The Author(s), under exclusive license to Springer Nature Switzerland AG 2023
H. Lu et al. (Eds.): ICIG 2023, LNCS 14357, pp. 138–149, 2023.
https://doi.org/10.1007/978-3-031-46311-2_12

Like the most influential work SMPL [4], our A-MeshNet effectively disentangles the shape and pose information from a given human mesh and accurately reconstructs input human mesh. By combining shape codes encoded by identity meshes and pose codes encoded by pose meshes, a new mesh is generated that preserves both the shape information of identity meshes and the pose information of pose meshes. However, disentangling shape and pose from meshes is an urgent task since meshes with pose or shape labels are difficult to gather. It is highly improbable to record two different humans displaying the same pose in real-world scenarios, resulting in datasets lacking different subjects in identical postures. To address this issue, deep learning techniques such as encoder-decoder based architectures have become increasingly popular and are widely used in deep 3D morphable models. Our proposed A-MeshNet shows promising results in accurately reconstructing input human meshes by separating them into shape and pose codes.

This work presents an innovative method that utilizes a multi-layer mesh auto-encoder and attention mechanism to encode the decoupled shape and pose latent variables of 3D mesh without supervision. Recent studies have demonstrated that the encoder-decoder based models have achieved remarkable performance in human body geometry by self-supervisedly encoding human meshes with low-dimensional vectors. Our A-MeshNet takes the vertex coordinates of three meshes as input, without any pose or shape annotations. Based on the mesh auto-encoder model, we introduce the AFA module for feature aggregation. The AFA module can effectively calculates the feature information between vertices of adjacent layers. In addition, we incorporate an ARAP deformer to ensure the shape of the reconstructed mesh remains consistent with the input mesh during training. Finally, we integrate the above modules into an end-to-end learning framework for ease of implementation.

We summarize the main contributions of this work are:

- We present A-MeshNet, an unsupervised mesh auto-encoder model designed to address the issue of disentanglement of human mesh problem in an end-to-end trainable manner.
- We introduce an Attentional Feature Aggregation(AFA) module into the mesh auto-encoder to enhance the aggregation of features from adjacent vertices. Our method achieves disentanglement of shape and pose latent variables without relying on corresponding annotations, and reconstructs high-precision meshes.
- The experimental results show that our A-MeshNet obtains superior performance than existing approaches in 3D vision tasks, including 3D human reconstruction from human mesh and 3D pose transfer.

2   Related Work

2.1   Deep Network on Meshes

Recently, numerous deep learning based approaches [10] have emerged for the analysis and reconstruction of 3D data. Bagautdinov *et al.* [11] proposed a multi-level VAE [12] architecture that can effectively model faces at global and local scales, exhibiting a strong generalization ability. MeshVAE [13] built a mesh VAE architecture to learn the deformation features of 3D mesh, but the model requires excessive computational resources due to the presence of linear layers. Ranjan *et al.* [14] introduced a multi-scale hierarchical structure, which combines graph convolutions [15] [16] and upsampling and downsampling operations to encode latent representation. The model can accurately reconstruct extreme facial expressions. To help the mesh autoencoder decrease reconstruction errors, DEMEA [17] adds an embedded deformation layer. However, the common issue of the above models is that they can not achieve disentanglement of shape and pose.

2.2 Deep Learning for Disentangled Representations

The motivation behind the disentanglement of human meshes is that it is often necessary to distinguish identity and pose information in many 3D tasks, including pose transfer, and pose and shape interpolation. Jiang *et al.* [18] introduced two VAE branches disentangle identity code and expression code separately, and fuse them to reconstruct the input mesh. Their method requires supervision with expression labels. Jiang *et al.* [19] presented an auto-encoder model to learn pose and shape embedding in a hierarchical manner, which improves the reconstruction accuracy. The method proposed in [20] trained on different subjects with identical motions in synthetic data, which is impossible to obtain in real-world scenarios. GDVAE [21], which computed the Laplace-Beltrami Operator spectrum of each mesh in correspondence, achieved unsupervised shape and pose disentanglement from point clouds.

2.3 Unsupervised Learning for 3D Shapes

Unsupervised learning has been widely applied for 3D shapes due to the lack of annotated 3D data. CorrNet3D [22] proposed the first unsupervised framework to learn dense correspondence for 3D point clouds. To alleviate the correspondence and interpolation problems, The method of [23] introduced effective geometric priors to the model, which allows training the model without any manual annotations. Zhou *et al.* [24] incorporated self-consistency and cross-consistency learning schemes to obtain disentangled shape and pose representations without supervision. The approach [24] used the pre-computed matrices in downsampling and upsampling, which limits the ability of feature aggregation. The method [25] proposed a GAN model to learn disentangled human mesh without annotations, but their approach [25] is very unstable to train and requires a significant amount of training time due to the characteristic of GAN [26]. In this paper, we incorporate attention mechanism [27], which helps feature aggregation, to encoder and decoder layers. Different from the cross-consistency learning scheme in method [24], our consistency learning scheme achieves effective shape and pose disentanglement.

3   Method

In this section, we present the overall network architecture of our proposed A-MeshNet, which utilizes a combination of Mesh Auto-encoder and AFA module to achieve unsupervised disentanglement of shape and pose. We will describe the details of the A-MeshNet, including the components of the Mesh Auto-encoder and AFA module.

3.1   Network Architecture

Our work is based on the classical mesh auto-encoder approach [24]. Given a 3D human mesh, the objective is to disentangle the shape and pose of the input mesh in an unsupervised manner and to reconstruct the input human mesh accurately. We propose an overall network architecture as illustrated in Fig. 1.

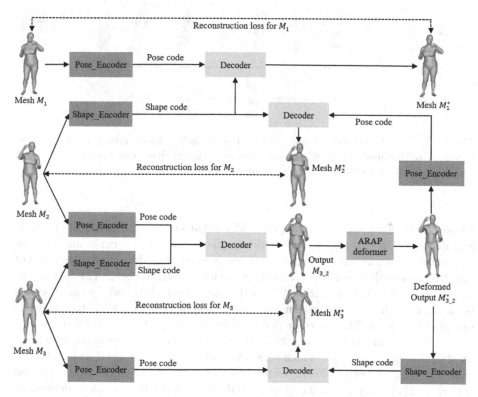

Fig. 1. An overview of our A-MeshNet. The model takes three meshes as input to extract shape codes and pose codes. These codes are then input into the decoder to recover the corresponding meshes, and three reconstruction errors are calculated accordingly.

Overview. Our A-MeshNet takes three meshes as input, namely M_1, M_2, and M_3. M_1 and M_2 correspond to different poses of the same subject, sharing the same shapes but with different poses; while M_3 has a different shape and pose from M_1 and M_2. First, we encode M_1 and M_2 using the Pose_Encoder and Shape_Encoder to obtain the corresponding latent vectors. The decoder is then utilized to reconstruct M_1^*, and the reconstruction error between M_1 and M_1^* is calculated to achieve shape and pose decoupling. Similarly, M_{3_2} is reconstructed using M_2 and M_3. During training, we add an ARAP deformer [28] to fine-tune the generated output to obtain $M_{3\_2}^*$. Then, the decoder is used to reconstruct M_2^* using the shape code of M_2 and the pose code of $M_{3\_2}^*$, and another decoder is used to reconstruct M_3^*. The reconstruction loss is adopted to confirm that the three reconstruction targets are satisfied: M_1 is approximately equal to M_1^*, M_2 is approximately equal to M_2^*, and M_3 is approximately equal to M_3^*.

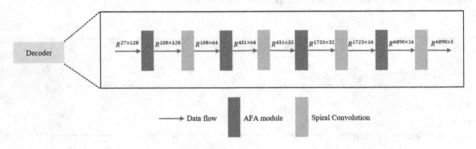

Fig. 2. The mesh decoder of our proposed A-MeshNet takes latent representation encoded by the mesh encoder as input. The decoder utilizes four Spiral convolution and AFA modules to reconstruct the input mesh.

Mesh Auto-Encoder. The proposed Mesh Auto-encoder consists of encoders and decoders. In this paper, We introduce the decoder as an example since the encoder has a symmetry architecture of the decoder. The decoder is composed of four Spiral convolution and AFA modules, as illustrated in Fig. 2. The core mechanism of the Spiral convolution [29] is the spiral convolutional operator, which is an operator for representation learning and generation on fixed-topology 3D morphable shapes. The operator defines the order of vertices using a spiral trajectory, which can be either clockwise or counterclockwise. The order is defined by the concept of "d-ring", which represents all vertices that are d distance away from the current vertex. For a vertex x on a mesh, its adjacent nodes can be sorted as $S(x) = x_1, x_2, ..., x_L$. The formula for spiral convolution is defined as $(f * g)_x = \sum_{l=1}^{L} g_l f(S_l(x))$, where f is similar to the pixel intensity of the image field, and g_l denotes the weights. For each spiral path, we define it as starting from x, traversing its adjacent nodes in a spiral shape until the neighborhood of radius h is reached. Compared to previous graph convolutional operators, the spiral convolutional operator offers stronger representation ability with less computational complexity.

3.2   The AFA Module

In Sect. 3.1, we discussed the decoder architecture of our proposed A-MeshNet, which is composed of spiral convolution and AFA module. We proposed AFA module, which aims to improve the feature aggregation of the model, including upsampling and downsampling. Feature aggregation was achieved by multiplying input feature with mapping matrix in existing models [14,24].

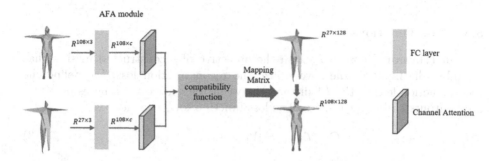

Fig. 3. The AFA module calculates mapping matrix between the key and query vectors.

Taking the downsampling operation in the encoder as an example. We can define the feature aggregation [14,24] as:

$$x_i^{(l)} = \sum_{j=1}^{n_{l-1}} m_{ij}^{(l-1\to l)} x_j^{(l-1)}, \tag{1}$$

where $x_i^{(l)}$ are vertex i features at level l and l is the numbers of encoder levels, $x_j^{(l-1)}$ are vertex j features at level $l-1$, $m_{ij}^{(l-1\to l)} \in \boldsymbol{M}^{(l-1\to l)}$ denote different aggregation weights used for upsampling or downsampling. In existing methods, the mapping matrix $\boldsymbol{M}^{(l-1\to l)}$ are obtained with mesh simplification and are fixed during training. Inspired by the work of [30], we introduce attention mechanisms to learn these mapping matrices used for down-sampling and up-sampling operations.

As shown in Fig. 3, the AFA module is obtained by applying a function to the query and corresponding key vectors to obtain the mapping matrix for aggregation weights. In contrast to [30], where the vertices are directly modeled as input query and key vectors, we first model the query and key vectors with a fully-connected layer and then calculate the relationships between vertices through a channel attention module. We define $\boldsymbol{q}_i^{(l)} \in \mathbb{R}^c$ and $\boldsymbol{k}_j^{(l-1)} \in \mathbb{R}^c$ as query vectors and key vectors. Then we adopt the cosine distance function to calculate the compatibility score between query vectors and key vectors as

$$s_{w,ij}^{(l-1\to l)} = cos(\boldsymbol{q}_i^{(l)}, \boldsymbol{k}_j^{(l-1)}), \tag{2}$$

which represents the matching degree between every two vertices in the two layers. However, we can not directly regard this score as the mapping matrix because any vertex is influenced by all vertices in the previous layer in this case. We adopt a mask operation by selecting a corresponding subset of the vertices in the previous layer for each vertex with top-k selection, then we calculate the weight score using the vertices in the corresponding subset. Finally, we acquire $M^{(l-1 \to l)}$ for feature aggregation in the encoder and decoder after normalizing the weight score.

3.3   Loss Functions

Reconstruction Loss. To attain the objective of reconstructed meshes that resemble the input meshes, we utilize the reconstruction loss. We define the reconstruction loss as the $L1$ distance between the vertex coordinates of generated outputs and input meshes. The loss function for M_1 as follows,

$$\mathcal{L}_{rec1} = \|V_1^* - V_1\|_1, \tag{3}$$

where V_1^* and $V_1 \in \mathbb{R}^{N_1 \times 3}$ are the vertex coordinates of M_1^* and M_1 respectively. N_1 is the vertex number. Similarly,

$$\mathcal{L}_{rec2} = \|V_2^* - V_2\|_1, \tag{4}$$

$$\mathcal{L}_{rec3} = \|V_3^* - V_3\|_1, \tag{5}$$

where V_2^* and $V_2 \in \mathbb{R}^{N_2 \times 3}$ are the vertex coordinates of M_2^* and M_2. V_3^* and $V_3 \in \mathbb{R}^{N_3 \times 3}$ are the vertex coordinates of M_3^* and M_3 respectively. N_2 and N_3 are the vertex number.

Normal Loss. To improve the reconstructed mesh surface smoother, we introduce the surface normal loss [31], which ensures that the normal vectors of output mesh are constant with ground truth. We formulate the loss function as follows:

$$\mathcal{L}_{normal} = \sum_f \sum_{\{p,q\} \subset f} |\langle \frac{\mathbf{v}_p - \mathbf{v}_q}{\|\mathbf{v}_p - \mathbf{v}_q\|_2}, n_f^* \rangle|, \tag{6}$$

where f and n_f^* denote triangle face and groundtruth of a normal vector of f, respectively. $\mathbf{v}_p$ and $\mathbf{v}_q$ is the pth and qth vertex.

Edge Loss. Since body parts like hands that have dense vertices, are prone to local optima and generate flying vertices during training. To solve this issue, we introduce edge length consistency loss [31], which helps smoothly recover edges of the human mesh. We formulate the loss function as follows:

$$\mathcal{L}_{edge} = \sum_f \sum_{\{p,q\} \subset f} |\|\mathbf{v}_p - \mathbf{v}_q\|_2 - \|\mathbf{v}_p^* - \mathbf{v}_q^*\|_2|, \tag{7}$$

where f and the asterisk denote triangle face and the groundtruth, respectively. $\mathbf{v}_p$ and $\mathbf{v}_q$ is the pth and qth vertex.

The overall objective for unsupervised 3D pose and shape disentanglement is,

$$\mathcal{L} = \lambda_{rec}(\mathcal{L}_{rec1} + \mathcal{L}_{rec2} + \mathcal{L}_{rec3}) + \lambda_n\mathcal{L}_{normal} + \lambda_e\mathcal{L}_{edge}, \tag{8}$$

where $\lambda_{rec} = 1$, $\lambda_n = 0.1$ and $\lambda_e = 20$.

4   Experiments

In this section, we present two datasets: AMASS dataset and COMA dataset. We then evaluate the performance of our proposed A-MeshNet by conducting pose transfer experiment on AMASS dataset [32] and expression extrapolation experiment on COMA dataset [14]. Moreover, we investigate the effectiveness of our AFA module through the ablation study. Finally, we provide qualitative results demonstrating the pose transfer of meshes from pose to identity.

4.1   Datasets

AMASS. The largest motion capture dataset for the human body, which uses SMPL model to uniformly parameterize multiple datasets and integrate them into a large dataset. The dataset covers more than 300 subjects and includes 10k motions. We follow the same splits as in [24].

COMA. The facial expression dataset proposed by Ranjan [14], consisting of 20K+ 3D face meshes from 12 different subjects. Every subject has twelve different kinds of expressions. We take the similar expression extrapolation setting as [14].

4.2   Quantitative Evaluation

3D Pose Transfer. To show the quantitative performance of our A-MeshNet, We show the results compared with relevant methods for 3D pose transfer reconstructions on AMASS dataset. Specifically, We calculate the L2 distances between vertices of the pose-transferred meshes and the pseudo-groundtruth meshes, which are generated by the SMPL [4] model since the AMASS dataset includes SMPL parameters. The two relevant methods are GDVAE [21], which achieves unsupervised shape and pose disentanglement from point clouds, and Zhou *et al.* [24] proposed method, which is a state-of-the-art approach that decouples human meshes without supervision. Table 1 shows that our A-MeshNet improves Mean Error by approximately 1.1 mm compared to Zhou *et al.* [24]. We can also observe that both our method and Zhou *et al.* [24] without ARAP deformer lead to degeneration, which proves the effectiveness of ARAP deformer [28]. Furthermore, we conduct an ablation study by removing the proposed AFA module and showing that the performance can be decreased by doing so. Overall, our results demonstrate the effectiveness of A-MeshNet for 3D pose transfer reconstruction.

Table 1. 3D pose transfer experimental results with relevant models on AMASS dataset. The numbers are calculated in millimeters.

Method	Mean Error
GDVAE	54.44
Zhou et al.'s	20.24
Zhou et al.'s without ARAP	22.59
Ours without ARAP	22.43
Ours without AFA	19.90
Ours	**19.16**

COMA Expression Extrapolation. The COMA dataset consists of 12 different kinds of expressions captured across 12 subjects. To evaluate the performance of our A-MeshNet, we adopt the same experimental setting as [14]. We present the results in Table 2 and compare our approach with FLAME [7], Zhou et al. [24] and Jiang et al. [18] methods. Our method uses 4-dimensional for shape and pose, while FLAME [7] employs 8-dimensional codes for shape and expression. We can observe that our A-MeshNet achieves the best performance compared with other approaches.

Table 2. Mean reconstruction error of extrapolation experiment. The numbers are calculated in millimeters.

Method	Mean Error
Flame	2.00
Jiang et al.'s	1.64
Zhou et al.'s	1.28
Ours	**1.12**

4.3   Qualitative Evaluation

3D Pose Transfer. In order to evaluate the effectiveness of our A-MeshNet for 3D pose transfer, we conducted an experiment where a set of pose meshes was transferred to a given shape mesh. In the event that our method achieved disentangled shape and pose, the generated mesh should maintain the shape of identity mesh while displaying the motion from the pose meshes. The generated outputs are shown in Fig. 4, we can observe that pose meshes effectively transfer pose to the identity mesh, and the generated outputs retained original shape.

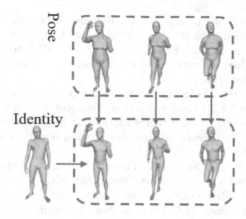

Fig. 4. Pose transfer from Pose meshes to Identity meshes.

5 Conclusion

This paper presents A-MeshNet, an innovative mesh encoder-decoder based model that enables unsupervised human mesh disentanglement. We incorporate AFA module into the encoder and decoder to aggregate vertex features. The experimental results show that A-MeshNet surpasses existing state-of-the-art approaches and exhibits better generalization capability. Our work has significant potential for advancing unsupervised shape and pose disentanglement, but there is still room for improvement. Our model currently requires meshes to be registered to a fix-topology data, and we plan to explore extending our method to handle un-registered data such as point clouds, in future work.

References

1. Pavlakos, G., et al.: Expressive body capture: 3D hands, face, and body from a single image. In: Proceedings of the IEEE/CVF Conference on Computer Vision and Pattern Recognition, pp. 10975–10985 (2019)
2. Osman, A.A.A., Bolkart, T., Black, M.J.: STAR: sparse trained articulated human body regressor. In: Vedaldi, A., Bischof, H., Brox, T., Frahm, J.-M. (eds.) ECCV 2020. LNCS, vol. 12351, pp. 598–613. Springer, Cham (2020). https://doi.org/10.1007/978-3-030-58539-6_36
3. Abdi, H., Williams, L.J.: Principal component analysis. Wiley Interdiscip. Rev.: Comput. Stat. **2**(4), 433–459 (2010)
4. Loper, M., Mahmood, N., Romero, J., Pons-Moll, G., Black, M.J.: Smpl: A skinned multi-person linear model. ACM Trans. Graph. (TOG), **34**(6), 1–16 (2015)
5. Joo, H., Simon, T., Sheikh, Y.: Total capture: A 3D deformation model for tracking faces, hands, and bodies. In: Proceedings of the IEEE Conference on Computer Vision and Pattern Recognition, pp. 8320–8329 (2018)
6. Romero, J., Tzionas, D., Black, M.J.: Embodied hands: Modeling and capturing hands and bodies together. arXiv preprint arXiv:2201.02610 (2022)

7. Li, T., Bolkart, T., Black, M.J., Li, H., Romero, J.: Learning a model of facial shape and expression from 4D scans. ACM Trans. Graph., **36**(6), 194–1 (2017)
8. Song, C., Wei, J., Li, R., Liu, F., Lin, G.: Unsupervised 3d pose transfer with cross consistency and dual reconstruction. IEEE Transactions on Pattern Analysis and Machine Intelligence (2023)
9. Zheng, X., Jiang, B., Zhang, J.: Deformation representation based convolutional mesh autoencoder for 3D hand generation. Neurocomputing **444**, 356–365 (2021)
10. Wu, Z.:. 3D shapenets: A deep representation for volumetric shapes. In: Proceedings of the IEEE Conference on Computer Vision and Pattern Recognition, pp. 1912–1920 (2015)
11. Bagautdinov, T., Wu, C., Saragih, J., Fua, P., Sheikh, Y.: Modeling facial geometry using compositional vaes. In: Proceedings of the IEEE Conference on Computer Vision and Pattern Recognition, pp. 3877–3886 (2018)
12. Kingma, D.P., Welling, M.: Auto-encoding variational bayes. arXiv preprint arXiv:1312.6114 (2013)
13. Tan, Q., Gao, L., Lai, Y.K., Xia, S.: Variational autoencoders for deforming 3D mesh models. In: Proceedings of the IEEE Conference on Computer Vision and Pattern Recognition, pp. 5841–5850 (2018)
14. Ranjan, A., Bolkart, T., Sanyal, S., Black, M.J.: Generating 3D faces using convolutional mesh autoencoders. In: Proceedings of the European Conference on Computer Vision (ECCV), pp. 704–720 (2018)
15. Bruna, J., Zaremba, W., Szlam, A., LeCun, Y.: Spectral networks and locally connected networks on graphs. arXiv preprint arXiv:1312.6203)(2013)
16. Shuman, D.I., Narang, S.K., Frossard, P., Ortega, A., Vandergheynst, P.: The emerging field of signal processing on graphs: Extending high-dimensional data analysis to networks and other irregular domains. IEEE Signal Process. Mag. **30**(3), 83–98 (2013)
17. Tretschk, E., Tewari, A., Zollhöfer, M., Golyanik, V., Theobalt, C.: DEMEA: deep mesh autoencoders for non-rigidly deforming objects. In: Vedaldi, A., Bischof, H., Brox, T., Frahm, J.-M. (eds.) ECCV 2020. LNCS, vol. 12349, pp. 601–617. Springer, Cham (2020). https://doi.org/10.1007/978-3-030-58548-8_35
18. Jiang, Z.H., Wu, Q., Chen, K., Zhang, J.: Disentangled representation learning for 3d face shape. In: Proceedings of the IEEE/CVF Conference on Computer Vision and Pattern Recognition, pp. 11957–11966 (2019)
19. Jiang, B., Zhang, J., Cai, J., Zheng, J.: Disentangled human body embedding based on deep hierarchical neural network. IEEE Trans. Visual Comput. Graph. **26**(8), 2560–2575 (2020)
20. Levinson, J., Sud, A., Makadia, A.: Latent feature disentanglement for 3D meshes. arXiv preprint arXiv:1906.03281 (2019)
21. Aumentado-Armstrong, T., Tsogkas, S., Jepson, A., Dickinson, S.: Geometric disentanglement for generative latent shape models. In: Proceedings of the IEEE/CVF International Conference on Computer Vision, pp. 8181–8190 (2019)
22. Zeng, Y., Qian, Y., Zhu, Z., Hou, J., Yuan, H., He, Y.: Corrnet3D: Unsupervised end-to-end learning of dense correspondence for 3d point clouds. In Proceedings of the IEEE/CVF Conference on Computer Vision and Pattern Recognition, pp. 6052–6061 (2021)
23. Eisenberger, M., et al.: Neuromorph: Unsupervised shape interpolation and correspondence in one go. In: Proceedings of the IEEE/CVF Conference on Computer Vision and Pattern Recognition, pp. 7473–7483 (2021)

24. Zhou, K., Bhatnagar, B.L., Pons-Moll, G.: Unsupervised shape and pose disentanglement for 3D meshes. In: Vedaldi, A., Bischof, H., Brox, T., Frahm, J.-M. (eds.) Computer Vision – ECCV 2020: 16th European Conference, Glasgow, UK, August 23–28, 2020, Proceedings, Part XXII, pp. 341–357. Springer, Cham (2020). https://doi.org/10.1007/978-3-030-58542-6_21

25. Chen, H., Tang, H., Shi, H., Peng, W., Sebe, N., Zhao, G.: Intrinsic-extrinsic preserved gans for unsupervised 3D pose transfer. In Proceedings of the IEEE/CVF International Conference on Computer Vision, pp. 8630–8639 (2021)

26. Creswell, A., White, T., Dumoulin, V., Arulkumaran, K., Sengupta, B., Bharath, A.A., et al.: Generative adversarial networks: An overview. IEEE Signal Process. Mag. 35(1), 53–65 (2018)

27. Vaswani, A., et al.: Attention is all you need. In: Advances in Neural Information Processing Systems, 30 (2017)

28. Sorkine, O., Alexa, M.: As-rigid-as-possible surface modeling. Symp. Geometry Process. 4, 109–116 (2007)

29. Bouritsas, G., Bokhnyak, S., Ploumpis, S., Bronstein, M., Zafeiriou, S.: Neural 3D morphable models: Spiral convolutional networks for 3d shape representation learning and generation. In: Proceedings of the IEEE/CVF International Conference on Computer Vision, pp. 7213–7222 (2019)

30. Chen, Z., Kim, T.K.: Learning feature aggregation for deep 3D morphable models. In: Proceedings of the IEEE/CVF Conference on Computer Vision and Pattern Recognition, pp. 13164–13173 (2021)

31. Wang, N., Zhang, Y., Li, Z., Fu, Y., Liu, W., Jiang, Y.G.: Pixel2mesh: Generating 3D mesh models from single RGB images. In: Proceedings of the European Conference on Computer Vision (ECCV), pp. 52–67 (2018)

32. Mahmood, N., Ghorbani, N., Troje, N.F., Pons-Moll, G., Black, M.J.: Amass: Archive of motion capture as surface shapes. In: Proceedings of the IEEE/CVF International Conference on Computer Vision, pp. 5442–5451 (2019)

Wavelet Knowledge Distillation via Decoupled Target for Scene Text Detection

Kefan Qu[1], Jianmin Lin[2]([✉]), Jinrong Li[2], Ming Yang[2],
and Wangpeng He[1]([✉])

[1] Xidian University, Xi'an, China
qukefan@stu.xidian.edu.cn, hewp@xidian.edu.cn
[2] CVTE Research, Guangzhou, China
{linjianmin,lijinrong,yangming}@cvte.com

Abstract. In this paper, we investigate the knowledge distillation strategy for training a compact student model for scene text detection, using a cumbersome teacher model that is too computational to apply on resource-constrained devices. We observed that the frequency domain information of the response map is different between the teacher and student models obviously, which can effectively guide the student model to learn more effective knowledge. Furtherly, we propose a wavelet knowledge distillation method via decoupled target for training accurate compact scene text detection networks. Specifically, we first use discrete wavelet transformation to decompose the probability map into different frequency bands which contain different characteristic components, transferring knowledge in the high-frequency band and low-frequency band respectively. In addition, we decouple the target to enhance the distillation effect of the corresponding region, by separating text and background regions through the ground truth mask. Extensive experiments demonstrate that our method consistently improves the F-measure of the student model and outperforms the other mainstream distillation methods.

Keywords: scene text detection · knowledge distillation · wavelet decomposition

1 Introduction

Scene text detection in the wild is a fundamental problem with numerous applications such as automatic driving, map navigation, and image search. In many scenarios, OCR systems need to run on embedded devices such as microprocessors, where the memory and processing power are restricted. However, the most advanced text detection networks [14,16,23] are not only computationally intensive but also have a large number of parameters, which limits their use on resource-constrained devices.

ⓒ The Author(s), under exclusive license to Springer Nature Switzerland AG 2023
H. Lu et al. (Eds.): ICIG 2023, LNCS 14357, pp. 150–161, 2023.
https://doi.org/10.1007/978-3-031-46311-2_13

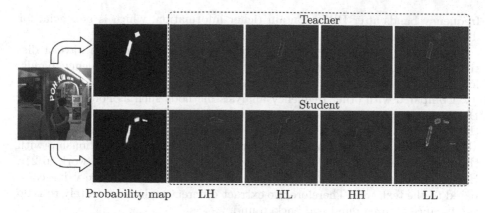

Fig. 1. Visualization of probability maps and frequency bands. Frequency bands from left to right include LH, HL, HH, and LL.

To address this problem, we use knowledge distillation [9] to transfer knowledge from a cumbersome teacher network to a compact student network. Compared with other model compression methods, knowledge distillation can simply and effectively improve the performance of small models. However, most knowledge distillation methods are developed for image classification, and some studies have shown that this may lead to insignificant improvements in different tasks [12, 15, 19].

Recently, Chen et al. [2] introduce the entropy map to transfer knowledge from the teacher network to the student network and achieve a state-of-the-art result. The entropy map reflects the model's uncertainty in predicting the text edge area, but it cannot distinguish the differences in text edges in different directions. In addition, calculating the entropy map may lose the main information of the text area.

Therefore, we propose to use Discrete Wavelet Transform (DWT) to decompose the predicted segmentation map into four frequency bands (LL, LH, HL, HH). The low-frequency band (LL) represents the low-frequency information of the probability map, while the three high-frequency bands (LH, HL, HH) represent vertical, horizontal, and diagonal edge features, respectively.

As shown in Fig. 1, the teacher model's probability map is more stable and confident, but the probability map of the student model is less confident. Analyzing the probability maps from the perspective of frequency, it can be observed that for the teacher model, the response of the frequency is more concentrated. However, the frequency bands of the student are more blurred. Especially for vertically arranged text, the differences in high-frequency features are more pronounced in the horizontal direction, and for horizontally arranged text, the differences are more significant in the vertical direction. In addition, the low-frequency band locates the text area and contains information about the angle, shape, and other characteristics of the text. Compared to the entropy map, the different frequency bands after DWT contain richer information, which is beneficial for distilling the knowledge from teachers to students.

Based on the above observation, we propose a method based on wavelet distillation, which mainly extracts the information of different frequency bands, forcing students to learn this knowledge and eventually improving generalizability. Compared with other frequency analysis methods such as Fourier analysis, DWT captures not only the spatial information in the probability map but also the frequency information. Furthermore, for the text detection task, the background also contains a lot of information and forms a complementary relationship with the target area, which has also been mentioned in some previous work [6,21]. However, the background has more pixel space and less responsive value compared to the text area. Therefore, we extract different regions separately to keep the balance of foreground and background

Specifically, our distillation algorithm consists of two parts during the training phase. First, we employ a simple and effective haar wavelet to decompose the response probability map into different frequency bands. Second, we generate two binary masks to separate text and background regions according to the ground truth, aligning each frequency band in all regions separately to force the student to learn this knowledge.

Our main contributions can be summarized as follows.

1. We study the knowledge distillation strategy for training accurate compact scene text detection networks.

2. We present a new response-based knowledge distillation scheme, which transfers knowledge in the frequency domain and separates text and background regions during distillation.

3. We have demonstrated that our method achieved state-of-the-art performance on each of the three benchmark datasets, with improvements of 4.03%, 2.11%, and 2.317% over the corresponding baselines for ICDAR2015 [10], MSRA-TD500 [22], and TotalText [3], respectively.

2 Related Work

2.1 Text Detection

Scene text detection methods are mainly divided into two categories according to different implementation principles: methods based on bounding-box regression and methods based on segmentation.

The methods based on bounding-box regression mainly improve based on the object detection framework. TextBoxes [13] and SegLink [18] are modified based on SSD. TextBoxes adjusts the scale of the convolution kernel and anchor points. SegLink predicts the bounding box and its links separately and obtains the complete text line through the merging algorithm. SSTD [8] introduces a text attention module to improve the robustness of text features. Regression-based methods use simpler post-processing algorithms, but the detection of irregularly shaped text is still a relatively difficult task.

Segmentation-based methods usually perform predictions at the pixel level while incorporating post-processing algorithms to detect text in different shapes. PixelLink [4] detected text regions by predicting two kinds of pixel-wise predictions, text/non-text prediction, and link prediction. PSENet [20] proposes a progressive scale expansion algorithm, which expands the small-scale kernel to the final text line size, effectively realizing the distinction between adjacent text lines. DBNet [14] proposes a differentiable binarization algorithm, which not only effectively simplifies the post-processing step, but also helps to distinguish text regions from the background.

2.2 Knowledge Distillation

Knowledge distillation is an effective method to achieve model compression. The concept was first proposed by Buciluǎ et al. [1] then generalized by Hinton et al. [9]. According to the different forms of knowledge, it can be categorized into response-based knowledge, feature-based knowledge, and relation-based knowledge. Hinton introduces a hyperparameter in softmax to soften the distribution of teacher logits. FitNet [17] proves that the intermediate features of the pre-trained teacher network can also effectively guide the students. AT [11] achieves knowledge transfer by using a simple strategy to extract attention from intermediate features. Yim et al. [24] proposed a flow of solution process (FSP), which summarizes the relations between pairs of feature maps, to transfer knowledge between two layers. WKD [25] first combines wavelet decomposition and knowledge distillation to enhance the image quality generated by the GAN network by extracting high-frequency information.

However, the effect of knowledge distillation on text detection has not been well-studied. Yuning [5] uses the CML framework to combine the mutual learning method with the teacher-student distillation framework to further improve the distillation effect. KDEM [2] introduces the concept of entropy into knowledge distillation, using the entropy of the probability map to promote the student network to learn information extracted by the teacher network. The knowledge distillation scheme proposed in this paper is innovative research aimed at the text detection task. It is different from previous methods in that it uses frequency domain features as the supervision information to more effectively guide the student model to learn from the teacher model. Moreover, it introduces the decoupled target method to better balance the differences between text and background regions, thus improving the effectiveness of knowledge distillation.

3   Methodology

In this section, we decompose the proposed method in detail. As shown in Fig. 1, the difference in detection ability between the teacher network and the student network is reflected in different frequency bands. By separately learning the frequency features of the teacher network, it helps to improve the performance of the student network. Therefore, we propose a distillation method based on wavelet decomposition. In addition, we decompose the text area and the background area through the mask generated by the ground truth and perform distillation separately. This can not only ensure the efficiency of knowledge transfer in probability maps but also help students learn complementary knowledge.

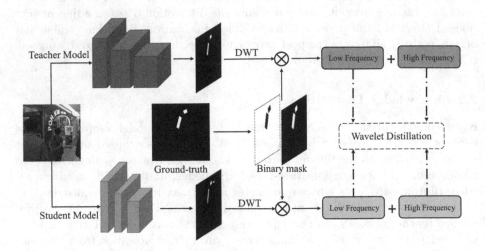

Fig. 2. The framework of Wavelet Distillation via Decoupled Target.

Figure 2 shows the framework of our proposed distillation method. The upper model is the pre-trained teacher network, and the lower model is the student network. During the training stage, our distillation method is divided into two parts: First, Perform discrete wavelet transform (DWT) on the probability map of the student and teacher respectively; Next, multiply the frequency bands by the binary mask to separate the features of the text area and the background area, and further strengthen the distillation effect of the background area, then calculate the distillation loss for each frequency band. During the inference stage, there is no need for an additional teacher model to provide supervision or calculate distillation loss. The independent student model can be directly used in practical scenarios for text detection.

3.1   Baseline Model

We use DBNet [14] as the baseline model, which is a text detection network based on the segmentation method. It consists of three parts: (a) the backbone, which is responsible for extracting image features and contains a large number of parameters; (b) FPN, which mainly realizes the connection between the backbone and the detection head and enhances the robustness of detecting targets of different sizes by fusing the feature maps of different levels of the backbone; (c) the detection head, which performs a differentiable binarization operation on the probability map and the threshold map to obtain an approximate binary map.

Referring DBNet, the overall loss L_{DB} of our detection model comprises three components: the probability map loss L_s, the binary map loss L_b, and the threshold map loss L_t. The total loss function can be expressed as:

$$L_{DB} = L_s + \alpha \times L_b + \beta \times L_t \tag{1}$$

where L_s is the binary cross-entropy loss, L_b and L_t are the Dice loss and L1 loss, respectively. α and β are set to 1.0 and 10 respectively.

3.2   Wavelet Knowledge Distillation

Based on previous observations, the disparity in response maps across frequency bands is caused by differences in the capabilities of the teacher network and the student network. The knowledge extracted through DWT can more effectively help the student network learn the generalizability of the teacher network. Specifically, we use a simple and effective wavelet transform, the Haar wavelet, which decomposes an image into components with different sizes, positions, and directions. For any image x, we denote the DWT of an image as $\Psi(x)$.

With DWT, we decompose the probability map into different frequency bands $\Psi(P) = \{LL_1, LH_1, HL_1, HH_1\}$, to extract richer high-frequency information, we use 4-level wavelet decomposition in all experiments. For all frequency bands, we mainly divided them into high-frequency $\Psi^H(P)$ and low-frequency $\Psi^L(P)$. $\Psi^L(P)$ indicates LL_4 band and $\Psi^H(P) = \{HL_n, LH_n, HH_n | n = 1, 2, 3, 4\}$.

Based on the above notations, we further introduce knowledge distillation based on wavelet decomposition. First, given a three-channel picture, the probability maps P^T and P^S are obtained through the teacher network and the student network. Next, with the above DWT, for different frequency bands, we calculate their L_1 losses separately to balance the weight between the high frequency and low frequency. Its loss function l_H, l_L can be formulated as:

$$l_H = \left\| \Psi^H\left(P^T\right) - \Psi^H\left(P^S\right) \right\|_1 \tag{2}$$

$$l_L = \left\| \Psi^L\left(P^T\right) - \Psi^L\left(P^S\right) \right\|_1 \tag{3}$$

3.3   Knowledge Distillation via Decoupled Target

Previously, target and background regions are usually treated equally. For the probability map of the teacher network and the student network, the (Kullback-Leibler) KL divergences are computed pixel by pixel. KDEM filters out useless information through the mask to ensure that only key information in the text area is extracted. However, the prediction of the background region can also complement the target region, further helping the student network to predict the text region, which is also mentioned in recent work [6,21]. Compared with the target area, the response probability of the background is smaller, forming a complementary relationship with the text area. We hope that the probability of the network responding to the background area is as low as possible, however, due to the limited learning ability of the student model and interference in complex scenes, it frequently makes incorrect judgments.

As a result, we propose a decoupled target distillation to separate text and background regions through the binary mask. We dilate the real text region B to ensure complete coverage of the text region and finally generate a binary mask M. According to the size of the frequency bands after DWT, M is down-sampled to the corresponding size $h \times w$:

$$M_{i,j} = 1[(i,j) \in B] \tag{4}$$

where $M \in \{0,1\}^{h \times w}$, the value of location (i,j) is 0 if it belongs to the background area, and 1 otherwise. Then, the above mask is used to separate the target and the background, respectively, as shown in Fig. 2, in different regions to minimize the loss of wavelet distillation.

The final wavelet distillation is formulated as:

$$L_H = \frac{1}{h \times w} \sum_{i=1}^{h} \sum_{j=1}^{w} (\gamma_{obj} \times M_{ij} \times l_H + \gamma_{bg} \times \omega \times (1 - M_{ij}) \times l_H) \tag{5}$$

$$L_L = \frac{1}{h \times w} \sum_{i=1}^{h} \sum_{j=1}^{w} (\gamma_{obj} \times M_{ij} \times l_L + \gamma_{bg} \times \omega \times (1 - M_{ij}) \times l_L) \tag{6}$$

$$L_{wkd} = \lambda_H \times L_H + \lambda_L \times L_L \tag{7}$$

where γ_{obj} and γ_{bg} are used to balance the weight of the distillation loss between the target region and the background region, while λ_H, λ_L are used to balance the weight of different frequency bands. These hyperparameters are set to $\{\lambda_H = 30, \lambda_L = 5, \gamma_{obj} = 2, \gamma_{bg} = 5\}$. ω is the proportional weight to control the influence of the background area which increases linearly from 0 to 1 with training iterations.

To sum up, we train the student network with the total loss as follows:

$$L = L_{DB} + L_{wkd} \tag{8}$$

4   Experiments

4.1   Datasets

SynthText [7]: SynthText is a synthetic dataset, containing more than 800k images. It is mainly used for text detection in natural scenes. In our experiments, this dataset is used for model pre-training.

MSRA-TD500 [22]: This dataset takes pictures from offices, shopping malls, and outdoor street scenes, and is mainly for multi-directional text detection tasks, with a resolution between 1296×864 and 1920×1280. The dataset contains

300 training images and 200 testing images, mixed with English text and Chinese text. Following the previous method [14], we include the additional 400 training pictures introduced by HUST-TR400.

ICDAR 2015 [10]: This dataset was proposed for the 2015 competition and consists of street-view images taken by wearable devices, including 1,000 training images and 500 testing images, all of which have an image size of 720 × 1280. Moreover, the data set is all English text, and the text area is given by four vertices. Image capture does not consider image quality, so factors such as blurring and occlusion increase the difficulty of this dataset.

Total-Text [3]: Total-Text is a dataset mainly for curved text, the images are mainly taken from street billboards and annotated as polygons with a variable number of vertices. The dataset contains 1255 training images and 300 test images, most of which are English text and a small amount of Chinese text.

4.2 Implementation Details

Model Structure. In this paper, the teacher network uses the original model of the DB algorithm, the backbone network uses ResNet50 with large parameters, and the FPN has 256 channels. Compared with the teacher model, the backbone network of the student model uses the lightweight network MobileNetV3-large. Besides the difference in the backbone network, we reduce the number of channels of the FPN from 256 to 96, further reducing the network parameters of the student.

Training Detail. We adopt the strategies of the DB algorithm. First, all networks are pre-trained on SynthText for 100k iterations and then fine-tuned on three datasets for 1200 epochs. Special attention is paid to masking blurred text. We choose the SGD optimizer with weight decay set to 0.0001. The initial learning rate is 0.007 and a polynomial learning rate adjustment strategy is adopted. Furthermore, all our experiments are run on the PyTorch deep learning framework and a single NVIDIA 1080TI GPU card.

During the training stage, three data augmentation strategies are used: random flipping and random cropping, random rotation between (-10, 10). Meanwhile, all training images are resized to 640 × 640. In the inference stage, we keep the aspect ratio of the test images and resize the input images by setting a suitable height for each dataset.

4.3 Ablation Study

Table 1 shows the ablation study of our distillation method, all the experiments are conducted on ICDAR 2015 dataset. First, we investigated the effect of different frequency bands on the distillation method. It can be seen from the table that the low frequency and high frequency bring an improvement of 0.981% and 2.455% on the F-measure. Compared with the low-frequency band, the high-frequency bands bring more significant improvement. As previously observed,

Table 1. Ablation study on ICDAR 2015.

Frequency		Mask		P	R	F
Low	High	obj	bg			
-	-	-	-	81.818	68.464	74.547
✓	-	-	-	81.218	70.582	75.528
-	✓	-	-	83.427	71.497	77.002
✓	✓	-	-	84.240	72.315	77.823
✓	✓	✓	-	82.415	74.241	78.115
✓	✓	✓	✓	84.572	73.375	78.577

the probability map of the student model is more confusing in the text edge areas, and the high-frequency bands information in these areas helps the student model to learn knowledge more effectively. Next, we implemented experiments on masks based on the wavelet distillation method. With learning only the target region, the F-measure improves by 0.292%, which proves that the method of target decoupling is effective. Further, separating the target and background regions brought a 0.462% improvement, which indicates that the background areas are complementary to the target knowledge. In conclusion, our experiments proved that the method based on wavelet distillation via decoupled targets can effectively enhance the generalization of students.

4.4   Compared with Previous Methods

In this section, we conduct experiments to compare our proposed distillation method with those proposed by other works on three datasets: ICDAR 2015, MSRA-TD500, and Total-Text. In our experiments, we not only included the only relevant state-of-the-art approach KDEM [2] for comparison but also included three classic knowledge distillation approaches ST [9], FitNet [17] and AT [11] for comparison, to validate our algorithm more thoroughly. ST distills the response results of the teacher probability map by adjusting them by temperature coefficients to obtain softening targets as supervised information. FitNet introduces the intermediate representations learned by the teacher as hints to improve the final performance of the student. AT adopts a simple scheme to transfer the attention maps for intermediate feature maps. KDEM makes full use of the entropy map of the segmentation map to promote the student network to learn the text edge information distilled by the teacher network.

The experimental results are shown in Table 2. Our method consistently improves the F-measure of the student model on all datasets. Specifically, F-measure has increased from 74.547% to 78.577% on the ICDAR 2015 dataset and has improved by 2.11% and 2.317% respectively on the corresponding MSRA-TD500 and Total-Text datasets. Our proposed knowledge distillation method outperforms three popular distillation methods (ST, FitNet, and AT). Notably, ST and FitNet showed performance decreases on certain datasets, indicating that

Table 2. Comparison with other distillation methods.

Method	ICDAR2015			MSRA-TD500			Total-Text		
	P	R	F	P	R	F	P	R	F
Teacher	87.689	83.678	85.636	90.403	80.927	85.403	88.038	82.150	84.993
Student	81.818	68.464	74.547	84.000	72.164	77.634	85.946	71.577	78.106
ST [9]	82.669	67.982	74.610	82.965	71.134	76.595	85.598	70.854	77.527
FitNet [17]	81.113	69.475	74.844	84.989	71.993	77.953	85.943	70.176	77.263
AT [11]	81.370	71.497	76.114	84.585	73.539	78.676	85.867	72.480	78.608
KDEM [2]	81.369	73.808	77.404	86.088	73.367	79.220	83.758	74.107	78.638
Ours	**84.572**	**73.375**	**78.577**	**85.019**	**75.085**	**79.744**	**86.082**	**75.463**	**80.423**

traditional distillation methods may not be suitable for segmentation-based text detection methods. In contrast, our proposed distillation algorithm fully considers the characteristics of text detection tasks and performs better than the state-of-the-art distillation method (KDEM) in scene text detection.

As shown in Fig. 3 of the qualitative results, our method effectively improves the ability of the student model to detect small and large targets in complex backgrounds.

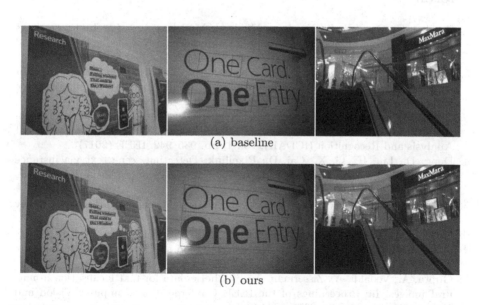

(a) baseline

(b) ours

Fig. 3. Some visualization results between baseline(original student model) and ours distillation

5 Conclusion

This paper proposes a distillation method via decoupled target and wavelet distillation for scene text detection. We analyze and reveal the important role of the high-frequency bands and the low-frequency band on the response map during the distillation process. Furthermore, we introduce the method of decoupling the text region and background region to enhance the distillation effect of the corresponding region. In practical applications, our model reduces the number of parameters from 25.9M to 3.1M compared to the larger teacher model, leading to a significant decrease in FLOPs from 38.12G to 5.29G. This effectively eases the limitations on resource-limited devices.

Besides, we conducted a series of experiments on three public datasets and compared the results, which demonstrated that our proposed algorithm significantly improves the F-measure of the student model compared to previous methods. However, knowledge distillation algorithms for text detection have not been fully researched. We hope that our work can inspire relevant researchers, and promote the development of the field of text detection. In our future work, we will explore combining self-distillation frameworks to design more efficient KD algorithms.

References

1. Buciluă, C., Caruana, R., Niculescu-Mizil, A.: Model compression. In: Proceedings of the 12th ACM SIGKDD International Conference on Knowledge Discovery and Data Mining, pp. 535–541 (2006)
2. Chen, J., Lai, Y., Zeng, Y., Yang, F.: Knowledge distillation via entropy map for scene text detection. In: 2021 16th International Conference on Computer Science and Education (ICCSE), pp. 506–511. IEEE, (2021)
3. Ch'ng, C.K., Chan, C.S.: Total-text: A comprehensive dataset for scene text detection and recognition. In: 2017 14th IAPR International Conference on Document Analysis and Recognition (ICDAR), vol. 1, pp. 935–942. IEEE (2017)
4. Deng, D., Liu, H., Li, X., Cai, D.: Pixellink: Detecting scene text via instance segmentation. In: Proceedings of the AAAI Conference on Artificial Intelligence, volume 32 (2018)
5. Du, Y., et al.: Pp-ocrv2: Bag of tricks for ultra lightweight OCR system. arXiv preprint arXiv:2109.03144 (2021)
6. Guo, J., et al.: Distilling object detectors via decoupled features. In: Proceedings of the IEEE/CVF Conference on Computer Vision and Pattern Recognition, pp. 2154–2164 (2021)
7. Gupta, A., Vedaldi, A., Zisserman, A.: Synthetic data for text localisation in natural images. In: Proceedings of the IEEE Conference on Computer Vision and Pattern Recognition, pp. 2315–2324 (2016)
8. He, P., Huang, W., He, T., Zhu, Q., Qiao, Y., Li, X.: Single shot text detector with regional attention. In: Proceedings of the IEEE International Conference on Computer Vision, pp. 3047–3055 (2017)
9. Hinton, G., Vinyals, O., Dean, J.: Distilling the knowledge in a neural network. arXiv preprint arXiv:1503.02531 (2015)

10. Karatzas, D., et al.: Icdar 2015 competition on robust reading. In: 2015 13th International Conference on Document Analysis and Recognition (ICDAR), pp. 1156–1160. IEEE (2015)
11. Komodakis, N., Zagoruyko, S.: Paying more attention to attention: improving the performance of convolutional neural networks via attention transfer. In: ICLR (2017)
12. Li, Q., Jin, S., Yan, J.: Mimicking very efficient network for object detection. In: Proceedings of the IEEE Conference on Computer Vision and Pattern Recognition, pp. 6356–6364 (2017)
13. Liao, M., Shi, B., Bai, X., Wang, X., Liu, W.: Textboxes: A fast text detector with a single deep neural network. In: Proceedings of the AAAI Conference on Artificial Intelligence, volume 31 (2017)
14. Liao, M., Wan, Z., Yao, C., Chen, K., Bai, X.: Real-time scene text detection with differentiable binarization. Proc. AAAI Conf. Artif. Intell. **34**, 11474–11481 (2020)
15. Liu, Y., Shu, C., Wang, J.: Structured knowledge distillation for dense prediction. IEEE Trans. Pattern Anal. Mach. Intell. (2020)
16. Qin, X., et al.: Mask is all you need: Rethinking mask R-CNN for dense and arbitrary-shaped scene text detection. In: Proceedings of the 29th ACM International Conference on Multimedia, pp. 414–423, 2021
17. Romero, A., Ballas, N., Kahou, S.E., Chassang, A., Gatta, C.,Bengio, Y.: Fitnets: Hints for thin deep nets. arXiv preprint arXiv:1412.6550 (2014)
18. Shi, B., Bai, X., Belongie, S.: Detecting oriented text in natural images by linking segments. In: Proceedings of the IEEE Conference on Computer Vision and Pattern Recognition, pp. 2550–2558 (2017)
19. Shu, C., Liu, Y., Gao, J., Yan, Z., Shen, C.: Channel-wise knowledge distillation for dense prediction. In: Proceedings of the IEEE/CVF International Conference on Computer Vision, pp. 5311–5320 (2021)
20. Wang, W., et al.: Shape robust text detection with progressive scale expansion network. In: Proceedings of the IEEE/CVF Conference on Computer Vision and Pattern Recognition, pp. 9336–9345 (2019)
21. Yang, Z., et al.: Focal and global knowledge distillation for detectors. In: Proceedings of the IEEE/CVF Conference on Computer Vision and Pattern Recognition, pp. 4643–4652 (2022)
22. Yao, C., Bai, X., Liu, W., Ma, Y., Tu, Z.: Detecting texts of arbitrary orientations in natural images. In: 2012 IEEE Conference on Computer Vision and Pattern Recognition, pp. 1083–1090. IEEE (2012)
23. Ye, J., Chen, Z., Liu, J., Bo, D.: Textfusenet: scene text detection with richer fused features. In IJCAI **20**, 516–522 (2020)
24. Yim, J., Joo, D., Bae, J., Kim, J.: A gift from knowledge distillation: Fast optimization, network minimization and transfer learning. In: Proceedings of the IEEE Conference on Computer Vision and Pattern Recognition, pp. 4133–4141 (2017)
25. Zhang, L., Chen, X., Tu, X., Wan, P., Xu, N., Ma, K.: Wavelet knowledge distillation: Towards efficient image-to-image translation. In: Proceedings of the IEEE/CVF Conference on Computer Vision and Pattern Recognition, pp. 12464–12474 (2022)

MGP-Net: Margin-Global Information Optimization-Prototype Network for Few-Shot Ancient Inscriptions Classification

Jiaxin Zhu, Xuelei He, Haonan Liu, and Xiaowei He[✉]

Xi'an Key Lab of Radiomics and Intelligent Perception,
School of Information Sciences and Technology, Northwest University,
Xi'an, Shaanxi, China
hexw@nwu.edu.cn

Abstract. This article focuses on the challenge of classifying bronze inscription rubbings, which have a limited number of samples and diverse characteristics. Traditional classification methods have failed to produce satisfactory results. With the emergence of meta-learning, few-shot image classification has become a popular research topic. This approach allows a classifier to recognize datasets outside the training set and complete classification with only a small number of samples. However, due to the existence of multiple categories in the ancient inscription dataset and the tendency for overfitting, existing prototype network structures have not achieved satisfactory prediction accuracy on ancient inscription datasets. To address this challenge, we propose two strategies. The first strategy is the Margin Prototype (MP), which expands the distribution of different class prototypes during the softmax operation. The second strategy is the global information optimization strategy (GioP), which reverses the prediction of support set samples to obtain more representative prototypes. Our proposed method achieves better accuracy without adding new parameters to the model. The end-to-end structural pattern remains unchanged.

Keywords: ancient inscriptions · few-shot-learning · prototype network · MGP-Net

1 Introduction

Ancient inscriptions play an important role in recording ancient history and culture. It provides important information and evidence for the study of ancient human life. Therefore, the understanding of ancient inscriptions is very meaningful. New inscriptions often require inscriptions experts to compare them with existing inscriptions, which is very cumbersome and unreasonable. Therefore, a more scientific approach is needed to classify the inscriptions.

ⓒ The Author(s), under exclusive license to Springer Nature Switzerland AG 2023
H. Lu et al. (Eds.): ICIG 2023, LNCS 14357, pp. 162–173, 2023.
https://doi.org/10.1007/978-3-031-46311-2_14

In recent years, various methods of deep learning have made significant progress in image classification and recognition [1–4]. Jaderberg [5] used synthetic data generation techniques to create a large number of single-character images and used convolutional networks to classify characters in natural scenes, which have high prediction accuracy for classification. However, there are still three problems: The first problem is that high prediction accuracy only applies to the categories in the training stage and cannot be transferred to categories not included in the training stage. This attribute makes it difficult for models to recognize new ancient inscriptions. The second problem is that a large number of samples are required for contribution during the training process. Last but not least, CNN model is prone to fall into the dilemma of overfitting for data sets with large categories and few samples. In addition, due to the age and preservation difficulties of ancient inscriptions, many rare characters have few inscriptions, resulting in only a few samples for most of the categories of ancient inscriptions. Therefore, the ancient inscription dataset has the characteristics of multiple categories and few samples. In this case, traditional CNN structures are no longer sufficient and small-sample recognition is required to solve these problems.

Few-shot learning involves learning to recognize novel classes from a small number of labeled examples. The goal is to generalize well to new classes, even with limited data [6]. In general,few shot learning methods can be divided into three categories: model based, metric based, and optimization based. The model-based approach aims to quickly update parameters on a small number of samples by designing the model structure, and directly establish mapping functions between input and predicted values [7,8]. The metric based method utilizes the concept of nearest neighbors to complete classification by measuring the distance between the samples in the query set and the support set [9]. The optimization based method considers that commonly used gradient descent methods are difficult to fit scenes with few shots, so the task is completed by adjusting the optimization methods.

Among these methods, metric based methods are more suitable for text image dataset classification. Finn [10], Abbeel, and Levine introduces a meta-learning called Model-Agnostic Meta-Learning (MAML), which aims to learn an initialization of the network parameters that can be quickly fine-tuned to new tasks with limited data. Sung et al. [11] presents a relation network for few-shot learning, which aims to learn a similarity metric between images in a way that allows for effective. Vinyals [12]presented a new type of neural network called Matching Networks, aimed at addressing the one-shot learning problem. These networks have high prediction accuracy on several benchmark datasets. Snell [13] propose a new neural network architecture called prototype network, which learns a metric space, where classification can be performed by calculating the distance to the prototype representation of each category. The prototype representation of a category is the average of the feature vectors that support examples for that category.

Although the prototype network has achieved very high prediction accuracy on omniglot, the prediction accuracy on other data sets can be difficult. In view of this, Weiyang Liu [14] proposed L-softmax, which decomposed the separability of samples into amplitude and Angle values with cosine similarity, and preset a constant M to generate Angle interval to increase the classification robustness. G. Cheng [15] used self-calibration (SC) and internal calibration (IC) to optimize the prototype in the process of remote sensing image classification. Liu [16] used the cosine similarity prototype network (CSPN) and deviation reduction (BD) methods to calibrate the prototype. Jaderberg [5] set the distance scaling strategy and class attention mechanism to improve the prediction accuracy, and J. Wang [17] added the prototype module to the Siamese network structure to learn the high-quality prototype representation of each class. Drawing inspiration from these works, we use Global information optimization (GioP) and Margin Prototype (MP) to improve the network without increasing the training parameters and model complexity.

Specifically, we propose two strategies: margin prototype strategy (MP) and global information optimization strategy (GioP). The first strategy is to increase the diversity between classes as much as possible, so as to encourage separability between classes. The essence of the prototype network is to project features into the prototype space, which means that similar features have similar distance measurements in the prototype space. MP aims to maximize the distance between these predicted samples and their corresponding prototypes, placing higher requirements on classification. Increasing the differences between classes in disguised form makes classification more accurate. The specific approach is to offset the prototype distance through simple multiplication in softmax calculation process by presetting the expanded proportionality constant m. The model learns the correct feature mapping relationship after the prototype deviation. It should be noted that the value of the proportionality constant m must be an appropriate value, otherwise the model will fall into the dilemma of overfitting. Experiments show that this method works better with more categories and 1-shot. Inspired by [15], we find that the prediction probability of the query set can be reversely calibrated to the prototype. Based on this, we propose the second strategy – the global prototype Pb reverse optimization strategy. pb can be regarded as the mean of the same category that carries the information of both the support set and the query set, and is used for reverse prediction optimization to improve the prototype p. In the process of reverse prediction of the support set sample, it is necessary to remove the contribution of the support set sample from pb to obtain PB. PB contains all the information in the class except the predicted support sample, and the cross entropy loss of its prediction is another auxiliary constraint. The experiment proves that this reverse optimization is effective. The model is trained with these two strategies. The experimental results show that these two strategies have good effects. In summary, we propose two strategies of margin prototype strategy (MP) and global information optimization (GioP) to improve the prototype network and make it more accurate in our dataset.

2   Related Work

In this section, we will briefly introduce the relevant knowledge of few-shot learning and metric learning, as well as explain the origin and characteristics of the ancient inscription dataset.

2.1   Self-built Ancient Inscriptions Dataset

The character images of ancient inscriptions are obtained by batch scanning and module segmentation of bronze inscriptions from the Shang Dynasty in China. The ancient inscription dataset consists of over a thousand different meanings of inscription characters. The ancient inscription dataset has two characteristics. Due to different engraving methods and large time spans, there is a significant difference in the font of the same character. The abstraction understanding is that there is a large inner class variance; The number categories of ancient inscriptions reach thousands, which leads to poor separability between categories. These two points caused the ancient inscription dataset to have large intra-class differences and large inter-class similarities. Therefore, compared with public text datasets, the classification of ancient inscriptions is more difficult.

2.2   Few-Shot-Learning and Metric Learning

The goal of few-shot-learning is to identify a large number of unlabeled new samples by giving only a few labeled samples. Few-shot-learning is the application of meta Learning in supervised learning [10–13].In recent years, with the application of metric learning in meta-learning, a large number of metric learning methods have emerged, which effectively measure the similarity between two instances by learning metric functions. For example, Koch et al. [18] introduced Siamese networks to learn basic measures on a base set by identifying whether input instance pairs belong to the same class. Sung [11] presents a relation network for few-shot learning, which aims to learn a cosine similarity metric between images in a way that allows for effective. Vinyals [12] presented Matching Networks, aimed at addressing the few-shot classification problem. Snell [13] proposed the prototype network, which learns a metric space, where classification can be performed by calculating the distance to the prototype representation of each category. In the future, how to better learn the similarity between two examples will still be a hot issue.

3   Method

3.1   Basic Knowledge

Prototype network: It is a measure-based few shot learning, whose purpose is to calculate the distance between the mean value of each category of support samples in the embedded space and the test samples for prediction to achieve classification [13].

Few-shot-learning: Existing few-shot-learning methods adopt episodic training manner. Generally speaking, the training set of few-shot learning contains many categories, and there are several samples in each category. During the training phase, the training assembly is randomly divided into thousands of meta-tasks. There are N categories in each meta-task and K samples in each category (N * K data in total), which are used as the support set input of the model. Then a batch of samples is extracted from the remaining data in the N classes as the prediction object of the model. That is, the model is required to learn how to distinguish N categories from N*K data. Such a task is called the n-way k-shot problem.

3.2   Method Overview

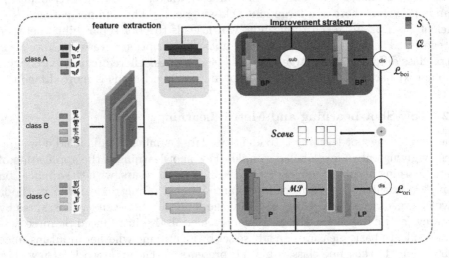

Fig. 1. Network Structure (Color figure online)

Figure 1 shows a simple 3-way, 2-shot meta-task. There are two Support samples and Query samples for each category. Our method is mainly based on the prototype network of CNN feature extraction. Support set and Query samples obtain corresponding features through the same feature extractor, and then predict the image of Query samples by calculating the distance between the feature distribution of Qurey sample and the spatial distribution of prototype.

In Fig. 1, our network structure consists of two modules. First, the feature extraction module, the yellow network layer is the feature extractor. It is composed of four convolutional blocks. Each block comprises a 64-fifilter 4 * 4 convolution, batch normalization layer, a ReLU nonlinearity and a 2 * 2 max-pooling layer.

The second module is the strategy improvement. This module contains the prototype margin prototype strategy (MP) (Green) and the global information optimization strategy(GioP) (Blue). The Green changes the original prototype space (P) by setting a constant m to obtain a pseudo prototype space (LP). During the training, through the training and learning of the classifier, the Query set can achieve more accurate prediction accuracy in the pseudo-prototype spatial distribution as far as possible. The distribution of Query set is more similar to the distribution of original prototype space, so the pseudo-prototype space has higher requirements for classification. However, the model needs to learn the correct feature mapping relationship after the prototype deviation, so it needs to fully consider the measurement distance between the prototype and the sample feature of the query set. Therefore, the value of M must be appropriate. Otherwise, the model will inevitably fall into the dilemma of overfitting. Inspired by [15], we find that the prediction probability of the query set can be reversely calibrated to the prototype. Therefore, the global information optimization strategy (GioP) is proposed. In this strategy, pb can be regarded as the same class mean carrying both support set and query set information, which is used for reverse prediction optimization to improve prototype P. In the process of reverse prediction of the support set sample, it is necessary to remove the contribution of the support set sample from pb to obtain PB, which contains all the information in the class except the predicted support sample. The predicted cross entropy loss is another auxiliary constraint Lboi, and the final constraint function is composed of this auxiliary constraint and its own constraint.

3.3   Margin Prototype Strategy (MP)

In this part, the prototype network is reviewed briefly, and the Margin Prototype strategy proposed in this paper is added in the review process.

For ancient inscriptions data set D, its internal samples are represented as D=(xi,yi), where x represents the vector, and y represents the classification label. In the meta-task of N-way and k-shot, K support samples are randomly generated from D, denoted as $S = (xi,yi)$. The prototype feature of this class is the arithmetic mean of K support set vectors, whose mathematical expression is as follows: where $f_\theta()$ represents a feature extraction function with learnable parameters.

$$P_i = \frac{1}{K} \sum f_\theta \ (x_i) \qquad (1)$$

The prototype c_k is obtained from Eq. 1, and similar to the generation of the support set S, the query set Q is generated by randomly selecting n sample points from the total sample set for each category. Accordingly, it is also necessary to generate coding for the sample of the query set to further calculate the distance between the query set and the prototype. The ultimate goal of the prototype network is to derive the probability distribution that the current sample x belongs to each category. Computing mode using softmax:

$$p_\varphi(y = k \mid x) = \frac{\exp\left(-d\left(f_\theta(x), c_k\right)\right)}{\sum_{k'} \exp\left(-d\left(f_\theta(x), c'_k\right)\right)} \qquad (2)$$

The margin prototype strategy (MP) Presets an expansion constant m, In softmax calculations, the distribution of the pseudo prototype space can be obtained by multiplying the distance d and the expansion constant m. The formula is as follows, where c_k is the category prototype from Eq. 2.

$$p_\varphi(y = k \mid x) = \frac{\exp\left(-m * d\left(f_\theta(x), c_k\right)\right)}{\exp\left(-m * d\left(f_\theta(x), c_k\right)\right) + \sum_{k'}^{k' \neq k} \exp\left(-d\left(f_\theta(x), c_{k'}\right)\right)} \tag{3}$$

Here is a brief description of the pseudo-prototype space. For an N-way-K-shot problem, MP broadens the distance between the query sample and the corresponding prototype, making it more difficult to predict the query sample during the prediction process. Therefore, higher requirements are put forward for correct classification in the pseudo prototype space, which makes the prototypes of different classes generate stricter isolation boundaries and improves the prediction accuracy in the real prototype space. However, it should be noted that in order for the model to learn the correct feature mapping relationship after the prototype deviation, the similarity between the prototype and the query set must be fully considered. Therefore, the value of the expansion constant m must be an appropriate value, otherwise the model is bound to fall into the dilemma of overfitting. In summary, the final loss function is as follows, which is the first part of the global loss.

$$J_\delta = -\log P_\delta(y = k \mid x) \tag{4}$$

3.4   Global Information Optimization Strategy (GioP)

According to [15], category mean Pb of query set can be used to reversely predict support set samples to realize prototype calibration. Among them, The mean of the query set cannot reflect global supervision information within the class, so this paper proposes a strategy to reversely predict support set samples by using global characteristics. To be specific, the mean value of all samples in the class is taken as the base prototype of the class, which is called Pb. However, in the process of reverse prediction, the contribution of the predicted sample to the base prototype needs to be removed to get pb'. Let the internal representation of this class sample be $S = (x_i, y_i)$. There are S samples in total. The sample of support set that requires reverse prediction is x_k, and code where $f_\theta()$ represents a feature extraction function with learnable parameters. The base class prototype is represented as follows:

$$Pb_i = \frac{S}{S-1}\left(\frac{\sum f_\theta(x_i)}{S} - \frac{x_k}{S}\right) \tag{5}$$

Based on the Eqs. 2, 5, the predicted probability distribution of sample x_k is as follow:

$$p_\delta(y = k \mid x) = \frac{\exp\left(-m * d\left(f_\theta(x), pb_k\right)\right)}{\exp\left(-m * d\left(f_\theta(x), pb_k\right)\right) + \sum_{k'}^{k' \neq k} \exp\left(-d\left(f_\theta(x), p'_{b_k}\right)\right)} \tag{6}$$

where m is the expanded proportionality constant $(m > 1)$, and is the prototype of the base class derived from Eqs. 2, 5. Thus, the final global supervision auxiliary constraint can be obtained:

$$J_\delta = -\log P_\delta(y = k \mid x) \tag{7}$$

The overall loss function is a linear combination of and

$$J_{glo} = J_\varphi + \lambda J_\delta \tag{8}$$

4 Experiments

In this section, we evaluated our two strategies on the self built ancient inscription dataset and the public dataset omniglot [19], and verified the effectiveness of our improvement by comparing the final classification success rate. The number of samples for each category in the two datasets is 20, and the Support set and Query set are randomly divided. For example, in the 5-way5-shot experiment, each category contains 15 Query set and 5 Support sets. Finally, ablation experiments were conducted. Evaluate the impact of each strategy on the model separately. All models are trained end-to-end from scratch. After 100 epochs, the model with the highest prediction accuracy in the validation set was recorded and saved. We reported the experimental results of 5way-5shot, 5-way-1-shot, 20-way-1shot, and 20-way-shot on two datasets during the testing phase.

4.1 Inscription Dataset Few-Shot Classification

The character images of ancient inscriptions are obtained by batch scanning and module segmentation of bronze inscriptions from the Shang Dynasty in China. The ancient inscription dataset consists of over a thousand different meanings of inscription characters. We preprocess the sample set, including flipping, translating, and blurring to enhance the dataset.

During the testing phase, we randomly selected 100 categories of ancient inscriptions, each containing corresponding support and query images. A total of 200 episodes were used to obtain the results, which can verify the effectiveness of our strategy. We have chosen several state-of-the-art methods for comparison. Our strategy performs best on all four tasks. The experimental results are shown in Table 1. From Table 1, it can be seen that our model performs better on 1-shot tasks. Compared to the baseline, there was an increase of 3.4% and 2.9%in the 5-way and 20-way scenarios, respectively.

Table 1. Few-shot classification accuracies (%) under the Inscription Dataset.

Method	FN	5way-5shot	5way-1shot	20way-5shot	20way-1shot
MN [12]	N	84.17 ± 0.64	64.43 ± 0.89	62.45 ± 0.54	43.64 ± 0.94
MAML [10]	Y	87.15 ± 0.44	68.54 ± 0.79	67.83 ± 0.34	44.94 ± 0.87
RN [11]	N	83.51 ± 0.15	65.85 ± 0.46	63.67 ± 0.17	42.48 ± 1.08
PN [13]	N	86.51 ± 0.47	69.43 ± 0.84	69.13 ± 0.25	45.77 ± 0.58
PN*(SC) [15]	N	86.91 ± 045	70.28 ± 0.67	68.79 ± 0.36	45.61 ± 0.71
Mp (ours)	N	88.01 ± 0.43	72.43 ± 0.28	70.13 ± 0.31	47.78 ± 0.54
GioP (ours)	N	87.23 ± 0.54	70.45 ± 1.24	69.97 ± 0.17	46.47 ± 0.48
MGP (ours)	N	88.31 ± 0.35	73.64 ± 0.84	70.34 ± 0.38	70.43 ± 0.51

4.2 Omniglot Few-Shot Classifification

Omniglot [19] is a dataset of 1623 handwritten characters collected from 50 letters. Each character has 20 samples. In order to present our method more prominently, we differ from Snell [13] in randomly partitioning datasets. We classified the dataset and found that the feature distributions of the data samples in each major category were more similar. During the testing phase, only test sets belonging to the same major category were used for each test. For a simple 2-way task, a model can more easily classify Korean and Japanese characters, but it is difficult to correctly classify two similar Japanese characters. The test set we selected consists of 150 types of images, including 3 major categories. The average values were obtained in three batches and the final results were reported in Table 2 below. Compared to the baseline, in the one shot task, the prediction accuracy of 5-way and 20-way improved by 3.9% and 3.8%, respectively.

Table 2. Few-shot classification accuracies (%) under the omniglot.

Method	FN	5way-5shot	5way-1shot	20way-5shot	20way-1shot
MN [12]	N	97.7	89.8	92.9	78.2
MAML [10]	Y	98.2	90.1	93.4	79.0
RN [11]	N	97.9	89.9	91.8	77.9
PN [13]	N	98.1	90.1	93.3	79.2
PN*(SC) [15]	N	98.1	90.3	93.5	79.4
Mp (ours)	N	98.4	93.2	94.8	82.5
GioP (ours)	N	98.0	90.3	93.6	80.6
MGP (ours)	N	98.3	94.1	95.1	83.6

5 Ablation Experiment

This section mainly includes exploring the impact of hyperparameter on few shot classification and demonstrating the effectiveness of our strategy by visualizing the distribution within the class. First, explore M and λ The impact on the model. A large number of tests were conducted under the task of 5way-5shot, when m belongs to [1.05, 1.15], λ belongs to [0.5, 3], A large number of combinatorial explorations were conducted, as Shown some representative combinations in Fig. 2. Under the combination of [1.105, 0.7], the model has the best effect; the experimental results also tell us that the setting of M has a significant impact on the model. When M reaches 10, regardless of λ The success rate of the model is already very low, indicating that the large scaling constant prevents the model from learning the correct mapping.

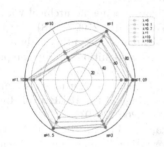

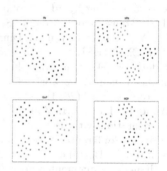

Fig. 2. Hyperparameter distribution

Fig. 3. t-SNE visualization for PN, MP, GioP, and MGP of 5 classes on Inscription dataset

In the Experiment stage, We have demonstrated the effectiveness of our two strategies through a comparison of prediction accuracy. In this section, we focus on visualizing the distribution, and visually shows the role of two strategies. In Fig. 3, without losing generality, T-sne [21] was randomly used to visualize the sample distribution of five different types of query sets in a 5way-5shot task on the ancient inscription dataset. From the distribution of features, our three methods clearly make different categories more borderline. It increases the distance between classes partly, and Improve model robustness. The characteristics of MGP species to some extent inherit the characteristics of MP and GioP, which has fully verified the effectiveness of our strategy.

6 Conclusion

In this paper, we have proposed two strategies to improve the prototype network, the first strategy is the Margin Prototype (MP), which expands the distribution of different class prototypes during the softmax operation. The second strategy is the global information optimization strategy (GioP), which reverses the prediction of support set samples to obtain more representative prototypes. The experimental results on the two character datasets show its effectiveness and competitiveness. The ablation experiments show the effectiveness of each module.

References

1. Ma, M., Mei, S., Wan, S., Hou, J., Wang, Z., Feng, D.D.: Video summarization via block sparse dictionary selection. Neurocomputing **378**, 197–209 (2020)
2. Cheng, G., Yang, C., Yao, X., Guo, L., Han, J.: When deep learning meets metric learning: remote sensing image scene classification via learning discriminative CNNs. IEEE Trans. Geosci. Remote Sens. **56**(5), 2811–2821 (2018)
3. Mei, S., Ji, J., Geng, Y., Zhang, Z., Li, X., Du, Q.: Unsupervised spatial-spectral feature learning by 3d convolutional autoencoder for hyperspectral classification. IEEE Trans. Geosci. Remote Sens. **57**(9), 6808–6820 (2019)
4. Liu, Y., Suen, C.Y., Liu, Y., Ding, L.: Scene classification using hierarchical Wasserstein CNN. IEEE Trans. Geosci. Remote Sens. **57**(5), 2494–2509 (2018)
5. Jaderberg, M., Simonyan, K., Vedaldi, A., Zisserman, A.: Synthetic data and artificial neural networks for natural scene text recognition. arXiv preprint arXiv:1406.2227 (2014)
6. Wang, K., Liew, J.H., Zou, Y., Zhou, D., Feng, J.: Panet: few-shot image semantic segmentation with prototype alignment. In: proceedings of the IEEE/CVF International Conference on Computer Vision, pp. 9197–9206 (2019)
7. Santoro, A., Bartunov, S., Botvinick, M., Wierstra, D., Lillicrap, T.: Meta-learning with memory-augmented neural networks. In: International Conference on Machine Learning, pp. 1842–1850. PMLR (2016)
8. Zhang, S., Zhou, Z., Huang, Z., Wei, Z.: Few-shot classification on graphs with structural regularized GCNs (2019)
9. Munkhdalai, T., Yu, H.: Meta networks. In: International Conference on Machine Learning, pp. 2554–2563. PMLR (2017)
10. Finn, C., Abbeel, P., Levine, S.: Model-agnostic meta-learning for fast adaptation of deep networks. In: International Conference on Machine Learning, pp. 1126–1135. PMLR (2017)
11. Sung, F., Yang, Y., Zhang, L., Xiang, T., Torr, P.H., Hospedales, T.M.: Learning to compare: relation network for few-shot learning. In: Proceedings of the IEEE Conference on Computer Vision and Pattern Recognition, pp. 1199–1208 (2018)
12. Vinyals, O., Blundell, C., Lillicrap, T., Wierstra, D., et al.: Matching networks for one shot learning. In: Advances in Neural Information Processing Systems, vol. 29 (2016)
13. Snell, J., Swersky, K., Zemel, R.: Prototypical networks for few-shot learning. In: Advances in Neural Information Processing Systems, vol. 30 (2017)
14. Liu, W., Wen, Y., Yu, Z., Yang, M.: Large-margin softmax loss for convolutional neural networks. arXiv preprint arXiv:1612.02295 (2016)
15. Cheng, G., et al.: SPnet: Siamese-prototype network for few-shot remote sensing image scene classification. IEEE Trans. Geosci. Remote Sens. **60**, 1–11 (2021)
16. Liu, J., Song, L., Qin, Y.: Prototype rectification for few-shot learning. In: Vedaldi, A., Bischof, H., Brox, T., Frahm, J.-M. (eds.) ECCV 2020. LNCS, vol. 12346, pp. 741–756. Springer, Cham (2020). https://doi.org/10.1007/978-3-030-58452-8_43

17. Wang, J., Zhai, Y.: Prototypical Siamese networks for few-shot learning. In: 2020 IEEE 10th International Conference on Electronics Information and Emergency Communication (ICEIEC), pp. 178–181. IEEE (2020)
18. Koch, G., Zemel, R., Salakhutdinov, R., et al.: Siamese neural networks for one-shot image recognition. In: ICML Deep Learning Workshop, vol. 2. Lille (2015)
19. Lake, B., Salakhutdinov, R., Gross, J., Tenenbaum, J.: One shot learning of simple visual concepts. In: Proceedings of the Annual Meeting of the Cognitive Science Society, vol. 33 (2011)
20. Ji, Z., Chai, X., Yu, Y., Pang, Y., Zhang, Z.: Improved prototypical networks for few-shot learning. Pattern Recogn. Lett. **140**, 81–87 (2020)
21. Van der Maaten, L., Hinton, G.: Visualizing data using t-SNE. J. Mach. Learn. Res. **9**(11) (2008)

Structure-Aware Point Cloud Completion

Zhihua Cheng and Xuejin Chen[(✉)] [ID]

NEL-BITA, University of Science and Technology of China, Hefei, Auhui, China
`czh666@mail.ustc.edu.cn`, `xjchen99@ustc.edu.cn`

Abstract. Structure plays a crucial role in point cloud completion. While many efforts have been made to recover geometric details of the target shape, it is non-trivial to recover global structures, especially when large areas are missing in the input partial point cloud. In this paper, we propose a novel point cloud completion approach named SAPCNet to reconstruct complete 3D shapes in a global structure-aware manner. To establish long-range dependencies within the global scope and efficiently capture the object structure, we propose a structure-aware enhancement module by introducing global attention to the seed point generation process. To explicitly enforce the category-specific structure recovery, we design a classification-supervised training strategy to enable the network to generate structures more consistent with object category properties. Moreover, we design a category-guided adaptive seed selection module to generate seed points in the first stage. A redundant structure elimination loss is also introduced to reduce the ill-posed generation of heavily missing regions in the incomplete point cloud. Qualitative and quantitative evaluations on the PCN dataset demonstrate that our method outperforms state-of-the-art completion approaches.

Keywords: Point cloud completion · Structure-aware · Classification-supervised

1 Introduction

3D vision is drawing more and more attention in both academia and industry, owing to its wide applications in areas such as autonomous driving, robotics, scene modeling, and virtual/augmented reality. Point cloud is a simple and efficient 3D data structure to represent object shapes in 3D vision. The acquisition of point clouds has become easier with the popularity of 3D scanning devices such as LiDAR and depth cameras. However, the scanned point clouds are usually incomplete and uneven due to inevitable self-occlusion, light reflection, limited sensor resolution, etc. The consequential absence of geometric and structural information in these incomplete point clouds will seriously affect the downstream

This work was supported by the National Natural Science Foundation of China under Grant 62076230.

ⓒ The Author(s), under exclusive license to Springer Nature Switzerland AG 2023
H. Lu et al. (Eds.): ICIG 2023, LNCS 14357, pp. 174–185, 2023.
https://doi.org/10.1007/978-3-031-46311-2_15

3D tasks. Therefore, recovering complete point clouds has become an indispensable step with ever-growing significance for many point cloud understanding tasks.

Most existing point cloud completion approaches [4,12,14,18,19,21] employ an encoder-decoder architecture to generate dense complete point clouds in a coarse-to-fine manner. However, these approaches mainly focus on enhancing local shape details but have difficulty in fully capturing the global structures, leading to the lack of structure rationality and realism of the completion results. Specifically, the structure is the crucial factor in determining the shape of an object since 3D objects are composed of low-level and high-level configurations, including surfaces, semantic parts, and geometrical elements. Therefore, how to efficiently utilize structural correlation between local regions becomes a key factor of point cloud completion. Either folding-based decoders [12,16–18] or MLP-based decoders [4,7,14] attempt to process each point independently by splitting one target point into more, while transformer-based decoders [21] integrate local information into the generation process by aggregating neighboring points. These decoder designs could only take the information from a single point or a local neighborhood into account but fail to effectively exploit global structure information from a broader region or the whole object.

While it is challenging to capture global structure directly from point clouds with a large missing area, the structural prior of a specific object category could provide valuable structure clues. Therefore, we enforce our completion pipeline to convey category-specific information by modifying the training strategy and the seed point generation stage. Based on the above two motivations, we propose a novel Structure-Aware Point cloud Completion Network (SAPCNet) to reconstruct a more reasonable structure with long-range dependency and preserve the category-specific object structure.

Our method especially focuses on the decoding process to complete partial point clouds, which is usually divided into two stages: seed generation and iterative coarse-to-fine refinement with upsampling layers. For both the coarse-grained seed generation and fine-grained completion, we propose a classification-supervised training strategy to provide category-aware structural priors using a pre-trained point cloud classifier, mitigating the generation of incorrect object structures. In the first seed generation stage, we propose a category-guided adaptive seed selection module to integrate the incomplete patch features from the encoder and the initial seed features to adaptively generate new seed features representing the coarse-grained complete shape by scoring, ranking, and selecting operations. Through this seed regeneration step, we expect the network to adaptively correct the wrong prediction of object categories by adjusting the distribution of patch seeds and features at the initial stage. Next, a structure-aware enhancement (SAE) module is proposed in the coarse-to-fine point cloud generation stage. More specifically, at each upsampling layer, the SAE employs a global attention mechanism to incorporate global structural information into the generation process by establishing long-range dependencies between different patches. Finally, a new loss function for eliminating redundant structures is designed in the training stage. Our SAPCNet achieves a superior completion performance compared with the state-of-the-art methods on the widely used PCN dataset [18].

In summary, our main contributions include:

- We propose a novel SAPCNet for point cloud completion, which greatly improves the completion performance concerning structural rationality and fidelity.
- We design a structure-aware enhancement module to exploit the global structural correlation between different parts and regions for shape completion.
- We introduce a classification-supervised training strategy and a category-guided adaptive seed selection module to generate structures that are more consistent with their category property.

2 Related Work

With the development of deep neural networks in recent years, researchers prefer to use learning-based methods to solve the point cloud completion problem. PCN [18] is the pioneering work of directly operating on raw point clouds. It generates complete 3D shapes from partial observation in a coarse-to-fine manner by first extracting a global feature to generate a coarse-grained point cloud and then refining it to a dense one using a folding-based network [16]. TopNet [7] elaborates a decoder with a hierarchical rooted tree structure to generate structured point clouds. CRN [9] is a cascaded refinement network that iteratively boosts the generated point clouds to recover shape details with an adversarial training scheme. Just like CRN [9], PF-Net [4] also utilizes a multi-stage generation pipeline to generate the missing part of the object at multiple scales and employs the adversarial loss to enhance the fidelity of the generated shapes. NSFA [19] aggregates multi-level features instead of using a global feature to recover a complete model. GRNet [15] and VE-PCN [10] achieve point cloud completion using differentiable gridding and gridding reverse operations for transformation between points and 3D grids and adopt 3D CNN to preserve the context of point clouds.

As the transformer [8] achieves great success in various fields of deep learning, transformer-based point cloud completion methods have drawn more and more attention. PoinTr [17] first applies transformer architecture to point cloud completion. SnowflakeNet [14] models the progressive generation process as a snowflake-like growth of points. A transformer-based network is applied to the decoder to capture geometric details in a local region. Moreover, SeedFormer [21] introduces the patch seeds to replace global features and designs a transformer-style point splitting operation, which improves the ability of detail preservation and recovery. However, existing methods mainly put effort into preserving local shape details, neglecting the recovery of global structure. In comparison, our SAPCNet exploits more global structural priors to complete partial point clouds.

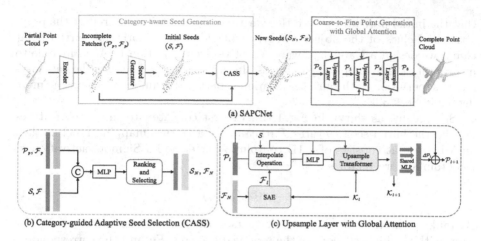

Fig. 1. The overview of our method. (a) The pipeline of our SAPCNet. (b) The Category-guided Adaptive Seed Selection (CASS) module. (c) The upsampling layer with our Structure-aware Enhancement (SAE) module.

3 Our Method

The overall architecture of our SAPCNet is shown in Fig. 1 (a), which consists of two key modules: Category-aware Seed Generation and Coarse-to-fine Point Generation with Global Attention. We also design a novel training strategy to enhance the category-aware structures in these two modules. In the first seed generation stage, we design a category-aware seed selection method to generate a set of seed points to represent the overall object structure at a coarse level. Then in the second stage, we follow a common coarse-to-fine point generation pipeline but with a newly designed transformer model with global attention to utilize long-range dependency between seed points.

3.1 Category-Aware Seed Generation

Denote $\mathcal{P} = \{\mathbf{p}_i | i = 1, 2, ..., N\}$ as the input partial point cloud, where N is the number of points and $\mathbf{p}_i$ denotes the 3D coordinate of each point. Following [14], the partial point cloud $\mathcal{P}$ is fed into an encoder comprised of point transformer [20] and set abstraction layers [6] to get a set of patch center points $\mathcal{P}_p \in \mathbb{R}^{N_P \times 3}$ and the corresponding patch features $\mathcal{F}_p \in \mathbb{R}^{N_P \times C_P}$. Then the patch center point set $\mathcal{P}_p$ and the patch features $\mathcal{F}_p$ are input to a seed generator [21] to obtain the initial set of seed points $\mathcal{S} \in \mathbb{R}^{N_s \times 3}$ and seed features $\mathcal{F}_s \in \mathbb{R}^{N_s \times C_s}$. Here, we set $C_s = C_p$.

Existing methods [14,21] are prone to object category confusion of the input point cloud when facing heavily incomplete point clouds, thus generating structures that do not belong to the correct object class. This category confusion problem tends to appear in the stage of seed point generation. Taking into account that the initial patches $\mathcal{P}_p$ with their features $\mathcal{F}_p$ can faithfully reflect the properties and clues of the object category embedded in the original partial point cloud, we design a Category-aware Adaptive Seed Selection (CASS) module to incorporate the incomplete patches as alternatives to seeds under the category-aware supervision with our classification-supervised training mechanism (more details in Sect. 3.3).

Specifically, as shown in Fig. 1 (b), we first concatenate the patch features $\mathcal{F}_p$ and the initial seed features $\mathcal{F}$, then apply a feature mapping function, i.e., an MLP ϕ that consists of a 1D convolution layer and a Sigmoid activation σ, to obtain a score vector $\mathbf{s} \in \mathbb{R}^{(N_s + N_p) \times 1}$ as

$$\mathbf{s} = \sigma(\phi(\mathcal{F}_p, \mathcal{F})). \tag{1}$$

By ranking the value $\mathbf{s}_i$ of all the elements in the score vector, we select N_s features with the highest score as the new seed features $\mathcal{F}_N$ and the corresponding coordinates as the new seed points $\mathcal{S}_N$. During training, we add a point cloud classifier to predict the object category of the enhanced seed points $\mathcal{S}_N$ as input and calculate the classification loss so that the CASS module can sufficiently exploit the category cues in the input partial point cloud under the guidance of the category prior and re-select seeds with structures belonging to the correct category.

3.2 Coarse-to-Fine Point Generation with Global Attention

After we get an initial set of seed points that coarsely depict the complete overall shape, we follow existing methods [14,16,21] to add shape details progressively in a coarse-to-fine manner. In each upsampling layer, previous methods [14,21] learn the geometric pattern in a local neighborhood based on the correlations between each point to its k-nearest neighbors to produce new points around each seed point. However, when facing a sizeable missing area, this local aggregation [21] strategy is insufficient to complete the missing large-scale structure. In contrast, we enhance the seed point features with a global cross-attention between all points at each upsampling layer to exploit long-range dependency in structure completion.

As Fig. 1 (c) shows, we add a Structure-Aware Enhancement (SAE) module for the seed features with global structural correlations in each upsampling layer while following the point splitting pipeline in SeedFormer. To upsample the point cloud $\mathcal{P}_l$ to $\mathcal{P}_{l+1}$ with an upsampling rate r_l in the l-th layer, we enhance the seed point features $\mathcal{F}_N$ globally before the local feature interpolation to take long-range correlations between patches. Specifically, we enhance the seed feature $\mathcal{F}_N$ based on their correlations between the point features $\mathcal{K}_l$ using multi-head global attention [8]. Taking the seed features $\mathcal{F}_N$ as queries and point features $\mathcal{K}_l$ as keys and values, a series of linear projections are applied to obtain a new group of queries $\mathcal{Q}_{hl} = \{\mathbf{q}_i^{hl}\}_{i=1}^{N_s}$, keys $\mathcal{K}_{hl} = \{\mathbf{k}_i^{hl}\}_{i=1}^{N_l}$, and values $\mathcal{V}_{hl} = \{\mathbf{v}_i^{hl}\}_{i=1}^{N_l}$ for $h = 1, 2, \ldots, M$ where M is the number of heads and N_l denotes the number of points of $\mathbf{P}_l$ of each upsampling layer.

The enhanced feature for each point is calculated as:

$$\mathbf{f}_i^{hl} = \sum_{j \in N_l} \rho\left(\frac{1}{\sqrt{d_k}} \mathbf{q}_i^{hl} \cdot \mathbf{k}_j^{hl}\right) \mathbf{v}_j^{hl}, \tag{2}$$

where ρ is the softmax function which normalizes the weights to $(0, 1)$. The enhanced seed feature $\mathbf{f}_i^l$ of each point is obtained by channel-wise concatenation of the $\mathbf{f}_i^{hl}$ of the M heads.

We apply the SAE module to each upsampling layer before the linear feature interpolation. For the first upsampling layer ($l = 0$), there is no point features input from the previous layer. Instead of $\mathcal{K}_0$, we use $\mathcal{F}_N$ as queries, keys and values for calculation. In the l-th upsampling layer, given the enhanced $\mathcal{F}_l = \{\mathbf{f}_i^l\}_{i=1}^{N_s}$ generated by our SAE and the point cloud $\mathcal{P}_l$, we spread $\mathcal{F}_l$ to each point $\mathbf{p}_i \in \mathcal{P}_l$ by interpolating feature values from its k nearest seed points in the new seed set $\mathcal{S}_N$. The interpolated features are then concatenated with the point cloud $\mathcal{P}_l$ and fed into an MLP to form the queries for the subsequent Upsample Transformer [21] to produce the point features $\mathcal{K}_{l+1}$ and the higher-resolution point cloud $\mathcal{P}_{l+1}$. After introducing the SAE module to the upsampling layers, the attention range of each point is expanded to the global scope rather than a local neighborhood.

3.3   Classification-Supervised Training

While most existing methods [14,17,21] use Chamfer distance as the geometric supervision to train the completion network, they tend to generate shapes with ambiguous category-ware structure from a heavily incomplete point cloud. Therefore, we propose to train our generation modules with explicit category supervision to enforce the network to complement point clouds based on the structure prior associated with the object category. The overall training loss is composed of two parts, i.e., classification loss and geometric loss.

Classification Loss. During training, we append a pre-trained point cloud classification network, such as PCT [3], to the new seed points $\mathcal{S}_N$ generated at the first stage and the final generated complete point cloud $\mathcal{P}_c$ to predict their object categories. Using cross entropy as the classification loss, we have the classification-supervised loss L_{cls}

$$\mathcal{L}_{cls} = -\sum_{k=1}^{K} (\hat{y}_k \log y_k^s + \hat{y}_k \log y_k^c), \tag{3}$$

where K is the total number of object categories, $\hat{y}_t$ is the ground-truth category of the point cloud, y_t^s and y_t^c are the category probability of the initial seeds and completed point cloud predicted by the classifier.

Geometry Loss. We use Chamfer distance as our primary loss function to measure the reconstruction error of the generated point cloud $\mathcal{P}_l$ compared with the ground truth point cloud $\mathcal{P}_{gt}$

$$CD(\mathcal{P}_l, \mathcal{P}_{gt}) = \frac{1}{|\mathcal{P}_l|} \sum_{\mathbf{x} \in \mathcal{P}_l} \min_{\mathbf{y} \in \mathcal{P}_{gt}} \|\mathbf{x} - \mathbf{y}\|_2 + \frac{1}{|\mathcal{P}_{gt}|} \sum_{\mathbf{y} \in \mathcal{P}_{gt}} \min_{\mathbf{x} \in \mathcal{P}_l} \|\mathbf{y} - \mathbf{x}\|_2. \qquad (4)$$

The above CD formulation is the symmetric version where the first term enforces the recovered points to lie close to the ground truth points and the second term ensures the ground truth points are covered by the predicted points. To explicitly constrain point clouds generated in the seed generation and the coarse-to-fine stage, we down-sample the ground truth point clouds to the same point number with $\mathcal{S}_N, \mathcal{P}_1, \mathcal{P}_2$ and compute the corresponding CD losses respectively. We define the sum of the above three CD losses as the completion loss $\mathcal{L}_{comp}$. Besides, we also apply the partial matching loss [11] $\mathcal{L}_{pm}$, which restricts the partial point cloud to be covered by the generated complete point cloud, to preserve the geometry and structure of the input point cloud. However, the symmetric version of CD will cause the problem of generating extra structures and noisy points that do not exist in the ground truth when facing a large missing area.

While the input partial point cloud has large missing regions, the network tends to generate a set of chaotic and disordered points to fit the complete point cloud but without any relevant structure clues. Therefore, we propose to weigh more on the Chamfer distance from the generated point clouds at each level $\mathcal{P}_l$ to the ground truth to avoid noisy points. We introduce a hyperparameter $\lambda > 0.5$ into the traditional symmetric CD, resulting in an asymmetric version of CD

$$CD_{weight}(\mathcal{P}_l, \mathcal{P}_{gt}) = \lambda \frac{1}{|\mathcal{P}_l|} \sum_{\mathbf{x} \in \mathcal{P}_l} \min_{\mathbf{y} \in \mathcal{P}_{gt}} \|\mathbf{x} - \mathbf{y}\|_2 + (1 - \lambda) \frac{1}{|\mathcal{P}_{gt}|} \sum_{\mathbf{y} \in \mathcal{P}_{gt}} \min_{\mathbf{x} \in \mathcal{P}_l} \|\mathbf{y} - \mathbf{x}\|_2.$$
$$(5)$$

By combining the asymmetric CD between the predicted point clouds at each step $\mathcal{P}_l$, in the coarse-to-fine stage with the ground-truth $\mathcal{P}_{gt}$, we have our Redundant Structure Elimination loss

$$\mathcal{L}_{RSE} = \sum_l CD_{weight}(\mathcal{P}_l, \mathcal{P}_{gt}). \qquad (6)$$

This $\mathcal{L}_{RSE}$ increases the penalty of extra points in the completed point cloud, thus avoiding redundant structures and the presense of chaotic points, effectively improving the performance of shape completion.

4   Experiments

To fully prove the effectiveness of our SAPCNet, we conduct comprehensive experiments and ablation studies under the widely used PCN dataset [18]. It is a subset of 30,974 models of eight categories from the ShapeNet dataset [1]. For each model, eight partial point clouds are generated by back-projecting the depth maps generated from the 3D model under eight randomly sampled viewpoints. Each complete point cloud contains 16,384 points evenly sampled from the mesh surface as the Ground-Truth (GT). We follow the same split setting with PCN [18] for comparison. For evaluation, we adopt CD-ℓ_1 and F-Score@1% as our metrics.

4.1 Comparison with State-of-the-Art Methods

We compare our method with a series of existing point cloud completion methods, including the latest PoinTr [17], SnowflakeNet [14], and SeedFormer [21]. Table 1 shows the quantitative comparison results on the PCN dataset. Our SAPCNet achieves the best results on most categories in terms of CD-ℓ_1 and F-Score@1%, demonstrating the superiority of our method over the others. In particular, compared with the state-of-the-art SeedFormer [21], our SAPCNet reduces the average CD-ℓ_1 by 6.82%. Figure 2 shows a group of completion results of our method, PoinTr [17], SnowflakeNet [14] and SeedFormer [21] for four object categories. We can see that our SAPCNet generates more plausible structures and geometric details. Taking the fourth row as an example, only our SAPCNet successfully recovers the symmetric and indented top of the table while other methods generate a flat top.

Table 1. Results of our SAPCNet and existing methods on the PCN dataset. The reported CD-ℓ_1 is multiplied by 1000 (lower is better).

Methods	Avg CD-ℓ_1	Plane	Cabinet	Car	Chair	Lamp	Couch	Table	Boat	F-Score@1%
FoldingNet [16]	14.31	9.49	15.80	12.61	15.55	16.41	15.97	13.65	14.99	0.322
TopNet [7]	12.15	7.61	13.31	10.90	13.82	14.44	14.78	11.22	11.12	0.503
AtlasNet [2]	10.85	6.37	11.94	10.10	12.06	12.37	12.99	10.33	10.61	0.616
PCN [18]	9.63	5.50	22.70	10.63	8.70	11.00	11.34	11.68	8.59	0.695
MSN [5]	10.00	5.60	11.90	10.30	10.20	10.70	11.60	9.60	9.90	0.705
GRNet [15]	8.83	6.45	10.37	9.45	9.41	7.96	10.51	8.44	8.04	0.708
CRN [9]	8.51	4.79	9.97	8.31	9.49	8.94	10.69	7.81	8.05	–
NSFA [19]	8.06	4.76	10.18	8.63	8.53	7.03	10.53	7.35	7.48	–
PMP-Net [13]	8.73	5.65	11.24	9.64	9.51	6.95	10.83	8.72	7.25	–
PoinTr [17]	8.38	4.75	10.47	8.68	9.39	7.75	10.93	7.78	7.29	0.745
SnowflakeNet [14]	7.21	4.29	9.16	8.08	7.89	6.07	9.23	6.55	6.40	–
SeedFormer [21]	6.74	3.85	9.05	**8.06**	7.06	5.21	8.85	6.05	5.85	0.818
Ours	**6.28**	**3.73**	**8.22**	8.10	**6.61**	**4.79**	**7.59**	**5.79**	**5.41**	**0.849**

4.2 Ablation Studies

To verify the effectiveness of each module in our SAPCNet, We adopt Seed-Former [21] as the baseline and develop three network variations by adding each design into the baseline step by step. Table 2 reports the quantitative results. Model-A, which adds the SAE module to the baseline, reduces the average CD-ℓ_1 by 0.22, 3.26% lower than the baseline's results (6.52 vs 6.74). Model-B continues to incorporate the Redundant Structure Elimination loss $\mathcal{L}_{RSE}$ into Model-A

Table 2. Effect of each design in SAPCNet.

Methods	SAE	$\mathcal{L}_{RSE}$	CST	CASS	Avg CD-ℓ_1
SeedFormer					6.74
Model-A	✓				6.52
Model-B	✓	✓			6.41
Model-C	✓	✓	✓		6.37
Our SAPCNet	✓	✓	✓	✓	**6.28**

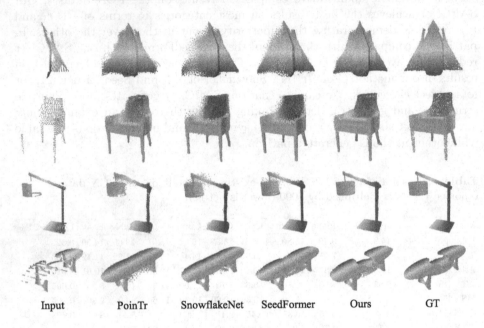

Input   PoinTr   SnowflakeNet   SeedFormer   Ours   GT

Fig. 2. Comparison of completion results from four categories in the PCN dataset.

and the CD-ℓ_1 is further reduced by 0.11, showing that the asymmetric $\mathcal{L}_{RSE}$ is effective to eliminate redundant structures and noisy points for point cloud completion. Integrating the classification-supervised training strategy (CST) with Model-B, Model-C decreases the CD-ℓ_1 by 0.04. Finally, our SAPCNet adds the CASS module to Model-C and achieves the best performance (6.28) of the CD-ℓ_1, which is 1.41% lower than Model-C (6.37). It proves that introducing category-aware structural prior and supervision can effectively avoid the production of ambigous structures belonging to wrong categories, thus greatly improving the overall completion performance.

We also visualize some completion results and demonstrate the effectives of each design in our method in Fig. 3. First, as shown in Fig. 3 (a), SAPCNet can recover more faithful structures for the aircraft tail fins and chair legs. We infer that this improvement comes from the SAE module which can effectively exploit structural correlations like symmetry to help recover the structure of

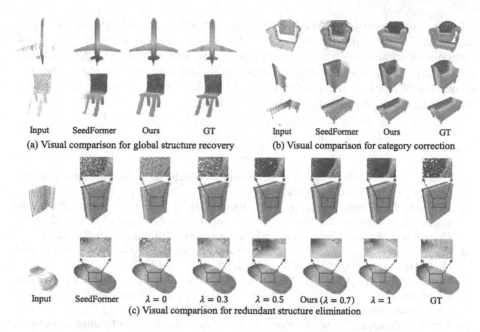

(a) Visual comparison for global structure recovery

(b) Visual comparison for category correction

(c) Visual comparison for redundant structure elimination

Fig. 3. (a) Visual comparison for shape completion with long-range dependency. (b) Visual comparison for category correction. (c) Visual comparison for redundant structure elimination.

the missing part from visible parts. From Fig. 3 (b), we can see that, with the category-guided adaptive seed selection and classification supervised training, our method is able to complete the shapes with structures of right category while SeedFormer misunderstands the chair and sofa input as cabinet and table respectively. In Fig. 3 (c), we visualize different results produced by our SAPCNet with different λ for $\mathcal{L}_{RSE}$. When $\lambda \leq 0.5$, the number of noisy points increases as λ decreases; when $\lambda = 1$, the overall completion performance is heavily affected. But when $\lambda = 1$, the point density is uneven in the completion results. We use $\lambda = 0.7$ in our SAPCNet, eliminating redundant structures and noise points in the predicted point clouds.

5   Conclusion

In this paper, we propose a novel point cloud completion method, namely SAPCNet. In order to capture global structure correlation more effectively, we design a structure-aware enhancement (SAE) module to enhance the seed features with long-range attentions. To alleviate the problem of generating redundant and noisy points while preserving correct object structure, we introduce a classification-supervised training strategy to provide category-aware structural priors for the completion network. Since the coarse-grained complete point cloud is better in representing the global structure, we design the category-guided adaptive seed selection (CASS) module to generate reasonable global structures at the initial stage. Furthermore, we introduce a Redundant Structure Elimination loss to alleviate the ill-posed generation problem derived from heavily partial inputs. Comprehensive experimental results demonstrate the superiority of our SAPCNet in recovering the global structure and fine shape details over state-of-the-art point cloud completion methods.

References

1. Chang, A.X., et al.: ShapeNet: an information-rich 3D model repository. arXiv preprint arXiv:1512.03012 (2015)
2. Groueix, T., Fisher, M., Kim, V.G., Russell, B.C., Aubry, M.: A papier-mâché approach to learning 3D surface generation. In: Proceedings of the IEEE/CVF Conference on Computer Vision and Pattern Recognition, pp. 216–224 (2018)
3. Guo, M.H., Cai, J.X., Liu, Z.N., Mu, T.J., Martin, R.R., Hu, S.M.: PCT: point cloud transformer. Comput. Visual Media **7**, 187–199 (2021)
4. Huang, Z., Yu, Y., Xu, J., Ni, F., Le, X.: PF-net: point fractal network for 3D point cloud completion. In: Proceedings of the IEEE/CVF Conference on Computer Vision and Pattern Recognition, pp. 7662–7670 (2020)
5. Liu, M., Sheng, L., Yang, S., Shao, J., Hu, S.M.: Morphing and sampling network for dense point cloud completion. In: Proceedings of the AAAI Conference on Artificial Intelligence, vol. 34, pp. 11596–11603 (2020)
6. Qi, C.R., Yi, L., Su, H., Guibas, L.J.: PointNet++: deep hierarchical feature learning on point sets in a metric space. arXiv preprint arXiv:1706.02413 (2017)
7. Tchapmi, L.P., Kosaraju, V., Rezatofighi, S.H., Reid, I., Savarese, S.: TopNet: structural point cloud decoder. In: Proceedings of the IEEE/CVF International Conference on Computer Vision (2019)
8. Vaswani, A., et al.: Attention is all you need. In: Advances in Neural Information Processing Systems, vol. 30 (2017)
9. Wang, X., M.H.A.J., Lee, G.H.: Cascaded refinement network for point cloud completion. In: Proceedings of the IEEE/CVF Conference on Computer Vision and Pattern Recognition, June 2020
10. Wang, X., Ang, M.H., Lee, G.H.: Voxel-based network for shape completion by leveraging edge generation. In: Proceedings of the IEEE/CVF International Conference on Computer Vision, pp. 13189–13198 (2021)
11. Wen, X., Han, Z., Cao, Y.P., Wan, P., Zheng, W., Liu, Y.S.: Cycle4Completion: unpaired point cloud completion using cycle transformation with missing region coding. In: Proceedings of the IEEE/CVF Conference on Computer Vision and Pattern Recognition, pp. 13075–13084 (2021)
12. Wen, X., Li, T., Han, Z., Liu, Y.S.: Point cloud completion by skip-attention network with hierarchical folding. In: Proceedings of the IEEE/CVF Conference on Computer Vision and Pattern Recognition, pp. 1939–1948 (2020)
13. Wen, X., et al.: PMP-net: point cloud completion by learning multi-step point moving paths. In: Proceedings of the IEEE/CVF Conference on Computer Vision and Pattern Recognition, pp. 7443–7452 (2021)
14. Xiang, P., et al.: SnowflakeNet: point cloud completion by snowflake point deconvolution with skip-transformer. In: Proceedings of the IEEE/CVF International Conference on Computer Vision, pp. 5499–5509 (October 2021)

15. Xie, H., Yao, H., Zhou, S., Mao, J., Zhang, S., Sun, W.: GRNet: gridding residual network for dense point cloud completion. In: Vedaldi, A., Bischof, H., Brox, T., Frahm, J.-M. (eds.) ECCV 2020. LNCS, vol. 12354, pp. 365–381. Springer, Cham (2020). https://doi.org/10.1007/978-3-030-58545-7_21

16. Yang, Y., Feng, C., Shen, Y., Tian, D.: FoldingNet: point cloud auto-encoder via deep grid deformation. In: Proceedings of the IEEE/CVF Conference on Computer Vision and Pattern Recognition, pp. 206–215 (2018)

17. Yu, X., Rao, Y., Wang, Z., Liu, Z., Lu, J., Zhou, J.: PoinTr: diverse point cloud completion with geometry-aware transformers. In: Proceedings of the IEEE/CVF International Conference on Computer Vision, pp. 12498–12507 (2021)

18. Yuan, W., Khot, T., Held, D., Mertz, C., Hebert, M.: PCN: point completion network. In: 3D Vision (3DV) (2018)

19. Zhang, W., Yan, Q., Xiao, C.: Detail preserved point cloud completion via separated feature aggregation. In: Vedaldi, A., Bischof, H., Brox, T., Frahm, J.-M. (eds.) ECCV 2020. LNCS, vol. 12370, pp. 512–528. Springer, Cham (2020). https://doi.org/10.1007/978-3-030-58595-2_31

20. Zhao, H., Jiang, L., Jia, J., Torr, P.H., Koltun, V.: Point transformer. In: Proceedings of the IEEE/CVF International Conference on Computer Vision, pp. 16259–16268 (2021)

21. Zhou, H., et al.: SeedFormer: patch seeds based point cloud completion with upsample transformer. In: Avidan, S., Brostow, G., Cissé, M., Farinella, G.M., Hassner, T. (eds.) ECCV 2022. LNCS, vol. 13663, pp. 416–432. Springer, Cham (2022). https://doi.org/10.1007/978-3-031-20062-5_24

Foreign Object Detection Based on Compositional Scene Modeling

Bingfei Fu[1], Lin Zhu[2], and Xiangyang Xue[1(✉)]

[1] Fudan University, Shanghai, China
{18110240021,xyxyue}@fudan.edu.cn
[2] Lenovo Research, Beijing, China
zhulin4@lenovo.com

Abstract. We are dedicated to researching the problem of foreign object detection in industrial production. Due to dynamic interference such as occlusion, lighting, and color difference in scenes in industrial production, it is difficult for many anomaly detection methods to maintain high performance. We propose a foreign object detection method based on compositional scene modeling, which includes a background denoising module and a foreground reconstruction module. In the background denoising module, we model dynamic disturbances in the scene into the background representation via a deep generative model. In the foreground reconstruction module, we use an autoencoder to learn abnormal foreground representations to achieve foreign object detection. To verify the effectiveness of our method, we simulate an industrial production environment and construct a synthetic dataset in a circuit board assembly scenario. Experiments show that our proposed architecture has good performance on both synthetic dataset and real dataset. While maintaining a low false detection rate, all abnormal objects are detected, with a miss detection rate of 0% in real dataset.

Keywords: foreign object detection · abnormal detection · compositional scene modeling

1 Introduction

Foreign object detection is a crucial task in the realm of computer vision with numerous real-world applications such as foreign object debris detection [1–5], video surveillance [6], and medical diagnosis [7–9]. It involves detecting and localizing abnormal objects within an image, and serves as an essential component of abnormal detection. While anomaly detection aims to identify whether there is any abnormality in the entire image, foreign object detection specifically targets the detection and positioning of anomalous objects within the image. Detecting foreign objects in real-world scenarios is a complex task due to the inherent complexities present in visual data, such as variations in illumination, pixel-level noise, and a wide range of potential interferences like occlusion and deformation. Achieving a balance between accuracy and generalization is crucial for developing effective foreign object detection models. Such models can significantly impact industrial and medical diagnostics, improving their efficiency and practical applications.

© The Author(s), under exclusive license to Springer Nature Switzerland AG 2023
H. Lu et al. (Eds.): ICIG 2023, LNCS 14357, pp. 186–198, 2023.
https://doi.org/10.1007/978-3-031-46311-2_16

Due to the conceptual relationship between foreign object detection and anomaly detection, most anomaly detection methods apply to foreign object detection studies. Anomaly detection approaches based on deep learning can be broadly categorized into pre-trained-based methods and generative model-based methods. Pre-trained-based methods involve training a feature extractor on large datasets and using these features to discriminate between anomalous and normal samples. This approach aims to further enhance the feature differences between anomalous and normal samples to achieve anomaly detection. On the other hand, generative model-based methods use autoencoder or GAN networks to reconstruct anomalous regions into normal regions and perform anomaly detection using the segmentation results.

However, in real-world scenarios, pre-training-based anomaly detection methods face challenges in maintaining high performance when dealing with significant differences in data distribution, while deep generative model-based methods may struggle to produce accurate reconstruction results in the presence of complex scenes.

Our method develops a foreign object detection method based on compositional scene modeling for the problem of foreign object detection in realistic scenes. The method consists of two modules: Background Denoising Module (BDM) and Foreground Reconstruction Module (FRM). BDM encodes the input image and reconstructs the areas of the image that may have anomalies into normal areas to obtain a reconstructed background image. FRM encodes the anomalous regions of the image to learn the latent representations (appearance, shape, location, and prediction) of multiple anomalous objects through slot-attention [10] and reconstructs the entire image through compositional scene modeling.

The main contributions of this paper are as follows:

(1) This paper addresses the need for foreign object detection in industrial production, and this paper proposes a foreign object detection method based on compositional scene modeling, which aims to detect anomalous objects in realistic scenes without annotation information.

(2) This method comprises two key components: Background Denoising Module (BDM) and Foreground Reconstruction Module (FRM). The primary function of BDM is to reconstruct a background image free from anomalous objects. On the other hand, FRM is responsible for learning the representation of anomalous objects and detecting them.

(3) This paper designs a synthetic dataset that is specifically designed for foreign object detection. The aim of the dataset is to simulate the open scene problem in industrial production settings. we use this synthetic dataset to train and evaluate our foreign object detection model.

The remainder of the paper is structured as follows: Sect. 2 describes recent research related to our method. Section 3 describes in detail the structure of our model. Section 4 shows the experimental setup, dataset, experimental results, and analysis related to the experiments. The fifth section provides a concluding summary and outlook.

2　Related work

2.1　Anomaly Detection Based on Deep Learning

Anomaly detection based on deep learning methods can be broadly divided into two paradigms: methods based on deep pre-trained models and methods based on generative models. Pre-trained model-based approaches [11–16] mostly train to obtain feature extractors through large datasets and then process anomalous sample features and normal sample features to achieve anomaly detection. SPADE [11] combines multi-scale feature pyramids to achieve anomaly detection by aligning sample features at different resolutions. CFLOW-AD [15] used a multi-scale pyramid structure to obtain global and local semantic information for anomaly detection through conditional normalizing flows. In addition to post-processing the features, [14, 17–19] performed knowledge distillation on pre-trained models to estimate anomalies by comparing differences in anomalous region features between teacher and student networks. In addition, Cutpaste [16] uses a data enhancement strategy to cut and paste image patches at random locations in the image to learn anomaly representations in a self-supervised manner.

Generative model-based methods typically encode images into low-dimensional representations to describe the distribution of observations, by which we can distinguish the normal and abnormal data. Based on the Variational AutoEncoder (VAE) model, Dehaene et al. [20] used gradient descent to project the energy function by the autoencoder, projecting the samples onto the data stream learned by the autoencoder and iteratively reconstructing the normal samples. Dehaene et al. [21] used VAE to reconstruct normal samples with different feature dimensions and detected abnormalities by deviations from normal samples. Hou et al. [22] also modeled normal samples by VAEs, while building a multi-scale memory module to store features of different resolutions and introducing adversarial learning to improve anomaly detection performance. Recently, some GAN-based generative models [23–25] emerged, which compare input images with the normal images generated in the generative network. The presence or absence of anomalies is assessed by discriminating the network.

As can be seen, the generative model-based approach is less dependent on the dataset than the pre-trained model-based approach and has a greater advantage when faced with realistic scenarios. Therefore, this paper investigates the problem of foreign object detection for circuit board assembly in industrial production along the lines of generative model-based approaches.

2.2　Compositional Scene Modeling with Object-Centric Representations

The core idea of the object-centric representation approach is that a visual scene image can be modeled as a composition of multiple objects. By learning the representation of each object in the visual scene, a representation of the whole visual scene can be obtained. Most existing object-centric representation learning methods use spatial mixture models or weighted summation methods to model visual scenes [10, 26–28]. CST-VAE [26] and AIR [27] use an attention mechanism to extract the representation of each object in the image in turn. Slot-Attention [10] initialize the representations of all objects and then perform iterative updates of the representations through a competition mechanism.

Our approach follows the idea of compositional scene modeling and draws on GMIOO's approach of modeling background and foreground separately, combined with generative model-based anomaly detection methods, to design a Foreign Object Detection method based on Compositional Scene Modeling (FOD-CSM).

3 Method

3.1 GMIOO

GMIOO [28] learns potential representations of multiple objects in an image in an unsupervised scenario, decouples properties such as location, shape, and appearance, and implements recombination of multiple objects and compositional modeling of the whole image. GMIOO firstly inputs image x into the background encoder to obtain the reconstructed background $\hat{x}^{bck}$, and then inputs image x, reconstructed background $\hat{x}^{bck}$ and initial mask into the foreground encoder, decoupling the potential representation of foreground objects into three latent variables (shape, appearance, and prediction), while inferring the overlapping occlusion problem that exists for multiple foreground objects, and finally reconstructing multiple foreground objects through the foreground decoder to achieve the compositional reconstruction of the whole image in unsupervised scenes.

GMIOO processes an image through background and foreground pathways separately. The former consists of a Long Short-Term Memory (LSTM) network and a multi-layer convolutional network, which encodes the input image x to obtain the reconstructed background $\hat{x}^{bck}$. The latter consists of Spatial Transformation Network and the Encoder and Decoder for foreground objects, which encodes the input image x to obtain the appearance, shape and prediction representations $(\hat{x}^{apc}_{1:K}, \hat{x}^{shp}_{1:K}, \hat{x}^{pre}_{1:K})$ of foreground objects and the final reconstructed image $\hat{x}$.

3.2 Foreign Object Detection Based on Compositional Scene Modeling (FOD-CSM)

Our method, based on GMIOO [28], proposes a deep learning model based on compositional scene modeling (shown in Fig. 1), which can be applied in realistic scenes. The model consists of two main modules: Background Denoising Module (BDM) and Foreground Reconstruction Module (FRM). In BDM, we treat the possible anomalous foreground as "noise" and encode the input image to remove the "noise", thus reconstructing a clean background image. In FRM, we take the reconstructed background and the original image as input, encode the image into latent variables using compositional modeling, and determine whether abnormal foregrounds exist in the image by sampling latent variables. After that, we use the decoder to reconstruct abnormal foregrounds and detect anomalies.

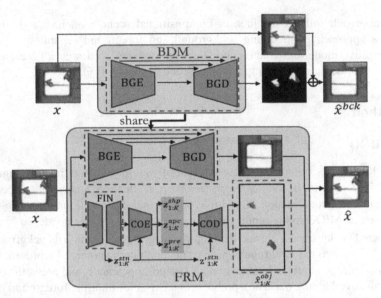

Fig. 1. The overall framework of FOD-CSM

3.3 Background Denoising Module (BDM)

BDM uses U-net-like structure, consisting of BackGround Encoder (BGE) and Back-Ground Decoder (BGD). The input image x is passed through BDM to obtain a clean background $\hat{x}^{bck}$.

(1) BGE: To encode the input image x, BGE uses multi-layer convolution layer to perform a non-linear transformation of the image, which consists of 2d convolution layer (Conv2d), normalization layer (Norm) and Rectified Layer Units (ReLU), as follows:

$$z^{bck} = f_{enc}^{bck}(x)$$

where x is input image, z^{bck} is the background latent variable obtained by BGE.

(2) BGD: After obtaining z^{bck}, we use BGD to gain the background image without anomalous objects. BGD consists of interpolate and skip-connect to restore the background latent variable to the dimensions of the original image and outputs the reconstructed representation $\tilde{x}$ and the reconstructed region $\tilde{x}^{mask}$, which is:

$$\tilde{x}, \tilde{x}^{mask} = f_{dec}^{bck}(z^{bck})$$

The reconstructed background $\hat{x}^{bck}$ that contains no anomalous foreground can be calculated by $\tilde{x}$ and $\tilde{x}^{mask}$, which as follows:

$$\hat{x}^{bck} = \tilde{x} \times \tilde{x}^{mask} + x \times \left(1 - \tilde{x}^{mask}\right)$$

BDM is based on the reconstruction method to generate the background $\hat{x}^{bck}$, but occlusion, noise, reflection, and deformation commonly exist in natural scenes. To gain better reconstruction results, the model increases the reconstruction area $\tilde{x}^{mask}$. However, larger reconstruction area makes it more difficult for the model to learn possible anomalous foregrounds during the foreground reconstruction phase. Thus, we redesigned the loss function of BDM, which is shown below:

$$L_{BGD} = L_{bck} + \alpha_1 L_{area}$$

$$L_{bck} = \|x, \hat{x}^{bck}\|^2,$$

$L_{area} = argmin(S_{recon}^{bck})$, where S_{recon}^{bck} is the activation area of $\tilde{x}^{mask}$

As can be seen, L_{area} allows the model to focus on reconstructing potentially anomalous background regions by constraining the activation area of the reconstructed region $\tilde{x}^{mask}$. L_{bck} achieves an overall constraint on the image through pixel-level reconstruction, allowing the model to have a better reconstruction effect while having a better generalization performance to real scenes.

3.4 Foreground Reconstruction Module (FRM)

FRM consists of the Full Image Network (FIN), Spatial Transformation Network (STN), Crop Object Encoder (COE) and Crop Object Decoder (COE). The image x, the reconstructed background $\hat{x}^{bck}$ and the initial mask $\tilde{x}^{mask}$ are fed into FRM to obtain the appearance, shape and anomaly prediction representations of foreground objects $\left\{\hat{x}_{1:K}^{apc}, \hat{x}_{1:K}^{shp}, \hat{x}_{1:K}^{pre}\right\}$. With these three representations, the reconstructing foreground object $\hat{x}_k^{obj}$ is as follows:

$$\hat{x}_k^{obj} = \hat{x}_k^{apc} \times \hat{x}_k^{shp} \times \hat{x}_k^{pre}$$

Similarly, the final reconstructed image $\hat{x}$ is represented as:

$$\hat{x} = \hat{x}^{bck} \times \left(1 - \sum_{k=1}^{K} \hat{x}_k^{shp} \hat{x}_k^{pre}\right) + \sum_{k=1}^{K} \hat{x}_k^{obj}$$

Typically, when using a generative model, the loss function only considers the reconstruction loss of the entire image. However, in the case of FRM, the background pathway parameters are initialized from the well-performing BDM. To improve the model's ability to learn the representation of foreground objects, we calculate separate foreground and background losses for the FRM, which is shown as follows:

$$L_{recon} = L_{image} + \alpha_2 L_{local}$$

$$L_{image} = \|x, \hat{x}\|^2$$

$$L_{local} = \sum_{k=1}^{K} \|x_k^{crop}, \hat{x}_k^{apc} \times \hat{x}_k^{shp} \times \hat{x}_k^{pre}\|^2$$

By leveraging L_{local}, FRM can apply additional constraints directly to foreground objects, resulting in more precise reconstructions. Furthermore, when combined with L_{image}, FRM can effectively reconstruct both foreground objects and the background image, yielding impressive results.

4 Experiments

4.1 Dataset dDefinition and Evaluation Methods

Dataset Definition. Real-world scenes are subject to interferences such as lighting, obstructions and noise, which cannot be covered all in closed sets. To simulate this issue, we randomly selected 6–10 images for each scene through 5507 pictures (including 9 abnormal scenes) provided by Lenovo. Then we combined the randomly selected data with 17 abnormal prospects through data synthesis to construct the training dataset and the validation dataset. The remaining images have been designated as the test dataset. The specific synthesis process and rules are shown in the Fig. 2:

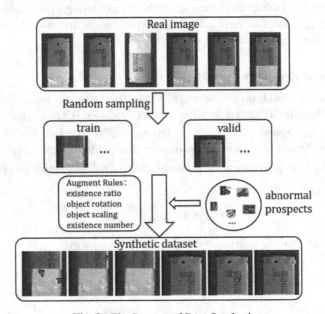

Fig. 2. The Process of Data Synthesis

The rules for data synthesis include the number of abnormal prospects, rotation angles, and scale et al. 20,000 synthetic images were generated, with a train-to-test dataset ratio of 5:5.

Evaluation Methods. The evaluation metrics for foreign object detection in this paper are based on the classification confusion matrix for anomaly detection (shown in Table 1), using the miss and false detection rates of greater interest to the industry.

Miss Detection Rate (MDR): reflects the proportion of abnormal samples that are detected as normal among abnormal samples, can be calculated as follows

$$MDR = \frac{FP}{FP + TN}$$

False Detection Rate (FDR): reflects the proportion of false detected samples in total samples, can be calculated as follows:

$$FDR = \frac{FP + FN}{TP + FP + FP + TN}$$

Table 1. The classification confusion matrix for anomaly detection

True category	Detection normal	Detection abnormal
normal	TP	FN
abnormal	FP	TN

4.2 Experimental Parameters

Experimental Environment. This experiment is based on the Ubuntu environment, using the Python language, and the model is built in the Linux environment. The main hardware parameters of the platform are CPU with Intel Xeon E5–2603, 16G memory, GPU with GTX 1080 with 11G memory.

Training Parameters. The model is trained in two stages, background denoising and foreground reconstruction, with the training parameters set as shown in Table 2:

Table 2. The parameters of training

True category	Iteration	Batch size	K	α_1	α_2
background denoising	10000	128	2	5	-
foreground reconstruction	12000	128	2	-	5

Network Structure. The model is divided into BDM and FRM, each with the network structure shown in Table 3 and Table 4:

Table 3. The neural network structure of BDM

Module Name	network structure
BGE	4 × convolution layer (Conv2d, Norm, ReLU)
BGD	4 × (interpolate + skip-connect)

Table 4. The neural network structure of FRM

Module Name	network structure
FIN	LSTM + LinearBlock(Linear layer + LinearNorm)
COE	LSTM + LinearBlock(Linear layer + LinearNorm)
COD	4 × (interpolate + convolution layer)
	4 × LinearBlock(Linear layer + LinearNorm)

4.3 Experiment results

Experiments for Background Denoising. Figure 3 shows the denoising effect of the background denoising module on the test set (images never seen during the training phase). The first column of the figure represents the original input images and the second column represents the locally reconstructed images that may have been noisy. It is noteworthy that the model is able to effectively denoise the images while using only 6–10 real images per scene as the training set. These results demonstrate the model's good robustness and generalization in the background denoising stage.

After adding L_{area} to the background denoising stage, the model's reconstruction loss for the whole image is reduced from 25.83 to 3.62, which indicates that L_{area} can better assist the model in achieving a clean background reconstruction.

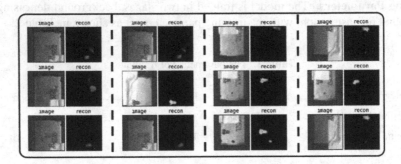

Fig. 3. The origin image and the reconstructed area of BDM

Experiments for Foreground Reconstruction. Figure 4 shows the foreign object detection performance of the foreground reconstruction module for nine different scenarios on the synthetic and real dataset. As can be seen, our model maintains strong detection performance on the previously unseen real dataset.

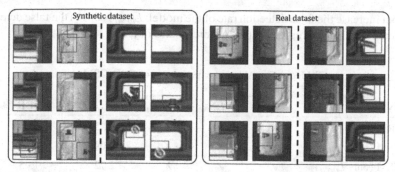

Fig. 4. The foreign object detection results in Synthetic dataset and Real dataset

Table 5 shows the foreign object detection results for nine different scenarios. It can be seen that the model has a 0% missed detection rate and a 4.55% false detection rate in the nine scenes. The false detection rate of 4.55% indicates that the model identified all the anomalous objects in the nine scenes without supervised information. Although the overall false detection rate of the model is 4.55%, the missed detection rate is more critical for foreign object detection. A relatively high false detection rate is acceptable when the missed detection rate is guaranteed to be 0.

Moreover, we compare FOD-CSM with Padim [12] and GANomaly [23]. In order to ensure the effect of existing works, we use some real data to train the two models, but the experimental results show that the MDR of Padim is 18.4%, and the MDR of GANomaly is 13.2%, both of which are higher than the method proposed in this paper. These methods are difficult to accurately distinguish the difference between normal samples and abnormal samples when faced with small abnormal objects.

Table 5. The performance of FOD-CSM method

	scene 1 (%)	scene 2 (%)	scene 3(%)	scene 4 (%)	scene 5 (%)	scene 6 (%)	scene 7 (%)	scene 8 (%)	scene 9 (%)	**Total**
MDR	0	0	0	0	0	0	0	0	0	0
FDR	1.2	12.8	5.9	2.4	3.1	3.4	3.1	0	6.9	4.55

Ablation Experiments. To verify the effectiveness of different modules in the model, a multi-stage ablation experiment has been performed:

(1) FOD-FRM: represents the model only with FRM.
(2) FOD-CSM (no extra loss): represents the model without additional constraints.
(3) FOD-CSM (only L_{area}): represents the model only has L_{area} constraints.
(4) FOD-CSM: represents the final model.

As can be seen from the ablation experiment (Table 6), BDM can greatly increase the performance of the model. L_{area} can significantly reduce the miss detection rate of the model but increase the false detection rate of the model. L_{local} reduces the false detection rate by constraining the representation of foreground objects.

Table 6. The Ablation experiments of FOD-CSM

Model Name	BDM	L_{area}	L_{local}	MDR (%)	FDR (%)
FOD-FRM	✗	✗	✗	21.54	35.62
FOD-CSM (no extra loss)	✓	✗	✗	9.09	2.17
FOD-CSM (only L_{area})	✓	✓	✗	2.72	13.5
FOD-CSM	✓	✓	✓	0	4.55

Effect of Data Augmentation on Experiments. Table 7 shows that, when adding rotation to the foreground object in data augmentation, the performance of FOD-CSM improves; when rotating the background, the performance of FOD-CSM decreases. This indicates that anomaly detection methods based on compositional modeling have poor performance in the face of drastic environmental changes.

Table 7. The effect of Data Augmentation on results

Model	foreground rotation	background rotation	MDR (%)	FDR (%)
FOD-CSM	✗	✗	0	5.87
FOD-CSM	✓	✗	0	4.55
FOD-CSM	✓	✓	5.68	8.79

5 Conclusion

In this paper, we propose a foreign object detection framework based on compositional scene modeling. The method is divided into two modules: background denoising and foreground reconstruction. The background denoising module focuses on reconstructing background while the foreground reconstruction module focuses on learning abnormal foreground representations. Experimental results show that the model is suitable for foreign object detection without large number of manual annotations. Therefore, our FOD-CSM can cope with foreign object detection tasks in actual industrial production.

References

1. Noroozi, M., Shah, A.: Towards optimal foreign object debris detection in an airport environment. Expert Syst. Appl. **213**, 118829 (2023)

2. Jing, Y., Zheng, H., Zheng, W., Dong, K.: A pixel-wise foreign object debris detection method based on multi-scale feature inpainting. Aerospace **9**(9), 480 (2022)

3. Munyer, T., Brinkman, D., Zhong, X., Huang, C., Konstantzos, I.: Foreign Object Debris Detection for Airport Pavement Images based on Self-supervised Localization and Vision Transformer. arXiv preprint arXiv:2210.16901 (2022)

4. Liu, J., Lu, Y.L: A lightweight foreign object debris detection algorithm for airport runway. In: Proceedings of the 5th International Conference on Computer Science and Software Engineering (2022)

5. Duygu, K.A.Y.A.: Examining the effect of different networks on foreign object debris detection. Bitlis Eren Üniversitesi Fen Bilimleri Dergisi **12**(1), 151–157 (2023)

6. Nawaratne, R., Alahakoon, D., De Silva, D., Yu, X.: Spatiotemporal anomaly detection using deep learning for real-time video surveillance. IEEE Trans. Industr. Inf. **16**(1), 393–402 (2019)

7. Baur, C., Wiestler, B., Albarqouni, S., Navab, N.: Deep autoencoding models for unsupervised anomaly segmentation in brain MR images. In: Crimi, A., Bakas, S., Kuijf, H., Keyvan, F., Reyes, M., van Walsum, T. (eds.) Brainlesion: Glioma, Multiple Sclerosis, Stroke and Traumatic Brain. LNCS, vol. 11383, pp. 161–169. Springer, Cham (2019). https://doi.org/10.1007/978-3-030-11723-8_16

8. Zhao, C., Yao, X.: Progressive line processing of global and local real-time anomaly detection in hyperspectral images. J. Real-Time Image Proc. **16**, 2289–2303 (2019)

9. Wyatt, J., Leach, A., Schmon, S.M., Willcocks, C.G.: AnoDDPM: anomaly detection with denoising diffusion probabilistic models using simplex noise. In: Proceedings of the IEEE/CVF Conference on Computer Vision and Pattern Recognition (2022)

10. Locatello, F., et al.: Object-centric learning with slot attention. Adv. Neural Inf. Process. Syst. **33**, 11525–11538 (2020)

11. Cohen, N., Hoshen, Y.: Sub-image anomaly detection with deep pyramid correspondences. arXiv preprint arXiv:2005.02357 (2020)

12. Defard, T., Setkov, A., Loesch, A., Audigier, R.: Padim: a patch distribution modeling framework for anomaly detection and localization. In: Del Bimbo, A., et al. (eds.) Pattern Recognition. ICPR International Workshops and Challenges. LNCS, vol. 12664, pp. 475–489. Springer, Cham (2021). https://doi.org/10.1007/978-3-030-68799-1_35

13. Roth, K., Pemula, L., Zepeda, J., Schölkopf, B., Brox, T., Gehler, P.: Towards total recall in industrial anomaly detection. In: Proceedings of the IEEE/CVF Conference on Computer Vision and Pattern Recognition, pp. 14318–14328 (2022)

14. Deng, H., Li, X.: Anomaly detection via reverse distillation from one-class embedding. In: Proceedings of the IEEE/CVF Conference on Computer Vision and Pattern Recognition (2022)

15. Gudovskiy, D., Ishizaka, S., Kozuka, K.: CFLOW-AD: real-time unsupervised anomaly detection with localization via conditional normalizing flows. In: Proceedings of the IEEE/CVF Winter Conference on Applications of Computer Vision (2022)

16. Li, C. L., Sohn, K., Yoon, J., Pfister, T.: CutPaste: self-supervised learning for anomaly detection and localization. In: Proceedings of the IEEE/CVF Conference on Computer Vision and Pattern Recognition, pp. 9664–9674 (2021)

17. Bergmann, P., Fauser, M., Sattlegger, D., Steger, C.: Uninformed students: student-teacher anomaly detection with discriminative latent embeddings. In: Proceedings of the IEEE/CVF Conference on Computer Vision and Pattern Recognition (2020)

18. Salehi, M., Sadjadi, N., Baselizadeh, S., Rohban, M.H., Rabiee, H.R.: Multiresolution knowledge distillation for anomaly detection. In: Proceedings of the IEEE/CVF Conference on Computer Vision and Pattern Recognition (2021)

19. Wang, G., Han, S., Ding, E., Huang, D.: Student-teacher feature pyramid matching for anomaly detection. arXiv preprint arXiv:2103.04257 (2021)

20. Dehaene, D., Frigo, O., Combrexelle, S., Eline, P.: Iterative energy-based projection on a normal data manifold for anomaly localization. arXiv preprint arXiv:2002.03734 (2020)
21. Dehaene, D., Eline, P.: Anomaly localization by modeling perceptual features. arXiv preprint arXiv:2008.05369 (2020)
22. Hou, J., Zhang, Y., Zhong, Q., Xie, D., Pu, S., Zhou, H.: Divide-and-assemble: Learning block-wise memory for unsupervised anomaly detection. In: Proceedings of the IEEE/CVF International Conference on Computer Vision (2021)
23. Akcay, S., Atapour-Abarghouei, A., Breckon, T.P.: Ganomaly: Semi-supervised anomaly detection via adversarial training. In: Jawahar, C.V., Li, H., Mori, G., Schindler, K. (eds.) Computer Vision – ACCV 2018. LNCS, vol. 11363, pp. 622–637. Springer, Cham (2019). https://doi.org/10.1007/978-3-030-20893-6_39
24. Gong, D., et al.: Memorizing normality to detect anomaly: Memory-augmented deep autoencoder for unsupervised anomaly detection. In: Proceedings of the IEEE/CVF International Conference on Computer Vision (2019)
25. Schlegl, T., Seeböck, P., Waldstein, S.M., Schmidt-Erfurth, U., Langs, G.: Unsupervised anomaly detection with generative adversarial networks to guide marker discovery. In: Niethammer, M., et al. (eds.) Information Processing in Medical Imaging. LNCS, vol. 10265, pp. 146–157. Springer, Cham (2017). https://doi.org/10.1007/978-3-319-59050-9_12
26. Huang, J., Murphy, K.: Efficient inference in occlusion-aware generative models of images. arXiv preprint arXiv:1511.06362 (2015)
27. Eslami, S.M., Heess, N., Weber, T., Tassa, Y., Szepesvari, D., Hinton, G.E.: Attend, infer, repeat: Fast scene understanding with generative models. In: Advances in Neural Information Processing Systems, vol. 29 (2016)
28. Yuan, J., Li, B., Xue, X.: Generative modeling of infinite occluded objects for compositional scene representation. In: International Conference on Machine Learning, pp. 7222–7231. PMLR (2019)

Computer Graphics and Visualization

Geometric Encoding-Based Attention Mechanism for Point Cloud Registration Network

Xuheng Liu⬤, Zhengyao Bai⁽✉⁾⬤, Jiajin Du⬤, Yihan Zhang⬤, and Zekai Li⬤

School of Information Science and Engineering, Yunnan University, 650050 Kunming, China
liuxuheng@mail.ynu.edu.cn, baizhy@ynu.edu.cn

Abstract. We propose a novel point cloud registration network called GEANet, which overcomes the issues of disregarding point cloud geometry information and inadequate utilization of geometric information by utilizing an attention mechanism-based approach and point cloud geometry encoding. Our approach starts by extracting point cloud features using Graph Neural Network (GNN) and feeding them into a point cloud geometry encoder to obtain geometric encoding. The encoding is then jointly input into the attention mechanism for feature interaction. Next, virtual point pairs and weight values are obtained by jointly calculating the point cloud features and point cloud spatial information features, such as Euclidean distance and direction vectors, and the required rigid transformation is solved through SVD. Our experimental results on the ModelNet40 dataset, including unseen point clouds, unseen point cloud categories, and Gaussian noise, demonstrate that the MSE for rotation matrices were reduced to 1.97, 1.68, and 3.70, and for translation to 0.015, 0.013, and 0.018. The findings suggest that our GEANet approach achieves higher accuracy and greater robustness than point cloud registration networks that solely rely on Transformer and do not utilize point cloud geometry encoding.

Keywords: Point Cloud Registration · Geometric Encoding · Transformer

1 Introduction

Point cloud, as a type of three-dimensional data in the real world, have diverse representations and wide applications, which offer numerous research directions, such as point cloud registration, point cloud super-resolution, point cloud completion, and point cloud segmentation [1]. This article focuses on the research topic of point cloud registration. Point cloud registration is a critical task in various applications, including 3D reconstruction, augmented reality, and robotics. The acquisition of object point clouds is often plagued by occlusion and uneven sampling, resulting in incomplete data that only represents partial surfaces. Consequently, point cloud registration is required to align these partial point clouds into a common coordinate system by finding the optimal rotation matrix and translation vector. Despite the numerous existing approaches for point cloud registration, many rely on simplistic measures of similarity, such as inner products

© The Author(s), under exclusive license to Springer Nature Switzerland AG 2023
H. Lu et al. (Eds.): ICIG 2023, LNCS 14357, pp. 201–212, 2023.
https://doi.org/10.1007/978-3-031-46311-2_17

or Euclidean distances, which suffer from low accuracy and can be easily influenced by the presence of outliers. Moreover, while the use of Transformers has shown promising results in fusing contextual information in point cloud features, the potential benefits of incorporating geometric information remain largely unexplored.

To address these challenges, Our proposed approach for point cloud registration involves a novel combination of several modules, including geometric encoding, feature extraction, and transformer. Initially, we leverage a GNN [2] to extract independent features of point clouds, followed by a geometry encoder to obtain geometric encodings. To capture contextual information within and between point clouds, we employ a Transformer model. To improve registration efficiency and accuracy, we introduce a key point extraction module to identify salient features, which are represented as a similarity matrix. Subsequently, a 1D CNN is utilized to extract a $N \times N \times 32$ matrix of features, and a confidence calculation module assigns weights to the similarity matrix. The correspondence is represented as a 1D matrix, which is then input into a weighted SVD to calculate R and t. Furthermore, to refine the accuracy of registration, an iterative approach is employed to refine R and t at the key points and solve the transformation matrix again.

Experimental results demonstrate that the proposed method achieves improved registration efficiency and accuracy compared to state-of-the-art methods on benchmark datasets. The proposed method is also robust to noise and outliers.

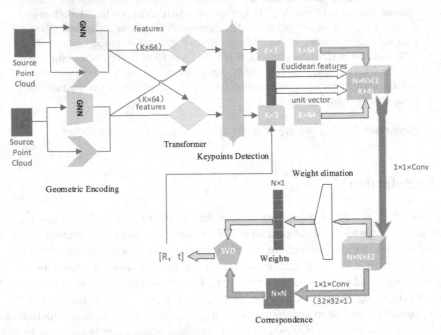

Fig. 1. Diagram of model components.

2 Method

2.1 Geometric Encoding

After extracting point cloud features using Graph Neural Networks (GNNs), the original point cloud is also input into the point cloud geometric encoder to obtain rich geometric information. The model architecture is shown in Fig. 1. Inspired by OGMM [3] and UTOPIC [4], this paper proposes a point cloud geometric encoding gij using the Point-wise Euclidean distance, maximum triplet-wise-angle, and triangle perimeter difference between points and the centroid of the point cloud. $gi, j = CAT[\rho x, c; \alpha c, i; \eta i, j]$. Where CAT[;] represents the concatenation operation. The formula is shown in the Fig. 2, where nc is the centroid of multiple point clouds, calculated by $nc = \sum_{i=1}^{N} ni$.

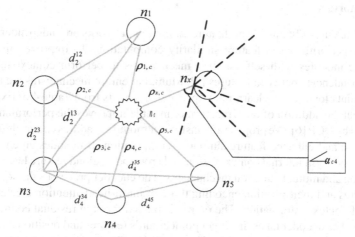

Fig. 2. The encoding of geometric positions in point clouds.

Point-Wise Euclidean Distance. After selecting neighboring points using K-nearest neighbors (KNN) centered at a specific point, the centroid of these points is computed. The distance between each point in the point cloud and the centroid is then calculated by $\|nx - nc\|_2$ and used to extract features through 1D-CNN φ.It can be represented using formula (1).

$$\rho x, c = \varphi(\|nx - nc\|_2) \tag{1}$$

Maximum Triplet-Wise-Angle. To extract features from a point cloud based on triplet-wise angles, we first select a point near the centroid and define it as the reference point "nx". Next, for each point "nx", we calculate the angle "αci" between the vectors "$nx - nc$" and "$nx - ni$". It can be represented using $\angle(nx - nc, nx - ni)$. We repeat this process for all pairs of points and select the maximum angle as the feature "$\max\{\alpha ci\}$". Finally, we use φ to extract features from "$\max\{\alpha ci\}$".It can be represented using formula (2).

$$\alpha ci = \varphi(\angle(nx - nc, nx - ni)) \tag{2}$$

Triangle Perimeter Difference. The approach involves calculating the perimeter of each triangle and subtracting the length of its sides. we select n1 and n3 as the neighboring points for n2 to form one triangle $(d_2^{12} + d_2^{23} + d_2^{13})$, and n3 and n5 for n4 to form another triangle $(d_4^{34} + d_4^{45} + d_4^{35})$. The distance between n1 and n2 is denoted as d_2^{12} and expressed using $d_2^{12} = \|n1 - n2\|_2$. The edges of the triangle formed by n2 as the vertex and n1, n3 as its edges can be represented using formula $d_2^{12} = \|n1 - n2\|_2$ and expressed as the distance between n1 and n2. The difference between the two triangles is computed using the formula (3).

$$\eta 24 = (d_2^{12} + d_2^{23} + d_2^{13}) - (d_4^{34} + d_4^{45} + d_4^{35}) \tag{3}$$

2.2 Transformer

Point cloud features obtained from feature extraction networks are independent, resulting in poor performance in feature similarity computation. To improve this, we use Transformer modules with self-attention mechanisms to perform context fusion and capture dependencies between features [5]. Mutual attention mechanisms are also used for cross-point cloud feature learning. Experimental results from Table 4 of Experiment 4.3 show that the addition of our Transformer module improves the performance.

Inspired by DCP [6]. We propose a Transformer module to address point cloud feature independence and enhance feature similarity computation. It includes an encoder and decoder that perform internal context fusion and cross-point cloud feature learning using self-attention and mutual attention mechanisms. The encoder processes the source point cloud features and their position encoding through multi-head attention mechanisms to capture self-context information. The output is passed through residual connections to the decoder. The decoder takes the target point cloud's features and position encoding as input, undergoes self-attention again to learn context information between point clouds, and then combines the output with the output of the second multi-head attention mechanism to enable cross-attention between different point clouds. To maintain consistency between input features and output, we add the output of the proposed module to the source point cloud features. The formula for calculation is given as Eq. (4), where Θ_1 is the output of the attention mechanism. Figure 3 depicts the schematic representation of the Transformer.

$$\begin{aligned} \Psi x &= \Phi x + \Theta_1(\Phi_X, \Phi_Y) \\ \Psi y &= \Phi y + \Theta_2(\Phi_Y, \Phi_X) \end{aligned} \tag{4}$$

2.3 Keypoints Extraction

In point cloud registration, reading and registering each point cloud individually can lead to inefficiencies such as longer registration time, higher GPU memory usage, and susceptibility to interference from outliers, ultimately resulting in registration failure. To mitigate these issues, this study proposes a keypoints extraction module that extracts more robust feature representations to improve registration efficiency. The module, illustrated

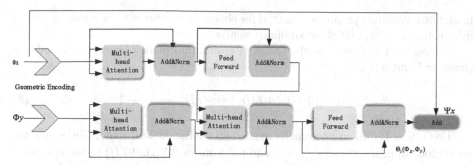

Fig. 3. Diagram illustrating the Transformer architecture.

in Fig. 4, utilizes MLP with fully connected layers and the ReLU activation function, progressively reducing features from 64 dimensions to a one-dimensional importance score. The higher the score, the more representative the point. K points with the highest scores are selected for subsequent processing, and their spatial and feature information is extracted. After the module, the original point cloud and point cloud features are transformed from (N × 3) to (K × 3) and from (N × 64) to (K × 64), represented $\Phi S(i)$ as spatial coordinates and represented $\Phi T(j)$ as features. The model diagram is illustrated in Fig. 4.

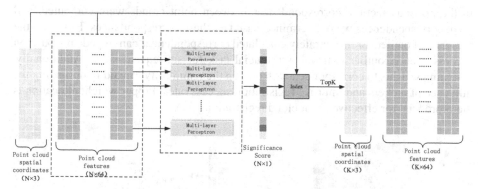

Fig. 4. Schematic Diagram of Key Point Extraction Module

2.4   Correspondence Search

The purpose of this module is to establish correspondences between two point clouds. Conventionally, correspondences are determined by calculating the inner product or Euclidean distance of features. However, this method has two major drawbacks. Firstly, it may lead to issues such as an increased number of outliers and low registration accuracy. Secondly, for specific objects, feature-similar but non-corresponding points may exist within the point cloud, particularly for symmetrical structures. Analyzing only feature similarity may result in confusion between left and right sides. To address these limitations, this study proposes a method for obtaining correspondence based on spatial information using a point cloud similarity matrix.

The matrix T is defined as the fusion of spatial information from point clouds, as shown in formula (5).

$$T[i,j] = [\Phi S(i), \Phi T(j), \|ni - nj\|, \frac{ni - nj}{\|ni - nj\|}] \tag{5}$$

This $(2K + 4)$-dimensional matrix aggregates the Euclidean distances $\|ni - nj\|$, the point cloud direction vectors $\frac{ni-nj}{\|ni-nj\|}$, and the features $\Phi S(i)$, $\Phi T(j)$ of the two point clouds. The 2K-dimensional matrix corresponds to the feature dimensions of the source and target point clouds, while the 4-dimensional matrix represents the Euclidean distance and direction vectors between them. A two-dimensional convolution is used to extract features, resulting in a 1-dimensional matrix denoted as S.. The convolution is implemented using a multi-layer perceptron (MLP) with a network depth of (32,32,32,32,1). The resulting matrix is subjected to a Softmax operation to obtain a probability matrix named $S[i,j]$, referred to as the similarity matrix. The $S[i,j]$ represents the probability that the i-th point in the source point cloud and the j-th point in the target point cloud correspond to each other.

2.5   Correspondences Credibility Computation

In the previous section, correspondences between point clouds were computed, and point correspondences were determined based on these correspondences. However, the presence of outliers or inaccurately calculated correspondences can impede registration success. Hence, outlier removal is a crucial task for subsequent steps. Additionally, assigning weights to correspondences based on their similarity can aid in mitigating the influence of outliers and improve registration success rates. Proper weight allocation is therefore vital for effective point cloud registration.

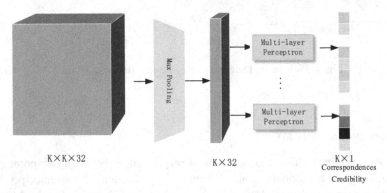

Fig. 5. Schematic Diagram of Confidence Estimation Module

We have proposed a model that incorporates a confidence calculation module to determine the weights of correspondences between point clouds. The model architecture is depicted in Fig. 5. The similarity matrix is first fused into a 32-dimensional vector and then transformed to an M × 1 × 32 matrix through a maximum pooling operation. A fully connected (FC) layer is subsequently applied to produce an M × 1 × 1 matrix, which is normalized to derive weight information denoted as $c(i)$. We calculate the weight information using Eq. 6, where function $[\![c(i) \geq median(c)]\!]$ evaluates whether weights exceed the median score.

$$wi = \frac{c(i) \cdot [\![c(i) \geq median(c)]\!]}{\sum_i c(i) \cdot [\![c(i) \geq median(c)]\!]} \tag{6}$$

After obtaining the weight values for different point pairs, a rigid transformation matrix can be calculated using weighted singular value decomposition (SVD). The specific formula for this calculation is presented in Eq. (7).

$$R, t = \underset{R,t}{\arg\min} \sum_i wi \| RpS(i) + t - pT(j^*) \| \tag{7}$$

2.6 Loss function

The loss function comprises two components: the iterative loss function, which is based on Reference [7], and the registration loss function.

Iterative Loss Function
The iterative loss function consists of three parts: 1) Point Matching Loss, 2) Keypoints Loss, and 3) Credibility Computation Loss.

Point Matching Loss. The point matching loss is shown in Eq. (8).

$$L_{match}(S, T, R^*, t^*) = \frac{1}{M} \sum_{i=1}^{M} -\log(S^{(n)}(i, j^*)) \cdot \left[\left\| R^* pi + t^* - q^i \right\|^2 \leq r^2 \right] \tag{8}$$

where

$$j^* = \underset{1 \leq j \leq M}{\arg\min} \| R^* pi + t^* - qj \|^2$$

the closest point in the target point cloud βT to each point in the source point cloud βS is computed based on the ground truth transformation, using the Euclidean distance $\| \|^2$. The hyper-parameter r is used to determine the minimum radius for correspondence and to exclude points with a distance greater than r from supervision. The point matching loss is the average of all iterations and evaluates the model's performance in matching points between the two point clouds. Minimizing this loss aids in the development of effective point cloud registration features.

Keypoints Loss. This loss is utilized to train Keypoints elimination. The formula is given in Eq. (9).

$$L_{Keypoints}^{(n)}(S, T, R^*, t^*) = \frac{1}{M} \sum_{i=1}^{M} \left| s(i) - \sum_{j=1}^{M} S^{(n)}(i, j) \log(S^{(n)}(i, j)) \right|^2 \tag{9}$$

where s(i) is the significant score for the ith point in βS. We only use this loss for the first iteration, as shape features are more important than Euclidean features early on.

Credibility Computation Loss. To train the hybrid point elimination, a similar mutual supervision idea can be applied [7]. The key difference is that the hybrid elimination takes into account the point pair information, while the hard point elimination only considers individual points. As a result, the mutual supervision signal is much more apparent for hybrid point elimination. The probability that there exists a point in βT which is the correspondence of point pi $\in \beta S$ is used as the supervision signal for the credibility score vi. Instead of explicitly computing the probability, the hybrid elimination loss for the nth iteration is defined as:

$$L_{Credibility}^{(n)}(S, T, R^*, t^*) = \frac{1}{M} \sum_{i=1}^{M} -\prod_i \cdot \log(vi) - (1 - \prod_i) \cdot \log(1 - vi) \tag{10}$$

where $\prod_i$ is defined as:

$$\prod_i = \left[\left[\left\| R^* pi + t^* - q_{\arg \max_j s^{(n)}(i,j)} \right\|^2 \le r^2 \right]\right]$$

In essence, this loss assigns a positive label of 1 to points in βS that correctly match, and a negative label of 0 to those that do not. Subsequently, pairs with high likelihoods of correct matching acquire higher validity scores.

Registration Loss. The second part of the loss function is designed to calculate the discrepancy between the true rigid transformation and the predicted rigid transformation obtained via the neural network, which is called the registration loss function and is represented by Eq. (11).

$$Lregistration = \left\| R_{GT}^T R - I \right\|^2 + \|t_{GT} - t\|^2 \tag{11}$$

3 Experiments

This paper presents an experimental study on point cloud registration using the ModelNet40 dataset [8]. The performance of the proposed GEANet model is compared with several math-based point cloud registration algorithms, including ICP [9], FPFH + RANSAC and Go-ICP [10], as well as end-to-end point cloud registration networks, including PointNetLK [11], DCP,FGR [12],PRNET [13], FPFH + IDAM [7], and GNN + IDAM, all of which were trained and tested using the ModelNet40 dataset. To comprehensively evaluate the performance of GEANet, three experiments were conducted to examine its robustness under various scenarios, including unseen point cloud, unseen point cloud categories, and Gaussian noise. The evaluation metrics used in this study include the root mean square error (RMSE) and the mean absolute error (MAE).The results demonstrate that GEANet outperforms the other algorithms in terms of registration accuracy and efficiency. The experiments in this study were conducted on a server equipped with a GeForce GTX 3090 GPU, using the Pytorch framework. ADAM optimizer was employed with specific experimental parameters, including a learning rate of 0.0001, decay rate of 0.0001, and a drop-out rate of 0.5.

3.1   Unseen Shapes

In the point cloud unseen Shape experiment, the model was evaluated on the complete official training/test set. 9843 data points were used for training the network, and 2468 data points were used for testing. GEANet was compared with multiple models, and the experimental results are shown in Table 1. The registration result was visualized using the Open3D [14] library, as shown in Fig. 6. To demonstrate the effectiveness of point cloud geometry encoding design in reducing the difficulty of registering symmetric point clouds, we choose to present registration results of symmetric point clouds. As the data preprocessing method was the same as reference 15, the experimental data of the other models in the table were also obtained from reference 15. The model exhibited improvement in RMSE metrics with reduced errors of 15.46% and 6.25%.

Table 1. Results on unseen point cloud.

Model	RMSE(R)	MAE(R)	RMSE(t)	MAE(t)
ICP	33.68	25.05	0.29	0.25
FPFH + RANSAC	2.33	1.96	0.015	0.013
FGR	11.24	2.83	0.030	0.008
GO-ICP	14.0	3.17	0.033	0.012
PointNetLK	16.74	7.55	0.045	0.025
DCP	6.71	4.45	0.027	0.020
PRNet	3.20	1.45	0.016	0.010
FPFH + IDAM	2.46	**0.56**	0.016	**0.003**
GNN + IDAM	2.95	0.76	0.021	0.005
Ours	**1.97**	0.62	**0.015**	0.004

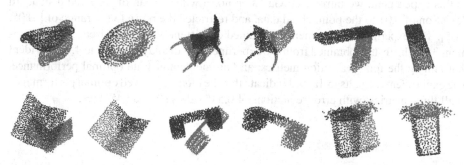

Fig. 6. Illustration of the experimental results on the ModelNet40 dataset, depicting the effects of registration on point cloud for 6 distinct object categories

3.2 Unseen Categories

Our second experiment focused on training the model using the first 20 categories in the ModelNet40 training set and evaluating it on the test set's remaining 20 categories. This test was designed to assess the model's ability to generalize to point clouds of unseen categories. The experimental findings are presented in Table 2. The results in Table 2 show that all four indicators are at their optimal values, with error values decreasing by 20.38%, 6.56%, 13.33%, and 25%.

Table 2. Results on unseen categories.

Model	RMSE(R)	MAE(R)	RMSE(t)	MAE(t)
ICP	34.89	25.46	0.29	0.25
FPFH + RANSAC	2.11	1.82	0.015	0.013
FGR	9.93	1.95	0.038	0.007
GO-ICP	12.53	2.94	0.031	0.010
PointNetLK	22.94	9.66	0.061	0.033
DCP	9.77	6.95	0.034	0.025
PRNet	4.99	2.33	0.021	0.015
FPFH + IDAM	3.04	0.61	0.019	0.004
GNN + IDAM	3.42	0.93	0.022	0.005
Ours	**1.68**	**0.57**	**0.013**	**0.003**

3.3 Gaussian Noise

In this experiment, we introduced Gaussian noise with a mean of zero and a standard deviation of 0.01 to the point cloud data, and restricted the noise to the range of [-0.05, 0.05]. The experimental parameters remained consistent with those used in the experiment 3.1. The results obtained from the experiment are displayed in Table 4. It is evident that among the four evaluation metrics, all but one demonstrate optimal performance. The experimental results in Table 3 indicate that the model achieved optimal performance in all three metrics, with error reductions of 0.54%, 28.11%, and 45.45%,

Table 3. Results on point clouds corrupted with white Gaussian noise

Model	RMSE(R)	MAE(R)	RMSE(t)	MAE(t)
ICP	35.07	25.56	0.29	0.25
FPFH + RANSAC	5.06	4.19	0.021	0.018
FGR	27.67	13.79	0.070	0.039
GO-ICP	12.26	2.85	0.028	0.029
PointNetLK	19.94	9.08	0.057	0.032
DCP	6.88	4.53	0.028	0.021
PRNet	4.32	2.05	**0.017**	0.012
FPFH + IDAM	14.21	7.52	0.067	0.042
GNN + IDAM	3.72	1.85	0.023	0.011
Ours	**3.70**	**1.33**	0.018	**0.006**

3.4 Ablation Study

To verify the positive effects of adding a global loss function, attention mechanism on feature fusion, and positional encoding to the model, The experimental results are shown in Table 4, which shows that the experimental results using Transformer, Geoencoding, and Global-loss achieved optimal values in all four evaluation metrics.

Table 4. Ablation study on Modelnet40

encoding	transformer	Global-loss	RMSE(R)	MAE(R)	RMSE(t)	MAE(t)
	✓	✓	1.91	0.49	0.014	0.003
✓		✓	2.20	0.63	0.018	0.004
✓	✓		2.71	0.83	0.018	0.005
✓	✓	✓	**1.68**	**0.57**	**0.013**	**0.003**

4 Conclusion

We proposes a GEANet, an attention-based point cloud registration network that utilizes geometric position encoding information. Multiple experiments conducted on the Modelnet40 dataset demonstrate the positive effect of using point cloud geometric position encoding on model performance. Furthermore, ablation experiments show that attention mechanism, point cloud geometric position encoding, and two-stage loss function all contribute to the improved model performance. However, it is observed that the model performs suboptimally under Gaussian noise with limited improvement. Therefore, future research should focus on enhancing the model's robustness against noise interference.

References

1. Zhong, F., Bai, Z.: 3D point cloud super-resolution with dynamic residual graph convolutional networks. J. ZheJiang Univ. (Eng. Sci.) **56**(11), 2251–2259 (2022)
2. Monti, F., Boscaini, D., Masci, J., et al.: Geometric deep learning on graphs and manifolds using mixture model CNNs. In: 2017 IEEE Conference on Computer Vision and Pattern Recognition (CVPR). Hawaii, USA, 21–26 July 2017, pp. 5425–5434. IEEE, Piscataway, NJ (2017)
3. Mei, G., Poiesi, F., Saltori, C., et al.: Overlap-guided Gaussian mixture models for point cloud registration. In: Proceedings of the IEEE/CVF Winter Conference on Applications of Computer Vision, pp. 4511–4520 (2023)
4. Chen, Z., Chen, H., Gong, L., et al.: UTOPIC: Uncertainty-aware Overlap Prediction Network for Partial Point Cloud Registration. arXiv preprint arXiv:2208.02712 (2022)
5. Vaswani, A., Shazeer, N., Parmar, N., et al.: Attention is all you need. In: Advances in Neural Information Processing Systems, vol. 30 (2017)
6. Wang, Y., Solomon, J.M.: Deep closest point: Learning representations for point cloud registration. In: Proceedings of the IEEE/CVF International Conference on Computer Vision, pp. 3523–3532 (2019)
7. Li, J., Zhang, C., Xu, Z., Zhou, H., Zhang, C.: Iterative distance-aware similarity matrix convolution with mutual-supervised point elimination for efficient point cloud registration. In: Vedaldi, A., Bischof, H., Brox, T., Frahm, J.-M. (eds.) Computer Vision – ECCV 2020. LNCS, vol. 12369, pp. 378–394. Springer, Cham (2020). https://doi.org/10.1007/978-3-030-58586-0_23
8. Wu, Z., Song, S., Khosla, A., et al.: 3d shapenets: a deep representation for volumetric shapes. In: Proceedings of the IEEE Conference on Computer Vision and Pattern Recognition, pp. 1912–1920 (2015)
9. Besl, P.J., Mckay, N.D.: Method for registration of 3-D shapes. In: Sensor fusion IV: control paradigms and data structures. Boston, USA, 12–15 November 1992, pp. 586–606. SPIE (1992)
10. Yang, J., Li, H., Campbell, D., Jia, Y.: Go-ICP: a globally optimal solution to 3D ICP point-set registration. IEEE Trans. Pattern Anal. Mach. Intell. **38**(11), 2241–2254 (2016). https://doi.org/10.1109/TPAMI.2015.2513405
11. Aoki, Y., Goforth, H., Srivatsan, R.A., et al.: Pointnetlk: robust & efficient point cloud registration using pointnet. In: Proceedings of the IEEE/CVF Conference on Computer Vision and Pattern Recognition. Long Beach, USA, June 16–20, 2019. Piscataway, NJ, pp. 7163–7172. IEEE (2019)
12. Zhou, Q.-Y., Park, J., Koltun, V.: Fast global registration. In: Leibe, B., Matas, J., Sebe, N., Welling, M. (eds.) Computer Vision – ECCV 2016. LNCS, vol. 9906, pp. 766–782. Springer, Cham (2016). https://doi.org/10.1007/978-3-319-46475-6_47
13. Wang, Y., Solomon, J.M.: PRNET: self-supervised learning for partial-to-partial registration. In: Advances in Neural Information Processing Systems, pp. 8812–8824 (2019)
14. Zhou, Q.Y., Park, J., Koltun, V.: Open3D: a modern library for 3D data processing. arXiv preprint arXiv:1801.09847 (2018)

End-To-End Phase Retrieval from Single-Shot Fringe Image for 3D Face Reconstruction

Xiao Zhang[1,4], Zhi sheng You[1], Jiangping Zhu[1,2], Di You[1], and Peng Cheng[1,3]([✉])

[1] National Key Laboratory of Fundamental Science on Synthetic Vision, Sichuan University, Chengdu, China
chengpeng_scu@163.com
[2] College of Computer Science, Sichuan University, Chengdu, China
[3] School of Aeronautics and Astronautics, Sichuan University, Chengdu, China
[4] Chengdu Aeronautic Polytechnic, Chengdu, China

Abstract. Phase retrieval is a critical aspect of structured light projection-based three-dimensional (3D) face imaging. The accurate extraction of desired phase information from a minimal number of fringe images without motion blur distortion remains a major challenge. Deep learning has gained attention in solving various optical measurement tasks, and in this study, we propose a deep learning-based dual-generator neural network (DGNET) that consists of two generators in series. The first generator filters interference caused by invalid regions, while the second converts valid regions in the fringe pattern into the final unwrapped phase. Moreover, the DGNET utilizes a single fringe image as input, which enhances the measurement speed and eliminates the impact of pose changes. Experimental results confirm the accuracy and feasibility of performing a phase-retrieval task from a single fringe pattern using the proposed DGNET.

Keywords: Phase retrieval · 3D face measurement · fringe pattern · deep learning

1 Introduction

Passive 3D measurement technology [1] can be utilized for 3D facial modeling under natural outdoor lighting. However, its modeling accuracy is poor, particularly in high-precision, close-range 3D face modeling [2]. To overcome this limitation, active 3D shape measurement technology [3] enhances the feature information of the face surface by introducing additional structural light sources and significantly improves measurement accuracy. Fringe projection profilometry (FPP), an active 3D measurement technology, has become a mainstream method due to its non-contact measurements, high precision, fast speed, strong versatility, and robustness [4–7]. In the FPP system, the phase information can be converted into a real 3D point cloud using the calibration parameters of the system [8, 9]. Therefore, phase retrieval is a critical step, and its accuracy plays a decisive role in the accuracy of the 3D model.

Previous studies of phase retrieval focused on two methods: the Phase-Shifting Method (PSP) [10–12] and the Spatial Phase-Demodulation Method (FTP) [13–16]. PSP

© The Author(s), under exclusive license to Springer Nature Switzerland AG 2023
H. Lu et al. (Eds.): ICIG 2023, LNCS 14357, pp. 213–223, 2023.
https://doi.org/10.1007/978-3-031-46311-2_18

requires multiple fringe images and utilizes the phase information of multi-frequency fringes for step-by-step phase retrieval, which is suitable for static target measurement. The Triple-Frequency Heterodyne Method [17], Multi-Frequency Method [18], and Dual-Frequency Method [19] are typical PSP algorithms. FTP enables phase retrieval from a single fringe image, but is prone to introducing cumulative errors, especially phase dislocations caused by spatially discontinuous objects and occlusions, such as isolated surfaces on the measured face like glasses. To address this problem, Hu et al. [20] combined a pseudo-correlator and maximum phase gradient map to obtain quality evaluation criteria. Goldstein et al. [21] proposed the branch-cutting method, and Zhang et al. [22] improved the branch-cutting method to enhance the cutting efficiency and success rate during phase unwrapping.

In recent years, learning-based methods have been shown to outperform physical-model-based algorithms [23], deep neural networks have been used to improve the performance of FPP. Feng et al. [24] proposed a deep neural network with two different convolutional neural networks to enhance the accuracy of the phase demodulation from a single fringe pattern. They also proposed a "one-to-many" deep learning technique that could analyze non-sinusoidal fringe images resulting from different non-sinusoidal factors and the coupling of these factors[25]. However, neither of the aforementioned methods [23, 24] can obtain the final unwrapped phase. They only predict the ideal numerator $M(x,y)$ and denominator $D(x,y)$ of the arctangent function, which needs to be fed into the subsequent arctangent function to obtain the wrapped and unwrapped phases to finish the phase retrieval. Spoorthi et al. [26] proposed PhaseNet, which reformulated the phase unwrapping problem as an image semantic segmentation problem, achieving significantly better results than quality-guided phase-unwrapping. Furthermore, Spoorthi et al. [27] proposed PhaseNet 2.0, which transformed the phase unwrapping problem into a dense classification problem and trained a fully convolutional DenseNet-based neural network to predict the wrap count at each pixel from the wrapped phase maps. Wang et al. [28] proposed a one-step deep learning phase-unwrapping method and successfully unwrapped the phase fields of living mouse osteoblasts and dynamic candle flames obtained by off-axis digital holography using a Mach-Zehnder interferometer. Zhang et al. [29] proposed a quantitative indicator to measure the amount of prior information contained in a wrapped phase map and an edge-enhanced self-attention network for two-dimensional phase unwrapping. However, the aforementioned methods [25–28] only went from the wrapped phase to the unwrapped phase, with the wrapped phase required to be calculated in advance. Zheng et al.[30] proposed a method to directly extract 3D geometry from a single-shot fringe image. They also built a digital twin of an FPP system and performed virtual scanning using computer graphics to save cost and labor.

In this paper, we propose a deep-learning-based dual-generator neural network (DGNET) that links two generators in series to enhance the phase-retrieval technique. The first generator filters out interference from invalid regions such as edges, glasses, tex-tures, and shadows, allowing the gradient information fed back into the second generator to focus on the valid regions, improving modeling accuracy in those areas. Our research shows that for the first time, the proposed DGNET completes the conversion from the fringe image to the unwrapped phase in one step, eliminating the need to calculate the wrapped phase and simplifying the operation process while reducing delay. Additionally, it only requires a single fringe image as input, improving measurement speed and avoiding the effects of pose changes. The training goal of DGNET is to learn statistically the mapping between individual stripes and their corresponding unfolding stages. The training process only needs to be executed once, and the network can then accurately generate unwrapped phase images. Evaluation results demonstrate the effectiveness of the proposed method.

2 Proposed Method

DGNET is a novel fringe phase retrieval method that utilizes two generators in series, enabling an end-to-end single-shot process. The first generator, G1, was designed to exclude invalid regions on the face by distinguishing between valid and invalid areas. Each fringe image was initially fed into G1, generating a corresponding mask image. The mask images consist of pixel values of either 0 or 1, where the latter represents the valid regions of the fringe image, and the former represents the invalid regions. The fringe image and mask were then dot-multiplied to produce the input for the second generator (G2). The output of G2 was also dot-multiplied with the mask before calculating the gradient feedback. This approach ensured that the feedback gradient information of G2 was focused more on the valid areas, leading to improved modeling accuracy in these regions. In this study, we utilized an extended U-Net [31] as our deep neural network architecture (Fig. 1).

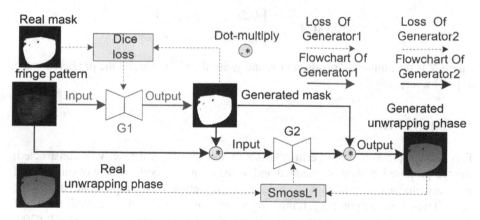

Fig. 1. Flowchart of proposed DGNET.

Figure 2 shows the architectures of G1 and G2, which are similar and consist of a contraction path on the left, an expansion path on the right, and a bridge path in the middle. G1's output layer uses sigmoid as the activation function, while G2's output layer uses Tanh. G1's goal is to minimize the following loss function$\mathcal{L}_1$:

$$\mathcal{L}_1 = 1 - \text{DiceCoefficient}, \tag{1}$$

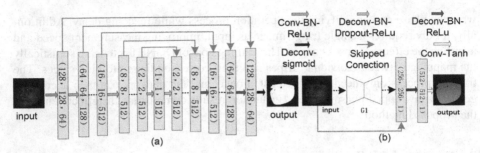

Fig. 2. Architecture of (a) G1 and (b) G2.

DiceCoefficient [32] calculates the similarity of two samples and is defined as:

$$DiceCoefficient = \frac{2|x \cap y| + 1}{|x| + |y| + 1}, \qquad (2)$$

where x represents the Ground Truth(GT) value and y represents the predicted value. The goal of G2 is to minimize the following loss function $\mathcal{L}_2$:

$$\mathcal{L}_2 = \frac{1}{N} \sum_{i=0}^{N} SmoothL_1(x_i - y_i), \qquad (3)$$

where

$$SmoothL_1(\varepsilon) = \begin{cases} 0.5\varepsilon^2, & if\,|\varepsilon| < 1 \\ |\varepsilon| - 0.5, & otherwise \end{cases}, \qquad (4)$$

where N is the number of pixels, and x_i and y_i are the GT value and the predicted value of pixel i, respectively.

3 Experiment

This section presents the experimental setup and results. A dataset was constructed, and the proposed method was trained and tested on it. The performance of our method was evaluated and compared with some classical methods. The implementation of our method was done in Python 3.7.1, utilizing the PyTorch framework with version 1.6.0 of Torch. The algorithm was executed in a Windows 10 environment with a core-i7-8700, 8 GB RAM, and NVIDIA GeForce GTX 1660 Ti. The structured-light illumination system comprised a DLP 4500 (9121140) projector and two industrial cameras (Daheng MER2, 1280 × 1024).

3.1 Dataset

To evaluate the accuracy of our method's unwrapped phase image, we created a face dataset consisting of 700 triples (fringe image, binary mask image, and unwrapped phase image). The dataset contains approximately 50% left and 50% right faces, and about 40% of the faces wore glasses. The distance between the acquisition system and the target was between 600–1000 mm. The data collection involved 100 individuals.

We employed the light-field projection module and projected them onto the face. Simultaneously, the industrial camera captured the modulated fringe image of the face. We used the high-frequency fringe image (corresponding to 64 fringes) to obtain the face fringe image that served as the input for constructing the dataset. The groundtruth of unwrapped phase image was obtained using a four-step phase-shifting algorithm with three frequencies (corresponding to 1, 8, and 64 fringes). The groundtruth of mask is marked manually.

3.2 Implementation Details

For both G1 and G2, we used convolutional and deconvolutional filters with a size of 4, stride of 2, and padding of 1 for down-sampling and up-sampling. The Adam optimizer with momentum parameters $\beta1 = 0.5$, $\beta2 = 0.999$, a fixed learning rate of 0.0001, and a batch size of 4 were employed. All face images were cropped to 256×256 pixels. Since G2 requires the output of G1, we first trained G1 with 1200 epochs and then G2 with 1200 epochs, both using the same aforementioned parameters.

3.3 Results

To assess the effectiveness of our proposed method, we selected two triplets that were not included in the training dataset: one without glasses (Fig. 3(a-c)) and another with glasses with isolated spaces (Fig. 7(a-c)).

We evaluated the performance of our method and compared it with the classic single-frame fringe analysis approach. Additionally, we performed ablation studies using U-Net with the same structure as G2 to analyze the effectiveness of our G1. For the classic single-frame approach, we adopted FT [33] (Fourier-transform) to demodulate the wrapped phase and QG [34] (quality guide phase unwrapping) to obtain the unwrapped phase. We compared the results of each method within the valid region of the mask to ensure a fair comparison.

Table 1 shows the mean absolute errors (MAE) for each method. Results using only a single U-Net showed prominent phase distortion with MAEs of 12.0540 mm (face with glasses) and 21.7915 mm (face without glasses), indicating the inefficiency of a single U-Net to map a single fringe image to an unwrapped phase image in the presence of interference due to invalid regions. Our proposed DGNET outperformed U-Net and achieved a minimum error of 0.5281 mm (face with glasses) and 0.6552 mm (face

Table 1. The MAE Results(mm) of different methods.

	DG-NET(Ours) U-Net FT + QG
face without glasses	0.6552 21.7915 0.7674
face with glasses	0.5281 12.0540 489.6408

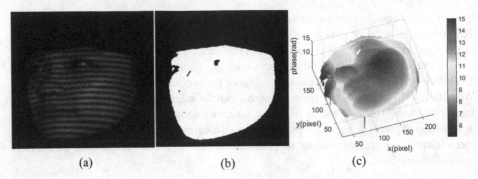

Fig. 3. Triple of face without glasses. (a) Input fringe image, (b) Mask, (c) GT.

without glasses), demonstrating its superiority in shielding against interference from invalid areas when solving such problems. While the result of the classic single-frame FT + QG approach for the face without glasses was close to that of DGNET, the result for the face with glasses was poor due to the presence of isolated regions.

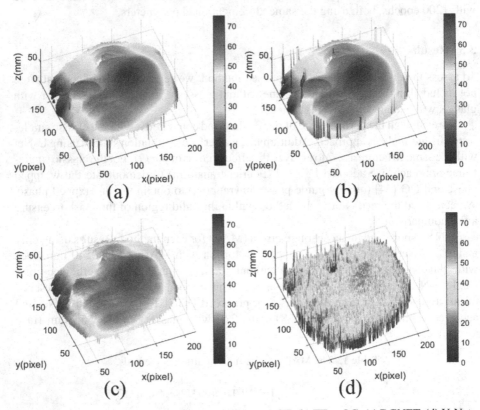

Fig. 4. 3D reconstruction of a face without glasses. (a) GT, (b) FT + QG, (c) DGNET, (d) U-Net.

When we used Fig. 3(a) as input to train G1, and predicted a mask similar to Fig. 3(b). Then we used the point multiplication of Fig. 3(a) and the mask to train G2, which predicted the final unwrapping phase, similar to that in Fig. 3(c). We calculated the phase error against Fig. 3(c), and the results for each approach are shown in Fig. 4(b-d). To compare the results in detail, we show the phase intensity of a row and its magnified view for the selected regions in Fig. 5(a-b). The phase error maps of each approach are shown in Fig. 6(a-c). Using only a single U-Net showed poor results under the interference of the invalid region, as shown in Fig. 4(d). Compared to DGNET, the surface shape recovered by the traditional method is smoother and performs well near the starting point of phase unwrapping, but the error gradually increases away from the starting point as shown in Figs. 5 and 6(a).

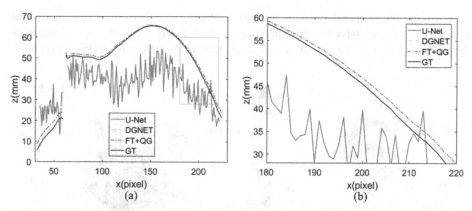

Fig. 5. (a) Depth error of the 133rd row in Fig. 6, (b) magnified view of the green-highlighted region in (a)

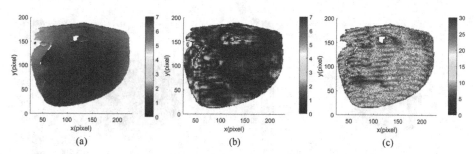

Fig. 6. Phase error map (for a face without glasses) for (a) FT + QG, (b) DGNET, (c) U-Net.

To further demonstrate the effectiveness of DGNET on isolated surfaces, we conducted a test on a face wearing glasses as shown in Fig. 7(a). The mask generated by G1 is shown in Fig. 7(b), while Fig. 7(c) shows the ground truth (GT). Due to the occlusion of the glasses, the face contains completely isolated regions, resulting in obvious phase jumps in the discontinuous regions when using the classical single-frame method, as shown in Fig. 8(b). The cumulative error also increases away from the starting point,

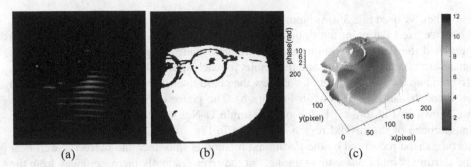

Fig. 7. Triple of a face without glasses. (a) Input fringe image, (b) Mask, (c) GT for G2.

as shown in Figs. 9(a) and 10(a). In contrast, a single U-Net does not mask the invalid area, resulting in excessive loss error and inaccurate mapping to the unwrapped phase, as shown in Figs. 9 and 10(c). Its phase-retrieval effect is also poor, as shown in Fig. 8(d).

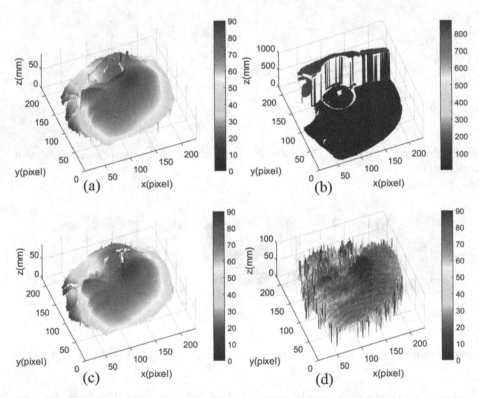

Fig. 8. 3D reconstruction of a face with glasses. (a) GT, (b) FT plus QG, (c) DGNET, (d) U-Net.

However, DGNET adopts point-to-point mapping with no phase jump in isolated spaces, as shown in Fig. 8(c). When away from the starting point of phase unwrapping, the mean absolute error is less than that of FT + QG because of the absence of error

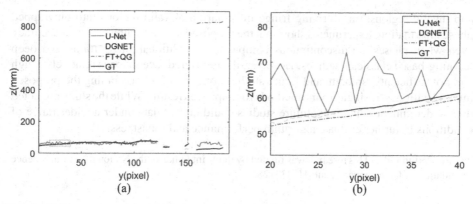

Fig. 9. (a) Phase error of the 55th column in Fig. 10, (b) magnified view of the green-highlighted region of (a).

accumulation, as shown in Fig. 9(b). These results further confirm the superiority of DGNET in shielding against the interference of invalid areas and achieving accurate phase retrieval, even in challenging scenarios such as those involving isolated surfaces.

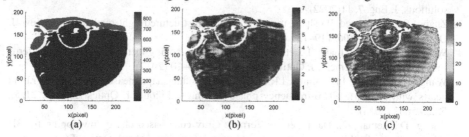

Fig. 10. Phase error map for modeling of face with glasses via (a) FT plus QG, (b) DGNET, (c) U-Net.

The experiments conducted in this study demonstrate the effectiveness of the proposed deep learning method in avoiding error accumulation and phase jump issues encountered in the classical single-frame method. By masking the impact of invalid regions, the proposed method maps the face fringe image to the unwrapped phase image with high accuracy. However, the recovered face shape using the deep learning method appeared to be less smooth and relatively rough. In future studies, a possible approach is to combine the deep learning method with the classical single-frame method to improve the results further.

4 Conclusion

This study proposes a deep learning-based method for phase retrieval of single face fringe images using a two-extended U-Net cascade. By masking the invalid regions, the proposed method improves modeling accuracy in the valid regions and effectively solves the problem of phase jumps caused by isolated regions. The method segments valid and invalid regions, transforming fringe information of valid regions into unwrapped phase information. Experiments show that the proposed method achieves higher accuracy even when phases are discontinuous compared to traditional single-frame and deep learning-based classical methods. However, the recovered face shape is relatively rough and not sufficiently smooth, and future studies could consider combining the proposed method with classic single-frame methods for improved results. While the study collected data under similar conditions, future studies could collect data under a wider range of conditions to further evaluate algorithm performance and robustness.

Acknowledgments. This research was funded by the Joint Funds of the National Natural Science Foundation of China under Grant -U1833128.

References

1. Raja, U.T., Ye, M., Cao, Z., et al.: passive intermodulation measurement of radiofrequency interference shielding gasket. In: 2019 International Applied Computational Electromagnetics Society Symposium-China (ACES). IEEE (2019)
2. Cai, Z., Liu, L., Paulis, F.D., et al.: Passive intermodulation measurement: challenges and solutions. J. Eng. **7**, 11(2022)
3. Zhang, S.: High-speed 3D shape measurement with structured light methods: A review. J. Optics Lasers Eng. **106**, 119–131 (2018)
4. Wang, Y., Chen, X., Huang, L., et al.: Improved phase-coding methods with fewer patterns for 3D shape measurement. J. Optics Commun. **401**, 6–10 (2017)
5. Wang, Y., Laughner, J.I., Efimov, I.R., et al.: 3D absolute shape measurement of live rabbit hearts with a superfast two-frequency phase-shifting technique. J. Optics Express. **21**(5), 5822–5832 (2013)
6. Zheng, D., Kemao, Q., Da, F., et al.: Ternary Gray code-based phase unwrapping for 3D measurement using binary patterns with projector defocusing. J. Appl. Optics. **56**(13), 3660–3665 (2017)
7. Zuo, C., Tao, T., Feng, S., et al.: Micro Fourier Transform Profilometry (μ FTP): 3D shape measurement at 10,000 frames per second. J. Optics Lasers Eng. **102**, 70–91 (2018)
8. Zhang, S., Huang, P.S.: Novel method for structured light system calibration. J. Optical Engineering. **45**(8), 083601 (2006)
9. Wang, Y., Wang, Y., Liu, Lu., et al.: Defocused camera calibration with a conventional periodic target based on fourier transform. J. Opt Lett. **44**(13):3254–3257(2019)
10. Zuo, C., Chen, Q., Gu, G., et al.: High-speed three-dimensional profilometry for multiple objects with complex shapes. J. Opt. Express. **20**(17), 19493–19510 (2012)
11. Tao, T., Chen, Q., Da, J., et al.: Real-time 3-D shape measurement with composite phase-shifting fringes and multi-view system. J. Opt Express. **24**(18), 20253–20269 (2016)
12. Zhang, Z., Catherine, E., Towers, et al.: Time efficient color fringe projection system for 3d shape and color using optimum 3-frequency selection. J. Opt Express. **14**(14), 6444–6455 (2006)
13. Su, X., Chen, W.: Fourier transform profilometry:a review. J. Opt Lasers Eng. **35**(5), 263–284 (2001)
14. Guo, H., Huang, P.S.: Absolute phase technique for the Fourier transform method. J. Opt Eng. **48**(4), 043609 (2009)
15. Hu, Y., Chen, Q., Zhang, Y., et al.: Dynamic microscopic 3D shape measurement based on marker-embedded Fourier transform profilometry. J. Appl Opt. **57**(4), 772–780 (2018)

16. Li, B., An, Y., Zhang, S.: Single-shot absolute 3D shape measurement with Fourier transform profilometry. J. Appl Opt. **55**(19), 5219–5225 (2016)
17. Ohtsuka, Y.: Real-time electro-optical heterodyne signal processors. J. Opto-electronics. **6**(3), 235–241(1974)
18. Chen, L., Deng, W., Lou, X.: Phase unwrapping method base on multi-frequencyinterferometry. J. Optical Tech. **38**(01), 73–78 (2012)
19. Li, J., Su, H., Su, X.: Two-frequency grating used in phase-measuring profilometry. J. Appl. Optics. **36**(1), 277–280 (1997)
20. Lu, Y., Wang, X., Zhong, X., et al.: A new quality map for quality-guided phase unwrapping. J. Chinese Optics Lett. 698–700(2004)
21. Richard, M.G., Howard, A.Z., Charles, L.W.: Satellite radar interferometry: two-dimensional phase unwrapping. J. Radio Science. **23**(4), 713–720 (1988)
22. Zhang, Y., Feng, D., Qu, X., et al.: Application of a Novel Branch-Cut Algorithm in Phase Unwrapping. J. J. Univ. Electron. Sci. Technol. China. **42**(4), 555–558 (2013)
23. Zuo, C., Feng, S., Zhang, X., et al.: Deep learning based computationali maging status challenges and future. J. Acta Optica Sinica. **40**(1), 0111003–1 – 0111003–26 (2020)
24. Feng, S., Chen, Q., Gu, G., et al.: Fringe pattern analysis using deep learning. J. Adv. Photonics. **1**(2), 25001–1 – 025001–7(2019)
25. Feng, S., Zuo, C., Zhang, L., et al.: Generalized framework for non-sinusoidal fringe analysis using deep learning. J. Photonics Res. **9**(6), 1084–1098 (2021)
26. Spoorthi, G.E., Gorthi, S., Gorthi, R.: PhaseNet: A deep convolutional neural network for two-dimensional phase unwrapping. J. IEEE Signal Proc. Let. **26**(1), 54–58 (2019)
27. Spoorthi, G.E., Gorthi, R., Gorthi, S.: PhaseNet 2.0: Phase unwrapping of noisy data based on deep learning approach. J. IEEE Trans. Image Process. **29**. 4862–4872 (2020)
28. Wang, K., Li, Y., Kemao, Q., et al.: One-step robust deep learning phase unwrapping. J. Optics Express **27**(10), 15100–15115 (2019)
29. Zhang, J., Li, Q.: EESANet: edge-enhanced self-attention network for two-dimensional phase unwrapping. J. Optics Express. **7**(30), 10470–10490 (2022)
30. Zheng, Y., Wang, S., Li, Q., et al.: Fringe projection profilometry by conducting deep learning from its digital twin. J. Optics Express. **28**(24), 36568–36583 (2020)
31. Lin, Y., Ling, S., Fu, K., et al.: An identity-preserved model for face sketch-photo synthesis. J. Latex Class Files. **14**(8), 1–5 (2015)
32. Li, X., Sun, X., Meng, Y., et al.: Dice Loss for Data-imbalanced NLP Tasks. J. Comput. Lang. (2019)
33. Mitsuo, T., Hideki, I., Seiji, K.: Fourier-transform method of fringe-pattern analysis for computer-based topography and interferometry. J. Optical Society Am. (1982)
34. Zhao, W.: Research on quality maps used in two dimensional phase unwrapping. D. School of Management and Engineering Nanjing University (2011)

Multi-modal Stream Fusion for Skeleton-Based Action Recognition

Ruixuan Pang, Rongchang Li, Tianyang Xu, Xiaoning Song,
and Xiao-Jun Wu[✉]

Jiangnan University, Wuxi 214122, China
{1033200405,li_rongchang}@stu.jiangnan.edu.cn,
{tianyang.xu,x.song,wu_xiaojun}@jiangnan.edu.cn

Abstract. In recent years, graph convolution networks (GCN) have
been widely used in skeleton-based action recognition to pursue higher
accuracy. In general, traditional approaches directly integrate different
modalities together using uniform fusion weights, which results in inadequate information fusion across modalities, sacrificing flexibility and
robustness. In this paper, we explore the potential of adaptively fusing
different modalities, and deliver a new fusion algorithm, coined Multi-
modal Stream Fusion GCN (MSF-GCN). In principle, our proposed algorithm consists of three branches: JS-GCN, BS-GCN, and MS-GCN, corresponding to joint, bone, and motion modeling, respectively. In our
design, the motion patterns between the joint and bone modalities are
dynamically fused using an MLP layer. After conducting typical motion
modeling, the static joint and bone branches are accompanied to perform
the final fusion for the category predictions. Our MSF-GCN emphasizes static and dynamic fusion simultaneously, which greatly increases
the interaction degree between the information of each modality, with
improved flexibility. The proposed fusion strategy is applicable to different backbones, exhibiting the power to boost performance with marginal
computation increase. Extensive experiments on a widely-used NTU-
RGB+D dataset demonstrate that our model can achieve better or comparable results to current solutions, reflecting the merit of our fusion
strategy.

Keywords: Skeleton-based Action Recognition · Multi-modal Stream
Fusion · GCN

1 Introduction

Human action recognition occupies an important position in computer vision,
which has attracted increasing attention in recent years. One typical action

This work is supported in part by the National Natural Science Foundation of China
(Grant No. 62106089, 62020106012).

© The Author(s), under exclusive license to Springer Nature Switzerland AG 2023
H. Lu et al. (Eds.): ICIG 2023, LNCS 14357, pp. 224–234, 2023.
https://doi.org/10.1007/978-3-031-46311-2_19

recognition task is skeleton-based human recognition. It focuses on recognizing human actions using the human skeleton as input, which own the advantages of less computation burden compared to the video-based solutions, with promising model robustness and wide application scenarios. In general, current skeleton-based human recognition methods mostly involve four modalities: joint, bone, joint motion, and bone motion. Joint information is the most commonly used modality for skeleton-based action recognition, because the joint provides basic position information of the human body parts, which is easy to collect from sensors. This is the most used modality in many skeleton-based action recognition methods, such as Spatial-Temporal Graph Convolutional Networks (ST-GCN) [1]. Specifically, ST-GCN makes it possible for spatial and temporal patterns to be automatically learned and trained from data based on the joint modality. Joint-based methods are efficient and robust, with the ability to capture the human pose and motion. However, the joint is sensitive to coordinate noise and occlusions between joints. Instead, bone information contains information about the connection between joints, which can effectively reduce the impact of noise and occlusions, thus helping to capture the structure and topology of the human skeleton. The bone modality is less expressive than the joint as it can not reflect the exact position of joints. Therefore, bone-based methods are often used as an additional branch to improve the recognition accuracy of joint-based methods. To combine the advantages of both modalities, joint and bone, Shi *et al.* [2] proposed Two-Stream Adaptive Graph Convolutional Networks (2s-AGCN), which introduces an end-to-end learning approach that uses a data-driven method to model both joint and bone information. Soon after, Shi *et al.* [3] proposed the Multi-Stream Adaptive Graph Convolutional Networks (MS-AGCN), adding two modalities, joint motion, and bone motion, to the network for training as well, which is the first attempt to achieve the fusion of four modalities. Joint motion information reflects the change of joint positions over time, containing more detailed temporal information which captures dynamic patterns more directly. Similarly, bone motion information reflects the change of bone positions over time, which can be used to capture the dynamic changes in human bones. Bone motion-based methods can also provide additional temporal information for better action recognition. These four modalities describe a human action from different perspectives and therefore, most of the methods after MS-AGCN adopt the strategy that aggregates the results after training the four modalities individually. However, in the final multi-stream fusion, uniform fusion weights are mostly used, and the information obtained between the streams cannot be fully integrated. First, fixed weights may not be optimal in all cases, and depending on the complexity and characteristics of the target action, different modalities may have different degrees of correlations and contributions to the final recognition performance, so they can not provide consistent fusion ratios for different samples. Secondly, under a fixed fusion mode, the interaction between modalities is missing, neglecting the complex dependencies among different modalities. Thirdly, when one modality contains noise or irrelevant features, its corresponding branch may lead to worse prediction, which can not be adjusted in the fixed fusion manner.

To address the above issues, we propose a solution (multi-modal stream fusion) that can flexibly and efficiently fuse the information of various streams. Specifically, our proposed approach includes three distinct branches, each of which utilizes GCN (graph convolutional networks) to model different aspects of the skeletal data. These branches are named Joint Stream GCN (JS-GCN), Bone Stream GCN (BS-GCN), and Motion Stream GCN (MS-GCN), and they focus on modeling joints, bones, and motion, respectively. In MS-GCN, the joint motion and bone motion modalities are dynamically fused by a learnable MLP layer, which increases the interactivity between the motion information and thus the flexibility of selecting the fusion weights. In addition, the results of the three models are summed by specific weights at the end to take advantage of each flow. In particular, for the motion stream, we concatenate the results of joint-motion and bone-motion training and fuse them through a fully connected layer to obtain a motion score. Finally, the final score derived from the motion score, joint score, and bone score are aggregated with the weights to obtain the prediction.

To summarise, the main contributions of the proposed method include:

- We propose a Multi-modal Stream Fusion Graph Convolutional Network (MSF-GCN) to learn the correlation between different modality streams and efficiently aggregate scores in different streams for skeleton-based action recognition. Our approach can effectively combine the advantages of each stream.
- We validated the validity of our model on two publicly available datasets, NTU RGB+D [4] and NTU RGB+D 120 [5] and our method can achieve better or comparable performance.

2   Related Work

Skeleton-Based Action Recognition. In recent years, action recognition has gained significant attention. Initially, hand-crafted feature-based approaches [6, 7] were used to simulate human motion. However, with the advent of deep learning, numerous neural network structures are popular in this field. RNN-based methods [8–10] consider skeleton data as time series, while CNN-based methods [11–15] have higher efficiency by converting skeleton coordinates into three channels and using network models to extract features for classification. Nevertheless, both RNNs and CNNs are not capable of fully representing the structure of skeleton data, as it is in the form of graphics rather than vector sequences or 2D image meshes. Yan *et al.* [1] implemented the first application of graph convolutional network to skeleton action recognition. Better performance is achieved by using graph convolution, which does not require manual rules. ST-GCN has been built upon by 2s-AGCN, CTR-GCN, TCA-GCN, and others, enabling the modeling of diversified topologies in spatial and temporal domains, fully extracting feature information, and achieving significant performance improvements.

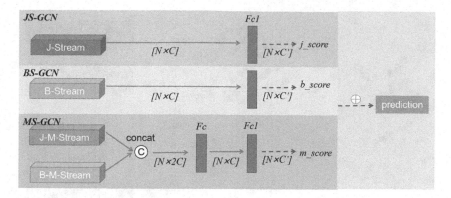

Fig. 1. Illustration of the proposed network structure, MSF-GCN. The final prediction scores are obtained by fusing the weighted sum of scores from three branches. J, B, and M provide joint, bone, and motion information, respectively. Fc and Fc1 are fully connected layers.

Graph Convolutional Neural Networks. Convolutional Neural Networks (CNNs) are typically used for regular grids with low dimensions such as images, audio, and video. However, they are not ideal for modeling irregular graphical data. The application of neural networks to data with graph structures that are non-Euclidean has gradually become mainstream in recent years. Graph Neural Networks (GNN) have become a popular method for processing such data, and they are commonly divided into two streams: spectral and spatial perspectives. Spectral GNN draws on the eigenvectors and eigenvalues in the Tulaplacian matrix and thus applies convolution in the spectral domain. It assumes that the adjacency between all samples is fixed and subject to certain restrictions. On the other hand, spatial GNN directly convolves the vertices of the graph and their neighbors, applying local feature fusion and activation for each node to update the features layer by layer. However, the order of vertices and edges in the spatial GNN domain usually follows the manually designed rules. Spatial perspective stream is what most GCN-based methods for skeleton-based action recognition would choose, and they construct a spatial-temporal map based on skeleton data, using convolution in neighborhoods for feature aggregation and layer-by-layer updates.

3   The Proposed Approach

In this section, we present our method for skeleton-based action recognition, as illustrated in Fig. 1. We begin with the related preparations in Sect. 3.1, which focuses on the representation of the data. We then describe in Sect. 3.2 the specific architecture of the JS (joint stream), BS (bone stream), and MS (motion stream) branches utilized and how they are fused by our proposed fusion algorithm. Finally, in Sect. 3.3, we compute overhead and compare them, the conclusion is the increase in overhead is little.

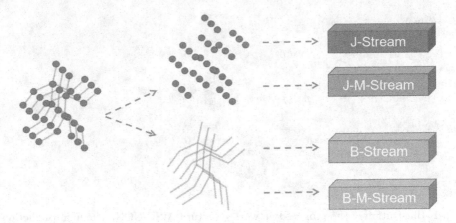

Fig. 2. Inputs of different modalities.

3.1 Preliminaries

Joint and Bone Data. In the representation of a graph over a sequence of human skeletons, we denote the set of vertices and edges by V and E, respectively. We represent each bone with a vector representation from the source joint pointing to the target joint, where the source and target joints are set by joints closer to and away from the skeleton's center of gravity, respectively. For instance, in a given frame t, the bone from source joint $v_{i,t} = (\ x_{i,t},\ y_{i,t},\ z_{i,t})$ to target joint $v_{j,t} = (\ x_{j,t},\ y_{j,t},\ z_{j,t})$, by the vector $e_{i,j} = (\ x_{j,t} - x_{i,t},\ y_{j,t} - y_{i,t},\ z_{j,t} - z_{i,t}\ )$. All joints except the root joint are assigned one-to-one to the bone as its unique target joint, so the number of joints and bones differs by one. To maintain equal numbers of joints and bones without complicating the network, we assign an empty bone with a value of zero to the root joint. Thus, the shape and network of the bone can be designed to be identical to the joint. We use J stream, B stream, JM stream, and BM stream to represent joints, bones, and networks of their respective motion information, as shown in Fig. 2.

Motion Data. The motion information is computed by calculating the difference between the same joints or bones in two consecutive frames. For instance, given the joint $v_{i,t}$ in frame t, and the same joint $v_{i,t+1}$ in frame $t+1$, the motion information is expressed as $m_{i,t,t+1} = (\ x_{i,t+1} - x_{i,t},\ y_{i,t+1} - y_{i,t},\ z_{i,t+1} - z_{i,t}\ )$.

3.2 Multi-modal Stream Fusion

JS and BS Branch. For joint modality and bone modality, the focus is on spatial modeling, which allows for more accurate recognition of human actions. The JS and BS branches contain graph convolutional networks based on the CTR-GCN model to extract features from joint and bone modalities, respectively.

Specifically, the JS branch and the BS branch each use a graph convolutional network to model joint connections and bone connections, respectively. Both branches produce feature maps encoding the spatial and structural information of the skeleton, of size $N \times C$. These feature maps are then fed into the fully connected layer to produce scores of joints and bones, of size $N \times C'$, and finally await fusion with the scores of the MS branch. The JS branch specifically focuses on recognizing actions such as pointing to something with a finger, reaching into a pocket, and wearing a shoe. On the other hand, the BS branch is designed to recognize actions based on bones, which can provide valuable information for action recognition. By analyzing the movement of different bones, the BS branch can accurately recognize actions such as lifting an object or opening a door. So these two branches are given greater weight when fusing information from different sources, as they provide more essential information for most actions.

MS Branch. To fully capture the spatio-temporal information of human actions, we propose to fuse the joint motion and bone motion modalities to a total motion branch. Specifically, the joint motion and bone motion results are concatenated along the feature dimension to form a single multi-modal input, which is then passed through a linear layer for fusion. First, by concatenating the joint motion and bone motion results, we can effectively capture both the fine-grained spatial details of the joints and the coarse-grained spatial information of the bones. This leads to a more complete representation of the human body and enables more accurate action recognition. Second, by applying a linear layer fusion, we can learn a set of weights to balance the contributions of the joint motion and bone motion modalities. This allows us to flexibly adjust the importance of each modality for specific actions. For example, if an action involves fine-grained hand movements, the joint motion modality may be given more weight, while if an action involves large body movements, the bone motion modality may be more important. Finally, by concatenating and fusing the joint motion and bone motion modalities, we can effectively combine their complementary strengths and mitigate their individual weaknesses. For example, the joint motion modality may struggle to capture large body movements, while the bone motion modality may struggle to capture fine-grained hand movements. By fusing the two modalities, we can overcome these limitations and achieve more accurate action recognition. Overall, our proposed approach of concatenating and fusing the joint motion and bone motion modalities using linear layer fusion is a powerful method for capturing spatio-temporal information in human actions.

Finally, we fuse these three branches. Specifically, we use a fixed weight of 0.4 for the MS branch and a weight of 0.6 for the BS and JS branches. This weighting scheme is based on empirical observations from our experiments on the data set. The fused features are then passed through a multi-layer perception (MLP) for classification. Our proposed approach aims to improve the accuracy of skeleton-based action recognition by leveraging both bone motion and joint motion information, and by using a learnable skeleton representation for more effective feature fusion.

3.3 Overhead Analysis

Our model is based on CTR-GCN. In the preliminary stage, we use the pre-trained CTR-GCN model to extract the features of each branch in MSF-GCN and get the output features of dimension C. In the fusion stage, CTR-GCN simply lets each modality go through the classification layer separately for prediction to get the analogous probability vector, whose dimension is the category number C'. So the computation of each modality in CTR–GCN is $C \times C'$ and the total computation is $4 \times C \times C'$. In the MSF-GCN, the JS branch and the BS branch are both computed as $C \times C'$ because they go through a classification layer. And for the MS branch, a linear layer is also used to fuse the features of two motion modalities and transform their dimension from $2C$ to C before the classification layer, so the computation is $2C \times C + C \times C'$. So the total computation of MSF-GCN is $C \times \left(2C + 3C'\right)$, which is $C \times \left(2C - C'\right)$ more than CTR-GCN. In the experiment, C is 256 and C' is 60 or 120, so the increase in inference overhead is very little.

4 Experimental Results

4.1 Datasets

We evaluate the proposed method on two publicly available data sets, i.e., NTU-RGB+D [4] and NTU-RGB+D 120 [5]. Following the convention, we report the Top-1 accuracy on NTU-RGB+D and NTU-RGB+D 120.

NTU-RGB+D. NTU-RGB+D [4] is a large-scale human action recognition dataset that contains 60 action classes performed by 40 different volunteers. The dataset includes both RGB and depth data, which are captured by a Microsoft Kinect v2 sensor at various camera angles. It is divided using two criteria recommended by the dataset: (1) cross-subject (X-sub): all samples from 40 subjects are used for training and the remaining 20 subjects are used for testing. (2) cross-view (X-view): the dataset is split into two parts based on the camera view angle, and samples from one part are used for training while the other part is used for testing.

NTU-RGB+D 120. NTU-RGB+D 120 [5] is currently the largest and most widely used human motion 3D joint dataset. The dataset is an extension of the NTU-RGB+D dataset, which contains 120 action classes and 114480 action samples. It was also captured using Microsoft Kinect v2 sensors from different angles. It is divided into two subsets: (1) the cross-subject (X-sub): it contains 20 training-testing splits, each of which covers 70 individuals for training and

Table 1. Ablation studies on NTU-RGB+D XSub

Methods	NTU60-XSub
baseline (fixed weights)	92.4
MSF-GCN	92.8
BS branch+MS branch	92.0
JS branch+MS branch	91.1
JS branch+BS branch	89.4

36 individuals for testing. (2) the cross-view (X-set): the data contains three training-testing splits, each of which uses samples from two camera views for training and samples from the remaining view for testing. The NTU-RGB+D 120 dataset has been widely used in various human action recognition research studies.

4.2 Implementation Details

We use pretrained CTR-GCN models [16] to extract features for each branch in MSF-GCN and only the later fusion part is trained. In the subsequent stream fusion part, the model is trained using SGD with a momentum of 0.9 and weight decay of 0.0004. The training epoch is set to 15, the learning rate is set to 0.1, and the learning rate is decayed by a factor of 0.1 at epoch 8 and 12. All experiments were conducted on an RTX 3080 TI GPU using the PyTorch deep learning framework.

4.3 Ablation Study

To further investigate the effectiveness of our proposed model, we conducted ablation experiments to explore the contributions of different components. Table 1 reports the performance on the X-Sub of the NTU-RGB+D dataset. Specifically, we compared the performance of our full model with that of several modified versions, each with one component removed. Our baseline is the CTR-GCN.

The Impact of JS Branch. To assess the impact of the JS branch, we removed the JS branch from our full model and trained the model on the remaining data. The results showed that the model without the JS branch achieved an accuracy of 92.0%, which is 0.8% lower than our full model's accuracy of 92.8%. This suggests that the JS branch provides important spatial information that helps the model better recognize human actions.

The Impact of BS Branch. Next, we evaluated the contribution of the BS branch by removing it from the full model. The results showed that the model

Table 2. Classification accuracy comparisons with state-of-the-art methods on NTU-RGB+D and NTU-RGB+D 120

	NTU60-XSub	NTU60-XView	NTU120-XSub	NTU120-XSet
ST-GCN [1]	81.5	88.3	70.7	73.2
2s-AGCN [2]	88.5	95.1	82.9	84.9
SGN [17]	89.0	94.5	79.2	81.5
Shift+GCN [18]	90.7	96.5	85.9	87.6
DSTA-Net [19]	91.5	96.4	86.6	89.0
DC-GCN+ADG [20]	90.8	96.6	86.5	88.1
MST-G3D [21]	91.5	96.2	86.9	88.4
Dynamic GCN [22]	91.5	96.0	87.3	88.6
TCA-GCN [23]	92.8	97.0	89.4	90.8
CTR-GCN [16]	92.4	96.8	88.9	90.6
MSF-GCN	92.8	96.9	89.0	90.6

without the BS branch achieved an accuracy of 91.1%, which is 1.7% lower than the accuracy of our full model. This indicates that the bone modality stream provides important information on the spatial relationship between joints, which is critical for accurate action recognition.

The Impact of MS Branch. We also evaluated the impact of the MS branch by removing this component from our full model. The results showed that the model without an MS branch achieved an accuracy of 89.4%, which is 3.4% lower than our full model's accuracy. This suggests that the MS module enables the model to better integrate joint motion and bone motion information, leading to improved recognition performance.

In addition, we set the final fusion method to additive and multiplicative, respectively, and compare their results, and the results show that the additive method is more effective than the multiplicative method.

Overall, the ablation experiments demonstrate the importance of each component in our proposed model and highlight the benefits of combining joint-motion and bone-motion modalities. The results show that our proposed method achieves a better performance than CTR-GCN.

4.4   Comparison to State-of-the-Art

To reflect our modeling merits, we compare the proposed method with the state-of-the-art skeleton-based action recognition methods on both the NTU-RGB+D dataset and NTU-RGB+D 120 dataset. The results are reported in Table 2. Our model is based on CTR-GCN. It can be seen from the table that on the NTU-RGB+D dataset, the performance of the proposed method is 0.4% and 0.1%

higher than that of CTR-GCN on the X-Sub and X-View standards, respectively. On the NTU-RGB+D dataset, the performance of the proposed method is 0.1% higher than that of CTR-GCN on the X-Sub standard, but the accuracy rate is unchanged on the X-set standard, so the proposed method has no great advantage on this dataset.

5   Conclusion

In this paper, we propose a late-fusion network that fuses multi-modal stream modality outputs in a learnable manner. The network can diversify and effectively integrate the information of each stream, so that the typical representations of each stream can be fully utilized. The experimental results indicate that our fusion algorithm can improve the performance with marginal introduced computation, achieving competitive performance to the current approaches on standard skeleton-based action recognition benchmarks.

References

1. Yan, S., Xiong, Y., Lin, D.: Spatial temporal graph convolutional networks for skeleton-based action recognition. arXiv preprint arXiv:1801.07455 (2018)
2. Shi, L., Zhang, Y., Cheng, J., Lu, H.: Two-stream adaptive graph convolutional networks for skeleton-based action recognition. In: Proceedings of the IEEE Conference on Computer Vision and Pattern Recognition, pp. 12018–12027 (2019)
3. Shi, L., Zhang, Y., Cheng, J., Lu, H.: Skeleton-based action recognition with multi-stream adaptive graph convolutional networks. In: Proceedings of the IEEE Conference on Computer Vision and Pattern Recognition (2019)
4. Shahroudy, A., Liu, J., Ng, T.-T., Wang, G.: NTU RGB+D: a large scale dataset for 3D human activity analysis. In: Proceedings of the IEEE Conference on Computer Vision and Pattern Recognition, pp. 1010–1019 (2016)
5. Liu, J., Shahroudy, A., Perez, M.L., Wang, G., Duan, L.-Y., Chichung, A.K.: NTU RGB+D 120: a large-scale benchmark for 3D human activity understanding. IEEE Trans. Pattern Anal. Mach. Intell. (2019)
6. Vemulapalli, R., Arrate, F., Chellappa, R.: Human action recognition by representing 3D skeletons as points in a lie group. In: IEEE Conference on Computer Vision and Pattern Recognition, pp. 588–595 (2014)
7. Fernando, B., Gavves, E., Oramas, J., Ghodrati, A., Tuytelaars, T.: Modeling video evolution for action recognition. In: IEEE Conference on Computer Vision and Pattern Recognition, pp. 5378–5387 (2015)
8. Du, Y., Wang, W., Wang, L.: Hierarchical recurrent neural network for skeleton based action recognition. In: Proceedings of the IEEE Conference on Computer Vision and Pattern Recognition, pp. 1110–1118 (2015)
9. Li, W., Wen, L., Chang, M.-C., Lim, S.-N., Lyu, S.: Adaptive RNN tree for large-scale human action recognition. In: IEEE International Conference on Computer Vision, pp. 1453–1461(2017)
10. Liu, J., Shahroudy, A., Xu, D., Wang, G.: Spatio-temporal LSTM with trust gates for 3D human action recognition. In: Leibe, B., Matas, J., Sebe, N., Welling, M. (eds.) ECCV 2016. LNCS, vol. 9907, pp. 816–833. Springer, Cham (2016). https://doi.org/10.1007/978-3-319-46487-9_50

11. Liu, H., Tu, J., Liu, M.: Two-stream 3D convolutional neural network for skeleton-based action recognition. arXiv preprint arXiv:1705.08106 (2017)
12. Kim, T.S., Reiter, A.: Interpretable 3D human action analysis with temporal convolutional networks. In: IEEE Conference on Computer Vision and Pattern Recognition Workshops (CVPRW), pp. 1623–1631 (2017)
13. Ke, Q., Bennamoun, S.A., Sohel, F., Boussaïd, F.: A new representation of skeleton sequences for 3D action recognition. In: IEEE Conference on Computer Vision and Pattern Recognition (CVPR), pp. 4570–4579 (2017)
14. Liu, M., Liu, H., Chen, C.: Enhanced skeleton visualization for view invariant human action recognition. Pattern Recogn. **68**, 346–362 (2017). The Journal of the Pattern Recognition Society
15. Xu, T., Feng, Z., Wu, X.-J., Kittler, J.: Toward robust visual object tracking with independent target-agnostic detection and effective Siamese cross-task interaction. IEEE Trans. Image Process. **32**, 1541–1554 (2023)
16. Chen, Y., Zhang, Z., Yuan, C., Li, B., Deng, Y., Hu, W.: Channel-wise topology refinement graph convolution for skeleton-based action recognition. In: IEEE/CVF International Conference on Computer Vision (ICCV), pp. 13339–13348(2021)
17. Zhang, P., Lan, C., Zeng, W., Xing, J., Xue, J., Zheng, N.: Semantics-guided neural networks for efficient skeleton-based human action recognition. In: Proceedings of the IEEE/CVF Conference on Computer Vision and Pattern Recognition, pp. 1112–1121 (2020)
18. Cheng, K., Zhang, Y., He, X., Chen, W., Cheng, J., Lu, H.: Skeleton-based action recognition with shift graph convolutional network. In: Proceedings of the IEEE/CVF Conference on Computer Vision and Pattern Recognition, pp. 183–192 (2020)
19. Shi, L., Zhang, Y., Cheng, J., Lu, H.: Decoupled spatial-temporal attention network for skeleton-based action recognition. arXiv:abs/2007.03263 (2020)
20. Cheng, K., Zhang, Y., Cao, C., Shi, L., Cheng, J., Lu, H.: Decoupling GCN with DropGraph module for skeleton-based action recognition. In: Vedaldi, A., Bischof, H., Brox, T., Frahm, J.-M. (eds.) ECCV 2020. LNCS, vol. 12369, pp. 536–553. Springer, Cham (2020). https://doi.org/10.1007/978-3-030-58586-0_32
21. Liu, Z., Zhang, H., Chen, Z., Wang, Z., Ouyang, W.: Disentangling and unifying graph convolutions for skeleton-based action recognition. In: Proceedings of the IEEE/CVF Conference on Computer Vision and Pattern Recognition, pp. 143–152 (2020)
22. Ye, F., Pu, S., Zhong, Q., Li, C., Xie, D., Tang, H.: Dynamic GCN: context-enriched topology learning for skeleton-based action recognition. In: Proceedings of the 28th ACM International Conference on Multimedia, pp. 55–63 (2020)
23. Wang, S., Zhang, Y., Wei, F., Wang, K., Zhao, M., Jiang, Y.: Skeleton-based action recognition via temporal-channel aggregation. arXiv:abs/2205.15936 (2022)

3D Object Recognition Based on Point Cloud Geometry Construction and Embeddable Attention

Jingshan Shi[1,2], Zhuyan Guo[1,2], Shujia Cheng[1,2], Yuhan Liu[1,2], Mandun Zhang[1,2(✉)], and Zhidong Xiao[3]

[1] School of Artificial Intelligence, Hebei University of Technology, Tianjin 300401, China
zhangmandun@scse.hebut.edu.cn
[2] Tianjin International Joint Center for Virtual Reality and Visual Computing, Tianjin 300401, China
[3] Faculty of Media and Communication, Bournemouth University, Bournemouth BH12 5BB, UK

Abstract. A point cloud is a collection of disordered and discrete points with irregularity, and it lacks of topological structure. The number of discrete points in the point cloud is huge, and how to capture the key features from the large amount of points is crucial to improve the accuracy of model recognition. In this paper, based on point cloud geometry construction and embeddable attention, a 3D object recognition algorithm is proposed. By constructing triangular geometries between points, topological structure information to the point cloud is stored for points' geometric construction module. The embeddable attention module uses an improved attention mechanism with feature bias and nonlinear mapping to enable focused attention to capture key features. In addition, a combination of max and average pooling to aggregate global feature has been applied to avoid situations when using only one method would ignore other key information. In comparison with other state-of-the-art methods using ModelNet40 and ScanObjectNN, the proposed method shows significant improvements in identifying both mAcc and OA. The experiments also demonstrate the effectiveness of the modules in this algorithm.

Keywords: 3D object recognition · Point cloud · Convolutional Neural Network · Geometric construction · Embeddable attention

1 Introduction

In recent year, 3D object recognition has become a research hotspot in the field of computer vision with great research prospects. Such as autonomous driving [1], intelligent robotics [2], virtual reality [3], etc.

The research of classification in pattern recognition based on point cloud has received wide attention from researchers around the world, and the accuracy

© The Author(s) under exclusive license to Springer Nature Switzerland AG 2023
H. Lu et al. (Eds.): ICIG 2023, LNCS 14357, pp. 235–246, 2023.
https://doi.org/10.1007/978-3-031-46311-2_20

of classification in pattern recognition has been significantly improved over the past years. However, due to the fact that each point cloud model contains a large number of discrete points, it may cause information overload. In addition, point clouds are aggregated from disordered discrete points without topological structure, and it lacks geometric information. According to the analysis of the above deficiencies, this paper proposes a 3D object recognition algorithm based on point cloud geometry construction and embeddable attention. The algorithm mainly includes three steps, i.e., point cloud data pre-processing, feature extraction and classification in pattern recognition. In the stage of point cloud pre-processing, the point cloud is randomly sampled from a uniform distribution to reduce the number of discrete points in each point cloud to avoid information redundancy and to simplify the computational complexity. Feature extraction is the key step, which gradually expands the perceptual field through local feature extraction and finally aggregates to obtain a global shape descriptor with rich semantic information. Finally, the class of each point cloud model is obtained by the classifier.

In summary, the main contributions of this paper are as follows:

- Point geometry construction module (PGCM) is proposed to construct triangular geometric structures for sampled points and their two nearest neighboring points. The topological structure information is attached to the point cloud to make up for the shortage of geometric information, so that the extracted point cloud shape descriptors are closer to the real shape of 3D objects.
- During the deep feature extraction of point clouds, an embeddable attention module (EAM) is introduced to achieve focused attention on key information. Meanwhile, the module is embeddable and can be ported to other network structures. By applying a combination of max pooling and average pooling, global features are aggregated for avoiding situations where critical information is overlooked.
- According to the experimental results, the proposed method shows significant improvements over other advanced algorithms from point cloud benchmark datasets ModelNet40 and ScanObjectNN.

The rest of this paper is structured as follows. A brief review of the related work is presented in Sect. 2. Then, the various parts of the proposed algorithm are presented in Sect. 3. Section 4 presents the specific configuration of the experiments and the comparison of the experimental results with other algorithms. Finally, the conclusions of this paper are presented in Sect. 5.

2   Related Work

Along with the iterative update of GPU computing power and the emergence of large 3D model data in the computer field, point cloud classification methods based on deep learning have gradually taken a dominant position, and in this section we mainly introduce several point cloud classification methods related to our algorithm.

In 2017, Qi et al. [4] proposed a groundbreaking method called PointNet, which is directly applied to point cloud learning. It learns features of individual points using a Multi-Layer Perceptron (MLP) and resolves the disorder found in point clouds by using a symmetric function called max pooling; A three-dimensional spatial transformer network is used to solve the problem of rotation invariance of point clouds; Geometric and feature transformations are performed on the input point clouds, and max pooling aggregated point features are used to solve the problem of point cloud substitution invariance. Although PointNet provides a new idea for learning point clouds, it only captures the information of individual points and global points when extracting features, and does not fully consider the interaction of neighboring points and does not extract the local shape information. Without knowing the local shapes, it is difficult for point cloud learning. To learn from local structures, we define a point cloud geometric construction module with discrete and explicit locality, with additional triangular geometry shape information to complement the Cartesian coordinate information of the points.

Convolutional Neural Networks (CNN) have also achieved good results in the classification and recognition task of point clouds. Although traditional CNNs can exploit spatial local correlation, applying them directly to irregular point clouds will not only lose point cloud shape information, but also suffer from point cloud disorder. Li et al. [7] proposed the X-transformation transform convolution operator in PointCNN, which solves the problem of disorder of point clouds to some extent. The KPConv proposed by Thomas H. et al. [9] provides variable convolution operators that use a set of kernel points to define the region applied to each kernel weight. In the proposed method, we use symmetric function max pooling to solve the disorder of point clouds, and apply a 1×1 convolution operation along with batch normalization and activation functions to implement MLP. Other researchers have applied attention mechanisms to point cloud classification. Attentional mechanisms enable the system to focus on primary information and ignore secondary information. Guo et al. [11] proposed a point cloud transformer network (PCT) for point cloud learning by borrowing the transformer structure in the field of natural language processing, and used stacked offset attention modules in the encoder part to improve the accuracy of classification and recognition of point clouds. In this paper, we also propose an embeddable attention module that uses feature bias and nonlinear mapping to improve the self-attention mechanism. The key information is focused and the network model is optimized.

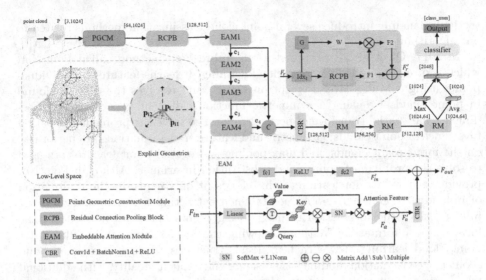

Fig. 1. Network structure of our algorithm. 1024 points are randomly and uniformly selected from the point cloud. And we use only the coordinates information $P = \{p_i | i = 1, ..., 1024\} \in \mathbb{R}^3$ as the input to the network.

3   Deep Hierarchical Network for Point Clouds

3.1   Point Geometric Construction Module

In contrast to existing research programs, we intend to provide some clues about the low-level geometry for the network, rather than repeating similar information for each layer. Point cloud data, although easy to collect, lacks geometric information compared to well-constructed mesh or voxel data. To remedy this drawback and better capture the geometric feature information of point clouds for representing 3D objects adequately, we explicitly enrich the geometric information of points in the low-level space, and apply the MLP-based hierarchy in the high-level feature space to implicitly learn the local geometric context of points and the global feature information between points. For a particular 3D object, we only provide the coordinate information of the 3D point cloud model as a priori knowledge of the network. However, this is not sufficient to describe the local geometry. By forming physically explicit geometric relationships in the low-level space, we are able to attach geometric information to the representation of the point cloud. And the richer low-level geometric cues are provided for better implicit geometric feature learning in the subsequent high-level space.

Inspired by the triangular mesh in computer graphics, the KNN method is used to find two nearest neighbors p_{i1}, p_{i2} for any sampled point $p_i, i = 1, ..., 1024$ to form a triangle in 3D space, as shown in Fig. 1. The triangular mesh can flexibly present continuous and complex 3D shapes, and then the features of the triangular mesh are used to explicitly enhance the low-level geometric relationships between discrete points and the extracted new geometric descriptor p_i'

corresponding to p_i. This geometric descriptor p_i' contains 1) the global position information of point p_i, 2) the vector information from two neighboring points p_{i1} and p_{i2} to point p_i, 3) the side lengths from two points p_{i1} and p_{i2} to point p_i in the triangular mesh, 4) the normals of the triangular mesh, 5) and the center of mass obtained through the intersection of the three medians. The specific formulas are shown below:

$$p_i' = (p_i, edge_1, edge_2, length_1, length_2, normal, centroid); p_i' \in \mathbb{R}^{17} \quad (1)$$

$$p_i = (x_i, y_i, z_i), p_{i1} = (x_{i1}, y_{i1}, z_{i1}), p_{i2} = (x_{i2}, y_{i2}, z_{i2}); p_i, p_{i1}, p_{i2} \in \mathbb{R}^3 \quad (2)$$

$$centroid = (\frac{x_i + x_{i1} + x_{i2}}{3}, \frac{y_i + y_{i1} + y_{i2}}{3}); centroid \in \mathbb{R}^3 \quad (3)$$

$$edge_1 = p_{i1} - p_i, edge_2 = p_{i2} - p_i; edge_1, edge_2 \in \mathbb{R}^3 \quad (4)$$

$$length_1 = |edge_1|, length_2 = |edge_2|; length_1, length_2 \in \mathbb{R}^1 \quad (5)$$

$$normal = edge_1 \times edge_2; normal \in \mathbb{R}^3 \quad (6)$$

p_i' extends the features of p_i from 3 dimensions containing only coordinates to 17 dimensions containing additional geometric information, combining the location and geometric information. The topological structure information between points is enriched. In the point geometry construction module, the obtained new geometric descriptor p_i' is subjected to further feature extraction by MLP to make the feature representation of the point more expressive. The MLP is expressed as a channel fully connected layer. In our experiments, we implement MLP by performing a 1×1 convolution operation on the feature map of the point cloud, as well as batch normalization and activation functions, as shown in the following equations:

$$M(p_i') := \tau(BN(c_{1\times1}(p_i'))) \quad (7)$$

where M is the MLP, τ is the activation function, BN is the batch normalization, and $c_{1\times1}$ is the convolution, and its subscript indicates the size of the convolution kernel.

3.2 Embeddable Attention Module

The human brain's attention is the process of selectively focusing on a small portion of relevant information from a large amount of input, filtering out a significant amount of irrelevant information, and thus addressing the problem of information overload. The proposed embeddable attention module is established based on this mechanism. It enables the neural network to automatically select channel features containing key information for enhancement from a large amount of input information. It helps to improve the ability of data processing in neural network. The limited computational resources will be well utilized for processing more important information and solving the information redundancy problem. To extend its applicability, the module has been designed with the same dimensionalities for both input and output parameters, and it can be directly embedded into other network architectures, as shown in Fig. 1.

The embeddable attention module uses the query-key-value model to map the input features F_1 to three different spaces using different linear transformations to obtain the query matrix Q, the key matrix K and the value matrix V. The linear mapping process is shown below:

$$Q = F_1 W_q \in \mathbb{R}^{D_k \times N} \tag{8}$$

$$K = F_1 W_k \in \mathbb{R}^{D_k \times N} \tag{9}$$

$$V = F_1 W_v \in \mathbb{R}^{D_v \times N} \tag{10}$$

where W_q, W_k, W_v are shared learnable linear transformations, D_k is the dimension of query matrix and key matrix, D_v is the dimension of value matrix, and D_k is not necessarily equal to D_v. Firstly, we use the query matrix and the key matrix to calculate the attention weights by matrix dot product:

$$A^{'} = (\alpha^{'})_{i,j} = Q \cdot K^T \tag{11}$$

The attention distribution is obtained by normalizing the weights using the softmax operator and the L_1 parametrization:

$$\alpha_{i,j} = \frac{\alpha^{''}_{i,j}}{\sum_k \alpha^{''}_{i,j}}, \alpha^{''}_{i,j} = softmax(\alpha^{'}_{i,j}) = \frac{exp(\alpha^{'}_{i,j})}{\sum_k exp(\alpha^{'}_{i,j})} \tag{12}$$

Then the weighted sum of the input information is calculated based on the attention distribution and the value matrix to obtain the attention feature F_a:

$$F_a = A \cdot V = (\alpha)_{i,j} \cdot V \tag{13}$$

In order to obtain the output features F_{out} of the embeddable attention module, first of all, the channel attention feature $F^{'}_{in}$ is achieved by mapping, the input feature F_{in} nonlinearly through the fully connected layer fc_1, the activation function ReLU and the fully connected layer fc_2. Then, similar to the Laplace operator, by calculation of element subtraction, the attention feature F_a is replaced by the offset $F^{'}_a$ between the input F_{in} of the attention module and the attention feature F_a. Finally, the matrix sum of $F^{'}_a$ processed by the convolution layer and the channel attention features $F^{'}_{in}$ is the output features. The equations are shown below:

$$F^{'}_{in} = fc_2(ReLU(BN(fc_1(F_{in})))) \tag{14}$$

$$F_{out} = CBR(F^{'}_a) + F^{'}_{in} = CBR(F_{in} - F_a) + F^{'}_{in} \tag{15}$$

In our designed attention module, softmax operator is used in the first dimension and the L_1 parametrization is applied in the second dimension to normalize the attention mapping, which improves the attention weight and reduces the effect of noise. The offset between the input F_{in} of the attention module and the attention feature F_a is also calculated for replacing the attention feature F_a in order to prevent its happening where the absolute coordinates of the same object

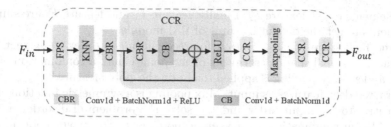

Fig. 2. Residual Connection Pooling Block

are completely different under strict transformation. Since the query matrix, key matrix and value matrix are jointly determined by the corresponding linear transformation matrix and the input features $F_{in} \in \mathbb{R}^{N \times d_e}$, they are all order-independent. Moreover, the softmax operator and the weighted sum are both permutation-independent operators. Therefore, the whole attention process is alignment invariant and is well suited for disordered and irregular regions presented by point clouds. The process of nonlinearly mapping of the input features F_{in} to obtain the channel attention features F'_{in} enables our network more adaptive to different channel features and more robust. In our network structure, we also applied stacked EAMs for controlling and optimizing the outputs, based on the global context, fine-grained attention features are generated for the input features and transformed into a high-dimensional feature space which can characterize the semantic similarity between points, as shown in the following equations:

$$F_1 = EAM^1(F_{in}) \tag{16}$$

$$F_i = EAM^i(F_{i-1}); i = 2, 3, 4 \tag{17}$$

$$F_{final} = MLP(concat(F_1, F_2, F_3, F_4)) \tag{18}$$

3.3 Deep Feature Extraction

As illustrated in Fig. 1, for deep feature extraction, the stacked RMs gradually expand the receptive field and aggregate the local feature information and global relationship information of the point cloud. The RM module initially contains a residual connection pooling block (RCPB). As is shown in Fig. 2, RCPB is a small residual network that improves the information propagation efficiency by adding directly connected edges to the nonlinear convolutional layer, while obtaining a new feature descriptor p'_i for each sampling point p_i. The local geometric context and feature context are fused based on the geometric relation between points. RCPB aggregates the local structure relationships of the point cloud to obtain the local feature F_1. Meanwhile, in order to increase the global relationship information between points, the global relationship matrix G between each point and other points is constructed using the same down-sampling index set Idx_1 as RCPB. Then it is converted into a weight matrix W and multiplied with feature

F_1 by elements to get feature F_2. Finally, feature F_1 and feature F_2 are summed by elements to get the output features of RM module.

In the final stage of classification for recognition, in order to extract more representative global shape descriptors of the point cloud, a combination of max pooling and average pooling is applied to obtain the global feature by aggregating the extracted deep features as input. Max pooling is a symmetric function, which is insensitive to the input order and can solve the problem of disorder in point clouds. Also in combination with average pooling, it can avoid ignoring other critical information. To classify point clouds into multiple object classes (e.g., tables, desks, chairs, etc.), we input global features to a classifier. The classifier consists of two cascaded feedforward neural networks with a dropout of 0.5 for each layer, which is finally determined by the linear layer. The class with the highest score in the final predicted classification score is the class of the point cloud.

4   Experiment

We evaluated the performance of our proposed network model on two datasets, ModelNet40 and ScanObjectNN, and compared it with other state-of-the-art methods. The effectiveness and superiority of the modules in this algorithm are demonstrated by ablation experiments.

4.1   Evaluation Indicators

For the evaluation metrics, we use the average accuracy(mAcc) on each category and the overall accuracy(OA) on all categories to evaluate the experimental results, as expressed by the following equations:

$$mAcc = \frac{\sum_{i=1}^{K} \frac{T_i}{N_i}}{K}, OA = \frac{T}{N} \tag{19}$$

where T is the number of correctly predicted point clouds. $T = \sum_{i=1}^{K} T_i$, T_i is the number of correctly predicted point clouds in class i. K is the number of classes in the dataset. N is the number of all point clouds in the dataset. $N = \sum_{i=1}^{K} N_i$, N_i is the number of point clouds in class i.

4.2   Classification on the ModelNet40 Dataset

The ModelNet40 dataset contains 12311 noise-free shape models from 40 classes, 9843 training models and 2468 test models. The experimental batch size is 32, and the initial learning rate is 0.1. The learning rate is adjusted using CosineAnnealingLR. The optimizer is SGD with a weight decay of 0.0002. 300 epochs were trained for the experiment. The experiment was run on GPU 3090 and CPU AMD epyc 7543.

Table 1. Comparison with the latest methods on the ModelNet40 classification dataset. All cited results are taken from the cited papers. P = points, N = normals. The best is marked in bold.

Method	Input	#Points	mAcc (%)	OA (%)
PointNet [4]	P	1k	86.0	89.2
PointNet++ [5]	P	1k	–	90.7
PointNet++ [5]	P+N	5k	–	91.9
PointCNN [7]	P	1k	88.1	92.5
PCNN [13]	P	1k	–	92.3
PointConv [8]	P+N	1k	–	92.5
Point2Sequence [14]	P	1k	90.4	92.6
RS-CNN [15]	P	1k	–	92.9
DGCNN [10]	P	1k	90.2	92.9
CAA [16]	P	1k	91.0	93.8
PointASNL [18]	P	1k	–	92.9
Point Trans. [17]	P	1k	–	92.8
PosPool [18]	P	5k	–	93.2
MLMSPT [19]	P	1k	–	92.9
PCT [11]	P	1k	–	93.2
Point Trans. [20]	P	1k	90.6	93.7
RepSurf-T [21]	P	1k	91.1	94.0
SGCNN [22]	P	1k	90.4	93.4
3DCTN [23]	P+N	1k	91.2	93.3
ours	P	1k	**91.7**	**94.5**

The experimental results are shown in Table 1. Compared with the Transformer-based PointTrans. [20] method, the mAcc improved by 1.1% and OA improved by 0.8%; Compared with CAA, the mAcc improved by 0.7% and OA improved by 0.7%. The mAcc improved by 1.5% and OA improved by 1.6% over the graph convolution-based method DGCNN; The mAcc improved by 3.6% and OA improved by 2.0% over the point convolution-based method PointCNN; The mAcc improved by 1.3% and OA improved by 1.9% over the attention-based method Point2Sequence. Our method obtains higher mAcc value and more competitive OA value, indicating that our method has robust classification performance for different types of point clouds.

4.3 Classification on the ScanObjectNN Dataset

The ScanObjectNN dataset is the first real-world dataset for point cloud classification, containing 15,000 point cloud models in 15 categories. There are 2902 corresponding unique object instances with background, noise and occlusion. The

experimental batch size is 32. The initial learning rate is 0.01. The optimizer is
SGD. The weights are decayed by 0.0001, and 200 epochs are trained.

Compared to the current state of the art, our method outperforms all methods with significant improvements in both mAcc and OA. As shown in Table 2, our mAcc and OA are 5.5% and 3.8% higher than PRANet, respectively. Furthermore, we note that our method achieves the smallest gap between mAcc and OA. This phenomenon indicates that our method is not biased towards a particular class and shows a fairly good robustness.

Table 2. Comparison with the latest methods on the ScanObjectNN classification dataset. All cited results are taken from the cited papers. The best one is marked in bold.

Method	mAcc (%)	OA (%)
PointNet [4]	63.4	68.2
PointNet++ [5]	75.4	77.9
PointCNN [7]	75.1	78.5
SpiderCNN [24]	69.8	73.7
DGCNN [10]	73.6	78.1
BGA-PA++ [25]	77.5	80.2
BGA-DGCNN [25]	75.7	79.7
Simple View [26]	–	80.5 ± 0.3
GBNet [16]	77.8	80.5
DRNet [27]	78.0	80.3
PRANet [28]	79.1	82.1
MVTN [29]	–	82.8
RepSurf-T [21]	81.2	84.1
ours	**84.6**	**85.9**

Table 3. Ablation experiments for the proposed network on ModelNet40. GRM indicates global relation matrix.

PGCM	EAM	GRM	Max	Max+Avg	mAcc (%)	OA (%)
✗	✓	✓	✗	✓	91.0	93.6
✓	✗	✓	✗	✓	90.4	93.1
✓	✓	✗	✗	✓	91.4	94.0
✓	✓	✓	✓	✗	91.3	93.7
✓	✓	✓	✗	✓	91.7	94.5

4.4   Ablation Studies

The results of the ablation experiments performed on ModelNet40 are shown in Table 3. As can be seen from the first row of data, the removal of the point geometric construction block resulted in a 0.7% decrease in mAcc and a 0.9% decrease in OA. The second row of data shows a 1.3% decrease in mAcc and a 1.4% decrease in OA after removing the embeddable attention module. As can be seen from the third row of data, after removing the global relationship matrix, mAcc decreases by 0.3% and OA decreases by 0.5%. As can be seen from the fourth row of data, using only maximum pooling when performing global feature aggregation, the mAcc decreases by 0.4% and the OA decreases by 0.8%. In summary, each component of the network is effective for point cloud classification recognition.

5   Conclusion

In this study, by constructing triangular geometries between points with stacked attention modules focus on the key information, a 3D object recognition algorithm based on point cloud geometry construction and embeddable attention is proposed. To enhance the robustness and effectiveness of the neural network, a combination of max pooling and average pooling is also applied to aggregate global shape descriptors. Due to the advantages of this algorithm, the proposed method has outperformed the most state-of-the-art methods by evaluating ModelNet40 and ScanObjectNN datasets. The proposed method has achieved higher accuracy and has shown good performance in 3D object recognition. Similarly, this framework can also be applied to point cloud semantic segmentation, which involves assigning semantic labels to each point. By adding additional layers or modules to the final layer of the framework, it can be extended from a classification model to a segmentation model. In this way, during the training process, the model can simultaneously learn the semantic labels for each point and output point-level semantic segmentation results.

Acknowledgements. This work is supported by Natural Science Foundation of Hebei Province (F2019202054).

References

1. Chiang, C.H., Kuo, C.H., Lin, C.C., Chiang, H.T.: 3D point cloud classification for autonomous driving via dense-residual fusion network. IEEE Access **8**, 163775–163783 (2020)
2. Yang, L., Liu, Y., Peng, J., Liang, Z.: A novel system for off-line 3D seam extraction and path planning based on point cloud segmentation for arc welding robot. Robot. Comput. Integr. Manuf. **64**(3), 101929 (2020)
3. Bolkas, D., Chiampi, J., Chapman, J., Pavill, V.F.: Creating a virtual reality environment with a fusion of sUAS and TLS point-clouds. Int. J. Image Data Fusion **1**, 1–26 (2020)
4. Qi, C.R., Su, H., Mo, K., Guibas, L.J.: PointNet: deep learning on point sets for 3D classification and segmentation. IEEE (2017)
5. Qi, C.R., Li, Y., Hao, S., Guibas, L.J.: PointNet++: deep hierarchical feature learning on point sets in a metric space (2017)

6. Yan, X., Zheng, C., Li, Z., Wang, S., Cui, S.: PointASNL: robust point clouds processing using nonlocal neural networks with adaptive sampling. IEEE (2020)
7. Li, Y., Bu, R., Sun, M., Wu, W., Di, X., Chen, B.: PointCNN: convolution on x-transformed points. In: Neural Information Processing Systems (2018)
8. Wu, W., Qi, Z., Li, F.: PointConv: deep convolutional networks on 3D point clouds. In: 2019 IEEE/CVF Conference on Computer Vision and Pattern Recognition (CVPR) (2019)
9. Thomas, H., Qi, C.R., Deschaud, J.E., Marcotegui, B., Guibas, L.J.: KpConv: flexible and deformable convolution for point clouds (2019)
10. Yan, S., et al.: Implicit autoencoder for point cloud self-supervised representation learning. arXiv e-prints (2022)
11. Guo, M.H., Cai, J.X., Liu, Z.N., Mu, T.J., Martin, R.R., Hu, S.M.: PCT: point cloud transformer. Comput. Visual Media **7**(2), 13 (2021)
12. Wu, Z., et al.: 3D ShapeNets: a deep representation for volumetric shapes. In: 2015 IEEE Conference on Computer Vision and Pattern Recognition (CVPR) (2015)
13. Atzmon, M., Maron, H., Lipman, Y.: Point convolutional neural networks by extension operators. ACM Trans. Graph. **37**(4CD), 71.1– 71.12 (2018)
14. Liu, X., Han, Z., Liu, Y.S., Zwicker, M.: Point2Sequence: learning the shape representation of 3D point clouds with an attention-based sequence to sequence network. Proc. AAAI Conf. Artif. Intell. **33**, 8778–8785 (2019)
15. Fan, B., Pan, C., Xiang, S., Liu, Y.: Relation-shape convolutional neural network for point cloud analysis (2019)
16. Qiu, S., Anwar, S., Barnes, N.: Geometric back-projection network for point cloud classification (2019)
17. Engel, N., Belagiannis, V., Dietmayer, K.: Point transformer (2020)
18. Liu, Z., Hu, H., Cao, Y., Zhang, Z., Tong, X.: A closer look at local aggregation operators in point cloud analysis (2020)
19. Han, X.F., Kuang, Y.J., Xiao, G.Q.: Point cloud learning with transformer (2021)
20. Zhao, H., Jiang, L., Jia, J., Torr, P., Koltun, V.: Point transformer (2020)
21. Ran, H., Liu, J., Wang, C.: Surface representation for point clouds (2022)
22. Liu, S., Liu, D., Chen, C., Xu, C.: SGCNN for 3D point cloud classification. In: 2022 14th International Conference on Machine Learning and Computing (ICMLC) (2022)
23. Lu, D., Xie, Q., Xu, L., Li, J.: 3DCTN: 3D convolution-transformer network for point cloud classification (2022)
24. Xu, Y., Fan, T., Xu, M., Long, Z., Yu, Q.: SpiderCNN: deep learning on point sets with parameterized convolutional filters (2018)
25. Uy, M.A., Pham, Q.H., Hua, B.S., Nguyen, T., Yeung, S.K.: Revisiting point cloud classification: a new benchmark dataset and classification model on real-world data. IEEE (2020)
26. Goyal, A., Law, H., Liu, B., Newell, A., Deng, J.: Revisiting point cloud shape classification with a simple and effective baseline (2021)
27. Qiu, S., Anwar, S., Barnes, N.: Dense-resolution network for point cloud classification and segmentation (2020)
28. Cheng, S., Chen, X., He, X., Liu, Z., Bai, X.: PRA-Net: point relation-aware network for 3D point cloud analysis. IEEE Trans. Image Process. **30**, 4436–4448 (2021)
29. Hamdi, A., Giancola, S., Li, B., Thabet, A., Ghanem, B.: MVTN: multi-view transformation network for 3D shape recognition (2020)
30. Klokov, R., Lempitsky, V.: Escape from cells: deep Kd-networks for the recognition of 3D point cloud models. IEEE (2017)

The Research Landscape of Site-Specific Art in Public Art Map Quantification Based on Citespace

Yun Zhang[1] and Cheeyong Kim[2(✉)]

[1] Department of Storytelling, Graduate School Dong-Eui University, Seoul, Korea
[2] College of ICT, Digital Contents Game Engineering, University, Seoul, Korea
kimchee@deu.ac.kr

Abstract. Public art has attracted attention from researchers in various fields due to its wide research scope. However, there has been relatively little research on specific fields within the development process of public art and specific artistic phenomena in these fields. Understanding and grasping the context of this phenomenon from a macro perspective is not an easy task. This paper utilizes the advantages of Citespace, a literature-based visualization software, to conduct data visualization analysis on research literature in the specific field of public art over the past two decades. The results show that: (1) The number of publications on specific fields within public art in both the Web of Science (WOS) and CNKI (China National Knowledge Infrastructure) platforms has experienced two stages of research. (2) By analyzing the cooperation networks of authors and research institutions, the research status and influence of national institutions and journals on this topic in the last 20 years can be observed. The research institutions on the WOS platform exhibit a pattern of broad collaboration and exchange, while those on the CNKI platform tend to have smaller group collaborations. (3) Through keyword clustering analysis, nine clusters were identified. On the WOS platform, they were summarized into two main research directions: the specificity of public art locations and their relationship with art, and the practical approaches within specific fields of public art. On the CNKI platform, they were summarized into three main research directions: public art and publicness, the regional nature of specific fields, and the artistic forms within specific fields. (4) Based on the high-frequency keyword table and keyword timeline graph, research content and trends on the WOS platform focus more on identity, cultural heritage, location, contemporary art, community, and other related research questions. On the CNKI platform, more attention is given to research questions about publicness, artistry, urban landscapes, urban memory, art intervention, field specificity, contemporary art, and public participation. This paper visually analyzes the research frontier network relationship in the field of urban public art through graph visualization, providing theoretical support for the practice, theoretical development, research hotspots, and knowledge structure of public art.

Keywords: Public art · Specific site · Citespace · Knowledge map · Art development

© The Author(s), under exclusive license to Springer Nature Switzerland AG 2023
H. Lu et al. (Eds.): ICIG 2023, LNCS 14357, pp. 247–261, 2023.
https://doi.org/10.1007/978-3-031-46311-2_21

1 Introduction

It was initially referred to as "art in spaces" until the Art-in-City Percent for Art program was passed in Philadelphia, USA, in 1959, which officially established public art as an important tool for cities. The realization of publicness in public art relies on two key factors. Firstly, it involves the artistic expression, encompassing various creative methods across different media. Secondly, it is characterized by its specificity to certain locations, known as site-specific art. Site-specific art refers to artworks created for and existing within specific places, often taking into consideration the physical features, history, natural environment, and cultural background of the location. The current state of research on site-specific art is continually evolving, with scholars and artists continually presenting new perspectives and viewpoints, which forms the core of this study.

This research focuses on the dimension of site-specificity, using relevant literature from the past two decades as the research object to summarize the research questions, hotspots, and trends within urban public art's site-specific art (referred to as "specific field art" hereafter). This exploration aims to contribute to a better understanding of the current state of site-specific art in urban public art.blic art, specific fields, Cite-Space, knowledge graph, artistic development.

2 Research Methods and Data Interpretation

Cite-Space is one of the most popular tools for analyzing co-citation networks in studies, which is able to visualize research citation history and citation structure in a subject area in a graphical mode. [1] The integration and assistance of Cite-Space software improve time efficiency and allow for a more intuitive, objective, and comprehensive presentation of systematic research in the field, minimizing potential biases in the research process.

Cite-Space 5.8.R3 was used as the analysis software for this study. To ensure the scientificity and completeness of the data sources, the Web of Science Core Collection database (WOSCC) was selected as the literature data platform, as it is considered an ideal data source for bibliometric surveys. [2] However, one major concern with using WOSCC is its English -centric and dominant focus. [3] To ensure the breadth and authority of the literature data, this study also collected data from the China National Knowledge Infrastructure (CNKI), a Chinese core data source for academic literature.

The research spanned from 2002 to 2022, focusing on the field of Site-Specific Art. The term "Site-Specific Art" was defined and encompassed by scholar Miwon Kwon in the book "One place after another: Site-specific art and locational identity" (MIT Press, 2004). Other scholars have extended the concept around the notions of site and art. Thus, the key search terms used in this study were "public art" and "site."The search parameters were set as follows: TS = ("site en public art") to capture the literature information in titles, abstracts, authors, keywords, and keyword plus fields containing the terms "site" and "public art." Only peer-reviewed articles were chosen as the document type, as they represent original scientific developments.After conducting the search, a preliminary retrieval yielded 731 records from WOS and 267 records from CNKI, resulting in a total of 838 valid records after removing duplicates and irrelevant data. Further analysis was conducted on a subset of relevant literature, consisting of 658 records from WOS and 267 records from CNKI.

2.1 Current Status of Public Art Research

Contemporary public art was first born in the United States in the late 1950s and early 1960s. Public art is a dynamic concept, and its conceptual connotation, work form, operation mechanism and value function are constantly changing and expanding. Public art ranges from urban architectural decoration to intervention in public places, thereby participating in new public art in urban planning, and then to new types of public art that connect communities. Public art has been extended from a cultural welfare policy to a universal cultural concept and artistic spirit, which represents a new value orientation of the relationship between art and the city, art and the public, art and society, and ultimately points to the The realization of a modern civil society that is open, public and democratic. This study focuses on the literature trend of specific fields in public art. Previous research reviews are basically completed through subjective analysis. This kind of comment based only on words is not as intuitive as images, and has certain limitations. Cite-space provides researchers with an objective analysis perspective.

Although the research paradigm of site-specific art comes from the category of Western art, the development of site-specific art occurs in different ways in different countries because it is influenced by various cultural, social and political factors. Therefore, the value of this study lies in the comparative analysis of WOS, the core literature data of Western studies, and CNKI, the Chinese literature research data. Taking the data characteristics of the retrieved 925 documents as the main research object, statistical analysis was carried out from the perspectives of the annual distribution of the number of documents, journals, high-yield authors and co-authors, high-frequency downloads and cited documents, etc., and summarized the field of urban public art The current status of the research, and the trend chart of the published papers is obtained by counting the number of each year.

2.1.1 Post Trend

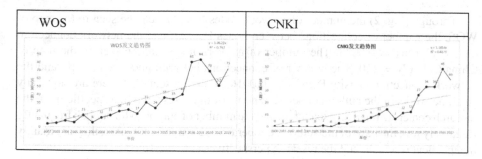

Fig. 1. Published Trend Chart

The annual publication volume in the research field is an important indicator to measure the development of scientific research. By drawing a quantitative map of Times Cited and Publications over time as shown in Fig. 1, we can understand the development status and development trend of art research in a specific field. According to the changes in the number of articles published throughout the search years, the research on site-specific art has shown an upward trend in the past 20 years. It can be seen from the number of published documents in WOS: research in related fields has begun in 2002, but the number of publications is within 4–40; in 2018, the enthusiasm for research gradually increased, and about 80 papers were published every year, and the number of papers showed a zigzag increase the trend of. The research on site-specific art in China's CNKI literature started in 2006, and showed a prominent upward trend in 2018, reaching an annual publication volume of 41 in 2021. From the growth trend of published papers, it can be seen that this field has become a global research hotspot in 2018 and the research scope is constantly expanding. The results show that the overall research level and attention in this field are constantly improving, and it can be seen from the number of published papers that it is an emerging research field.

2.1.2 Literature Author Visual Analysis

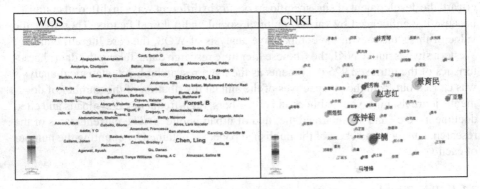

Fig. 2. Literature author collaboration visualization

Through (Fig. 2) the number of network nodes $N = 127$ can be seen in the map of WOS, the number of connections between nodes $E = 27$, and the network connection density Density $= 0.0034$. The number of network nodes can be seen in the map of China CNKI $N = 150$, The number of connections between nodes is $E = 18$, and the network connection density Density $= 0.0016$. It can be seen that there are not many small networks in the author cooperation network of art research in a specific field, the research content is relatively scattered, and the number of authors who publish frequently Relatively few, the base of the author's cooperative research is not large, they are mainly independent research, and the research perspectives are diversified.

2.1.3 Literature Author Visual Analysis

An effective analysis of the issuing institutions and their cooperative relations will help to grasp the core research institutions in the field of art research in a specific field as a whole. As shown in Fig. 3, each node in the map represents a research institution, and the connection between nodes reflects the cooperative relationship between different

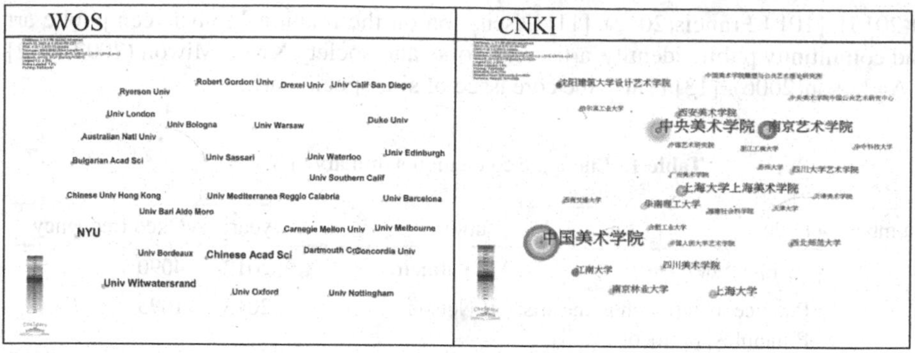

Fig. 3. Network visualization of research institutions cooperation

institutions. The running result of Wos is the number of nodes N = 132, the number of connections E = 27, and the network density Density = 0.0031. It can be seen from the figure that NYU, Chinese Acad Sci, Univ Witwatersrand, Univ Barcelona, Robert Gordon Univ, Univ Sassari, Univ Bari Aldo Moro, Univ Melbourne, Univ Oxford, and Duke Univ are the top ten institutions in this field. From the graph, it can be observed that the institutional density is relatively high, indicating significant contributions from both national and institutional entities to this field. Moreover, there exists a close collaborative relationship among them, suggesting a relatively high level of communication and cooperation.The result of CNKI operation is that the number of nodes N = 115, the number of connections E = 15, and the network density Density = 0.0023. It can be seen from the figure that the institutions with relatively high research centrality are mainly the Chinese Academy of Fine Arts. Secondly, it can be seen that some academies have established public art research centers and theoretical research institutes, including the China Academy of Art, the Central Academy of Fine Arts, and Nanjing Art Academy. The academy and the Shanghai Academy of Fine Arts of Shanghai University have published a relatively large amount of papers. It can be seen from the map that although the number of research institutions is increasing, the density is relatively low, which indicates that there is a lack of close cooperation between institutions and the degree of communication is relatively low. It can be seen that in the process of global urbanization, each country faces different problems and focuses differently.

2.1.4 Document Co-citation Analysis

The number of co-citations of documents can be seen as hot spots in the research field. The top ten articles with the most co-citations are listed through statistics. As shown in Table 1, it can be seen that the cited documents are researched from multiple dimensions. Discussion needs to explore the relationship with art from other fields. Among them, as a study discussing artistic practice methods, the authors of the cited literature refer to M Palmeira (2012), [4] R Nelson (2013), [5] He focuses on art in a collaborative way as a practical method. Human geography related to place and field D Ley(2014), [6] K Yusoff (2011), [7] has a relatively high number of citations, involving public art and urban research literature T Hall(2001), [8] D Atkinson(1998) [9] McGillivray

D(2015), [10] J Francis(2012), [11] Discussion on the relationship between public art and community public identity, artist and works and society Kwon Miwon (2002), [12] S Anderson(2006), [13] is also the core issue of site-specific art.

Table 1. Literature co-citation summary of WOS

number	topic	author	years	Cited frequency
1	Artificial hellsrar	M Palmeira	2012	4090
2	Practice as research in the arts: Principles, protocols, pedagogies, resistances	R Nelson	2013	1093
3	Creating sense of community: The role of public space	J Francis	2012	767
4	Social & Cultural Geography	D Ley	2014	619
5	Public art and urban regeneration: advocacy, claims and critical debates	T Hall, I Robertson	2001	426
6	Climate change and the imagination	K Yusoff	2011	348
7	Urban rhetoric and embodied identities: city, nation, and empire at the Vittorio Emanuele II monument in Rome, 1870–1945	D Atkinson	1998	317
8	One place after another	Kwon Miwon	2002	280
9	Imagined communities	S Anderson	2006	254
10	Urban studies	McGillivray D	2015	250

From the perspective of the number of published articles, the research trend of public art in China has shown an upward trend in recent years. The research status of site-specific art in China is different from that in the West. The research content and trends are summarized from the researchers and the types of articles published. Based on the author co-citation graph above, this study retrieves the top ten authors with the highest frequency of publications and the most cited documents in CNKI, and summarizes their research field dimensions and research contents in the following Table 2, it can be seen that many researchers are sorting out the development of public art in China, such as: Jing Yumin(2012), [14] Zhao Zhihong (2007), [15] Ding Yahui (2019), [16] and researchers discussing the problems and strategies of public art in the development of Chinese cities, Wang Donghui (2012), [17] Ma Zengfeng(2011), [18] Zhou Xiumei (2013), [19] Wang Zhong (2015),[20] a researcher from the perspective of education, Li Nan(2013), [21] who researched from the ontology of public art creation Lin Xiuqin (2014), [22] and from Zhang Zhongtao, a researcher who discusses the relationship between public art and digital capital from a critical perspective(2022), [23] it can be seen that the research on field development in public art in China is mainly based on conceptual history, strategy and ontology research.

Table 2. Literature co-citation summary of CNKI

number	topic	author	years	Cited frequency
1	The Cultural Logic of Digital Capitalism:" Participation" from Artistic Critique to Data Production	Zhang Z	2022	411
2	Application Research of Qin and Han Culture in Xi'an Metro Public Art	Li Nan	2013	658
3	The Symbol of Urban Spirit——The Development of Public Art in China	Jing Yumin	2012	411
4	The Discourse Transformation of Art in Public Space——The Change of the Concept of Public Art	Zhao Zhihong	2007	619
5	Research on the Integral Design of Public Art from the Perspective of Urban Culture	Zhou Xiume	2013	11764
6	Research on the planning of public art activities in urban blocks	Ma Zengfeng	2011	348
7	Public Art and Aesthetic Intervention	Lin Xiuqin	2014	755
8	One place after another	Kwon Miwon	2002	280
9	Imagined communities	S Anderson	2006	254
10	The Current Situation and Development Strategies of Public Art Education in China	Wang Zhong	2015	592

3   Analysis of Research Hotspots and Research Trends

By summarizing the content of the clusters in the keyword map, combined with the frequency of keywords, betweenness centrality and the above analysis, we can understand and summarize the main content and hot topics of the research on the specific field of public art published by WOS in the past 20 years, and then use Cite-Space's salient value detection function finds out the key nodes of research and research directions that have attracted much attention in recent years.

3.1   Research Hotspots

Keywords are the vocabulary refined by the author to summarize the theme of the article. They are the author's high-level summary and refinement of the author's academic thoughts, research topics and research content for a specific research. Keywords can also become a way and method to analyze the research topic. At the same time, by examining the frequency of keywords in this field, we can understand and grasp the research hotspots in this field, and judge the update speed of research content in this field and the vitality of subject research. Through the cluster analysis and word frequency analysis functions of keywords, it is possible to clarify the development context, hot areas and important themes of research on specific fields of public art. The knowledge graph of keyword co-occurrence can reflect research hotspots over time, while burst keywords (keywords are frequently cited over a period of time) can indicate cutting-edge research topics. The high-frequency keywords are analyzed by CiteSpace, and Fig. 4 lists the top 10 keywords according to frequency and centrality.

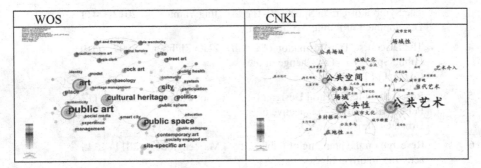

Fig. 4. Keyword co-occurrence graph

From the WOS literature data in Table 3, among the top 10 high-frequency keywords, "public art" appears most frequently, followed by "public space, cultural heritage, city, politics, site-specific art, place, contemporary art". It can be seen that field-specific research involves core fields such as public space, cities, cultural history, politics, and contemporary art practice. In terms of betweenness centrality, if the centrality of a keyword exceeds 0.1, it means that there are many studies around this keyword. It can be seen from Table 3 that "archaeology" (0.19), "public space" (0.15), and "cultural heritage" (0.13) all have high centrality, indicating that the research centrality around the field is mainly based on "regional cultural history " and "public space" are two core points, which have become research hotspots and trends. In the China CNKI document data platform, the top 10 high-frequency keywords in Table 4 are "public art, publicity, public space, public field, locality, contemporary art, intervention, public participation, rural revitalization", it can be seen that Chinese researchers pay more attention to the realization of publicity through field art in public art, and pay attention to the methods and purposes of art practice.

3.2 Development and Trend of the Research Field

3.2.1 Keyword Cluster Analysis

Based on the data processing results of keyword clustering analysis, a high-frequency keyword clustering knowledge map for the research on public art in specific fields from

Table 3. Top10 keywords in terms of counts and centrality of WOS

Rank	Frequency	Keywords	Centrality	Keywords
1	57	public art	0.19	archaeology
2	28	art	0.18	art
3	26	public space	0.16	city
4	20	cultural heritage	0.15	public space
5	14	city	0.13	cultural heritage
6	9	politics	0.1	politics
7	8	site-specific art	0.08	public sphere
8	7	rock art	0.08	urban common
9	7	place	0.07	site
10	6	contemporary art	0.06	experience

Table 4. Top10 keywords in terms of counts and centrality of CNKI

Rank	Frequency	Keywords	Centrality	Keywords
1	120	public art	0.83	public art
2	28	publicity	0.75	publicity
3	26	public space	0.52	public space
4	12	field	0.15	contemporary art
5	8	public space	0.13	public space
6	7	Locality	0.11	intervention
7	7	contemporary art	0.11	City
8	7	intervention	0.08	city image
9	6	public participation	0.08	rural revitalization
10	6	rural revitalization	0.08	participate

2002 to 2022 was generated using CiteSpace. The clarity of the network structure and clustering in CiteSpace is evaluated using two indicators: Modularity value (Q-value) and Average silhouette value (S-value). These indicators serve as criteria for assessing the effectiveness of the knowledge map. Generally, Q-value within the range of 0.1 is acceptable, and Q > 0.3 indicates a significant clustering structure. A silhouette value (S-value) of 0.7 indicates high efficiency of clustering, and above 0.5 is generally considered reasonable for clustering structure. [24] A silhouette value (S-value) of 0.7 indicates high efficiency of clustering, and above 0.5 is generally considered reasonable for clustering. The Q-value calculated from the WOS data platform is 0.7857 (>0.3), indicating a significant clustering structure, and the S-value is 0.9464 (>0.7), indicating high efficiency and convincing clustering. Similarly, the Q-value from the CNKI data platform is 0.7719 (>0.3), showing significant clustering structure, and the S-value is 0.9625 (>0.7), indicating high efficiency and convincing clustering. These results suggest that the generated knowledge maps have a significant clustering structure, high efficiency, and reliability, providing valuable insights into the development and trends in the research on public art in specific fields over the years.

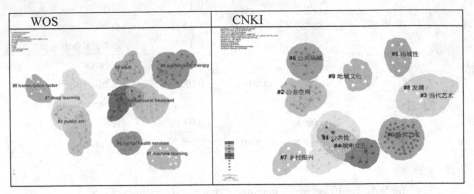

Fig. 5. Keyword co-occurrence graph

As shown in Fig. 5, there are 9 clusters of high-frequency keywords in the research field in the WOS data platform. The cluster numbers start from 0 according to the cluster size. The largest cluster #0public art has a contour value of 0.915, the number of nodes is 15, including important keywords (cultural heritage; architecture; virtual reality; smart cities), the second largest cluster is #1 public engagement with a contour value of 0.988, the number of nodes is 15, including important keywords (art inquiry; decolonisation; inter dependency; social inclusivity), the third largest cluster #3artificial intelligence, the contour value is 1, the number of nodes is 13, including important keywords (deep learning; internet of things; twitter; sentiment analysis); the largest in CNKI data platform The cluster #0 public art, the contour value is 0.995, the number of nodes is 40, contains important keywords (publicity; space; public space; contemporary art), the second largest cluster is #1 publicity, the contour value is 0.93, The number of nodes is 25, including important keywords (public participation; artistry; locality; urban space aesthetics), the third largest cluster #3 public space, the contour value is 0.993, the number of nodes is 18, including important keywords (public art; urban public art; place remodeling; subway station); As a result, each cluster presents a list of keywords extracted based on the TF*IDF weighted algorithm. Citespace provides an automatic clustering function using spectral clustering algorithm and offers three algorithms to extract cluster theme words from clustered citing literature. The default automatic label words are generated using the TF-IDF weighted algorithm. [25] The importance of each cluster is arranged from the largest to the smallest, from left to right. Analyzing the arrangement of keywords in clusters, it can be summarized that the research hotspots and key areas of urban public art revolve around urban spatial design planning, urban policies, public spaces, and public participation in urban issues, which extend the research scope and disciplinary boundaries of public art.

3.2.2 Development and Evolution

Select the timeline view in Cite-Space to get the keyword timeline visualization knowledge map Fig. 6, from which you can get the clustering information of keywords, discover the dynamic development law of the research field, and clearly present the relationship between the research topics.

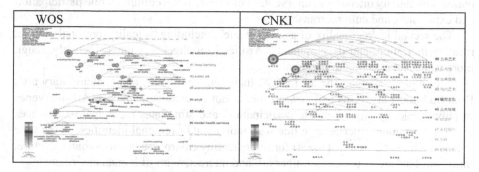

Fig. 6. Keyword timeline visualization

It can be seen from Fig. 5 that the first nine clustering labels in the keyword timeline visualization knowledge map in the WOS data platform are "public art", "public engagement", "artificial intelligence", "public space", and "culture for sustainable development", "independent spaces", "public pedagogy", "rock art", "art museums". According to the clustering labels and the structural characteristics of the public art research field, this study distilled nine clustering labels into three major research fields. The three major research areas are also hot spots in the field of research on specific fields of public art.

The first one is "Specificity of Public Art Sites and Art", including "public art", "public space", "independent spaces", "culture for sustainable development", "rock art", and "art museums". The field research in public art revolves around the physical form, which can also be said to be the public space. At the same time, the research on the non-material field includes the public field of culture and history. The two are in parallel. Therefore, the physical space Public art, sustainable development in the cultural field, public education, and art museums are the focus of research.

The second is "Practical methods of public art in specific sites", including "public engagement", "artificial intelligence", "#6 risk factors", the "Art Percentage" project in Philadelphia, USA regards the entire city and its processes as artistic intervention The practice of field, the combination with the city from the perspective of art has become the trend of regional development research. Among them, public participation, the construction of regional identity through art, and the use of new digital technology and artificial intelligence methods actively endow public art with more value and meaning.

The first nine cluster labels in the timeline map of China CNKI data platform are "public art, publicity, public space, contemporary art, urban culture, public field, field, rural revitalization, development, and regional culture". According to the clustering tags and the structural characteristics of the public art research field, this study distills nine clustering tags into three major research fields, and summarizes the hotspots in the field of public art research.

The first one is "public art and publicity", including "publicity, public space, public field, and urban culture". Chinese scholars focus more on the field of public art and publicity, and discuss the scope of public space and public field from the aspects of public space function, civic culture, aesthetic public welfare, public discourse, public participation, community interaction, intervention methods, urban culture, public participation and expression, and cultural transmission.

The second is "regionality of a specific site", including "siteality, regional culture, rural revitalization, and development". Artificial intelligence methods actively assign more value and meaning to public art.

The third is "site-specific art forms", including "public art and contemporary art". Both traditional art forms and new art media can be creative elements. Art intervenes in public space, promotes public participation, and stimulates individual experiences to form a common experience in line with individual or regional identities. In the time zone map, it can be seen that the art forms are mainly environmental art, urban sculpture, mural art, land art, paper-cut art, fiber art, and interactive art of human environment.

3.2.3 Research Hotspots and Trends

The salient words extracted from keywords show the evolution of hot content in the research field. For example, in a certain time period of the research time, when and what kind of articles appeared, changed the direction of the research field, or changed the original development direction, or greatly promoted the development of the next research. It is possible to do Burst detection through metrological methods. After further processing the above keyword co-occurrence map, the WOS data platform finally obtained 17 keywords with high emergent value for the research on specific fields of public art from 2002 to 2022. In the CNKI data platform, 19 keywords with high emergent value for the research on the specific field of public art from 2002 to 2022 were finally obtained. Arrange these high-emergence keywords in order from far to near according to the age of emergence start, and the following figure is obtained. In the figure, "Strength" indicates the emergence strength, "Begin" and "End" are the start and end times of the emergence, and the red line represents the start and end time period of the emergence.

From the WOS data platform on the left side of Fig. 7, it can be seen that the research on site-specific art in public art shows its strength from the keyword "identity" in 2005, and the practice and theoretical research of site-specific art revolves around the regional identity of artists and the public. In 2012, the study of regional cultural heritage became the focus of research on the dematerialization of the field. In 2018, research hotspots and trends emerged in site-specific art, and continued to extend to the present. The research hotspots "addresses, contemporary art, and communities" that have emerged since 2020 are all extensions of site research. In addition, along with the characteristics of field art projects, business management, public health, political science, and cultural relics management have also become areas of concern for researchers. From 2020 to 2021, street art and contemporary art, which are carried out with the study of art ontology, have always been the focus of public art research.

WOS	CNKI

Top 17 Keywords with the Strongest Citation Bursts

Keywords	Year	Strength	Begin	End	2002 - 2022
identity	2005	1.98	2005	2006	
cultural heritage	2012	2.74	2012	2018	
public space	2013	1.88	2013	2015	
art	2005	1.77	2015	2017	
site-specific art	2018	3.35	2018	2019	
public pedagogy	2018	1.72	2018	2018	
socially engaged art	2018	1.65	2018	2019	
place	2019	2.4	2019	2019	
management	2019	2.14	2019	2020	
community	2019	1.62	2019	2019	
authenticity	2019	1.62	2019	2019	
site	2007	2.1	2020	2022	
street art	2020	1.84	2020	2022	
politics	2002	1.8	2020	2020	
public health	2021	1.92	2021	2022	
heritage management	2021	1.83	2021	2022	
contemporary art	2010	1.57	2021	2022	

Top 19 Keywords with the Strongest Citation Bursts

Keywords	Year	Strength	Begin	End	2008 - 2022
城市雕塑	2009	1.14	2009	2015	
公共性	2010	1.97	2012	2014	
艺术性	2012	1.29	2012	2012	
城市文化	2013	2.11	2013	2017	
公共场域	2012	1.23	2014	2017	
城市景观	2015	1.82	2015	2016	
城市记忆	2015	1.21	2015	2016	
当代艺术	2008	2.13	2018	2019	
艺术介入	2018	1.57	2018	2018	
场域性	2008	1.26	2018	2018	
公众参与	2018	1.22	2018	2020	
空间	2018	1.18	2018	2018	
景观	2018	1.18	2018	2018	
公共领域	2019	1.21	2019	2019	
乡村振兴	2020	1.71	2020	2022	
社区	2020	1.21	2020	2020	
场域	2012	2.58	2021	2022	
地域文化	2012	1.41	2021	2022	
艺术	2021	1.12	2021	2022	

Fig. 7. Salient word map

On the right side of Fig. 6, it can be seen from the CNKI data platform literature that the research on this field began from 2009 to 2015. The traditional form of sculpture art attached to urban architecture is the core of public art. From 2010 to 2016, it revolves around the basic characteristics of public art. It is an artistic practice and theoretical analysis around publicity and artistry. In addition, 2013–2016 public art is the main content of urban research, exploring the relationship between public art and the city from the aspects of urban culture, public field, urban landscape, and urban memory. In 2018, the research on site-specific art became a hot spot, and researchers paid more attention to the relationship between art and society and the field, such as art intervention, site-specificity, contemporary art, and public participation. Since 2020, scholars have paid more attention to the relationship between public art and local art, and rural revitalization, community, and regional culture are the destinations of public art research. Of course, the field research in public art is still in a continuous state, and it is developing towards multi-disciplinary, multi-field, multi-dimensional and multi-level.

4   Conclusion

Through the use of cite space to analyze the research field of specific fields of public art, the research objects are WOS literature data and CNKI literature data, and the trend of published papers, author citations, literature co-citations, cooperative institutions, and research hotspots are clustered, Research hotspots and trends and other content analysis, and make relevant visual maps.

The results show that: (1) There are two research stages in the number of research publications in the field of public art in the specific field of public art on the WOS literature platform. From 2002 to 2018, the annual publication volume is less than 50. A sharp increase trend, up to 84 articles. The CNKI platform data shows that there are two research phases in the number of research publications in the specific field of public art. From 2006 to 2014, the number of publications increased slowly, until 2021, the number of publications was 41 and continued to grow. It can be seen that the research field of the specific field of public art is a new research field and is a current research hotspot.(2) Through the cooperation network of authors and research institutions, we can see the research status and influence of national institutions and journals on this topic in the past 20 years; research institutions in the WOS data platform present multi-scope cooperation and exchanges, and CNKI data platform Research institutions and researchers tend to work in small groups.(3) Nine clusters were obtained through keyword cluster analysis, and the WOS data platform was summarized into two major research directions, namely the specificity of public art sites and the practice of art and public art in specific fields. The CNKI data platform is summarized into three research directions: public art and publicity, regionality of specific sites, and art forms of specific sites. According to the high-frequency keyword table and keyword timeline diagram, the research keywords and evolution paths of urban public art research in different periods from 2000 to 2022 are extracted; the research content and trends in the WOS data platform pay more attention to identity, cultural heritage, address, contemporary Art, community, etc. research questions. The research content and trends in the CNKI data platform pay more attention to research issues such as publicity, artistry, urban landscape, urban memory, art intervention, field, contemporary art, and public participation. Through map visualization, we can gain a more macroscopic understanding of the international research frontier network relationship in the field of public art research, and provide scientific, accurate, and convenient research ideas and methods for the practice of public art, theoretical trends in the research field, research hotspots, and knowledge structures.

References

1. Deci, E.L., Ryan, R.M.: Instrinsic motivation and self-determinati on in human behavior. New York Plenum Publishing (1985)
2. Chen, C.: CiteSpace II: detecting and visualizing emerging trends and transient patterns in scientific literature. J. Am. Society Inform. Sci. Technol. **57**(3), 359–377 (2006)
3. Zebracki, M., Xiao, M.: The landscape of public art research: a knowledge map analysis. Professional Geograph. **73**(3), 481–495 (2021)
4. Palmeira, M.: Artificial hells. Arte & Ensaios, vol.25, No.25, pp.203–205 (2012)
5. Nelson R.: Practice as research in the arts: Principles, protocols, pedagogies, resistances [M]. Springer (2013)
6. Ley, D., Samuels, M.: Humanistic Geography (RLE Social & Cultural Geography): Problems and Prospects. Routledge (2014)
7. Yusoff, K., Gabrys, J.: Climate change and the imagination. Wiley Interdisciplinary Reviews: Climate Change **2**(4), 516–534(2011)
8. Hall, T., Robertson, I.: Public art and urban regeneration: advocacy, claims and critical debates (2001)
9. Atkinson, D., Cosgrove, D.: Urban rhetoric and embodied identities: city, nation, and empire at the Vittorio Emanuele II monument in Rome, 1870–1945[J]. Ann. Assoc. Am. Geogr. **88**(1), 28–49 (1998)
10. Encyclopedia of urban studies. Sage (2010)

11. Francis, J., Giles-Corti, B., Wood, L., et al.: Creating sense of community: The role of public space. J. Environ. Psychol. **32**(4), 401–409 (2012)

12. Kwon, M.: One place after another. Massachusetts and London, Cambridge (2002)

13. Anderson's, S.: Imagined communities. Literary Criticism and Cultural Theory (2006)

14. Jing, Y.: The symbol of urban spirit——the development of public art in China. Northern Art: J. Tianjin Acad. Fine Arts **3**, 28–32 (2008)

15. Zhao, Z., Huang, Z.: The discourse transformation of art in public space——the change of the concept of public art. Art Obser. **11**, 103–107 (2007)

16. Ding, Y.: Clues in the Agitation. Central Academy of Fine Arts (2019)

17. Wang, D.: The Current Situation, Problems and Countermeasures of Chinese Contemporary Public Art. China National Academy of Arts (2012)

18. Ma, Z.: Research on the planning of public art activities in urban blocks. South China University of Technology (2020)

19. Zhou, X.: Research on the integral design of public art from the perspective of urban culture. Wuhan University, Available from Cnki (2013)

20. Wang, Z.: The current situation and development strategies of public art education in China. Decoration **11**, 14–19 (2015)

21. Li, N.: Application research of Qin and Han culture in Xi'an metro public art. Master's Degree Thesis of Xi'an University of Architecture and Technology (2013)

22. Lin, X.: Public Art and Aesthetic Intervention.**5**, 219–227 (2014)

23. Chen, Y.: Citational Space Analysis: Principles and Applications. Science Press (2014)

24. Zhang, Z.: The cultural logic of digital capitalism: "participation" from artistic critique to data production. Theor. Stud. Lit. Art **40**(4), 188–194 (2020)

25. Chen, Y., Chen, C., Liu, Z., et al.: Methodological functions of CiteSpace knowledge graph. Sci. Res. **33**(2), 242–253(2015)

Research on Emotional Classification and Literary Narrative Visualization Based on Graph Convolutional Neural Network

Shi Zhuo[1,2]([✉]), Wang Meng[1], Chen Wei[2], and Luo Xiaonan[1]

[1] Guilin University of Electronic Science and Technology, Guilin, China
shzh@guet.edu.cn
[2] State Key Lab of CAD&CG, Zhejiang University, Hangzhou, China

Abstract. Watching a movie for three minutes has become a popular term in contemporary life, and people also hope to spend less time understanding the emotional direction and general plot of long novels. Currently, research on emotional analysis in novels mainly focuses on foreign languages. This article introduces Graph Convolutional Neural networks into the text emotion classification of novels. Text GCN is used to conduct emotion analysis on Ba Jin's novel "The Rapids Trilogy", and iStoryline is used to visualize the storyline of literary works. Visual coding adjustments are made based on the results of emotion analysis in the generated storyline, where line aggregation and dispersion represent whether the characters appear in the same scene, The brighter the color of the lines, the more positive the emotions, making the visualization more vivid, full, and beautiful. The experimental results indicate that this method enables readers to easily grasp the overall direction of the novel's plot and have a clearer understanding of the emotional changes of the characters. In addition, the accuracy of the Text GCN model is superior to traditional sentiment classification methods on Chinese datasets. This method provides a new approach for emotional analysis and narrative visualization research in literary works, and can be extended to other fields of digital entertainment.

Keywords: Emotional classification · Graph convolutional neural network · Narrative visualization · iStoryline

1 Introduction

Text sentiment analysis, also known as opinion mining, refers to the analysis of subjective texts with emotional colors, mining the emotional tendencies contained within them, and dividing the emotional states into different levels. Currently, research on sentiment analysis in novels mainly focuses on foreign novels, while there is still relatively little research on sentiment analysis in Chinese classic novels. Narrative visualization has always been an effective way to convey information and knowledge, and is currently crucial in various industries and activities such as education, teaching, management, culture, history, and marketing. Nowadays, narrative visualization mostly ignores the role of emotions in it, which may lead to some errors in readers' understanding of novels or movies.

© The Author(s), under exclusive license to Springer Nature Switzerland AG 2023
H. Lu et al. (Eds.): ICIG 2023, LNCS 14357, pp. 262–272, 2023.
https://doi.org/10.1007/978-3-031-46311-2_22

Li Yuqing et al. [1] proposed a multi emotion category analysis method based on bilingual dictionaries, which can effectively capture the opinions of groups. CAI Y et al. [2] proposed a three-layer emotion dictionary to reduce multiple meanings. Zhao Yanyan et al. [3] constructed a large-scale emotional dictionary of 100000 words based on a large amount of Weibo data. And using it as a feature for sentiment classification, this method has significant improvement in sentiment classification performance. Fei Jiang et al. [4] proposed the emoticon space model (ESM), which effectively utilizes emoticon signals and outperforms previous state-of-the-art strategies and benchmark tests for optimal performance. H. Jelodar et al. [5] used the natural language processing method of automatically extracting COVID-19 related discussions from social media and topic based modeling to find various problems related to COVID-19 from public opinion. Graph convolution neural network (GCN) [6] has received a lot of attention from researchers since it was proposed, and graph convolution neural network has also been widely used in the field of natural language processing. Bastings et al. [7] integrated syntactic structure into the neural attention based machine translation encoder model. Use the predicted syntactic dependency tree of the source statement to generate word representations that are sensitive to its syntactic neighborhood Graph Convolution takes word representation as input and generates words as output, which has made substantial improvements in translation work in various languages Beck et al. [8] combined gating graph neural networks with transform inputs, which solved the problem of having too many parameters Nguyen et al. [9] studied a dependency tree based convolutional neural network for event detection. This method relies on entity references to aggregate convolutional vectors. Yao et al. [10] constructed a co word network and document relationship network, proposed a Text GCN text classification model, and applied GCN to text classification tasks, achieving better results compared to other text classification models. Currently, GCN's application in sentiment analysis is mainly on existing datasets such as MR and Weibo comments, and there is still relatively little research on GCN in the field of Chinese novel sentiment classification.

With the rapid development of computer technology, visualization technology has gradually become popular, and researchers have begun to consider visualizing stories. So narrative visualization techniques similar to storytelling emerged. Chen et al. [11] proposed an expressive narrative visualization scheme to describe NBA games, which comprehensively explains three levels of detail of NBA games: season level, game level and conversation level. Reorganize a basketball game into a series of conversations to depict the state of the game and intense confrontations. Shi et al. developed MeetingVis [12], which is a narrative based visualization of meeting elements to help participants remember the content and background of previous meetings. Tang et al. developed iStoryline, a creative tool used to integrate advanced user interaction into optimization algorithms and achieve a balance between hand drawn storylines and automatic layout iStoryline allows users to easily create novel storyline visualizations based on their preferences by modifying the automatically generated layout. At present, narrative visualization mostly creates storylines based on characters, time, scenes, etc., often ignoring the emotional elements of characters in novels or movies. Adding emotional elements can clearly help readers understand the relationship between characters and the plot of the story.

Most classic literary works have complex content, while traditional text visualization methods are mostly limited to using front-end web pages to display manually processed data. The accuracy is only based on the subjective judgment of researchers and cannot effectively assist readers in reading these classic literary works. This article applies graph convolutional neural networks to the emotional analysis of novel texts, assisting readers in reading Mr. Ba Jin's 'Trilogy of the Rapids' – 'Home', 'Spring', and 'Autumn'. The beautiful and clear storylines generated by iStoryline, as well as suggestive symbols and text, can greatly attract readers' interest in reading, help readers strengthen their memory and understanding of the plot of the 'Trilogy of the Rapids', and help improve reading efficiency and reduce reading difficulty.

This article introduces Graph Convolutional Neural network technology into the field of sentiment analysis in Chinese novel texts, and uses Text-GCN to conduct sentiment analysis on the "Rapids Trilogy" as the research object. Research has found that the accuracy of this model is superior to traditional sentiment classification methods on Chinese datasets. Adding emotional elements can make the entire narrative more vivid, full, and visually appealing. Using iStoryline to visualize the storyline of literary works, visual encoding adjustments are made based on the emotional analysis results of the storyline generated by iStoryline, optimizing the generation results of iStoryline, allowing readers to easily grasp the overall story. This provides a new method for emotional analysis and narrative visualization research in literary works.

2 Research Design

This study is based on the classic novel text "The Rapids Trilogy", utilizing graph Convolutional Neural Networks and narrative visualization related theories and techniques to classify emotions in the novel text and visualize the novel storyline through narrative visualization. It is mainly divided into three parts: text preprocessing, sentiment classification using Text GCN, and iStoryline visualization of storyline.

(1) Text Preprocessing

Obtain the electronic text of the 'Rapids Trilogy' from the internet, process and organize it, remove any errors, extract emotional statements from it, construct a datasets, and perform operations such as word segmentation and word removal on the data.

(2) Text-GCN Sentiment Classification

Using Text-GCN for sentiment classification of processed datasets, firstly construct a text graph, and then train using GCN based on the constructed text graph.

(3) IStoryline Visualization Storyline

Intensive reading of text, recording data such as characters' appearance and exit times, appearance scenes, etc. Use iStoryline tools to visualize novel storylines. Adjust the visual encoding of the generated storylines based on emotional classification results, and optimize iStoryline generation results.

3 Experimental Design

3.1 Text Preprocessing

Obtain the electronic text of the "Rapids Trilogy" online, process and organize it, remove errors, and extract emotional statements to construct a dataset which preprocessing the original text in the datasets, as Chinese data is used, spaces cannot be directly used for word segmentation like English data This article uses the jieba.cut() method to segment text and remove stop words in Chinese, there are some meaningless words, such as auxiliary words, conjunctions, modal particles, etc., which are called stop words. We usually filter out stop words. We can add or remove some words from the disabled vocabulary according to the different processing objects. Filtering out inactive words can purify the processing results.

3.2 Text-GCN Sentiment Classification

3.2.1 Construct Text Map

Text GCN [10] constructs a heterogeneous graph with two types of nodes in the graph network: text document and word, which are no repeating words in the document. There are two types of edges: word of document type and word of word type. Each edge has weights, and the weights on the edges are defined by Eq. (1).

$$A_{ij} = \begin{cases} PMI(i,j) & i,j \ are \ words, \ PMI(i,j) > 0 \\ TF - IDF_{ij} & i \ is \ document, \ j \ is \ word \\ 1 & i = j \\ 0 & otherwise \end{cases} \quad (1)$$

The edge weights of document word are defined through TF-IDF, while the edge weights of word are defined through PMI (point wise mutual information).

The main function of PMI is to measure the correlation between two words, and the calculation method of $PMI(i,j)$ is as follows:

$$PMI(i,j) = log \frac{p(i,j)}{p(i)p(j)} \quad (2)$$

$$p(i,j) = \frac{\#W(i,j)}{\#W} \quad (3)$$

$$p(i) = \frac{\#W(i)}{\#W} \quad (4)$$

Among them, $\#W(i)$ represents the number of word nodes i in all sliding windows $\#W(i,j)$ represents the number of word nodes i and j in all sliding windows $\#W$ is the total number of window slides.

A regular PMI value indicates a high semantic correlation between two words, while a negative PMI value indicates a low correlation. Therefore, in the final graph construction process, only the edges composed of positive word node pairs were retained.

3.2.2 Graph Convolutional Network

Graph Convolutional Network (GCN) is a model that can process graph data for deep learning. For a graph $G = (V, E)$, V represents the set of nodes in the graph, and E represents the set of edges. The core calculation process of GCN is to set up a batch of graphical data, containing N nodes, each with its own feature information, such as the neighbors of the nodes. Construct an N using the characteristics of this batch of nodes × D-dimensional matrix X, and the relationships between each node will form an N × N-dimensional matrix A, A is called adjacency matrix. The neural network model of the graph can be represented by $f(X, A)$, X and A as inputs to the GCN model. A multi-layer GCN which propagates rules layer by layer, and the propagation between layers is as follows:

$$H^{l+1} = \sigma(\tilde{D}^{-\frac{1}{2}}\tilde{A}\tilde{D}^{-\frac{1}{2}}H^{(l)}W^{(l)}) \tag{5}$$

$$\tilde{D} = \sum j\tilde{A}_{ij} \tag{6}$$

where $\tilde{A}$ is equal to $A+I_N$ (I_N is the identity matrix), $\tilde{D}$ is the degree matrix of $\tilde{A}$. . The formula is (1), where $H^{(l)}$ is the activation matrix of layer l, and $W^{(l)}$ ϭ is the trainable weight matrix of the specified layer, ϭ(•)is a nonlinear activation function, such as ReLU.

The Text GCN model is based on the GCN model and a text map is constructed. The loss function of the model is as follows.

$$L = -\sum_{l\in Y_L}\sum_{f=1}^{F} Y_{lf}\ln Z_{lf} \tag{7}$$

In Eq. (7), Y is the index of the labeled document, F is the dimension of the output feature. For example, for a binary task of text, the output dimension is 2, while for a triple task of text, the output dimension is 3. Y is the matrix of the label indicator, Z is the output of the classifier, and the output function of the specific Text-GCN classifier is as follows:

$$Z = \text{softmax}(\hat{A}\,\text{ReLU}(\hat{A}XW^{(0)})W^{(1)}) \tag{8}$$

In formula (8), Z is a two-layer GCN model, softmax function is also called normalized exponential function, which is widely used in classification problems. A is the normalized symmetric adjacency matrix, ReLU method is the activation function, and X is the characteristic matrix composed of the eigenvectors of all nodes, $W^{(0)}$, $W^{(1)}$is the weight matrix.

3.2.3 Experimental Results

The datasets used in this article is sentiment statements extracted from the 'Rapids Trilogy', with a total of 2439 pieces of data, including 1324 positive data and 1115 negative data.

The model used in this paper is GCN [6] proposed by KIPF et al., the learning rate is 0.04, and the activation function uses ReLU function.

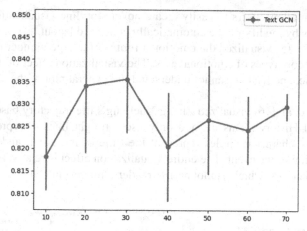

Fig. 1. Test accuracy under different embedding dimensions

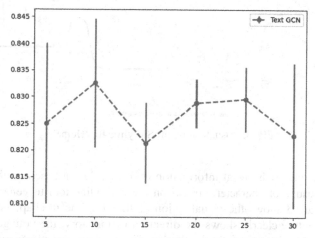

Fig. 2. Test accuracy under different sliding window sizes

Figures 1 and 2 indicate that when the embedding dimensions are 20 and the sliding window size is 10, the test accuracy is the highest, at 0.84163 better than the classical emotion classification algorithm LSTM with an accuracy of 0.74.

3.3 iStoryline

People are accustomed to and enjoy telling and listening to stories. But once the story becomes complex, with numerous characters and frequent scene switching, it becomes particularly difficult to tell a good story, movie, or novel. Therefore, this article uses the iStoryline [13] tool to visualize the storyline of the novel text.

IStoryline is a creative tool used to integrate advanced user interaction into optimization algorithms and achieve a balance between hand drawn storylines and automatic layout iStoryline allows users to easily create novel storyline visualizations based on their preferences by modifying the automatically generated layout.

Reagan et al. [15] visualized the emotional routes of a large number of stories and summarized six core types of emotional arcs. The visualization effect of this method is relatively chaotic, and readers cannot understand the general plot of the story based on the charts.

Wang Ruan et al. [16] visualized Zhang Xueliang's life trajectory based on 'Zhang Xueliang's Oral History'. This method only uses straight lines to represent the life trajectory of any character, circles represent the time of the event, and below is the textual description of the event. The entire visualization effect is relatively flat, lacking undulations and colors, which cannot arouse readers' interest in reading.

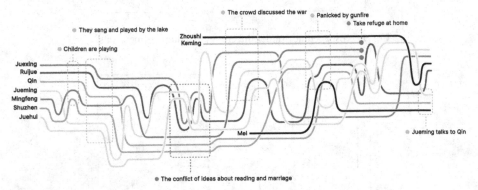

Fig. 3. Visualization of iStoryline for 'Home'

This article adds rich visual information encoding design based on the emotional classification results of characters, based on the iStoryline tool to generate narrative storylines. Figure 3 shows the visualization of the storyline in chapters 19 to 25 of 'Home'. The picture clearly shows the direction of the story: the younger generation of the Gao family went to play in the Shuige, Shuzhen was afraid of ghosts pestering Mingfeng, and the Juehui Juemin brothers played with them. Everyone took a boat to sing and play the flute in the lake, and then there was a heated discussion about the issue of 'foot binding', such as marriage and reading. At this moment, news came that Captain Zhang's army had attacked, causing everyone to panic. Cousin Mei, Qin, and Mrs. Zhang all came to seek refuge. As the war became increasingly tense, the Gao family became the wealthiest in the area, with people from three, four, and five families seeking refuge at relatives' homes. After the war, everything was restored to peace. Ruijue and Mei became friends at first sight, and they chatted openly. The relationship between Juemin and Qin also quickly heated up.

Figure 4 shows the visualization effect of the storyline in chapters 28 to 31 of 'Spring'. On Shuhua's birthday, Shuying, Juexin, and others came to pay her respects. Afterwards, Mrs. Zhou brought the two sisters Hui and Yun, and everyone welcomed them greatly. Although Hui's face was haggard, everyone still had a lively and enjoyable time. Every-one suggested appreciating osmanthus flowers in the garden, and everyone had fun. A

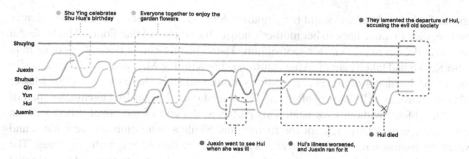

Fig. 4. Visualization of the iStoryline for 'Spring'

few days after Hui returned, bad news came out: Hui had fallen ill again with a severe fever. Jue Xin went to visit him, but Hui's condition worsened day by day. Even the traditional Chinese medicine doctors who tried to treat Hui repeatedly failed to alleviate her condition However, Hui's father Zhou Botao strongly opposed the use of Western medicine, believing that Western medicine could only treat surgery, delaying the opportunity for treatment. In the end, Hui passed away in the hospital bed. This section is the plot of the death of characters in the novel, with a heavy atmosphere. Most of the characters are powerless to the current situation, and the lines present a grayish tone. Through emotional analysis, Juemin, Qin, Shuhua, and Shuying have new ideas and oppose the old society, presenting bright and vibrant colors.

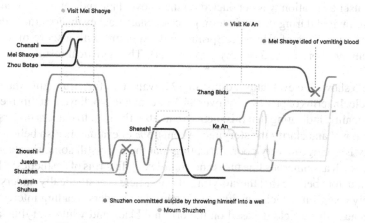

Fig. 5. Visualization of the iStoryline for 'Autumn'

Figure 5 shows the visualization of the storyline in chapters 41–46 of Autumn Master Mei was seriously ill, and Chen, Zhou Botao, Zhou, and Juexin came to visit him one after another. Chen blamed Zhou Botao for breaking the cup and waking Mei up. Mei continued to vomit blood, and Zhou Botao became angry with embarrassment. The two of them left one after another. That night, Shuzhen committed suicide by throwing herself into a well because she couldn't bear the beating and scolding of her mother, Shen Shi. After Shuzhen's death, Shen was deeply saddened and regretted all the actions she had taken to beat and scold her daughter. She was disheartened by the Gao family and decided to move back to her mother's house. Juemin heard that Fourth Uncle Ke An was ill and went to his mansion to visit him. There, he met Zhang Bixiu, the young man who Ke An had taken care of. After returning, Jue Xin, Jue Min, and Shu Hua excitedly discussed the matter of Shu Hua attending school. Suddenly, there was news that Master Mei was critically ill. Shortly after Jue Xin rushed over, Master Mei eventually died of vomiting blood without treatment. This part is at the end of the novel, filled with an oppressive atmosphere. Except for Juemin and Shuhua, who embrace new ideas and yearn for innovation, all other characters are bound by the old era, with gray lines. The passing of one character after another also reflects the ineffectiveness of old ideas at that time. Zhou Botao and others also delayed Mei's treatment opportunity due to their lack of faith in Western medicine. These characters were all victims of old era concepts.

4 User Evaluation

In order to evaluate the effectiveness of this method in assisting in reading long novels, three evaluation indicators (T1–T3) were proposed

T1: Practicality (can the novel content be well displayed)
T2: Aesthetics (can it arouse readers' interest in reading)
T3: Recommendation (whether willing to recommend others to use this method to assist in reading a novel)

Visual user evaluation was conducted on the above three indicators. A total of evaluators were invited during the evaluation process. Statistical evaluators rated the visual effect of the storylines of 'Home', 'Spring' and 'Autumn' with a score of 1–5 points (1 = extremely poor effect, 5 = very good effect). The statistical results are shown in Fig. 6:

Figure 6 shows the evaluation results of 124 evaluators for visualizing the storyline of this article. In terms of practicality, over 84% of evaluators believe that this method has good practicality, indicating that this method can effectively help readers understand the plot of the novel and clarify the storyline. About 15% of evaluators also believe that the practicality is average or very poor, indicating that there are still some shortcomings in this article, such as numerous line turns and complexity. In terms of aesthetics: More than 90% of evaluators believe that the storyline of this article is aesthetically understandable or relatively beautiful, which can effectively stimulate readers' reading interest. This is mainly because this article is based on the original black and white storyline and uses visual encoding adjustments, supplemented by easy to understand symbols and text, to beautify the visual representation of the storyline. About 13% of evaluators believe that it is very unattractive, relatively simple, or plain, indicating that there is still room for improvement in beautifying the storyline. In terms of recommendation: The vast majority of evaluators highly recommend or compare the storyline visualization results of this study to be used for the plot analysis of long novels, which greatly recognizes the research in this article and indicates that this study has played a positive role in assisting the reading of Chinese classical literature.

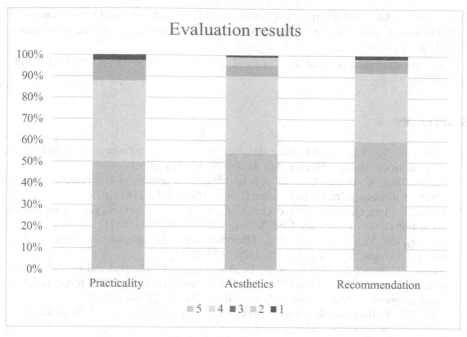

Fig. 6. Evaluation Results

Overall, most evaluators are satisfied with the visualization results of the storyline in this article, which can effectively save readers' reading time, grasp the rough plot of the novel, and enhance the expressive power of narrative visualization.

5   Conclusion

This study firstly uses natural language processing technology to create a novel text emotional sentence datasets, and uses Chinese word segmentation, stop words removal and other technologies to preprocess the data. Secondly, graph convolution neural network is introduced into novel text emotion analysis, and the parameters are adjusted. Text GCN is used to conduct emotion analysis with "torrent trilogy" as the research object. Research has found that the accuracy of this model is superior to traditional sentiment classification methods on Chinese datasets, and the classified results serve as the basis for encoding visual information in iStoryline. Adding emotional elements can make the automatically generated storyline more vivid, full, and beautiful. Using iStoryline to visualize the storyline of literary works, visual information encoding adjustments are made based on emotional analysis results, and the generation results of iStoryline are optimized, allowing readers to easily grasp the overall story.

Overall, this article introduces GCN into the field of sentiment analysis in novel texts, constructing rich and colorful storylines of classic literary works, reducing obstacles for readers to clearly read classics and gaining a deeper and more intuitive understanding of the works. It is a new attempt to apply machine learning to classical Chinese literature.

There is still significant room for improvement in the interaction and beautification of storyline visualization. In the future, we will continue to conduct research on narrative visualization.

This project is supported by National Natural Science Foundation of China (61862018).

References

1. Yuqing, L., Xin, L., et al.: A bilingual dictionary based method for analyzing multiple types of emotions on Weibo. J. Electron. Sci. **44**(09), 2068–2073 (2016)
2. Cai, Y., Yang, K., Huang, D., et al.: A hybrid model for opinion mining based on domain sentiment dictionary. Int. J. Mach. Learn. Cybern. **10**(8), 2131–2142 (2019)
3. Yanyan, Z., Bing, Q., et al.: Construction of a large-scale emotion dictionary and its application in emotion classification. Chin. J. Inf. Technol. **31**(02), 187–193 (2017)
4. Jiang, F., Liu, Y.Q., Luan, H.B., et al.: Microblog sentiment analysis with emoticon space model. J. Comput. Sci. Technol. **30**(5), 1120–1129 (2015)
5. Jelodar, H., Wang, Y., Orji, R., et al.: Deep sentiment classification and topic discovery on novel coronavirus or COVID-19 online discussions: NLP using LSTM recurrent neural network approach. IEEE J. Biomed. Health Inform. **24**(10), 2733–2742 (2020)
6. Kipf, T.N., Welling, M.: Semi-supervised classification with graph convolutional networks. arXiv preprint arXiv:1609.02907 (2016)
7. Bastings, J., Titov, .I, Aziz, W., et al. Graph convolutional encoders for syntax-aware neural machine translation. arXiv preprint arXiv:1704.04675 (2017)
8. Beck, D., Haffari, G., Cohn, T.: Graph-to-sequence learning using gated graph neural networks. arXiv preprint arXiv:1806.09835 (2018)
9. Nguyen, T., Grishman, R.: Graph convolutional networks with argument-aware pooling for event detection. In: 32nd Proceedings of the AAAI Conference on Artificial Intelligence (2018)
10. Yao, L., Mao, C., Luo, Y.: Graph convolutional networks for text classification. Proc. AAAI Conf. Artif. Intell. **33**(01), 7370–7377 (2019)
11. Chen, W., Lao, T., Xia, J., et al.: Gameflow: narrative visualization of NBA basketball games. IEEE Trans. Multimedia **18**(11), 2247–2256 (2016)
12. Shi, Y., Bryan, C., Bhamidipati, S., et al.: MeetingVis: visual narratives to assist in recalling meeting context and content. IEEE Trans. Vis. Comput. Graph. **24**(6), 1918–1929 (2018)
13. Tang, T., Rubab, S., Lai, J., et al.: IStoryline: Effective convergence to hand-drawn storylines. IEEE Trans. Vis. Comput. Graph. **25**(1), 769–778 (2018)
14. Tang, T., Li, R., Wu, X., et al.: Plotthread: Creating expressive storyline visualizations using reinforcement learning. IEEE Trans. Vis. Comput. Graph. **27**(2), 294–303 (2020)
15. Reagan, A.J., Mitchell, L., Kiley, D., et al.: The emotional arcs of stories are dominated by six basic shapes. EPJ Data Sci. **5**(1), 1–12 (2016)
16. Ruan, W., Jun, D.: Exploring the Construction and Visualization, Emotionalization, and Scenarioization of Storylines: Taking "Zhang Xueliang's Oral History" as an Example. Library and Information Work (2022)

Novel 3D Model Zero-Watermarking Using Geometrical and Statistical Features

Hanxue Li[1], Jianping Hu[1], Xiaochao Wang[2], and Qi Xie[1](✉)

[1] Northeast Electric Power University, Jilin 132012, Jilin, China
xieqi_19820302@126.com
[2] Tiangong University, Tianjin 300387, China

Abstract. In order to prevent illegal dissemination and misappropriation of 3D models, this paper presents a novel 3D model zero-watermarking method using geometrical and statistical features. It firstly obtains some feature vertices according to an adaptive sampling scheme based on the Gaussian curvature of an input 3D model. Such vertices can describe the basic shape of the model. And then, it uses FPFH (fast point feature histograms) to generate a multidimensional histogram descriptor representing the statistical characteristics of the neighborhood of the feature vertices. After that, a binary watermark information can be generated to achieve the aim of copyright protection for the input 3D model. Experimental results show that the proposed method has good robustness against various attacks including similarity transformation, element reordering, noise, simplification, smoothing, cropping attacks, etc. Furthermore, it is very competitive with the state-of-the-art watermarking methods for 3D models.

Keywords: 3D models · Copyright protection · Zero-watermarking · Fast point feature histogram · Robustness

1 Introduction

With the advancement of the Internet and digital signal processing technology, digital media products including music, images and videos, are widely used in many fields, such as medicine, business, and entertainment. Digital watermarking technology is considered an effective tool for solving the problem of copyright protection for digital products. At present, 3D models have also become an emerging digital product after music, images and video. The study of 3D model watermarking technology has received increasing attention from researchers.

In 1997, Ohbuchi et al. involved digital watermarking technology to 3D models [1], which is considered the pioneer of digital watermarking technology for 3D models. The traditional 3D embedding watermarking consists of two parts: watermarking embedding and watermarking detection [1–9]. Watermarking embedding inserts the watermarking information into the 3D host model, and the watermark is extracted from the 3D model to be detected by the watermarking detection method when needed. Embedded watermarking inevitably changes the original data when embedding the watermarking into the

© The Author(s), under exclusive license to Springer Nature Switzerland AG 2023
H. Lu et al. (Eds.): ICIG 2023, LNCS 14357, pp. 273–284, 2023.
https://doi.org/10.1007/978-3-031-46311-2_23

3D model data, resulting in a certain deviation of the model. To solve these problems, some researchers have made some attempts on the zero-watermarking technique for 3D models [10–16]. Zhang et al. [10] constructed a 3D zero-watermarking algorithm by the local planar parameterization and singular value decomposition. Wang and Zhan [11] first partitioned the vertex set of the 3D model by arranging the vertex distances from smallest to largest. And then, they obtained a zero-watermarking method according to the relationship between the number of vertices and the magnitude of the mean value in each vertex partition. Su and Shen [12] generated a watermark based on the presence or absence of intermediate layer nodes of the 3D model by the lossless octree theory. Cui et al. [13] proposed a zero-watermarking method based on spherical integral invariants. Such method first splits up the vertices of the 3D model according to the ray-based method, and then constructs neighboring spheres for each group of vertex data and calculates their integral invariants to generate the final watermark. Lee et al. [14] proposed a zero-watermarking method based on spherical coordinates and skewness measurements. It firstly partitions the vertices according to the vertex norm, and then calculates the skewness value of the latitude coordinates of each partitioned vertex set to obtain the watermark information. However, it is less robust to cropping attacks. Liu et al. [15] selected vertices with medium area size as a candidate set based on the area of the one-loop neighborhood of vertices in the model, and then used the Beamlet transform to construct a watermark image. Wang and Zhan [16] performed the watermarking construction by calculating the bias coefficients of the vertex norm number, SDF, and the vertex number ratio for each vertex partition. This idea can enhance the robustness of 3D watermarking methods under smoothing attacks and cropping attacks, but it is vulnerable to noise attacks.

Although the aforementioned methods have made many attempts in 3D zero-watermarking, it is still a challenge to construct robust watermarks for 3D models against multiple types of attacks due to the possible complicated structure of 3D models. In this paper, we propose a novel 3D model zero-watermarking method using geometrical and statistical features. It firstly selects stable feature points to represent the basic shape of the model by an adaptive vertex sampling strategy. And then, it uses FPFH (fast point feature histograms) to generate a multidimensional histogram descriptor representing the statistical characteristics of the neighborhood of the feature vertices. After that, a binary watermark information can be generated to achieve the aim of copyright protection for the input 3D model. Experimental results show that the proposed method has good robustness against various attacks including similarity transformation, element reordering, noise, simplification, smoothing, cropping attacks, etc. Furthermore, it is very competitive with the state-of-the-art watermarking methods for 3D models.

2 Proposed 3D Zero-Watermarking Method

Let M represent a 3D model (triangular mesh or point cloud), denote the set of vertices of the 3D model as $P = \left\{ \boldsymbol{p}_i = (x_i, y_i, z_i) \in R^3 \middle| 0 \leq i \leq N_p - 1 \right\}$ where N_p is the number of vertices, and the bit number of the watermark is represented by N_w. The proposed 3D zero-watermarking method first transforms the 3D model to obtain a normalized scale model and uses an adaptive vertex sampling strategy to describe the basic shape of the model. And then, it calculates a multidimensional histogram descriptor to illustrate the geometric statistical properties of the neighborhood of the feature points by FPFH. Finally, it constructs the watermarking information through the binomial norm of the feature descriptor. The overall flowchart of the proposed method is shown in Fig. 1.

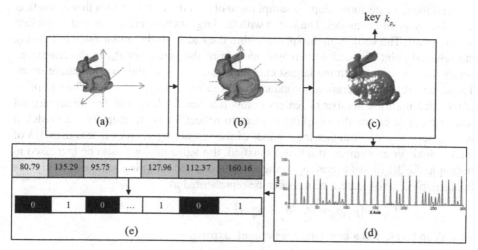

Fig. 1. The flowchart of the proposed 3D zero-watermarking method. (a) Original 3D model. (b) Preprocessing. (c) Vertex sampling based on shape feature description. (d) Computation of FPFH of feature vertices. (e) Construction of the binary watermark.

2.1 Preprocessing

In order to ensure that the attacked 3D model is still in the same coordinate system with the original model, we conduct a preprocessing for the input model. It can translate and scale the input model to get a standardized scale model as follows:

(1) Calculate the translation transformation from the centroid of the original model to the coordinate origin.
(2) Calculate the scaling transformation of the translated model into a standardized scale model. It uses the distance between the farthest vertex and the centroid in the translated model as the scaling factor. In our experiments, we set the standardized scale into 12.

2.2 Vertex Sampling Based on Shape Feature Description

Considering that the curvature of vertices can reflect the shape characteristics of a 3D model, we use it to perform adaptive sampling to obtain a set of feature vertices. They can describe the basic shape of the model, and can be retained well under simplification attack.

Specifically, we first calculate the Gaussian curvature of all vertices of the 3D model, and sort all vertices according to the values of Gaussian curvature from largest to smallest as follows:

$$P_s = \{p_i | s_{p_i} > s_{p_{i+1}}, \ i = 0, \cdots, N_p - 1\}. \tag{1}$$

And then, we perform adaptive sampling to obtain the feature points that can reflect the basic shape of the model. The vertex with the largest curvature is selected as the first feature point. The vertices in the sphere within the radius d (the initial value is 1) using the selected point as the center are excluded from the vertex set P_s. In the remaining vertex set, the vertex with the largest curvature is selected as the second feature point. The same exclusion operation is conducted on the remaining vertex set. The sampling is repeated until the number of feature points reaches the length of the watermark bit N_w. In order to ensure the sampling vertices to reflect the basic shape of the model, it is necessary to judge whether the number of the remaining vertices is less than 1/3 of the original vertex number. If it is not satisfied, the value of d needs to be increased to resample the 3D model according to the aforementioned sampling scheme. Finally, the final sampled set of feature vertices can be represented as

$$P_w = \{p_q | p_q \in P_s, |p_q - p_{q+1}| > d, q = 0, \cdots, N_w - 1\}, \tag{2}$$

which can be used as a key during watermark extraction.

(a)   (b)   (c)   (d)   (e)

Fig. 2. Vertex sampling results based on the proposed adaptive sampling scheme. (a) Bunny model (up) and Dragon model (down). (b) Gaussian curvature. (c) 36 feature points. (d) 72 feature points. (e) 128 feature points.

By using the proposed adaptive sample scheme, both the feature information of the vertices and the distribution of the vertices in the 3D model are considered. Undoubtedly, more feature points can represent the model shape better, but they need more storage space to conduct watermark extraction. It is necessary to simultaneously describe the basic shape of the model and have small storage space when selecting the number of feature points. Figure 2 shows the results of selecting the number of sampling points of 32, 72 and 128 for the Bunny and Dragon model, respectively. As can be seen, when the number of selected points is 72, the obtained feature points can represent the basic shape of the model well. Therefore, 72 feature points are used to generate a 3D zero-watermarking information in our experiments.

2.3 Zero-Watermarking Generation

In order to construct a watermark containing the local property of the 3D model without losing the overall characteristics, we consider to use a point feature histogram to represent the statistical characteristics of the neighborhood of each sampled feature vertex. PFH (Point Feature Histogram) [17] is a feature descriptor based on the normal relationship between vertices and neighboring points. It can calculate the spatial difference between a vertex and its neighborhood points to take into account the geometric characteristics of the point and the geometric distribution within the neighborhood. FPFH [18] is an improvement of PFH that retains the main geometric description of PFH and significantly reduces the computational complexity. Therefore, we adopt FPFH to generate the statistical features of the input 3D model.

For each feature point p_q and the points p_{ki}, $i = 1, ..., k$ in its k-neighborhood of the input 3D model, the relationship between the vertices p_q, p_{ki} and their corresponding normal directions can be described by three angle features. Each angle feature is divided into 11 intervals, and the 11 intervals divided by the three feature operators are directly connected to form 33 intervals. The number of vertices falling on each interval is counted to obtain the statistical histogram $SPFH(p_q)$ with the dimension 33. The other points p_{ki}, $i = 1, ..., k$ in the neighborhood of p_q are found outward to obtain the statistical histogram $SPFH(p_{ki})$, and finally the FPFH of the vertex p_q is obtained by the following formula:

$$FPFH(p_q) = SPFH(p_q) + \frac{1}{k} \sum_{i=1}^{k} \frac{1}{\|p_q - p_{ki}\|} SPFH(p_{ki}), \quad (3)$$

which can be regarded as a vector with the dimension 33.

Once the statistical histograms of all feature points are computed, we can use their 2-norms d_q, $q = 0, \cdots, N_w-1$ to generate a binary watermark. Let $\overline{d}$ denote the mean of all d_q, $q = 0, \cdots, N_w-1$. If d_q is larger than the mean $\overline{d}$, we construct the watermark "1" in the q-th watermark bit. If d_q is smaller than the mean $\overline{d}$, we construct the watermark "0" in the q-th watermark bit, i.e.

$$w_q = \begin{cases} 0, & d_q < \overline{d} \\ 1, & d_q \geq \overline{d} \end{cases}. \quad (4)$$

The binary watermark data $W = (w_0, w_1, \cdots, w_{N_w-1})$ of the input 3D model obtained by the above formula can be registered in a third-party authority's IPR intellectual property information database to achieve the copyright protection role.

2.4 Zero-Watermarking Detection

The zero-watermarking detection is required to validate the copyright of the 3D models. The 3D model to be detected may be subjected to some attacks, which can change the positions of the original feature points. For this reason, we use the set of feature vertices sampled during watermarking construction to align with the 3D model to be detected before watermark extraction [19]. Each feature point after alignment is selected as the nearest point in the model to be witnessed to obtain the feature point set P'_w. The watermark information W' of the model to be detected is obtained using the same steps in the watermarking construction. The correlation between the extracted watermark and the original watermark registered in the copyright database is computed by

$$Corr = \frac{\sum_{q=0}^{N_w-1} (w'_q - \overline{w'}) \cdot (w_q - \overline{w})}{\sqrt{\sum_{q=0}^{N_{w'}-1} (w'_q - \overline{w'})^2 \sum_{q=0}^{N_w-1} (w_q - \overline{w})^2}}, \tag{5}$$

where w_q is the q-th bit of the original watermark, $\overline{w}$ is the mean value of the original watermark, w'_q is the q-th bit of the watermark extracted from the model to be detected, and $\overline{w'}$ is the mean value of the extracted watermark. The value of $Corr$ is in the range of $[-1, 1]$. If it is much closer to 1, two watermarks have much correlation. When the correlation value is negative, it indicates that two watermarks are not related. Usually, a threshold can be predefined by the user to conduct the copyright protection.

3 Experimental Results and Analysis

In our experiments, we test the proposed method on several common 3D models in the research of 3D watermarking, including Bunny, Dragon, Rabbit, Horse, and Venus, as shown in Fig. 3. The number of constructed watermark bits N_w is set into 72, which can obtain a good balance between shape description and storage space of the key. In order to illustrate the feasibility and effectiveness of the proposed method, we conduct the following relevance and robustness experiments, and make some comparisons with several state-of-the-art 3D model watermarking methods.

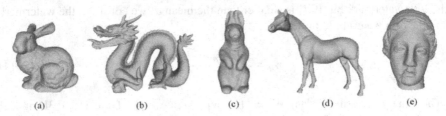

(a)   (b)   (c)   (d)   (e)

Fig. 3. 3D models in our experiments. (a) Bunny. (b) Dragon. (c) Rabbit. (d) Horse. (e) Venus.

3.1 Relevance Experiments

Table 1 gives the correlation results of the proposed method between the watermarks constructed on all the tested models in Fig. 3. As can be seen, the correlation between the watermarks constructed by different 3D models is very low. It means that the proposed 3D model zero-watermarking method has good feasibility.

Table 1. Watermark correlation results of the proposed method on all the tested 3D models.

Corr	Bunny	Dragon	Rabbit	Horse	Venus
Bunny	1	-0.036	0.023	−0.026	−0.003
Dragon	−0.036	1	-0.045	−0.164	−0.036
Rabbit	0.023	−0.045	1	0.002	0.079
Horse	−0.026	−0.164	0.002	1	0.085
Venus	−0.003	−0.036	0.079	0.085	1

3.2 Robustness Experiments

Robustness is measured by detecting the correlation between the watermark extracted from the attacked 3D model and the original watermark. The attacked 3D model is simulated and implemented using the 3D Mesh Watermarking Benchmark [20], an attack software developed in the Liris lab. It includes various attack types including similarity transformation, element reordering, noise, simplification, smoothing, and cropping attacks. The Bunny models under different attacks are given in Fig. 4.

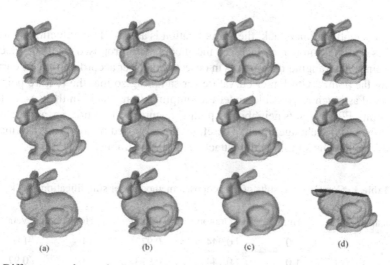

Fig. 4. Different attacks on the Bunny model. (a) Noise attack with intensity 0.1% (top), 0.3% (middle), and 0.5% (bottom). (b) Simplification attack with simplification rate 10% (top), 30% (middle) and 50% (bottom). (c) Smoothing attack with iteration number 10 (top), 30 (middle) and 50 (bottom). (d) Cropping attack with cropping rate 10% (top), 20% (middle) and 30% (bottom).

For the similarity transformation attack and vertex reordering attack, the proposed method can extract the watermark with a correlation coefficient of 1. In this paper, alignment operation ensures the consistency of the feature points selected after similarity transformation and the feature points during watermarking construction. The vertex reordering also does not affect the selection of feature points, and the watermark can be extracted from the attacked model in the same way as the original model.

As the noise intensity increases, the impact on the geometric features of the 3D model becomes more and more apparent. Table 2 shows the correlation between the watermark extracted by the proposed method and the original watermark after the 3D model suffers from noise attack. It can be seen that the proposed method still achieves good results when the noise intensity reaches 0.5%. Although the noise attack will affect the normal direction of the vertices and there will be deviations in the calculation of the three operators, the number of vertices falling in each subinterval does not change much after dividing it into subintervals. Therefore, the proposed method has high robustness under noise attacks.

Table 2. Correlation results of the proposed method under noise attack

Noise intensity	Bunny	Dragon	Rabbit	Horse	Venus
0.1%	1.0	0.972	1.0	1.0	1.0
0.3%	0.972	0.972	0.944	1.0	1.0
0.5%	0.972	0.972	0.944	0.944	0.916

For the simplification attack, the simplification is achieved by reducing the number of vertices and the number of faces of the model. The proposed method selects the feature points by arranging the vertices in descending order according to their curvature and fixing the points with larger curvature for sampling so that the feature points can be preserved as much as possible under the simplification attack. In the case of loss of feature points, FPFH counts neighboring points' features by partitioning, and the normal distribution does not change much. Therefore, the proposed method can also maintain robustness against the simplification attack, as shown in Table 3.

Table 3. Correlation results of the proposed method under simplification attack.

Simplification rate	Bunny	Dragon	Rabbit	Horse	Venus
10%	1.0	0.944	0.973	1.0	1.0
30%	1.0	0.944	0.973	1.0	0.972
50%	1.0	0.944	0.973	1.0	0.945

For the smoothing attack, the surface details of the 3D model are gradually lost as the number of iterations increases. In the meanwhile, the normal directions of adjacent vertices gradually converge, which weakens the influence brought by the vertex's normal directions. Experiments show that the extracted watermark of the proposed method still maintains a high correlation with the original watermark when the number of iterations is 50, as shown in Table 4.

Table 4. Correlation results of the proposed method under smoothing attack.

Iteration number	Bunny	Dragon	Rabbit	Horse	Venus
10	0.944	0.943	0.917	1.0	1.0
30	0.890	0.943	0.890	1.0	0.944
50	0.835	0.943	0.890	1.0	0.805

For cropping attacks, more feature points may be lost as the cropping proportion increases. Consequently, the correlation of the extracted watermark of the proposed method gradually decreases. Even so, it is still above 0.7 at 30% cropping rate for all test models as shown in Table 5.

Table 5. Correlation results of the proposed method under cropping attack.

Cropping rate	Bunny	Dragon	Rabbit	Horse	Venus
10%	0.919	0.972	0.946	0.946	0.919
20%	0.795	0.972	0.846	0.893	0.817
30%	0.724	0.763	0.776	0.811	0.734

3.3 Comparison with the State-of-the-Art 3D Watermarking Methods

To further illustrate the effectiveness of the proposed method, we compare the proposed method with several state-of-the-art 3D watermarking methods, including the optimized multiple histograms-based mesh watermarking method(OMH) [9], the spherical integral invariant-based zero-watermarking method (SII) [13], the spherical coordinate and skewness measurement-based zero-watermarking method (SCSM) [14] and the multi-feature-based zero-watermarking method (MF) [16]. Figure 5 demonstrates the correlation results of these methods on the Bunny, Dragon, and Horse models against various attacks. Here the results of the compared methods are directly copied from their corresponding papers and some data are missed since they are not reported in their experimental results. As for the Bunny model, the proposed method can better resist the simplification attack, the smoothing attack and the cropping attack than the other methods. It also achieves close results with the SII method under the noise attack (Fig. 5(a)). As for the models with more complex structures like the Dragon and Horse models, the proposed method can obtain better results than the SII and MF methods under various attacks (Fig. 5(b) (c)). Although the SCSM method can generate close results on the Dragon model with the proposed method under the noise attack and the smooth attack, it gets lower correlation values under the other attacks (Fig. 5(b). Consequently, the proposed method is very competitive with the compared state-of-the-art 3D watermarking methods.

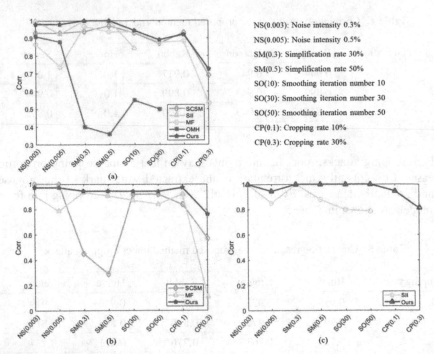

NS(0.003): Noise intensity 0.3%
NS(0.005): Noise intensity 0.5%
SM(0.3): Simplification rate 30%
SM(0.5): Simplification rate 50%
SO(10): Smoothing iteration number 10
SO(30): Smoothing iteration number 30
SO(50): Smoothing iteration number 50
CP(0.1): Cropping rate 10%
CP(0.3): Cropping rate 30%

Fig. 5. Correlation comparison with the state-of-the-art 3D watermarking methods. (a) Bunny. (b) Dragon. (c) Horse.

4   Conclusion

In this paper, we propose a novel 3D model zero-watermarking method using geometrical and statistical features. It first adaptively samples the 3D model according to the Gaussian curvature to obtain the feature vertices describing the basic shape of the model. Such feature vertices can be well preserved under the simplification attack. And then, it constructs a binary watermark by using a histogram-based statistical method. Such scheme not only describes the local features of the 3D model, but also considers the overall property of the 3D model. The experimental results show that the proposed method is not affected by the similarity transform attack and vertex reordering attack. It also has good robustness under noise attack, simplification attack, smoothing attack, and cropping attack. Moreover, compared with several state-of-the-art 3D watermarking methods, it can obtain competitive results.

It should be noted that the proposed method uses the feature points of 3D model to construct the watermark information. If these feature vertices are greatly affected by some attacks, such as the cropping attack missing most feature vertices, the robustness of the proposed method will be reduced accordingly. It is one of our next tasks in the near future to further enhance the robustness of the proposed 3D zero-watermarking method.

Acknowledgements. We would like to thank the anonymous reviewers for their helpful comments. This work is supported by Natural Science Foundation of Jilin Province in China (No. 20210101472JC).

References

1. Ohbuchi, R., Masuda, H., Aono, M.: Watermarking three-dimensional polygonal models. In: 1997 ACM International Conference on Multimedia, Seattle, WA, USA, pp. 261–272 (1997)
2. Choi, H.Y., Jang, H.U., Son, J., Lee, H.K.: Blind 3D mesh watermarking based on cropping resilient synchronization. Multimedia Tools Appl. **76**(24), 26695–26721 (2017)
3. Delmotte, A., Tanaka, K., Kubo, H., Funatomi, T., Mukaigawa, Y.: Blind watermarking for 3-D printed objects by locally modifying layer thickness. IEEE Trans. Multimedia **22**(11), 2780–2791 (2019)
4. Sayahi, I., Elkefi, A., Amar, C.B.: Crypto-watermarking system for safe transmission of 3D multiresolution meshes. Multimedia Tools Appl. **78**(10), 13877–13903 (2019)
5. Peng, F., Long, B., Long, M.: A general region nesting-based semi-fragile reversible watermarking for authenticating 3D mesh models. IEEE Trans. Circ. Syst. Video Technol. **31**(11), 4538–4553 (2021)
6. Medimegh, N., Belaid, S., Atri. M., Werghi, N.: 3D mesh watermarking using salient points. Multimedia Tools Appl. **77**(24), 32287–32309 (2018)
7. Narendra, M., Valarmathi, M.L., Anbarasi, L.J.: Optimization of 3D triangular mesh watermarking using ACO-Weber's law. KSII Trans. Internet Inf. Syst. (TIIS) **14**(10), 4042–4059 (2020)
8. Lu, Z., Guo, J., Xiao, J., Wang, Y., Zhang, X., Yan, D.M.: Extracting cycle-aware feature curve networks from 3D models. Comput. Aided Des. **131**, 102949 (2021)
9. Kashida, N., Hasegawa, K., Uto, T.: 3-D mesh watermarking based on optimized multiple histograms. In: 2020 35th International Technical Conference on Circuits/Systems, Computers and Communications (ITC-CSCC), pp. 363–366. IEEE (2020)
10. Zhang, J.W., Pan, G., Jiang, C., Zhou, X.Z.: A locatable zero watermarking scheme and visualization for 3D mesh models. In: International Conference on Computer Graphics, pp. 510–515. IEEE Computer Society (2009)
11. Wang, X., Zhan, Y.: Robust zero watermarking scheme for 3D point model. Comput. Appl. Eng. Educ. **47**(28), 7–11 (2011)
12. Su, C., Shen, X.: Octree-based robust watermarking for 3D model. J. Multimed. **6**(1), 83–90 (2011)
13. Cui, C., Ni, R., Zhao, Y.: Robust zero watermarking for 3D triangular mesh models based on spherical integral invariants. In: Digital Forensics and Watermarking: 16th International Workshop, IWDW 2017, Magdeburg, Germany, pp. 318–330 (2017)
14. Lee, J.S., Liu, C., Chen, Y.C., Hung, W.C., Li, B.: Robust 3D mesh zero-watermarking based on spherical coordinate and skewness measurement. Multimedia Tools Appl. **80**(17), 1–16 (2021)
15. Liu, G., Wang, Q., Wu, L., Pan, R., Wan, B., Tian, Y.: Zero-watermarking method for resisting rotation attack in 3D models. Neurocomputing **421**, 39–50 (2021)
16. Wang, X., Zhan, Y.: A zero-watermarking scheme for three-dimensional mesh models based on multi-features. Multimedia Tools Appl. **78**(19), 27001–27028 (2019)
17. Rusu, R.B., Martoh, Z.C, Blodow, N., Beetz, M.: Persistent point feature histograms for 3D point clouds. In: Proceedings of the 10th International Conference on Intelligent Autonomous Systems (IAS-10), Baden-Baden, Germany, pp. 119–128 (2008)

18. Rusu, R.B., Blodow, N., Beetz, M.: Fast point feature histograms (FPFH) for 3D registration. In: 2009 IEEE International Conference on Robotics and Automation, pp. 3212–3217. IEEE (2009)

19. Gojcic, Z., Zhou, C.F., Wegner, J.D., Wieser, A.: The perfect match: 3D point cloud matching with smoothed densities. In: 16 Proceedings of the IEEE Conference on Computer Vision and Pattern Recognition, pp. 5545–5554 (2019)

20. Wang, K., Lavoue, G., Denis, F., Baskurt, A., He, X.Y.: A benchmark for 3D mesh watermarking. In: 2010 Shape Modeling International Conference, pp. 231–235. IEEE (2010)

Compression, Transmission, Retrieval

Edge-Guided Interpretable Neural Network for Image Compressive Sensing Reconstruction

Xinlu Wang[1], Lijun Zhao[1(✉)] (ID), Jinjing Zhang[2], Yufeng Zhang[1], and Anhong Wang[1]

[1] Taiyuan University of Science and Technology, Taiyuan 030024, China
zlj_ty@163.com, s202215210574@stu.tyust.edu.cn
[2] North University of China, Jiancaoping District, Taiyuan 030051, China
zjj_ginger@nuc.edu.cn

Abstract. In recent years, interpretable Compressive Sensing (CS) technology has received more and more attention. Although these CS reconstruction methods can obtain good interpretability, they ignore the importance of edge information, which greatly limits the representation ability of their reconstruction models. Therefore, this paper reasonably embeds the boundary consistency constraint to the CS optimization model and proposes a CS reconstruction model with boundary constraint. This model can be expanded into Edge-Guided Interpretable Neural Network (EGINNet) for image CS reconstruction. In particular, in order to solve the problem of information loss in the iterative process, we introduce a multiple-memory enhancement mechanism to explore the feature dependency of EGINNet across different iterative stages. At the same time, we design a parallel-cross fusion module, which can selectively fuse boundary features and image features. Qualitative and quantitative experimental results show that compared with the state-of-the-art explainable CS reconstruction methods, the proposed EGINNet has better reconstruction performance while maintaining the network interpretability, especially on the restoration of boundary information.

Keywords: Compressive sensing · Image recovery · Interpretable network · Feature fusion

1 Introduction

Compressive Sensing (CS) theory [1] has shown that, if a signal is compressible or sparse in a certain orthogonal space, this signal can be sampled at a lower ratio which is much smaller than the Nyquist sampling ratio, and this signal can be reconstructed with high probability. Mathematically, given the natural signal x and the linear random projection matrix $\Phi \in R^{M \times N}$, the purpose of CS reconstruction is to estimate the natural signal $x \in R^N$ from the CS measurement value by $y = \Phi x (y \in R^M)$. This inverse problem is ill-posed because of M

© The Author(s), under exclusive license to Springer Nature Switzerland AG 2023
H. Lu et al. (Eds.): ICIG 2023, LNCS 14357, pp. 287–298, 2023.
https://doi.org/10.1007/978-3-031-46311-2_24

is far smaller than N. In practice, CS reconstruction can be converted into the following optimization problem:

$$\min_x \frac{1}{2}\|\Phi x - y\|_2^2 + \lambda\|F(x)\|_1, \tag{1}$$

where a sparsity-inducing regularization function of $F(\cdot)$ is used to sparsely represent natural images, and λ is a hyper-parameter to make a trade-off between data-fidelity term and regularization term.

Since traditional CS methods with high model interpretability cannot achieve high-quality reconstruction and there is no theoretical support for the designs of deep neural networks with high accuracy, a series of interpretable CS reconstruction methods based on neural networks have been proposed to make up for the shortcomings of each other. For example, inspired by the Iterative Shrinkage Threshold Algorithm (ISTA), *Zhang et al.* [2] unfolded this algorithm into ISTA-Net. In order to further improve the performance of CS reconstruction, they imposed orthogonal constraint and binary constraint on sampling matrix simultaneously [3]. Considering that these methods lost some information during the transmission between different phases, *Song et al.* used memory enhancement networks to reduce information loss within and between different stages [4]. Recently, *You et al.* proposed a Random Projection Augmentation (RPA) strategy to achieve arbitrary sampling [5]. To further improve the network reconstruction performance, *Mou et al.* [6] integrated the gradient estimation strategy into the proximal gradient descent algorithm, and then expanded this algorithm into DGUNet. Because traditional algorithms updated and transmitted images in the image domain and did not make full use of feature information, *Chen et al.* proposed to transmit information phase by phase in feature space [7]. These methods build upon traditional optimization solvers, which make deep unfolding networks with good interpretability. However, these methods do not take into account the important role of edge information in the image reconstruction process, resulting in poor performance of the restored image at the boundaries.

Inspired by multi-task deep learning with the help of edge loss [8], we propose a boundary-constrained image CS reconstruction model. The main contributions of the proposed method are summarized as follows: 1) We propose an optimization model with boundary constraints, and expand it into an Edge Guided Interpretable Neural Network (EGINNet) for image CS reconstruction. 2) According to the alternative-iterative optimization of the proposed method, the EGINNet has three essential parts: edge-aware feature-extraction module, edge guided intermediate-variable updating module and intermediate-variable guided image reconstruction module. 3) We design a multiple-memory enhancement mechanism to alleviate the problem of information loss between stages and explore the feature dependency of our network across different iteration stages. Meanwhile, we also design a parallel-cross fusion module, which can selectively fuse edge features and image features. 4) As far as we know, our network is the first method to introduce the edge information of the image into the CS interpretable reconstruction. Due to explicit edge constrain, the proposed method can well preserve image edges and details. Above all, our EGINNet has high interpretability for high-quality CS reconstruction.

The rest of this paper is organized as follows. First, we introduce the proposed method in detail in Sect. 2. Secondly, we provide extensive experimental results in Sect. 3. Finally, we draw conclusions in Sect. 4.

2   The Proposed Method

2.1   Problem Formulation

In the proposed method, the edge map $f(x)$ is got by edge convolution on the original image x, namely $f(x) = E * x$. E represents the edge detection operator. We assume that the prior distribution of the edge map $f(x)$ is $P(f(x)) \propto e^{-\alpha g(f(x))}$, and the implicit prior distribution of x guided by the edge map $f(x)$ is $P(x|f(x)) \propto e^{-\mu \Omega(x|f(x))}$. $\Omega(x|f(x))$ is the energy function related to x and $f(x)$, and μ is the weight parameter. Therefore, the probability of variable $f(x)$, given condition x, and the probability of variable x, given conditions y and $f(x)$, can be computed by the Bayes formula:

$$P(f(x)|x) = \frac{P(f(x))P(x|f(x))}{P(x)}, \tag{2}$$

$$P(x|y, f(x)) = \frac{P(y|x)P(x|f(x))}{P(y|f(x))}. \tag{3}$$

Among them, $P(x)$ is the probability distribution of x, which is independent of $f(x)$. $P(y|f(x))$ is the marginal distribution of y, independent of x. We use the maximum a posteriori principle to maximize the log posterior probability $P(f(x)|x)$ and $P(x|y, f(x))$ to obtain the final $f(x)$ and x. Equation (2) and Eq. (3) can be re-written as the following optimization problem:

$$\arg \max_{f(x)} \log P(x|f(x)) + \log P(f(x)), \tag{4}$$

$$\arg \max_{x} \log P(y|x) + \log P(x|f(x)). \tag{5}$$

By performing a negative logarithmic transformation, Eq. (4) and Eq. (5) can be reformulated as an energy minimization model:

$$\arg \min_{f(x)} \frac{1}{2} \|f(x) - Ex\|_2^2 + \alpha g(f(x)), \tag{6}$$

$$\arg \min_{x} \frac{1}{2} \|\Phi x - y\|_2^2 + \lambda \|F(x)\|_1 + \mu \Omega(x|f(x)), \tag{7}$$

where $g(f(x))$ represents a priori term and α is the trade-off parameter. Equation (6) and Eq. (7) are the optimization models for image x and edge map $f(x)$.

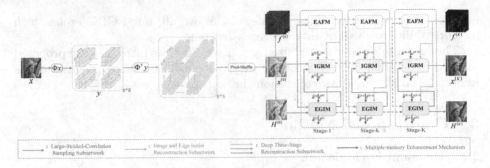

Fig. 1. The diagram of the proposed EGINNet.

We use the Proximal Gradient Descent (PGD) algorithm to solve Eq. (6), whose iterative updation equations can be written as:

$$
\begin{cases}
z^{(k)} = f^{(k)}(x^{(k-1)}) - \delta_1(f^{(k)}(x^{(k-1)}) - Ex^{(k)}), \\
f^{(k+1)}(x^{(k)}) = prox_{\alpha,g}(z^{(k)}),
\end{cases}
\tag{8}
$$

where k represents the k-th iteration step, δ_1 is the learnable step parameter and $prox(\cdot)$ is the proximal operator. Next, we use half quadratic splitting algorithm to solve the optimization problem in Eq. (7). We introduce an auxiliary variable H to solve the optimization problem in Eq. (7), that is,

$$
\arg\min_{x,H} \frac{1}{2}\|\Phi x - y\|_2^2 + \lambda\|F(x)\|_1 + \frac{\mu_1}{2}\|H - x\|_2^2 + \mu\Omega(H|f(x)),
\tag{9}
$$

where μ_1 is a penalty parameter. Equation (9) can be decomposed into two subproblems for alternative solution, that is,

$$
\arg\min_{H} \frac{\mu_1}{2}\|H - x\|_2^2 + \mu\Omega(H|f(x)),
\tag{10}
$$

$$
\arg\min_{x} \frac{1}{2}\|\Phi x - y\|_2^2 + \lambda\|F(x)\|_1 + \frac{\mu_1}{2}\|H - x\|_2^2.
\tag{11}
$$

Next, we use the PGD algorithm to alternately solve Eq. (10) and Eq. (11),

$$
\begin{cases}
h^{(k)} = H^{(k)} - \delta_2(H^{(k)} - x^{(k)}), \\
H^{(k+1)} = prox_{\mu,\Omega}(h^{(k)}),
\end{cases}
\tag{12}
$$

$$
\begin{cases}
r^{(k)} = x^{(k)} - \delta_3[\Phi^T(\Phi x^{(k)} - y) - \mu_1(H^{(k+1)} - x^{(k)})], \\
x^{(k+1)} = prox_{\lambda,F}(r^{(k)}),
\end{cases}
\tag{13}
$$

where k represents the k-th iteration step. δ_2 and δ_3 are two learnable step parameters and $prox(\cdot)$ is the proximal operator.

2.2 Edge Guided Interpretable Neural Network (EGINNet)

In this section, we jointly unfold Eq. (6) and Eq. (7) into an interpretable CS deep network of EGINNet based on the iterative algorithm. Figure 1 shows the overall network framework of EGINNet. The network is composed of three sub-networks, namely, the large-strided-convolution sampling subnetwork, the image and edge initial reconstruction subnetwork and the deep three-stage reconstruction subnetwork. Next, we will introduce the design of these subnetworks.

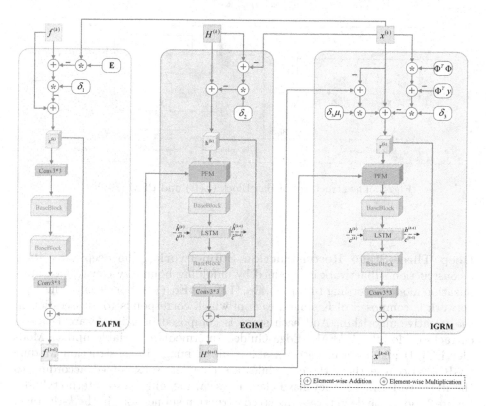

Fig. 2. The architecture of k-th stage of the proposed EGINNet.

Large-Strided-Convolution Sampling Subnetwork. In the large-strided-convolution sampling subnetwork, an image $x \in R^{H \times W}$ is divided into $\frac{H}{\sqrt{N}} \times \frac{W}{\sqrt{N}}$ non-overlapping image block $\hat{x}$ with a size of $\sqrt{N} \times \sqrt{N}$. And then each of $\hat{x}$ can be reshaped to a new vector $\hat{x} \in R^N$. $\hat{y} \in R^M$ represents the linear measurement of image block and measurement vector can be got by $\hat{y} = \Phi\hat{x}$, where $\Phi \in R^{M \times N}$ is the sampling matrix. Figure 1 shows the sampling operation of image x with a sampling rate of 25%. The large-strided-convolution sampling subnetwork uses filter kernels to obtain measurement values $\hat{y}$ from the $\hat{x}$.

Image and Edge Initial Reconstruction Subnetwork. The image and edge initial reconstruction subnetwork uses $\hat{x}^{(0)} = \Phi^T \hat{y}$ to initialize the image block $\hat{x}$ in EGINNet. Then, we use the pixel-shuffle layer to obtain the final initialization image $x^{(0)}$. Since H in the proposed method is an approximation of image x, we use $H^{(0)} = x^{(0)}$ as the initialization of H in EGINNet. The initialization of edge map $f^{(0)}$ in EGINNet is obtained by convolving the initial image of $x^{(0)}$ with eight gradient convolutional kernels, and they can be aggregated by the operations of concatenation and the convolution.

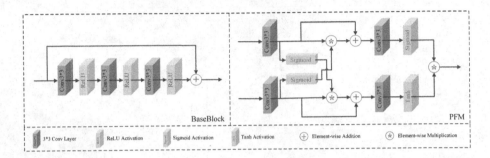

Fig. 3. The structures of BaseBlock (Left) and PFM (Right).

Deep Three-Stage Reconstruction Subnetwork. The deep three-stage reconstruction subnetwork is obtained by unfolding boundary-constrained optimization model according to Eq. (8), Eq. (12) and Eq. (13). Specifically, this subnetwork is composed of K stages, each of which corresponds to an iteration in the iterative algorithm. And each stage is composed of Edge-Aware Feature-extraction Module (EAFM), Edge Guided Intermediate variable update Module (EGIM) and Intermediate variable Guided image Reconstruction Module (IGRM). Because these three modules are completely expanded according to the iterative formulas, they have clear physical meanings and interpretability. Figure 2 shows the deep three-stage reconstruction subnetwork in the k-th stage.

In this network, we use the BaseBlock to extract features. The BaseBlock consists of three groups of convolution and activation operations. Generally, different features can be fused in a manner of addition/concatenation to enrich the information of features. However, these methods can not fully explore the relationship between edge features and image features, which limits the performance of image reconstruction. In order to integrate the boundary information into the image reconstruction process, we define a Parallel-cross Fusion Module (PFM). The proposed PFM can selectively fuse boundary features and image features. The structures of the BaseBlock and the PFM are shown in Fig. 3. Meanwhile, in order to strengthen the short-term memory of the network and reduce the loss of information between stages, we design a multiple-memory enhancement mechanism to explore the feature dependency of our network across different iteration stages. And the reconstruction performance of this module is improved by adding the Long Short Term Memory (LSTM) units into EGIM and IGRM. In the whole network, we also add several residual connections to enhance the representation ability of this network.

2.3 Loss Function

Given training dataset $\{(x_i)\}_{i=1}^{N_b}$ of image and the dataset $\{(f_i)\}_{i=1}^{N_b}$ of edge map, our aim is to reduce the differences between original image x_i and reconstructed image $x_i^{(K)}$, as well as between original edge map f_i and reconstructed edge map $f_i^{(K)}$, so we use L_1-norm data loss to regularize image reconstruction, namely:

$$\mathcal{L}_{rec} = \frac{1}{N_a N_b} \sum_{i=1}^{N_b} \|x_i - x_i^{(K)}\|_1, \tag{14}$$

$$\mathcal{L}_{edge} = \frac{1}{N_a N_b} \sum_{i=1}^{N_b} \|f_i - f_i^{(K)}\|_1, \tag{15}$$

where N_a is the pixel number of each image, N_b is the number of training images, and K is the whole stage number of EGINNet. Finally, the total loss function can be written as:

$$\mathcal{L}(\Theta) = \mathcal{L}_{rec} + \mu \mathcal{L}_{edge}, \tag{16}$$

where $\Theta = \{\Phi, \delta_1, \delta_2, \delta_3, \mu_1\}_{k=1}^{K}$ is the learnable parameter set in EGINNet and μ is the trade-off hyper parameter.

3 Experimental Results

3.1 Training Details

During the training phase, we use the same 91 image dataset as the one used in [3]. First, the luminance components of 88912 image blocks of size 33×33 are randomly extracted to obtain the training dataset $\{(x_i)\}_{i=1}^{N_b}$, that is, $N = 1089$ and $N_b = 88912$ in EGINNet. And five EGINNet models are trained when the CS ratio was $\{10\%, 25\%, 30\%, 40\%, 50\%\}$. Our experiments are all trained and tested on NVIDIA RTX A6000. During training, the block size of training images is 33×33, the feature channel number is 32, the number of stages K is 9, the batch size is set to 64, and the convolution kernel size is set to 3×3. Our model is trained by 50 epochs. The Adam [9] optimizer is used to optimize the proposed network. The initial learning rate is 2e−4, and the learning rate is reduced to 1e−4 until the 31st epoch is reached. For testing, we use three publicly available testing datasets, including Set11 [10], CBSD68 [11] and Urban100 [12]. We use two commonly used image evaluation criteria, namely Peak Signal-to-Noise Ratio (PSNR) and Structural Similarity (SSIM) for the performance comparison of CS reconstruction.

Table 1. The average PSNR/SSIM comparison of interpretable CS methods on Set11, CBSD68 and Urban100 datasets. (The best results are shown in bold, and the second best results are shown in underline.)

Datasets	Methods	CS Ratio				
		10%	25%	30%	40%	50%
Set11	ISTA-Net+ [2]	26.53/0.8066	32.44/0.9239	33.77/0.9388	35.99/0.9580	38.03/0.9704
	OPINE-Net+ [3]	29.81/0.8902	34.83/0.9514	36.04/0.9601	38.24/0.9721	40.20/0.9799
	MADUN [4]	27.87/0.8470	33.28/0.9373	34.66/0.9494	36.85/0.9644	38.60/0.9739
	COAST [5]	28.67/0.8608	-	35.07/0.9507	37.22/0.9655	39.03/0.9749
	DGUNet+ [6]	28.86/0.8791	31.53/0.9266	34.26/0.9508	36.44/0.9662	39.13/0.9782
	FSOINet [7]	29.80/0.8911	34.84/0.9526	36.18/0.9618	38.29/0.9727	40.17/0.9806
	EGINNet	30.01/0.8939	35.25/0.9550	36.46/0.9632	38.64/0.9742	40.60/0.9813
CBSD68	ISTA-Net+ [2]	25.33/0.7011	29.29/0.8505	30.34/0.8777	32.18/0.9161	34.02/0.9423
	OPINE-Net+ [3]	27.81/0.8047	31.49/0.9064	32.51/0.9238	34.41/0.9487	36.32/0.9657
	MADUN [4]	25.52/0.7191	29.35/0.8575	30.46/0.8837	32.22/0.9183	33.94/0.9424
	COAST [5]	26.42/0.7434	-	31.15/0.8939	33.02/0.9273	34.82/0.9502
	DGUNet+ [6]	26.89/0.7824	28.68/0.8639	30.97/0.9063	32.82/0.9351	35.09/0.9592
	FSOINet [7]	27.64/0.8021	31.22/0.9025	32.32/0.9217	34.24/0.9474	36.03/0.9640
	EGINNet	27.90/0.8076	31.75/0.9110	32.76/0.9282	34.75/0.9528	36.65/0.9684
Urban100	ISTA-Net+ [2]	23.52/0.7218	28.84/0.8830	30.17/0.9073	32.31/0.9371	34.41/0.9574
	OPINE-Net+ [3]	26.64/0.8375	31.44/0.9280	32.59/0.9417	34.69/0.9602	36.67/0.9728
	MADUN [4]	25.08/0.7870	30.23/0.9079	31.53/0.9265	33.48/0.9483	35.28/0.9634
	COAST [5]	25.80/0.8012	-	31.93/0.9305	34.11/0.9528	35.97/0.9670
	DGUNet+ [6]	25.61/0.8152	28.99/0.9020	30.86/0.9278	32.96/0.9501	35.24/0.9674
	FSOINet [7]	26.56/0.8412	31.49/0.9303	32.66/0.9438	34.77/0.9618	36.55/0.9728
	EGINNet	26.83/0.8438	31.88/0.9341	32.95/0.9460	35.11/0.9635	37.02/0.9746

3.2   Comparison with Interpretable CS Methods

We compare the proposed explicable method with six state-of-the-art interpretable CS reconstruction approaches, including ISTA-Net+ [2], OPINE-Net+ [3], MADUN [4], COAST [5], DGUNet+ [6] and FSOINet [7]. The implementations of all those competing methods can be obtained from their projects. For a fair comparison, we retrain these six methods on NVIDIA RTX A6000 to get the best performance. We use the source codes given by the author, and use the same training dataset to train all the comparative methods. Table 1 shows the comparison of average PSNR/SSIM of several methods on Set11, CBSD68 and Urban100 datasets under five CS sampling rates. From this table, it can be found that under different sampling rates, the PSNR/SSIM of the proposed EGINNet is superior to that of several newest CS reconstruction methods.

It is worth noting that EGINNet is far superior to ISTA-Net+, MADUN, COAST and DGUNet+. Among them, the reconstruction performance of ISTA-Net+ is the worst, because the ISTA-Net+ loses a lot of information when transmitting information phase by phase. The MADUN adds HSM and CLM mechanisms to alleviate the problem of information loss within and between phases, so the reconstruction performance is slightly better than that of ISTA-Net+. COAST uses plug-and-play deblocking strategy to eliminate artifacts, and DGUNet+ network adds inter stage information path to reduce information loss, so the reconstruction performance of these two methods has been further improved. OPINE-Net⁺ and FSOINet are second only as compared to the proposed method. OPINE-Net⁺ adds orthogonal constraint and binary constraint of the sampling matrix on the basis of ISTA-Net⁺ to improve the reconstruction performance. FSOINet supplements the measurement information in the feature space and makes full use of the feature representation capability of CNN, but both methods ignore the importance of edge information. So we add the edge information of the image to EGINNet, so that the reconstructed image can better restore the edge features, that is, the SSIM value is higher. Meanwhile, the PSNR value is also improved. After comparison, it can be found that the reconstruction performance of the proposed EGINNet is better than that of several state-of-the-art image CS methods.

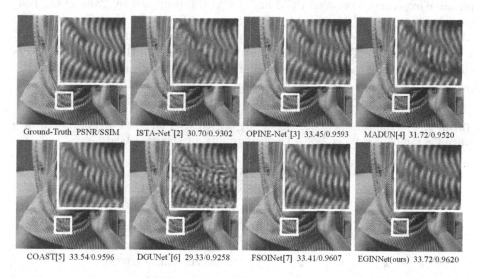

Fig. 4. The visual comparison between the proposed method and several recent interpretable CS methods to restore the image named "Barbara" on the Set11 dataset.

To further evaluate the performance of the proposed EGINNet, Fig. 4 shows the visual comparison of several methods on Set11 dataset. From this figure, we can observe that when CS sampling ratio = 30%, the reconstructed images by ISTA-Net⁺, MADUN and DGUNet⁺ have different degrees of artifact distortions. And the reconstructed images by OPINE-Net⁺, COAST and FSOINet are blurry at the boundary. Obviously, compared with other interpretable CS methods, the image restored by the proposed method retains more details and restores clearer edges, which clearly verifies the advantages of the proposed EGINNet.

3.3   Ablation Study

In order to better evaluate the impact of each module of EGINNet on the reconstruction performance, we provide several variants of the proposed model. Some of the modules are selectively discarded or replaced. Table 2 shows the ablation results of EGINNet on Set11 [10] and Set14 [13] datasets. Here, we consider the effects of EAFM, EGIM and IGRM. It should be noted that when EAFM is discarded, we will also remove the PFM when removing the module. When the EGIM or IGRM is discarded, in order to maintain the integrity of the network, we use simple 'Conv+ResidualBlock+Conv' to replace the original network. We can observe from Table 2 that the different gains can be achieved by adding the three modules of EAFM, EGIM and IGRM.

In order to verify the effectiveness of the proposed PFM, we conduct a comparative experiment between PFM and MFM [14] proposed by *Zhou et al.*, Feature Aggregation [15] proposed by *Cui et al.*, and Fusion Block [16] proposed by *Ye et al.* The ablation results of these four fusion modules are shown in Table 3. It can be seen from Table 3 that the fusion performance of the proposed PFM is superior to that of the other three fusion methods. This clearly verifies that the proposed PFM can better fuse edge features and image features.

Table 2. The comparison of ablation study of EGINNet on Set11 and Set14 datasets when CS sampling ratio = 25%. (The best results are shown in bold.)

EAFM	EGIM	IGRM	Set11	Set14
			PSNR/SSIM	PSNR/SSIM
✗	✗	✗	31.16/0.9167	30.61/0.8875
✓	✗	✗	34.64/0.9500	32.95/0.9186
✗	✓	✗	27.79/0.8315	27.81/0.8089
✗	✗	✓	35.10/0.9539	33.32/0.9225
✓	✓	✗	34.36/0.9482	32.83/0.9178
✓	✗	✓	35.19/0.9544	33.41/0.9233
✗	✓	✓	35.15/0.9543	33.39/0.9229
✓	✓	✓	**35.25/0.9550**	**33.46/0.9241**

Table 3. Ablation results of four fusion modules when CS sampling ratio = 25%. (The best results are shown in bold.)

Datasets	Fusion Module			
	MFM [14]	Feature Aggregation [15]	Fusion Block [16]	The proposed PFM
Set11	32.91/0.9401	35.06/0.9536	34.94/0.9533	**35.25/0.9550**
Set14	30.91/0.9002	33.38/0.9233	33.29/0.9224	**33.46/0.9241**

4 Conclusion

In this paper, we propose an interpretable end-to-end CS network EGINNet to improve the performance of image reconstruction. First, we propose an optimization model with boundary constraints and unfold it into a network to restore more image edges and details. Then, we divide the model into two-subproblem to optimize edge features and image features in sequence. Finally, considering the problem of information loss between stages, we propose a multiple-memory enhancement mechanism to retain more information. At the same time, in order to achieve effective fusion of edge features and image features, we design a PFM, which can selectively fuse edge features and image features. Comprehensive experimental results show that our method can recover more clear edge details than many of the most advanced CS methods. In the future work, we will study CS reconstruction in frequency domain such as wavelet domain or fourier domain according to the design of our EGINNet.

Acknowledgements. This work was supported by National Natural Science Foundation of China Youth Science Foundation Project (No. 62202323), Fundamental Research Program of Shanxi Province (No. 202103021223284), Taiyuan University of Science and Technology Scientific Research Initial Funding (No. 20192023, No. 20192055), Graduate Education Innovation Project of Taiyuan University of Science and Technology in 2022 (SY2022027), National Natural Science Foundation of China (No. 62072325).

References

1. Donoho, D.L.: Compressed sensing. IEEE Trans. Inf. Theory **52**(4), 1289–1306 (2006)
2. Zhang, J., Ghanem, B.: ISTA-Net: interpretable optimization-inspired deep network for image compressive sensing. In: Proceedings of the IEEE Conference on Computer Vision and Pattern Recognition, pp. 1828–1837 (2018)
3. Zhang, J., Zhao, C., Gao, W.: Optimization-inspired compact deep compressive sensing. IEEE J. Sel. Top. Sign. Process. **14**(4), 765–774 (2020)
4. Song, J., Chen, B., Zhang, J.: Memory-augmented deep unfolding network for compressive sensing. In: Proceedings of the 29th ACM International Conference on Multimedia, pp. 4249–4258 (2021)
5. You, D., Zhang, J., Xie, J., Chen, B., Ma, S.: COAST: controllable arbitrary-sampling network for compressive sensing. IEEE Trans. Image Process. **30**(1), 6066–6080 (2021)
6. Mou, C., Wang, Q., Zhang, J.: Deep generalized unfolding networks for image restoration. In: Proceedings of the IEEE/CVF Conference on Computer Vision and Pattern Recognition, pp. 17399–17410 (2022)
7. Chen, W., Yang, C., Yang, X.: FSOINET: feature-space optimization-inspired network for image compressive sensing. In: ICASSP 2022–2022 IEEE International Conference on Acoustics, Speech and Signal Processing (ICASSP), pp. 2460–2464. IEEE (2022)
8. Wang, C., et al.: EAA-Net: a novel edge assisted attention network for single image dehazing. Knowl.-Based Syst. **228**(1), 107279 (2021)

9. Kingma, D.P., Ba, J.: Adam: a method for stochastic optimization. arXiv preprint arXiv:1412.6980 1(1), 1–15 (2014)
10. Kulkarni, K., Lohit, S., Turaga, P., Kerviche, R., Ashok, A.: ReconNet: non-iterative reconstruction of images from compressively sensed measurements, pp. 449–458 (2016)
11. Martin, D., Fowlkes, C., Tal, D., Malik, J.: A database of human segmented natural images and its application to evaluating segmentation algorithms and measuring ecological statistics. In: Proceedings Eighth IEEE International Conference on Computer Vision, ICCV 2001, vol. 2, pp. 416–423. IEEE (2001)
12. Huang, J.B., Singh, A., Ahuja, N.: Single image super-resolution from transformed self-exemplars. In: Proceedings of the IEEE Conference on Computer Vision and Pattern Recognition, pp. 5197–5206 (2015)
13. Cui, W., Xu, H., Gao, X., Zhang, S., Jiang, F., Zhao, D.: An efficient deep convolutional Laplacian pyramid architecture for CS reconstruction at low sampling ratios. In: 2018 IEEE International Conference on Acoustics, Speech and Signal Processing (ICASSP), pp. 1748–1752. IEEE (2018)
14. Zhou, W., Dong, S., Xu, C., Qian, Y.: Edge-aware guidance fusion network for RGB thermal scene parsing. ArXiv abs/2112.05144 (2022)
15. Cui, W., Liu, S., Zhao, D.: Fast hierarchical deep unfolding network for image compressed sensing. In: Proceedings of the 30th ACM International Conference on Multimedia, pp. 2739–2748 (2022)
16. Ye, X., et al.: PMBANet: progressive multi-branch aggregation network for scene depth super-resolution. IEEE Trans. Image Process. 29, 7427–7442 (2020)

Patch-Wise LiDAR Point Cloud Geometry Compression Based on Autoencoder

Runnan Huang and Miaohui Wang[✉]

Guangdong Key Laboratory of Intelligent Information Processing, Shenzhen University, Shenzhen, People's Republic of China
wang.miaohui@gmail.com

Abstract. Point cloud compression plays a critical role in efficient point cloud storage and transmission. This paper focuses on the lossy geometric compression of LiDAR point clouds, which have been widely used in various autonomous driving systems. Based on the data characteristics of the LiDAR point cloud, we propose an ordered partition algorithm for patch-wise LiDAR point cloud compression. The proposed algorithm has several advantages: (1) all patches are free of duplicate points and retain the original points; (2) each patch has an equal number of points, facilitating easy parallelization; (3) the partitioning process is swift and therefore can be well performed online during the training phase. Experiments on the benchmark SemanticKITTI dataset demonstrate that our patch-wise compression model can reconstruct point clouds with a spatial distribution that more closely resembles the original ones compared with existing representative methods.

Keywords: LiDAR point cloud · Compression · Autoencoder

1 Introduction

The application of 3D sensors in various scenarios [11,15,17] results in the increasing amount of 3D point cloud data and the concomitantly growing demand for point cloud's transmission and storage. To store and transmit 3D point clouds more efficiently, it is necessary to compress them. Representative point cloud compression methods are Geometry-based Point Cloud Compression (G-PCC) and Video-based Point Cloud Compression (V-PCC) proposed by the Moving Picture Experts Group (MPEG) [16], which are used to compress static and dynamic point clouds, respectively. However, G-PCC and V-PCC rely on hand-crafted features and have certain performance bottlenecks. Recently, the

This work was supported in part by Natural Science Foundation of Guangdong Province under Grant 2022A1515011245 and Grant 2021A1515011877, and in part by Natural Science Foundation of Shenzhen City under Grant 20220809160139001.

© The Author(s), under exclusive license to Springer Nature Switzerland AG 2023
H. Lu et al. (Eds.): ICIG 2023, LNCS 14357, pp. 299–310, 2023.
https://doi.org/10.1007/978-3-031-46311-2_25

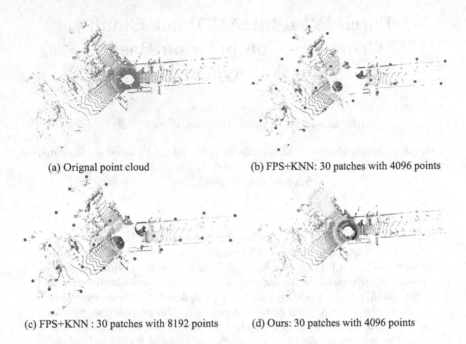

(a) Orignal point cloud   (b) FPS+KNN: 30 patches with 4096 points

(c) FPS+KNN : 30 patches with 8192 points   (d) Ours: 30 patches with 4096 points

Fig. 1. Visualized results of various partitioning methods. (a) is the original point cloud with 120K+ points; (b) and (c) are the visualization of patches based on FPS and KNN: (b) shows 30 patches with 4096 points; (c) shows 30 patches with 8192 points; the red dots are sampling points. (d) visualizes the 30 patches with 4096 points generated from our ordered partition algorithm. (Color figure online)

end-to-end compression model based on autoencoder has outperformed traditional methods in image compression tasks and is continuously improving its performance [1,2,7,28,29], demonstrating a potential data compression paradigm. Therefore, it is necessary to explore more advanced and effective point cloud compression methods based on autoencoder.

Typical point clouds include small-scale object point clouds sampled from 3D models and large-scale LiDAR point clouds scanned by vehicular LiDAR sensors [3,4,21]. For object point clouds, there are many methods [5,8,10,22,25] that use point-based deep models [6,13,14,26] as encoders and propose point cloud compression methods based on autoencoder, which outperform G-PCC in some compression ratios. However, these methods are more suitable for small-scale point clouds. For large-scale LiDAR point clouds, these models may be limited by hardware conditions and are difficult to process and reconstruct the entire original point cloud.

To enable the compression model to process large-scale LiDAR point clouds efficiently, an effective approach is to divide the input point clouds into patches, and then compress and reconstruct them patch by patch. In our opinion, the following factors should be taken into consideration when the point cloud is partitioned: (1) Each patch should contain the same number of points, making it easier to process them in parallel. (2) There should be few, if any, repeated points between each patch, and the total number of points in all patches should be similar to that of the original point cloud. This ensures that no data points are missing or redundant. (3) The partition algorithm should not be too complex, otherwise, it will significantly increase the training times. Although it is possible to make patch datasets offline, this also takes up a lot of computer memory and cannot arbitrarily modify the parameters of the partition algorithm.

The recent works [23,24] proposed a patch-based deep autoencoder for point cloud compression and its improvement version IPDAE, based on k-nearest neighbors (KNN) and farthest point sampling (FPS). They use FPS to sample the original point cloud, and then use KNN centered on each sample point to obtain patches of the original point cloud with an equal number of points. However, this method is only suitable for uniformly distributed object point clouds, but not for unevenly distributed LiDAR point clouds. As shown in Fig. 1(b), and Fig. 1(c), the patches obtained by this method cannot cover the original point cloud, and each patch has repeated points. Even if the total number of points in all the patches is close to double that of the original point cloud, the loss of points cannot be avoided, and this results in more duplicate points. In addition, FPS and KNN take a lot of time.

This paper focuses on lossy geometric intra-frame compression of LiDAR point clouds [18] and proposes an ordered partition algorithm for the patch-wise point cloud compression model based on autoencoder. The ordered partition algorithm first divides the point clouds according to their data characteristics, including the distance of each point to the origin and the yaw angle of each point, then generate their local center points according to the point coordinates in each patch. Its advantages include: all patches have no duplicate points and almost no loss of original points, as shown in Fig. 1(d); each patch has the same number of points, which is easy to parallelize; partitioning is fast and can be done online well during the training phase.

Experiments on the SemanticKITTI dataset [3] demonstrate that our proposed patch-wise LiDAR point cloud compression model can reconstruct point clouds with a spatial distribution that is closer to the original compared to IPDAE and G-PCC.

2   Proposed Method

This section will introduce our proposed patch-wise LiDAR point cloud compression method. Section 2.1 provides an overview of our model; Sect. 2.2 introduces our LiDAR point cloud partition algorithm; Sect. 2.3 describes the details of the encoder and decoder.

2.1   Overview

Autoencoder-based compression method [1,24] learns the information-dense potential representation of the original data in the code space by autoencoder

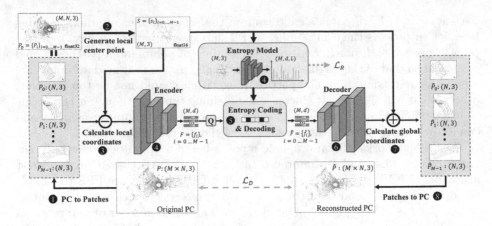

Fig. 2. The framework of the proposed method. PC denotes point cloud; Q denotes quantization.

and further compresses the potential representation lossless by entropy coding guided by the entropy model. Our model framework is shown in Fig. 2. At the transmitting end, the entire input point cloud P is first divided into M patches P_p by our proposed ordered partition algorithm, and meanwhile, the local central points S are generated. Then, each patch P_m is subtracted by the corresponding local central point s_m to obtain local coordinates and input to the encoder to get the potential feature F. At the same time, the sampling points S are input into the entropy model to obtain the probability distribution of each potential feature, which will be used for entropy coding of the quantized potential feature $\hat{F}$. We use the same quantification method and entropy model as [24].

At the receiving end, the half-float-type sampling points S are received and fed into the entropy model to obtain the distribution of potential features, which are then used for entropy decoding to obtain the reconstructed features from the bit stream. The reconstructed features $\hat{F}$ are then input to the decoder to predict the offset of each point in the patch relative to its local center point. Adding each offset to the corresponding center point will yield the reconstructed patch $\hat{P}_m$. Finally, all the reconstructed patches are combined to obtain a completely reconstructed point cloud $\hat{P}$.

The distortion loss is measured as the chamfer distance between the reconstructed point cloud $\hat{P}$ and the original one P, while the rate loss is measured as the entropy of the output distribution of the entropy model. The rate-distortion loss function is constructed by combining these two losses and is used to train the model:

$$\min_{\theta} \quad \mathcal{L}_D(P, \hat{P}) + \lambda \cdot \mathcal{L}_R(S), \tag{1}$$

where θ is the parameter of the model; λ is the constant weight. Note that entropy encoding and decoding are skipped during the training phase.

Algorithm 1: Ordered Partition

Input: The number of patches to be partitioned, $M = R \times C$; The number of
points in each patch, N; LiDAR point cloud with N_{ori} points,
$P_{ori} = \{p_0, p_1, ..., p_{N_{ori}-1}\}$, where $p_i = (x_i, y_i, z_i)$.

Output: M patches , $P_p = \{P_0, P_1, ..., P_{M-1}\}$ and the corresponding local
center points $S = \{s_0, s_1, \cdots, s_{M-1}\}$

1 Sample (only in the training phase) or pad P_{ori} by random selecting points
from itself to make: $P = \{p_0, p_1, ..., p_{M \cdot N-1}\}$.

2 Calculate the distance from all points $p_i \in P$ to the origin:
$d(p_i) = \sqrt{x_i^2 + y_i^2 + z_i^2}$;

3 Rearrange P in order of distance from smallest to largest:

$$P' = \{p_0', p_1', ..., p_{M \cdot N-1}'\}, \text{where} \quad d(p_i') < d(p_j'), \text{if} \quad i < j.$$

4 Initialize $P_p = \{\}, m = 0$.

5 **for** $r = 0$ to $R - 1$ **do**

6   Select an annular point cloud : $P_a = P'[r \cdot C \cdot N : (r+1) \cdot C \cdot N]$;

7   Calculate the yaw angle of each point $p_i \in P_a$: $\theta(p_i) = \arctan(y_i/x_i)$;

8   Rearrange P_a in order of yaw angle from smallest to largest:

$$P_a' = \{p_0', p_1', ..., p_{N-1}'\}, \text{where} \quad \theta(p_i') < \theta(p_j'), \text{if} \quad i < j.$$

9   **for** $c = 0$ to $C - 1$ **do**

10   Get a patch: $P_m = P_a'[c \cdot N : (c+1) \cdot N] = \{p_{m,0}, p_{m,1}, ..., p_{m,N-1}\}$;

11   Append P_m to P_p;

12         $m = m + 1$;

13 Calculate the mean value of point coordinates in each patch:

$$\mu_m = (\frac{1}{N} \sum_{k=0}^{N-1} x_{m,k}, \frac{1}{N} \sum_{k=0}^{N-1} y_{m,k}, \frac{1}{N} \sum_{k=0}^{N-1} z_{m,k}), m = 0, 1, 2, ..., M - 1.$$

14 Find the nearest neighbor point s_m of u_m in P as the local center point of each
patch: $S = \{s_0, s_1, \cdots, s_{M-1}\}$.

15 Return P_p, S.

2.2 Point Cloud Partition Method

We propose an ordered partition algorithm for patch-wise LiDAR point cloud
compression based on their data characteristics. Unlike recent approaches [23,
24], which first sample the original point cloud and then generate patches around
the sampling points, our method first divides the point cloud into patches based
on the distance and angle information of the points and then generates local
center points from each patch.

Algorithm 1 outlines the steps of the partition algorithm. To obtain patches
containing N points with a specified number of patches M, we randomly select
points from the original point cloud to either sample (if the number of points is
greater than $M \times N$) or pad (if the number of points is less than $M \times N$) the

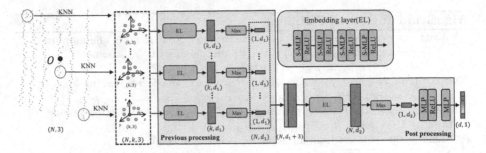

Fig. 3. The structure of the encoder. $O = (0,0,0)$.

original point cloud. Note that in the test phase, we set $M = N_{ori}//N + 1$ to avoid losing the original points. The sample step only takes place during training.

Next, we calculate the Euclidean distance between all points in the original point cloud P and the original point and then sort them in ascending order. We then divide the sorted points P' into multiple annular point clouds with a specified number of points. Within each annular point cloud P_a, we sort the points according to their yaw angle and further divide them into multiple patches.

Once we obtain each patch P_m, we calculate the mean coordinates μ_m of the points within it and find the nearest neighbor s_m of the mean coordinates μ_m from the original point cloud. Finally, these nearest neighbors S serve as the local central point of each patch.

2.3   Autoencoder

This section will describe the detail of the encoder and decoder in our model.
Encoder. Figure 3 illustrates the structure of our encoder, which can be divided into a pre-processing stage and a post-processing stage. In the pre-processing stage, we first use KNN to obtain the $(N, k, 3)$ local point group centered on each point in the patch. Then, we use an embedding layer with shared multi-layer perceptron (S-MLP) layer [13,14] to extract features of the $(k, 3)$ points in each group and obtain the (N, d) local grouping features through max pooling. After concatenating the (N, d) feature and the $(N, 3)$ input patch, it is input to the post-processing stage. In this stage, we use the embedding layer to get the (N, d_2) features. We then use the maximum function to aggregate features and obtain the $(1, d_2)$ potential feature. Finally, the potential feature is transformed into the $(d_2, 1)$ final potential feature through the MLP layers.
Decoder. As shown in Fig. 4. The decoder first uses multiple MLP layers to map the $(d, 1)$ reconstructed feature to $(N \times D, 1)$ and then reshapes it into the (N, D) feature with the same dimension as the point cloud. Then the (N, D) feature is concatenated with the reconstructed features and input to the multi-layer S-MLP with Instance Normalization (IN) [20] to obtain the final $(N, 3)$ offset.

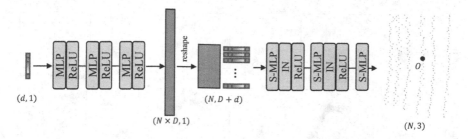

Fig. 4. The structure of the decoder. $O = (0, 0, 0)$

3   Experiments

This section will introduce the experience setting in Sect. 3.1 and the experience result in Sect. 3.2.

3.1   Experiment Setting

Dataset. We conducted experiments on 00 to 10 sequences in the SemanticKITTI dataset, where sequence 08 is used for testing, and the others are used for training. Due to the small difference between adjacent point clouds in the sequence, we obtained a test set with 1018 samples from the 08 sequence by a step size of 4. And point clouds with a point number less than 110K in the training set were discarded.

Experimental Details. Our model was implemented by *PyTorch* and experienced on *NVIDIA Titan RTX* and *Intel Xeon W-2265*. We used the Adam [9] optimizer to train the model with a learning rate of 0.001 and 40K iterative. We achieve different bpp by adjusting the number of patches. λ is set to 0 in the first 4000 iterations, and 0.001 in subsequent iterations. For the encoder, decoder, and entropy model, we set $k = 8, d_1 = 128, d_2 = 64, d = 8, D = 32$, and $L = 25$. We use *torchac* [12] for entropy encoding and *Open3D* [27] for visualization.

Baseline. We compared our model with G-PCC and IPDAE. For G-PCC, we merged duplicate points at the same location, leaving only valid points. For IPDAE and our method, normalization and learning rate decay were not used in the training phase, and sampling points were transmitted using a half-float type.

Metrics. The evaluation of a compression algorithm is a trade-off between compression ratio and distortion. For the compression ratio of lossy compression, we use bit per valid reconstruction point:

$$\text{bpp} = \frac{\text{bit}}{\min(N_{in}, N_{rec})}, \tag{2}$$

where bpp is the bit num of bitstream after compression, N_{in} and N_{rec} are the point num of the input point cloud and the reconstruction one respectively.

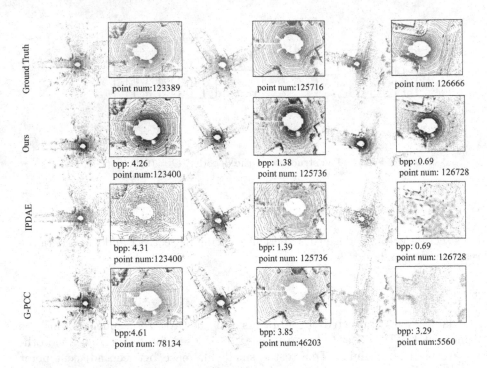

Fig. 5. Reconstruction results on the 08-000000, 08-000804, and 08-001600 (left to right) in the SemanticKITTI dataset. From top to down is the ground truth point cloud, our method, IPDAE, and G-PCC.

Unlike the uniform object point clouds, the distribution of LiDAR point clouds is uneven, with higher density near and lower density far away. However, PSNR which is commonly used to evaluate reconstructed object point clouds [5,8,22, 25], calculates errors at the nearest points. This makes it difficult for PSNR to evaluate the spatial distribution similarity between the reconstructed point cloud and the original point cloud because the original points can also find relatively nearby points in the uniform reconstruction. Considering the unevenness of the LiDAR point cloud, we sort the points in both the original and reconstructed point clouds based on their distances from the origin and calculate the symmetric PSNR separately for the near (2/3 points) point cloud P_{near}, $\hat{P}_{near}$ and far (1/3 points) point cloud P_{far}, $\hat{P}_{far}$. We then average the two values to obtain the final distortion metric:

$$\mathrm{PSNR}_{\mathrm{n-f}}\left(P, \hat{P}\right) = \frac{1}{2}(10\log_{10}\frac{p_{near}^2}{\max\{e(P_{near}, \hat{P}_{near}), e(\hat{P}_{near}, P_{near})\}}$$

$$+ 10\log_{10}\frac{p_{far}^2}{\max\{e(P_{far}, \hat{P}_{far}), e(\hat{P}_{far}, P_{far})\}}) \tag{3}$$

where $e(\cdot, \cdot)$ is the point-to-point or point-to-plane error [19] calculated at the nearest neighbor point; p_{near} and p_{far} is the maximum nearest neighbor distance

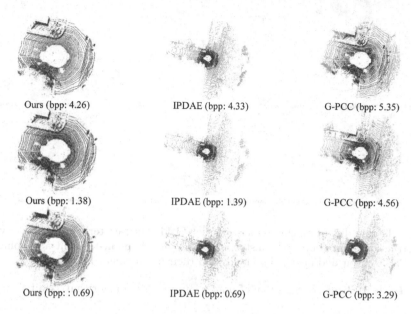

Ours (bpp: 4.26)	IPDAE (bpp: 4.33)	G-PCC (bpp: 5.35)
Ours (bpp: 1.38)	IPDAE (bpp: 1.39)	G-PCC (bpp: 4.56)
Ours (bpp: : 0.69)	IPDAE (bpp: 0.69)	G-PCC (bpp: 3.29)

Fig. 6. The nearest 2/3 points of the original (blue-green) and reconstructed (orange) point clouds of 08-001600 in the SemanticKITTI dataset. (Color figure online)

of the points in near and far point clouds respectively. We use the software provided by [19] to calculate this metric.

3.2   Experiment Result

Compression Performance Comparison. Figure 5 shows the reconstructed point cloud visualization results of our method and the baseline methods. The geometric compression of G-PCC is based on the octree, the points of the original point cloud in the same octant of the octree will be merged into a single point. When the constructed octree is shallow, a large number of the original points will be lost. This also results in the reconstructed point cloud will be interspersed with some grid lines. For IPDAE, since its sampling points are obtained by FPS and evenly cover the entire original point cloud, the reconstructed point cloud takes the sampling points as local center points will lose the characteristic of LiDAR point clouds that are dense near and sparse far away. Compared with these two methods, the point clouds reconstructed by our method can maintain the characteristics of dense near and sparse far. In addition, our method will not lose the points of the original point clouds.

To further demonstrate that the point cloud reconstructed by our method can maintain the spatial distribution of the LiDAR point cloud, we visualized the near point cloud which accounts for 2/3 of the whole point cloud of the reconstructed point cloud and the original point cloud. As shown in Fig. 6, the range of the near point clouds on each bpp reconstructed by our method is almost the

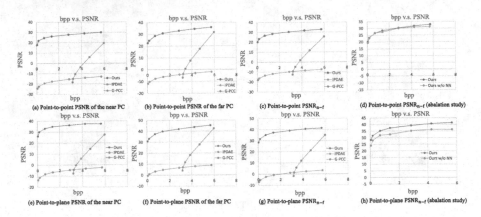

Fig. 7. The rate-distortion curves on SemanticKITTI. The rate term is the bit per valid reconstruction point (bpp). The distortion terms include point-to-point and point-to-plane PSNR of far and near point clouds and their mean values $PSNR_{n-f}$.

Table 1. Time consumption of point cloud partition algorithm. (Unit:s)

Method	(M, N)					
	(64,2000)	(256,500)	(1024,124)	(2048,62)	(4096,30)	(6400,20)
FPS+KNN	0.124	0.388	1.578	2.832	5.631	8.802
FPS+KNN (GPU)	2.066	1.138	0.973	1.026	1.150	1.320
Ours	0.043	0.077	0.222	0.403	0.743	1.18
Ours w/o NN	0.022	0.026	0.035	0.044	0.065	0.091

same as the original. In contrast, point clouds reconstructed by other methods are more uniform than the original point clouds or lose the original point, which results in significant differences in the range of the near point cloud. Figure 7(a)–(c) and Fig. 7(e)–(g) respectively show the rate-distortion performance on the SemanticKITTI dataset. It can be seen that our method outperforms the baseline methods in terms of PSNR at the listed bpp.

Time Complexity of Partition Algorithm. Table 1 shows the time consumption using our partitioning method and FPS+KNN partitioning algorithm for different numbers of patches. It can be seen that for different patch numbers, our partition algorithm requires only a very short time, while the FPS+KNN partitioning algorithm increases significantly with the number of patches. Even with GPU, the FPS+KNN partition algorithm takes longer than ours.

Ablation Study on Partition Algorithm. Table 1 also shows that using the nearest neighbor (NN) point as the local center point will increase the partitioning time of our method. To demonstrate the gain effect of the nearest neighbor point, we perform an ablation study on it. As shown in Fig. 7(d) and Fig. 7(h), the nearest neighbor point can significantly improve the quality of reconstructed point clouds in terms of point-to-plane $PSNR_{n-f}$.

4   Conclusion

This paper proposes an ordered partition algorithm for patch-wise LiDAR point cloud compression based on the autoencoder. The algorithm leverages the data characteristics of LiDAR point clouds and has several advantages, including the absence of duplicate points, the retention of original points, equal point num in patches, and efficient online performance. Experiments on the SemanticKITTI dataset demonstrate that our patch-wise compression model can reconstruct point clouds with a spatial distribution that more closely resembles the original ones compared with G-PCC and IPDAE.

References

1. Ballé, J., Laparra, V., Simoncelli, E.P.: End-to-end optimized image compression. In: International Conference on Learning Representations (ICLR), pp. 1–12 (2017)
2. Ballé, J., Minnen, D., Singh, S., Hwang, S.J., Johnston, N.: Variational image compression with a scale hyperprior. In: International Conference on Learning Representations (ICLR), pp. 1–13 (2018)
3. Behley, J., et al.: SemanticKITTI: a dataset for semantic scene understanding of lidar sequences. In: IEEE/CVF International Conference on Computer Vision (ICCV), pp. 9297–9307 (2019)
4. Chang, A.X., et al.: ShapeNet: an information-rich 3d model repository. arXiv preprint arXiv:1512.03012 (2015)
5. Gao, L., Fan, T., Wan, J., Xu, Y., Sun, J., Ma, Z.: Point cloud geometry compression via neural graph sampling. In: IEEE International Conference on Image Processing (ICIP), pp. 3373–3377 (2021)
6. Guo, M.H., Cai, J.X., Liu, Z.N., Mu, T.J., Martin, R.R., Hu, S.M.: PCT: point cloud transformer. Comput. Visual Media **7**(1), 187–199 (2021). https://doi.org/10.1007/s41095-021-0229-5
7. He, D., Yang, Z., Peng, W., Ma, R., Qin, H., Wang, Y.: ELIC: efficient learned image compression with unevenly grouped space-channel contextual adaptive coding. In: IEEE/CVF Conference on Computer Vision and Pattern Recognition (CVPR), pp. 5718–5727 (2022)
8. Huang, T., Liu, Y.: 3D point cloud geometry compression on deep learning. In: ACM International Conference on Multimedia (ACMMM), pp. 890–898 (2019)
9. Kingma, D.P., Ba, J.: Adam: a method for stochastic optimization. arXiv preprint arXiv:1412.6980, pp. 1–11 (2014)
10. Liang, Z., Liang, F.: TransPCC: towards deep point cloud compression via transformers. In: International Conference on Multimedia Retrieval (ICMR), pp. 1–5 (2022)
11. Liu, M.: Robotic online path planning on point cloud. IEEE Trans. Cybern. **46**(5), 1217–1228 (2015). https://doi.org/10.1109/TCYB.2015.2430526
12. Mentzer, F., Agustsson, E., Tschannen, M., Timofte, R., Gool, L.V.: Practical full resolution learned lossless image compression. In: IEEE/CVF Conference on Computer Vision and Pattern Recognition (CVPR), pp. 10629–10638 (2019)
13. Qi, C.R., Su, H., Mo, K., Guibas, L.J.: PointNet: deep learning on point sets for 3D classification and segmentation. In: IEEE/CVF Conference on Computer Vision and Pattern Recognition (CVPR), pp. 652–660 (2017)

14. Qi, C.R., Yi, L., Su, H., Guibas, L.J.: PointNet++ deep hierarchical feature learning on point sets in a metric space. In: International Conference on Neural Information Processing Systems (NeurIPS), pp. 5105–5114 (2017)

15. Quach, M., Pang, J., Tian, D., Valenzise, G., Dufaux, F.: Survey on deep learning-based point cloud compression. Frontiers Sig. Process. **2**(1), 19 (2022). https://doi.org/10.3389/frsip.2022.846972

16. Schwarz, S., et al.: Emerging MPEG standards for point cloud compression. IEEE J. Emerg. Sel. Top. Circuits Syst. **9**(1), 133–148 (2018). https://doi.org/10.1109/JETCAS.2018.2885981

17. Sun, X., Wang, M., Du, J., Sun, Y., Cheng, S.S., Xie, W.: A task-driven scene-aware LiDAR point cloud coding framework for autonomous vehicles. IEEE Trans. Industr. Inf. **1**(1), 1–11 (2022). https://doi.org/10.1109/TII.2022.3221222

18. Sun, X., Wang, S., Wang, M., Cheng, S.S., Liu, M.: An advanced LiDAR point cloud sequence coding scheme for autonomous driving. In: ACM International Conference on Multimedia (ACM MM), pp. 2793–2801 (2020)

19. Tian, D., Ochimizu, H., Feng, C., Cohen, R., Vetro, A.: Geometric distortion metrics for point cloud compression. In: IEEE International Conference on Image Processing (ICIP), pp. 3460–3464 (2017). https://doi.org/10.1109/ICIP.2017.8296925

20. Ulyanov, D., Vedaldi, A., Lempitsky, V.: Instance normalization: the missing ingredient for fast stylization. arXiv preprint arXiv:1607.08022, pp. 1–6 (2016)

21. Wu, Z., et al.: 3D ShapeNets: a deep representation for volumetric shapes. In: IEEE/CVF Conference on Computer Vision and Pattern Recognition (CVPR), pp. 1912–1920 (2015)

22. Yan, W., Liu, S., Li, T.H., Li, Z., Li, G., et al.: Deep autoencoder-based lossy geometry compression for point clouds. arXiv preprint arXiv:1905.03691, pp. 4321–4328 (2019)

23. You, K., Gao, P.: Patch-based deep autoencoder for point cloud geometry compression. In: ACM Multimedia Asia (MMAsia), pp. 1–7 (2021)

24. You, K., Gao, P., Li, Q.: IPDAE: improved patch-based deep autoencoder for lossy point cloud geometry compression. In: International Workshop on Advances in Point Cloud Compression, Processing and Analysis (APCCPA), pp. 1–10 (2022)

25. Zhang, J., Liu, G., Ding, D., Ma, Z.: Transformer and upsampling-based point cloud compression. In: International Workshop on Advances in Point Cloud Compression, Processing and Analysis (APCCPA), pp. 33–39 (2022)

26. Zhao, H., Jiang, L., Jia, J., Torr, P.H., Koltun, V.: Point transformer. In: IEEE/CVF International Conference on Computer Vision (ICCV), pp. 16259–16268 (2021)

27. Zhou, Q.Y., Park, J., Koltun, V.: Open3D: a modern library for 3D data processing. arXiv preprint arXiv:1801.09847, pp. 1–6 (2018)

28. Zhu, X., Song, J., Gao, L., Zheng, F., Shen, H.T.: Unified multivariate gaussian mixture for efficient neural image compression. In: IEEE/CVF Conference on Computer Vision and Pattern Recognition (CVPR), pp. 17612–17621 (2022)

29. Zhu, Y., Yang, Y., Cohen, T.: Transformer-based transform coding. In: International Conference on Learning Representations (ICLR), pp. 1–14 (2022)

Astronomical Image Coding Based on Graph Fourier Transform

Lingshan Li, Yan Zhao$^{(\boxtimes)}$, and Shigang Wang

Jilin University, Changchun, China
lils20@mails.jlu.edu.cn, {zhao_y,wangsg}@jlu.edu.cn

Abstract. In recent years, astronomical image coding has attracted increasing attention. The existing image compression algorithms are usually developed for ordinary images, which ignore the image characteristics and storage purpose of astronomical image itself, resulting in low compression efficiency. Aiming at the existing problems, we proposed an astronomical image compression algorithm based graph Fourier transform (GFT), which is mainly devoted to the high performance compression of the astronomical image with a deep space background taken by the ground astronomical telescope. The algorithm not only improves the compression ratio of the image, but also better preserves the information of the targets, so as to realize the storage of a large number of high-resolution astronomical maps in the limited storage space. Firstly, the GTF basis dictionary is constructed according to the result of the classification of astronomical image blocks by Weisfeiler-Lehman (W-L) subtree kernel. Then, during image block coding, the transform basis of the same kind of images is selected for GFT according to the calculation of image similarity, and different quantization matrices are adopted for quantization operation. Finally, the quantized transformation coefficients and the dictionary indexes are encoded by run length encoding and Huffman coding. By comparing with the image coding standard, it is verified that the proposed algorithm has higher peak signal-noise ratio and structural similarity index at low pixel depth than the existing image and video coding standards, and has better compression performance.

Keywords: Image coding · Astronomical image · Graph Fourier Transform · Graph kernel

1 Introduction

In recent years, with the improvement of people's understanding of image source characteristics and human visual system characteristics, image coding technology has been developed rapidly. Many image compression algorithms with good performance have been proposed. Although the compression performance of these algorithms has achieved remarkable results on natural images, the performance on astronomical images is not up to expectations because of the difference between astronomical images and natural images. Astronomical image has the characteristics of dense content, single background, complex noise and high resolution. To better target the above characteristics, researchers

© The Author(s), under exclusive license to Springer Nature Switzerland AG 2023
H. Lu et al. (Eds.): ICIG 2023, LNCS 14357, pp. 311–322, 2023.
https://doi.org/10.1007/978-3-031-46311-2_26

have proposed some astronomical image coding algorithms such as proposing a novel minimum total variation with block adaptive sensing to reconstruct astronomical images [1], a multiscale cubic B-spline wavelet compressor [2] and a region of interest compression algorithm under the deep learning self-encoder framework [3]. Due to the dense content and single background of astronomical images, the compression algorithm for natural images cannot make full use of the redundant information in astronomical images, resulting in low compression efficiency. Therefore, researchers generally have two ways to solve this problem. One is to adopte different coding methods for different image content regions in order to make full use of redundant information in different regions and achieve better compression performance. The other is to try a variety of transformation methods, seeking a more suitable transformation method for astronomical image.

In this paper, we aim to find a new coding algorithm dedicated to high performance compression of astronomical images taken by terrestrial astronomical telescopes with deep space as the background. GFT is a transformation method based on graph structure in graph theory, which is derived from the analogy of Fourier transform. By replacing the Fourier transform basis with the transform basis composed of the feature vectors of the graph Laplace matrix, GFT maps the graph signal to graph frequency domain. Therefore, we propose an astronomical image coding algorithm based on GFT. Specifically, in order to reduce the cost of storing the GFT basis, the astronomical image blocks are classified by the W-L subtree kernel, and then the GFT basis dictionary is constructed. In the process of using GFT to encode, we select the transform basis of the same kind of image block to transform according to the calculation of the similarity of the image. Then, we design a quantization matrix more suitable for the transform coefficients of astronomical images to further reduce the compressed bit stream. Finally, the quantized transform coefficients and the indexes of the basis dictionary are encoded by run length encoding and Huffman coding.

The rest of this paper is structured as follows: Sect. 2 introduces the related work about our method including astronomical image coding GFT and W-L subtree kernel. In Sect. 3, we describe the proposed method. The experimental results of the method are provided in Sect. 4. At last, we conclude the whole work in Sect. 5

2 Related Work

2.1 Astronomical Image Coding

With the development of astronomical observation technology, the amount of astronomical images keeps increasing. In order to reduce the bit stream required for the transmission or storage of astronomical images, a series of astronomical image coding algorithms are proposed. Zhou proposed a compression reconstruction algorithm for astronomical images based on compressed sensing technology, and proposed a novel minimum total variation with block adaptive sensing to reconstruct astronomical images [1]. V.V.Kitaeff demonstrated the viability of JPEG2000 compression for storing and distributing radio astronomy images[4]. EF Khanjer created an image compression method based on Five Modulus Method (FMM)[5]. Jesus Pulido proposed a new lossy image compression method which contains a multiscale cubic B-spline wavelet compressor [2]. Karadeniz proposed an improvement of Zlib for astronomical images based on polynomial curve fitting [6]. Anasuodei M proposed an techniques for satellite image compression based hybrid Discrete Wavelet Transform, Discrete Cosine Transform and Singular Value Decomposition [7]. Maireles-González Ò proved JPEG-LS, LZMA and NDZIP yield the best compression ratio results for 16-bit data, floating-point data and radio data [8]. Zhang proposed a region of interest (ROI) compression algorithm under the deep learning self-encoder framework to improve the reconstruction performance of the image and reduce the distortion of the ROI [3].

2.2 Graph Fourier Transform

Graph Signal Processing combines the knowledge of algebraic theory and graph theory to calculate the image from the perspective of graph structure, so as to achieve better processing effect of graph signal. As a kind of transformation method widely used in graph signal processing, the essence of GFT is the projection of graph signal on the GFT basis with the graph Laplacian matrix eigenvector as the column. Hu proposed to compress the PWS images using suitable GFTs to minimize the total signal representation cost of each pixel block [9]. Then Hu proposed an optimized transform for the prediction residual, based on a generalized version of GFT [10]. Xu proposed a novel point cloud compression method for attributes, based on geometric clustering and Normal Weighted Graph Fourier Transform (NWGFT) [11].

2.3 Weisfeiler-Lehman Subtree Kernel

Graph kernel is a method to calculate the similarity between graphs, which has become an important branch of structured data learning rapidly in recent years [12]. W-L subtree kernel [13] is a graph calculation method based on subtree which uses the idea of label propagation for reference, so that the graph similarity is calculated by the graph core obtained in the process of multiple iterations. Bastian Rieck leveraged propagated node label information and transform unweighted graphs into metric ones to extract the topological features of graphs [14]. D H Nguyen proposed a method to learn the weights of subtree patterns in the framework of Wasserstein Weisfeiler-Lehman (WWL) kernels to enhance the classification result [15].

3 Method

The framework of our proposed method is shown in Fig. 1. The method we proposed is divided into the following steps. Firstly, the astronomical image blocks are classified using the W-L subtree kernel, and the GFT basis dictionary is constructed according to the classification results. In this process, the feature vectors of the images are arranged according to the ascending order of the corresponding graph frequency, which is convenient for the subsequent feature analysis of the transform coefficients. Secondly, in the process of using GFT to encode, we select the transform basis of the same kind of image block to transform according to the calculation of the similarity of the image, and different quantization matrices are adopted for quantization of the transform coefficients. Finally, run length coding and Huffman coding are used to encode the quantized transform coefficients and the basis dictionary indexes.

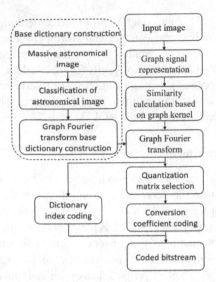

Fig. 1. Framework of our proposed method

3.1 Graph Classification Based on Weisfeiler-Lehman Subtree Kernel

W-L subtree kernel uses the idea of label propagation for reference, and carries out multiple iterations on the graph structure. In each iteration, the current node is updated according to the label after the last iteration of the adjacent nodes, and the updated graph kernel is calculated through the new label of each node. The graph similarity is obtained by comprehensive calculation of graph kernel in the process of multiple iterations.

W-L subtree kernel algorithm is an effective method to judge whether two graphs are isomorphic, and its operation is mainly divided into two steps. Firstly, the labels of the current node v and its adjacent nodes are recorded and collected. Secondly, the statistics recorded before are mapped to a new label by using the hash function and assigned it to current node v. By iterating the above two steps for several times, we judge whether all node labels of the two graphs are the same according to the final mapping results. If they are the same, the two graphs are considered to be isomorphic. Otherwise, the two graphs are considered to be non-isomorphic.

If it is assumed that the label representing node v is h(v), the update formula of the node label can be expressed as follow.

$$h^{(t)}(v) = HASH\left(h^{(t-1)}(v), F\left\{h^{(t-1)}(u)|u \in N(v)\right\}\right) \tag{1}$$

where t represents the number of iterations, F represents the function that counts the adjacent nodes of the current node, and $N(v)$ represents the set of the adjacent nodes of node v in the graph. For the graph $G = \{V,E,I\}$, node set V and edge set E remain unchanged in the iteration, and label set I changes with the iteration of W-L subtree kernel algorithm. Finally, whether the two graphs are isomorphic structure is determined by calculating the label set.

The W-L subtree kernel of graph G_1 and G_2 after hth iterations is defined as follow.

$$W_{WLsub}^{(h)}(G_1, G_2) = \langle \varnothing_{WLsub}^{(h)}(G_1), \varnothing_{WLsub}^{(h)}(G_2) \rangle \qquad (2)$$

$$\varnothing_{WLsub}^{(h)}(G_1) = \left(c_0(G_1, \sigma_{01}), \ldots, c_0\left(G_1, \sigma_{0|\Sigma_0|}\right), \ldots, c_h(G_1, \sigma_{h1}), \ldots, c_h\left(G_1, \sigma_{h|\Sigma_h|}\right) \right) \qquad (3)$$

$$\varnothing_{WLsub}^{(h)}(G_2) = \left(c_0(G_2, \sigma_{01}), \ldots, c_0\left(G_2, \sigma_{0|\Sigma_0|}\right), \ldots, c_h(G_2, \sigma_{h1}), \ldots, c_h\left(G_2, \sigma_{h|\Sigma_h|}\right) \right) \qquad (4)$$

where $\Sigma_i = \left\{ \sigma_{i1}, \sigma_{i2}, \ldots, \sigma_{i|\Sigma_i|} \right\}$ is ordered and represents the node label set of the graph after the hth iteration of the W-L subtree kernel. Define the map $c : \{G, G\prime\} \times \Sigma_i \to N$ so that $c_i\left(G, \sigma_{ij}\right)$ represents the number of label σ_{ij} appears in graph G.

3.2 The Construction of Graph Fourier Transform Base Dictionary

GFT maps the graph signal to graph frequency domain by replacing the Fourier transform basis with the transform basis composed of the feature vectors of the graph Laplace matrix, so as to facilitate the further processing of the graph signal.

The Laplacian matrix of the graph is expressed as $L = D\text{-}W$, where W is the adjacency matrix, representing the connection relation of each vertex in the graph. D is the degree matrix of the graph, and is expressed as a diagonal matrix, where the ith diagonal element is the sum of all the elements in the ith row of the adjacency matrix.

$$D_{i,i} = \sum_{j=1}^{N} \omega_{i,j} \qquad (5)$$

The Laplacian matrix is a real symmetric matrix, and it has an orthonormal eigenvector set U. The Laplacian matrix can be eigen-decomposed into the following formula:

$$L = U \wedge U^T \qquad (6)$$

where $\wedge$ is the diagonal matrix whose eigenvalue λ_k of Laplacian matrix is the diagonal element, and U is an eigenmatrix with orthogonal eigenvector u_i as columns. The structure of the graph determines the value of the Laplacian matrix of graph, so different graph structures correspond to different Laplacian matrices.

Taking the eigenvector u_i of the Laplacian matrix as the basis for GFT, the GFT of image blocks with the size of $\sqrt{N} \times \sqrt{N}$ can be expressed as follow.

$$\hat{f}(k) = \sum_{n=1}^{N} f(n)u_k^*(n), \ k = 0, 1, \ldots, N-1 \qquad (7)$$

And the inverse GFT of the graph is expressed as following formula:

$$f(n) = \sum_{k=0}^{N-1} \hat{f}(k)u_k(n), \ n = 1, 2, \ldots, N \qquad (8)$$

where $f(n)$ represents the image signal, which is a one-dimensional vector of length N transformed by a $\sqrt{N} \times \sqrt{N}$ image block. $\hat{f}(k)$ represents the transform coefficients of graph signals on the k eigenvector.

3.3 Design of Quantization Matrix

Because the distribution of the transform coefficients after GFT is different from that after discrete cosine transform (DCT), the existing quantization matrix designed based on DCT is not applicable to the transform coefficients after GFT. Therefore, according to the mathematical characteristics of the transform coefficients of astronomical images after GFT, a quantization matrix which is more suitable for GFT is designed.

Firstly, the quantization matrix is divided into two parts for the background region and the target region according to the different relationship between the transform coefficients and the eigenvalues.

The Fig. 2 is the relationship between the transform coefficients after GFT and their corresponding eigenvalues, in which the resolution of the astronomical image is 8 × 8. In Fig. 2 (a), we use the astronomical image which contains only the background region. And Fig. 2 (b) is the result of an astronomical image which contains the target.

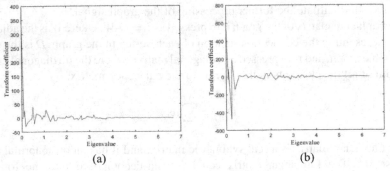

(a)   (b)

Fig. 2. The relationship between transform coefficients and their corresponding eigenvalues. The result of the astronomical image which contains only the background region is shown in (a). The result of the astronomical image which contains the target area is shown in (b).

According to the analysis in Fig. 2, the transform coefficients of the background region and the target region of the astronomical image have different distribution characteristics. The transform coefficients of the background region mainly include the larger DC coefficient corresponding to eigenvalue 0 and the smaller transform coefficients corresponding to other eigenvalues. And the transform coefficients of the target region mainly includes the larger transform coefficients corresponding to the small eigenvalues and the smaller transform coefficients corresponding to other eigenvalues. Therefore, this paper will adopt different coding schemes for different image content to encode the image.

After dividing astronomical image data into equal image blocks, threshold segmentation is used to divide it into two parts including target region and background region. According to the image similarity, the transform basis of the same kind of image is selected as the GFT basis.

Taking background region of the astronomical image block as an example, 4072 image blocks with the resolution of 8 × 8 were preliminarily obtained after threshold detection. Each image block can obtain 64 transform coefficients after GFT, which correspond to 64 image frequencies respectively. The Fig. 3 shows the transform coefficients corresponding to the same image frequency of different images. Figure 3 (a) shows the transform coefficients corresponding to the first image frequency of different images. And Fig. 3 (b) shows the transform coefficients corresponding to the fifth image frequency of different images. According to Fig. 3, the transform coefficients corresponding to the same graph frequency have the characteristic of centralized distribution.

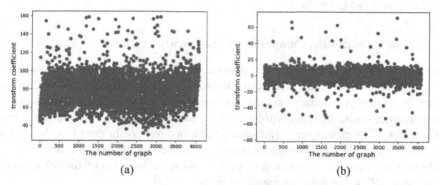

             (a)   (b)

Fig. 3. The transform coefficients corresponding to the same image frequency of different images. The transform coefficients corresponding to the first image frequency is shown in (a). The transform coefficients corresponding to the fifth image frequency is shown in (b).

Mean value and variance are commonly used mathematical features. Mean value reflects the central tendency of data and describes the average condition characteristics of random variables. The variance reflects the degree of dispersion of a set of data and describes the degree of deviation between a random variable and its mean value.

In this paper, mean value and variance are used for statistical analysis of the transform coefficients, and different quantization matrices are designed according to the characteristics of the two kinds of transform coefficients.

Taking n image blocks with the resolution of 8×8 as an example, the transform coefficients can be expressed as a two-dimensional matrix with the size of $n \times 64$, and the elements in each row represent the transform coefficients of a block, and the elements in each column represent the transform coefficients of different image blocks corresponding to the same image frequency. After calculating the mean value of the transform coefficients in each column, the transform coefficients with large deviation from the mean value is screened and removed, and the variance of the screened transform coefficients is taken as the quantized value of the corresponding graph frequency. Finally, a two-dimensional quantization matrix with the size of 8×8 can be obtained by converting the obtained one-dimensional quantization value.

4 Experiments

The experimental data are the astronomical images taken by the ground telescope of Changchun Satellite Observation Station of National Astronomical Observatories, Chinese Academy of Sciences. All experiments are implemented on a desktop machine equipped with an Inter(R) Core(TM) i5-9400F CPU @ 2.90GHz and 16.0 GB RAM. The proposed algorithm and the JPEG were executed using Python 3.9 in Pycharm 2021 compiler, HEVC is executed in Microsoft Visual Studio 2017 using C + +, JPEG2000 is implemented in Matlab 2018a.

4.1 Graph Classification Comparison Experiments

The existing astronomical images were divided into 8*8 image blocks, and three images of the same type and different type were selected through the calculation of W-L subtree kernel for further preliminary experimental verification. The image is encoded by its own transform basis, the transform basis of the similar image and the transform basis of the different species image. After setting the transform coefficients less than the set threshold as zero, the transform coefficients are encoded by run length coding.

Figure 4 shows the comparison of peak signal-to-noise ratio of the astronomical image after GFT using different transform basis.

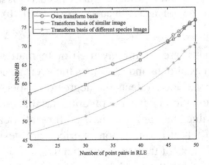

Fig. 4. The comparison of peak signal-to-noise ratio.

It can be seen from Fig. 4 that it is feasible to use the same transform basis for GFT of the images classified into the same class by W-L subtree kernel. Although there are more bitstreams using the transform basis of the similar image than the bitstreams using its own transform basis, it is far less than the bitstreams required for encoding and transmitting the transform basis, and the peak signal-to-noise ratio of the decoded image after inverse transformation is almost the same. Compared with using the transform basis of the different species image, the quality of the decoded image which encoded by the transform basis of the similar image after the inverse transformation is much higher than that of using the transform basis of different species image.

By classifying astronomical images with W-L subtree kernel, 2531 categories of image blocks are obtained. The transform basis dictionary consists of the transform basis of these images, and the feature vectors of each image block are sorted according to the ascending order of corresponding graph frequency during the construction of the basis dictionary. Thus a GFT basis dictionary containing 2531 categories is obtained.

4.2 Experiments Results of Quantization Matrix

Figure 5 shows the bpp-PSNR curve that uses the original quantization matrix in JPEG and the quantization matrix designed in this paper to encode astronomical images with different resolutions respectively.

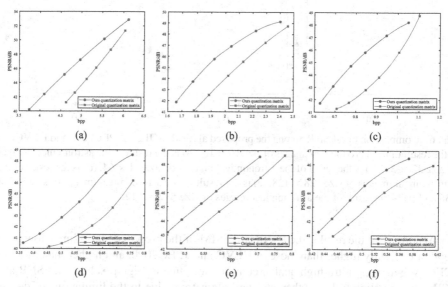

(a)   (b)   (c)

(d)   (e)   (f)

Fig. 5. Comparison bpp-PSNR among different quantization matrix, (a) is the result of the astronomical images of size 16×16, (b) is the result of the astronomical images of size 32×32, (c) is the result of the astronomical images of size 64×64, (d) is the result of the astronomical images of size 128×128, (e) is the result of the astronomical images of size 256×256 and (f) is the result of the astronomical images of size 512×512.

As can be seen from Fig. 5, the quantization matrix designed in this paper has a higher peak signal-to-noise ratio compared with the original quantization matrix in JPEG, so it is more suitable for the distribution characteristics of the transform coefficients after GFT compared with the original quantization matrix.

4.3 Astronomical Image Coding Based on GFT

In the experiment, astronomical images with various resolutions were used as experimental data, and the proposed algorithm is compared with the standard algorithms from two perspectives of subjective visual quality and objective indicators.

In terms of objective indicators, we compare the decoded image of astronomical images of different resolutions among the proposed algorithm, JPEG, JPEG2000 and HEVC in Fig. 6. And Fig. 7.

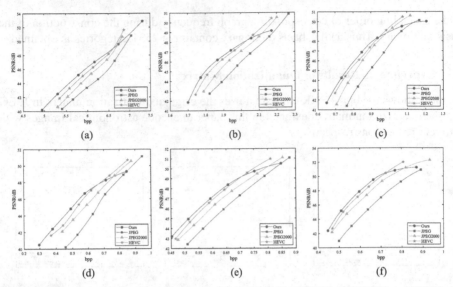

Fig. 6. Comparison bpp-PSNR among the proposed algorithm, JPEG, JPEG2000 and HEVC. (a) is the result of the astronomical images of size 16 × 16, (b) is the result of the astronomical images of size 32 × 32, (c) is the result of the astronomical images of size 64 × 64, (d) is the result of the astronomical images of size 128 × 128, (e) is the result of the astronomical images of size 256 × 256 and (f) is the result of the astronomical images of size 512 × 512.

According to the results, the PSNR and SSIM of the proposed algorithm at low pixel depth are slightly higher than those of HEVC and JPEG2000, and higher than those of JPEG. When using ultra-high quality compression, that is, high pixel depth, PSNR and SSIM will be slightly lower than standard algorithms due to the limitations of design quantization matrix. At the same time, the performance of the proposed algorithm in SSIM is better than that in PSNR, which proves that the algorithm in this paper has a better retention effect on image details.

In terms of subjective visual quality, Fig. 8 shows the comparison of the subjective visual quality of the decoded images using different algorithms at the same peak signal-to-noise ratio.

By observing the three triangular distributed small target areas in Fig. 8, it can be seen that the target shape and brightness of the small target area in the decoded image corresponding to JPEG have distortion, while the halo of the large target area in the decoded image corresponding to HEVC has fuzzy distortion. By comparing the decoded images, the decoded image of the proposed algorithm is closer to the origi-nal image. It has better subjective visual quality.

From the experimental results, the PSNR and SSIM of the proposed algorithm at low pixel depth are slightly higher than other standard algorithms in astronomical images. Meanwhile, the proposed algorithm can better retain the details of the target and obtain better subjective visual quality of the reconstructed image.

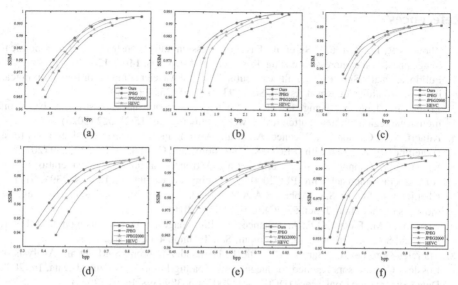

Fig. 7. Comparison bpp-SSIM among the proposed algorithm, JPEG, JPEG2000 and HEVC. (a) is the result of the astronomical images of size 16 × 16, (b) is the result of the astronomical images of size 32 × 32, (c) is the result of the astronomical images of size 64 × 64, (d) is the result of the astronomical images of size 128 × 128, (e) is the result of the astronomical images of size 256 × 256 and (f) is the result of the astronomical images of size 512 × 512.

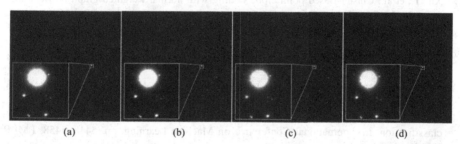

Fig. 8. The subjective visual quality of the decoded images. The original picture is shown in (a), the decoded image of HEVC is shown in (b), (c) is the decoded image of JPEG and the decoded image of the proposed algorithm is shown in (d)

5 Conclusion

In this paper, we propose an astronomical image coding algorithm based on GFT. The GFT basis dictionary is constructed based on W-L subtree kernel, and transform basis of the same kind of images is selected from the basis dictionary for GFT. Different quantization matrices are adopted for different regions. Finally, the basis dictionary indexes and the quantized transform coefficients are further encoded. By comparing subjective visual quality and objective indicators, such as PSNR and SSIM, the proposed algorithm based GFT has higher PSNR and SSIM at low pixel depth than other standard algorithms, and has better compression performance.

References

1. Zhou, W.P., Li, Y., Liu, Q.S., et al.: Fast compression and reconstruction of astronomical images based on compressed sensing. Res. Astron. Astrophys. **14**(9), 120 (2014)
2. Pulido, J., et al.: SnowPac: a multiscale cubic B-spline wavelet compressor for astronomical images. Monthly Not. Royal Astron. Soc. **493**(2), 2545–2555 (2020)
3. Zhang, J., Zhang, S., Wang, H., et al.: Image compression network structure based on multiscale region of interest attention network. Remote Sens. **15**(2), 522 (2023)
4. Kitaeff, V.V., Cannon, A., Wicenec, A., et al.: Astronomical imagery: considerations for a contemporary approach with JPEG2000. Astronomy and Computing **12**, 229–239 (2015)
5. Kitaeff, V.V., Cannon, A., Wicenec, A., et al.: Astronomical imagery: considerations for a contemporary approach with JPEG2000. Astronomy and Computing **12**, 229–239 (2015)
6. Khanjer, E.F., Shnain, S.K., Abbas, B.A.A.R.: Compression of astronomical image using five modulus method. Iraqi J. Sci. **57**(2C), 1566–1571 (2016)
7. Anasuodei, M., Eleonu, O.F.: An enhanced satellite image compression using hybrid (DWT, DCT and SVD) algorithm. Am. J. Comput. Sci. Technol. **4**(1), 1–10 (2021)
8. Maireles-González, Ò., Bartrina-Rapesta, J., Hernández-Cabronero, M., et al.: Analysis of Lossless Compressors Applied to Integer and Floating-Point Astronomical Data. In: 2002 Data Compression Conference (DCC), vol. 2002, pp, 389–398. IEEE (2022)
9. Hu, W., Cheung, G., Ortega, A., et al.: Multiresolution graph fourier transform for compression of piecewise smooth images. IEEE Trans. Image Process. Public. IEEE Signal Process. Soc. **24**(1), 419–433 (2015)
10. Hu, W., Cheung, G., Ortega, A.: Intra-Prediction and generalized graph fourier transform for image coding. IEEE Signal Process. Lett. **22**(11), 1913–1917 (2015)
11. Xu, Y., et al.: Cluster-Based point cloud coding with normal weighted graph fourier transform. In: 2018 IEEE International Conference on Acoustics, Speech and Signal Processing (ICASSP), Calgary, AB, Canada, pp. 1753–1757 (2018). https://doi.org/10.1109/ICASSP.2018.8462684
12. Shervashidze, N., Borgwardt, K.: Fast subtree kernels on graphs. Adv. Neural. Inf. Process. Syst. **22**, 1660–1668 (2009)
13. Shervashidze, N., Schweitzer, P., Jan, E., et al.: Weisfeiler-Lehman graph kernels. J. Mach. Learn. Res. **12**(3), 2539–2561 (2011)
14. Rieck, B., Bock, C., Borgwardt, K.: A persistent Weisfeiler-Lehman procedure for graph classification. In: International Conference on Machine Learning, pp. 5448–5458. PMLR (2019)
15. Nguyen, D.H., Nguyen, C.H., Mamitsuka, H.: Learning subtree pattern importance for Weisfeiler-Lehman based graph kernels. Mach. Learn. **110**, 1585–1607 (2021)

A Novel Homogenized Chaotic System of Compressed Sensing Image Encryption Algorithm

Zijie Zhou, Liyong Bao$^{(\boxtimes)}$, Hongwei Ding, and Xiao Yang

Information School, Yunnan University, Kunming 650500, China
bly.yx@163.com

Abstract. Aimed at the problems of limited range, uneven distribution, and insufficient complexity of traditional one-dimensional chaotic mapping. In this paper, a method for constructing chaotic measurement matrices is presented. An experimental analysis of the chaotic properties of the proposed map is presented. Firstly, the Chebyshev map is homogeneously reconstructed, and the distributional characteristics of the original sequences are altered, in order to make the generated time series more consistent with information security requirements. Second, the Lyapunov exponent, information entropy, spectral entropy, and the NIST randomness test of pseudo random sequences are analyzed, and the results of the analysis show that the newly generated sequences have a good homogenized distribution, complex pseudo random sequences, and good ergodic properties. Then, based on that mapping, a measurement matrix for compressed sensing is generated. Finally, based on this measurement matrix, the image is compressed and encrypted. Simulation results show that the system has improved image reconstruction capability and complexity, and can withstand statistical and other common adversarial attacks.

Keywords: Measurement matrix · Distribution characteristics · Compressive sensing · Chaos

1 Introduction

The rapid development of technology and multimedia means that people are paying increasing attention to information security because of the increasing convenience of obtaining information [1]. Because of the its sensitivity of chaotic systems to initial value and traversal, it is gradually being used in the area of image encryption.

In recent years, many image encryption schemes based on chaotic systems [2–4], deep learning [5, 6] and Deoxyribonucleic Acid (DNA) sequences [7–9] have been proposed. However, the transmission after direct encryption of the image will increase the amount of data and hardware requirements, and compressed sensing can realize image compression and encryption at the same time, reducing the amount of data in the transmission process.

© The Author(s), under exclusive license to Springer Nature Switzerland AG 2023
H. Lu et al. (Eds.): ICIG 2023, LNCS 14357, pp. 323–335, 2023.
https://doi.org/10.1007/978-3-031-46311-2_27

In 2006, compressed sensing [10] was proposed, and subsequently, researchers demonstrated that pseudo-random measurement matrices constructed by chaotic sequences satisfy Restricted Isometry Property (RIP) with overwhelming probability [11], after which chaotic systems have been applied to compressed sensing [12]. There are two main strategies for common image compression and encryption schemes. The first is to construct a chaotic system, and the other is the structural design of the encryption algorithm. Excellent chaotic systems can not only improve the reconstruction quality of images, but also resist various common attacks, so the construction of chaotic systems is the most concerned problem for researchers. Yaqin Xie et al. [13] proposed a new three-dimensional chaotic system, which has a large key space, but the chaotic region of the system is small according to the bifurcation map of three-dimensional chaos, and the Lyapunov exponent is low and the sequences complexity is not enough, so the security is not high. Liu, J.L. et al. [14] proposed an optimization algorithm for a five-dimensional chaotic system and a compressed perceptual measurement matrix. First, high-dimensional chaos generates chaotic sequences, then the relationship between sequences is broken by logistic map to reduce the correlation between matrix columns, and finally, the plaintext images are compressed and then dislocated and diffused. This algorithm is not only effective in improving the image reconstruction quality but also in resisting various common attacks. Gong, L.H. et al. [15] proposed a compressed encryption algorithm that first performs the Arnold transform on the plaintext image and then compresses and encrypts the image. The sequences of the measurement matrix and the XOR operation in the paper consists of chaotic sequences generated by the Logistic map. The Lyapunov exponent of the one-dimensional logistic chaotic map is low, the sequences complexity is not enough, and the Arnold transform of the plaintext image increases the encryption time, and the efficiency of the algorithm needs to be improved. Zhang, T.F. et al. [16] proposed a method to construct a 1D chaotic system by first parallelizing and then cascading the Tent chaotic map, Logistic chaotic map, and Sine chaotic map. Although the improved chaotic map has better uniform distribution characteristics and larger key space, the improved PSNR value does not get much improvement and the reconstruction quality of the picture is not satisfactory.

In this paper, we propose a method for homogenizing a one-dimensional chaotic system of measurement matrix, providing an idea to construct a homogenized chaotic measurement matrix that overcomes the problems of non-uniform distribution and low sequence complexity of one-dimensional chaotic system. The experimental results show that the algorithm in this paper has good reconstruction performance and security for images.

2 Construction and Analysis of Homogeneous Chebyshev Mapping Model

2.1 Definition

The definition of Chebyshev:

$$u(i+1) = \cos(k * \arccos(u(i))); -1 \le u(i) \le 1 \tag{1}$$

For the requirement that the iterated values of the chaotic mapping are homogeneously distributed throughout the interval, the method of mathematically deriving the probability density of the Chebyshev mapping is used to derive the random variable function.

According to the definition of homogeneous distribution, if the probability density function of the random variable y satisfies the homogeneous distribution, the following equation can be obtained:

$$y(i+1) = \frac{2}{\pi}\sin^{-1}(u(i)) + C \tag{2}$$

where $u(i)$ is the chaotic sequences generated by Eq. (1) and C is the constant term in the solution after solving the differential equation, and $C = 0$ in this paper.

Then substitute Eq. (1) into Eq. (2) yields a random variable y that follows a uniform distribution in the interval $[-1, 1]$:

$$\begin{cases} u(i+1) = cos(k * arccos(u(i))) - 1 \leq u(i) \leq 1 \\ y(i) = u(i+1) \\ y(i+1) = \frac{2}{\pi}sin^{-1}(y(i)) \qquad -1 \leq y_{(i)} \leq 1 \\ u(i) = y(i+1) \end{cases} \tag{3}$$

where $y(i)$ is the chaotic sequence generated by the Chebyshev map and $y(i+1)$ is the homogenized sequence.

2.2 Fork Chart and Histograms

The chaotic behavior of a chaotic system can be analyzed by describing the chaotic sequences produced by chaotic mapping. Figure 1 (a) is a split diagram after mapping homogenization. If $k > 2$, mapping can achieve a good state of chaos, the chaotic region of the system is larger and the map has no periodic window. The sequence histogram can show the distribution of a sequence in each interval. Figure 1 (b) shows the histogram of the Chebyshev sequence, which shows that the chaotic sequence distribution is U-shaped. Figure 1 (c) is the histogram of the homogenized sequence. From Fig. 1 (c), the homogenized Chebyshev mapping has a better uniform distribution.

2.3 Lyapunov Exponent

The Lyapunov exponent is an important indicator to determine whether the system is in a chaotic state. If the system's Lyapunov exponent is positive, the system is in a chaotic state. The larger the Lyapunov exponent, the more sensitive the chaotic system is to the initial value. The Lyapunov exponent calculation formula is as follows:

$$\lambda = \lim_{n\to\infty} \frac{1}{n}\sum_{i=1}^{n-1} \ln|f'(y_i)| \tag{4}$$

where $f(y_i)$ is the chaotic sequences y_{n+1}, therefore $f'(y_i) = \frac{df(y)}{dy}|_{y=y_i}$.

In order to analyze the chaotic characteristics of the one-dimensional map homogenization. The initial value $u = 0.7577$ of a one-dimensional chaotic map with parameter k in the range of [0, 100] was controlled and the Lyapunov exponential of the map was calculated. As shown in Fig. 1 (d), when $k > 1.08$, Lyapunov exponent is positive, and the Lyapunov exponent increases with k, so the uniform chaotic system presented in this paper can be considered to have good chaotic properties and high sensitivity to initial values.

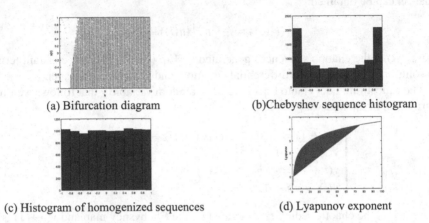

(a) Bifurcation diagram	(b)Chebyshev sequence histogram
(c) Histogram of homogenized sequences	(d) Lyapunov exponent

Fig. 1. Homogeneity and chaotic characteristics analysis

2.4 Uniformity and Complexity

Information Entropy.   The degree of chaos in a sequence is characterized by the information entropy. In other words, the closer the information entropy of the chaotic sequences is to the maximum information entropy, the better the uniformity of the system will be expected to be. The information entropy is calculated as follows:

$$H(s) = \sum_{i=0}^{2^n-1} p(s_i)\log_2\frac{1}{p(s_i)} \tag{5}$$

where s_i is the chaotic sequences and $p(s_i)$ is the probability of occurrence of s_i.

The number of iterations of chaos is $n = 100000$, the initial value is 0.7577, the sequences value is divided into different intervals M and the information entropy is calculated separately. As can be seen from the results in Table 1. Comparison of the Chebyshev mapping with the uniform mapping, and the information entropy of the homogenized mapping is close to the maximum of the information entropy. The sequences generated by the homogenized chaotic system in this paper can thus be viewed as having good homogenized distributional properties.

Spectral Entropy.   The spectral entropy of a sequence reflects the distribution characteristics of the power spectrum. The larger the spectral entropy of the sequences,

Table 1. Two chaotic mappings contrasted

Number of intervals M	Chebyshev mapping	Homogenized chaotic	Maximum information entropy
50	5.3668	5.6437	5.6439
100	6.3425	6.6433	6.6439
200	7.3241	7.6427	7.6439
500	8.6297	8.9624	8.9658

the greater the complexity, the smaller the spectral entropy value of the sequences, the smaller the complexity. The spectral entropy is calculated as follows:

$$se = - \sum_{k=0}^{\frac{n}{2}-1} p_k \ln p_k \tag{6}$$

where p_k is the relative power spectral density and n is the sequences length.

The spectral entropy of the uniform chaotic system was calculated. The calculation results are shown in Table 2, the longer the sequences, the greater the spectral entropy and gradually approaching the ideal value. After one-dimensional chaos homogenization, the longer chaotic sequences still have good sequence complexity and can be used for compressed encryption.

Table 2. Spectral entropy

Sequences length L	Spectral entropy
500	0.9266
1000	0.9293
2000	0.9393
3000	0.9396
4000	0.9447

2.5 The Randomness of the Sequences

The purpose of this paper is to use the NIST SP 800–22 norm to test the randomness of the sequences generated by the homogenized chaotic system. This standard consists of 15 tests, which compare the p value calculated by the test with a given significance level to determine the sequences generated by the system. When $P - value > 0.01$ the inspection is qualified and the results of the tests are shown in Table 3.

Table 3. Test Results of NIST SP800–22

Test index	P-value	Pass/Fail
Frequency	0.224821	Pass
Block Frequency	0.678686	Pass
Cumulative Sums	0.719747	Pass
Runs	0.514124	Pass
Longest Run	0.262249	Pass
Rank	0.249284	Pass
FFT	0.616305	Pass
Non-Overlapping Template	0.946308	Pass
Overlapping Template	0.759756	Pass
Universal	0.514124	Pass
Approximate Entropy	0.978072	Pass
Serial	0.455937	Pass
Linear Complexity	0.019188	Pass
Random Excursions	0.595549	Pass
Random Excursions Variant	0.834308	Pass

3 Compressed Sensing

Compressed Sensing is a novel sampling and reconstruction technique that has been developed. In CS theory, if the signal is sparse within a certain domain, sampling at less than twice the highest frequency of the signal can still successfully reconstruct the signal. A finite length signal X of size $N \times 1$, it can be represented by the sparse basis $\Psi(N \times N)$:

$$X = \Psi S \tag{7}$$

In CS, the signal X can be compressed with the measurement matrix $\Phi(M \times N)$:

$$Y = \Phi X = \Phi \Psi S = \Theta S \tag{8}$$

where Θ is the sensing matrix with size $M \times N (M < N)$.

In order to recover the signal from a small amount of Y, the matrix Φ must satisfy RIP. Specific conditions are as follows:

$$(1 - \delta_k)\|f\|_2^2 \leq \|\Phi f\|_2^2 \leq (1 + \delta_k)\|f\|_2^2 \tag{9}$$

where $\delta_k \in (0, 1)$, denotes the constraint isometric constant.

The RIP of the measurement matrix Φ is an NP-hard, but the RIP of matrix is equivalent to the incoherent measurement matrix Φ and the sparse basis Ψ.

Find the sparsest solution and recover signal X from measurement Y.

$$\min \|S\|_0 \, subject to, \, Y = \Theta S \tag{10}$$

The sparse transform used in this article is the Discrete Wavelet Transform (DWT), the measurement matrix is a matrix composed of chaotic sequences that obey a homogenized distribution, and the reconstruction algorithm used is the OMP.

4   The Key Stream for the Encryption Process

The random sequences used in this article for encryption is generated by the Lorenz hyper-chaos system, which is a classic chaos map defined as follows:

$$\begin{cases} \frac{dx}{dt} = a(y - x) + w \\ \frac{dy}{dt} = cx - y - xz \\ \frac{dz}{dt} = xy - bz \\ \frac{dw}{dt} = rw - yz \end{cases} \tag{11}$$

where $a = 10$, $b = 8/3$, $c = 28$, $r \in [-1.52, -0.06]$, and the system has two positive Lyapunov exponent, $LE1 = 0.3381$, $LE2 = 0.1586$, the system is in a state of hyper-chaotic. Iterative hyper-chaotic mapping produces pseudorandom sequences with $W = \{w_1, w_2, \ldots, w_n\}$, $X = \{x_1, x_2, \ldots, x_n\}$, $Y = \{y_1, y_2, \ldots, y_n\}$, $Z = \{z_1, z_2, \ldots, z_n\}$, representing four sequences.

5   The Process of Image Compression and Encryption.

5.1   Compression and Encryption of Image

The homogenized chaotic sequences are used to construct the measurement matrix Φ, and the hyper-chaotic Lorenz system encrypts the compressed image again. The flowchart of the encryption is given in Fig. 2.

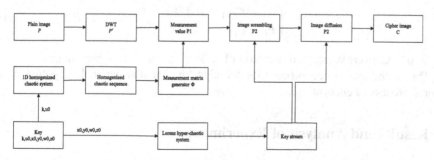

Fig. 2. Flowchart of the proposed scheme

If the size of plain image P is $N \times N$, the compression steps are as follows:

Step 1: Image sparse representation. Using DWT for plain images, a sparse coefficient matrix $P\prime$ is obtained with a size of $N \times N$.

Step 2: Set the initial condition $u0$ and parameter k of the Chebyshev map to eliminate transients by rounding out the first 800 iterations generated by the system. The resulting key stream is homogenized and then formed into a measurement matrix with a size of $M \times N (M < N, M = CR \times N)$, CR is the plain image compression ratio:

$$CR = \frac{C_{height} \times C_{width}}{P_{height} \times P_{width}} \tag{12}$$

Step 3: The measurement matrix Φ is used to compress the sparse matrix $P\prime$, and the expression of a compressed matrix $P1 = \Phi P\prime$.

Where $P1$ has a size of $M \times N$, and the original image is compressed because $M < N$.

Step 4: Set the initial conditions of the Lorenz hyper-chaotic system w_0, x_0, y_0, z_0, to eliminate transients, the first 300 iterations generated by the system are discarded for the dislocation and diffusion of image P1. Chaotic sequences are divided into sequences I, I_1, I_2.

Step 5: Image P1 for the scrambling operation. The principle of scrambling is shown below:

$$\begin{cases} P1'(I(i)) = v \\ P1'(I(M \times N - i + 1)) = P1'(I(i)) \\ v = P1'(I(M \times N - i + 1)) \end{cases} \tag{13}$$

Step 6: Diffusion algorithm based on XOR operation. After diffusion of the 1D vector $P2$, the cipher image C is finally obtained, where ciphertext C is also a 1D vector. The principle of forward diffusion and reverse diffusion is shown below:

Let C and I be cryptographic vectors, i from 1 to $M \times N$:

$$\begin{cases} C_i = C_{i-1} \oplus I_i \oplus P2_i \\ P_i = C_{i-1} \oplus C_i \oplus I_i \end{cases} \tag{14}$$

Same as above, i from $M \times N$ to 1:

$$\begin{cases} C_i = C_{i+1} \oplus I_i \oplus P2_i \\ P_i = C_{i+1} \oplus C_i \oplus I_i \end{cases} \tag{15}$$

Step 7: Convert vector C to a matrix of $M \times N$ to obtain a cipher image.

This is the encryption process for the algorithm of this paper. Decryption is the reverse process of encryption.

6 Results and Analysis of Experiments

This section presents an analysis of the compression performance and defense against the attack performance of the system in this paper. In this paper, the size of the plain image is selected as 256×256.

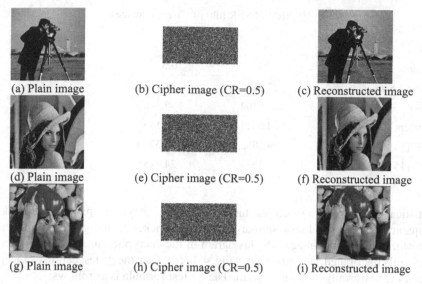

Fig. 3. Encryption and decryption results

6.1 Experimental Results

This paper verifies the performance of the proposed encryption scheme using Camera-man, Lena, and Peppers standard grayscale images. The key settings of the encryption system are as follows: $u0 = 0.7577, w0 = 3.705, x2 = 5.216, y3 = 7.863, z4 = 6.724, k = 5$. Figure 3 shows the results of the image compression encryption.

Compression Performance Analysis. The Peak Signal to Noise Ratio (PSNR) is used to assess the performance of the compression method. The PSNR between plain image P and reconstructed image $P\prime$ is calculated as follows:

$$MSE = \frac{1}{N^2} \sum_{i=1}^{N} \sum_{j=1}^{N} \left[P(i,j) - P'(i,j) \right]^2 \tag{16}$$

$$PSNR = 10 \times log_{10} \left(\frac{255 \times 255}{MSE} \right) \tag{17}$$

where $P(i,j)$ is plain images and $P'(i,j)$ is reconstruction images. The test image is of size $N \times N$.

In order to benchmark the compression performance of our algorithm against other approaches, PSNR values of reconstructed images under different compression methods are listed in Table 4. For the same compression ratio, the proposed algorithm is able to achieve better image recovery quality.

6.2 Safety Analysis

Histogram Analysis. Each pixel in the histogram may reflect its frequency. Plain images are often uneven, and an attacker can recover plaintext information through

Table 4. PSNR (db) of different images

CR Images	0.25	0.5	0.75
Cameraman	22.8296	28.2672	32.2672
Lena	24.5262	30.3486	34.8732
Peppers	24.5628	30.1467	34.0103
Ref. [14] (Lena)	24.2852	33.5780	33.4708
Ref. [15] (Peppers)	19.1615	24.8485	31.2463

statistical analysis. As a result, the histogram of the encrypted image should make the frequency of each pixel look similar so that the attacker cannot get valid information to restore the original image. The histogram of the encryption image is approximately uniformly distributed, as can be seen in Fig. 4. In addition, the χ^2 test can also objectively check the uniformity of the histogram. The χ^2 test formula is as follows:

$$\chi^2 = \sum_{i=0}^{255} \frac{(f_i - g)^2}{g} \tag{18}$$

where $g = M \times N/256$, f_i is the frequency at which the pixel value i appears on the image. When the significance level $\alpha = 0.05$, the critical value is $\chi^2_{0.05} = 293.24783$. When $\chi^2 < 293.24783$, the histogram can be considered uniform. The χ^2 values of Cameraman, Lena and Peppers are calculated to be 244.0208, 203.9479, 225.9271. The histogram of the cipher image is uniformly distributed.

Adjacent Pixel Correlation. Plain images contain a great deal of information, causing the correlation coefficient between neighboring pixels to typically be close to 1. The correlation between adjacent pixels in the image can be removed by a good encryption algorithm, and the correlation coefficient is closer to 0. In this paper, 2000 pairs of adjacent pixels are chosen at random from both plaintext and ciphertext images, and correlation coefficients are computed from horizontal, vertical, and diagonal directions. The correlation calculation formula is as follows:

$$r_{xy} = \frac{cov(x, y)}{\sqrt{D(x)D(y)}} \tag{19}$$

where $cov(x, y) = \frac{1}{N} \sum_{i=1}^{N} [(x_i - E(x)][y_i - E(y)]$, $D(x) = \frac{1}{N} \sum_{i=1}^{N} [x_i - \frac{1}{N} \sum_{i=1}^{N} x_i]^2$, x and y are the neighboring pixel values of the same image.

Calculations are shown in Table 5. After encryption, the correlation of cipher image in all directions is nearly 0. The proposed algorithm reduces the relevance of the original image. It can be seen from the results of the proposed algorithm that it effectively eliminates the close relationship between adjacent pixels in the original image.

Information Entropy. Information entropy is a standard used to reflect randomness or uncertainty in an image. As the randomness of the image increases, its information

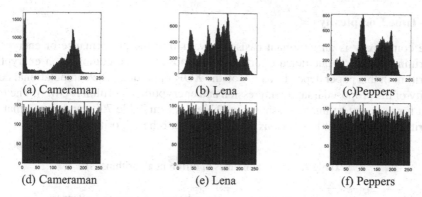

Fig. 4. Histograms of plain images and cipher images

Table 5. Lena image correlation coefficients with different algorithms

Direction	Horizontal	Vertical	Diagonal
The plain image of "Lena"	0.9669	0.9442	0.9225
The cipher image of "Lena"	−0.0053	−0.0126	0.0246
Ref. [14] (Lena)	0.0031	0.0076	−0.026

entropy approaches the theoretical value of the mathematics. The information entropy is computed as follows:

$$H(x) = \sum_{t=0}^{T-1} p(x_i) log \frac{1}{p(x_i)} \tag{20}$$

where $p(x_i)$ is the probability of grayscale value x_i occurring, T represents grayscale, and the theoretical value of information entropy is 8.

Table 6 shows the information entropy for Cameraman, Lena, and Peppers. Comparing [14] and [15], the encryption algorithm of this paper has relatively ideal information entropy results and is able to withstand attacks on the information entropy.

Table 6. Information entropy

Images	Cameraman	Lena	Peppers	Ref. [14] (Lena)	Ref. [14] (Cameraman)	Ref. [15] (Peppers)
Information entropy	7.9950	7.9942	7.9940	7.9858	7.9868	7.9970

6.3 Time Complexity

Time complexity is an important basis for evaluating the performance of encryption algorithms. The computational effort of the proposed image compression encryption algorithm in this paper depends mainly on the XOR operation. The computational complexity of the proposed image compression and encryption algorithm is $O(n^2)$. The time spent for various test images is shown in Table 7. From Table 7, it can be seen that the algorithm in this paper has obvious advantages over other algorithms.

Table 7. Encryption times of different algorithms (s)

Algorithms	Cameraman	Lena	Peppers
Ours	0.2354	0.1372	0.1503
[14]	–	0.6563	–
[16]	≈ 6.32	≈ 6.32	–

7 Conclusion

Compressed sensing uses low-complexity sampling to achieve digital image compression and encryption, which is computationally secure. This paper proposes a method to construct a homogenized measurement matrix. There are three advantages to this algorithm, firstly, the measurement matrix in the algorithm is generated by homogenizing the mapping, which increases the key space and transmission efficiency. Secondly, homogenized mapping has a higher sequence complexity, enhancing the safety of the system. Finally, the Lorenz hyper-chaos system is used to scramble and diffuse the compressed images, which further enhances the security of the system. Security and experimental results show that the algorithm has advantages in terms of compression performance, key space, key sensitivity, and can withstand statistical attacks, brute-force attacks, information entropy attacks, and other common ones.

References

1. Iwamoto, M., Ohta, K., Shikata, J.: Security formalizations and their relationships for encryption and key agreement in information-theoretic cryptography. IEEE Trans. Inf. Theory **64**, 654–685 (2018)
2. Erkan, U., Toktas, A., Lai, Q.: 2D hyperchaotic system based on schaffer function for image encryption. Expert Syst. Appl. **213**, 12 (2023)
3. Tao, L.M., Liang, X.K., Hu, B., Han, L.D.: Compound encryption of multiple images by utilizing a novel chaos and nonlinear transform. Neural Comput. Appl. **14** https://doi.org/10.1007/s00521-022-07849-3
4. Xian, Y.J., Wang, X.Y., Wang, X.Y., Li, Q., Yan, X.P.: Spiral-transform-based fractal sorting matrix for chaotic image encryption. IEEE Trans. Circuits Syst. I-Regul. Pap. **69**, 3320–3327 (2022)

5. Zhou, S., Zhao, Z.P., Wang, X.Y.: Novel chaotic color image cryptosystem with deep learning. Chaos Solitons Fractals **161**, 13 (2022)
6. Erkan, U., Toktas, A., Enginoglu, S., Akbacak, E., Thanh, D.N.H.: An image encryption scheme based on chaotic logarithmic map and key generation using deep CNN. Multimedia Tools Appli. **81**, 7365–7391 (2022)
7. Tang, Z., Yin, Z.X., Wang, R.S., Wang, X.Y., Yang, J., Cui, J.Z.: A double-layer image encryption scheme based on chaotic maps and DNA strand displacement. J. Chem. **2022**, 10 (2022)
8. Wang, X.Y., Liu, L.: Image encryption based on hash table scrambling and DNA substitution. IEEE Access **8**, 68533–68547 (2020)
9. Cun, Q.Q., Tong, X.J., Wang, Z., Zhang, M.: A new chaotic image encryption algorithm based on dynamic DNA coding and RNA computing. Visual Compute. **20** https://doi.org/10.1007/s00371-022-02750-5
10. Donoho, D.L.: Compressed sensing. IEEE Trans. Inf. Theory **52**, 1289–1306 (2006). https://doi.org/10.1109/TIT.2006.871582
11. Yu, L., Barbot, J.P., Zheng, G., Sun, H.: Compressive sensing with chaotic sequence. IEEE Signal Process. Lett. **17**, 731–734 (2010)
12. Wei, J., Zhang, M., Tong, X.: Multi-Image compression-encryption algorithm based on compressed sensing and optical encryption. Entropy **24**, 784 (2022)
13. Xie, Y.Q., Yu, J.Y., Guo, S.Y., Ding, Q., Wang, E.F.: Image encryption scheme with compressed sensing based on new three-dimensional chaotic system. Entropy **21**, 17 (2019)
14. Liu, J.L., Zhang, M., Tong, X.J., Wang, Z.: Image compression and encryption algorithm based on compressive sensing and nonlinear diffusion. Multimedia Tools and Appli. **80**, 25433–25452 (2021)
15. Gong, L.H., Qiu, K.D., Deng, C.Z., Zhou, N.R.: An image compression and encryption algorithm based on chaotic system and compressive sensing. Opt. Laser Technol. **115**, 257–267 (2019)
16. Zhang, T.F., Li, S.L., Ge, R.J., Yuan, M., Ma, Y.D.: A novel 1D hybrid chaotic map-based image compression and encryption using compressed sensing and fibonacci-lucas transform. Math. Problems Eng. (2016)

Reversible Data Hiding in Encrypted Images Based on Quantization Prediction Error

Ruihua Liu, Quan Zhou$^{(\boxtimes)}$, Yanlang Hu, Juanni Liu, Yi Zhang, and Jiayuan Wei

Xi'an Institute of Space Radio Technology, 710000 Xi'an, China
zhouq97@cast504.com

Abstract. Reversible data hiding in encrypted images (RDH-EI) can simultaneously protect secret data and the content of transmission carriers, so it has important applications in cloud computing, medicine, and other fields involving data privacy. Aiming at the problem of low embedding capacity in current RDH-EI algorithms, a separate algorithm based on interpolation prediction error quantization is proposed. First, we down-sample the cover image to obtain the sampled pixels. Then interpolate and predict non-sampled pixels to obtain auxiliary data such as prediction errors and classify the auxiliary data. By introducing a quantitative prediction error loss factor, auxiliary data can be compressed to various degrees, reducing the amount of auxiliary data. Next, auxiliary data is embedded into sampled pixels through reversible data hiding (RDH) technology, and the partial of non-sampled pixels. Finally, according to the hiding key, the mark data and secret data are embedded in the encrypted image. At the receiver, a legitimate user extracts secret data and recovers the cover image with owned keys. Experimental results show that the proposed algorithm can ensure the error-free extraction of secret data and provide lossy and lossless versions of the cover image. In lossy versions, the maximum embedding rate can be around 4bpp. Compared to other advanced algorithms, the proposed algorithm has the advantages of more flexibility, a high embedding rate, and recovery quality.

Keywords: Reversible Data Hiding in Encrypted Images · Interpolation Prediction · Quantization Error · Separability

1 Introduction

In recent years, for military, medicine, trade, and other application scenarios, the protection of carriers has also become an urgent need. To ensure the security of data transmission, reversible data hiding in encrypted images (RDH-EI) has been developed. It embeds secret data in encrypted images, and all data is invisible during transmission, which greatly improves security.

According to the order of encryption and hidden space generation, existing algorithms are generally based on two types of frameworks: vacating room after encryption (VRAE) and reserving room before encryption (RRBE).

In the algorithms [1–9] based on the VRAE framework, the sender first encrypts the image and then makes space by flipping bits [1–3], compressing [6, 7], predicting [8, 9],

© The Author(s), under exclusive license to Springer Nature Switzerland AG 2023
H. Lu et al. (Eds.): ICIG 2023, LNCS 14357, pp. 336–348, 2023.
https://doi.org/10.1007/978-3-031-46311-2_28

etc. This framework, originally proposed by [1], realized data embedding by flipping the lower three bits of encrypted pixels. But the embedding rate is low and the extracted data has errors. The works [2, 3] designed a new wave function to improve the estimation accuracy of data recovery. To increase the capacity, the lossless compression in a block was used in [4, 5]. In [6, 7], block cryptography was adopted to provide a correlation suitable for hiding. The works [8, 9] improved the accuracy of prediction to vacate space. The difficulty of the VRAE algorithm is that the image after encryption loses relevance and leaves less space.

To improve performance, the work [10] proposed the RRBE framework. The sender preprocesses the cover image before encryption and then embeds the data. In [11], the image is divided into blocks of different scales, and then the average value is taken as a reference to reserve the lowest two bits of each pixel. The works [12–14] adopted compression technology, such as Huffman coding[13] and absolute moment block truncation coding [14]. Prediction technology [15–19] is also a vital technology for reservation space. An adaptive block-level prediction error extension method was adopted in [15]. In [16, 17], auxiliary correction data was used to improve the accuracy of the prediction. Interpolation was introduced in [18, 19]. It was applied to restore pixel combining with prediction error [18] and estimate whether the position can be used for embedding [19]. In general, RRBE algorithms utilize the correlation of images, so the performance has been improved to a certain extent.

According to the above scheme analysis, we found it challenging to hide data in encrypted images. Compression [6, 7, 12–14] and prediction [8, 9, 15–19] are all important technologies for mining space, but the embedding capacity and recovery quality are also affected by compression ability and prediction accuracy. In addition, [1–3, 9] and other algorithms adopt the joint scheme with low complexity and simple operation, while [5, 11, 12, 18] and other algorithms adopt the separable scheme, which is helpful for the receiver to operate and increase flexibility. To improve performance, this paper proposes an RDH-EI algorithm based on quantization prediction error under the RRBE framework. The sampled image and auxiliary data are generated by pre-processing. Then quantization interpolation error loss factor is used to compress the auxiliary data. The recovery quality of the receiver is controllable. In the lossy and lossless versions, the performance of the algorithm has been greatly improved.

2 The Proposed Algorithm

The algorithm framework is shown in Fig. 1. At the sender, the image owner downsamples the image and uses an interpolation technique to obtain the predicted value of the non-sampled pixels. Then, according to the threshold, the predicted values are classified and processed to obtain the location map and auxiliary data. Next, some auxiliary data is embedded into the sampled pixels and part of the space of non-sampled pixels. Finally, the secret data is embedded into the reserved space after encryption according to the key and mark data. At the receiver, the legitimate user can extract data according to the hiding key and also can use the decryption key to process the received image. Finally, the cover image can be recovered losslessly.

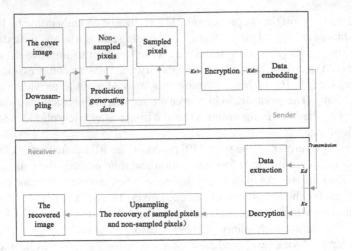

Fig. 1 The proposed algorithm.

2.1 RRBE

Down-Sampling. As shown in Fig. 1, input cover image I with size $M*N$. Suppose the pixel of the original image is $f(i,j)$, The pixel after the sampled image is:

$$f'(i,j) = f(i, 2*j), i[1, M], i[1, N] \tag{1}$$

As a result, a down-sampled image with a size of $M * N/2$ is obtained.

Pixel Classification and Data Generation. All pixels in the down-sampled image are sampled pixels, while $f(i,2*j)$ in the original image are non-sampled pixels. To recover the cover image with high quality at the receiver, it is necessary to process the values of non-sampled pixels. In the cover image I, the non-sampled pixel is adjacent to the sampled pixel, so it can be predicted by the sampled pixel. Let the left side of the non-sampled pixel x_2 be x_1 and the right side be x_3, then their relationship can be expressed as (2):

$$delta = round((x_1 + x_3)/2) - x_2 \tag{2}$$

$delta$ represents the prediction error generated by the prediction of adjacent sampled pixels and the non-sampled pixels and also represents the precision of pixel recovery. For the last column of non-sampled pixels, there is no adjacent pixel x_3 to the right, so only x_1 can be used to predict.

Then, the threshold value T is set to classify all $deltas$ and generate a location map with a size of $M*N/2$. The specific method is as follows: if the absolute value of the $delta$ is not bigger than T, the location map is set as 1. Otherwise, it is set to 0.

We also need to record the $deltas$ as auxiliary data. If the absolute value of $delta$ is within T, it is stored as PE_1. The data generated by each $delta$ costs Nb_1 bits:

$$Nb_1 = 1 + \log_2(T + 1) - Eb(\text{bits}) \tag{3}$$

where Eb is the quantization prediction error loss factor. When Eb is 0, the auxiliary data *delta* is lossless, otherwise, it is lossy. When in a lossy version, quantization tables can be produced to guide data generation and recovery.

Table 1. Quantization table

New Value	0	1	2	...	T
$Eb = 0$	0	1	2	...	T
$Eb = 1$	[0, 1]	[2, 3]	[4, 5]	...	[$(T$-1$), T$]
$Eb = 2$	[0, 3]	[4, 7]	[8, 11]	...	[$(T$-3$), T$]
...					
$Eb = \log2(T + 1)$	[0,(2^{Eb}-1)]	[$2^{Eb}, 2^{Eb+1}$-1]	...	...	[T-(2^{Eb}-1$), T$]

In Table 1, the first row in the table represents the new code after Eb quantization, and the data in the table represents the original quantization interval corresponding to the new value.

Data with the absolute value of *delta* bigger than T is denoted as PE_2. The data generated by each *delta* is denoted by Nb_2. Since there is little data bigger than T, and the cost of storing the value is high, the original pixel value is adopted, then $Nb_2 = 8$.

In this step, we get the location map, prediction error, and other auxiliary data. The auxiliary data after processing can also be compressed according to the value of Eb.

Reversible Data Hiding (RDH) in Sampled Images. To maximize capacity and recovery quality, we use RDH in sampled images. Traditional RDH techniques such as HS and DE can be used, while the capacity of the sampled image is relatively low. Therefore, an improved HS algorithm based on prediction errors is used here. The details can be seen in [20].

After hiding the data, the sampled image is placed on the left, with rows 1 to M and columns 1 to $N/2$. Then embed the rest of the data in the right space, with rows 1 to M and columns $(N/2) + 1$ to N. We place the map in the LSB bit of the pixel in the right space and then embed auxiliary data in the upper 7 bits. In the beginning, total data length, T, and Eb are embedded. According to theoretical calculation, the total length of data is fixed at 20 bits. The T range is set as [1, 63] and the length is 7 bits. The cost of Eb is 3 bits. After these fixed bits, the data is embedded.

At this step, all other remaining space is reserved for secret data. The cover image I is pre-processed as I_1.

2.2 Encryption

Stream cipher encryption is used here. Let the range of pixel gray value $x(i, j)$ at position (i, j) in I_1 be [0, 255]. Let the bit of each pixel be $b_{i,j,1}$, $b_{i,j,2},...$ $b_{i,j,8}$, and the relationship between the bit of each pixel and $x(i, j)$ is shown in Eqs. (4) and (5):

$$b_{i,j,k} = \left\lfloor \frac{x(i, j)}{2^{k-1}} \right\rfloor \bmod 2, k = 1, ...8 \tag{4}$$

$$x(i, j) = \sum_{k=1}^{8} (b_{i,j,k} * 2^{k-1}) \tag{5}$$

A pseudo-random binary array is generated using the key Ke, and then $r_{i,j,k}$ performs xor with $b_{i,j,k}$ bit by bit. As shown in Eq. (6):

$$I_{2i,j,k} = b_{i,j,k} \oplus r_{i,j,k} \tag{6}$$

where I_2 is the encrypted image.

2.3 Secret Data Embedding

This step is to embed data in I_2, which is completed by the data hiding key Kd. Based on the space reserved in 2.1. The front rows of the right of I_2 are auxiliary data. To facilitate extraction, we embed the secret data length and secret data in the upper 7 bits from back to front on the right of I_2. Among them, according to the calculation of the maximum embedding capacity of the algorithm, a fixed 20 bits can be used as the marker of the secret data length. Finally, we obtain the encrypted image containing the secret data for transmission.

2.4 Data Extraction and Recovery

At the receiver, we use a separable method for data extraction and cover image recovery.

(1) The hiding key Kd.

Used to extract secret data. According to the hiding key Kd, divide the received image into left and right parts. The length and content of the secret data are then extracted in the order of back to front.

(2) The decryption key Ke.

First, use key Ke to decrypt the received image to get D_0. Then divide D_0 into left and right parts. The left part is the sampled image processed by RDH technology, and the right part is the auxiliary data and location map. Next, the left image is reversibly restored, part of the auxiliary data is extracted, and the recovered sampled image D_1 is obtained. The size of D_1 is M rows and $N/2$ columns.

Finally, the cover image recovery is performed. If the location map is 0, the non-sampled pixels are obtained by PE_2. Otherwise, D_1 provides adjacent pixels, and auxiliary data provides interpolation prediction error PE_1. The non-sampled pixel value can be calculated according to Eq. (7):

$$value = 2^{E_b} * (PE_1) + 2^{E_b - 1} - 1 \qquad (7)$$

To reduce the overall error, we choose $2^{Eb-1}-1$ to assist pixel recovery.

(3) The hiding key Kd and the decryption key Ke.

In the algorithm, the cover image recovery and data extraction are separable. In addition, it can be seen from step (2) that the data in step (1) is not used in the recovery part. Therefore, the decrypted image in (2) is also the final recovery quality.

Through the above steps, we get the recovered image.

3 Experimental Results and Discussion

To verify the performance of the proposed algorithm, we experiment with a software platform. Configuration: Intel(R) Core(TM) i7–8700 CPU, 16 GB memory, Windows 10 operating system, and Matlab2019b. As shown in Fig. 2, Lena, Airplane, Peppers, and Baboon [21] are used for testing, with the size of 512 * 512, the format of BMP. Figure 2 and Fig. 3 show the process of test images at each stage of the algorithm.

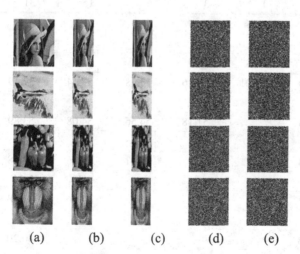

Fig. 2 Different processing stages at the sender. Column (a): the cover image; Column (b): the sampled image; Column (c): the sampled image after RDH; Column (d): the encrypted image; Column (e): the encrypted image with secret data.

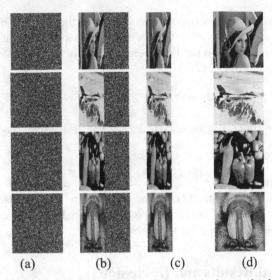

(a)   (b)   (c)   (d)

Fig. 3 Different processing stages at the receiver. Column (a): the received image; Column (b): the initially decrypted image; Column (c): the recovered sampled image; Column (d): the cover image after up-sampling.

Table 2. Experimental results of Lena: embedding rate(er) and peak signal-to-noise ratio(psnr)

Eb	T	1	3	7	15	31	63
0	er/bpp	0.55	1.15	1.30	1.00	0.55	0.06
	psnr/dB	inf	inf	inf	inf	inf	inf
1	er/bpp	0.88	1.47	1.74	1.48	1.05	0.56
	psnr/dB	61.01	58.96	57.98	57.64	57.49	57.45
2	er/bpp		2.11	2.18	1.96	1.54	1.06
	psnr/dB		51.18	54.56	54.08	53.89	53.85
3	er/bpp			3.05	2.44	2.04	1.56
	psnr/dB			45.41	49.96	49.68	49.62
4	er/bpp				3.40	2.54	2.06
	psnr/dB				42.06	41.58	41.55
5	er/bpp					3.53	2.56
	psnr/dB					40.20	33.15
6	er/bpp						3.56

(*continued*)

Table 2. (*continued*)

Eb	T	1	3	7	15	31	63
	psnr/dB						39.86
8	er/bpp						4.06
	psnr/dB						39.86

Table 3. Experimental results of Airplane

Eb	T	1	3	7	15	31	63
0	er/bpp	1.03	1.47	1.38	1.03	0.58	0.08
	psnr/dB	inf	inf	inf	inf	inf	inf
1	er/bpp	1.52	1.85	1.83	1.51	1.07	0.58
	psnr/dB	59.87	58.59	57.98	57.71	57.59	57.54
2	er/bpp		2.61	2.28	1.99	1.57	1.08
	psnr/dB		51.79	55.78	55.31	55.10	55.04
3	er/bpp			3.18	2.48	2.06	1.58
	psnr/dB			46.95	50.25	50.00	49.94
4	er/bpp				3.44	2.56	2.08
	psnr/dB				43.30	41.13	41.10
5	er/bpp					3.55	2.58
	psnr/dB					41.33	33.10
6	er/bpp						3.58
	psnr/dB						40.79
8	er/bpp						4.09
	psnr/dB						40.77

3.1 Embedding Capacity Analysis

The embedding rates under different T are given in Table 2, 3, 4 and 5. Theoretically, the larger T is, the more non-sampled pixels are available, but the number of prediction errors also increases. We assume Eb is 2, and can find that there are two characteristics of the data: (1) With the increase of T, the embedding rate increases first and then decreases; (2) The appropriate T is different for each image. For images of Airplane, Lena, and Peppers with smooth textures, they reach the maximum capacity when T is small (7 and 3), while it is large (15) for images of Baboon.

Eb is mainly used to compress the auxiliary data and control the recovery quality of the cover image. When $Eb = 0$, there is no loss. At this point, the maximum embedding rates achieved are 1.30 bpp, 1.47 bpp, 1.22bpp, and 0.68 bpp, respectively. Image. Assume $T = 63$ in each table. We can find that the embedding rate increases gradually

Table 4. Experimental results of Peppers

Eb	T	1	3	7	15	31	63
0	er/bpp	0.34	0.90	1.22	1.00	0.54	0.05
	psnr/dB	inf	inf	inf	inf	inf	inf
1	er/bpp	0.60	1.17	1.64	1.48	1.04	0.55
	psnr/dB	61.99	59.62	58.08	57.56	57.45	57.42
2	er/bpp		1.72	2.06	1.96	1.53	1.05
	psnr/dB		51.57	54.31	53.69	53.56	53.52
3	er/bpp			2.90	2.45	2.03	1.55
	psnr/dB			44.32	49.14	48.96	48.92
4	er/bpp				3.41	2.52	2.04
	psnr/dB				40.63	42.18	42.14
5	er/bpp					3.52	2.54
	psnr/dB					39.53	33.78
6	er/bpp						3.54
	psnr/dB						39.24
8	er/bpp						4.05
	psnr/dB						39.15

with the increase of Eb. This is because the quantization loss increases, resulting in a decrease in the amount of auxiliary data for pixel recovery (i.e., PE_1), thus vacating more reserved space. When $Eb = 8$, the embedding capacity is the sum of the space provided by the down-sampled image under the RDH technique and half of the cover image. Therefore, the maximum embedding rate can reach around 4bpp.

3.2 Recovery Performance Analysis

The proposed algorithm belongs to a separate algorithm under the RRBE framework. Since the receiver directly decrypts the down-sampled image, the size of which is $M * N/2$, it needs to be up-sampled to become $M*N$. The final decryption image is obtained by combining the prediction error with the sampled pixel, which is also the recovery of the cover image. Therefore, the decryption quality in this algorithm is consistent with the cover image recovery quality.

According to the experimental results, when Eb is fixed, the recovery quality decreases with the increase of T, which is because the amount of embedded data keeps increasing, however, the quantization loss is fixed, and the recovery quality only depends on the number of available spaces. Therefore, different T has less effect on recovery quality.

When T is fixed, the recovery quality decreases with the increase of Eb. Theoretically, the greater the quantization error, the less accurate the recovery. This point can also be

Table 5. Experimental results of Baboon

Eb	T	1	3	7	15	31	63
0	er/bpp		0.25	0.58	0.68	0.45	0.01
	psnr/dB		inf	inf	inf	inf	inf
1	er/bpp	0.05	0.39	0.84	1.07	0.92	0.51
	psnr/dB	64.78	62.04	59.74	58.25	57.48	57.24
2	er/bpp		0.69	1.11	1.45	1.39	1.01
	psnr/dB		53.72	55.61	53.96	53.14	52.88
3	er/bpp			1.64	1.84	1.86	1.51
	psnr/dB			44.96	48.95	47.98	47.68
4	er/bpp				2.62	2.33	2.01
	psnr/dB				38.33	42.17	41.84
5	er/bpp					3.27	2.50
	psnr/dB					35.15	34.82
6	er/bpp						3.50
	psnr/dB						35.15
8	er/bpp						4.01
	psnr/dB						34.43

Table 6. Maximum embedding capability comparison of algorithms (bpp)

image	Zhang [1]	Hong [2]	Xu [7]	Ma [10]	Wu [11]	Qin [12]	Xiao [19]	Proposed (lossless)	Proposed (lossy)
Lena	0.024	0.015	0.811	0.886	1.192	0.0325	0.492	1.30	4.06
Airplane	0.019	0.015	0.796	0.918	1.22	0.0325	0.492	1.47	4.10
Peppers	0.016	0.015	0.663	0.624	1.173	0.0325	0.492	1.22	4.05
Baboon	0.005	0.015	0.377	0.741	0.316	0.0325	0.471	0.68	4.02

known from the calculation of the psnr, the larger the quantization error, the larger the square of MSE, and the smaller the PSNR value. In addition, it should be noted that when $Eb = 0$, it means that the cover image can be recovered losslessly. When Eb increased from 1 to 8, quantization loss gradually increased, and the cover image could achieve high-quality recovery. When $Eb = 8$, quantization loss reaches the maximum, and the recovery quality is only determined by the down-sampled image. They are 39.86 dB, 40.77 dB, 39.15 dB, and 34.43 dB, respectively. It is generally believed that the visual quality is good when the PSNR value is greater than 30 dB. In practical applications, parameters can be designed and selected according to the performance requirements of the users.

3.3 Compare with Other Algorithms

We compared the maximum embedding capability with the various methods in Table 6. In the lossless version, the capacity of the proposed algorithm is superior to other algorithms. However, for Baboon, the embedding rate is slightly lower than [10]. In the lossy version, the maximum embedding capability can be achieved when $Eb = 8$ according to the parameter configuration in Table 2, 3, 4, 5 and 6. Because the sampled image is half the size of the original cover image, any image can be embedded about 4bpp, and the secret data can be recovered without error.

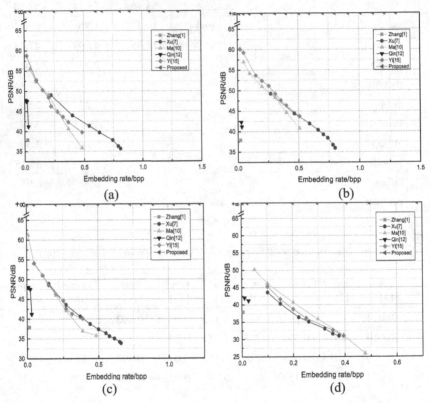

Fig. 4 Relationship between decryption performance and embedding rate. (a) Lena; (b) Airplane; (c) Peppers; (d) Baboon.

Figure 4 shows the cover image decryption performance under different embedding rates. According to the data, the psnr of other schemes gradually decreases with the increase of the embedding rate, which is consistent with the theoretical analysis. However, due to the separability and the design of the auxiliary data embedding strategy, both the decrypted image and the recovered image can be completely lossless, realizing the full reversibility of any cover image. At the same time, the data in Table 2, 3, 4, 5 and 6 also show that even in the lossy version, the embedding capacity of about 4 bpp, and the recovery quality still can reach 30 dB +. The recovery quality of most images is around 40 dB, except for images with complex textures.

4   Conclusion

This paper proposes a separable RDH-EI algorithm based on quantization prediction error, which can achieve high embedding capacity while ensuring complete reversibility. At the sender, the interpolation technique is applied to predict the values of non-sampled pixels, and then a quantized prediction error factor is introduced to compress auxiliary data, thereby increasing the capacity of reserved space. At the receiver, the user can extract secret data by a hiding key, or completely recover the cover image with a decryption key. In this algorithm, two versions of lossy recovery and lossless recovery are provided through different parameter settings, and the cover recovery quality is controllable completely. In the lossy version, when the embedding rate is at a maximum of about 4bpp, the recovery quality of most cover images is close to around 40dB. The performance is suitable for scenarios with large capacity and high-quality recovery requirements. In the lossless version, experimental data show that both high embedding rate and lossless decryption quality have advantages over related algorithms. Therefore, the performance of the proposed algorithm is superior to related algorithms. Future research can consider further compressing auxiliary data, improving the capacity of RDH technology, and other aspects.

References

1. Zhang, X.P.: Reversible data hiding in encrypted image. IEEE Signal Process. Lett. **18**(4), 255–258 (2011)
2. Hong, W., Chen, T.S., Wu, H.Y.: An improved reversible data hiding in encrypted images using side match. IEEE Signal Process. Lett. **19**(4), 199–202 (2012)
3. Liao, X., Shu, C.W.: Reversible data hiding in encrypted images based on absolute mean difference of multiple neighboring pixels. J. Vis. Commun. Image Represent.Commun. Image Represent. **28**, 21–27 (2015)
4. Wang, Y.M., Cai, Z.C., He, W.G.: High capacity reversible data hiding in encrypted image based on intra-block lossless compression. IEEE Trans. Multimedia **23**, 1466–1473 (2021)
5. Zhang, X.P.: Separable reversible data hiding in encrypted image. IEEE Trans. Inf. Forensics Secur. **7**(2), 826–832 (2012)
6. Anushiadevi, R.: Separable reversible data hiding in an encrypted image using the adjacency pixel difference histogram. J. Inform. Sec. Appli. **72**, 103407 (2023)
7. Xu, D.W., Su, S.B.: Reversible data hiding in encrypted images with separability and high embedding capacity. Signal Process. Image Commun. **95**, 116274 (2021)
8. Chen, K.M., Chang, C.C.: Error-free separable reversible data hiding in encrypted images using linear regression and prediction error map. Multimedia Tools Appli. **78**(22), 31441–31465 (2019)
9. Qiu, Y.Q., Cai, C.H., Zeng, H.Q., et al.: Joint reversible data hiding in encrypted images with the self-correcting ability. J. Xidian Univ. **48**(1), 107–116 (2021)
10. Ma, K.D., Zhang, W.M., Zhao, X.F., et al.: Reversible data hiding in encrypted images by reserving room before encryption. IEEE Trans. Inf. Forensics Secur.Secur. **8**(3), 553–562 (2013)

11. Wu, H.B., Li, F.Y., Qin, C., et al.: Separable reversible data hiding in encrypted images based on scalable blocks. Multimedia Tools Applic. **78**(18), 25349–25372 (2019)
12. Qin, C., Zhang, W., Cao, F., et al.: Separable reversible data hiding in encrypted images via adaptive embedding strategy with block selection. Signal Process. **153**, 109–122 (2018)
13. Chen, F., Yuan, Y., He, H.J., et al.: Multi-msb compression based reversible data hiding scheme in encrypted images. IEEE Trans. Circuits Syst. Video Technol. **31**(3), 905–916 (2021)
14. Nguyen, T.S., Chang, C.C., Lin, C.C.: High capacity reversible data hiding scheme based on AMBTC for encrypted images. J. Internet Technol. **23**(2), 255–266 (2022)
15. Yi, S., Zhou, Y.C., Hua, Z.Y.: Reversible data hiding in encrypted images using adaptive block-level prediction-error expansion. Signal Process. Image Commun. **64**, 78–88 (2018)
16. Zhou, X., Wu, F.H., Chen, Z.L., Ren, S.: All bit planes reversible data hiding for images with high-embedding-rate in ciphertext field. J. Image Graph. **26**(05), 1147–1156 (2021)
17. Mohammadi, A.: A general framework for reversible data hiding in encrypted images by reserving room before encryption. J. Vis. Commun. Image Represent.Commun. Image Represent. **85**, 103478 (2022)
18. Wang, J.J., Li, G.X., Xia, G.E., et al.: A separable and reversible data hiding algorithm in encrypted domain based on image interpolation space. Acta Electronic Sinica **48**(1), 92–100 (2020)
19. Xiao, D., Wang, Y., Xiang, T., et al.: High-payload completely reversible data hiding in encrypted images by an interpolation technique. Front. Inform. Technol. Elect. Eng. **18**(11), 1732–1743 (2017)
20. Jia, Y.J., Yin, Z.X., Zhang, X.P., et al.: Reversible data hiding based on reducing invalid shifting of pixels in histogram shifting. Signal Process. **163**, 238–246 (2019)
21. https://ccia.ugr.es/cvg/index2.php.

Improving Text Image Super-Resolution Using Optimal Transport

Fan Wu and Xiangyang Liu[✉]

College of Science, Hohai University, Nanjing, China
`liuxy@hhu.edu.cn`

Abstract. Text images in natural scene captured by handheld devices like mobile phone are usually faced with low resolution problems, making optical character recognition task and other detection tasks more difficult. To address this problem, super-resolution is used as a preprocessing procedure to generate super-resolution text images. However, existing image super-resolution methods are usually to enhance the visual performance of images. These methods can not perform well on text images since that for text images, we pay more attention to the semantic features of text in images in order to reduce the difficulty of subsequent recognition tasks. In this paper, we employ a metric, which we call the optimal transport based energy distance. It combines optimal transport in primal form with an energy distance defined in an adversarially learned feature space. This combination results in a highly discriminative distance function that can maintain the spatial structure of texts with unbiased sample gradients during network optimization. To achieve better performance of our model, we propose a generative adversarial network(GAN) architecture for text image super-resolution so that the results of the super-resolution(SR) model can be closer to the natural manifold. Experiments show that our method performs well and boosts the performance of the text image super-resolution result in optical character recognition(OCR).

Keywords: Optimal Transport · Super Resolution · Generative Adversarial Network

1 Introduction

Text images usually carry rich semantic information, some content-based applications have to extract the information of the text images. Howerver, due to the camera blur, Internet transmission, compression and so on, the degradations usually result in a low-resolution of the text image. The low-resolution(LR) problem brings great difficulties to extracting the information from the images, such as the optical character recognition task [3,14]. One of the effective solutions is that we use ths SR technique as a preprocessing procedure to generate super-resolution text images with high-resolution(HR) text patterns by learning the mapping between low-resolution images and high-resolution images. Then the generated super-resolution images are used to perform the optical character

ⓒ The Author(s), under exclusive license to Springer Nature Switzerland AG 2023
H. Lu et al. (Eds.): ICIG 2023, LNCS 14357, pp. 349–360, 2023.
https://doi.org/10.1007/978-3-031-46311-2_29

recognition task and other subsequent detection tasks. Generally, a SR framework is a network which learns the mapping between low-resolution images and high-resolution images.

In recent years, the convolutional neural networks have been widely used in the single image super-resolution field [5,9,10,13,18]. A series of MSE loss guided SR models were proposed to reach state-of-the-art PSNR performance [13,19, 20]. However, the results of the SR models usually fail in visual performance. Therefore, SRGAN [11] was presented with a described perceptual loss which can better describe the visual difference between the super-resolution images and their corresponding high resolution images achieved visual pleasant results. Some further work of the SRGAN were also made by [21,22]. For the text image super-resolution, it is straightforward to directly employ the existing SR models for the text images. Zhang et al. [26] proposed a model adapted from the VDSR network [9] to text image super-resolution. However, the MSE loss and the perceptual loss used in traditional SR models are both not appropriate for the text images with rich semantic information. Therefore, Geng et al. [6] proposed a new text super-resolution framework using Sinkhorn distance defined in a learned feature space as the measure which can maintain more accurate semantic information and is robust against the semantic shift. We are inspired by their work that the optimal transport theory can be used in the field of text image super-resolution and will significantly improve the results. However, a disadvantage of the Sinkhorn distance is that it does not satisfy the property of unbiased sample gradients, which will be discussed in Sect. 3.1. Therefore, directly using Sinkhorn distance as a measure may results in non-convergence or convergence to inaccurate values during the network training. Therefore we made corresponding improvements and proposed our method.

In this paper, we proposed a new text image super-resolution GAN model and employed a new metric proposed by the OT-GAN [17] to measure the similarity between images. The metric is called the optimal transport based energy distance. This metric is combined by Sinkhorn distance between mini-batches defined in the feature space learned by the critic of our network. This combination results in a highly discriminative metric with unbiased mini-batch gradients in our SR model to achieve better text image super-resolution results.

Our contributions can be summarized as follows: we employed a metric in our model which not only can maintain the advantage of the Sinkhorn distance that can maintain more useful semantic information, but also can better use the Sinkhorn distance in the text image super-resolution GAN with better probabilistic properties. In the super-resolution experiments, our method achieves the stat-of-the-art performance over the OCR text image dataset and improves the text image super-resolution results with a high accuracy in OCR.

2   Related Works

Single Image Super-Resolution. Single Image Super-Resolution has developed a lot since the work of SRCNN [5]. A series of deep convolution neural network(CNN) framework have brought excellent developments in the super-resolution field [9,10,13,18]. Furthermore, to achieve better visual results, the generative adversarial network is usually employed as loss supervisions to push the solutions generated by the generator closer to the natural manifold, some super-resolution framework based on GAN achieved better results than the CNN framework [11,21,22]. As for the loss function of the super-resolution task, the MSE loss is often used so that high Peak Signal Noise Ratio(PSNR) can be achieved. However, these PSNR oriented method can not well reconstruct results with good visual quality. The perceptual loss presented by the SRGAN [11] is to address this issue. ESRGAN and Real-ESRGAN were also proposed to achieve better results [21,22].

While the text image super-resolution field has not been well researched and very limited results have been reported. Wang et al. [23] presented a cGAN model using channel attention and spatial attention. Xue et al. [25] improved the model presented by Wang et al. and achieved better results. While Geng et al. [6] employed the Sinkhorn distance in their SR model, which inspired us to present our SR framework.

Apply Optimal Transport to Image Generation Tasks. GAN [7] suffers from the model collapse and unstable training [1]. WGAN is introduced to deal with the issue with the application of optimal transport theory [1]. Salimans et al. [17] proposed a OT-GAN framework which further improve the training stability. The presented metric defined in optimal transport is employed by us to improve the text image super-resolution results. Gyntaek et al. [15] presented the OT-cycleGAN for the acceleration of MRI which can reconstruct high resolution MR images. While in the field of super-resolution, Goswami et al. [8] employed optimal transport to improve the super-resolution of real faces with an architecture of GAN. As we can see, optimal transport is usually used in GANs for image generation tasks. Therefore, we also present a GAN model for text image super-resolution.

3 Text Image SR Model Using Optimal Transport

In this paper, we propose a text image super-resolution GAN framework to generate text image with more texture information and introduce an optimal transport based energy distance to measure the difference between the super-resolved text images and ground truth text images. Section 3.1 presents some basic information of the optimal transport theory and tells why we use optimal transport based energy distance instead of directly using the Sinkhorn distance. In Sect. 3.2, we introduce the network architecture which is shown in Fig. 1. Finally, Sect. 3.3 presents the formulation of our loss function. The energy distance used as loss function can generate more accurate texture details so that better OCR accuracy can be achieved.

3.1   Optimal Transport and the Energy Distance

When comparing the difference between two probability measures, optimal transport can be more accurate and efficient than commonly used measures such as KL divergence. Now the optimal transport theory has been widely used in machine learning [12], deep learning [17], natural language processing [24] and computer vision [15].

For discrete optimal transport problem, It involves solving the Wasserstein distance as follows:

$$W(\mu, \nu) = min_{\gamma \in \Sigma(\mu,\nu)} \langle c, \gamma \rangle, \tag{1}$$

where μ and ν are two empirical probability distribution, $W(\mu, \nu)$ denotes the Wasserstein distance between μ and ν, $c = [c_{ij}] \in \mathbf{R}_+^{m \times n}$ is the cost function matrix, c_{ij} denotes the distance between i-th support point of μ and j-th support point of ν, γ is the transport matrix. $\Sigma(\mu, \nu)$ is the coupling of the two probability distributions:

$$\Sigma(\mu, \nu) = \left\{ \gamma \in \mathbf{R}_+^{m \times n} : \gamma 1_m = \mu, \gamma^T 1_n = \nu \right\}$$

where 1_m represents n-dimensional vector of ones, $\langle \cdot, \cdot \rangle$ denotes the Frobenius dot-product.

Geng et al. [6] has shown that the Wasserstein distance can give a more accurate measure when comparing the difference between two text images against the semantic shift. If we reshuffle the locations of pixels of two images, the Euclidean distance and KL divergence between them stay unchanged. Only the Wasserstein distance changes because it uses the information of pixels' locations in their calculation.

Though the Wasserstein distance has excellent properties, its application in real life has been limited due to its high computational complexity. In order to reduce the computational burden, the Sinkhorn distance proposed by Cuturi is usually used to approximate the Wasserstein distance in the field of machine learning.

Cuturi [4] proposed a regularized variation of (1), (1) then turns into solving an entropy regularization problem:

$$W_\epsilon(\mu, \nu) = min_{\gamma \in \Sigma(\mu,\nu)} \langle c, \gamma \rangle + \epsilon h(\gamma), \tag{2}$$

where ϵ is the entropy regularized parameter, $\epsilon > 0$. $h(\gamma) = \Sigma_{ij} \gamma_{ij} ln \gamma_{ij}$.

The result of this problem can be efficiently computed using the Sinkhorn algorithm:

$$a^{(l+1)} = \frac{\mu}{Kb^{(l)}}, b^{(l+1)} = \frac{\nu}{K^T a^{(l+1)}},$$

where $b^{(0)} = \frac{1}{n} 1_n$, $K = [K_{ij}]$, $K_{ij} = e^{-c_{ij}/\epsilon}$.

Then the approximate solution $\gamma^{(l)}$ is obtained, $\gamma_{ij}^{(l)} = a_i^{(l)} K_{ij} b_j^{(l)}$. Assuming that the γ^* is the exact solution of problem (1),Then we have that $lim_{l \to +\infty} \gamma^{(l)} = \gamma^*$. The approximate solution computed by the Sinkhorn algorithm is called the Sinkhorn distance.

However, in generative models, the Sinkhorn distance is inappropriate to be directly used as a measure between empirical distributions due to a disadvantage of mini-batch Sinkhorn distance that the expectation of mini-batch Sinkhorn distance is no longer a valid measure between probability distributions. Viewed another way, the gradient of the mini-batch Sinkhorn distance is no longer an unbiased estimator of the gradients of the original optimal transport problem. The unbiased sample gradients are defined as follows:

Theorem 1. *[2]Let $X_m := X_1, ...X_m$ be independent samples from the target distribution P. Since the distribution P can not be directly obtained, we define the empirical distribution based on these samples $P'_m := \frac{1}{m}\sum_{i=1}^{m} \delta_{X_i}$. The δ_x is the Dirac funtions at different values of x. We need to generate a distribution Q_η to be close to the target distribution P as possible as we can. Q_η is a distribution parametrized by η. Therefore we define the sample loss $\eta x \mapsto d\left(P'_m, Q_\eta\right)$, we say that d has the unbiased sample gradients when the expected gradient of the sample loss equals the gradient of the true loss for P and m:*

$$\mathop{E}\limits_{X_m} \nabla_\eta d\left(P'_m, Q_\eta\right) = \nabla_\eta d\left(P, Q_\eta\right).$$

This property is very important for the training of neural networks. If a defined loss does not satisfy this property, Gradients are no longer accurate when using optimization algorithms based on gradient descent, which may result in non-convergence or convergence to inaccurate values. Satisfying this property enables the metric to be a proper scoring rule.

Therefore,we need to employ a metric based on the Wasserstein distance to measure the difference between images which possess the property of unbiased sample gradients. We choose the mini-batch energy distance used in OT-GAN [17] as our metric, we call it the optimal transport based energy distance in our method, combining optimal transport in primal form with an energy distance defined in an adversarially learned feature space. This combination results in a highly discriminative metric with unbiased mini-batch gradients. Therefore, it can be understood as using OT-GAN [17] in the field of text image super-resolution.

The generalized optimal transport based energy distance is as follows [17]:

$$D_{oted}(p, q) = \sqrt{2E\left[W\left(X, Y\right)\right] - E\left[W\left(X, X'\right)\right] - E\left[W\left(Y, Y'\right)\right]}$$

where X, X' are two independent samples from target distribution p and Y, Y' are two independent samples from generated distribution q. W is the Wasserstain distance. $D_{oted}(p, q)$ is a metric since the Wasserstein distance is a metric. Note that we also need to use the Sinkhorn distance to approximate the Wasserstein distance. The optimal transport based energy distance is a much stronger discriminative metric with unbiased gradients between individual mini-batches, which leads to a better super-resolution results in our experiments.

3.2   Network Architecture

Our proposed network architecture includes two parts: generator and critic, as shown in Fig. 1. We use the EDSR [13] network as the generator. It uses residual blocks as the basic module to generate SR images from LR images. It removes the batch normalization layers from the SRResnet [11] and can get better super-resolution result. In the critic, we employ the corresponding architecture of OT-GAN [17] as the basis of our model. The critic is employed to map both the SR images and HR images into a learned latent space, so that the energy distance between them can be computed efficiently. Note that the network architecture we use is simple and effective so that the advantages of the proposed loss function can be demonstrated.

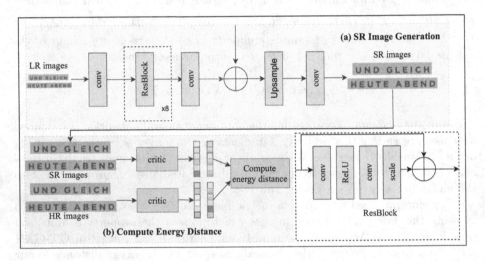

Fig. 1. The training pipeline of our method. We randomly sample a pair of LR images from the dataset. (a) The SR image generation procedure will use the EDSR model to generate the corresponding SR images from the LR images. (b)For SR images and their corresponding HR images, we use a critic network to map all of them to a learned space. Then we compute the optimal transport based energy distance by computing the Sinkhorn distance between them.

3.3   Loss Function

The loss function in our network divides into two parts: MSE loss and the energy loss, the total loss can be formulated as:

$$L_{total} = \omega_1 L_{mse} + \omega_2 L_{energy},$$

Note that since the energy loss is formulated in the terms of mini-batches, the MSE loss is calculated by the sum of the pair of the images in the mini-batches.

Assuming that S_1, S_2 are the two SR images of the mini-batches generated by the network from two LR images sampled from the training set.The MSE loss part of the network is formulated as:

$$L_{mse} = L_{mse1} + L_{mse2},$$

where L_{mse1} and L_{mse2} are the MSE loss of S_1, S_2 and their ground truth HR images.

As for the energy loss, we employ a new metric measuring the difference between the super-resolved text images and their ground truth high-resolution images. This metric has been used in basic image generation task and performed well, we will also employ the strategy which has been used in OT-GAN [17] to use this metric well. In each step in our training procedure, we samples two low-resolution text image from the training set and use the generator to generator two super-resolution images. Then we use the critic network to map both super-resolution images and their ground truth high-resolution images into a learned latent space to easily compute the Sinkhorn distance so that the optimal transport based energy distance can be computed as well. In the learned latent space, the cost matrix defined below instead of the Euclidean distance is used as the transport cost matrix [17]:

$$c_\delta\left(x,y\right) = 1 - \frac{\delta\left(x\right)\delta\left(y\right)}{\left\|\delta\left(x\right)\right\|_2 \left\|\delta\left(y\right)\right\|_2},$$

where x, y are two images in our mini-batch, δ is a neural network that maps the images into a learned latent space.

Therefore, the energy loss is formulated as:

$$L_{energy} = W_{c_\delta}\left(S_1, G_1\right) + W_{c_\delta}\left(S_1, G_2\right) + W_{c_\delta}\left(S_2, G_1\right)$$
$$+ W_{c_\delta}\left(S_2, G_2\right) - 2W_{c_\delta}\left(S_1, S_2\right) - 2W_{c_\delta}\left(G_1, G_2\right),$$

where W_{c_δ} is the Wasserstein distance between two images which is computed in a space learned by the critic using the cost matrix c_δ. G_1, G_2 are the corresponding ground truth images. During the network training, the Wasserstein distance is approximated by the Sinkhorn distance.

For the MSE loss, while achieving particularly high PSNR score, results of MSE optimization often lack spatial structure and texture information which leads to poor performance in OCR. Therefore, the ω_1 is set to relatively small while ω_2 is set to relatively large.Note that when training, the critic is trained to maximize the energy loss L_{energy}. While the generator is trained to minimize the total loss L_{total}.

4   Experimental Results

4.1   Dataset

We use the ICDAR 2015 TextSR dataset [16], which is the standard dataset provided by the ICDAR 2015 Competition on Text Image Super-Resolution.This dataset extracted from French TV videos which consists of a training set and a test set. The training set contains 567 images and the test set has 141 images. The dataset downsamples the HD images by factors of ×2 and ×4 to create HR-LR and HD-LR pairs respectively for two scales' super-resolution tasks.

4.2 Evaluation Protocol

We employ two different categories of measures for the text image super-resolution task. (1) Peak Signal to Noise Ratio (PSNR) and Structural Similarity (SSIM); (2) The OCR accuracy score of the SR images.The OCR accuracy is measured by using the Tesseract OCR engine 3.02:

$$OCR = 1 - \frac{1}{T} \sum_{i=1}^{N} (E_i), \tag{3}$$

where N is the number of testing images and T is the total number of characters of these text images. E_i is the edit distance between the SR text image OCR result of the i-th test images and its corresponding ground truth.

4.3 Implementation Details

Our experiments were based on a model of the PyTorch framework on a single RTX-2080 GPU. Instead of cropping the images to produce training samples at first, we use the protocol of online data augmentation. In each we train batch, we randomly crop the HR images to 18×18 and LR images to 9×9 from the original training set. Then we augment the training set by randomly flipping the crops horizontally or vertically or rotating them by 90°. We use the Adam optimizer to train our network, β_1 is set to 0.9 and β_2 is set to 0.999. The learning rate is set to 0.0001 and the batch size is set to 32. We train a total of 2500 epochs. And we folow a standard training protocol which has been used in OT-GAN. The generator is trained more often than the critic, then the generator and the critic can become stronger together gradually. In our experiments, we train the generator for three epochs then the critic for a single epoch.

Table 1. Results of EDSR, Geng et al. and our method on the ICDAR 2015 TextSR dataset, Bold numbers indicate the best performances. By using optimal transport based energy distance as a metric,our method achieves the best performance in OCR.

Method	PSNR	SSIM	OCR(%)
EDSR	**34.91**	0.989	77.94
Geng et al.	34.89	0.989	78.56
Ours	34.73	**0.991**	**78.90**

4.4   Effectiveness of the Optimal Transport Based Energy Distance

Since our method and Geng et al. [6]. both use the EDSR [13] network as the backbone to generate the SR images from LR images, it can be seen as using different metric on a same generating network. Therefore, we compare the results of the three methods first to illustrate that the optimal transport based energy distance we use is a better metric. Table 1 shows the results of the three methods on the ICDAR 2015 TextSR dataset. In Table 1, the EDSR achieves the best performance on PSNR while its accuracy in OCR is relative low. Geng et al. suffers a small decrease on PSNR score and equal to EDSR on SSIM score, but its performance in OCR is increased by 0.62% from the result of EDSR. Our method results in 0.16 decrease on PSNR score compared with the Geng et al. But the SSIM score is increased by 0.002 and especially the accuracy in OCR is increased by 0.34%. As we can see, Using the Sinkhorn distance and optimal transport distance as the metric both results in decrease on PSNR score and increase th accuracy in OCR. At the same time, our method achieves better performance in OCR for its better property.This demonstrates that the optimal transport based energy distance is a better metric to evaluate the difference between the SR images and their corresponding ground truth HR images so that SR images with more useful information for OCR can be generated.

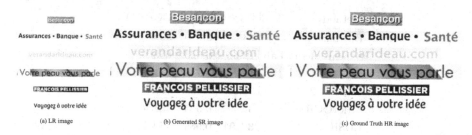

     (a) LR image   (b) Generated SR image   (c) Ground Truth HR image

Fig. 2. Some examples of text image super-resolution results by our method

4.5   Comparision with State-of-the-Art Methods

To further verify the performances of our proposed method, We compare the performances of the proposed method with some state-of-the-art image super-resolution methods. SRCNN-1 [5] and SRCNN-2 [5] is the best results in ICDAR 2015 Competition on Text Image Super-Resolution. SRforOCR [26] obtains a good result for text image super-resolution. EDSR [13] can achieve significant improvement in terms of PSNR and SSIM. Geng et al. [6] is based on EDSR, which introduce the sinkhorn distance to the text image super-resolution field, can achieve a better result for OCR compared with the EDSR. Wang et al. [23] used channel attention and spatial attention to improve the SR model. Xue et al. [25] explored the advantages and disadvantages of Wang et al. and made corresponding improvements and achieved better results.

We evaluate the performances of the proposed method with some state-of-the-art methods on the pair of LR-HR images corresponding to a scaling factor ×2 in Table 2. EDSR, Geng et al. and our method can achieve significant improvement in terms of PSNR, SSIM and OCR accuracy compared with the other methods. This proves the effectiveness of EDSR to be our backbone. Meanwhile, though our method can not achieve a higher PSNR score, we can get the best result in OCR compared with the other state-of-the-art methods. In Fig. 2, we provide the visual results of the SR images generating by our method. We can observe that our method is robust to generate SR images from different LR images with high quality.

To further demonstrate the effectiveness of our method, we also compare the performances of our method with som top state-of-the-art methods on the pairs of LR-HD images with a scaling factor ×4 in Table 3. Compared with the results of Geng et al., though suffering with a decrease of PSNR score, the performance of our method on the scale factor ×4 also achieve a better performance in OCR. Even compared with some models with more complex generative networks, our model can still achieve state-of-the-art results.

Table 2. Comparison of the performance with some other method with scaling factor ×2 on the ICDAR 2015 TextSR dataset.

Method	PSNR	SSIM	OCR(%)
Bicubic	23.50	0.879	60.64
Synchromedia Lab	12.66	0.623	65.93
SRCNN-1	31.75	0.980	77.19
SRCNN-2	31.99	0.981	76.10
SRforOCR	32.42	0.984	78.10
EDSR	**34.91**	0.989	77.94
Geng et al.	34.89	0.989	78.56
Ours	34.73	**0.991**	**78.90**

Table 3. Comparison of the performance with some other method with scaling factor ×4 on the ICDAR 2015 TextSR dataset.

Method	PSNR	SSIM	OCR(%)
LapSRN	29.98	0.942	80.95
EDSR	30.36	0.945	81.12
RDN	30.64	0.949	81.53
Wang et al.	30.92	0.950	81.73
Geng et al.	31.02	0.948	81.71
Xue et al.	**31.61**	0.951	81.89
Ours	30.80	**0.956**	**81.97**

5 Conclusion

In this paper, we present a new super-resolution framework using generative adversarial network and employ a new metric in the super-resolution field. The metric combines optimal transport in primal form with an energy distance defined in an adversarially learned feature space. The critic network used to compute the optimal transport based energy distance helps to push the generator to generate super-resolution results with more semantic information. Experiments show that our method achieve the state-of-the-art results with high accuracy in optical character recognition.

References

1. Arjovsky, M., Chintala, S., Bottou, L.: Wasserstein generative adversarial networks. In: International Conference on Machine Learning, pp. 214–223. PMLR (2017)
2. Bellemare, M.G., et al.: The cramer distance as a solution to biased wasserstein gradients. arXiv preprint arXiv:1705.10743 (2017)
3. Chaudhuri, A., Mandaviya, K., Badelia, P., Ghosh, S.K.: Optical character recognition systems. In: Optical Character Recognition Systems for Different Languages with Soft Computing. SFSC, vol. 352, pp. 9–41. Springer, Cham (2017). https://doi.org/10.1007/978-3-319-50252-6_2
4. Cuturi, M.: Sinkhorn distances: Lightspeed computation of optimal transport. In: Advances in Neural Information Processing Systems 26 (2013)
5. Dong, C., Loy, C.C., He, K., Tang, X.: Learning a deep convolutional network for image super-resolution. In: Fleet, D., Pajdla, T., Schiele, B., Tuytelaars, T. (eds.) ECCV 2014. LNCS, vol. 8692, pp. 184–199. Springer, Cham (2014). https://doi.org/10.1007/978-3-319-10593-2_13
6. Geng, C., Chen, L., Zhang, X., Gao, Z.: Adversarial text image super-resolution using sinkhorn distance. In: ICASSP 2020–2020 IEEE International Conference on Acoustics, Speech and Signal Processing (ICASSP), pp. 2663–2667. IEEE (2020)
7. Goodfellow, I., et al.: Generative adversarial nets. In: Advances in neural information processing systems 27 (2014)
8. Goswami, S., Rajagopalan, A., et al.: Robust super-resolution of real faces using smooth features. In: European Conference on Computer Vision. pp. 169–185. Springer (2020). https://doi.org/10.1007/978-3-030-66415-2_11
9. Kim, J., Lee, J.K., Lee, K.M.: Accurate image super-resolution using very deep convolutional networks. In: Proceedings of the IEEE Conference on Computer Vision and Pattern Recognition, pp. 1646–1654 (2016)
10. Lai, W.S., Huang, J.B., Ahuja, N., Yang, M.H.: Deep Laplacian pyramid networks for fast and accurate super-resolution. In: Proceedings of the IEEE Conference on Computer Vision and Pattern Recognition, pp. 624–632 (2017)
11. Ledig, C., et al.: Photo-realistic single image super-resolution using a generative adversarial network. In: Proceedings of the IEEE Conference on Computer Vision and Pattern Recognition, pp. 4681–4690 (2017)
12. Li, W., Montúfar, G.: Natural gradient via optimal transport. Inf. Geom. $1(2)$, 181–214 (2018)
13. Lim, B., Son, S., Kim, H., Nah, S., Mu Lee, K.: Enhanced deep residual networks for single image super-resolution. In: Proceedings of the IEEE Conference on Computer Vision and Pattern Recognition Workshops, pp. 136–144 (2017)

14. Long, S., He, X., Yao, C.: Scene text detection and recognition: the deep learning era. Int. J. Comput. Vision **129**(1), 161–184 (2021)
15. Oh, G., Sim, B., Chung, H., Sunwoo, L., Ye, J.C.: Unpaired deep learning for accelerated MRI using optimal transport driven Cyclegan. IEEE Trans. Comput. Imaging **6**, 1285–1296 (2020)
16. Peyrard, C., Baccouche, M., Mamalet, F., Garcia, C.: ICDAR 2015 competition on text image super-resolution. In: 2015 13th International Conference on Document Analysis and Recognition (ICDAR), pp. 1201–1205. IEEE (2015)
17. Salimans, T., Zhang, H., Radford, A., Metaxas, D.: Improving GANs using optimal transport. arXiv preprint arXiv:1803.05573 (2018)
18. Shi, W., et al.: Real-time single image and video super-resolution using an efficient sub-pixel convolutional neural network. In: Proceedings of the IEEE Conference on Computer Vision and Pattern Recognition, pp. 1874–1883 (2016)
19. Tai, Y., Yang, J., Liu, X.: Image super-resolution via deep recursive residual network. In: Proceedings of the IEEE Conference on Computer Vision and Pattern Recognition, pp. 3147–3155 (2017)
20. Tai, Y., Yang, J., Liu, X., Xu, C.: MemNet: a persistent memory network for image restoration. In: Proceedings of the IEEE international conference on computer vision. pp. 4539–4547 (2017)
21. Wang, X., Xie, L., Dong, C., Shan, Y.: Real-ESRGAN: training real-world blind super-resolution with pure synthetic data. In: Proceedings of the IEEE/CVF International Conference on Computer Vision, pp. 1905–1914 (2021)
22. Wang, X., et al.: ESRGAN: enhanced super-resolution generative adversarial networks. In: Proceedings of the European Conference on Computer Vision (ECCV) Workshops (2018)
23. Wang, Y., Su, F., Qian, Y.: Text-attentional conditional generative adversarial network for super-resolution of text images. In: 2019 IEEE International Conference on Multimedia and Expo (ICME), pp. 1024–1029. IEEE (2019)
24. Xu, J., Zhou, H., Gan, C., Zheng, Z., Li, L.: Vocabulary learning via optimal transport for neural machine translation. arXiv preprint arXiv:2012.15671 (2020)
25. Xue, M., Huang, Z., Liu, R.Z., Lu, T.: A novel attention enhanced residual-in-residual dense network for text image super-resolution. In: 2021 IEEE International Conference on Multimedia and Expo (ICME), pp. 1–6. IEEE (2021)
26. Zhang, H., Liu, D., Xiong, Z.: CNN-based text image super-resolution tailored for OCR. In: 2017 IEEE Visual Communications and Image Processing (VCIP), pp. 1–4. IEEE (2017)

GAN-Based Image Compression with Improved RDO Process

Fanxin Xia[1], Jian Jin[2(✉)], Lili Meng[1(✉)], Feng Ding[1], and Huaxiang Zhang[1]

[1] Information Science and Engineering, Shandong Normal University, Jinan 250014, China
mengll_83@hotmail.com
[2] Computer Science and Engineering, Nanyang Technological University, 639798 Singapore, Singapore
jian.jin@ntu.edu.sg

Abstract. GAN-based image compression schemes have shown remarkable progress lately due to their high perceptual quality at low bit rates. However, there are two main issues, including 1) the reconstructed image perceptual degeneration in color, texture, and structure as well as 2) the inaccurate entropy model. In this paper, we present a novel GAN-based image compression approach with improved rate-distortion optimization (RDO) process. To achieve this, we utilize the DISTS and MS-SSIM metrics to measure perceptual degeneration in color, texture, and structure. Besides, we absorb the discretized gaussian-laplacian-logistic mixture model (GLLMM) for entropy modeling to improve the accuracy in estimating the probability distributions of the latent representation. During the evaluation process, instead of evaluating the perceptual quality of the reconstructed image via IQA metrics, we directly conduct the Mean Opinion Score (MOS) experiment among different codecs, which fully reflects the actual perceptual results of humans. Experimental results demonstrate that the proposed method outperforms the existing GAN-based methods and the state-of-the-art hybrid codec (*i.e.*, VVC).

Keywords: Perceptual image compression · GAN-based method

1 Introduction

Image compression is an essential technique for effective image representation, storage, transmission, and so on. With the great successes of deep learning in computer vision and signal processing, many learning based image compression schemes have been developed recently. Toderici *et al.* [24] proposed a learnable image compression method based on the recurrent neural network (RNN) to disentangle thumbnail image compression. After that, Ballé *et al.* [3] developed the first end-to-end image compression framework, which was mainly made up of convolutional autoencoder and mixed with Generalized Divisive Normalization (GDN) [5]. Besides, Ballé *et al.* [4] further developed a hyperprior model

ⓒ The Author(s), under exclusive license to Springer Nature Switzerland AG 2023
H. Lu et al. (Eds.): ICIG 2023, LNCS 14357, pp. 361–372, 2023.
https://doi.org/10.1007/978-3-031-46311-2_30

Original (bpp↓/MOS↓)   Ours(0.198/1.30)

HIFIC [18] (0.220/2.08)   VVC(0.22/3.69)

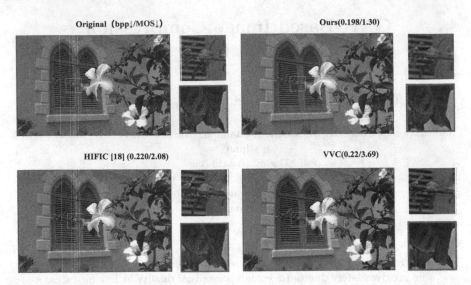

Fig. 1. Visual comparison among the original image, compressed images with our method, HIFIC [21] (state-of-the-art GAN-based image compression method), and VVC [6] (state-of-the-art hybrid image codec). The bpp and MOS values of each compressed image are exhibited as well.

to extract side information for estimating the probability of the latent representation. Although image compression schemes like [8,9,22,23] have made significant advancements in PSNR and MS-SSIM, the biggest challenge still focuses on achieving high perceptual quality image reconstruction, especially for image compression under the low bit rates.

To overcome this problem, some works [1,10,16,21] tried to utilize the Generative Adversarial Network (GAN) [13] to replace the decoder for reconstructing high perceptual quality images. For example, Agustsson et al. [1] proposed a method that used GAN to achieve image compression at extremely low bit rates and demonstrated satisfactory results. However, this method did not adequately consider the perceptual quality degeneration [17] in the reconstructed image. Fabian et al. [21] proposed a perceptual image compression model that incorporated LIPIS [28] together with MSE into the RDO loss function. However, LIPIS overlooked the essential factor of color, which caused the perceptual quality degradation of the reconstructed image in color and texture. Besides, MSE is commonly used for maintaining the fidelity of signal, which overlooked the structure information of reconstructed image[14]. It has been demonstrated in [25] that structure information is one of the most sensitivity factors for the perceptual quality of humans vision. Hence, more suitable perceptual metrics are expected to be utilized for perceiving the distortion in the reconstructed image.

In addition, the entropy model, used for estimate bit rate cost in the RDO, is also an important part of GAN-based image compression. However, the accuracy of entropy model in most of existing GAN-based image compression works was low, which also affect the performance of image compression. For instance, the discretized Gaussian mixture model (GMM) and zero-mean Gaussian distribution model were used in [10,16] and [21] for entropy modeling, which were difficult to accurately estimate the probability distribution of each image. Therefore, a more accurate probability model is expected to be used for entropy modeling.

In this paper, our main contributions are as follows:

- We integrate DISTS and MS-SSIM into the RDO loss function, which provides a comprehensive assessment of distortion in the reconstructed image in terms of color, texture, and structure.
- We absorb a discretized GLLMM probability model for entropy modeling and achieve higher accuracy in estimating the probability distributions of the latent representation, reducing the reconstruction error attributed to imprecise entropy estimation.
- Subjective tests demonstrate the proposed method has better perceptual quality and lower BPP cost compared with the existing state-of-the-art GAN-based image codec and the hybrid one (i.e., VVC), as shown in Fig. 1.

2   GAN-Based Image Compression Method Review

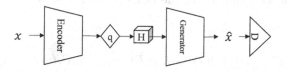

Fig. 2. The framework of the GAN-based image compression. The image x to be compressed is fed into the encoder at first. Then, it is represented with latent y. Afterward, y is quantized and entropy coded to $\omega = H(q(y))$. Then, it is decoded by the generator to reconstruct the image $\hat{x}$. The input image x and its corresponding reconstructed one $\hat{x}$ are alternately fed into a discriminator to improve its discriminative capability. Meanwhile, to fool the discriminator, the generator is further improved to produce higher-quality images.

2.1   GAN

GAN typically consists of two components, one is the generator and the other is the discriminator. The objective function of the GAN model is as follows.

$$\min_{G} \max_{D} V(D,G) = E[log(1 - D(G(z)))] + E[log(D(x))], \tag{1}$$

where x and z denote the real image and the latent representation, respectively. $E[log(1 - D(G(z)))]$ is the objective function for the generator, which is used to produce examples that has genuine and authentic content to the original ones.

$E[log(D(x))]$ is the objective function for the discriminator, which is used to train a powerful discriminator to distinguish the generated examples from the original ones. By combining these two items, the generator is able to generate examples that are close enough to the original ones. Hence, GAN technology has been applied to a range of tasks in recent years, including image-inpainting [27], image deblurring [19], image compression [16], and so on.

2.2 GAN-Based Image Compression

Figure 2 illustrates the framework of a typical GAN-based image compression method, which is mainly made up of an encoder, a generator, a discriminator, and an entropy model. The goal of integrating GAN into the learning-based image compression method was to utilize its powerful generator for high-quality image reconstruction. Such as [20], the authors incorporated GAN into the original structure as a reconstruction enhancement method to improve the perceptual reconstruction capability. Furthermore, GAN's strong generation capability has made it a common choice for image compression methods [2,18,26] targeting extremely low bitrates to overcome the problem of insufficient details in low bitrates.

The optimization process still follows the RDO, but the incorporated GAN needs additional adversarial losses to optimize the generator and discriminator, respectively. The loss function of the GAN-based image codec is formulated as follows.

$$\min_{E,G} \max_D V(D,G) = E[f(D(x))] + E[g(D(G(z)))] + \lambda E(d(x,G(z)) + \beta H(\hat{y}), \quad (2)$$

which four items. The first two items refer to the GAN losses for discriminator and generator, respectively. $E(d(x,G(z)))$ and $H(\hat{y})$ are the rate-distortion loss based on Shannon theory [12]. To make the training of GAN stable, the instability of GAN network training, the $d(x,G(z))$ term often needs MSE to avoid mode collapse.

3   Method

3.1   Network Architecture

The framework of our proposed method is shown in Fig. 3(a), which is a variant of the state-of-the-art GAN-based image compression method [21]. It contains an encoder, a generator, a discriminator, and a hyperprior coding model. The detailed structure is as follows.

Encoder and Generator. The encoder is made up of six convolution layers, and the generator contains five residual blocks and the de-convolution layers.

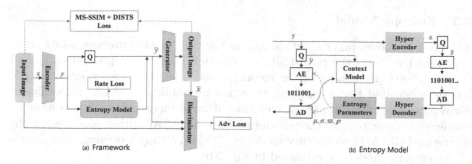

(a) Framework   (b) Entropy Model

Fig. 3. The framework of the proposed method. First, image x is fed into the encoder to achieve latent representation y. Then, y is quantized into $\hat{y}$ through rounding. Meanwhile, y is fed into the entropy model to estimate the probability distribution of each entry. Next, $\hat{y}$ is fed into the generator for image reconstruction. Finally, $\hat{y}$ is fed into the discriminator along with the original image x and the reconstructed image $\hat{x}$. Q, AE, and AD are a quantizer, an arithmetic encoder and an arithmetic decoder, respectively.

Meanwhile, the ChannelNorm is carried out after each layer of encoder and generator to reduce the darkening artifacts. Instead of directly using the activation function "Relu" in the encoder and the generator in [21], "Leaky-Relu" is used to expand the scope of features processing, makes data processing more accurate, and enables the network to accelerate convergence.

Discriminator. The purpose of the discriminator is to help the generator produce more realistic images. As shown in Fig. 3(a), we feed $\hat{y}$ together with the original image x and its corresponding reconstructed one $\hat{x}$ into the discriminator, which is made up of five convolution layers (Table 1).

Table 1. The network struct we used, where all the layers use Leaky-Relu as activation function except for the last layer with no activation.

Encoder	Generator	Discriminator
Conv 7×7×60 Norm	Norm Conv 960 Norm	Conv 12 - NN 16
Conv 120 s2 Norm	ResBlock(×5): Conv 960 Norm	Conv 4×4×64 s2
Conv 240 s2 Norm	Conv 480 s2 Norm	Conv 4×4×128 s2
Conv 480 s2 Norm	Conv 240 s2 Norm	Conv 4×4×256 s2
Conv 960 s2 Norm	Conv 120 s2 Norm	Conv 4×4×512
Conv 220	Conv 60 s2 Norm	Conv 1×1×1 Sigmoid
	Conv 7×7×3	

3.2   Entropy Model

The entropy model plays a critical role in the compression process, as its accuracy directly affects the probability distribution of each compressed entry and further affects the quality of the reconstructed images. A recent study in [15] has demonstrated that a single distribution probability model is not sufficient for representing the complex distribution of large images. In order to improve the accuracy, we replace the zero-mean Gaussian distribution model with the discretized GLLMM probability model in [15] for entropy modeling. The details of the entropy model are exhibited in Fig. 3(b).

Here, the probability of each entry in core latent representation $\hat{y}$ and the side information $\hat{z}$ are to be estimated. To achieve this, we use a non-parametric and fully factorized density model in [4] to estimate the probability of $\hat{z}$, which is formulated as,

$$p_{\hat{z}|\psi}(\hat{z}|\psi) = \prod_i (p_{z_i}|\psi(\psi) * U(-\frac{1}{2}, \frac{1}{2}))(\hat{z}_i), \tag{3}$$

where z_i is the i-th entry of the side information z, i-th represents the location index in the feature tensor. ψ is the parameters of each univariate distribution $p_{z_i}|\psi$.

For quantized latent representation $\hat{y}$, the discretized GLLMM probability model with different mean and variance is used for estimation. The entropy model is thus formulated as

$$\begin{aligned} P_{\hat{y}|\hat{z}}(\hat{y}_i|\hat{z}) = [p_0 \sum_{k=1}^{K} \omega_i^k N(\mu_i^{(k)}, \sigma_i^{2(k)}) \\ + p_1 \sum_{m=1}^{M} \omega_i^m Lap(\mu_i^{(m)}, \sigma_i^{2(m)}) \\ + p_2 \sum_{n=1}^{N} \omega_i^n Log(\mu_i^{(n)}, \sigma_i^{2(n)})\,] * U(-\frac{1}{2}, \frac{1}{2}) \\ = c(\hat{y}_i + \frac{1}{2}) - c(\hat{y}_i - \frac{1}{2}), \end{aligned} \tag{4}$$

where $N(\cdot)$ represents the uniform distribution, $Lap(\cdot)$ represents the Laplacian distribution, $Log(\cdot)$ represents the Logistic distribution, and each distribution has four related parameters $i.e.$ $p_i, \omega_i, \mu_i, \sigma_i$, and the value of K, M, and N are set to 3. $c(\cdot)$ is the cumulative function.

3.3   Loss Function

As mentioned in Subsect. 2.2, the commonly used loss function of GAN-based image compression scheme contains RDO loss and GAN loss. In this paper, the objective function is defined as follows:

$$\mathcal{L}_{(E,H,G)} = E[d(x, \hat{x}) + \lambda(R(\hat{y}) + R(\hat{z})) + \beta log D(G(y), y)], \quad (5)$$

$$\mathcal{L}_D = E[-log(1 - D(\hat{x}, y))] + E[-log(D(x, y))], \quad (6)$$

where G and D represent the generator and discriminator. $R(\hat{y})$ and $R(\hat{z})$ are the entropy of the latent representation and hyper latent representation. $d(x, \hat{x})$ denotes the distortion term, which is a combination of MS-SSIM and DISTS.

$$\mathcal{L}_d^{ms} = E[1 - MS - SSIM(x, \hat{x})], \quad (7)$$

$$\mathcal{L}_d^{dists} = E[DISTS(x, \hat{x})], \quad (8)$$

$$\mathcal{L}_d = k\_ms\, \mathcal{L}_{ms} + k\_di\, \mathcal{L}_{dists}, \quad (9)$$

where k_ms and k_di are two hyperparameters, used for balancing $\mathcal{L}_{ms}$ and $\mathcal{L}_{dists}$.

Different from MSE, MS-SSIM not only considers the differences between pixel levels but also incorporates structural information of images at multiple scales. This makes MS-SSIM particularly effective in evaluating the quality degradation of images, especially for structural degradation. As aforementioned, the main degradation in GAN-based reconstructed images is structure degradation. Hence, it is quite suitable for measuring the degradation that exists in GAN-based reconstructed images.

DISTS is a newly developed metric for evaluating the perceptual quality of images, taking various image characteristics, including color, texture, and structure into account. Through a detailed analysis of these features, DISTS accurately quantifies image similarity and generates more precise evaluation results. Unlike other metrics, DISTS also incorporates local texture information, which allows for a more comprehensive assessment of image quality by evaluating both global and local characteristics. Its robustness to texture and high correlation with human perception makes it suitable for measuring the degradation of reconstructed images in RDO as well.

4   Experiments

4.1   Training Setting

Dataset. The COCO2017 dataset is used to train our model. It contains 118,282 images with different resolutions. At the beginning of the training, each image is scaled to the corresponding proportion and randomly cropped to the size of 256 × 256. Besides, all these data are normalized in [−1,1] before they are trained.

Training Parameters. In this paper, we use λ to control the rate. We set $\lambda = \{2, 1, 0.5\}$ and obtained compressed images with three different bpp. We select the AMD optimizer with a batch size of 4 during training. Besides, for the rest of hyper-prameters, we set $k\_ms = 765 \times 2^{-5}$, $k\_di = 1$, and $\beta = 0.15$

Training Strategy. As shown in Eq. (2), the loss function consists of five components. It is difficult to achieve global optimization for each component through end-to-end training. Besides, it's also challenging to achieve a good balance among different components. Here, we adopt a two-stage training strategy.

In the initial stage, we train the fundamental compression components, which include the encoder, generator, and entropy coding model. The loss function in this stage is the rate-distortion optimization function, $i.e.$ $\mathcal{L}_{E,H,G} = d(x, G(y)) + R(\hat{y}) + R(\hat{z})$. The second stage is based on the previous one, the weights of all the components above are imported for fine-tuning. In the second stage, we train the whole framework of the proposed method (including the discriminator). Meanwhile, the GAN loss is incorporated with the rate-distortion optimization function to help with training. In addition, the training process follows the rule that training discriminator and generator in an alternate way.

Fig. 4. Qualitative results of *kodim*10 from Kodak dataset

Such a training strategy can avoid optimizing five components at the same time. In the second stage, it is no longer prepared from scratch when training the discriminator, which means the generator has acquired a certain capability to generate relevant images.

4.2 Experiment Setting

To better reflect the actual perceptual quality of users, we set a subjective test based on MOS (Mean Opinion Score) experiments. MOS experiments are a standardized method that evaluates image quality through human visual perception, thus it is believed the most convincing test for subjective quality assessment. For more details on the setting of the experimental environment, refer to the ITU-R BT.500-11 criterion [7].

We tested our method against the three anchors (including the state-of-the-art GAN-based image compression method [21], the state-of-the-art hybrid image codec VVC-4:2:0, and a commonly used learning-based image codec method [11]) at the Kodak dataset, which contains 24 images. To this end, we compress all these 24 images with four different image codecs mentioned above under three different bpp (low, mid, and high). Then, we release 4 image pairs to each subject per test. For each image pair, the original image and its corresponding reconstructed image (generated with the image codec mentioned above) are exhibited on the right and left of the screen. All the compressed images in the 4 image pairs above have the same bpp. Then, the subject is asked to rate the score of the reconstructed image with reference to the original image. The score ranges from 1 (best) to 4 (worst). Hence, there are 24×3 tests for each subject. To minimize the potential influence of other factors, we maximized the screen size of these two images. A total of 13 subjects take part in the experiment and the average score of all 13 subjects is used for comparison, namely MOS. The detailed MOS scores are exhibited in Subsect. 4.3.

Table 2. The MOS of Kodak Dataset. "Mean" denotes the average of the scores, and "Std" is its associated standard deviation.

	Low (0.23 bpp)				Mid (0.33 bpp)				High (0.48 bpp)			
	Ours	Cheng [11]	HIFIC [21]	VVC	Ours	Cheng [11]	HIFIC [21]	VVC	Ours	Cheng [11]	HIFIC [21]	VVC
P1	1.67	2.88	2.04	3.42	2.04	2.79	2.21	2.96	1.79	2.46	2.21	3.54
P2	2.17	2.50	2.42	2.92	1.83	2.88	2.29	3.00	1.96	2.71	2.25	3.08
P3	2.04	2.58	2.42	2.88	2.13	2.88	2.29	2.71	1.88	2.33	2.42	3.38
P4	2.21	2.58	2.08	3.13	1.71	2.33	2.58	3.38	1.71	2.08	2.58	3.63
P5	2.04	2.75	2.08	3.13	1.88	2.63	2.00	3.50	1.75	2.42	2.13	3.71
P6	1.67	2.88	1.79	3.58	1.88	2.71	1.71	3.67	1.58	2.67	2.00	3.67
P7	2.08	2.42	2.38	3.13	1.79	2.58	2.50	3.13	1.79	2.63	2.79	2.79
P8	2.17	2.54	2.29	3.00	2.13	2.71	2.17	3.00	2.17	2.46	2.29	3.08
P9	1.54	2.17	2.38	3.92	1.83	1.96	2.25	3.96	1.88	2.83	2.04	3.25
P10	1.83	2.63	2.17	3.38	1.92	2.58	2.33	3.21	1.83	2.25	2.38	3.54
P11	1.96	2.88	2.13	3.04	1.67	2.79	2.42	3.13	1.88	2.83	2.04	3.25
P12	1.83	2.71	2.25	3.21	1.83	2.50	2.25	3.42	1.75	2.25	2.50	3.50
P13	1.88	2.75	2.21	3.17	1.96	2.54	2.25	3.25	1.83	2.50	2.33	3.33
Mean	1.93	2.63	2.20	3.22	1.89	2.61	2.25	3.25	1.83	2.49	2.30	3.37
Std	0.21	0.20	0.17	0.28	0.14	0.24	0.21	0.32	0.13	0.22	0.22	0.26

4.3   Experimental Results

MOS. The result of the MOS is shown in Table 2 and Table 3. A lower score indicates a better perceptual quality of the reconstructed image. It can be seen that our method achieves the best results in the low, mid, and high bpp, respectively. The results above demonstrate the proposed method is able to achieve a better perceptual quality image reconstruction under the same bpp.

Detail Comparison. Figure 4 shows the original image of *kodim10*, it associated reconstructed images with different methods and bpp. Our method outperforms the anchor methods in reconstructing detailed texture and structure, as shown in Fig. 4, particularly in the region of sailboats and seawater. Additionally, Fig. 5 also indicates that our method achieves good performance in color

Table 3. The average MOS of different methods at three different bbp.

	Ours	Cheng [11]	HIFIC [21]	VVC
P1	1.83	2.71	2.15	3.31
P2	1.99	2.69	2.32	3.00
P3	2.01	2.60	2.38	2.99
P4	1.88	2.33	2.42	3.38
P5	1.89	2.60	2.07	3.44
P6	1.71	2.75	1.83	3.64
P7	1.89	2.54	2.56	3.01
P8	2.15	2.57	2.25	3.03
P9	1.75	2.32	2.22	3.71
P10	1.86	2.49	2.29	3.38
P11	1.83	2.83	2.19	3.14
P12	1.81	2.49	2.33	3.38
P13	1.89	2.60	2.26	3.25
Mean	1.88	2.58	2.25	3.28
Std	0.21	0.20	0.17	0.28

Original   Ours(0.323bpp)   HIFIC[17](0.335bpp)

Fig. 5. Qualitative results of *kodim20* from Kodak dataset

fidelity compared with the state-of-the-art GAN-based method HIFIC [21], such as the text on the plane, which should be blue instead of gray.

5 Conclusion

In this paper, we have optimized the state-of-the-art GAN-based image codec by improving its RDO process. To achieve this, we integrate the DISTS and MS-SSIM metrics to measure perceptual degeneration in color, texture, and structure. Meanwhile, we also absorb the GLLMM to improve the accuracy of entropy modeling, which further promotes the probability distribution estimation of the latent representation. To evaluate that the proposed method can achieve higher perceptual quality image reconstruction, the MOS experiment is performed among different codecs, which is believed as the most accurate subjective test experiment that highly reflects the actual perceptual quality of human vision. Experimental results show that our method outperforms the state-of-the-art GAN-based image codecs and hybrid image one (*e.g.*, VVC).

Acknowledgements. This work was supported in part by the NSF of Shandong Province under Grant ZR2020MF042 and Grant ZR2022MF346.

References

1. Agustsson, E., Tschannen, M., Mentzer, F., Timofte, R., Van Gool, L.: Generative adversarial networks for extreme learned image compression. In: Proceedings of the IEEE/CVF International Conference on Computer Vision, pp. 221–231 (2019)
2. Akutsu, H., Suzuki, A., Zhong, Z., Aizawa, K.: Ultra low bitrate learned image compression by selective detail decoding. In: Proceedings of the IEEE/CVF Conference on Computer Vision and Pattern Recognition Workshops, pp. 118–119 (2020)
3. Ballé, J., Laparra, V., Simoncelli, E.P.: End-to-end optimized image compression. arXiv preprint arXiv:1611.01704 (2016)
4. Ballé, J., Minnen, D., Singh, S., Hwang, S.J., Johnston, N.: Variational image compression with a scale hyperprior. arXiv preprint arXiv:1802.01436 (2018)
5. Ballé, J., Laparra, V., Simoncelli, E.P.: Density modeling of images using a generalized normalization transformation. arXiv (2015)
6. Bross, B., et al.: Overview of the versatile video coding (vvc) standard and its applications. IEEE Trans. Circuits Syst. Video Technol. **31**(10), 3736–3764 (2021)
7. Recommendation ITU-R BT. Methodology for the subjective assessment of the quality of television pictures. International Telecommunication Union (2002)
8. Cao, J., Yao, X., Zhang, H., Jin, J., Zhang, Y., Ling, B.W.-K.: Slimmable multi-task image compression for human and machine vision. IEEE Access **11**, 29946–29958 (2023)
9. Chen, S., et al.: A new image codec paradigm for human and machine uses. arXiv preprint arXiv:2112.10071 (2021)
10. Cheng, Z., et al.: Perceptual image compression using relativistic average least squares gans. In: Proceedings of the IEEE/CVF Conference on Computer Vision and Pattern Recognition, pp. 1895–1900 (2021)

11. Cheng, Z., Sun, H., Takeuchi, M., Katto, J.: Learned image compression with discretized gaussian mixture likelihoods and attention modules. In: Proceedings of the IEEE/CVF Conference on Computer Vision and Pattern Recognition, pp. 7939–7948 (2020)
12. Cover, T.M.: Elements of Information Theory. John Wiley & Sons, Hoboken (1999)
13. Creswell, A., White, T., Dumoulin, V., Arulkumaran, K., Sengupta, B., Bharath, A.A.: Generative adversarial networks: an overview. IEEE Signal Process. Maga. **35**(1), 53–65 (2018)
14. Ding, F., Jin, J., Meng, L., Lin, W.: Jnd-based perceptual optimization for learned image compression. arXiv preprint arXiv:2302.13092 (2023)
15. Fu, H., et al.: Learned image compression with discretized gaussian-laplacian-logistic mixture model and concatenated residual modules. arXiv preprint arXiv:2107.06463 (2021)
16. Iwai, S., Miyazaki, T., Sugaya, Y., Omachi, S.: Fidelity-controllable extreme image compression with generative adversarial networks. In: 2020 25th International Conference on Pattern Recognition (ICPR), pp. 8235–8242. IEEE (2021)
17. Jin, J., Yu, D., Lin, W., Meng, L., Wang, H., Zhang, H.: Full rgb just noticeable difference (jnd) modelling. arXiv preprint arXiv:2203.00629 (2022)
18. Kim, Y., Cho, S., Lee, J., Jeong, S.Y., Choi, J.S., Do, J.: Towards the perceptual quality enhancement of low bit-rate compressed images. In: Proceedings of the IEEE/CVF Conference on Computer Vision and Pattern Recognition Workshops, pp. 136–137 (2020)
19. Kupyn, O., Budzan, V., Mykhailych, M., Mishkin, D., Matas, J.: Deblurgan: blind motion deblurring using conditional adversarial networks. In: Proceedings of the IEEE Conference on Computer Vision and Pattern Recognition, pp. 8183–8192 (2018)
20. Lee, J., Kim, D., Kim, Y., Kwon, H., Kim, J., Lee, T.: A training method for image compression networks to improve perceptual quality of reconstructions. In: 2020 IEEE/CVF Conference on Computer Vision and Pattern Recognition Workshops (CVPRW), pp. 585–589 (2020)
21. Mentzer, F., Toderici, G.D., Tschannen, M., Agustsson, E.: High-fidelity generative image compression. Adv. Neural Inf. Process. Syst. **33**, 11913–11924 (2020)
22. Minnen, D., Ballé, J., Toderici, G.D.: Joint autoregressive and hierarchical priors for learned image compression. Adv. Neural Inf. Process. Syst. **31** (2018)
23. Theis, L., Shi, W., Cunningham, A., Huszár, F.: Lossy image compression with compressive autoencoders. arXiv preprint arXiv:1703.00395 (2017)
24. Toderici, G., et al.: Variable rate image compression with recurrent neural networks. arXiv preprint arXiv:1511.06085 (2015)
25. Wang, Z., Bovik, A.C., Sheikh, H.R., Simoncelli, E.P.: Image quality assessment: from error visibility to structural similarity. IEEE Trans. Image Process. **13**(4), 600–612 (2004)
26. Wu, L., Huang, K, Shen, H.: A gan-based tunable image compression system. In: 2020 IEEE Winter Conference on Applications of Computer Vision (WACV), pp. 2323–2331 (2020)
27. Yu, J., Lin, Z., Yang, J., Shen, X., Lu, X., Huang, T.S.: Free-form image inpainting with gated convolution. In: Proceedings of the IEEE/CVF International Conference on Computer Vision, pp. 4471–4480 (2019)
28. Zhang, R., Isola, P., Efros, A.A., Shechtman, E., Wang, O.: The unreasonable effectiveness of deep features as a perceptual metric. In: IEEE/CVF Conference on Computer Vision & Pattern Recognition (2018)

Video Coding for Machines Based on Motion Assisted Saliency Analysis

Hui Chen[1,2] and Yuanyuan Xu[1,2(✉)]

[1] Key Laboratory of Water Big Data Technology of Ministry of Water Resources,
Hohai University, Nanjing 211100, China
{hui_c,yuanyuan_xu}@hhu.edu.cn
[2] College of Computer and Information, Hohai University, Nanjing 211100, China

Abstract. With an increasing amount of video content analyzed automatically by computer vision algorithms, video coding for machines has received growing attention. With saliency analysis for machine vision, video coding scheme can be designed to preserve key information for machine tasks during compression. In this paper, based on versatile video coding (VVC), we propose a video coding scheme for machines using motion assisted saliency analysis. Taking multi-object tracking as an example task, Grad-CAM, a deep learning visualization method, is used to conduct saliency analysis for key video frames. Considering the complexity of saliency analysis and to improve association performance of multi-object tracking, a motion assisted saliency analysis has been designed for non-key frames, whose saliency maps are predicted using motion vectors and saliency maps of key frames. With saliency maps of all the frames, a coding tree unit (CTU)-level QP adjustment scheme has been derived, which prioritizes salient regions concerning machine vision during bitrate allocation. Experimental results show that, compared with VVC, the proposed scheme can achieve at least 20.3% of bitrate saving with the same tracking accuracy.

Keywords: Video Coding for Machines · Saliency analysis · Multi-object tracking

1 Introduction

In recent years, deep learning-based computer vision has made great progress, and thus more and more videos are processed automatically by machines. The majority of traditional video coding schemes are designed for human visual system (HVS). However, machine vision and human vision have different characteristics. For example, human vision focuses on area with high contrast, while machine vision is more task-oriented. Therefore, it is necessary to design a video coding scheme for machine vision, to preserve key information for machines during compression. Moving Picture Experts Group (MPEG) has launched the exploration of video coding for machine (VCM) in 2019 [8].

© The Author(s), under exclusive license to Springer Nature Switzerland AG 2023
H. Lu et al. (Eds.): ICIG 2023, LNCS 14501, pp. 373–384, 2023.
https://doi.org/10.1007/978-3-031-46311-2_31

To design machine vision-oriented video coding, we need to conduct saliency analysis for machine vision, which measure the importance of different regions on the machine analysis task. Results of machine vision tasks can be utilized to indicate salient regions. Fischer et al. [7] used output bounding boxes of Yolo [15] as regions of interest in the images, and designed an image coding for machines based on Versatile Video Coding (VVC) [3]. A reinforcement learning approach has been designed to determine quantization parameter (QP) for each CTU in High Efficiency Video Coding (HEVC), where task-driven semantic distortion metrics were integrated in the coding optimization [18]. Some works developed their own saliency analysis schemes. Distortion metrics calculated in the feature space extracted by the first layers of a deep neural network model was used in [6], to replace pixel-based distortion in rate-distortion optimization. Huang et al. [9] evaluated the importance of each coding tree unit (CTU) utilizing the generated bounding boxes before non-maximum suppression, and a CTU-level bitrate allocation scheme has been designed accordingly for VVC intra coding. Explanation methods of neural networks, e.g., the Gradient-weighted Class Activation Mapping (Grad-CAM) [17], can be used to perform salient analysis as well. The class-discriminative visualization of Grad-CAM is obtained from the gradient backpropagation of target concept flowing into the final convolutional layer. The work in [12] used Grad-CAM to generate semantic importance maps, and designed task-driven coding scheme via reinforcement learning.

The above works mainly focus on either image coding or intra coding for videos. Cai et al. [4] proposed a back propagation based method to analyze the influence of each pixel for object detection, and designed a bitrate allocation scheme for HEVC with evaluation conducted on video sequences. However, saliency for machine vision is calculated separately for each video frame which introduces a high complexity. Furthermore, without considering temporal correlation, variations in separately generated saliency maps for neighboring frames affect performance of machine vision tasks on videos, e.g., the association performance for multi-object tracking.

In this paper, we propose a video coding scheme for machine vision based on motion assisted saliency analysis, using multi-object tracking as the target task. For key frames, saliency maps for each object can be obtained using Grad-CAM, and multiple saliency maps for all detected objects are then merged into one for each key frame. For other frames, a low-complexity motion assisted saliency analysis has been designed, which predicts saliency maps using motion vectors (MVs) and saliency information of key frames. Based on the proposed saliency analysis, an adaptive CTU-level QP adjustment scheme has been derived, allocating more bits to areas that are more important for machine vision. Experimental results verify the effectiveness of the proposed scheme.

2   Proposed Method

Figure 1 shows the overall framework of the proposed method. Firstly, saliency detection is performed on key frame in each Group of picture (GOP), obtaining saliency maps for each detected object. Then, multiple saliency maps are merged into one map representing all detected objects. Key frames are coded with QP decisions guided by merged saliency map. Then, for coding of other frames, MV and saliency map of previous frame is used to obtain saliency for current CTU. Guided by saliency maps, the sequence is coded with a CTU-level QP selection scheme.

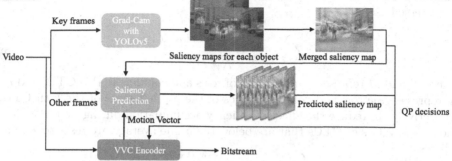

Fig. 1. Illustration of the proposed framework. For key frames, Grad-CAM with Yolov5 is used to generate the saliency maps for each object, which are then merged into one map for each frame. For other frames, saliency maps are predicted using motion vectors and saliency maps of the key frames. The sequence is coded with a CTU-level QP selection scheme

In this work, multi-object tracking is used as an example task. Multi-object tracking involves detecting and assigning IDs to multiple objects in a video for trajectory tracking, without prior knowledge of the number of objects. Multi-object tracking mainly consists of detection and association. The detection part detects potential objects in each frame, while the associating part assigns and updates the detected objects to the corresponding trajectories, i.e., the Re-ID task.

2.1 Saliency Analysis for Key Frames

The beginning frame in each GOP is selected as key frames. Instead of interacting with video machine vision task, detection results produced by Yolov5 are considered in saliency analysis for key frames to reduce the complexity. Grad-CAM [17] uses the gradients of the convolutional layers before the Detect head in Yolov5 to generate saliency maps for detection. The Detect head in Yolov5 contains three detectors for detecting objects of multiple scales. Since Grad-CAM produces one heatmap for each object, multiple maps have to be merged into one map to reflect the overall importance. Saliency maps are merged as follows

$$S'_{i,j} = \sum_k w_k S_{i,j,k}, \tag{1}$$

where $S'_{i,j}$, $S_{i,j,k}$ and w_k are the values of the pixel in i-th row and j-th column in the merged saliency map and the k-th saliency map, and weight for the k-th saliency map, respectively. The weights for the first detector and other two detectors are set to 0.75 and 1, respectively, paying attention to object detection results with medium and larger scales. The merged map $S'_{i,j}$ is normalized to ensure that each salient weight is within the range of $[0, 1]$, where the normalized map is denoted as $S_{i,j}$.

Then the saliency weight of each CTU can be represented as the average value of pixels in the CTU. The saliency weight of the k-th CTU, denoted as S'_k, is expressed as:

$$S'_k = \frac{\sum_{i=0}^{N-1} \sum_{j=0}^{M-1} S_{i_k+i, j_k+j}}{N * M}, \tag{2}$$

where N and M represent the number of rows and columns in this CTU, and i_k, j_k represent the row and column indices of the top-left pixel of the k-th CTU, respectively. To reduce the effect of saliency accumulation during map merging, the salient values of CTUs that are below the frame average are reset to zero as follows.

$$S_k = \begin{cases} 0 & if \quad S'_k < \frac{\sum_{i=0}^{W-1} \sum_{j=0}^{H-1} S_i S_j}{W * H}, \\ S'_k & else \end{cases} \tag{3}$$

where W and H represent the number of rows and columns of the image, respectively. Figure 2 shows an example of saliency analysis for a key frame.

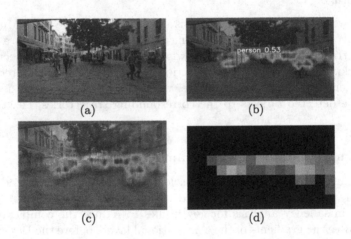

Fig. 2. An example of saliency analysis for a key frame using Grad-CAM with Yolov5: (a) original frame; (b) a saliency map for one object; (c) merged saliency map; (d) CTU-level weight map

2.2 Motion Assisted Saliency Analysis for Other Frames

In hybrid video coding framework [3,19,20], motion estimation and compensation are performed to reduce temporal redundancy. Similarly, saliency maps for video frames exhibit temporal redundancy as well. Therefore, a motion assisted saliency analysis has been designed to predict saliency maps for non-key frames. Specifically, motion estimation is performed to obtain coding unit (CU)-level motion vector, denoted as $MV = \{cur, ref, x, y, w, h, mv_x, mv_y\}$, where x, y, w and h represent the x-axis, y-axis coordinates of the upper-left pixel, and width and height of the current block, respectively. mv_x and mv_y represent the displacement on the x-axis and y-axis between the current block and the predicted block. cur and ref represent the frame indices for the current frame and the reference frame, respectively. The saliency value for a pixel in the current CU is predicted as follows,

$$S_{cur}(i, j) = S_{ref}(i + mv_x, j + mv_y), x \leq i < x + w, \text{ and } y \leq j < y + h, \quad (4)$$

Saliency weights for some CUs at the edge or intra-coded CU cannot be obtained using the above method. For CUs at the edge whose motion goes beyond the range of the previous frame, saliency values from the corresponding position of the previous frame are copied. For intra-coded CUs without MV information, saliency weights from neighboring CU blocks are filled in.

2.3 Bitrate Allocation with Predicted Saliency

With predicted video saliency, video coding for machine vision can be represented by minimizing semantic-weighted distortion under a total bit-rate constraint, which can be expressed as:

$$\min \sum_k D_k^* = \sum (1 + \alpha * S_k) D_k \quad s.t. \sum_k R_k < R_c, \quad (5)$$

where D_k^*, D_k, R_k and S_k denote the semantic-weighted distortion, distortion, bitrate, and saliency value of the k-th CTU, respectively. R_c is the total bit rate constraint, and α is the weight value for saliency.

The constrained optimization problem can be converted into an unconstrained optimization problem by introducing Lagrange multipliers as follows:

$$\min J = \sum_k D_k^* + \lambda \sum_k R_k, \quad (6)$$

where λ is the Lagrange multiplier, and the first term represents the semantic weighted distortion, while the second term represents the rate constraint. The optimal value of λ can be obtained with

$$\frac{\partial J}{\partial R_k} = \frac{\partial (1 + \alpha * S_k) D_k + \partial (\lambda R_k)}{\partial R_k} = 0; \quad (7)$$

$$\lambda = -(1 + \alpha * S_k) \frac{\partial D_k}{\partial R_k}. \quad (8)$$

As the saliency value S_k is independent of the coding process, if $\lambda_k = -\frac{\partial D_k}{\partial R_k}$, we can derive:

$$\lambda = (1 + \alpha * S_k) \lambda_k. \quad (9)$$

λ is determined by QP in the reference software of both HEVC and VVC with $\lambda = c * 2^{(QP-12)/3}$, where c is a frame-level parameter related to the coding structure. The optimal QP value of the kth CTU, QP_k, can be calculated as:

$$QP_k = QP_{base} - 3 * \log_2(1 + \alpha * S_k), \tag{10}$$

where QP_{base} is the QP corresponding to the global Lagrangian factor λ in a frame. In the cases of performing multiple-QP optimization, a linear relationship between $ln(\lambda)$ and QP has been found in [11] as follows to refine QP of HEVC,

$$QP = 4.2005 * \ln(\lambda) + 13.7122 \tag{11}$$

which can also be used for common used coding structure in other codecs. Therefore, this relationship is used in this work to refine the optimal QP, with

$$QP_k = QP_{base} - 4.2005 * \ln(1 + \alpha * S_k). \tag{12}$$

3   Experiments and Results

3.1   Experimental Settings

To validate the effectiveness of the proposed method, seven video sequences from the training set of MOT17 [14] are used, which have ground truth annotations for multiple people tracking. The sequences have a resolution of 1920×1080 except one with a resolution of 640×480. The number of total frames for these sequences varies within the range of $[525, 1050]$, with a frame rate of 30 frames per second (fps) except two with 14 and 25 fps, respectively. All the frames in each sequence are coded during simulation. The bitrate is normalized according to a framerate of 30 fps.

The proposed coding scheme is implemented in the VVC reference software VTM 16.0 in the setting of Low Delay P(LDP). The GOP size is 8, and the first frame of each GOP is a key frame in saliency analysis. A pretrained Yolov5s is used saliency analysis of key frames. GradCam is used to interpret results of Yolov5s, where the resulting heatmaps are viewed and verified to eliminate abnormal ones. Motion estimation with pixel accuracy is used in saliency prediction for non-key frames. MMtracking [5] is used to perform multi-object tracking, and the code from [10] is used for calculating different metrics. Performance of multi-object tracking can be evaluated using HOTA [13], MOTA [1], where object detection accuracy can be represented by mAp or HOTA's sub-metric DetA, and association performance is represented by IDF1 [16] or HOTA's sub-metric AssA. The peak signal-to-noise ratio (PSNR) metric in the Bjontegaard rate (BDrate) [2] is replaced by HOTA, MOTA, mAp and IDF1.

3.2   Performance with Varying Weights for Saliency

The coding performance with varying weight for saliency is investigated, which is the α in Eq. (12). A larger value of α results in a larger difference between

QP_k and QP_{base} with the same salient value, and more bitrate are allocated to saliency regions. Figure 3 shows the BD-rate of the proposed scheme compared with VVC with varying saliency weights. Since the improvement of accuracy is not significant at high bitrates, $QP_{base} \in \{35, 40, 45, 50\}$ is selected for BD-rate calculation. It can be seen that the proposed scheme has the largest BD-rate reduction in terms of all the evaluation metrics when α is set to 4. Therefore, in the following experiment, α is set to 4. It can be seen from the figure that, when α equals 4, the IDF1 metric has the largest bitrate reduction among all the metrics, which indicates improvement in association performance.

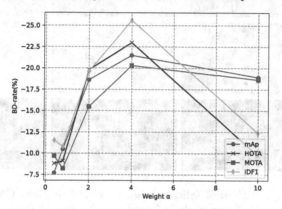

Fig. 3. BD-rate compared with VVC for varying weight for saliency

3.3 Performance Comparison

To show the effectiveness of the proposed motion-assisted saliency analysis, the proposed scheme is compared with a counterpart which conducts separated saliency analysis using Grad-CAM and Yolov5s for every frame. On the contrary, the proposed scheme only performs saliency detection on the first frame of a GOP, while the saliency of the remaining seven frames is obtained through the proposed saliency prediction scheme, which significantly reduces the computational cost of saliency detection. A visual comparison of saliency maps produced by Grad-CAM and the proposed motion-assisted saliency analysis for non-key frames is shown in Fig. 4. It can be seen that difference between maps produced by the two schemes is small, and it slightly increases as the frame is further away from the key frame.

The rate-accuracy comparison is shown in Fig. 5. For $QP_{base} \in \{35, 40, 45, 50\}$, using VVC as the anchor, the BD-rates of coding schemes with the proposed saliency prediction and separate analysis by Grad-CAM are shown in Table 1. It can be observed that, compared with VVC, the proposed scheme and its counterpart achieve at least 18.9% and 20.3% bitrate saving with the same accuracy. With a lower complexity for saliency analysis, the proposed scheme with saliency prediction achieves almost the same or slightly better performance than its counterpart with all saliency maps produced by GradCam, especially in terms of HOTA and IDF1. This is because the proposed scheme using motion

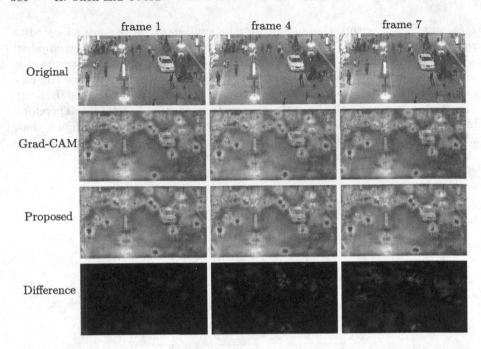

Fig. 4. A visual comparison of saliency maps produced by Grad-CAM and the proposed motion-assisted saliency analysis for non-key frames. The rows from top to bottom show the original picture, saliency maps generated by Grad-CAM, saliency maps generated by the proposed saliency prediction scheme, and difference between maps of two schemes. The columns from left to right show the 2nd frame, 5th frame, and 8th frame within the first GOP, respectively, where frame 0 is the key frame in saliency analysis

assisted saliency analysis maintains consistent saliency across frames, which is beneficial for the association metrics.

Figure 6 presents a visual comparison of the proposed scheme and the VVC scheme in detection part of multi-object tracking, and average bitrate, HOTA, AssA and DetA for the whole sequence are presented as well. Compared to VVC, multi-object tracking using the reconstructed videos of the proposed scheme

Table 1. BD-rate comparison of coding schemes using the proposed saliency prediction, and separate saliency analysis using Grad-CAM, where VVC is used as an anchor

Metrics	Separate analysis by GradCAM	With saliency prediction
HOTA	−19.4%	−23.0%
MOTA	−18.9%	−20.3%
mAp	−19.8%	−21.5%
IDF1	−23.2%	−25.6%

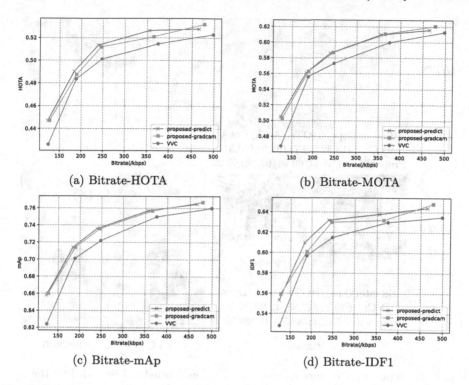

(a) Bitrate-HOTA

(b) Bitrate-MOTA

(c) Bitrate-mAp

(d) Bitrate-IDF1

Fig. 5. Rate-accuracy comparison of the proposed scheme with saliency prediction, the scheme with all saliency maps produced by GradCam, and VVC

with a lower coding rate can identify objects that were missed or misdetected in reconstructed videos of VVC. The visual comparison of the proposed scheme and the VVC scheme on the association task is shown in Fig. 7. As shown in the figure, multi-object tracking using the reconstructed video coded by VVC fails to detect the girl at the background at frame 412, and has an ID switch for the same girl at frame 419, whose ID is changed from 49 to a new ID of 56. In contrast, multi-object tracking using the reconstructed video coded by the proposed scheme correctly detects and associates the same target, and the coding rate of the proposed scheme is lower. The reason is that the proposed scheme prioritizes semantic important information for machine vision during bitrate allocation.

MOT04

Bitrate(kbps)/HOTA/AssA/DetA
VVC: 213.32/60.71/61.96/60.51
Proposed: 176.93/60.96/62.36/60.29

MOT09

Bitrate(kbps)/HOTA/AssA/DetA
VVC: 639.78/47.65/42.92/53.20
Proposed: 580.35/49.57/46.58/53.02

Original   VVC   Proposed

Fig. 6. Detection performance comparison of reconstructed videos coded by the proposed scheme and VVC

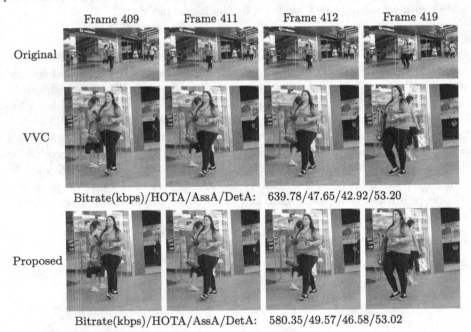

Frame 409   Frame 411   Frame 412   Frame 419

Original

VVC

Bitrate(kbps)/HOTA/AssA/DetA: 639.78/47.65/42.92/53.20

Proposed

Bitrate(kbps)/HOTA/AssA/DetA: 580.35/49.57/46.58/53.02

Fig. 7. Association performance comparison of reconstructed videos coded by the proposed scheme and VVC. Frames 409, 411, 411 and 419 of the *MOT09* are displayed

4 Conclusion

In this paper, in view of complexity in video saliency analysis and improve the association performance, a video coding scheme for machines has been proposed based on motion assisted video saliency analysis. For key frames, saliency maps are generated by merging results from a black-box explanation method of neural networks, Grad-CAM. For other frames, saliency maps can be obtained using motion vectors and saliency of previous frames. Furthermore, a CTU-level QP adjustment scheme has been designed to prioritize areas of interest for machine vision. Taking multi-object tracking as an example task, experimental results show that the proposed scheme can at least reduce the bitrate of VVC by 20.3% with the same tracking accuracy.

References

1. Bernardin, K., Stiefelhagen, R.: Evaluating multiple object tracking performance: the clear mot metrics. EURASIP J. Image Video Process. **2008**, 1–10 (2008)
2. Bjontegaard, G.: Calculation of average psnr differences between rd-curves. ITU SG16 Doc. VCEG-M33 (2001)
3. Bross, B., Chen, J., Ohm, J.R., Sullivan, G.J., Wang, Y.K.: Developments in international video coding standardization after avc, with an overview of versatile video coding (VVC). Proc. IEEE **109**(9), 1463–1493 (2021)
4. Cai, Q., Chen, Z., Wu, D.O., Liu, S., Li, X.: A novel video coding strategy in HEVC for object detection. IEEE Trans. Circ. Syst. Video Technol. **31**(12), 4924–4937 (2021)
5. Contributors, M.: MMTracking: OpenMMLab video perception toolbox and benchmark (2020). https://github.com/open-mmlab/mmtracking
6. Fischer, K., Brand, F., Herglotz, C., Kaup, A.: Video coding for machines with feature-based rate-distortion optimization. In: IEEE International Workshop on Multimedia Signal Processing, pp. 1–6. IEEE (2020)
7. Fischer, K., Fleckenstein, F., Herglotz, C., Kaup, A.: Saliency-driven versatile video coding for neural object detection. In: IEEE International Conference on Acoustics, Speech and Signal Processing, pp. 1505–1509. IEEE (2021)
8. Gao, W., Liu, S., Xu, X., Rafie, M., Zhang, Y., Curcio, I.: Recent standard development activities on video coding for machines. arXiv preprint arXiv:2105.12653 (2021)
9. Huang, Z., Jia, C., Wang, S., Ma, S.: Visual analysis motivated rate-distortion model for image coding. In: IEEE International Conference on Multimedia and Expo, pp. 1–6. IEEE (2021)
10. Jonathon Luiten, A.H.: Trackeval (2020). https://github.com/JonathonLuiten/TrackEval
11. Li, B., Xu, J., Zhang, D., Li, H.: QP refinement according to Lagrange multiplier for high efficiency video coding. In: IEEE International Symposium on Circuits and Systems, pp. 477–480. IEEE (2013)
12. Li, X., Shi, J., Chen, Z.: Task-driven semantic coding via reinforcement learning. IEEE Trans. Image Process. **30**, 6307–6320 (2021)
13. Luiten, J., et al.: Hota: a higher order metric for evaluating multi-object tracking. Int. J. Comput. Vision **129**, 548–578 (2021)

14. Milan, A., Leal-Taixé, L., Reid, I., Roth, S., Schindler, K.: Mot16: a benchmark for multi-object tracking. arXiv preprint arXiv:1603.00831 (2016)
15. Redmon, J., Divvala, S., Girshick, R., Farhadi, A.: You only look once: unified, real-time object detection. In: Proceedings of the IEEE Conference on Computer Vision and Pattern Recognition, pp. 779–788. IEEE Computer Society (2016)
16. Ristani, E., Solera, F., Zou, R., Cucchiara, R., Tomasi, C.: Performance measures and a data set for multi-target, multi-camera tracking. In: Hua, G., Jégou, H. (eds.) ECCV 2016. LNCS, vol. 9914, pp. 17–35. Springer, Cham (2016). https://doi.org/10.1007/978-3-319-48881-3_2
17. Selvaraju, R.R., Cogswell, M., Das, A., Vedantam, R., Parikh, D., Batra, D.: Gradcam: visual explanations from deep networks via gradient-based localization. In: Proceedings of the IEEE International Conference on Computer Vision, pp. 618–626 (2017)
18. Shi, J., Chen, Z.: Reinforced bit allocation under task-driven semantic distortion metrics. In: IEEE International Symposium on Circuits and Systems, pp. 1–5. IEEE (2020)
19. Sullivan, G.J., Ohm, J.R., Han, W.J., Wiegand, T.: Overview of the high efficiency video coding (HEVC) standard. IEEE Trans. Circ. Syst. Video Technol. **22**(12), 1649–1668 (2012)
20. Wiegand, T., Sullivan, G.J., Bjontegaard, G., Luthra, A.: Overview of the H.264/AVC video coding standard. IEEE Trans. Circ. Syst. Video Technol. **13**(7), 560–576 (2003)

CSDNet: Contrastive Similarity Distillation Network for Multi-lingual Image-Text Retrieval

Shichen Lu[1], Longteng Guo[2], Xingjian He[2], Xinxin Zhu[2], Jing Liu[2], and Si Liu[3(✉)]

[1] School of Computer Science and Engineering, Beihang University,
Beijing 100191, China
sclu2020@buaa.edu.cn
[2] The Laboratory of Cognition and Decision Intelligence for Complex
Systems, Institute of Automation, Chinese Academy of Sciences,
Beijing 100080, China
{longteng.guo,xingjian.he,xinxin.zhu,xinxin.zhu}@nlpr.ia.ac.cn
[3] Institute of Artificial Intelligence, Beihang University, Beijing 100191, China
liusi@buaa.edu.cn

Abstract. Cross-modal image-text retrieval is a crucial task in the field of vision and language, aimed at retrieving the relevant samples from one modality as per the given user expressed in another modality. While most methods developed for this task have focused on English, recent advances expanded the scope of this task to the Multi-lingual domain. However, these methods face challenges due to the limited availability of annotated data in non-English languages. In this work, we propose a novel method that leverages an English pre-training model as a teacher to improve Multi-lingual image-text retrieval performance. Our method trains a student model that produces better Multi-lingual image-text similarity scores by learning from the English image-text similarity scores of the trained teacher. We introduce the contrastive loss to align the two different representations of the image and text, and the Contrastive Similarity Distillation loss to align the Multi-lingual image-text distribution of the student with that of the English teacher. We evaluate our method on two popular datasets, i.e., MS-COCO and Flickr-30K, and achieve state-of-the-art performance. Our approach shows significant improvement over existing methods and has potential for practical applications.

Keywords: Image-Text Retrieval · Multi-Lingual · Knowledge Distillation

1 Introduction

Image-text retrieval is a fundamental task in the field of vision and language [16]. Its objective is to effectively retrieve the most similar samples to the given query of text (or images) from a database of images (or texts). With the increasing

© The Author(s), under exclusive license to Springer Nature Switzerland AG 2023
H. Lu et al. (Eds.): ICIG 2023, LNCS 14357, pp. 385–395, 2023.
https://doi.org/10.1007/978-3-031-46311-2_32

number of images uploaded to the internet, this task is becoming increasingly important. While tremendous success has been realized in multimodal research with the advent of vision-and-language pre-training, most methods developed for this task are trained and evaluated only with English text. So, most of the current multimodal pre-training models can only be used for image and English text retrieval tasks, and cannot be applied to other languages. Compared to image-English text retrieval, Multi-lingual image retrieval tasks are more universal and necessary. Recently, the success of the self-supervised language model with multimodal pre-training [6,7,32,35,37] has expanded to the Multi-lingual domain [3,9,18,21,28,30]. Meanwhile, advances in Multi-lingual pre-training enable cutting-edge language technology to benefit a much broader group of users, including non-English speakers. Our work focuses on improving the performance of Multi-lingual image-text retrieval.

The multi-modal pre-training models and multi-lingual pre-training models get successful performance depending on the availability of large amounts of parallel data. However, there exist only a few multi-lingual multi-modal corpora and their language coverage is also limited. Current multi-modal Multi-lingual pre-training models can only use machine translation models to translate English texts into other languages to obtain training data in those languages. The problem with this approach is that the quality of the pre-training model training largely depends on the performance of the machine translation model. Two pioneering works, M^3P [23] and UC^2 [36], propose to pivot either on English texts or images to align multi-lingual multi-modal representations. Both of them introduce a number of new objectives to make use of the anchor for alignment. While these methods have led to improvements in Multi-lingual image-text retrieval, the performance for English is typically higher than for other languages. We speculate that this could be due to two main reasons. Firstly, there is often a significantly larger amount of English data during the training of the Multi-lingual model compared to data in other languages. Secondly, the quality of English data is often superior to that of other languages as data in other languages may be obtained through English translation, which can potentially introduce errors.

In this work, to address the gap in performance between English and Multilingual image-text retrieval. Our CSDNet is used to train the student model to acquire the ability to align representation of image and text, and utilize an English pre-training model as the teacher to enhance the performance of our multi-modal multi-lingual model in Multi-lingual image-text retrieval. Specifically, we train a student model to learn better Multi-lingual image-text similarity scores by leveraging the English image-text scores of the trained and frozen teacher. We introduce a Contrastive Similarity Distillation Loss between the student's Multi-lingual image-text distribution and the teacher's English image-text distribution. This loss encourages the student's distribution to be more aligned with the English distribution, thus improving the overall Multi-lingual image-text retrieval performance.

To evaluate the effectiveness of our approach, we test our model following the proposed Multi-lingual model XLM-R [5] and multimodal model Clip [26] on two image-text retrieval datasets: Flickr-30K [34] and MS-COCO [2]. Our experimental results demonstrate that our method achieves state-of-the-art performance on these datasets. Furthermore, we evaluate our model's capability in a zero-shot setting and show that it outperforms previous methods in this scenario.

In summary, our contribution is: We propose the Contrastive Similarity Distillation Network (CSDNet) for Multi-lingual Image-Text Retrieval, which guides a student model to learn better Multi-lingual image-text similarity distribution by learning from the image-text distribution of teachers using English text translations as input. Our method achieves state-of-the-art performance on two Multi-lingual image-text retrieval datasets, demonstrating its effectiveness in improving the performance of Multi-lingual image-text retrieval.

2   Related Work

2.1   Image-Text Retrieval

Image-Text Retrieval (ITR) has been a popular research topic in the multi-modal community. Traditional approaches to ITR utilized Convolutional Neural Networks (CNNs) [1] to encode images and texts separately [8,31]. Recently, transformer-based models and large-scale language-image pre-training have gained popularity [13,20,22,29]. In those models, the pretraining typically consists of three types of tasks: 1) masked language modeling, 2) masked region modeling, and 3) text-image matching. By exploiting the multi-modal attention and being pretrained on large-scale datasets. These models have achieved state-of-the-art performance on various ITR benchmarks by leveraging multi-modal attention and being pre-trained on large-scale datasets. However, most of these models are limited to a single language (usually English) and the image or video domain.

2.2   Multi-lingual Learning

Multi-lingual pre-trained language models [31,32] are capable of encoding text from multiple languages simultaneously. Notably, Multi-lingual BERT [6] employs the same model structure and training objective as BERT, but it was pre-trained on more than 100 languages from Wikipedia. Later, XLM [15], XLM-R [5], and Unicoder [11] introduced new objectives, including translation language modeling (TLM), multi-lingual word recovery, and multi-lingual paraphrase classification, to enhance Multi-lingual pre-training. Recently, MAD-X [25] and InfoXLM [4] have further improved Multi-lingual pre-training using adapter [10] and contrastive learning techniques.

2.3   Multi-lingual Multi-modal Pre-training

Multi-lingual multi-modal pre-training aims to make multi-modal models applicable to non-English texts by multi-lingual transfer. In this paper, we mainly consider multi-modal in the vision-language context. The key difficulty of multi-lingual multi-modal pre-training is the lack of non-English image-text pairs. M^3P [23] introduces the first pre-training framework that alternatively optimizes the model on multimodal monolingual corpus and mono-modal Multi-lingual corpus. While M^3P achieves better performance compared to task-specific methods, the alignment between vision and Non-English languages is hard to capture, as the model is learned via using English as the anchor point. To strengthen the alignment between vision and all languages, UC^2 [36] proposes to pre-train a unified architecture where sentences in different languages are grounded on shared visual context. Our CSDNet uses a limited amount of Multi-lingual image-text pairs and utilizes the superior English image-text retrieval ability as a teacher to guide the student model's learning, thereby further improving the model's performance in Multi-lingual image-text retrieval.

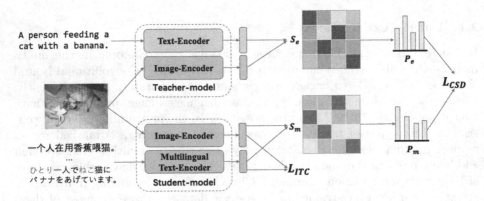

Fig. 1. The Framework of our Contrastive Similarity Distillation Network (CSDNet). A Multi-lingual student model computes image-text similarity scores for a batch of image and text inputs, while the teacher model processes the same image and corresponding English captions. Our model is trained with two losses.L_{ITC} (described in Sect. 3.2)trains the model align image and Multi-lingual text representations.L_{CSD} (described in Sect. 3.3) distills the knowledge from the teacher image-English test scores

3   Method

3.1   Overview

Our model, illustrated in Fig. 1, is comprised of two components: (1)Teacher model has an English text encoder and an image encoder (2)Student model has a Multilingual text encoder and an image encoder which is the same as teacher model. Next, we describe the framework in detail.

Image Encoder. In our method, we use a pre-trained CLIP-ViT image encoder to extract the image embeddings. Given an image V, we reshape the image $\mathbf{x} \in \mathbb{R}^{H \times W \times C}$ into a sequence of flattened 2D patches $\mathbf{x}_p \in \mathbb{R}^{N \times (P^2 \cdot C)}$, where H, W is the resolution of the original image, C is the number of channels, (P, P) is the resolution of each image patch, and $N = HW/P^2$ is the resulting number of patches, which also serves as the effective input sequence length for the Transformer. Then we get the image embedding $\mathbf{F_v} \in \mathbb{R}^{N \times D}$ where D denote the embedding dimensions. It is noteworthy that the image encoder parameters of our teacher model and student model are not shared. We will discuss this further in the experimental Section.

Text Encoder. Let the corresponding inputs English text caption be E and Multi-lingual text caption M. We use the pre-trained CLIP-ViT text encoder to convert the English text caption into a sequence of embeddings $F_e \in \mathbb{R}^{p \times d_e}$ where p denote the lengths of English text and d_e denote the embedding dimensions. For the student model, we use the pre-trained XLM-R for Multi-lingual texts. Similar to the CLIP model, the Multi-lingual text caption is converted into a sequence of embeddings $F_m \in \mathbb{R}^{q \times d_m}$ where q denote the lengths of Multi-lingual text and d_m denote the embedding dimensions.

3.2   Contrastive Learning

For the first step, we freeze the teacher model and for student model use the Info Noise-Contrastive Estimation loss (InfoNCE) [24] to mutual information $I(F_v, F_m)$ measures dependencies between the two different views of data point, which can be either an image-English pair or an image-Multi-lingual pair. In this case, we will show our model maximizes a lower bound of $I(F_v, F_t)$ for multi-lingual multi-modal pre-training by minimizing the InfoNCE loss defined as:

$$\mathcal{L}_{\text{ITC}} = -\mathbb{E}_{p(F_v, F_m)} \left[\log \frac{\exp\left(f_\theta(F_v, f_m)\right)}{\sum_{\tilde{f}_m \in \tilde{F}_m} \exp\left(f_\theta(F_v, \tilde{f}_m)\right)} \right] \quad (1)$$

where $f_\theta \in \mathbb{R}$ is a function parameterized by θ and $\tilde{F}_m$ contains the positive sample f_m and $|\tilde{F}_m| - 1$ negative samples.

3.3   Contrastive Similarity Distillation Loss

Although $\mathcal{L}_{\text{ITC}}$ can be used to learn Multi-lingual image-text representations, the performance for English image-text retrieval is usually higher than for other languages, as mentioned in the introduction. This implies that the English image-text similarity scores are the most accurate among all the languages. To address this issue, we introduce a distillation objective that encourages the student's Multi-lingual image-text similarity scores to be similar to the teacher's image-English text scores. In each batch of images and Multi-lingual text, both teacher and student are simultaneously provided with the image and English text as input. Both teacher and student produce an image-text similarity matrix S_e and S_m. Then we can get two probability distribution P_e and P_m by normalized image-text similarity score in S_e and S_m:

$$P = \frac{\exp(\mathbf{S_{ij}}/\tau)}{\sum_{k=1}^{N} \exp(\mathbf{S_{ik}}/\tau)} \tag{2}$$

We apply the relative entropy loss between P_e and P_m:

$$\mathcal{L}_{\text{CSD}} = \sum_i P_m \log \frac{P_m}{P_e} \tag{3}$$

We apply $\mathcal{L}_{\text{CSD}}$ to each of the student image-text similarity matrices using text in different languages, the final loss is given by:

$$\mathcal{L}_{\text{total}} = \alpha \mathcal{L}_{\text{ITC}} + (1 - \alpha)\mathcal{L}_{\text{CSD}} \tag{4}$$

α is a coefficient of balance. Others have also observed that the contrastive loss may be too strict in a multi-modal setting and have proposed complementary objectives such as captioning [33] and clustering [34,35]. However, we use the contrastive loss in a multi-modal setting with target distributions generated from the image-text similarity scores of the teacher model.

4   Experiments

4.1   Datasets

Multi-modal Training Data. We pre-train our CSDNet on the image-caption pairs. For these data, we follow the practice of UC^2 and use their released translation-augmented version of CC3M dataset. It contains the original CC3M image-caption pairs [27] and then uses machine-translated captions in five languages (German, French, Czech, Japanese, and Chinese). Because some links to the images are broken, we are unable to obtain the complete CC3M dataset. For our work, we have used a total of 2.83 million images. Additionally, each image corresponds to six different language translations, including English.

Test Data for Evaluation. We use the MS-COCO caption dataset and translate the captions into Japanese [33] and Chinese [17]. These two language subsets consist of 820K Japanese captions and 20K Chinese captions (JA and ZH). Following previous work, we use the same training and test split for English and Japanese as defined in Karpathy and Li [14]. As for Chinese, we use the COCO-CN split [17]. The second is Flickr-30K, this dataset extended Flickr-30K from English to German, French and Czech (note as DE, FR and CS). It contains 31,783 images and provides five captions per image in English and German, and only one caption for French and Czech per image. Datasets splits are defined as the original Flickr-30K.

We compute Recall@K (recall of top K candidates) for both image-to-text retrieval and text-to-image retrieval with $K = 1/5/10$. The Average Recall is used as the final evaluation metric.

4.2   Implementation Details

We initialize the teacher model by Clip-ViT/Base-16 [26], which has 12 layers of Transformer blocks and each block has 768 hidden units, 12 self-attention heads in the text encoder. As for the student model we use XLM-R as our Multi-lingual text encoder. Both our teacher and student image encoders were initialized with ViT-base/16, which takes images with a resolution of 224*224 as input. We set the maximum sequence length to 30 for image-caption pairs and used a batch size of 512. The training procedure took 1 day for 30 epochs on 8 40GB Nvidia A100 GPUs. We employed the AdamW [19] optimizer with a weight decay of 0.01 and warmed up the learning rate from $1e^{-5}$ to $1e^{-4}$ in the first 2000 steps. The temperature coefficient $\tau = 1$ and balance $\alpha = 0.3$. For the evaluation procedure, we fine-tuned the student model for 10 epochs on each dataset without the teacher model.

Table 1. Evaluation results on Multi-Lingual Image-Text Retrieval over Flickr-30K and MC-COCO datasets across different languages in the zero-shot task. We compute the average Recall @K for both image-to-text retrieval with $K = 1/5/10$, as the evaluation metric.

Method	Flickr-30K (1K)				MS-COCO (1K)			MS-COCO (5K)		
	EN	DE	FR	CS	EN	ZH	JA	EN	ZH	JA
Zero-shot										
M^3P [23]	57.9	36.8	27.1	20.4	63.1	32.3	33.3	–	–	
ALIGN-base [13]	83.3	78.9	78.3	71.1	79.5	–	70.9	59.6	–	51.9
MURAL-base [12]	80.9	76.0	75.7	68.2	78.1		72.5	58.0	–	49.7
Ours	**84.5**	**79.2**	**78.5**	**72.2**	**81.3**	**76.5**	**76.1**	**64.5**	**54.3**	**55.3**

4.3   Results on Multi-lingual Image-Text Retrieval

In Table 1, we report the results of our proposed approach and previous results on Flickr-30K and MS-coco datasets both zero-shot settings. First, for zero-shot multi-lingual transfer results, we can see that our method outperforms all compared models by a substantial margin while pre-trained on the same multi-modal data. Specifically, compared to ALIGN-base [13] which trained in Alt-Text dataset [27]and MURAL-base [12] which trained in translate CC12m (ALIGN and MURAL-large is larger than our model and is pre-trained on much more 450× image-text pairs), our method obtains an average improvement of 4.3% Multi-lingual image-text retrieval. This demonstrates that the teacher model we introduced can leverage its powerful zero-shot capabilities to help the student model better align multi-lingual multi-modal representations.

In Table 2, we report the fine-tuning of target languages or the combination of all languages yields consistent improvements. The improvements are not as significant as that for UC^2 and M^3P, which is probably because the zero-shot multi-lingual transfer ability of our method is strong enough and the performance of our models is already saturating. Note that we did not use the teacher model during the fine-tuning process. Nevertheless, our method still substantially outperforms prior state-of-the-art by 7.4% and 3.6% averaged recall across five languages when fine-tuned on target languages or the combination of all languages, respectively. Moreover, our approach outperforms the state-of-the-art model, MURAL-base, in the all-language fine-tuning setting by achieving a 1.2% average recall improvement across six languages.

Table 2. Multi-Lingual Image-Text Retrieval results on Flickr-30K and MS-COCO datasets after 10 epochs fine-tuning. The metric is the average Recall @K for both image-to-text retrieval retrieval with $K = 1, 5, 10$.

Method	Flickr-30K (1K)				MS-COCO (1K)			MS-COCO (5K)		
	EN	DE	FR	CS	EN	ZH	JA	EN	ZH	JA
Only-English Fine-tune										
M^3P [23]	87.4	58.5	46.0	36.8	88.6	56.0	53.8	–	–	–
UC^2 [36]	87.2	74.9	74.0	67.9	88.1	82.0	71.7	–	–	–
Ours	**92.6**	**75.6**	**74.6**	**69.1**	**91.2**	**78.5**	**79.3**	**82.7**	**69.5**	**76.0**
ALL-Language Fine-tune										
M^3P [23]	87.7	82.7	73.9	72.2	88.6	87.9	86.2	–	–	–
UC^2 [36]	88.2	84.5	83.9	81.2	88.1	89.8	87.5	–	–	–
ALIGN-base [13]	92.3	88.3	78.8	81.4	89.2	–	86.7	76.1	–	74.1
MURAL-base [12]	91.0	87.3	86.4	82.4	89.4	–	87.4	73.7	–	71.9
Ours	**92.6**	**88.6**	**87.0**	**82.7**	**91.5**	**89.9**	**88.4**	**82.6**	**80.5**	**81.2**

4.4   Ablation Studies and Analysis

We also conduct an in-depth ablation study to investigate the role of different design choices in our method, including contrastive loss, teacher model and bias α. We pre-train 4 ablated variants models where Contrastive Similarity Distillation Loss, parallel sentence pairs(text-text contrastive loss), share image-encoder with frozen parameters or not. All compared models are pre-trained with the same CC3M data for 30 epochs to ensure a fair comparison. The results are shown in Table 3. First, we observed that the guidance of the teacher model to the student model is very practical, not only in English but also in improving the retrieval performance of Multi-lingual retrieval. This confirms our hypothesis that we can guide the learning of the student model in Multi-lingual retrieval tasks by distilling the guidance provided by the teacher model in English image-text retrieval. Then, we obtain training between text pairs without introducing new data has little effect on the Multi-lingual image-text retrieval, while introducing new training targets (parallel sentence pairs) may cause a decline in model performance. When training both teacher and student model with a shared image encoder the teacher model loses its excellent English image-text retrieval capability, which in turn makes it ineffective in guiding the student model's learning.

Table 3. Ablation study results. The best results with statistical significance are marked in bold.

	MS-COCO (5K)		
	EN	ZH	JA
Ours	**82.6**	**80.5**	**81.2**
w/o CSD loss	80.1	77.6	78.3
w/o TTC loss	82.2	80.2	80.7
w share train	73.1	67.5	68.3
w share fix	81.5	78.3	79.6

5   Conclusion

In this paper, we present Contrastive Similarity Distillation Network for the Multi-lingual Image-Text Retrieval task. Our method is designed to enhance the performance of Multi-lingual image-text retrieval. Our approach is motivated by the observation that English retrieval outperforms other languages, and we train a student model to output similar image-text similarity scores to teachers using input English text, but using input Multi-lingual text instead. We use relative entropy to distill the multi-modal knowledge from the teacher model, which helps the student model to acquire better Multi-lingual image-text retrieval ability. We apply our method to two datasets and observe an improvement in Multi-lingual image-text retrieval performance across languages and domains. Furthermore, our cross-view language modeling framework has the potential to unify more modalities, such as speech and video, with the same architectures and objectives. We leave this as future work.

Acknowledgments. This work was supported by the National Key Research and Development Program of China (No.2020AAA0106400), National Natural Science Foundation of China (U21B204362102416).

References

1. Bengio, Y., LeCun, Y., Henderson, D.: Globally trained handwritten word recognizer using spatial representation, convolutional neural networks, and hidden markov models. Adv. Neural Inf. Process. Syst. **6**, 1–8 (1993)
2. Chen, X., et al.: Microsoft coco captions: Data collection and evaluation server. arXiv preprint arXiv:1504.00325 (2015)

3. Chen, Y.-C., et al.: UNITER: UNiversal image-TExt representation learning. In: Vedaldi, A., Bischof, H., Brox, T., Frahm, J.-M. (eds.) ECCV 2020. LNCS, vol. 12375, pp. 104–120. Springer, Cham (2020). https://doi.org/10.1007/978-3-030-58577-8_7

4. Chi, Z., et al.: Infoxlm: an information-theoretic framework for cross-lingual language model pre-training. arXiv preprint arXiv:2007.07834 (2020)

5. Conneau, A., et al.: Unsupervised cross-lingual representation learning at scale. arXiv preprint arXiv:1911.02116 (2019)

6. Devlin, J., Chang, M.W., Lee, K., Toutanova, K.: Bert: pre-training of deep bidirectional transformers for language understanding. arXiv preprint arXiv:1810.04805 (2018)

7. Dong, L., et al.: Unified language model pre-training for natural language understanding and generation. Adv. Neural Inf. Process. Syst. **32**, 1–13 (2019)

8. Faghri, F., Fleet, D.J., Kiros, J.R., Fidler, S.: Vse++: improving visual-semantic embeddings with hard negatives. arXiv preprint arXiv:1707.05612 (2017)

9. Guo, L., Liu, J., Zhu, X., Yao, P., Lu, S., Lu, H.: Normalized and geometry-aware self-attention network for image captioning. In: Proceedings of the IEEE/CVF Conference on Computer Vision and Pattern Recognition, pp. 10327–10336 (2020)

10. Houlsby, N., et al.: Parameter-efficient transfer learning for nlp. In: International Conference on Machine Learning, pp. 2790–2799. PMLR (2019)

11. Huang, H., et al.: Unicoder: a universal language encoder by pre-training with multiple cross-lingual tasks. arXiv preprint arXiv:1909.00964 (2019)

12. Jain, A., et al.: Mural: multimodal, multitask retrieval across languages. arXiv preprint arXiv:2109.05125 (2021)

13. Jia, C., et al.: Scaling up visual and vision-language representation learning with noisy text supervision. In: International Conference on Machine Learning, pp. 4904–4916. PMLR (2021)

14. Karpathy, A., Fei-Fei, L.: Deep visual-semantic alignments for generating image descriptions. In: Proceedings of the IEEE Conference on Computer Vision and Pattern Recognition, pp. 3128–3137 (2015)

15. Lample, G., Conneau, A.: Cross-lingual language model pretraining. arXiv preprint arXiv:1901.07291 (2019)

16. Li, F., et al.: Vision-language intelligence: tasks, representation learning, and large models. arXiv preprint arXiv:2203.01922 (2022)

17. Li, X., et al.: COCO-CN for cross-lingual image tagging, captioning, and retrieval. IEEE Trans. Multimedia **21**(9), 2347–2360 (2019)

18. Liu, W., Chen, S., Guo, L., Zhu, X., Liu, J.: CPTR: full transformer network for image captioning. arXiv preprint arXiv:2101.10804 (2021)

19. Loshchilov, I., Hutter, F.: Decoupled weight decay regularization. arXiv preprint arXiv:1711.05101 (2017)

20. Lu, H., Fei, N., Huo, Y., Gao, Y., Lu, Z., Wen, J.R.: Cots: collaborative two-stream vision-language pre-training model for cross-modal retrieval. In: Proceedings of the IEEE/CVF Conference on Computer Vision and Pattern Recognition, pp. 15692–15701 (2022)

21. Lu, J., Batra, D., Parikh, D., Lee, S.: Vilbert: pretraining task-agnostic visiolinguistic representations for vision-and-language tasks. Adv. Neural Inf. Process. Syst. **32**, 1–11 (2019)

22. Luo, Z., Xi, Y., Zhang, R., Li, G., Zhao, Z., Ma, J.: Conditioned masked language and image modeling for image-text dense retrieval. In: Findings of the Association for Computational Linguistics: EMNLP 2022, pp. 130–140 (2022)

23. Ni, M., et al.: M3p: learning universal representations via multitask multilingual multimodal pre-training. In: Proceedings of the IEEE/CVF Conference on Computer Vision and Pattern Recognition, pp. 3977–3986 (2021)

24. Oord, A.V.D., Li, Y., Vinyals, O.: Representation learning with contrastive predictive coding. arXiv preprint arXiv:1807.03748 (2018)

25. Pfeiffer, J., Vulić, I., Gurevych, I., Ruder, S.: Mad-x: an adapter-based framework for multi-task cross-lingual transfer. arXiv preprint arXiv:2005.00052 (2020)

26. Radford, A., et al.: Learning transferable visual models from natural language supervision. In: International Conference on Machine Learning, pp. 8748–8763. PMLR (2021)

27. Sharma, P., Ding, N., Goodman, S., Soricut, R.: Conceptual captions: a cleaned, hypernymed, image alt-text dataset for automatic image captioning. In: Proceedings of the 56th Annual Meeting of the Association for Computational Linguistics, vol. 1: Long Papers, pp. 2556–2565 (2018)

28. Su, W., et al.: Vl-bert: pre-training of generic visual-linguistic representations. arXiv preprint arXiv:1908.08530 (2019)

29. Sun, S., Chen, Y.C., Li, L., Wang, S., Fang, Y., Liu, J.: Lightningdot: pre-training visual-semantic embeddings for real-time image-text retrieval. In: Proceedings of the 2021 Conference of the North American Chapter of the Association for Computational Linguistics: Human Language Technologies, pp. 982–997 (2021)

30. Tan, H., Bansal, M.: Lxmert: learning cross-modality encoder representations from transformers. arXiv preprint arXiv:1908.07490 (2019)

31. Wang, L., Li, Y., Huang, J., Lazebnik, S.: Learning two-branch neural networks for image-text matching tasks. IEEE Trans. Pattern Anal. Mach. Intell. **41**(2), 394–407 (2018)

32. Xu, C., Zhou, W., Ge, T., Wei, F., Zhou, M.: Bert-of-theseus: compressing bert by progressive module replacing. arXiv preprint arXiv:2002.02925 (2020)

33. Yoshikawa, Y., Shigeto, Y., Takeuchi, A.: Stair captions: constructing a large-scale Japanese image caption dataset. arXiv preprint arXiv:1705.00823 (2017)

34. Young, P., Lai, A., Hodosh, M., Hockenmaier, J.: From image descriptions to visual denotations: new similarity metrics for semantic inference over event descriptions. Trans. Assoc. Comput. Linguist. **2**, 67–78 (2014)

35. Zhao, Z., Guo, L., He, X., Shao, S., Yuan, Z., Liu, J.: Mamo: masked multimodal modeling for fine-grained vision-language representation learning. arXiv preprint arXiv:2210.04183 (2022)

36. Zhou, M., et al.: Uc2: universal cross-lingual cross-modal vision-and-language pre-training. In: Proceedings of the IEEE/CVF Conference on Computer Vision and Pattern Recognition, pp. 4155–4165 (2021)

37. Zhou, W., Lee, D.H., Selvam, R.K., Lee, S., Lin, B.Y., Ren, X.: Pre-training text-to-text transformers for concept-centric common sense. arXiv preprint arXiv:2011.07956 (2020)

Flexible Hierarchical Parallel Processing for AVS3 Video Coding

Hannong Zheng[1]([✉]), Yuhuai Zhang[2], Jian Zhang[1], Hengyu Man[3],
Xuan Deng[3], and Siwei Ma[2,3]

[1] Peking University Shenzhen Graduate School, Shenzhen, China
zhenghannong@stu.pku.edu.cn, zhangjian.sz@pku.edu.cn
[2] Peking University, Beijing, China
{yhzhangvcl,swma}@pku.edu.cn
[3] Pengcheng Laboratory, Shenzhen, China
20B903061@stu.hit.edu.cn

Abstract. Video coding standards adopt a series of time-consuming techniques to improve coding performance. Acceleration is vital to the application of real-time video coding. However, conventional frame-level parallelisms usually fail to accelerate effectively, since the coding order is barely adjusted. This motivates more fine-grained parallelisms adopted in industry codecs, while the coding performance loss is inevitably introduced due to the coding restrictions. To benefit parallelism in Random Access (RA) configuration, we propose a novel parallel strategy named Flexible Hierarchical Parallel Processing (FHPP). Based on level order traversal, FHPP achieves cross-GOP and cross-intra-period parallelism in a flexible and hierarchical way. Furthermore, we analyze the upper bound of the FHPP speedup ratio theoretically. Extensive experimental results on the AVS3 standard show that FHPP can achieve an average acceleration of 10 times for 4K sequences under 16 threads, and the maximum acceleration can exceed 12 times, which is significantly better than the traditional frame-level parallelisms.

Keywords: Video coding · Frame-level parallelism · Coding order

1 Introduction

The Audio and Video coding Standard (AVS) workgroup of China, which was established in 2002, has been dedicated to advancing and innovating the digital audio-video industry with highly efficient and economical encoding/decoding technologies, and a series of prestigious video coding standards and extensions, including AVS1 [8], AVS2 [17], and AVS3 [26], have been published and standardized [18].

As a new standard, AVS3 has adopted many novel coding techniques and has achieved a significant reduction in bit-rate compared with AVS2 and HEVC under 4K resolution sequences [26]. For coding unit partition, AVS3 adopts

© The Author(s), under exclusive license to Springer Nature Switzerland AG 2023
H. Lu et al. (Eds.): ICIG 2023, LNCS 14357, pp. 396–406, 2023.
https://doi.org/10.1007/978-3-031-46311-2_33

Binary Tree (BT) partition [21] and Extended QuadTree (EQT) partition [23], which can provide more flexible partition types than that in AVS2. By assuming the linear correlation between the prediction results of luma and chroma components, Two-Step Cross-component Prediction Mode (TSCPM) [13,14] is designed for eliminating cross-component redundancy in chroma coding. To achieve a more complex motion representation, affine motion prediction is proposed and combined with the direct mode [3] and inter mode [15]. In AVS3, Position-Based Transform (PBT) [22] is used to residual blocks in the transform processing of the first phase. Moreover, Implicit Selection of Transform (IST) [27] is adopted in the second phase which introduces DST-VII as a transform candidate, and an implicit indication method is incorporated to save the signaling bits of transform type. The entropy coding of the first phase of AVS3 is consistent with AVS2, while in the second phase, Scan Region-based Coefficient Coding (SRCC) [16] is applied to reduce coding bits of zero-coefficients. Enhanced Cross-Component Sample Adaptive Offset (CCSAO) [10,11] is introduced to filter based on Sample Adaptive Offset (SAO).

All these advanced techniques contribute to the coding performance improvement [1] with the expense of the heavy encoder computational burden, bringing obstacles to real-world applications. To speed up the encoding process, fast algorithms have also been proposed, such as fast CU partition based on frequency coefficients [25], early termination of mode decision [24], and accelerating transform processing [9]. Nevertheless, they are all defective due to the cost of performance losses. Parallelism is an alternative solution to accelerate. Frame-level parallelism is simple to implement and gains significant time-savings without coding performance losses. However, conventional frame-level parallelisms [5] usually fail to accelerate sufficiently, since the traditional coding order in Random Access (RA) configuration is not friendly to parallelism. This may be a universal problem existing in many encoders, such as uavs3e [2]. As a result, more fine-grained parallelisms are applied in these encoders, such as Wavefront Parallel Processing (WPP). However, the shortcomings of WPP are obvious. Because of the wavefront dependencies, the rows of Coding Tree Block (CTB) cannot start encoding simultaneously, such that they will not finish at the same time and cause parallelization inefficiencies [6]. Many other parallelisms are also defective because of the performance losses caused by breaking the references. Besides, although GOP-level parallelisms have been proposed in All Intra (AI) and Low Delay (LD) configurations [19], they are not bounded with frame-level parallelisms in RA configuration. Therefore, conventional frame-level parallelisms are usually adopted within the Group Of Pictures (GOP) such that they cannot make full use of the independence between intra-periods.

Herein, we design a new parallel strategy named Flexible Hierarchical Parallel Processing (FHPP) for frame-level parallelism on AVS3 reference software HPM-12.0 [12]. By focusing on coding order, FHPP achieves cross-GOP and cross-intra-period parallelism flexibly and hierarchically, thereby achieving ultrafast coding. To our best knowledge, this is the first work that achieves the flexible hierarchical parallel processing for frame-level parallelism in AVS3.

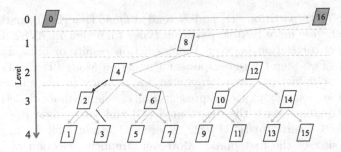

Fig. 1. Traditional hierarchical referencing structure of the first GOP [7], where numbers denote display order and light green arrows indicate the coding order. The coding order is the preorder traversal of the binary tree structure, which is not friendly to frame-level parallelism

2   Flexible Hierarchical Parallel Processing

2.1   Background

For the traditional coding order of Random Access (RA) configuration with a GOP sized 16, the hierarchical picture referencing structure of the first GOP is shown in Fig. 1, where the numbers denote display order and the light green arrows indicate the coding order [7]. The hierarchical structure implies the referencing relationship. Any frame (except for frame 16, to some extent it belongs to the next GOP) always refers to ones in the lower levels, but will not refer to a higher one or the one in the same level.

2.2   Motivation

As shown in Fig. 1, after encoding frames 0 and 16, frames 1 to 15 are arranged in a binary tree structure, and the coding order is the preorder traversal of it. After encoding frame 32, frames 17 to 31 go through a similar binary tree structure. The preorder traversal can reduce the delay between coding and display, due to the frames playing first will be encoded as early as possible. However, for multi-thread coding, this order becomes the main factor that restricts the efficiency of parallelism.

Multi-thread allows the encoding of more frames simultaneously, while only for the independent ones. In the traditional coding order, successive frames are usually dependent, which leads to thread waits. For example, when 3 threads are applied for frame-level parallelism, the encoder can load and encode 3 successive frames in parallel. However, when dealing with frames 8, 4, and 2 simultaneously, there are referencing relationships between them (frame 4 refers to frame 8, and frame 2 refers to frame 4). Therefore, the threads of frames 4 and 2 are suspended to wait, while only frame 8 is encoded. This phenomenon influences the whole coding process, and greatly affects the degree of parallelism or causes a waste of threads. These thread waits are not necessary and can be eliminated by changing

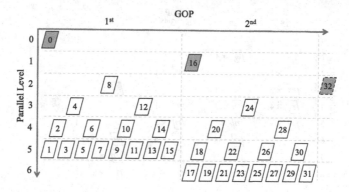

Fig. 2. Our proposed hierarchical structure of the first 2 GOPs. The structure of each GOP is consistent with Fig. 1. The second GOP starts at Parallel Level (PL) 1, such that frame 16 fills in the blank PL reserved in the first GOP

the coding order. For example, when frame 4 is encoded, frames 12 and 32 can be encoded simultaneously. It is important to further accelerate by coding more frames that are independent of each other simultaneously.

2.3 Proposed Method

Inspired by the structure in Fig. 1, all frames in the same level are independent of each other. If frames of the whole sequence can be separated into several levels, while all frames in the same level only refer to the frames in the lower levels, then there will be no thread waits when encoding them level by level. This can be proved by induction:

- For level 0, all frames can be encoded immediately at any time, because they do not refer to any frame.
- If levels 0 to n are finished, then all frames of level $(n + 1)$ (if exists) can be encoded immediately since all its reference frames are ready.

In this strategy, we define Parallel Level (PL) to denote the global level of a frame for the whole sequence. As shown in Fig. 2, for the first GOP, the PLs of each frame are basically consistent with the levels in Fig. 1, except for the special frame 16, which bridges the first and second GOP. As a result, a blank PL (PL 1 in Fig. 2) is inserted between frames 0 and 8, reserved for frame 16 in the second GOP. Therefore, frame 16 starts at PL 1, and the rest of the frames in the second GOP are arranged similarly. Iterate this process for the first 4 GOPs as an intra-period stage, as shown in Fig. 3. GOPs are arranged progressively, and they only take up $l_0 = 9$ PLs in total. In this way, cross-GOP parallelism is achieved.

Moreover, since any intra-period stage can be encoded independently, cross-intra-period parallelism is available by piling up multiple intra-period structures in Fig. 3. The fastest coding process is to start coding all intra-period stages at

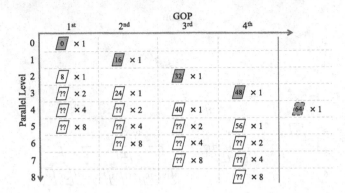

Fig. 3. Our proposed hierarchical structure of the first intra-period, including 4 structures of GOP (each as Fig. 1) arranged in a progressive way. They take up $l_0 = 9$ PLs

the same time, but with the increasing of the stages, there will be numerous frames in a single PL. As mentioned above, all frames in the same PL should be encoded simultaneously. Otherwise, they block the coding process of higher PL and cause coding delay. It is unrealistic to encode innumerable frames simultaneously due to the limited cores. A more reasonable and flexible way is to define an incremental delay for each stage to guarantee the priority of the frames. Herein, we denote the increment as p and set every q intra-periods as a group. The first q intra-periods start simultaneously at PL 0, the second q intra-periods start simultaneously at PL p, and the third q intra-periods start simultaneously at PL $2p$. Any positive integer for p and q is legal, and p is no more than 4 which is reasonable since a larger one produces a gap between stages, incurring the redundant and meaningless delay. Figure 4 provides an example of $q = 1$ and $p = 1$, where any intra-period starts at one PL higher than the previous one. Because some of the I frames (frames 64, 128, 192, etc.) bridge different GOPs and are shared by them, the frames in higher PL (corresponding to the rightmost frame 64 in Fig. 3) are omitted in Fig. 4.

As mentioned above, coding these frames PL by PL is a parallel-friendly strategy. Theoretically, the orientation to go through each PL is insignificant in the ideal case where all frames of the same PL start to be encoded simultaneously. A left-to-right order is adopted here since it is easy to understand, as the light green arrows in Fig. 4. We name it Flexible Hierarchical Parallel Processing (FHPP) since parameters p and q show flexibility in different degrees of parallelism.

2.4 Acceleration Analysis

In this section, the theoretical acceleration of Flexible Hierarchical Parallel Processing (FHPP) is analyzed given parameters p and q. Then, the total Parallel

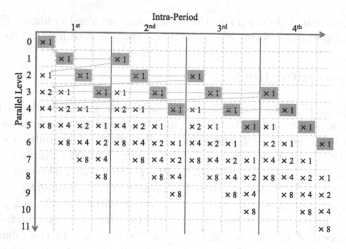

Fig. 4. Our proposed hierarchical structure of multiple intra-periods, where $p = 1$ and $q = 1$. Structures of intra-period (each as Fig. 3) are piled up to form the whole sequence. As is indicated by light green arrows, coding these frames PL by PL is called Flexible Hierarchical Parallel Processing (FHPP). Cross-GOP and cross-intra-period parallelisms are achieved

Levels (PLs) taken up can be derived as follows,

$$l = l_0 + p(\lceil \frac{n}{q} \rceil - 1) , \tag{1}$$

where l denotes PLs taken up by the whole sequence, p denotes the PL increment for each q intra-periods, n denotes the count of the intra-periods to be encoded, l_0 denotes PLs taken up by one GOP, and symbol $\lceil \cdot \rceil$ means rounding up. Because the frames in a lower level of the GOP are encoded under a lower Quantization Parameter (QP) to prevent passing the error to a higher level [20], they usually cost more time, especially for the bottom frames (colored orange in all figures) of each GOP. Considering this, the time consumption for each PL can be determined by the slowest frames. Suppose the time spent in any other frame is t on average, and the time spent in the slowest frames in each PL is $r \cdot t$ ($r > 1$) on average. When each intra-period contains 64 frames, the speedup ratio η can be derived as follow,

$$\eta = \frac{4n \cdot rt + 60n \cdot t}{l \cdot rt}$$
$$= \frac{4r + 60}{r} \cdot \frac{n}{l_0 + p(\lceil \frac{n}{q} \rceil - 1)} . \tag{2}$$

Furthermore, we assume the sequence is long enough. The ideal parallelism will approach the theoretical maximum,

$$\lim_{n \to \infty} \eta = \frac{4r + 60}{r} \cdot \frac{q}{p} . \tag{3}$$

In an ideal parallel condition, this is also the required count of CPU cores since a quickly-finished frame can yield its computing resource to the other.

3   Experimental Results

In this section, Flexible Hierarchical Parallel Processing (FHPP) is tested on AVS3 reference software HPM-12.0 [12], and the complexity performance is compared with the traditional frame-level parallelism [5]. The multicore platform consists of two Intel Xeon Gold 6354 CPUs at up to 3.00 GHz and 200 GB of RAM. The operating system is Windows 10 for ×86 64bit. The testing sequences are selected from the Common Test Conditions (CTC) sequences [4] of AVS3 in RA configuration. Since long sequences are required for efficient parallelization, each of the testing sequences is extended by alternately concatenating itself and the reversal of it, and choosing the first 2000 frames. In the following, any sequence refers to the extended one, and the thread count refers to the thread for frame-level parallelism unless otherwise specified.

First, all the 4K and 1080P sequences are picked to test for the overall performance when other factors are fixed. When $p, q = 1$ and the Quantization Parameter (QP) is 38, Table 1 shows the comparison between the traditional method

Table 1. Comparisons of speed ratios for various test sequences between the traditional method and proposed FHPP, on the condition of $p, q = 1$ and QP $= 38$, under different thread counts.

Parallelism Method	Resolution	Sequence	Thread Count for Frame-Level Parallelism							
			1	2	3	4	6	8	12	16
Traditional Frame-Level Parallelism	1080P	BasketballDrive	1.00	1.18	1.44	1.51	1.71	2.06	2.08	3.91
		Cactus	1.00	1.18	1.43	1.49	1.68	1.99	2.03	3.83
		MarketPlace	1.00	1.17	1.41	1.47	1.65	1.93	1.97	3.53
		RitualDance	1.00	1.21	1.51	1.58	1.83	2.17	2.22	4.09
		Average	1.00	1.18	1.45	1.51	1.72	2.04	2.08	3.84
	4K	Campfire	1.00	1.25	1.67	1.69	2.08	2.49	2.55	4.74
		DaylightRoad2	1.00	1.21	1.51	1.55	1.79	2.06	2.11	3.95
		ParkRunning3	1.00	1.14	1.32	1.38	1.54	1.87	1.90	3.55
		Tango2	1.00	1.21	1.46	1.53	1.71	2.04	2.07	3.84
		Average	1.00	1.20	1.49	1.54	1.78	2.12	2.16	4.02
FHPP	1080P	BasketballDrive	1.00	1.90	2.78	3.61	4.81	6.32	7.64	9.88
		Cactus	1.00	1.87	2.80	3.46	4.81	6.36	7.70	10.19
		MarketPlace	1.00	1.88	2.69	3.35	4.37	5.47	6.38	7.93
		RitualDance	1.00	1.92	2.78	3.61	4.87	6.39	8.03	10.35
		Average	1.00	1.89	2.76	3.51	4.72	6.13	7.44	9.59
	4K	Campfire	1.00	1.99	2.94	3.85	5.42	7.23	9.68	12.29
		DaylightRoad2	1.00	1.87	2.79	3.45	4.78	6.26	7.65	9.91
		ParkRunning3	1.00	1.91	2.76	3.49	4.54	6.08	7.11	9.86
		Tango2	1.00	1.88	2.76	3.48	4.63	6.05	7.25	9.53
		Average	1.00	1.91	2.81	3.57	4.84	6.41	7.92	10.40

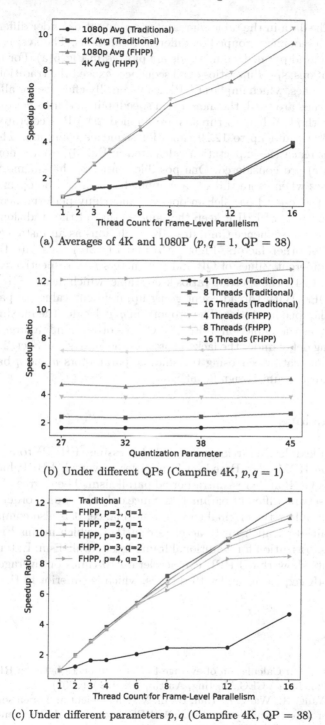

(a) Averages of 4K and 1080P ($p, q = 1$, QP $= 38$)

(b) Under different QPs (Campfire 4K, $p, q = 1$)

(c) Under different parameters p, q (Campfire 4K, QP $= 38$)

Fig. 5. Speedup ratios for different sequences, QPs, and parameters p, q, respectively

and FHPP. The data in the table represent speedup ratios under different thread counts, of each sequence grouped by different resolutions. The averages of different resolutions and parallelism methods are plotted in Fig. 5(a). For both 1080P and 4K resolutions, speedup ratios of all sequences exceed the traditional method by one or two times, which implies FHPP is universally effective for all sequences. The more threads are used, the more extra speedup it performs compared to the traditional method. When 16 threads are applied, FHPP accelerates about 10 times on average, and up to 12.29 times for sequence Campfire. This speedup ratio does not reach the expectation calculated in Eq. (3), even if non-ideal factors (such as r) are considered. One possible reason is that memory fragmentation increases when more threads are applied, which can be optimized in the future. Since frame-level parallelism does not incur any performance losses, the bitrates and outputs of FHPP keep the same as that of the traditional method.

Herein, we take sequence Campfire (4K resolution) as an instance to test for the influence of other factors. Figure 5(b) and Fig. 5(c) illustrate the speedup ratios under different values of QP and parameters p, q, respectively. When QP varies from 27 to 45, the speedup ratios keep stable, which means FHPP is robust to different QPs. With thread count going up, different values of parameters p and q affect the speedup ratios. The proportion q/p decides the maximum degree of parallelism, as the depiction in Eq. (3). On the other hand, a large proportion leads to coding delay under the lack of cores, as the analysis in Sect. 2. Therefore, in practical application, choosing the suitable parameters p and q based on the supported thread count is significant.

4   Conclusions

We propose Flexible Hierarchical Parallel Processing (FHPP) to achieve ultra-fast coding on HPM-12.0. Based on level order traversal, FHPP hierarchically achieves cross-GOP and cross-intra-period parallelism. The degree of parallelism is flexible by setting different parameters. Since only the coding order is changed, FHPP will not affect the original coding performance. It is also compatible with more fine-grained parallelisms to accelerate further, which means FHPP can be an awesome substitution for traditional frame-level parallelism. Extensive experimental results show that FHPP can accelerate 10 times on average and up to 12 times for 4K sequences under 16 threads, which is superior to the traditional method.

References

1. Bjontegarrd, G.: Calculation of average PSNR differences between RD-curves. In: VCEG-M33, 13th VCEG Meeting, Austin, TX, USA (2001)
2. Cai, Y., Wang, R., Wang, Z., Han, B., Li, X.: An efficient and open source encoder Uavs3e for video compression. In: 2021 IEEE International Conference on Multimedia and Expo (ICME), pp. 1–6. IEEE (2021)
3. Chen, H., Zhao, Y., Yang, H.: Affine skip mode. AVS workgroup Doc. M4643 (2019)

4. Chen, J.: Common test conditions AVS3-P2 v12.0. AVS workgroup Doc. N2926 (2020)
5. Chen, Y.K., Li, E.Q., Zhou, X., Ge, S.: Implementation of H.264 encoder and decoder on personal computers. J. Vis. Commun. Image Represent. **17**(2), 509–532 (2006)
6. Chi, C.C., et al.: Parallel scalability and efficiency of HEVC parallelization approaches. IEEE Trans. Circuits Syst. Video Technol. **22**(12), 1827–1838 (2012)
7. Enhorn, J., Sjöberg, R., Wennersten, P.: A temporal pre-filter for video coding based on bilateral filtering. In: 2020 IEEE International Conference on Image Processing (ICIP), pp. 1161–1165. IEEE (2020)
8. Fan, L., Ma, S., Wu, F.: Overview of AVS video standard. In: 2004 IEEE International Conference on Multimedia and Expo (ICME)(IEEE Cat. No. 04TH8763), vol. 1, pp. 423–426. IEEE (2004)
9. Guo, Y., Gao, W., Ma, S., Li, G.: Accelerating transform algorithm implementation for efficient intra coding of 8K UHD videos. ACM Trans. Multimedia Comput. Commun. Appl. (TOMM) **18**(4), 1–20 (2022)
10. Jian, Y., et al.: Enhanced cross component sample adaptive offset for AVS3. In: 2021 International Conference on Visual Communications and Image Processing (VCIP), pp. 1–5. IEEE (2021)
11. Kuo, C.W., et al.: Cross-component sample adaptive offset. In: 2022 Data Compression Conference (DCC), pp. 359–368. IEEE (2022)
12. Li, J., Chen, J., Zhao, Y.: HPM12.0 and HPM12.1 software maintenance report. AVS workgroup Doc. M6629 (2021)
13. Li, J., et al.: Chroma coding with two-step cross-component prediction. AVS workgroup Doc. M4632 (2018)
14. Li, J., et al.: Modified comparison logic for TSCPM. AVS workgroup Doc. M4726 (2019)
15. Lu, X., Yang, H.: Ce8: the integration progress report of affine motion model in TAVS3. AVS workgroup Doc. M4451 (2018)
16. Lv, Z., Piao, Y., Wu, Y., Choi, K., Choi, K.P.: Scan region-based coefficient coding in AVS3. In: 2020 IEEE International Conference on Multimedia Expo Workshops (ICMEW), pp. 1–5. IEEE (2020)
17. Ma, S., Huang, T., Reader, C., Gao, W.: AVS2 - making video coding smarter. IEEE Signal Process. Mag. **32**(2), 172–183 (2015)
18. Ma, S., et al.: Evolution of AVS video coding standards: twenty years of innovation and development. Sci. China Inf. Sci. **65**(9), 1–24 (2022)
19. Piñol, P., Migallón, H., López-Granado, O., Malumbres, M.P.: Parallel strategies analysis over the HEVC encoder. J. Supercomput. **70**(2), 671–683 (2014)
20. Schwarz, H., Marpe, D., Wiegand, T.: Analysis of hierarchical B pictures and MCTF. In: 2006 IEEE International Conference on Multimedia and Expo, pp. 1929–1932 (2006)
21. Wang, L., Niu, B., Wei, Z., Lei, M., Zhang, J.: Flexible block partitioning structure based on TAVS3 platform. AVS workgroup Doc. 4409 (2018)
22. Wang, L., Niu, B., Xiao, H., Wei, Z., He, Y.: CE4 : position based inter prediction residual transform method. AVS workgroup Doc. M4541 (2018)
23. Wang, M., et al.: Extended quad-tree partitions AVS3-P2. AVS workgroup Doc. M4507 (2018)
24. Wang, Y., Cao, J., Wang, J., Liang, F.: Gradient-based fast intra coding decision algorithm for HEVC. In: 2019 IEEE 4th International Conference on Signal and Image Processing (ICSIP), pp. 870–874 (2019)

25. Xu, C., Wu, Y., Chen, L., Liu, Z., Cao, C.: Fast cu partition decision algorithm for AVS3 based on frequency domain. In: 2022 21st International Symposium on Communications and Information Technologies (ISCIT), pp. 195–198. IEEE (2022)
26. Zhang, J., Jia, C., Lei, M., Wang, S., Ma, S., Gao, W.: Recent development of AVS video coding standard: AVS3. In: 2019 Picture Coding Symposium (PCS), pp. 1–5. IEEE (2019)
27. Zhang, Y., Zhang, K., Zhang, L., Wang, S., Gao, W.: Implicitly selected transform for AVS3. IEEE Trans. Image Process. **31**, 1298–1310 (2022)

Content-Adaptive Block Clustering for Improving VVC Adaptive Loop Filtering

Fan Ye, Li Li, and Dong Liu[✉]

University of Science and Technology of China, Hefei 230027, China
fanye@mail.ustc.edu.cn, {lil1,dongeliu}@ustc.edu.cn

Abstract. Adaptive loop filtering (ALF) is an important tool in the H.266/VVC standard, and offers significant compression efficiency gain. ALF adopts a set of linear filters to process the reconstructed samples of one picture, where the filter coefficients are adaptive to the picture, and the filter selection is based on classifying the samples at the granularity of 4×4 block. We investigate how to make ALF more adaptive by focusing on the sample classification. We argue that the classification may be replaced with kinds of clustering, since we perform the filter selection based on the clusters without requiring the definition of classes. Thus, we propose to cluster the samples, also at 4×4 block level, according to the content-based features extracted from the blocks. By an extensive set of experiments with different kinds of features, we observed that the proposed method achieves on average 0.69% BD-rate reduction than the H.266/VVC anchor on a number of 2K-resolution images.

Keywords: Adaptive loop filtering (ALF) · Block clustering · H.266/VVC

1 Introduction

The ITU-T Video Coding Experts Group (VCEG) and the ISO/IEC Moving Picture Experts Group (MPEG) have finalized the state-of-the-art H.266 Versatile Video Coding (VVC) standard [4]. In H.266/VVC, the quantization mechanism in lossy compression inevitably results in artifacts, which lead to the video quality degradation. The compression artifacts can be removed by using in-loop filtering technologies [14], which are used to post-process the reconstruction frames before they are used for inter-prediction as reference frames.

Adaptive Loop Filtering (ALF) [19] is a modern in-loop filtering function introduced in H.266/VVC. The main idea of ALF is to minimize the Mean Square Error (MSE) between the original samples and the reconstructed samples by using a set of wiener filters. Here, the wiener filter has been considered an optimal linear filter to improve the degraded picture. ALF is typically composed of a classification process and a filtering process. In the classification process, each

© The Author(s), under exclusive license to Springer Nature Switzerland AG 2023
H. Lu et al. (Eds.): ICIG 2023, LNCS 14357, pp. 407–417, 2023.
https://doi.org/10.1007/978-3-031-46311-2_34

4×4 block is classified into a class according to a gradient-based classification rule. In the filtering process, one set of filter coefficients is estimated to the corresponding one or more classes in the encoder frame by frame. Further, the estimated filter coefficients are encoded into the bitstream as side information so that the decoder can select the same filters according to the classes.

In recent years, ALF has been investigated as a promising research topic to further improve coding performance. In [6,7], reconstructed samples are assigned into two categories according to the local features, and each filter is applied to process the corresponding samples. However, a frame level filter switch does not take into account block level differences. Later on, to better achieve block level filtering, Block-based ALF (BALF) [8] and Quadtree-based ALF (QALF) [9] are proposed to indicate whether or not to use block level filters. Besides, to reduce time and computational complexity, Lim et al. [16] propose the sum-modified-laplacian operator to reduce the sample number needed to be used in the classification process. Those above studies mainly focus on spatial adaptation and computational complexity to improve the performance of ALF, paying little attention to optimizing the sample classification. However, the filters to process the reconstructed samples are directly connected to video quality, and the filter coefficients are adaptive to the picture, guided by the sample classification. So ALF essentially relies on the result of the sample classification. Therefore, it is necessary to make ALF more adaptive by focusing on sample classification to improve compression efficiency.

In the existing studies, there are mainly two technology routes to optimize the sample classification. (1) One is to increase the number of categories in [13,15]. These methods illustrate that more categories lead to higher quality, but more coding overhead of the filter coefficients is also needed. (2) The other is to extend multi-classification methods based on multi-features in [11,12]. Since the texture complexity in the natural picture is very diverse, it seems a difficult task to classify samples with limited classification methods.

Although H.266/VVC [10] ALF empirically defines the classes according to local gradient features, the class definition does not always apply to every image. Besides, the classes are only used to select different filters, without actual physical significance and characteristics. Therefore, we can consider sample classification as an unsupervised learning problem, which inspires us to utilize clustering for replacing the existing sample classification method. By block level clustering, we can use the features of all the blocks in one frame to consider the correlation between them, utilizing the context information effectively. Still, also we can perform filter selection based on the clusters without requiring the definition of classes. To achieve content-adaptive block clustering, we propose to cluster the block level samples on the basis of content-based features extracted from the blocks. In the first step, to utilize effective feature representation for each block, we extract different kinds of features in the picture. In the second step, we establish a content-adaptive mapping from features to categories by clustering based on different kinds of features, which leads to the determination of the most appropriate classification result. Our contribution can be summarized as follows:

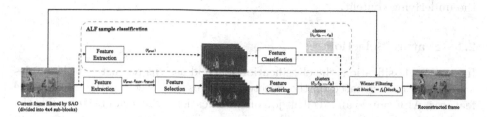

Fig. 1. Comparison between the ALF in H.266/VVC and our proposed method. At the decoder side, after applying SAO, one picture is divided into 4×4 blocks and for each block we select one wiener filter f_k from the filter pool. Traditionally (inside the dotted box), gradient-based features F_{grad} were extracted and used to classify the block as belonging to one of the 25 predefined classes; filter selection is based on the class (denoted by k). We propose to first extract different features (including gradient-based features F_{grad}, GLCM features F_{GLCM}, VQVAE features F_{VQVAE}), or select from different features (Sect. 2.1), and then cluster the blocks according to the features (Sect. 2.2); filter selection is based on the cluster index (also denoted by k)

- We propose to utilize content-adaptive block clustering to establish a mapping from features to categories without requiring the definition of classes.
- We can use all block features to consider the correlation between them by clustering, utilizing the context information effectively.
- We replace H.266/VVC ALF sample classification method with our proposed method and integrate it into VTM-10.0, further improving the performance of ALF.

The remainder of this article is organized as follows. In Sect. 2, we describe the main procedure of our proposed method. In Sect. 3, we show the experimental results and analyses. Finally, we conclude the entire paper in Sect. 4.

2   Proposed Method

This Section presents a detailed explanation of the content-adaptive clustering method. To illustrate the effectiveness of our proposed method, we provide a comparison with H.266/VVC ALF, as shown in Fig. 1. Our method differs from ALF in H.266/VVC in two ways. Firstly, we extract different types of features and select the most relevant features for clustering. Secondly, we utilize clustering algorithms to establish a mapping from features to categories by clustering, replacing the traditional class definition with clusters.

To begin, we discuss the importance of appropriate feature selection and explain our selection criteria in detail. Subsequently, we provide a step-by-step description of our content-adaptive clustering approach based on the selected features. By leveraging the rich information present in the selected features, we can cluster the blocks effectively and obtain a more accurate representation of the underlying content.

2.1 Feature Selection

In sample classification, the classification method assigns reconstructed samples to different classes based on the selected features. By selecting the appropriate features, ALF can do an excellent job of classification, which can better guide the coefficients estimation of wiener filters. The gradient feature is the most common feature because it represents the directional change and structural attributes of an image. In this paper, we decide to stick with the gradient features introduced in the existing ALF, including the four directional gradient features and an activity feature. The four directional gradient features consist of the vertical (g_v), the horizontal (g_h), the 45-degree diagonal (g_{d1}) and the 135-degree diagonal direction (g_{d2}) gradient features. And the activity feature A is calculated by summing the horizontal gradient and the vertical gradient values. Therefore, the four directional gradient features can describe the direction of the gradient, and the activity feature can describe the magnitude of the gradient.

However, in certain cases, such as when a block comprises of large smooth regions, the gradient features can be easily disrupted by noise samples, necessitating the selection of a subset of gradient features to better represent the content direction of the block. Additionally, to accommodate images with varying characteristics, we have extended the Gray-level Co-occurrence Matrix (GLCM) features [17] and depth features extracted by Vector Quantized Variational Autoencoders (VQVAE) [20] as optional features. GLCM is a predefined image feature that characterizes the texture variation, and the details of its feature extraction can be found in [17]. We calculate the GLCM features of each block and cluster them to obtain clusters. VQVAE is a neural network-based codec framework, in which the encoder and decoder share a set of codebooks, and the encoded feature vector is quantized to a standard feature in the codebook. We have set the number of codebook vectors to 25, so the index of the codebook vectors quantized by each feature can be expressed as the category.

2.2 Content-Adaptive Clustering

When we get the above features, we utilize these features to obtain a classification according to a classification algorithm; here, the classification algorithm can be considered as a function f that performs the mapping of block features to categories. In the H.266/VVC ALF classification, the parameters $\Theta = \{\theta_1, \theta_2, \ldots, \theta_N\}$ of function f are fixed in the basis of empirical theoretical analysis. Suppose we can get a set of features $\{x_1, x_2, \ldots, x_N\}$ from an image I , where the features are extracted from the granularity of 4×4 block, each feature vector x_k as the input of the function f will get the corresponding output category c_k, where $c_k \in \{1, \ldots, 25\}$. Therefore, the mapping of block features to classes can be represented by the following formula:

$$f(x_k; \Theta) = c_k, \quad x_k \in \{x_1, x_2, \ldots, x_N\} \tag{1}$$

By observing the formula, we can find that the category of the current block is only related to the feature vector of the current block. However, image content can vary from having a regular repeated structure to having multiple complex textures, it is not reasonable to design the fixed parameters $\Theta = \{\theta_1, \theta_2, \ldots, \theta_N\}$ for various images. Consequently, we propose to use a clustering algorithm to dynamically update the parameters $\hat{\Theta} = \{\hat{\theta}_1, \hat{\theta}_2, \ldots, \hat{\theta}_N\}$ of function f for each image, overcoming the limitations of the fixed parameters Θ used in ALF. The proposed clustering method to obtain cluster $\hat{c}_k$ can be expressed as:

$$f(x_k; \hat{\Theta}(x_1, x_2, \ldots, x_N)) = \hat{c}_k, \quad x_k \in \{x_1, x_2, \ldots, x_N\} \tag{2}$$

The function f aims to group the set of features into clusters so that the intra-category similarity is maximized while the inter-category similarity is minimized. So our optimization target is to minimize the sum of squared errors (SSE) expressed as:

$$SSE = \sum_{\hat{c}_k=1}^{25} \sum_{x_k \in \hat{c}_k} \|x_k - u_{\hat{c}_k}\|^2 \tag{3}$$

where $u_{\hat{c}_k}$ represents the mean feature vector of cluster $\hat{c}_k$. Through cluster-driven algorithm, the parameters $\hat{\Theta} = \{\hat{\theta}_1, \hat{\theta}_2, \ldots, \hat{\theta}_N\}$ can be updated according to the image content, and the context of different block features can be fully utilized.

The proposed content-adaptive clustering method consists of two main steps. The first step involves feature pre-processing, which entails the normalization of feature vectors. Specifically, we divide each dimension of the gradient features by a constant numeric value, which we refer to as the activity value, denoted by A. Extensive experiments have demonstrated that this normalization technique enhances the ability of clustering convergence, leading to better results.

In the second step, we employ the GMM algorithm to cluster the selected features. This decision is based on a comprehensive set of experiments reported in Sect. 3.1. As known to all, the GMM algorithm maximizes the likelihood estimation [18]. Unlike the common K-Means clustering algorithm, GMM calculates the probability that each sample belongs to each of the distribution, rather than assigning each sample directly to a class. Therefore, GMM is well-suited for data with highly dissimilar shapes and sizes. Thus, in this paper, we choose to utilize the GMM algorithm to cluster features.

3   Experimental Results and Analyses

This Section is devoted to evaluating the performance of the content-adaptive clustering method for ALF. We implemented the proposed method into

Table 1. BD-rate results of the proposed method than the H.266/VVC anchor using gradient-based features $\{g_v, g_h, g_{d1}, g_{d2}, A\}$ but different clustering algorithms (All-Intra configuration)

DIV2K Sequence	Bisecting K-Means			MiniBatch K-Means			K-Means			GMM		
	Y(%)	U(%)	V(%)	Y(%)	U(%)	V(%)	Y(%)	U(%)	V(%)	Y(%)	U(%)	V(%)
0038	0.04	0.06	0.06	−0.20	0.04	0.05	−0.12	0.03	0.03	**−0.74**	0.09	0.09
0043	0.37	−0.01	−0.01	0.36	0.00	0.01	0.20	0.03	0.04	**−0.30**	0.07	0.07
0132	0.70	0.00	−0.01	0.59	0.01	0.01	0.52	0.00	0.00	**−0.33**	0.03	0.03
0138	0.04	0.31	0.31	0.03	0.15	0.22	0.02	0.19	0.25	**−0.73**	0.29	0.36
0150	−0.36	0.01	0.02	−0.23	0.00	0.01	−0.38	0.09	0.10	**−0.40**	0.07	0.07
0154	0.27	0.05	0.05	0.23	0.05	0.05	0.17	0.05	0.04	**−0.70**	0.10	0.09
0170	0.67	0.07	0.07	0.57	0.05	0.05	0.55	0.07	0.07	**−0.67**	0.10	0.11
0188	−0.09	0.08	0.07	−0.15	0.06	0.06	−0.23	0.08	0.09	**−0.50**	0.12	0.12
0190	0.39	0.04	0.04	0.41	0.05	0.05	0.37	0.01	0.01	**−0.50**	0.13	0.13
0373	−0.14	0.11	0.11	−0.08	0.11	0.11	−0.26	0.14	0.14	**−1.34**	0.19	0.19
0392	−0.10	0.01	0.01	−0.16	0.02	0.01	−0.19	0.03	0.02	**−0.26**	0.03	0.02
0399	−0.29	0.03	0.03	−0.38	0.03	0.03	−0.40	0.02	0.02	**−0.51**	0.08	0.09
0457	−0.37	0.04	0.03	**−0.52**	0.09	0.08	−0.45	0.06	0.06	−0.49	0.07	0.06
0460	−0.32	0.04	0.05	**−0.32**	0.05	0.05	−0.28	0.05	0.05	−0.31	0.07	0.07
0493	0.58	0.13	0.13	0.50	0.09	0.09	0.25	0.10	0.09	**−0.73**	0.17	0.16
0520	0.26	0.11	0.11	0.36	0.05	0.05	0.14	0.11	0.11	**−0.68**	0.16	0.16
0562	−0.12	0.15	0.15	−0.25	0.14	0.14	−0.32	0.16	0.15	**−2.19**	0.15	0.15
0677	−0.31	−0.03	−0.02	0.74	−0.11	−0.11	−0.57	−0.02	−0.02	**−1.70**	0.08	0.09
0703	−0.26	0.02	0.02	−0.33	0.03	0.03	−0.31	0.04	0.04	**−0.38**	0.07	0.07
0762	−0.18	0.03	0.03	−0.26	0.03	0.03	−0.24	0.04	0.04	**−0.29**	0.07	0.07
All	0.04	0.06	0.06	0.05	0.05	0.05	−0.08	0.06	0.07	**−0.69**	0.11	0.11

H.266/VVC reference software VTM (version 10.0) [5] and compared it with the vanilla VTM. Specifically, we replace the ALF fixed classification rule with our proposed method. Because our proposal is designed for various image content, All-Intra coding configuration is used for the evaluation. The H.266/VVC bitstreams are generated using the five quantization parameter values 22, 27, 32, 37, and 42. Besides, BD-rate [2] is computed to quantify the bits saving between different methods.

In testing, we first conduct feature clustering on a small dataset and find that the proposed method did not perform well for all types of content, but there are still a number of images in favor of the proposed method, particularly those with smooth areas and repeated regular texture characteristics. Therefore, according to these image characteristics, we selected a subset of images from the high-quality DIV2K [1] dataset to be used as our testset. This dataset contains a diverse range of 2K resolution images with various image content. Figure 2 (a) showcases some examples of the images in our testset. We then evaluated the proposed method on this testset and presented the index numbers of selected images in Table 1. Additionally, we conducted experiments on H.266/VVC common test sequences [3] using different clustering algorithms, and the results are reported in Sect. 3.2.

3.1 Performance of DIV2K Images

1) *Results of Different Clustering Algorithms:* Table 1 summarizes the BD-rate results of four clustering algorithms including GMM and K-Means, with Bisecting K-Means and MiniBatch K-Means, all compared to the H.266/VVC anchor under All-Intra configuration. The selected features used for clustering are the gradient features $\{g_v, g_h, g_{d1}, g_{d2}, A\}$ mentioned in Sect. 2.1.

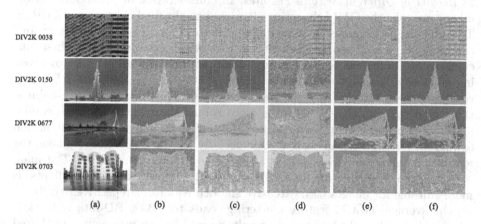

Fig. 2. (a) Original image. (b)–(f) Visualization of the classification or clustering results, where different colors represent different classes or different cluster indexes. (b) The ALF in H.266/VVC. (c)–(f) The proposed method using gradient-based features $\{g_v, g_h, g_{d1}, g_{d2}, A\}$ but different clustering algorithms. (c) Bisecting K-Means; (d) Mini-Batch K-Means; (e) K-Means; (f) GMM.

For luma component Y, we can find that GMM algorithm outperforms the other three algorithms, leading to an average 0.69% BD-rate reduction compared with the anchor. And the performance of GMM algorithms is consistently higher than those for the other three algorithms across all classes except for DIV2K 0457 image and DIV2K 0460 image. In particular, Mini Batch K-Means algorithm slightly outperforms GMM algorithm above the two images. The main reason behind the better classification results by Mini Batch K-Means algorithm may be the mechanism that only partially selected features are used for clustering makes which discards noisy feature samples and bad feature samples coincidentally. Similarly, if Mini Batch K-Means algorithm discards some useful feature samples, its performance can be greatly degraded, and this is also why the performance of DIV2K 0677 images is remarkably worse than the other three algorithms. To gain more insight from the experimental results, we show some DIV2K images and corresponding classification and clustering results in Fig. 2. We find that the GMM algorithm has a strong robustness ability to the noise points in the smooth region and can also distinguish the texture of the different details.

For chroma components U and V, the performances of the four clustering algorithms are slightly lower than the anchor. Because our proposed method is mainly designed for luma component and there is no algorithm optimization for chroma components, the PSNR of chroma components remains the same with the H.266/VVC anchor. Besides, the proposed method can affect the total number of bits due to the filter bitstream in luma component. When the overall bitrate of the proposed method is higher than the anchor, the BD-rate performance of the chroma components exhibits loss; otherwise, there will be coding gain on the chroma components.

2) *Results of Different Selected Features:* In consideration of the coding performance, we take the GMM clustering algorithm as our final clustering algorithm. To verify the performance between different feature combinations, we set up four combination cases based on gradient features, which are shown in the first four columns of Table 2. Those four feature combination cases all can improve coding efficiency, leading to on average 0.69%, 0.56%, 0.11%, and 0.04% BD-rate reduction, respectively. And the result shows conclusively that the combination of $\{g_v, g_h, g_{d1}, g_{d2}, A\}$ feature is more robust than the other three combinations regarding coding performance. But for some images, the combination of $\{g_v, g_h, g_{d1}, g_{d2}\}$ feature is better. Especially for the DIV2K 0150 image, the feature combination of $\{g_v, g_h\}$ is superior to other combinations. The main reason is that selecting appropriate features, instead of excessive gradients, is more suitable for images with extensive smooth regions or repetitive details.

On average, GLCM feature clustering leads to 0.33% BD-rate reduction, which is lower than the first column result. Several factors may have contributed to the performance of the GLCM feature clustering. On the one hand, GLCM feature uses the co-occurrence matrix to describe the texture attributes, which may not be representative enough to reflect the direction change of the image. On the other hand, high-dimensional GLCM features will increase the difficulty of clustering and affect the performance of clustering results.

VQVAE is less effective than the anchor, resulting in 1.22% BD-rate increment. We train and test the VQVAE network both on DIV2K dataset. Even though the data set and test set are identical, the performance is not ideal. The discrepancy between the nonlinear deep features and the linear Wiener filter is the main reason behind the suboptimal performance. The nonlinear features extracted by the VQVAE network do not conform to the assumptions of linearity that are inherent to the Wiener filter. As a result, the output of the filter does not fully exploit the potential of the nonlinear features, which ultimately results in decreased performance. This issue underscores the importance of designing filters that are better suited to the characteristics of the features being utilized, and points to the need for developing more sophisticated filtering techniques.

3.2   Performance of H.266/VVC Common Test Sequences

We have shown the experimental results of VVC common test sequences with different clustering algorithms based on our proposed method in Table 3, under All-Intra configuration. For luma component, it is observed that the content-adaptive block clustering method can achieve considerable coding gains for several test sequences, such as *BasketballDrive* and *RaceHorsesC*. Moreover, we

Table 2. BD-rate results of the proposed method than the H.266/VVC anchor using different features but the same clustering algorithm GMM, where GMM is not used for VQVAE (All-Intra configuration)

DIV2K Sequence	BD-rate performance of Y component(%)					
	$\{g_v, g_h, g_{d1}, g_{d2}, A\}$ (proposed)	$\{g_v, g_h, g_{d1}, g_{d2}\}$	$\{g_v, g_h\}$	$\{g_{d1}, g_{d2}\}$	GLCM	VQVAE
0038	**−0.74**	−0.49	0.08	−0.05	−0.38	2.08
0043	**−0.30**	−0.10	0.08	0.23	0.00	1.33
0132	**−0.33**	−0.28	0.32	0.37	0.09	1.40
0138	**−0.73**	−0.44	−0.63	0.02	0.33	2.62
0150	**−0.40**	−0.16	−0.49	0.04	−0.32	0.41
0154	**−0.70**	−0.06	0.34	−0.27	−0.30	1.42
0170	**−0.67**	−0.23	0.19	0.09	0.24	2.13
0188	**−0.50**	−0.23	0.02	−0.04	−0.30	1.13
0190	**−0.50**	−0.29	0.08	0.03	0.05	1.55
0373	**−1.34**	−1.28	−0.10	−0.35	−0.73	1.97
0392	**−0.26**	−0.25	−0.16	−0.01	−0.12	0.30
0399	−0.51	**−0.54**	−0.32	0.15	−0.33	0.57
0457	−0.49	**−0.52**	−0.48	0.23	−0.22	0.49
0460	−0.31	**−0.35**	−0.33	−0.05	−0.30	0.14
0493	−0.73	**−0.79**	0.23	−0.14	−0.31	1.21
0520	**−0.68**	−0.68	−0.22	0.16	−0.73	1.15
0562	**−2.19**	−2.04	−0.39	−0.85	−1.69	1.66
0677	−1.70	**−1.80**	0.25	−0.67	−1.14	2.09
0703	**−0.38**	−0.36	−0.36	0.10	−0.16	0.42
0762	−0.29	**−0.30**	−0.28	0.12	−0.21	0.40
All	**−0.69**	**−0.56**	**−0.11**	**−0.04**	**−0.33**	1.22

have provided the ratio of encoding time at the bottom of Table 3. The encoding complexity of K-Means clustering method is comparable to that of the anchor, and the algorithm complexity of optimized K-Means, such as Bisecting K-Means, demonstrates lower algorithm complexity as compared to the original K-Means. It should be noted that we use a plain implementation of GMM without any time complexity optimization, which offers scope for future work in optimizing the GMM algorithm and reducing its coding time complexity.

Therefore, all-in-all experiments demonstrate that the proposed method leads to significant performance gain and then further improves the performance of ALF. However, the proposed method is not general enough to adapt to all images, so we can set an RDO flag to control whether to use this method. In addition, the time complexity of the clustering algorithm is high, so we need to design the time optimization algorithm further.

Table 3. BD-rate results of the proposed method than the H.266/VVC anchor using gradient-based features $\{g_v, g_h, g_{d1}, g_{d2}, A\}$ under common test sequences but different clustering algorithms (All-Intra configuration)

Class	Sequence	Bisecting K-Means			MiniBatch K-Means			K-Means			GMM		
		Y(%)	U(%)	V(%)	Y(%)	U(%)	V(%)	Y(%)	U(%)	V(%)	Y(%)	U(%)	V(%)
A1	*Tango2*	−0.07	−0.09	−0.09	−0.10	−0.10	−0.10	−0.08	−0.08	−0.08	**−0.24**	0.05	0.06
	FoodMarket4	−0.19	0.00	0.01	−0.21	0.01	0.01	−0.21	0.00	0.00	**−0.21**	−0.02	−0.02
	Campfire	0.21	−0.05	−0.05	0.19	−0.04	−0.06	0.15	−0.03	−0.04	0.05	−0.02	−0.02
A2	*CatRobot1*	0.15	−0.08	−0.08	0.14	−0.05	−0.05	0.14	−0.07	−0.08	0.03	−0.06	−0.06
	DaylightRoad2	0.10	−0.03	−0.03	0.08	−0.04	−0.04	0.04	−0.03	−0.03	0.02	0.01	0.01
	ParkRunning3	0.05	0.00	0.00	0.01	0.00	0.00	0.01	0.00	0.00	**0.00**	0.00	0.00
B	*MarketPlace*	0.08	−0.01	−0.01	0.06	−0.02	−0.02	0.06	−0.02	−0.02	0.05	0.02	0.02
	RitualDance	0.14	−0.13	−0.12	0.18	−0.08	−0.07	0.14	−0.13	−0.11	0.08	−0.06	−0.05
	Cactus	0.13	−0.04	−0.05	0.13	−0.04	−0.05	0.11	−0.02	−0.03	0.05	0.01	0.00
	BasketballDrive	0.07	0.02	0.02	0.06	−0.01	0.06	−0.04	0.00	0.00	**−0.19**	0.10	0.09
	BQTerrace	−0.06	0.03	0.02	−0.12	0.03	0.03	−0.10	0.03	0.03	**−0.16**	0.03	0.03
C	*RaceHorsesC*	−0.12	0.14	0.16	**−0.13**	0.17	0.19	−0.10	0.12	0.14	−0.12	0.15	0.17
	BQMall	0.09	−0.16	−0.16	0.09	−0.01	−0.01	0.06	−0.11	−0.10	0.05	−0.04	−0.04
	PartyScene	0.12	−0.02	−0.02	0.07	−0.02	−0.02	0.07	0.02	0.01	0.01	0.03	0.03
	BasketballDrill	0.44	−0.17	−0.17	0.26	−0.20	−0.21	0.34	−0.25	−0.26	**−0.12**	0.15	0.17
D	*RaceHorses*	0.22	0.02	0.01	0.12	−0.08	−0.10	0.11	0.00	−0.01	0.07	−0.08	−0.10
	BQSquare	0.04	0.01	−0.01	0.04	0.15	0.13	0.03	−0.02	−0.02	0.00	0.02	0.00
	BlowingBubbles	0.18	0.17	0.16	0.16	0.21	0.20	0.23	0.19	0.17	0.17	0.28	0.27
	BasketballPass	0.29	0.22	0.26	0.32	0.24	0.27	0.30	0.24	0.28	0.19	0.40	0.42
E	*FourPeople*	0.11	0.10	0.10	0.11	0.02	0.02	0.06	0.02	0.02	0.04	0.11	0.11
	Johnny	0.30	−0.17	−0.15	0.26	−0.13	−0.12	0.18	0.02	0.03	**−0.03**	0.06	0.07
	KristenAndSara	0.06	−0.12	−0.12	0.08	−0.11	−0.11	0.03	−0.12	−0.12	0.01	0.06	0.06
F	*BasketballDrillText*	0.16	−0.17	−0.16	0.18	−0.17	−0.18	0.23	−0.10	−0.09	**−0.11**	−0.07	−0.06
	ChinaSpeed	0.14	−0.03	−0.03	0.06	0.00	0.00	0.13	0.03	0.03	0.06	0.02	0.02
	SlideEditing	−0.14	0.06	0.07	−0.15	0.04	0.05	**−0.21**	0.05	0.06	−0.10	−0.10	−0.10
	SlideShow	−0.03	0.00	0.00	−0.06	−0.01	0.00	−0.03	0.00	0.00	**−0.07**	−0.12	−0.13
Enc Time Ratio		100%			101%			102%			128%		

4   Conclusion

In this paper, a content-adaptive block clustering for the H.266/VVC ALF framework is proposed. Instead of having a clear class definition to group reconstructed samples, the proposed method based on feature clustering is tested. Test results show that for the selected DIV2K images, a coding gain of 0.69% is achievable for All-Intra configuration. Therefore, the proposed method has great potential to optimize the existing ALF method. And the results also show several limitations, and can be a starting point for further investigations. For future studies, more features may be investigated, and the clustering result of each one could be analyzed. Besides, we can explore more clustering algorithms. In the end, we plan to combine the feature clustering and filtering processes to design an adaptive algorithm that can update both simultaneously.

Acknowledgments. This work was supported by the Natural Science Foundation of China under Grants 62022075 and 61931014, and by the Fundamental Research Funds for the Central Universities under Grant WK3490000006.

References

1. Agustsson, E., Timofte, R.: NTIRE 2017 challenge on single image super-resolution: dataset and study. In: Computer Vision and Pattern Recognition Workshops (CVPRW) (2017)
2. Bjontegaard, G.: Calculation of average PSNR differences between RD-curves. VCEG-M33 (2001)
3. Boyce, J., Suehring, K., Li, X., et al.: JVET common test conditions and software reference configurations. In: JVET-J1010, San Diego (2018)
4. Bross, B., Wang, Y.K., Ye, Y., et al.: Overview of the versatile video coding (VVC) standard and its applications. IEEE Trans. Circuits Syst. Video Technol. **31**(10), 3736–3764 (2021)
5. Chen, J., Ye, Y., Kim, S.H.: Algorithm description for versatile video coding and test model 10 (VTM 10). In: Document JVET-S2002, Teleconference (2020)
6. Chiu, Y.J., Xu, L.: Adaptive (wiener) filter for video compression. In: ITU-T SG16 Contribution C437, Geneva (2008)
7. Chujoh, T., Tanizawa, A., Yamakage, T.: Adaptive loop filter for improving coding efficiency. In: ITU-T SG16 Contribution C402, Geneva (2008)
8. Chujoh, T., Tanizawa, A., Yamakage, T.: Block-based adaptive loop filter. In: VCEG-AJ13, ITU-T SG16, San Diego (2008)
9. Chujoh, T., Wada, N., Yasuda, G.: Quadtree-based adaptive loop filter. In: ITU-T SG16 Contribution C181, Geneva (2009)
10. Coban, M., Léannec, F.L., Liao, R.L., et al.: Algorithm description of enhanced compression model 7 (ECM 7). In: Document JVET-AB2025, Mainz (2022)
11. Erfurt, J., Lim, W.Q., Schwarz, H., et al.: Extended multiple feature-based classifications for adaptive loop filtering. APSIPA Trans. Signal Inf. Process. **8**, e28 (2019)
12. Erfurt, J., Lim, W.Q., Schwarz, H., et al.: Multiple feature-based classifications adaptive loop filter. In: Proceedings IEEE Picture Coding Symposium (PCS), pp. 91–95 (2018)
13. Karczewicz, M., Chen, P., Joshi, R., et al.: Video coding technology proposal by Qualcomm Inc. In: JCTVC-A121, ITU-T SG16, Dresden (2010)
14. Karczewicz, M., Hu, N., Taquet, J., et al.: VVC in-loop filters. IEEE Trans. Circuits Syst. Video Technol. **31**(10), 3907–3925 (2021)
15. Karczewicz, M., Zhang, L., Chien, W.J., et al.: Geometry transformation-based adaptive in-loop filter. In: Proceedings IEEE Picture Coding Symposium (PCS), pp. 1–5 (2016)
16. Lim, S.C., Kim, M., Kang, J., et al.: Subsampled sum-modified-laplacian for adaptive loop filter in versatile video coding. IEEE Access **8**, 176330–176342 (2020)
17. Mohanaiah, P., Sathyanarayana, P., GuruKumar, L.: Image texture feature extraction using GLCM approach. Int. J. Sci. Res. Publ. **3**(5), 1–5 (2013)
18. Su, T., Dy, J.G.: In search of deterministic methods for initializing k-means and gaussian mixture clustering. Intell. Data Anal. **11**(4), 319–338 (2007)
19. Tsai, C.Y., Chen, C.Y., Yamakage, T., et al.: Adaptive loop filtering for video coding. IEEE J. Sel. Top. Signal Process. **7**(6), 934–945 (2013)
20. Van Den Oord, A., Vinyals, O., et al.: Neural discrete representation learning. In: Advances in Neural Information Processing Systems, pp. 6306–6315 (2017)

Author Index

© The Editor(s) (if applicable) and The Author(s), under exclusive license
to Springer Nature Switzerland AG 2023
H. Lu et al. (Eds.): ICIG 2023, LNCS 14357, pp. 419–420, 2023.
https://doi.org/10.1007/978-3-031-46311-2

Printed in the United States
by Baker & Taylor Publisher Services